Examining the Evolution of Gaming and Its Impact on Social, Cultural, and Political Perspectives

Keri Duncan Valentine
West Virginia University, USA

Lucas John Jensen
Georgia Southern University, USA

A volume in the Advances in Human and Social
Aspects of Technology (AHSAT) Book Series

Information Science
REFERENCE
An Imprint of IGI Global

Published in the United States of America by
Information Science Reference (an imprint of IGI Global)
701 E. Chocolate Avenue
Hershey PA, USA 17033
Tel: 717-533-8845
Fax: 717-533-8661
E-mail: cust@igi-global.com
Web site: http://www.igi-global.com

Library of Congress Cataloging-in-Publication Data

Names: Valentine, Keri Duncan, editor. | Jensen, Lucas John, editor.
Title: Examining the evolution of gaming and its impact on social, cultural,
  and political perspectives / Keri Duncan Valentine and Lucas John Jensen,
  editors.
Description: Hershey, PA : Information Science Reference, 2016. | Includes
  bibliographical references.
Identifiers: LCCN 2016003164| ISBN 9781522502616 (hardcover) | ISBN
  9781522502623 (ebook)
Subjects: LCSH: Video games--Social aspects. | Video games--Political
  aspects. | Video gamers--Psychology.
Classification: LCC GV1469.34.S52 E93 2016 | DDC 794.8--dc23 LC record available at http://lccn.loc.gov/2016003164

This book is published in the IGI Global book series Advances in Human and Social Aspects of Technology (AHSAT) (ISSN: 2328-1316; eISSN: 2328-1324)

British Cataloguing in Publication Data
A Cataloguing in Publication record for this book is available from the British Library.

All work contributed to this book is new, previously-unpublished material. The views expressed in this book are those of the authors, but not necessarily of the publisher.

For electronic access to this publication, please contact: eresources@igi-global.com.

Advances in Human and Social Aspects of Technology (AHSAT) Book Series

Ashish Dwivedi
The University of Hull, UK

ISSN: 2328-1316
EISSN: 2328-1324

MISSION

In recent years, the societal impact of technology has been noted as we become increasingly more connected and are presented with more digital tools and devices. With the popularity of digital devices such as cell phones and tablets, it is crucial to consider the implications of our digital dependence and the presence of technology in our everyday lives.

The **Advances in Human and Social Aspects of Technology (AHSAT) Book Series** seeks to explore the ways in which society and human beings have been affected by technology and how the technological revolution has changed the way we conduct our lives as well as our behavior. The AHSAT book series aims to publish the most cutting-edge research on human behavior and interaction with technology and the ways in which the digital age is changing society.

COVERAGE

- Digital Identity
- Computer-Mediated Communication
- Public Access to ICTs
- Technology Adoption
- Gender and Technology
- ICTs and human empowerment
- Technology and Social Change
- Cyber Behavior
- Technology Dependence
- Human-Computer Interaction

IGI Global is currently accepting manuscripts for publication within this series. To submit a proposal for a volume in this series, please contact our Acquisition Editors at Acquisitions@igi-global.com or visit: http://www.igi-global.com/publish/.

Titles in this Series

For a list of additional titles in this series, please visit: www.igi-global.com

Defining Identity and the Changing Scope of Culture in the Digital Age
Alison Novak (Rowan University, USA) and Imaani Jamillah El-Burki (Lehigh University, USA)
Information Science Reference • copyright 2016 • 316pp • H/C (ISBN: 9781522502128) • US $185.00 (our price)

Gender Considerations in Online Consumption Behavior and Internet Use
Rebecca English (Queensland University of Technology, Australia) and Raechel Johns (University of Canberra, Australia)
Information Science Reference • copyright 2016 • 297pp • H/C (ISBN: 9781522500100) • US $165.00 (our price)

Analyzing Digital Discourse and Human Behavior in Modern Virtual Environments
Bobbe Gaines Baggio (American University, USA)
Information Science Reference • copyright 2016 • 320pp • H/C (ISBN: 9781466698994) • US $175.00 (our price)

Overcoming Gender Inequalities through Technology Integration
Joseph Wilson (University of Maiduguri, Nigeria) and Nuhu Diraso Gapsiso (University of Maiduguri, Nigeria)
Information Science Reference • copyright 2016 • 324pp • H/C (ISBN: 9781466697737) • US $185.00 (our price)

Cultural, Behavioral, and Social Considerations in Electronic Collaboration
Ayse Kok (Bogazici University, Turkey) and Hyunkyung Lee (Yonsei University, South Korea)
Business Science Reference • copyright 2016 • 374pp • H/C (ISBN: 9781466695566) • US $205.00 (our price)

Handbook of Research on Cultural and Economic Impacts of the Information Society
P.E. Thomas (Bharathiar University, India) M. Srihari (Bharathiar University, India) and Sandeep Kaur (Bharathiar University, India)
Information Science Reference • copyright 2015 • 618pp • H/C (ISBN: 9781466685987) • US $325.00 (our price)

Human Behavior, Psychology, and Social Interaction in the Digital Era
Anabela Mesquita (CICE – ISCAP/Polytechnic of Porto, Portugal & Algoritmi Centre, Minho University, Portugal) and Chia-Wen Tsai (Ming Chuan University, Taiwan)
Information Science Reference • copyright 2015 • 372pp • H/C (ISBN: 9781466684508) • US $200.00 (our price)

Rethinking Machine Ethics in the Age of Ubiquitous Technology
Jeffrey White (Korean Advanced Institute of Science and Technology, KAIST, South Korea) and Rick Searle (IEET, USA)
Information Science Reference • copyright 2015 • 331pp • H/C (ISBN: 9781466685925) • US $205.00 (our price)

www.igi-global.com

701 E. Chocolate Ave., Hershey, PA 17033
Order online at www.igi-global.com or call 717-533-8845 x100
To place a standing order for titles released in this series, contact: cust@igi-global.com
Mon-Fri 8:00 am - 5:00 pm (est) or fax 24 hours a day 717-533-8661

Editorial Advisory Board

Table of Contents

Foreword xvi

Preface xx

Acknowledgment xxxiv

Chapter 1
Toward Broader Definitions of "Video Games": Shifts in Narrative, Player Goals, Subject Matter,
and Digital Play Environments 1
    Lucas John Jensen, Georgia Southern University, USA
    Daisyane Barreto, University of North Carolina – Wilmington, USA
    Keri Duncan Valentine, West Virginia University, USA

Chapter 2
Telling Tales with Technology: Remediating Folklore and Myth through the Videogame *Alan
Wake* 38
    Dawn Catherine Stobbart, Lancaster University, UK

Chapter 3
"There Are No Observers Here": The Video Game Gaze in *Outlast* (2013) and *Outlast:
Whistleblower* (2014) 54
    Hazel E. Monforton, University of Durham, UK

Chapter 4
The Game Space of *Dear Esther* and Beyond: Perspective Shift and the Subversion of Player
Agency 73
    Harrington Weihl, Northwestern University, USA

Chapter 5
Apportioned Commodity Fetishism and the Transformative Power of Game Studies 95
    Ken S. McAllister, University of Arizona, USA
    Judd Ethan Ruggill, University of Arizona, USA
    Tobias Conradi, ZeM – Brandenburgisches Zentrum für Medienwissenschaften, Germany
    Steven Conway, Swinburne University of Technology, Australia
    Jennifer deWinter, Worcester Polytechnic Institute, USA
    Chris Hanson, Syracuse University, USA
    Carly A. Kocurek, Illinois Institute of Technology, USA
    Kevin A. Moberly, Old Dominion University, USA
    Randy Nichols, University of Washington Tacoma, USA
    Rolf F. Nohr, Hochschule für Bildende Künste Braunschweig, Germany
    Marc A. Ouellette, Old Dominion University, USA

Chapter 6
Co-Creation and the Distributed Authorship of Video Games 123
    Stephanie C Jennings, Rensselaer Polytechnic Institute, USA

Chapter 7
She Designs Therefore She Is? Evolving Understandings of Video Game Design 147
    Carolyn Michelle Cunningham, Gonzaga University, USA

Chapter 8
Gaming before E-Sports: Playing with Gender in Early Gaming Communities, 1993-2001 170
    Marley-Vincent Lindsey, Brown University, USA

Chapter 9
Serious Games Teaching Values: Discussing Games Dealing with Human Rights Issues 195
    Sonja Gabriel, KPH Vienna/Krems, Austria

Chapter 10
Affordances and Constraints of Analog Games for Ethics Education: Dilemmas and Dragons 219
    Spencer P. Greenhalgh, Michigan State University, USA

Chapter 11
Knowledge Production in E-Sports Culture: Learning with and from the Masters 238
    Robert James Hein, The Pennsylvania State University, USA
    Jason A. Engerman, The Pennsylvania State University, USA

Chapter 12
Gaming to Increase Reading Skills: A Case Study 258
    Laura Kieran, Drake University, USA
    Christine Anderson, Western Illinois University, USA

Chapter 13
Game/Write: Gameplay as a Factor in College-Level Literacy and Writing Ability 272
  Sandy Baldwin, Rochester Institute of Technology, USA
  Nicholas D. Bowman, West Virginia University, USA
  John Jones, West Virginia University, USA

Chapter 14
Implementing a Game-Based Instructional Design Strategy in the Eighth Grade Science
Classroom: Teaching Science the *Chutes and Ladders* Way! 292
  Angela Dowling, Suncrest Middle School, USA
  Terence C. Ahern, West Virginia University, USA

Chapter 15
Jamming Econo: The Phenomenon of Perspectival Shifts in Indie Video Games 309
  Keri Duncan Valentine, West Virginia University, USA
  Lucas John Jensen, Georgia Southern University, USA

Chapter 16
Playful Experiments: Conditions of "An Experience" in Touchscreen Games by a Non-
Hermeneutic Perspective 343
  Felippe Calazans Thomaz, Federal University of Bahia, Brazil
  Jorge Cardoso Filho, Federal University from Recôncavo of Bahia, Brazil

Chapter 17
Games People Play: A Trilateral Collaboration Researching Computer Gaming across Cultures 364
  Sandy Baldwin, Rochester Institute of Technology, USA
  Kwabena Opoku-Agyemang, West Virginia University, USA
  Dibyadyuti Roy, West Virginia University, USA

Chapter 18
Games Beyond the Screen: Festivals of Play Across the Western World 377
  William Zachary Wood, Stanford University, USA

Compilation of References 397

About the Contributors 446

Index 454

Detailed Table of Contents

Foreword xvi

Preface xx

Acknowledgment xxxiv

Chapter 1
Toward Broader Definitions of "Video Games": Shifts in Narrative, Player Goals, Subject Matter,
and Digital Play Environments 1
    Lucas John Jensen, Georgia Southern University, USA
    Daisyane Barreto, University of North Carolina – Wilmington, USA
    Keri Duncan Valentine, West Virginia University, USA

As video games grow in popularity, ambition, scope, and technological prowess, they also mature as an art form, shedding old definitions tethered to video games as simple, competitive exercises. Greater technological capabilities, in addition to years of experimentation and maturation, have expanded the ability of games to tell different kinds of stories, offering branching paths. The question of "what makes a game a game?" looms larger than ever in this era of video game storytelling. As plots and characters grow, branch, and develop, so, too, do the boundaries of what a game actually is. In traditional definitions of gaming, a set of rules and a victory condition were essential elements to a game. As game narratives and game mechanics grow in increasingly complex and experimental directions, new player goals have emerged. Now, gamers socialize, customize, nurture, kill, build, destroy, break, glitch, and explore as much as they work to win and accrue points. This chapter surveys the current landscape of video games, highlighting examples and trends that challenge more traditional notions and definitions of what it means to be a "video game." The broader definition presented here takes into account play, narrative, digital environments, and more, acknowledging the expanse of the video game experience.

Chapter 2
Telling Tales with Technology: Remediating Folklore and Myth through the Videogame *Alan
Wake* 38
    Dawn Catherine Stobbart, Lancaster University, UK

This chapter analyses the 2010 videogame *Alan Wake*, a narrative based videogame that makes frequent use of intertextuality. As well as using contemporary examples, the game also uses traditional international folklore in its narrative, with the antagonist Barbara Jagger being recognisable as the Russian folk tale character Baba Yaga, for example. Using the concepts proposed and elucidated by Vladimir Propp, Joseph

Campbell, the chapter will first establish that the videogame offers a remediation of several traditional mythical narratives in one contemporary videogame, before going on to use the classifications found in *The Morphology of the Folktale* and *The Hero with a Thousand Faces* to place this videogame within the folklore and mythical tradition. It will also serve to establish whether these classifications are suitable for the narratives found in videogames, and if they depart from them, where the scholar needs to establish new concepts and definitions for these traditional classifications.

Chapter 3

"There Are No Observers Here": The Video Game Gaze in *Outlast* (2013) and *Outlast: Whistleblower* (2014) 54
   Hazel E. Monforton, University of Durham, UK

As an emergent medium capable of telling complex stories, the video game gives us unique insight and challenges to established critical theory. This chapter will examine the ways 'the gaze' is expressed and utilized in video games, particularly the "survival horror" genre. It will discuss some of the ways 'the gaze' has been shaped by literary and filmic studies before turning to *Outlast* (2013) by Red Barrels Games as an example of the way the medium can rearticulate our understanding of watching and being watched. Through its player-driven diegesis, immersion and phenomenologically-situated avatar body, and an ability to stimulate emotional response through game mechanics, the video game gaze might be capable of engendering emotional sympathy rather than constructing hierarchical positions of mastery. With its narratives of state control and institutionalization, journalistic distance, and medical invasiveness, *Outlast* uses critical understandings of 'the gaze' to ask questions about privacy, complicity, and responsibility.

Chapter 4

The Game Space of *Dear Esther* and Beyond: Perspective Shift and the Subversion of Player Agency 73
   Harrington Weihl, Northwestern University, USA

This chapter argues that the spaces created by video games are central to the formulation of player agency in the game. More precisely, this chapter analyzes several recent independent and experimental games—*Dear Esther, Menagerie,* and the work of games collective Arcane Kids—to argue that the dislocation or alienation of player agency through the formal category of game space has political and aesthetic significance. The dislocation of player agency sees 'agency' taken away from the player and granted instead to the game space itself; players are placed at the mercy of the game space in such a way that their lack of agency is emphasized. The effect of this emphasis is to enable these games to critique the atomized, neoliberal undercurrents of contemporary cultural production.

Chapter 5
Apportioned Commodity Fetishism and the Transformative Power of Game Studies 95

Ken S. McAllister, University of Arizona, USA
Judd Ethan Ruggill, University of Arizona, USA
Tobias Conradi, ZeM – Brandenburgisches Zentrum für Medienwissenschaften, Germany
Steven Conway, Swinburne University of Technology, Australia
Jennifer deWinter, Worcester Polytechnic Institute, USA
Chris Hanson, Syracuse University, USA
Carly A. Kocurek, Illinois Institute of Technology, USA
Kevin A. Moberly, Old Dominion University, USA
Randy Nichols, University of Washington Tacoma, USA
Rolf F. Nohr, Hochschule für Bildende Künste Braunschweig, Germany
Marc A. Ouellette, Old Dominion University, USA

This chapter explores the ways in which the field of Game Studies helps shape popular understandings of player, play, and game, and specifically how the field alters the conceptual, linguistic, and discursive apparatuses that gamers use to contextualize, describe, and make sense of their experiences. The chapter deploys the concept of apportioned commodity fetishism to analyze the phenomena of discourse as practice, persona, the vagaries of game design, recursion, lexical formation, institutionalization, systems of self-effectiveness, theory as anti-theory, and commodification.

Chapter 6
Co-Creation and the Distributed Authorship of Video Games 123

Stephanie C Jennings, Rensselaer Polytechnic Institute, USA

This chapter reconceptualizes the authorship of video games through the development of a theory of distributed authorship. It defines distributed authorship as the interplay of negotiated capacities of a number of actors (including but not limited to developers, publishers, and players) to create the content, structures, form, and affordances of video game works. However, the theory does not assume that these actors always work together collaboratively or that capacities for authorship are shared equally among them. Rather, distributed authorship understands the authorship of video games as a relationship of power—the power to create, shape, and influence video game works.

Chapter 7
She Designs Therefore She Is? Evolving Understandings of Video Game Design 147

Carolyn Michelle Cunningham, Gonzaga University, USA

Girls and women play video games in equal number to boys, yet they continue to be under-represented in the video game industry. The goal of this chapter is to examine initiatives that encourage gender equality in video game design. This chapter argues that the process of becoming a video game designer may have the potential to shift girls' notions of identity. Drawing on research on girls and video game design, as well as analyses of informal programs that teach girls video game design, this chapter emphasizes the intersection of design and identity. This chapter offers directions and recommendations for future research, including the need for expanded understandings of the cultural and democratic benefits of video game design for girls.

Chapter 8

Gaming before E-Sports: Playing with Gender in Early Gaming Communities, 1993-2001 170
Marley-Vincent Lindsey, Brown University, USA

Discussions of competitive gaming often begin and end with the development of professional E-Sports. However, competitive gaming has a history that stretches back to the first days of networked play with first generation games like *Doom*, *Warcraft II* and Multi-User Dungeons (Henceforth MUDs). Within these games, digital communities became a prominent means of discourse and discussion, heavily reliant on gender as a habit of thought to describe inequality and disparities between players. Using an archive of Warcraft II histories, and forum threads for the game, this chapter describes a social history of this digital community with specific emphasis on the ways that gender was used.

Chapter 9

Serious Games Teaching Values: Discussing Games Dealing with Human Rights Issues 195
Sonja Gabriel, KPH Vienna/Krems, Austria

The number of serious games dealing with human right issues has increased in recent years. All of them want to teach/present certain values and make players think about the contents presented. Therefore, it is interesting to have a closer look at different ways of how these games try to integrate values. After discussing the development of human rights digital games in brief, this chapter is going to have a look at various game elements that can express and embody values. Several examples will illustrate how games might more or less successfully deal with human rights and values. Finally, some research results will be presented discussing what serious games might be able to achieve.

Chapter 10

Affordances and Constraints of Analog Games for Ethics Education: Dilemmas and Dragons 219
Spencer P. Greenhalgh, Michigan State University, USA

Today's students face a wide range of complex moral dilemmas, and games have the potential to represent these dilemmas, thereby supporting formal ethics education. The potential of digital games to contribute in this way is being increasingly recognized, but the author argues that those interested in the convergence of games, ethics, and education should more fully consider analog games (i.e., games without a digital component). This argument draws from a qualitative study that focused on the use of an analog roleplaying game in an undergraduate activity that explored ethical issues related to politics, society, and culture. The results of this study are examined through an educational technology lens, which suggests that games (like other educational resources) afford and constrain learning and teaching in certain ways. These results demonstrate that this game afforded and constrained ethics education in both ways similar to digital games and ways unique to analog games.

Chapter 11

Knowledge Production in E-Sports Culture: Learning with and from the Masters 238
Robert James Hein, The Pennsylvania State University, USA
Jason A. Engerman, The Pennsylvania State University, USA

Competitive video games, commonly referred to as "e-sports," are becoming increasingly popular among young. However, unlike more traditional, physical sports, these video games blur the lines between their participants and spectators, encouraging veterans and newcomers alike to become contributing members evolving, digital affinity spaces. Bolstered by the affordances of live-streaming technology, e-sports culture constantly gathers its experts and novices together to play, compete, and discuss in real time. These inclusive practices help to facilitate the rapid knowledge and skill acquisition of all of its community members. Consequently, this chapter will explore how and why e-sports culture successfully champions participation and mastery learning. Likewise, the authors will discuss what teachers can learn and apply from this culture's values.

Chapter 12
Gaming to Increase Reading Skills: A Case Study.. 258
    Laura Kieran, Drake University, USA
    Christine Anderson, Western Illinois University, USA

When considering instructional supports for struggling adolescent readers, scholars suggested that the interventions be comprehensive, include a variety of authentic reading and writing opportunities, and be based on varied assessment data. The researchers developed a schedule for Maya, an 8th grade student to work on vocabulary and reading comprehension via games that reviewed discreet skills as well as social media per Maya's preferences. The use of technology interventions for Maya allowed her to read, listen to, and think about meaningful texts, while maintaining balance with instruction in skills related to reading for a variety of purposes.

Chapter 13
Game/Write: Gameplay as a Factor in College-Level Literacy and Writing Ability......................... 272
    Sandy Baldwin, Rochester Institute of Technology, USA
    Nicholas D. Bowman, West Virginia University, USA
    John Jones, West Virginia University, USA

This chapter explores the potential correlation between college students' leisurely video game experience and their narrative composition writing ability in a first-semester university writing course. This exploratory survey data report moderate correlations between students' aggregated video game experience (years spent playing) and their ability to articulate tension and turn, and use proper organization in composition assignments, notably a diagnostic essay assigned on the first day of class, prior to formal instruction. Findings suggest that leisure gameplay might help develop competency with the same cognitive and creative skills related to written narrative ability by exposing players – in particular, adolescents – to elements of narrative through the gameplay process, facilitating the learning of these skills in the classroom. In conclusion, the authors suggest areas for future research on this topic.

Chapter 14
Implementing a Game-Based Instructional Design Strategy in the Eighth Grade Science
Classroom: Teaching Science the *Chutes and Ladders* Way!... 292
    Angela Dowling, Suncrest Middle School, USA
    Terence C. Ahern, West Virginia University, USA

This chapter examines the effects of a game-like environment on instructional activity design and learning outcomes in a middle school general science class. The authors investigated if science content can be designed and successfully delivered instructionally using a game-like learning environment. The authors also wanted to investigate if by utilizing a game-design method could class and student engagement be increased. The results indicated that the instructional design of the unit using a game-like environment was successful and students exhibited learning. The authors also address the challenges inherent in utilizing this instructional strategy.

Chapter 15

Jamming Econo: The Phenomenon of Perspectival Shifts in Indie Video Games 309

Keri Duncan Valentine, West Virginia University, USA

Lucas John Jensen, Georgia Southern University, USA

By their nature, video games create perspectival relationships between the game space, with its mechanics, characters, etc. and their players. Perspectival mechanics in games like *Monument Valley* and *Fez* require one to simultaneously transform the environment, the objects in the environment, and one's egocentric reference frames, illustrating the complex nature intrinsic to video game spaces. The authors seek to investigate the ways perspectival mechanics in video games are both created and experienced using postphenomenological inquiry. This investigation is situated within the indie genre of games in particular, a context where these mechanics are intentionally being explored. In addition, this chapter draws parallels between indie games and indie music, contexts where boundary pushing is the norm. In addition to explicating the phenomenon of perspectival shifts in indie games, the authors review research related to spatial thinking, conjecturing affordances of indie games as geometric gifts, possibly well positioned to support spatial thinking.

Chapter 16

Playful Experiments: Conditions of "An Experience" in Touchscreen Games by a Non-Hermeneutic Perspective 343

Felippe Calazans Thomaz, Federal University of Bahia, Brazil

Jorge Cardoso Filho, Federal University from Recôncavo of Bahia, Brazil

This study investigates the conditions to aesthetic experience in games for touchscreen devices from a non-hermeneutic perspective. For that reason, the body and the technical devices are taken as fundamental dimensions in the process of having "an experience", in which their material aspects are not indifferent. In other words, what is of interest is to analyze game situations and the mutual influence between player and game, in the sense of identifying elements that could lead to "an experience", taking as objects the games *Mountain* and *Monument Valley*. Moreover, concerns to understand how such titles contribute to the broadening of the technoludic experience. The article is sustained in the induction that from the moment in which characteristics of traditional games are tensioned, it seems that they assume an air of experimentation in their ways of calling to action. We argue that "an experience" can emerge from the articulation between "effects of presence" and "effects of meaning", so that the material constitution of the medium is not indifferent.

Chapter 17

Games People Play: A Trilateral Collaboration Researching Computer Gaming across Cultures 364

Sandy Baldwin, Rochester Institute of Technology, USA

Kwabena Opoku-Agyemang, West Virginia University, USA

Dibyadyuti Roy, West Virginia University, USA

The study of various choices made while producing and playing games allows little opportunity for interrogating video games as a transcultural convergence of multiple subjectivities and institutions. This chapter speaks to this topic by presenting the Computer Games Across Cultures (CGAC) project. CGAC involved humanities researchers from West Virginia University (USA), Bangor University (Wales), and Jawaharlal Nehru University (India) who over a two-year period sought to understand creative and cultural aspects of gaming. CGAC's researchers employed both qualitative and quantitative methodologies to bridge the gap between the academic explorations of gaming in tandem with industry-specific practices within such spaces. This chapter provides an overview of the resultant work through its analysis of a cross-section of games. Examining both Western mainstream games and lesser known games from places like India and Ghana helped interrogate representational politics in videogames and provide a broader view of the relationship between gaming and game making, in a socio-cultural context.

Chapter 18

Games Beyond the Screen: Festivals of Play Across the Western World... 377
  William Zachary Wood, Stanford University, USA

This chapter introduces a phenomenon that has gone largely unaddressed in research since its emergence in western countries in the last decade: festivals of games and play. The bulk of the chapter is drawn from interviews with people involved in these festivals, including founders, current organizers and game designers, using this data to build on the work of researchers on play and playfulness. Taking an autoethnographic stance, the author speaks from personal experience as a participant and game designer in order to convey these festivals' unique qualities and potential as sites for public play.

Compilation of References 397

About the Contributors 446

Index.. 454

Foreword

Introduction to the Evolution of Gaming

Writing an introduction to the "evolution" of games (videogames, non-digital games or otherwise) feels daunting. Actually, it is probably that I'm simply being difficult about it. As an anthropologist of game development, game developer and a player of games, I feel like I have a sense of their evolutionary flows. Yet my training comes from the strange interdisciplinary field of Science and Technology Studies, which, perhaps predictably, means that my first response isn't, "Indeed… Games have changed," but rather, "What is evolution anyway? Have games evolved?" Thus, I apologize in advance for what comes next.

I suspect that if I were to ask an Executive Producer at Electronic Arts, Nintendo or Sony if games have evolved, they would likely answer in a kind of resounding, "Yes, of course!" Evolution appeals to a kind of market-based logic that dominates the mainstream "triple-A" or "AAA" game industry. Market logics plug directly into the narrative of "natural selection" or that "the strong survive," which should not be equated to evolution by any means, though it is often how it is imagined. Shifts in computational power and the rise of technologies also, sort of, lend themselves to this kind of grand evolutionary narrative. Darwinism, as it is frequently argued, fits well into broader social and cultural conceptions of meritocracy and might makes right. Comfortable narratives of progress and infinite growth should probably make anyone nervous.

At this precise moment, it is that mainstream industry that is undergoing seismic tectonic shifts. I frequently tell students that the shifts we are seeing in the game industry, if we can even consider such a monolithic concept to even exist, parallel those of 1984-5. To which, I pose the question, what kind of evolution are we witnessing in that case? What species will emerge from this particular epoch? Because, the reality is that evolution is much more complicated than the overly simplified vision of it as a kind of capitalist market economy for DNA or a "survival of the fittest." Rather, something far more interesting is going on when we advance the idea that games have evolved and that the implications of those shifts have had broad social, cultural and political ramifications.

This is a perspective that others and I have advanced on numerous occasions: That games and the craft of game development have dramatic implications for society, culture and our political economic systems. I've gone so far as to say that games in/as/of/through culture ought to be how we understand this particular cultural form (Malaby, 2009; O'Donnell, 2014). So, I've clearly drunk the Kool-Aid that forms the foundation of many of the entries contained herein. But, what if we take the metaphor of evolution seriously in the context of this collected volume? Not the Darwinism as Market Capitalism metaphor, but rather a reading of evolution as one also rooted in epigenetics through which a variety of factors may come to influence the evolutionary traits passed down over the years.

I once quipped that evolution makes a really boring game mechanic, because like diffusion and all sorts of other natural processes, it just kind of happens. And the idea that there is a kind of guiding hand for evolution lands us quickly in the hands of people arguing for the teaching of "intelligent" design. Yet, we clearly do shape and are shaped by our own activities when you look at the current state of evolution. Monsanto is in the business of intelligent design. High-fructose corn syrup and the human (at least the American) body demands that we face the fact that we are manipulating these systems in ways we don't fully understand. To which I can then ask, what kind of monsters are we making (O'Donnell, 2015)?

Now, to be clear, I'm not sailing down an epigenetic stream where thoughts can cure cancer, but rather that genetic regulation and expression are complex factors subject to a wide array of factors. It allows us to think, in particular, about things like toxicology and the ways in which genetics, and thus evolution, have become imbricated by a complex heritage that implicates human activity and non-human activity in the future of evolutionary processes.

I don't know if I'd go so far as to call games a kind of "companion species," but that might be a reasonable starting point for thinking through from an evolutionary perspective where games have come from and where they are going. Not unlike dogs, games serve as a kind of "obligatory, constitutive, historical, protean relationship" with humanity (Haraway, 2003, p. 12). Games are part of us as much as our companion species, and while not biological in the same sense, they've kind of always been with us along the way and mutated, shifted, moved, grown and evolved along side us. And they have returned the favor, in all likelihood manipulating us as well.

In many ways, the metaphor works well for the evolution of games. Much like dog breeds, particular kinds of games have enjoyed more or less care over time. We have deliberately cultivated particular traits and neglected others. Some breeds have thrived and others have suffered under the less watchful eyes of their breeders. Mutts, mongrels, half-breeds and hybrid breeds have emerged for a variety of reasons. Not unlike dogs, games have served in both war and peace. They both reflect and reflect back on broader social and cultural shifts.

Which is why exploring the co-evolution of games makes particular sense at this moment in their (our) history (histories). Which is why asking questions about what are games is important. Our definition of what counts as a game or videogame is of crucial import. Calling attention to particularly important, compelling, notable or infamous games provides a compelling story for how we might want to think about our co-evolutionary existence with these things that are both simultaneously frivolous and incredibly meaningful.

Games implicate us in this co-evolutionary moment. As Monforton notes in this volume, "There are no observers here." Well, there are, but they too are implicated in this whole system. Twitch.tv has made what was always the case even more abundantly clear. We are playing even when we are observing. Certainly as someone who teaches at a "Division I" sports university, I can attest to the role that a spectator plays when they too step into the magic circles called "stadiums" where games like Basketball, Football (of the American variety) and Hockey are played. And yet, I can also recall quite fondly times spent watching my cousin play *The Legend of Zelda: A Link to the Past* on his Super Nintendo Entertainment System. I was the keeper of the strategy guide as he played along.

It also makes the role of Game Studies, as a field, if we can imagine that such a unified field exists, all the more critical. If games are evolving along with us, then they are a thing worth studying in their own right. Not simply because they can be "games for change" or "serious games" or "games for health."

Games are important. Part of the evolution of games is understanding them as important in their own right. Indeed, we can look to them for sites where formal or informal learning occurs, but that isn't why they're important. Games may be sites where we can understand how "effects" of games occur, but that isn't why they're important. They're important because they simultaneously mean something and mean nothing at all. The meaningful and meaninglessness of them intertwines in ways that make them special.

So too have games had strange entanglements with how we understand femininity and masculinity. The embodied nature of games and play often cannot be avoided. Even in "virtual" spaces we embody avatars that embody us, or not. This may even be more intense when we extend our understandings of games to sports. One might even argue that is one reason why scholars studying games have been recalcitrant in their pursuit of studying sports games. It is hard to avoid when videogames begin to become more sports-like. Competition is fierce in sports and bodies matter in ways that complicate our understanding of them, and yet games, precisely by their designed character, mean that often times we make uncomfortable choices about what counts and what doesn't.

But none of this is really new. It has been a part of the human experience all along. Games have moved with us and changed with the times. We can't say that only the text of a game matters, or that only players matter or that only the developers matter. In this complicated system all of the components matter. As researchers of games (or makers of games or those studying creators of games) we make decisions about which aspects of the system we examine, yet, all matter simultaneously. So, we continue to muddle through our study of them and of ourselves. Games both help and hinder our understanding of the world. They simultaneously over-complicate and simplify things. That is what makes them interesting.

While some might argue that games have "simply" changed to mirror the political-economic moment of the times, I think that neglects the kinship ties that games have with us and with themselves. They change how we think about a great many things. Education is one particularly salient more or less playful system that games have forced us to think quite differently about. I cannot help but look at the DNA (aka "structure") of the "big bad game industry" in 2008 and its subsequent mutations through 2014 implicated in what eventually became #GAMERGATE on Twitter (and in real life) (Chess & Shaw, 2015). The shifting structure of games and our relationship with them was under shift and change. Little wonder there were those who once defined and defended one "breed" over another would find discomfort in the "destruction" of a particular species. When what was ultimately happening was that the ecosystem was diversifying. But tell that to the species that feels under threat.

Games have evolved not because we've brought them along with us. Games have evolved because they've changed us as much as we've changed them. This volume seeks to take very seriously (or not, because that's part of the point) the broader social, political, economic, educational, fun, serious, silly, salient, designed, sad or otherwise role that games have in our current moment. This isn't a sign that games have "come of age," but rather that we, collectively, have come of age to understand the role that these systems have in our broader human, collective journey.

The window at the end of the hallway in which my office is located looks out on what I often refer to as, "the church of football." I transitioned from being a Georgia Bulldog to being a Michigan State Spartan in recent years, but both stadiums definitely border on religious. Think about how the game of football has changed even in recent history. College ball and "professional" ball are certainly related breeds, but also different in not unimportant ways. College ball is as much a professional endeavor for those that pursue it. I sat and watched this last year a Spartan football game up in the "nosebleed" seats and watched as three young athletes were micro-profiled on giant screens that also informed me that Mountain Dew was now the "official" beverage of the Spartan Nation. These screens informed me as to which videogames were these athletes favorite growing up: *The Legend of Zelda* (and I can only surmise that this was actually *Ocarina of Time* but I'll not split hairs), *Super Mario Kart* and *Golden Eye 007*. Clearly we have a Nintendo 64 generation on our hands. But this tells us something about games. They mean things to us.

This is why we study the evolution of games.

Casey O'Donnell
Michigan State University, USA

REFERENCES

Chess, S., & Shaw, A. (2015). A Conspiracy of Fishes, or, How We Learned to Stop Worrying About #GamerGate and Embrace Hegemonic Masculinity. *Journal of Broadcasting & Electronic Media, 59*(1), 208–220. doi:10.1080/08838151.2014.999917

Haraway, D. J. (2003). *The Companion Species Manifesto: Dogs, People, and Significant Otherness.* Chicago, IL: Prickly Paradigm Press.

Malaby, T. M. (2009). Anthropology and Play: The Contours of Playful Experience. *New Literary History, 40*(1), 205–218. doi:10.1353/nlh.0.0079

O'Donnell, C. (2014). On Balinese Cockfights: Deeply Extending Play. *Games and Culture, 9*(6), 406–416. doi:10.1177/1555412014545783

O'Donnell, C. (2015). In Search of Hopeful Monsters: A Special Issue from the International Conference on Meaningful Play. *International Journal of Gaming and Computer-Mediated Simulations, 7*(3), iv–vii.

Preface

THE TIME OUR KIDS CHEERED PROTEUS AND OTHER STORIES

It's beautiful - look at that! It's an asteroid belt. And the moon! Look at the shooting stars!

That was Matthew (names have been changed to protect the innocent), a cherubic young camper/game designer at a video game design-based summer youth program run by this book's editors. And he was not alone in his fascination with the strange 8-bit-gone-2D/3D world projected in front of the classroom, pastel colors flickering across his eyes. A group of mostly young boys, ages 11-17, yelled—in a complete abdication of the "inside voice" concept—directions at the poor, befuddled camper stuck guiding the first-person character via the mouse and keyboard controls.

Together, the class was playing *Proteus* (Key & Kanaga, 2013), a video game so experimental that its developer once had to take to the company blog to defend its very status as a game (Key, 2013). To describe *Proteus* is difficult; the player explores a randomly generated island with flat, forward-facing 2D objects that emit tones, pulses, and musical swells. It would be a dramatic understatement to call *Proteus's* narrative flow non-traditional. The game has no dialogue, no text beyond the menus, and no buttons with which to interact. The player advances the "story" by exploring this pixelated hybrid 2D/3D landscape that one camper described to us as "Atari 3D." The objects in *Proteus* look flat, chunky, and pixelated, all rendered in a smooth high-definition, first-person environment where objects always face forward.

Chase the frog...follow the wisp. Wait, you can crouch. How did you do that?

In the middle! In the middle! See all the gravestones? Go down! Look, they're (the wisps) going that way!

But the crystal light – they might lead you to possible death. You probably become one of the gravestones.

They're going in all directions! Where are they going? Go that way! Go that way! They're moving that direction – follow them!

Of course, games—even single-player video games—can be powerful participatory and shared experiences. Much like the author of the book's foreword, Casey O'Donnell, we grew up playing ostensible single-player games like *Metroid* (Nintendo, 1986b), the *Legend of Zelda* (Nintendo, 1986a), and *Super Mario Bros.* (Nintendo, 1985) as multiplayer participatory experiences, passing Nintendo Entertainment System controllers back and forth in a collaborative effort to defeat the games. As O'Donnell and others throughout this book note, games serve as a powerful social connector. One needs to look no further than the flourishing world of e-sports and video game streaming to witness the boundaries between video game playing and spectatorship collapsing.

E-sports and the communities that grow around video games provide the historical context for two of the chapters in this book. Chapter 8 examines the use of gendered, homophobic, and sexually violent insults in competitive gaming online communities before the arrival of professional e-sports. The authors of Chapter 11 argue that e-sports and the live-streaming of video games might create "affinity spaces" for cognitive apprenticeship, where novices learn from experts through communities built around each game's live stream.

We found a house! Forget the crystals, people! See if you can go inside. Oh, there's a door! See if you can go inside. No, you can't. Touch it. Follow the fairies (back to the fairies). They're everywhere. They froze. They're frozen. Oh, they're crowding around that area. Okay, they're moving! All the fairies – did you just get trapped? Turn around – it's right there – touch it! We're at the edge! So the farther away you go from that…Show him the fairy thingy – show him the gravestone circle. There's the house again. Go to the house and see if the leaves don't fall.

What makes this experience even more odd is that *Proteus* is a "de facto" music game: each pixelated frog, tree, or statue gives off a tone, so the randomly generated island is one giant ambient music generator. And yet the kids were cheering *Proteus* with the sound off because the speakers in the room were malfunctioning. Here is *Proteus*, one of the most infamous of a group of experimental games often tagged with the pejorative "walking simulator," games where exploration and experiencing the game world and/or narrative—and, to be sure, *Proteus's* narrative is quite opaque—is more important than the player scoring points or killing the bad guy or rescuing the princess. Because of *Proteus'* experimental art style and dearth of combat, dialogue, or goals, it made an unorthodox candidate for this shared, participatory experience. *Proteus* is a video game so inscrutable that academic and designer Ian Bogost (2013) approached this notorious "not a game" from three different "artisanal" angles in one review. For him, a game so "unusual"—or perhaps any video game—necessitates dissection using multiple critical lenses, much like a movie might be deconstructed on more than one level, from aesthetic and technical concerns like cinematography or screenwriting, to its symbolism or implicit political message.

Its unique approach to narrative and aesthetics has put *Proteus* at the forefront of debates about what makes a video game a "video game" and whether some video games are even games at all (Key,

2013). These young campers cheering *Proteus* like a spectator sport are not regular avant garde game enthusiasts. Their tastes, while diverse, still adhere to the most popular game series of the day: *Call of Duty*; *Minecraft*; *Smash Brothers*; *Minecraft*; *Grand Theft Auto*; *Minecraft*; *Pokémon*; and *Minecraft*. Boundary-pushing genre and indie games like *Portal* (Valve Corporation, 2007), and *Papers, Please* (Pope, 2013) are popular, but rarely do these campers' tastes veer into more experimental games where the notion of "winning" is subsumed by other concerns like storytelling or atmosphere. In *Proteus'* case, we observed its unusual aesthetic, with its "flat" 3D and dripping 8-bit trees, engaging the campers the most. These aesthetics stood in stark contrast to the sepia-toned shooters that occupied so much of their mental real estate.

Video games have matured and are offering trailblazing, challenging, and alternative perspectives and points-of-view, through idiosyncratic combinations of the social, interactive, audio, spatial, and visual aspects of video games. Chapter 1 surveys the new video game landscape and explores how these new experiences are changing our traditional notions of what a game can or should be. The independent game sphere precipitated much of this challenge to dominant industry paradigms, by introducing these novel and provocative aesthetics and player perspectives. Chapter 15 compares this to the classic hardcore, punk, DIY, and indie movements of the 80s and 90s and how those values are represented in the perspectival shifting game mechanics of games like *Monument Valley* (Ustwo, 2014), *Fez* (Polytron Corporation, 2012), and *Proteus*. Indie games *Outlast* (Red Barrels, 2013) and *Dear Esther* (The Chinese Room, 2012), discussed in Chapters 3 and 4, respectively, create much of their tension by subverting player agency. The player in *Dear Esther* canvasses a lonely randomly generated island, much like *Proteus*, in search of a narrative doled out in pieces out of the player's control. In *Outlast*, discussed at length in Chapter 3, the player uses a video camera to document the gruesome horrors at an insane asylum run amuck. The player-as-video camera serves as an effective and scary narrative hook as well as a proxy embodiment of the surveillance state.

GAMING WITHOUT GOALS: WALL OF MINECRAFT

How was your weekend, Colin?

Pretty good, I guess. I was super depressed and shaky, but then I realized I just needed to play some Minecraft.

This actual exchange with a student decked out in a *Minecraft* hoodie and t-shirt is the stuff of parental nightmares, a confirmation of all the alarmist news stories about video game addiction and gamers dying from dehydration in Internet cafes. Sometimes it feels like physical force is necessary to separate children (and some adults) from the infinite Lego sandbox that is *Minecraft* (Mojang, 2011), the video game phenomenon that fetched billions of dollars from Microsoft. Some play and game theorists have suggested that there are four types of play: play for progress; play for power; play for fantasy; and play for self (Pellegrini, 1995; Rieber, 1996; Sutton-Smith, 2009). Others have said that gamers can be killers, explorers, achievers, or socializers (Bartle, 1996). We have observed all of these behaviors among kids playing *Minecraft*, so perhaps the possibility space it creates scratches the idiosyncratic needs of its different players.

We witnessed this phenomenon ourselves, manifested in the Wall of *Minecraft*, six children who played nonstop *Minecraft* on a row of computers against a wall, impervious to outside influence and distractions. They swapped between various mods—player-created modifications to the game's core systems—and servers that housed different universes to explore, fluent not just in *Minecraft's* internal rules, but also in the "meta"-game of mods, servers, YouTube *Minecraft* celebrities, and more. Did we mention that kids today like *Minecraft*? One of us jokingly referred to *Minecraft* as "The Great Equalizer"—Southern children from different socioeconomic classes, ethnicities, and religions—all playing games for different reasons and in different ways, united under the banner of this blocky randomly-generated playground. A few of the Minecrafters enjoyed the crafting elements, discovering new tools and blocks. Others focus on the building mechanic itself. Another just liked to explore and view everyone else's creations. A couple were determined to beat the EnderDragon, the putative goal of *Minecraft*. One young girl approached *Minecraft* with the ethics of Sun Tzu, treating a non-competitive game as a competition, stealing or sabotaging everyone else's stuff when they were not looking.

Within the Wall of *Minecraft* alone, we had kids playing for all of the reasons listed above, to be killers and explorers, to play for progress and fantasy, and to play for self, as Colin recounted. We have often debated as to whether the kids' obsession with this world of never-ending Legos was a "good thing," in part because we wanted them to "go outside," so to speak, and experience new games and worlds beyond *Minecraft*. But, perhaps like all debates about whether something was a "good thing" or not, from *Dungeons & Dragons* (Gygax & Arneson, 1974) to *Grand Theft Auto* (DMA Design, 1997) before them, this is the wrong debate, and we should look to how a game like *Minecraft* satisfies so many needs of such a large, diverse group of players, young and old alike. Just like the Swedish-developed *Minecraft* can appeal to a diverse group of children in the United States, Chapter 17 holds up a mirror to the cultural dimensions of games and game design while examining video games' increasing global influence. Similarly, Chapter 18 considers the importance of public games across the world, emphasizing the global cultural importance of community play that is not always connected to a game controller or a screen. Even with its technological trappings, *Minecraft* increasingly resembles as much a community as a game, from the playground conversations and layers of meta-content around it, the numerous servers and mods, to the live-streaming of *Minecraft* on Twitch and YouTube. One can even find specialized *Minecraft* parkour videos on YouTube.

EXPLORING FLATLAND: JUXTAPOSING CASES AS ALTERNATIVE PERSPECTIVE

One of the editors is a former middle school mathematics teacher whose most pivotal moment was problematizing space and perspective with 5th – 8th graders, incited by the short film *Flatland: The Movie* (Caplan, Wallace, Travis, & Johnson, 2007). "Is there a fourth dimension?" is the typical initial question this film inspires, following the rotating 4-dimensional cube (aka, tesseract, hypercube) expanded during the last scene. Building on this experience, she designed a hypermedia site (https://spaceandperspective.com) to support eighth grade learners investigation of cases as alternative perspective (Valentine & Kopcha, in press). One set of cases focused on video games like *Asteroids* (Atari Inc., 1979), *Portal* (Valve Corporation, 2007), and *Super Paper Mario* (Intelligent Systems, 2007). These video game cases became "geometric gifts" to support learners problematization of geometric shape and the dimensional qualities of these worlds. Alistar, one of the students, recounted this time as one where he found his gamer identity shifting:

Before, I just liked games that were big, you know were fun, interesting — I didn't really care if they did anything new. And with indie games, a lot of them with their art styles and their mechanics like Fez kind feel like they're almost taken from like different perspectives in space where every game feels different in that regard.

A typical console, blockbuster-loving gamer became mesmerized by games that messed with space and perspective, especially *Fez* (Polytron Corporation, 2012). However, he didn't just play *Fez* for enjoyment, he wanted to re-skin *Fez* and tell the story of *Flatland* – a story about A. Square, a 4-sided polygon who lives on a plane. For Alistar, there were many parallels between A. Square's visit to the third dimension and Gomez's, the main character in *Fez*, ability to rotate his two-dimensional world in order to traverse the landscape.

So when I first bought Fez—this was right after the Space and Perspective class—I was interested and I had heard of this game before and I bought it. I played through the entire game and I thought it was great. Then I came across this guy on YouTube who had taken another game—like a space fighting game and made a modification where he actually converted the entire game and redesigned all the skins for everything—made all the different weapons for everything. And he made it a Star Wars game, which was kind of interesting. So what I've been trying to do is redesign Fez to kind of pretty much be Flatland.

Alistar is now in high school, taking classes in programming and video editing—anything that he sees helping him accomplish his goal to mod *Fez*. Not only is Alistar attune to the ability of games to mess with perspective, or create impossible perspectives, he is motivated by a desire to integrate the 1884 satire of *Flatland: A Romance of Many Dimensions* (Abbott, 1991) into an experience that only video games can accomplish. More about Alistar's experience is explicated in Chapter 15.

SIZING UP KATAMARIS

[Paraphrased from the original conversation]

So I can suck up that cat?

When you get bigger, yeah. As you get bigger, well, more like wider, you can pick up bigger things.

I want to suck up that cat.

Yeah, that feels good. I like to pick up cinder blocks. I don't know why. It's just cool to pull them out of the ground because they're so heavy.

{later in the level}

Oh, cool, I'm picking up trees. I was just bouncing off them.

Yeah, it kinda picks up steam as you get bigger. In the last level, you're picking up islands and clouds and stuff.

So I was just here when I was small and now I'm eating it?

Yeah.

That's [insert 'cool,' 'amazing,' 'awesome,' or whatever the kids are saying these days].

Truthfully, the exact superlative our camper used to describe *Katamari Damacy* (Namco, 2004) has been lost to the ages, but the look on his face displayed the mediation going on inside his brain, as he wrestled with the concepts. In his book, *The Meaning of Video Games*, Steven Jones (2008) attributes part of the *Katamari Damacy's* unique appeal to a consumerist post-Ebay collectible-obsessed world, and, to be sure, there was a bit of that "gotta collect them all" completism going on here. But what motivated Jason was the size and scale of it all, that his tiny little ball had now grown into a world-destroying monster boulder and that he could watch grow on the diameter meter with every tree that stuck to it. His brain was working through the cognitive dissonance of the greater size and how small everything now looked on screen as compared to the earlier experience of being smaller than mice, pencils, and playing cards. He was contemplating volume and mass, all while playing a resolutely unrealistic, absurdist videogame, similar to the artificial flatness of *Fez*. The worlds of these games had a powerful affect on young learners.

Educators are well aware of these informal game experiences to contribute to learning; some educators, researchers, and game designers even seek to formalize this type of learning, creating games like *Quest Atlantis* (Barab, Thomas, Dodge, Carteaux, & Tuzun, 2005). In this book, several chapters describe games as a means to motivate and advance conceptual understandings of young learners. For example, Chapter 14 explores research on teaching science in a game-like environment, describing the benefits (and considerations) for motivation and learning. Chapter 12 presents a case study that uses games and social media as a way to increase an adolescent's literacy skills. However, it is important to point out that using games for educative purposes is wrought with complexity—formalizing informal experiences is not always well received by learners, nor are games that focus on teaching concepts always well designed. In the journal, *Science*, editor-in-chief Bruce Alberts expressed dismay at the state of what passed for "science" questions in a recent edition of *Trivial Pursuit*, but also how closely it resembled the rote memorization and regurgitation of facts that characterizes much science education in schools (2012). Even though he calls *Trivial Pursuit* "merely a game," Alberts sees how the simplicity of *Trivial Pursuit*'s science section is reflected by poor science education and vice versa. Maybe the value lies not so much in the learning goals guiding these educative games as much as the game causing a shift in perspective, that leverages the sometimes educative value of video games. Whether through a perspective shift in identity, a reconsideration of dimensional landscapes and the physical nature of objects, or a shift in values from the consequences of in-game decisions, video games offer players a "safe space" to live, die, try, succeed, and fail at a range of activities and experiential phenomena.

GAMES THAT MADE US CRY

[Warning: semi-spoilers for *Brothers: A Tale of Two Sons* (Starbreeze Studios, 2013) and some other games ahead]

Why did you make me play this?

One of the editors came home to their significant other, sobbing in front of the TV, holding an Xbox 360 controller, the credits for the fifth episode of Telltale's *Walking Dead* (2012) rolling onscreen. She had been warned about this by her editor boyfriend, who had been reduced to a heaving, inconsolable wreck by the same game months before. She came to the game not so much a console video gamer, but rather a fan of the *Walking Dead's* zombie-filled universe in television and comic book form. That same world had the same emotional power in video game form, helped in no small part to that game's superior writing and voice acting. Still, this experience was similar to a lot of interactive fiction in that it mirrored cinema or television, even with its branching narratives and quick time events (QTEs).

sob

That was one of the editors of this book (*Ed. note: not Dr. Valentine*), at 2 o'clock in the morning, one hand on the controller, as he helped a young kid swim across a lake. *Brothers: A Tale of Two Sons* is a fantastical but gritty story of two brothers searching for medicine to save their dying father, is told through the actions of the two brothers, each mapped to a different analog stick on the controller and one of the triggers. Controlling the two brothers at the same time can be tricky, but you feel each one's personality through the sticks as you solve puzzles. The younger brother is impish and playful and can crawl through small places and be hoisted up. The older brother is more thoughtful and strong, represented by the player's other hand. The story plays out through this control scheme, so when one of the characters is…no longer there…*sniff*…that absence is felt via the controller.

This experience could only happen through video games because of the importance of the controller to the emotional response. The fractured video detective narrative of *Her Story* (Barlow, 2015), the exploratory house featured in *Gone Home* (Fullbright, 2013), or the metafictional game development commentary of *The Beginner's Guide* (Everything Unlimited Ltd., 2015) are only possible through video games' synthesis of interactivity and ability to tell non-linear stories. Though reports of crying because of video games have sprouted up here and there over the years—of particular note is the death of a certain character in *Final Fantasy VII* (Square, 1997)—it is only recently that games have become an accepted vehicle for delivering emotional content beyond "shooting that thing was pretty cool." Game designers and developers increasingly embrace more serious topics and craft stories and narrative structures tailored to video games and concerns of player embodiment. Chapter 16 explores this embodiment related to the game and controller use, with a particular focus on touchscreen games. Many of the other chapters in this book, such as Chapters 2, 3 and 4, deal with the emotional power of this new breed of games, and their ability to transform player perspectives through emotional resonance. More than that, some of these games play with narrative tropes, such as the unreliable narrator famously used by Edgar Allen Poe and employed in the cult classic, *Shadow of the Colossus* (Team Ico, 2005), as described by Alistar, a youth game designer:

...you play as this criminal guy sort of, who is – your girlfriend's been sacrificed...So you bring her to this forbidden land where there's this god who says, kills these 16 giant monsters and I'll bring her back. And um, the story at first is really simple, that's all it is. But each of these monsters – they're really huge and every one you fight is kind of a puzzle. So there's only 16 fights in the entire game. But also, you get this feeling that first of all, where you are, you're not supposed to be there. What you're doing is also wrong, because all of the things you fight never actually try and kill you – they only just defend themselves. They never really try and hurt you, so you kind of feel bad for killing them. And it's actually a giant – the developer himself made it as a big non-violence message. And it's a really beautiful game, it's just – the point of the game is you wake up in this temple; you have to find each one, just explore a place. There's not a single loading screen in the entire game. You just look around the land, trying to find each one. And then, I don't want to spoil it because I feel like you should look into this. It's a VERY, VERY cool game. Um, but the story does get deeper and as far as storytelling goes, there's no dialogue in the entire game besides this god talking to you and it still tells one of the greatest stories in games of all time...and the ending of the game is so beautiful and so sad.

This ninth grader's description of *Shadow of the Colossus* is a multitiered deconstruction of the game's message and central narrative. He notes the aesthetics of the world, the fact that it has no words, the final twist that subverted his perception of his in-game actions, and even what he had of heard of the game developer's message, that the game was intended to make a statement about non-violence. While still a ninth grader, this young gamer already viewed games on a number of cultural and political layers. This kind of exchange was what inspired the editors to propose this book, and it was similar conversations that most likely inspired the authors of Chapter 13 to explore the link between gamers and college-level literacy and writing ability. The editors' own video game youth programs feature quite a bit of writing, as it is an essential part of game design.

Although Alistar admits he is drawn to unique narrative games, it is possible that many gamers, even those attracted to the *Call of Duty* and *Grand Theft Auto* series, will try out the pre-packaged missions and develop a growing repertoire of the concepts of story—climax, anticipation, twists and turns – the elements upon which great stories are created. Chapter 2, for example, delves into the videogame *Alan Wake* and its embedded folklore as part of the game's narrative, problematizing the notion of traditional literary classification in this somewhat new narrative medium.

DESIGNING WAR GAMES AGAINST WAR

The inspiration for this book came from examples accumulated through our years working with game design in classrooms, summer camps, and after-school youth programs. During these programs, kids, typically middle- to high-school-aged, learn the basics and fundamentals of video and tabletop game design and development. At most of these camps, the kids work in groups on an original game design pitch, delivered to a group of experts, parents, and/or educators who offer frank, but constructive, feedback. The campers are required to generate these game ideas around loose educational design constraints, like make a game that addresses "economy" in some way, or "states of matter," or "biomes," or even "cicadas" (true story!). Despite the limited time allotted for this challenging design activity, the kids' game pitches are often thoughtful, ridiculous, humorous, detailed, innovative, and educational, however rough around the edges.

Because video games have the power to place us in impossible worlds, show us unique perspectives, and make us feel genuine emotion like in *Brothers: A Tale of Two Sons* or the *Walking Dead*, games might be used to address more "serious" topics. As educators, we have observed the term "serious game" bandied about for years, as if games before were "not serious" and not to be taken seriously. A "serious game" is ostensibly a game that educates about a topic, though many "edutainment" games often fall short (Michael & Chen, 2005).

It is not that games have not addressed nor been symptomatic of political, economic, and social issues of their times. The old standby *Monopoly*, for example, is often portrayed as a celebration of rags-to-riches capitalism, but its underpinnings are more complicated, and it can be seen as a satire of such. Its roots are tangled, lying further back in a critique of unregulated monopolistic business practices (Pilon, 2015; Wagner, 2015). Certainly, its main purpose is the complete derailment of any family gathering, but even a beloved classic such as *Monopoly*, *Life*, or even *Trivial Pursuit* can transmit political messages, however subtle. There are idiosyncratic and complex systems in every game design, no matter how simple it might appear. The authors of Chapters 5 and 6 delve into these complex webs that interconnect the game design process, the designers and developers, and the game themselves, as well as the players, how we study and discuss games, and the spaces wherein games are created and distributed.

Throughout this game design process, the kids play plenty of video games for "research," and over the years, we have observed their game preferences inform the designs of their game pitches, and vice versa. Nearly a decade ago, in the mid-2000s, our campers wanted to design grandiose unattainable wish fulfillment AAA blockbuster mega-budget games: "It's like *Gears of War* meets *Halo* meets *Grand Theft Auto* meets *Zelda* meets…" Since the rise of mobile, indie, and generally "smaller" games, our kids' perceptions of video games have changed, and so, too, have their designs, focusing on games with simpler mechanics and more specific goals. Our goal in sharing these stories is to elaborate upon the various phenomena that inspired us to reflect on games and their power to influence player perspectives.

Maybe it was something in the air or water that day, but one particular weekend game design workshop wrangled with complex sociopolitical issues, along lines of gender, race, imperialism, and poverty, to name a few.

You get points for showing the horrors of war.

Years ago, Nintendo released an adorable Nintendo 64 game about photographing Pokémon called *Pokémon Snap* (HAL Laboratory, 1999). *War Photographer* is sort of the polar opposite of that, and an example of a youth-designed political game. The three boys in the small group told me this game was designed explicitly to demonstrate the human cost of war. The player goes to various war zones on assignment for a magazine to take pictures of destroyed buildings, families grieving, and bodies on the ground. In a rather cynical twist (especially for 11-year-olds!) on "if it bleeds, it leads," the more gruesome the photograph, the more the war photographer gets paid and the more acclaim they get from their peers. Along the way they have to choose whether to involve themselves further in the conflict, saving lives in the process and treating people respectfully in the process, but also jeopardizing her/his budding photojournalistic career. This type of quandary is explored in Chapter 10 where the author assesses the educative affordances of analog games to place players in ethical and moral dilemmas, in much the same way the young creators of *War Photographer* imagined their titular hero finding him/herself trapped in a world of ethical gray areas.

You can't call a game 'Civil War Capers'.

And yet they did. Even after these nascent young white male game designers were told that the word "caper" suggested a comedy, and thus was a *tad* jaunty-sounding for a video game about the Underground Railroad, they went ahead and called their game idea "*Civil War Capers*" anyway. [Ed. note: years later, we also had to put the kibosh on a game concept called *Killer Kar Krash*]. They were also told that the premise of a game, wherein one of their actual real life best friends was sent back to a time before the Civil War and was sold into slavery might be perceived as…problematic to some.

Strip away the tone-deaf title and ridiculous time travel premise—that might be asking too much—and what these young designers created was a sincere, deep survival horror game idea. Their idea was steeped in actual historical events and shorn of the usual genre tropes like zombies, firearms, and doors that lock with magical amulets. This was *real* horror, the horror of escaped slaves along the Underground Railroad, foraging for food and supplies, trying to identify safe houses, escaping bounty hunters, dogs, local law enforcement, and the suspicious eyes of an often unsympathetic citizenry. Knock on the wrong door or eat the wrong plant, and it was peril. Their game design adhered to survival horror tropes, to be sure, but the situation was real. Now if they could just have changed the name….

These two examples parallel a recent rise in games that deal with heavy topics. For example, in the survival game *This War of Mine* (11 bit studios, 2014), players forage for food and supplies in a war zone based on the Balkan Wars. The greed of other humans represents as much of a threat as the war does. *Papers, Please* (Pope, 2013) tasks the player with being a border guard in a dystopian 1980s Soviet bloc-esque setting, where you check IDs and work visas for forgeries and imprison the huddled masses yearning to be free, all for a little bonus money to pay for medicine for your dying son. These video games are popular, despite dealing with decidedly "non-fun" subjects like the ravages of war. Chapter 9 discusses these two video games and other serious games from a human rights angle, what values they impart, and how games might be used to educate on human rights issues.

Like in those 'We Can Do It' posters….

It is no secret that games fall short in offering a diverse palette of characters and stories along racial and gender lines, so this is why it is no surprise that a compelling and fascinating game design idea to come out of a weekend workshop challenged the assumptions of one of gaming's most hoary tropes, the masculine, grim and gritty World War II shooter, which generally skew male in target demographic, to say nothing of all-male character portrayal. WWII games focus on the male soldiers with nary a woman in sight, unless they are a civilian to be rescued. *Homefront*, designed by some of our campers, subverts these clichés. The girls in the group were inspired by Rosie the Riveter, *A League of Their Own*, and research into "war wives." They demanded, to the chagrin of the boy in their group, that half the game feature the wife of a soldier, going to work in the factory, taking care of the children, selling war bonds, attending war rallies, rationing meat, almost like a high-consequence version of the Sims series. Depending on how the player did during the day, the wife wrote a letter to the soldier in the field depicting her mood. The reading of this letter affected the soldier's morale, determining his health and ability in the more generic—and less interesting—"shooter" portion of the game. The soldier's performance in combat elicited a letter in return that helped or hindered the wife, and so on. *Homefront* (not to be confused with any other Homefront movies, video games, or TV series), satisfied all three members of the group, in addition to shining a light on the importance of women to the war effort, seldom featured in video or tabletop games, even in the overused WWII setting. Chapter 7 wrestles directly with issues of unbalanced gender representation in the game industry, arguing for increased game design opportunities for girls, especially in the context of increasing female STEM participation. *Homefront* resembles few previous WWII video games in part because young women were given an opportunity to participate in the design process.

SUMMARY

This book surveys the current landscape of video (and non-video!) games, investigating recent trends in game narratives, gamer communities, sociopolitical gaming issues, educational gaming, and more. The authors of these book chapters examine the ways in which video games have broadened the definition of "video games" and the ways in which video games have caused perspective shifts in players by allowing them to embody and engage with unfamiliar, unusual, and uncomfortable scenarios. Video games, with their powerful integration of interactivity, storytelling, and aesthetics might be able to shift player perspectives on a number of social, cultural, and political concepts and issues, tackling topics as serious and diverse as living with depression (e.g. *Depression Quest*), LGBT issues and family dysfunction (e.g., *Gone Home*), the drudgery of bureaucratic work (e.g., *I Get This Call All the Time*), and working in an autocracy (e.g., *Papers, Please*), in addition to many of the games mentioned earlier in this preface. The chapters that follow turn a curious, critical, phenomenological, and educative gaze to the changing landscape of games, be they video, analogue, or somewhere in between.

I just want to be able to do anything.

Only one other game got the *Dead Poet's Society* "Oh Captain My Captain" treatment given to *Proteus* that same summer camp, and it was not even a game at all, and one that still has not seen official release, as of this writing. In this case, the mere viewing (again, with the sound off!) of the promotional trailer for the sprawling, computer-generated space exploration game *No Man's Sky* (Hello Games, 2016) sent the kids—and some counselors—into spasms of cheering and desk-climbing. *No Man's Sky* features a near-endless universe of trillions of stars and planet, each one teeming with colorful, unique foreign fauna, flora, and topography ready for exploration. The player who discovers a new species even gets her/his name appended to it as a bit of a reward, and there is crafting and spaceship-upgrading and robot shooting. "It would take a staggering 5 billion years to visit every single planet in its universe, even in you were exploring those planets for just a single second each" (King, 2015, p. 133). The developer has even alluded to targeting the *"Minecraft* generation" with *No Man's Sky*, meaning a generation of *No Man's Sky* will eschew traditional narratives and mission goals and structures in favor of exploration, though, like *Minecraft*, there is a nominal ending to the game. Even a video game featuring epic space battles is not immune to the "not a video game" debate, and, indeed, it has raged on Internet message boards everywhere since *No Man's Sky's* unveiling.

In fact, an argument in the hallway broke out between one of our counselors and an old-school gamer visitor about whether *No Man's Sky* had "enough to do," or "was even a game at all." This debate did not matter to the kids raised on infinite Legos, who cheered for the Atari 3D of Proteus. Back inside the room, these kids just asked to watch the video again, marveling at the near-infinite planets and perspectives that were possible within games.

Lucas John Jensen
Georgia Southern University, USA

Keri Duncan Valentine
West Virginia University, USA

REFERENCES

11 bit studios. (2014). *This war of mine* [Microsoft Windows/OS X/Linux video game]. Warsaw, Poland: 11 bit studios.

Abbott, E. A. (1991). *Flatland: A romance of many dimensions*. Princeton, NJ: Princeton University Press.

Alberts, B. (2012). Trivializing science education. *Science*, *335*(6066), 263–263. doi:10.1126/science.1218912 PMID:22267776

Atari Inc. (1979). *Asteroids* [Arcade video game]. Sunnyvale, CA: Atari Inc.

Banchoff, T. F. (1990). Dimension. In L. Steen (Ed.), *On the shoulders of giants: New approaches to numeracy* (pp. 11–59). Washington, D.C.: National Academy Press.

Barab, S., Thomas, M., Dodge, T., Carteaux, R., & Tuzun, H. (2005). Making learning fun: *Quest Atlantis*, a game without guns. *Educational Technology Research and Development*, *53*(1), 86–107. doi:10.1007/BF02504859

Barlow, S. (2015). *Her story* [Microsoft Windows/OS X/iOS video game].

Bartle, R. (1996). Hearts, clubs, diamonds, spades: Players who suit MUDs. *Journal of MUD Research*, *1*(1), 19.

Bogost, I. (2013, February 15). *Proteus*: A trio of artisanal game reviews: Three reviews as three lenses through which to approach and appreciate an unusual videogame. Retrieved March 29, 2016, from http://bogost.com/writing/proteus/

Caplan, S., & Wallace, W. (Producers), Travis, J., & Johnson, D. (Directors) (2007). *Flatland: The movie* [DVD]. United States: Flat World Productions.

Design, D. M. A. (1997). *Grand theft auto* [MS-Dos, Microsoft Windows, PlayStation, Game Boy Color video game]. New York, NY: Rockstar Games.

Everything Unlimited Ltd. (2015). *The beginner's guide* [Microsoft Windows, Os X, Linux video game]. Everything Unlimited Ltd.

Fullbright. (2013). *Gone home* [Windows, OS, Linux video game]. Portland, OR: Fullbright.

Gygax, G., & Arneson, D. (1974). *Dungeons & dragons* (1st ed.). Lake Geneva, WI: Tactical Studies Rules, Inc.

Hello Games. (2016). *No man's sky* [PlayStation 4, Microsoft Windows video game]. Guildford, UK: Hello Games.

Intelligent Systems. (2007). *Super paper mario* [Wii video game]. Kyoto, Japan: Nintendo.

Jones, S. E. (2008). *The meaning of video games: Gaming and textual strategies*. London, United Kingdom: Routledge.

Key, E. (2013, February 1). What are games [Blog]. Retrieved from http://www.visitproteus.com/

Key, E., & Kanaga, D. (2013). *Proteus* [Linus, OS, Windows, PS3, PS Vita video game]. Shippensburg, Pa.

King, R. (Ed.). (2015). *Game on! 2016*. New York, NY: Scholastic, Inc.

Laboratory, H. A. L. (1999). *Pokémon snap* [Nintendo 64 video game]. Kyoto, Japan: Nintendo.

Michael, D. R., & Chen, S. L. (2005). *Serious games: Games that educate, train, and inform*. Muska & Lipman/Premier-Trade.

Mojang. (2011). *Minecraft* [Windows, OS, Linux, Android, iOS video game]. Stockholm, Sweden: Mojang.

Namco. (2004). *Katamari damacy* [PlayStation 2 video game]. Tokyo, Japan: Namco.

Nintendo. (1985). *Super mario bros.* [NES/Famicom video game]. Kyoto, Japan: Nintendo.

Nintendo. (1986a). *Legend of zelda* [Nintendo Entertainment System video game]. Kyoto, Japan: Nintendo.

Nintendo. (1986b). *Metroid* [NES video game]. Kyoto, Japan: Nintendo.

Pellegrini, A. D. (1995). *The future of play theory: A multidisciplinary inquiry into the contributions of Brian Sutton-Smith*. SUNY Press.

Pilon, M. (2015). *The monopolists: Obsession, Fury, and the scandal behind the world's favorite board game*. Bloomsbury Publishing USA.

Polytron Corporation. (2012). *Fez* [Xbox 360 video game]. Montreal, Canada: Trapdoor.

Pope, L. (2013). *Papers, please* [Windows, OS X video game].

Red Barrels. (2013). *Outlast* [Microsoft Windows video game]. Red Barrels.

Rieber, L. P. (1996). Seriously considering play: Designing interactive learning environments based on the blending of microworlds, simulations, and games. *Educational Technology Research and Development*, *44*(2), 43–58. doi:10.1007/BF02300540

Square. (1997). *Final fantasy VII* [Playstation, Microsoft Windows, iOS video game]. Minato, Tokyo, Japan: Sony Computer Entertainment.

Starbreeze Studios. (2013). *Brothers: A tale of two sons* [Xbox 360/Microsoft Windows/PlayStation 3 video game]. Milan, Italy: 505 Games.

Sutton-Smith, B. (2009). *The ambiguity of play*. Harvard University Press.

Team Ico. (2005). *Shadow of the colossus* [PlayStation 2 video game]. Minato, Tokyo, Japan: Sony Computer Entertainment.

Telltale Games. (2012). *The walking dead* [PlayStation 3/Xbox 360 video game]. San Rafael, CA: Telltale Games.

The Chinese Room. (2012). *Dear esther* [Windows, OS X video game]. Brighton, United Kingdom: The Chinese Room.

Ustwo. (2014). *Monument valley* [IOS, Android video game]. Ustwo.

Valentine, K. D., & Kopcha, T. J. (2016). The embodiment of cases as alternative perspective in a mathematics hypermedia learning environment. *Educational Technology Research and Development*.

Valve Corporation. (2007). *Portal* [Windows, PS3, Xbox 360 video game]. Bellevue, WA: Valve Corporation.

Wagner, E. (2015, June 24). Do not pass go: the tangled roots of *Monopoly* [News]. Retrieved October 12, 2015, from http://www.newstatesman.com/culture/2015/06/do-not-pass-go-tangled-roots-monopoly

Acknowledgment

In addition to our many friends, family, teachers, and students, we extend a special thanks to our Editorial Advisory Board, our Editorial Assistant, Jessica Thomas, and the many reviewers that made this book possible: Mete Akcaoglu, Christine Anderson, Charles Baldwin, Jaime Banks, Daisyane Barreto, Maggie Behringer, Nicholas Bowman, Spencer Greenhalgh, Daniel Guimarães, Nicholas Hanford, Neo Hao, Stephanie Jennings, Theodore Kopcha, Laura Kieran, Larry McCalla, Evan Meaney, Casey O'Donnell, Lydia Olson, Adwoa Opoku-Agyemang, Kwabena Opoku-Agyemang, Felippe Thomaz, Frances Van Scoy, Harrington Weihl, Courtnie Wolfgang, and William Wood.

Chapter 1
Toward Broader Definitions of "Video Games":
Shifts in Narrative, Player Goals, Subject Matter, and Digital Play Environments

Lucas John Jensen
Georgia Southern University, USA

Daisyane Barreto
University of North Carolina – Wilmington, USA

Keri Duncan Valentine
West Virginia University, USA

ABSTRACT

As video games grow in popularity, ambition, scope, and technological prowess, they also mature as an art form, shedding old definitions tethered to video games as simple, competitive exercises. Greater technological capabilities, in addition to years of experimentation and maturation, have expanded the ability of games to tell different kinds of stories, offering branching paths. The question of "what makes a game a game?" looms larger than ever in this era of video game storytelling. As plots and characters grow, branch, and develop, so, too, do the boundaries of what a game actually is. In traditional definitions of gaming, a set of rules and a victory condition were essential elements to a game. As game narratives and game mechanics grow in increasingly complex and experimental directions, new player goals have emerged. Now, gamers socialize, customize, nurture, kill, build, destroy, break, glitch, and explore as much as they work to win and accrue points. This chapter surveys the current landscape of video games, highlighting examples and trends that challenge more traditional notions and definitions of what it means to be a "video game." The broader definition presented here takes into account play, narrative, digital environments, and more, acknowledging the expanse of the video game experience.

DOI: 10.4018/978-1-5225-0261-6.ch001

INTRODUCTION

As video games grow in popularity, ambition, scope, and technological prowess, they also mature as an art form, shedding old definitions tethered to video games as simple, competitive exercises. Over the last four decades, video games have made great narrative strides from the simpler days at the beginning of video gaming. In fact, those who view video games as an art form often point to game narrative and storytelling as a place where video games have not only matured, but have offered something different than other narrative experiences like literature or film. Video games can provide players with "a great deal of control over the pacing and sequence of events" (Schell, 2015, p. 12). Greater technological capabilities, in addition to years of experimentation and maturation, have expanded the ability of games to tell different kinds of stories, offering branching paths, fragmented narratives, experimental stories, and even the opportunity to create their own goals and games.

The question of "what makes a game a game?"—or "what makes a video game a video game"—looms larger than ever in this era of expanded video game storytelling options. The word "game" as a part of the phrase "video games" is a complicating factor in defining video games, to be sure. In traditional definitions of games and gaming, a set of rules and a victory condition/win scenario were essential elements to a game (Salen & Zimmerman, 2004; Schell, 2015). Because of this, many definitions of video games proffered by designers, developers, and academics still focus on the "game-y" aspects of it: rules, victories, systems, choices, and game mechanics (Salen & Zimmerman, 2004).

Game designer and writer Raph Koster (2013) finds fun to be crucial to gaming of any kind, but throughout this chapter, we will come across a number of video games, such as *Oases* (Gibson & Dziff, 2016), *That Dragon, Cancer* (Numinous Games, 2016) and *This War of Mine* (11 bit studios, 2014), that push against the notion of an inextricable link between play, games, and fun. These video games are not fun in a traditional sense (unless the idea of a child dying of cancer seems fun to you!), but they still offer players the opportunity to play and inhabit different spaces, perspectives, and worlds, while using the affordances of video games, such as mechanics, gameplay, and systems.

In the short time since the publication of *Rules of Play* (Salen & Zimmerman, 2004), video game narratives and game mechanics have grown in increasingly complex and experimental directions. The ostensible central goal of games—to win—has been subsumed or complemented by a variety of new player goals (Bateman, 2015; Juul, 2011; Karlsen, 2007). In today's video game landscape, video gamers socialize, customize, nurture, kill, build, destroy, break, glitch, and explore as much as they work to win and accrue points (Juul, 2011; McGonigal, 2011). Even traditional game-y aspects of video games—victory conditions, rules—have spurred off into new, often unexpected, directions, as evidenced by the rise in emergent gaming in sandbox games, in competitive video gaming activities like speedrunning and e-sports, and in the broadcasting of video game playing via outlets like Twitch, YouTube, and Let's Play's.

So-called "sandbox" and "open world" games often eschew narrative in favor of player-generated goals. The phenomenally popular Lego-esque sandbox game, *Minecraft* (Mojang, 2011) has a nominal ending wherein players defeat the Ender Dragon, but most players are participating to see what they can create with their infinite blocks and complex crafting system, not to see if they can "win." Nor are they playing a game like *Minecraft* to see any sort of story through to completion. These kinds of sandbox experiences, while not necessarily new, represent emergent gaming experiences, wherein the player pursues goals that are not necessarily the intended goal of the game programmers or the game itself, often created by the intersection of different game systems (Juul, 2011). *Grand Theft Auto* players spend hundreds of hours wreaking havoc in their mini-universe, all without ever pushing the central plot forward. For them and other "sandbox gamers," the reward is in the journey and the experience, accomplishing ad hoc goals that are player-created rather than created by the game developers. Still, other gamers prefer the social and customization aspects of the experience, evidenced in online games like *World of Warcraft* (Blizzard Entertainment, 2004), which exists simultaneously as a platform for self-expression, and a place to do battle with ogres (Rigby & Ryan, 2011).

This chapter surveys the current landscape of video games, highlighting examples and trends that challenge more traditional notions and definitions of what it means to be a "video game." We also trace the evolution of these trends, debates, and boundary-pushers, acknowledging bellwethers along the way. This is in no way meant to be an exhaustive or comprehensive list, and we avoid the narrative vs. ludology (or the study of games) debate as much as possible. To be sure, play remains a central goal for the current video game player, as much as winning does, and it is because of this that we propose broadening the definition of video games to refocus on the play aspect of the experience, while acknowledging that video games can very much still be "games" in the rawest sense. This broader definition takes into account play, narrative, digital environments, and more, acknowledging the expanse of the video game experience, instead of the (intentionally) narrower definitions offered by Salen & Zimmerman (2004), Schell (2015), Koster (2013), and others.

DO VIDEO GAMES HAVE TO BE FUN OR PLAYFUL?

"Games" seem to be a relatively simple concept, as we have been playing some variant of games since we were young children (e.g., games like tag, charades, and hide-and-seek). And games are a part of our cultural fabric, from families playing board games together to spectators watching professional football. The latter is a reminder that games are big business, and video games are no exception, as they were predicted to be a $91.5 billion global industry in 2015 (Sinclair, 2015).

The word "game," however, is loaded with different understandings and meanings of what a game actually is, complicating the term "video game" (Schell, 2015). According to Schell, there are four core elements that compose a game: (a) mechanics, (b) story, (c) aesthetics, and (d) technology.

Mechanics are the procedures and rules of a game that are unique to the game itself. For example, the mechanics and rules of *Tetris* (AcademySoft, 1986) are specific to that game; you couldn't rotate squares and L-shapes in *Plants vs. Zombies* (PopCap Games, 2009) or *Grand Theft Auto V* (Rockstar North, 2013). Mechanics are the foundation of the interactivity that sits at the core of video games. These rules and systems can be an essential part of games, and the structure of rules might be the reason that video games are fun (Bogost, 2008; Salen & Zimmerman, 2004). Common game mechanics include combat, building, resource management, and object collection.

Story in video games can be defined as a series of events that reveal the game's nature or underpinnings (Schell, 2015). Video game stories typically fit on a continuum between pre-scripted linear affairs or emergent narratives, depending on the game's design and mechanics. When playing games, players often interact with the game within a space and it is this space that provides context and dimensions for its story or narrative (Salen & Zimmerman, 2004; Juul, 2011). This affords video games the opportunity to disperse their stories in a non-linear fashion, sometimes at the behest of the player. A good example might be the search for clues in the empty house in *Gone Home* (Fullbright, 2013), told primarily through the player's interactions with objects in the environment. This kind of story stands in stark contrast to other forms of story-driven entertainment, such as television, film and literature, which are almost always intended to be experienced linearly.

Aesthetics encompass the artistic and audio/visual qualities of a video game, amplifying the players' sense of immersion, affecting "how the game looks, sounds, smells, tastes, and feels," providing "the most direct relationship to a player's experience" (Schell, 2015, p. 52). For Wark (2009), video games offer spaces of play that synthesize various other fields of art like fiction, film, animation, and music as part of their algorithms, much like the game mechanics. Aesthetics help video games create their fictions through the synchronicity of art style, game design, graphics, animation, audio, dialogue, sound effects, and mechanics (Juul, 2011; Schell, 2015; Wark, 2009).

The video game experience is also unusual in how it is affected by the functionality of the technology on which it is played. The affordances and limitations of a game's technology constrain the player's actions and shape their experience (Schell, 2015) as well as "any materials and interactions that make [the] game possible" (Tucker, 2012, p. 42). Just like a bad movie theater experience might shape one's impression of a movie, the functionality of a video game's technology influences a gamer's perception of that particular game. If a game features broken or glitchy gameplay then this could color the player's overall view of the game's quality and success at meeting its artistic goals, regardless of the quality of its core features, such as graphics, audio, story, or character design. This raises another distinction between video games and other storytelling media: a reader does not hold the author responsible for a paperback with a torn cover just like a moviegoer does not hold the director of a movie accountable when the projector bulb goes out in their movie theater. However, the video game's designers and developers are often held accountable for these technological flaws.

Chris Melissinos, curator of a Smithsonian exhibit on video games as an art form, argues that this need for functioning technology is one of the more unique of video gaming's three "voices," so to speak: the designer and developers' voice and intent; the player's voice; and then the voice of the game itself (Mustich, 2012). The interactivity between these three voices is something unusual that happens only with games, and allows for experiences different than experiencing other works of art like film, television, or literature. As Ian Bogost (Young, 2015) suggests, the technological affordances of video games allow for the designing of experiences and telling of stories that are endemic to the medium.

Even given the uniqueness of the technology, many video game definitions still rely on traditional notions of what games are at their core—a series of rules and systems. As Koster (2013) notes, game designers themselves define video games differently, sometimes at odds with each other. For example, video game designer Sid Meier once referred to games as a "series of meaningful choices," highlighting that video games offer their players agency and choice, for the most part, over how they engage with the video game space (Koster, 2013). These choices, though, are mostly prescriptive and created by the designers; the player engages the game through them. On the converse, *Sims* developer Wil Wright finds the most exciting part of gaming the emergent strategies that players develop from engaging with the game's rules. In the seminal game design book *Rules of Play*, Salen and Zimmerman (2004) offer this definition of games: "A game is a system in which players engage in an artificial conflict defined by rules, that results in a quantifiable outcome" (p. 81). The components of their definition—rules, conflict, outcomes—are all regular elements of what Juul calls the "classic game model," and, to be sure, most video games have these (2011, p. 22). Salen and Zimmerman synthesized this definition from a number of other definitions of "video games," looking for commonalities in all of them.

Jesper Juul (2011), in noting the changing of the "classic game model" in the new world of indie and experimental games, also states that many previous game studies fail to include the perspective of the player themselves. His more nuanced and modern take on video games asserts the following:

a game is a rule-based formal system with variable and quantifiable outcomes, where different outcomes are assigned different values, where the player exerts effort in order to influence the outcome, the player feels emotionally attached to the outcome, and the consequences of the activity are optional and negotiable. (p. 6-7)

For Juul (2011), the player's perspective and emotional attachment to the outcome of their decisions are core to the video game experience. He considers all of the features listed above as being necessary to define a phenomenon as a game. Other media might have some of these features, but only games come from the intersection of all of these. Juul (2011) sees most video games as sets of rules and as creators of fiction worlds.

A key underpinning to academic discussions of video game definitions, and something missing formally from definitions like Salen & Zimmerman's and Juul's, is the concept of play, which might do a better job of explaining video game player goals and activities than just rules. This is not meant as a criticism of Salen and Zimmerman, whose seminal book on game design principles, *Rules of Play* (2004), includes play in its title. It obviously gives great importance to the notion of play, noting that rules are essential to establishing a successful play environment. Juul (2011) takes player perspective into account, but only in terms of emotional attachment and not as a play experience.

Koster (2013) finds the concept of fun to be an integral aspect of games of all kinds and missing from a lot of the above definitions, even though many of these tend to be linked to notions of play. Though fun is the ostensible goal of most video games, many games fail at being fun because of poor design, high difficulty, or alignment with player preferences (Koster, 2013). Koster himself sees mastering puzzles as a key aspect of video games, concentrating on the ways in which these kinds of tasks can, and should, be fun.

"Fun," while an admirable goal for most video games, might not be the same thing as play or even a component of it, however inextricable they might be linked in our mind. Even if play were central to a video game experience, the presence of play does not necessarily equate to "fun," which might be idiosyncratic to the player. A video game might simply not be well-designed, as Koster (2013) notes, but the designers and developers of the game might not have intended for the game to be a fun experience. What if a game were designed without the explicit purpose of being fun but still involved play? *That Dragon, Cancer* (Numinous Games, 2016), discussed later in the chapter, tells the story of the death of the designers' young child from cancer in a video game-like manner. The game is capable of creating emotional resonance in players even making them cry (Shapiro, 2016; Sterling, 2016; Stuart, 2016), but no one would mistake this tribute to their dead son as a fun experience.

Play is a complicated concept to define, but is thought of as a state of being that is voluntary, contains some element of make-believe, and is pleasurable or motivating on its own (Csikszentmihalyi, 2000; Csikszentmihalyi & Rathunde, 1993; Pellegrini, 1995; Rieber, 1996; Sutton-Smith, 2009). Video games can act as play and possibility spaces, satisfying four aspects of play, depending on the combination of game and player(s): play as power; play as fantasy; play for self; and play for progress (Pellegrini, 1995; Rieber, 1996; Sutton-Smith, 2009). Obviously many video gamers play for power, to dominate their peers, to knock down records, and to win. Gamers use play as fantasy, embodying roles and possible selves (Lee & Hoadley, 2007) that they might not otherwise be able to occupy. Players also play games for self for a variety of reasons: relaxation, escapism, and socialization (Bartle, 1996). They play for progress and practice, to get better at games and meet internal intrinsic goals of their own making, probably most noteworthy in the emergent goals that pop up in *Minecraft* and other "sandbox" games. Juul calls emergence "a number of simple rules combining to form interesting variations," (2011, p. 5) and gamers, in search of some combination of power, fantasy, progress, and even self, explore the corners of *Minecraft* and *Grand Theft Auto V* for new strategies, social experiences, rewards, glitches, and the unexpected collisions of systems.

NEW NARRATIVE COMPLEXITY

It might be an understatement to say that narrative complexity was not a hallmark of the early days of video gaming, beyond text-based adventures and computer "adventure" and role-playing games like the *Kings Quest* (Mojang, 2011) and the *Ultima* series. Nobody would accuse games like *Ms. Pac-Man* (Bally Midway, 1982a), *Dig Dug* (Atari, Inc., 1982a), or *Donkey Kong* (Nintendo, 1981) of having rich, developed stories or characters. Plots of early games were non-existent or hung on simplified tropes like save the princess/female, although not much has changed in this regard (feministfrequency [Screen name], 2013). Even games based on movies, like *Tron* (Bally Midway, 1982b), *Krull* (Atari, Inc., 1983), or the infamous *ET* for the Atari 2600 (Atari, Inc., 1982b), were a series of simple skill challenges with a movie coat of paint, often bearing little resemblance to the properties that inspired them. Most games at the time were programmed by small teams of developers, and storytelling was not a major concern or focus of the gameplay.

Immersion in a story as a main character is a unique and powerful aspect of the play offered in video games (Lee & Hoadley, 2007; Mustich, 2012; Schell, 2015; Tucker, 2012), even games in the early history of video games offered players this immersive experience. *Zork* (Infocom, 1977) was a text adventure that allowed the player the opportunity to explore a fantasy world on their own, albeit one without graphics; rather than see a dark room with no light, the game spelled it out for the player, who then typed commands like "light torch" or "kill troll." The *Ultima* RPG series told long, nonlinear narratives, complete with separate cloth maps and runic alphabet decoders. These kinds of free-roaming experiences with branching paths were rather uncommon, and the games with heavy plots, particularly from the "adventure" genre (see *Kings Quest*, *Day of the Tentacle*) were generally linear experiences. The player went from Point A to Point B to Point C. Game series like *Metroid* (Nintendo, 1986) and *Castlevania* (Konami, 1986) removed some gameplay linearity by offering players the chance to backtrack and progress by garnering items and solving puzzles. Even so, their plots were relatively simple: get an item to open a door over here that leads to another item that opens another door. Also: shoot the bad guys. Role-playing games (RPGs) remained the game genre where longer tales were told.

As video capabilities in games increased, cinema exerted a greater influence on the growth of videogame narratives. The change to disc-based media in the 1990s allowed video in games, giving rise to "cut scenes," filmic breaks in gameplay that often pushed the story forward (Narcisse, 2010). Early examples of cut scenes in games like *Night Trap* (Digital Pictures, 1992) were often quite crude, using full-motion video of actual actors of questionable quality.

The era of low-quality cinematics is no longer the case, as large games now feature Hollywood production values, including quality writing and voice acting. In some games, cinematic cut scenes go on for tens of minutes, a rather notorious feature of the *Metal Gear* series. Furthermore, almost every big budget action, adventure, or first person shooter (FPS) video game contains a plot, backstory, and mythology.

Some of these big-budget titles attempt social critiques in much the same manner as their big-budgeted Hollywood brethren. The *Bioshock* series, between bouts of gruesome violence, offers critiques of Ayn Rand's objectivist philosophy, jingoism, American exceptionalism, and xenophobia (Adams, 2013; Meyer, 2013). *Red Dead Redemption* (Rockstar San Diego, 2010) takes players on a journey through a twisting 20 plus hour Western saga that includes everything from cattle herding to dramatic gunfights in Mexico, all in service of a story that tackles serious topics like American expansionism and father-son relationships.

Meanwhile, on the indie scene, much like the independent movie scene, there is a growing market for smaller, more experimental storytelling approaches. The aforementioned 2013 hit *Gone Home* (Fullbright, 2013) deals with highly personal issues of sexuality and family dysfunction, all told through picking up objects around a house. The developers of *That Dragon, Cancer* (Numinous Games, 2016) used their own loss of a child to cancer as the basis for the game's plot. These games challenge the notions of what it means to "play" and "win" within a game.

This is not to say that video game stories are generally good, at least by the standards of other media. Renowned game developer, Tim Shaffer, once lamented that video games only told a few types of stories even though there was a diverse range of stories out there to be told. The story that seems to be told more than most is the story of someone shooting someone else. The sequelitis and lack of imagination that drives so much Hollywood filmmaking goes double for the video game industry. For every interactive drama such as *Gone Home* or immersive narrative experience like the serene, solemn forest fire lookout drama *Firewatch* (Campo Santo, 2016), there is another beige military FPS whose setup is "man kills people." Even though recent successful critical and commercial games like *The Last of Us* (Naughty Dog, 2013) have given large video game development a measure of artistic credibility, video games are still often judged by their most egregious examples or misrepresented in the media, like when a *Fox News* guest erroneously accused the critically-acclaimed game *Mass Effect* (BioWare, 2007) of having graphic sexual content marketed to children (Schiesel, 2008). However, just as we do not judge the entirety of cinema by the likes of *Slumber Party Massacre II* (Cormon, Brock & Daniel, 1987) or the cinematic oeuvre of Uwe Boll, we should not paint video games with the broad brush of, say, *Night Trap* (Digital Pictures, 1992) or *Dead or Alive: Extreme Volleyball* (Team Ninja, 2003; Webster, 2016).

It is important to pause and note that stories and narratives, however complex, are not necessary to a video game's aesthetic success. After all, what is the story of *Tetris* (AcademySoft, 1986)? What's the plot of *Scrabble*? How invested are players in the character backstories of *Pac-Man* (Namco, 1980) or *Super Mario Bros.* (Nintendo, 1985)? Sports, music, and driving games are often narrative free and no less valid as game experiences. However, these days, even puzzle and strategy games like *Plants vs. Zombies* (PopCap Games, 2009) have well-developed quirky characters and a veneer of backstory to grab players' attention. The controversial cult hit *Catherine* (Atlus, 2011) even combines a dating simulator with a puzzle game.

THE UNRELIABLE NARRATOR-PLAYER

Being able to control a lead character allows users to assume a unique participant role in the characters they inhabit, guiding their actions, and sometimes even challenging their expectations of how they should play and how the story should progress. Player expectation, even in linear games, can be challenged through the use of the "unreliable narrator," or, in this case, the "unreliable player." Just like Edgar Allen Poe once employed this technique in classic short stories like "The Tell-Tale Heart" (Poe, 1843) and "The Cask of Amantillado" (Poe, 1846), video games often place the player in the role of a narrator-protagonist whose view of the proceedings might be a bit biased, skewed, or warped.

Shadow of the Colossus

Possibly the best example of an unreliable narrator-player technique is the revered Playstation 2 game *Shadow of the Colossus* (Team Ico, 2005). This nearly wordless game is unusual in that it features very few enemies to combat. Instead of hordes of repetitive enemies, the player takes on sixteen unique Colossi, each one different than the last. The first of these alone is a hundred feet tall, and the player-character has to climb the Colossus' fur to eventually kill it by driving a sword into its brain. If that sounds brutal, then, yes, it is, and over the course of fighting the 16 Colossi, the task becomes more difficult, from both a gameplay and moral perspective. The player's character is killing these giant, beautiful, one-of-a-kind creatures to give their power to a dead woman, presumably a lover. The death of each Colossus brings the player closer to his goal, but he starts to grow paler and more sinister, with horns peeking through his hair. By the end of the game, it is clear that the dead woman is dead because of something you, the player, did, and that *you* are the villain of the story, validating the sneaking suspicion that killing these Colossi – many of whom only attack in retaliation! – is not a good act.

Knights of the Old Republic

In Bioware's now-classic RPG, *Star Wars: Knights of the Old Republic* (2003), a player's dialogue choices and actions decide their relative morality and how they interact with other characters. The morality system, itself fairly novel, collides with the story in a shocking third act reveal, wherein the knowledge of the player-character's motives changes drastically, coloring the perception of previous events. For most of the game, the player is an amnesiac Jedi, piecing their past back together, assembling a crew, and stopping threats throughout the galaxy. Along the way, the player faces moral dilemmas that fall on either the Light Side (good) or the Dark Side (bad) and accrues morality points based on these decisions. Stop the muggers robbing the old man? Light Side. Decide to mug the man yourself? Dark Side. Your companions react to your decisions and might even refuse to work with you, given your choices. When *KOTOR* makes its big twist, it takes the decisions up to that point and asks the players to reevaluate whether they really ARE good or evil. After this revelation, you have to decide again how to play the game from that point on, based on this new information.

The Walking Dead

Player choices do not often make a difference in the static universes of video games, at least in terms of how they affect the narrative. 2012's episodic *The Walking Dead*, developed by Telltale Games (2012),

8

balances narrative concerns while emphasizing the importance of player choices. Based on the Robert Kirkman comic book series, itself the basis for the popular television show of the same name (Darabont et al., 2010), *The Walking Dead* is not a game that you can win, per se. It drops the player *in media res* into the character of Lee Everett, former University of Georgia professor charged with murder. You begin the game in the back of a police car at the beginning of the zombie apocalypse. What follows is a harrowing game of survival, one in which the player's decisions color the story itself. The paths that the player takes are fairly linear, but what happens based on their decisions is not. Throughout the game, the player is presented with a variety of choices, quite often driven by choosing conversation options. Whose side you choose, whom you choose to save, and what tone you take with your fellow survivors can drastically change how the story plays out, even if all of the games essentially end at the same place. The moral dilemmas quickly pile up: Do you help the person trapped in the bear trap? Do you steal food from the abandoned station wagon? Do you save the nerd or the journalist? In many cases, these choices are life and death and need to be made quickly; the player has to live with the unintended consequences of their choices and actions. Characters in the game remember what you say and do, and will bring it up in conversations later. The game is not about score or points, though it does compare the decisions you made to other players. Even if the story moves through similar beats, the dialogue and the progression of the story is the player's very specific version of it. The developers created a myriad of dialogue options; thus, the chance of two games being played the same is unlikely. Some players reported being too attached to the decisions they made to replay the game, choosing instead to follow the story wherever it went, even if favorite characters were killed.

MULTIPLE PROTAGONISTS

Some games challenge player expectations by featuring multiple protagonists, such as *Grand Theft Auto V* (Rockstar North, 2013), *Eternal Darkness: Sanity's Requiem* (Silicon Knights, 2002), and the recent interactive fiction horror game *Until Dawn* (Supermassive Games, 2015).

Eternal Darkness: Sanity's Requiem

Eternal Darkness: Sanity's Requiem, a horror game released in the early 2000s for the Nintendo Gamecube, is an antecedent of sorts to *Until Dawn* and other games that swap perspectives between protagonists. It featured a roster of characters of different ethnicities, genders, and historical backgrounds, piecing together a Lovecraftian mystery throughout the ages and across a number of locations on this astral plane and others. One of the more surprising moments in the game comes when the overweight architect character gets, well, squashed out of nowhere by a demon. Besides being shocking as jump-scare, this twist is made more compelling in that the character's death was intended by the game developers. Typically, the death or incapacitation of the main character in a story-driven game results in a "Game Over" screen and the loading of a previous save file. Because *Eternal Darkness* has multiple characters, the story does not hinge on a single character's survival, so it trundles on with the narrative consequence of this death. There is no player agency in this decision, but it is still surprising, as no one ever expects their own character to die.

Brothers: A Tale of Two Sons

Brothers: A Tale of Two Sons (Starbreeze Studios, 2013) goes one step further than games that feature multiple protagonists, requiring the player to control two characters at once. Two brothers, having lost their mother to drowning, must now set off to find medicine for their sick father. The titular brothers are each controlled by one of the controller's twin sticks and a corresponding trigger button on the right or left side. Each brother plays and acts according to his personality and age. The younger brother is lithe, more agile, and a bit precocious, while the older brother is stronger and wiser. The younger brother is scared of water while the older brother can swim. The player simultaneously controls each brother with each thumb stick as they solve puzzles during their journey, through magical forests and in the bloody aftermath of a war between giants. The controller scheme alone might make *Brothers* worth mentioning, but it is perhaps most notable in how it reveals much of its story, eschewing onscreen text or dialogue, through the player's interaction with the brothers through the controller. The brothers' actions are felt by the player through the vibrations of force feedback in the controller. Over the course of the game, each player's hand adapts to the differences between the two brothers and how they play, so—spoiler alert—when the absence of one of the brothers is there, it is felt immediately by the player, creating emotional story beats through the game mechanics and how the player interacts with the game. The absence felt in one's hand buttresses the tragedy that plays out onscreen, exacerbating that sense of loss.

OPEN WORLDS AND SANDBOXES

Missions, branching paths, and exploration are all ways that non-linear stories are told in video games, but many gamers choose to create their own experiences, using the tools that were given to them, whether they were meant to be used this way or not. The rise in computer processing power since the late 70s has brought more than just better graphics, music, cinematics, and generally higher production values. The greater power has given them the capacity to create larger, more realistic in-game universes. The increased horsepower means better artificial intelligence, more characters onscreen for a time, and larger playing areas. It also brings with it more play possibilities.

An older game like *Super Mario Bros.* was a mostly linear experience. The goal of SMB is pretty simple: move to the right, avoid obstacles, save the princess. By the mid-1980s, game series like *Ultima*, *Zelda*, *Castlevania*, and *Metroid* broke the mold, allowing players to progress through games in a (relatively) non-linear fashion. A game like *Excitebike* (Nintendo R&D1, 1984) might have included a level editing tool to create its own courses, but it still worked within strict parameters—and saving the levels was impossible.

Now many games are so-called "sandboxes" or "open worlds." Even if they have a story, they offer the player opportunities to roam and do things on their own terms, and, quite often, this exploration of these possibility spaces becomes the game's *raison d'etre*, whether it was intended or not. Players create ad hoc goals along the way, intrinsic goals that are not necessarily explicit or formalized in the video games rules, not unlike the "Free Parking" addition to so many Monopoly games. This is "emergence" or "emergent gaming;" the emergence here manifests itself in goals that the players create as they play.

Grand Theft Auto V

It is difficult to talk about open-world gaming without talking about perhaps the most popular and controversial game series of them all: *Grand Theft Auto*. The latest major iteration, *Grand Theft Auto V* (Rockstar North, 2013), otherwise known as *GTA V*, has shipped over 30 million copies. Let us note this up front: the games are extremely violent pseudo-satires that display a rare contempt for just about every group imaginable. They are also technical marvels, giant open sandboxes where players can do nearly anything, much of it criminal, of course. *GTA V* presents the player with a world the virtual size of a small state. It would take the players tens of minutes to drive across the world, at least. Beyond this, there is a golf course, pool halls, a stock market, property management, skydiving, and generally causing mayhem. So much of *GTA* is seeing what kinds of boundaries can be pushed. Can your motorcycle backfire set fire to gasoline? (Yes!). Can you stage a demolition derby on top of a skyscraper using a helicopter? (Yes!). And yet critics, Leigh Alexander (2013) and Garrett Martin (2013), while reviewing *Grand Theft Auto V*, lamented that the game featured a beautiful open world as the player's playground, but most of the missions boiled down to the usual: drive your vehicle from one place to another, shoot some people, escape, repeat. Martin (2013) noted that he felt more comfortable flying over the world then he did engaging in the bloodshed below.

Grand Theft Auto IV

Giving players too much gameplay freedom can clash with the narrative goals of a game's creators, in a concept referred to as *ludonarrative dissonance*, evidenced by Rockstar's hyper-popular *Grand Theft Auto IV* (Rockstar North, 2008). The player takes control of Niko Bellic, an immigrant—and possible war criminal—from a nameless Eastern European country. Early in the game, Niko laments killing, violence, and war, and speaks of starting a new life in America. Unfortunately, Niko's actions do not often match his words. He runs over innocent pedestrians on the sidewalk (often by accident!), shoots down helicopters, gets in high speed chases with the police, and other violent mischief and mayhem. Though the *Grand Theft Auto* series couches this hyper-violence in layers of satire and cultural critique, Niko's violent deeds often stand in repose to his need for redemption, and the narrative can be frustrating because of it. A classic *Penny Arcade* cartoon lampoons this game, depicting the main character picking up a date in a semi truck covered in blood and the corpses of pedestrians (Holkins & Krahulik, 2008). Though this might seem ridiculous, this kind of situation comes up frequently during the game with little punishment or consequence from your friends and romantic partners, who generally brush off your obvious sociopathy and wanton killing.

Minecraft

Scooped up by Microsoft for two billion dollars and the obsession of children everywhere (Ekaputra, Lim, & Eng, 2013; Grant, 2014), *Minecraft* is the elephant in the room, so to speak, in any discussion of sandbox games. *Minecraft* is a virtual construction playground, constrained only by imagination, work ethic, and the cubic tools. *Minecraft* also acts as a survival game, something of a social platform, to say nothing of the cottage industry of merchandise surrounding it. Kids—and adults, too—are Minecraft-obsessed, and, for many players, it is the only video game that they need to play. A brand new *Minecraft* game starts in a randomly generated *tabula rasa* of a world, a chunky, blocky series of hills, greenery, and cows waiting to be broken down and built back up into mansions, roller coasters, underground lairs, or whatever comes to the players imagination, providing they have crafted the necessary materials and stayed away from the zombie-like Creepers that menace players at night. *Minecraft* provides the player endless Legos wrapped up in an addictive crafting mechanic where they combine different elements in specific patterns to make newer items. And that is just the beginning: there are programmable logic blocks, the share-ability of levels, the socialization that happens as players migrate from server to server, and the availability of mods that change the core graphics and gameplay, featuring a passel of game types beyond "build build build" and "hide from the Creepers." It is possible to view *Minecraft* as its own platform, and yet the purported victory condition, killing the Enderdragon, is not what has transfixed so many players: it is the near-endless possibility space it offers.

GAMES AS OBJECTS D'ART

Part of *Minecraft*'s appeal lies in its blocky voxel-based aesthetic that resembles something of an 8-bit attempt at 3D, much like *Proteus*, mentioned below. This aesthetic internal consistency between the blocky aesthetics and the fact that the game involves stacking blocks could be part of its success: the aesthetics match the gameplay. The aesthetics of a video game–the synchronicity between the animation, character art, background graphics, music, and/or voice-acting–are more than mere window dressing. Aesthetics are important in increasing the immersion and the success of these possibility spaces (Bogost, 2008). Some games go further than just high-fidelity graphics, employing unique, compelling, or nontraditional art styles and aesthetics to hook the player further into their play environments. Radical aesthetic choices are mostly found in the independent game development scene, where limited resources push designers and developers toward interesting aesthetics, but large publisher and developers like Nintendo are known for their dedication to quirky design aesthetics. The recent *Yoshi's Woolly World* (Good-Feel, 2015) and *Kirby's Epic Yarn* (Good-Feel, 2010) used yarn, fabric, and crafting supplies as the drivers of their aesthetic world, with denim mountains stitched into the background and felt signs held up by push pins. *Yoshi's Story* (Nintendo EAD, 1998b) for the Nintendo 64 used a look that simulated clay and crafting supplies, and *Super Mario World 2: Yoshi's Island* (Nintendo EAD, 1995) deployed a hand-drawn aesthetic to give its world a playful, surreal character. The *Paper Mario* series (e.g., Intelligent Systems, 2007) presents a 3D world populated with 2D characters that look like papercraft, akin to a diorama. Even pushing this aesthetic to some of the game mechanics, wherein Paper Mario himself folds up into a paper airplane to cross chasms.

It is not just Nintendo that employs creative, holistic aesthetic sense for their games. *Tearaway* (Media Molecule, 2013) and *Unravel* (Coldwood Interactive, 2016) use torn paper and crocheted yarn aesthetics, respectively, to represent their worlds. The side-scrolling platformer *Apotheon* (Alientrap, 2015) takes place in the time of Greek mythology, so the game designers used an art style similar to the paintings from the side of Ancient Grecian urns and buildings to emphasize the game's setting. Some of these aesthetics might be a "coat of paint," but all affect the player's perception of the game and its mechanics. This aesthetic component is also something missing from a number of definitions of "video games," with their focus on games as rules, boundaries, and choices, first and foremost. *Sentris* (Timbre Interactive, 2015), discussed below, plays almost like a musical instrument combined with an art piece, as the beauty of its radial patterns and futuristic backgrounds combine with its music in an inextricable way. Not to wade too far into the "are games art?" debate (yes, they are), but some games can exist as objets d'art unto themselves, pieces of art to experience for their beauty as much as their gameplay.

Limbo

The aesthetic choices behind the graphic style of *Limbo* (Playdead, 2010) demonstrates how crucial aesthetics can be to narrative immersion (Schell, 2015; Wark, 2009). *Limbo,* which takes place in the purgatory of the same name, features a spooky black-and-white/grayscale aesthetic, leeched of color to symbolize this place that exists out of time and space between worlds. The lead character is a young boy in search of his lost (or dead?) sister in a world of shadow and silhouettes, where peril and sudden, bloody, often comically violent death, lurks at every turn. The mechanics of this side-scrolling 2D puzzle platformer seem simple at first, with only a few buttons used. Still, the game often tells its story environmentally, like many games mentioned in this chapter, through backgrounds, atmosphere, and wordless action. Without dialogue, only your interactions and encounters tell the story within this lonely universe. You lurk in the shadows, the only thing you can see are your eyes, blinking, right before you are eaten by a giant spider or beheaded in a bear trap. *Limbo* is a beautiful game on its own, but its atmosphere and aesthetics are intrinsic to the success of the narrative and gameplay, as it juxtaposes cuteness, a gothic setting, and an almost comical level of violence. Aesthetics can influence story and vice versa, and Limbo's aesthetics and level design are inextricable from the narrative.

Okami

Okami from Capcom (Clover Studio, 2006) takes place during the time of ancient Japanese lore and plays out in a similar fashion to a 3D Zelda game like *The Legend of Zelda: Ocarina of Time* (Nintendo EAD, 1998a), though its art style and game mechanics are tied in a way that set it apart from other 3D action-adventure titles. The player traverses a mystical ancient Japan as a wolf goddess who uses the power of a magical ink brush to solve puzzles, attack enemies, draw in bridges, and more. By gesturing on the screen with the controller, the player paints symbols like circles, X's, and slashes on the screen to accomplish these magical tasks. This Japanese ink brush aesthetic is more than just the magical power of the main characters, as it permeates the game, flowing back and forth within the cel-shaded environments and characters of the game, which themselves look like moving components in a Japanese ink painting/drawing. In the Wii version (Clover Studio, 2008), the player even uses the Wiimote controller to "paint" on the screen with motion controls. With *Okami*, the central mechanic is more than a gimmick, as it is informed by the art style and vice versa.

Journey and Flower

In the wordless game *Journey* (thatgamecompany, 2012), the player is a robed figure crossing a vast expanse of desert, only connecting with other players who happen to be online and at the same moment in the game. The player can only jump and communicate using a magical tone that transforms aspects of the landscape and lengthens the player's scarf, all adding color to the drab landscape in the process, and allowing the player to move forward in the game. Despite its short running time and its wordless narrative, *Journey* is regularly listed as one of the best games of all time and a regular source of ammunition in the "are video games art?" debate. A similar serene player experience can be found in the earlier wordless game *Flower* by the same developers thatgamecompany (2009). In *Flower*, the players are flower petals, surfing on the wind to reach their destination, an experience shorn of everything but the focus on riding the waves of air. There are no enemies and no obstacles other than nature and your own skill, in contrast to the general "kill the bad guys" vibe of so much of the video game market, which extends to many of the games here. These games value serenity and atmosphere as their key storytelling aspects, using their environments, and the player's navigation of them, as the media through which they tell their minimalist but affecting stories.

Oases

"My grandfather's plane was reported lost in 1960 during the Algeria Independence War, days before the birth of his first child. This is what I like to think happened to him." Beyond this introductory paragraph and a shot of a military plane crashing, there is little context to this brief, beautiful experimental video game. There is no winning in *Oases* (Gibson & Dziff, 2016), just the experience of exploration and flight in an impossible universe. Free-roaming exploration in flight simulators has some precedent, as evidenced by the Nintendo series *Pilotwings* (Nintendo EAD, 1991), but *Oases* makes the exploration of its dream-like universe its primary *raison d'être*. The player controls a ghostly white plane through a dreamy version of heaven where colors swirl around grasping spectral hands while purple vines twist into warped clouds. Throbbing ambient and electronic music plays as you fly through these randomly generated heavens, each one created anew when the game is restarted. In a sense, the experience of playing the game, from the graphics and universe it creates as a whole is the story itself, however brief, of the imagined continued adventures of a departed loved one in a world of endless, random beauty (Patrick Klepek, 2015).

GENERATING MUSIC THROUGH PLAY

The audio aspects of game interactivity are important, but often forgotten in larger discussions of visual aesthetics and gameplay. Music and sound are crucial components of video games, used for everything from emotional manipulation to indicators of on-screen activities that can be a mechanic or central part of a system. Most every video game has music and sound, but "music games" have usually meant games where players tap along to a rhythm or strum along to a song on a plastic guitar.

The music video game genre is a solid example of the notion of "play as fantasy" (Pellegrini, 1995; Rieber, 1996; Sutton-Smith, 2009), most recently represented in the plastic instruments of recent successes *Guitar Hero* (Harmonix, 2005) and *Rock Band* (Harmonix, 2007). The goals of these video games are to expose players to music and potentially encourage players to actually play real instruments and/ or become a musician. These games also serve as a chance for players to experience what music artists face in their profession: the mastering of an instrument, the coordination of a band, the playing of gigs, and (hopefully) the earning of fan adulation and money (McGonigal, 2011). Did we mention these games were fantasy? However, this is still just playing along with the music within the boundaries of the already-existing songs (Juul, 2007). When playing these games on their included plastic approximations of, players are not actually playing the music, but performing along with it in a sort of pantomime (Juul, 2007). For example, playing the guitar or bass on *Rock Band* or *Guitar Hero* does not require the same movements or notes of playing an actual guitar or bass. Players are actually expected to perform a series/sequence of movements (pressing buttons) to simulate the idea of playing guitar or bass (Juul, 2007). Deviating from the original work results in punishment, which includes losing fans.

The music game genre is expanding into new territory, moving on from its roots in plastic instruments that corresponded to indicators onscreen. Music video games with plastic instruments are restrictive in that they demand fidelity to the original piece of music, but a newer breed of video games generate their music and sounds in response to player choices and actions. *Proteus*, mentioned below, and its predecessor, the Brian Eno-scored *Spore* (Maxis, 2008), feature music snippets and sound clips that reacts to player actions and location. All of the games mentioned below emphasize sound and music generation as part of their core gameplay.

Proteus

Experimental game *Proteus* (Key & Kanaga, 2013) has earned a special place in the "what is a video game?" debate. Even though the game features video game-like mechanics, its lack of explicit goals and serene nature led to the developer having to defend *Proteus's* good name as a video game against a stream of "not a game's" (Key, 2013). In the unusual *Proteus*, the player explores an island made of pixelated 3D-by-way-of-2D objects, chasing pixelated frogs, wisps, and chickens in a world whose aesthetic recalls a past where early video game systems had 3D rendering capabilities. There is an implied narrative in the game, as the seasons pass and doom and gloom comes to the randomly generated island. *Proteus* features little in the way of explicit game mechanics other than exploration and looking around the environment. However, the environment and its exploration are all linked to a central mechanic: the player generates the music and sounds in the game by exploring the environment. *Proteus* is essentially one giant music creator, not dissimilar to the "generative music" work of musician Brian Eno, wherein a user or player need not know much about music to create (1996). Every thing and place on the island emits a tone, pulse, or synth pad, so the player's movement creates the soundtrack to the game, making each play-through slightly different. One might even argue that the emotions of the narrative are partially told through the music and sound of the game, as there is no dialogue in *Proteus* (a recurring theme in this chapter!).

Mini Metro

In the puzzle game *Mini Metro* (Dinosaur Polo Club, 2015), the player essentially plays a version of the iconic New York City subway map, as you drag subway lines between different shapes – squares, circles, triangles, diamonds, and more – to deposit similarly-shaped passengers at their station of choice. As the player progresses, more stations randomly pop up on the board and the flow of passengers increases. The game features minimalist iconography, intuitive controls, and a charming flat aesthetic that matches the subway maps from which it draws inspiration, but, along with the compelling art style, the game features a minimalist approach to sound and music. Composed by electronic music group Disasterpeace, each passenger, subway line, subway station, and player movement features a set of sounds that are generated by the playing of the boards themselves. The minimalist clicks, pops, whirrs, and swells of the beginning become more frantic and prominent as the map fills up. Because each game plays out randomly, even on the same map, each playthrough generates a unique soundtrack to the experience, composed of all the little bits of music assigned to each component and action in the game. Other games like *Spore* have used this kind of generative music based on player actions, but in *Mini Metro*, musical fragments serve as both the soundtrack and sound effects. In much the same way the dancers in some Merce Cunningham pieces create the music through their dancing, *Mini Metro* uses the player's actions and the game's reaction to them to fill the sonic space.

Sentris

Sentris, by developer Samantha Kalman (Timbre Interactive, 2015), seems closer to a tone matrix or step sequencer than a game on first appearance, as an inscrutable *Tron*-like radial pattern turns in front of icy, polygonal futurescapes. The player rotates and drops musical blocks on the constantly rotating and thrumming radial wheel, which symbolizes the length of the loop, and these arched blocks push other blocks down, adding sounds, rhythms, chords, and more. Colors need to be matched to complete certain levels, but there is no penalty for failing to achieve the task, and happy accidents can result in accidental melodies and rhythms. As the player progresses—again, at their own pace—the compositions become more complex. Though the game does offer you puzzles and levels to complete along the way, it is more concerned with exploration and creation, even offering the player a chance to export their songs, which usually sound like—in the authors' case—the work of experimental artist Nobukazu Takemura. Play for play's sake is itself the most central goal of the game, with its low-punishment tasks, gentle difficulty curve, and discovery-oriented design.

FRACTURED STORIES

The exploration of aesthetically compelling imagined universes is one of the ways in which video games can tell stories differently than other media. It can come from more than art style. Video game stories can reveal themselves as the players interact with the game world, mechanics, or characters. Video games can offer players the ability to engage with stories in a less linear fashion while still telling a central story. For example, large open-world role-playing games like *The Witcher* (CD Projekt RED, 2007), *The Elder Scrolls V: Skyrim* (Bethesda Game Studios, 2011), or *Dragon Age: Inquisition* (BioWare, 2014) offer some of this fragmentary narrative engagement by way of hundreds of side stories and missions to complete. Throughout a playthrough, new missions and side quests pop up on the map that the player might engage with, somewhat out of order. In general, these side stories are unlocked by completing other tasks or talking to non-player characters (NPCs), but there are usually main story quests that advance the plot forward. Because of this, there is still a nominal victory condition, even if players' time is mostly spent chasing down emergent goals, collecting items, leveling up, and completing the myriad side quests available to them.

Video games can also fracture a narrative and deliver it through objects that the player interacts with or through the player's exploration of the environment. Chris Melissinos, curator of the *Art of Video Games* exhibit at the Smithsonian American Art Museum, thinks that exploration-based narratives are what makes video games the most immersive medium:

In books, everything is laid before you...[t]here is nothing left for you to discover. Video games are the only forms of artistic expression that allow the authoritative voice of the author to remain true while allowing the observer to explore and experiment. (Mustich, 2012)

As discussed above, the aesthetics and perspectives offered by video games deepen the immersion, allowing the story to be told by background art or the exploration of an environment.

Bioshock (2K Boston, 2007) is an example of a narrative told through environmental details, like songs playing over loudspeakers, overheard conversations of enemies, posters on the wall, and audio recordings hidden throughout each level. These audio recordings compelled the player to discover bits of the story to flesh out the proceedings, but their placement in random trash cans and desks around an underwater city felt a little contrived. Contrivances aside, they encouraged the player to search every nook and cranny of the game to ferret out the entire story.

A more successful version of this was in the early 2000s first person adventure game *Metroid Prime* (Nintendo, 2002). Through the eyes of Samus Aran, intergalactic bounty hunter, the player used a computerized visor to scan the environment for clues to solve puzzles but also to learn backstories and scientific data about rock formations, space pirates, poisonous plants, weapon upgrades, and more. The game keeps track of these data scans and to achieve a 100% rating, the player must scan them all. Some visor scans are necessary to complete the game, but they feel like objects that Samus would want to analyze anyway: locked doors, a crack in a glass window, or the titular Metroids. The player has a choice to take the time to seek out optional scans or play through the game with less written backstory while not sacrificing too much immersion. The analysis of the environment fills in gaps in the story through one of the embodied character's core problem-solving skills.

Gone Home

An exemplar of exploration-based narrative is the popular–yet controversial–video game *Gone Home* (Fullbright, 2013). In *Gone Home*, you play—in the first person perspective—a young woman in the 1990s who has come home to find her house empty and her family gone, including a beloved sister. By examining various items and documents left around the house, the player pieces together what happened in whatever order they like, creating the narrative themselves through object manipulation. You discover your father's drinking problem and failed career as an author by finding liquor bottles and stacks of books in the closet. You find secret love letters written to your sister from her AWOL girlfriend. Each one of these discoveries might tell a piece of the story, but most of them are optional. Beyond the exploration-based narrative structure, *Gone Home* is non-violent and grounded in the real world. It addresses mature themes, but not in the usual sense of the word "mature" (e.g. sex, violence, and profanity). Throughout its relatively short running time, *Gone Home* addresses themes of isolation, gender identity, nostalgia, family, and homosexuality without ever shooting, killing, or punching anyone. *Gone Home* is a shining example of the growth of the medium, even as it eschews conventions like points.

Definitely not worth 20$. If you enjoy these kinds of experiences, that's fine, but there is not a shred of gameplay in this and for something so basic and limited to get a 5/5 is truly shocking.

I kind of think this was a waste of money. I got a LGBT agenda heartstring tugger in the guise of a spooky detective game.

This is BARELY a game. It's just a story.

This is NOT even a good fucking story.

I just think people expect games to be games. We can both elaborate on the topic and muse on theories how the possibilities of games are endless – but you must admit that there is a certain golden standard people instantly recognize, and this is the reason why sometimes titles like Gone Home cause people to take pause when describing them to friends as "games" and often times choosing to label them as "interactive stories" or whatnot instead.

...a game that isn't a game, an entertainment product devoid of any variety or fun, with a story that isn't exceptionally "well written" for an asking price that's regarded by the majority as "too much" should not get a single 5/5 review.

These are some of the many comments on popular video game website *Giant Bomb* decrying the independent first person exploration game *Gone Home*, which had just received a "perfect" 5 out of 5 score from reviewer Patrick Klepek (2013). *Gone Home* received much critical acclaim upon release in 2013, including another "perfect" score at fellow video game news site *Polygon*, where the tenor of the comments was much the same. Because *Gone Home* eschews points, victory, and winning in service of an explorative story—and its length was short and price tag deemed too high by some—it was tagged as "not a game" by a small but vocal portion of the commentariat on video game-related websites, message boards, and social media. The "not a game" tag has also been thrown at other so-called "walking simulators" like *Proteus* (Key & Kanaga, 2013) and *Dear Esther* (The Chinese Room, 2012), implying that a video game without traditional combat mechanics is somehow less than a "traditional" or "normal" video game, even though the similar 1990s exploratory game sensation, *Myst* (Cyan, 1993), is one of the best-selling games of all time. However, all of these video games, no matter how experimental, still feature mechanics, systems, interactivity, and aesthetics, all key components of video games (Bogost, 2008; Juul, 2011; Salen & Zimmerman, 2004; Schell, 2015; Tucker, 2012). Some of this criticism, as evidenced above, has to do with *Gone Home*'s engagement with homosexuality, a topic fairly verboten in gaming until recently. However, much of it has to do with player expectations of value, both aesthetic and monetary. Not to be too reductive, but gamers are used to shooting and blowing up things; to many of them, *that* is what a "video game" is. This is not to say that video games like *Gone Home* fit every gamer's preferences. Cinema fans might prefer a genre like film noir or romantic comedy. Book lovers may prefer mystery or graphic novels. Video gamers have similar genre preferences (e.g. FPS, adventure, RPG). For the most part, though, book and movie fans do not question the validity of their preferred art form if it lacks in quality or is in an unfamiliar or disliked genre. Even if a reader does not like a book, they do not question its existence as a book or the very definition of the concept of Book. *Gone Home* is arguably the most high profile example of this kind of game, or "walking simulator," and certainly one of the most acclaimed, so the backlash feels inevitable. The non-violent gameplay and exploration-driven story-telling of real world stories and human experience stands in contrast to the dominant strains of AAA video game development as well as indie games, which, however broad they may be in scope, still feature plenty of violence as the central reason for being.

Elegy for a Dead World

Wordless narratives, while boundary-pushing, challenging, and somewhat in vogue, are not the only ways in which game designers and developers can experiment with story-telling and game design. *Elegy for a Dead World*, by Dejobaan Games (2014), asks: what if a video game allowed you to write the story yourself? This video game, which is as much a writing exercise as a game that the player wins, appears, at first glance, to be a *Metroid*-style side-scrolling exploration game, as your jetpacked, spacesuited character descends into alien caverns, discovers ancient ruins, and overlooks interplanetary vistas, similar to the ones generated in *Oases*. However, this game is as much interactive fiction as anything; the player is asked to write in portions of the story at various points on each world. The painterly visuals in the background exist mostly as story inspirations, as it is up to the player to fill in blank words, phrases, or paragraphs of their own, rather than follow a pre-made story. There are pre-made templates that start the player-writer off with scenarios, but even those can be fully deleted. If *Elegy for a Dead World* lacks in the traditional gameplay department, its story is only limited by the imagination of the player and the images of alien worlds it presents, and the player can even save the story it spits out.

Her Story

The era of full-motion video from the 1990s, more commonly known as FMV, is not considered one of high-quality game development and storytelling, at least in hindsight. FMV games were not confined to one genre, but featured actual video and film of actors performing the dialogue and cutscenes in the game. FMV games were notorious for bad acting, production values, and rigid gameplay, perhaps most evident in the controversial and silly *Night Trap*. Despite FMV's questionable critical consensus, the games goofy charms have taken on a certain kitsch value in recent years. Despite this reputation, one of the most critically acclaimed games of 2015, *Her Story* (Barlow, 2015), was essentially an FMV game. *Her Story's* critical and commercial success is even more surprising given that it revolves around a single turgid-sounding game mechanic: searching a database for video clips to watch. The player "sits down" at an antiquated—by today's technology standards, at least—computer desktop that not coincidentally looks like something out of the FMV era of the 90s, complete with Windows 3.1-style Minesweeper-esque game underneath. In the search bar there is a word loaded up for you, the player: "murder." Onscreen, a woman answers an unseen police interviewer's questions in scrambled chunks of VHS video. Each time a search term is entered, the database retrieves the top five video clips. Because the database is supposedly corrupted, the interviewer is not shown, only the interviewee, who delivers cryptic bits of information in irregular video clips that take place over the course of months. The player plays investigator, combing through clips for new bits of information, using the search bar to dig deeper until they come to the game's rather arbitrary ending point. Retrieving information in different ways is part of the game's storytelling, meaning that the order in which players see the actress's responses colors how they view the game's twists and turns.

Cibele

Cibele, by indie game designer Nina Freeman (Star Maid Games, 2015), traces the awkward and all-too-real courtship and subsequent dissolution of a relationship via online multiplayer game. There is a game to play within *Cibele*, but the narrative is woven into instant messages and video chats sent between friends, all transmitted through a desktop computer motif, akin to the one in *Her Story*. *Cibele* painstakingly recreates a multiplayer online role-playing game (MMORPG) from the 2000s, which is played while chat windows pop up onscreen from other characters. As the player engages with these messages, the turbulent story follows the emotional swings of a whirlwind online relationship, but it also speaks to the social importance of these kinds of online communities. Because Freeman used actual chat logs from a similar relationship as some of the game's dialogue, the verisimilitude of some of the material presented can be bracing. Like *Her Story* and *Gone Home*, *Cibele*'s narrative unfolds through discovery and exploration of its environment, giving the story away in the fractured pieces, through the instant messages, the MMO gameplay, and even actual video starring Freeman herself. The MMORPG that you play in *Cibele* is really only one part of its story, as the whole narrative is embedded in the fastidious recreation of this digital environment. Falling for a person online requires sharing each other's identity in bits and pieces as the nature of the other person slowly emerges, and the narrative of *Cibele* is constructed to reveal itself to the player in much the same fashion.

BREAKING THE FOURTH WALL: GAMES AS METAFICTION

Both *Her Story* and *Cibele* house their games within the leitmotif of using a desktop computer as the portal to accessing the game content. These settings and aesthetic trappings are integral frame stories for each of these games, and *Cibele*, in particular, uses the trappings of a fictional MMO to tell its story. Some video games go beyond this narrative conceit, nesting video games within video games or using the rules and tropes of video games to comment on video games themselves.

There is some tradition to this sort of in-game commentary and breaking down the barriers between player and game. In the aforementioned game *Eternal Darkness* (Silicon Knights, 2002), the player experiences "insanity effects" as they encounter horrific monsters, each with a deleterious effect on the player's gameplay. A couple of these blur the boundaries between the "real world" of the player and the game itself. In one example, the game facetiously notifies the player that the controller has been unplugged, even while action continues behind the notification for a short period of time, often resulting in the player's death. One insanity effect tells the player that the save game has been corrupted while another simulates a game crash.

One of the more famous examples occurs during the "boss fight" with the character Psycho Mantis in *Metal Gear Solid* (Konami Computer Entertainment Japan, 1998). The character of Psycho Mantis uses his telepathic abilities to "read" the save games on the player's memory card and comment on whether the player had been playing other games from publisher Konami: "You like Castlevania, don't you?" *The Stanley Parable* and *Undertale* take these breaks in the fourth wall one step further, adding in-game narration and dialogue that reflect a bevy of player interactions and actions, including such mundane acts as restarting, saving, and loading.

The Magic Circle

In *The Magic Circle* (Question, 2015), the player is a protagonist trapped inside an unfinished fantasy game, at the mercy of the designers of this game, who act like vengeful gods, manipulating the player experience in much the way the animators meddled with Daffy Duck in the famous cartoon *Duck Amuck* (Selzer & Jones, 1953). The warped, glitched out, surrealistic landscapes in the game are meant to simulate the middle of the development process, when games are unfinished and not necessarily "fun," and the player works their way through the world by stealing development tools from the developer and remixing, destroying, or changing the game's rules to solve puzzles. The title of the game, which is a play on the sociological concept of the "magic circle," originated from Johan Huizinga's (1938) seminal work, *Homo Ludens*, and refers to an agreed-upon space among people where play "magically" happens

(Huizinga, 1938/2014; see also Zimmerman, 2012). To "win" *The Magic Circle*, the player must engage with game design and development itself.

Hack 'n' Slash

Hack 'n' Slash, from Double Fine Productions (2014) presents itself as something of a spiffed-up version of Nintendo's original Legend of Zelda game. In this case, the lead character is armed with a USB stick sword which plugs into ports throughout the game world, allowing the player to recode the world with a rudimentary version of the Lua programming language. If a rock is blocking your way, then recode it to move by resetting its X and Y position. Set an enemy's health to zero or spawn more helpful items, all using Boolean variables and coding syntax. With this and other games, the lines between designer, developer, and player are purposefully blurred as the meta-manipulation of the game rules themselves is essential to succeeding at the game's internal goals.

The Stanley Parable

In *The Stanley Parable* (Galactic Cafe, 2013), the player plays an office-working, clock-watching drone who discovers that all of his coworkers have disappeared. The game's dark premise is tinged with humor, embodied in the voice of the disembodied narrator, a droll British man who becomes increasingly annoyed with the player's inability to do what he says. It features a number of in-game jokes about the kinds of mundane tasks that games make us do, such as playing a repetitive, simple mini-game for a long period of time, only for the meager symbolic victory of an achievement point or trophy. Furthermore, its short running time of less than an hour encourages repeated playing of the game, wherein the narrator addresses the player's actions in previous playthroughs.

Undertale

The indie game sensation *Undertale* (tobyfox, 2015) offers an absurdist, fourth-wall-breaking take on bipolar video game morality systems, all while remembering your game actions and commenting on them, much in a similar way to *The Stanley Parable*. An underlying theme of the game is its emphasis on "humanizing" the non-player characters and enemies that you encounter along the way, causing the player to question whether the mindless killing in games is so mindless after all. *Undertale* rewards multiple playthroughs, as it comments on the actions in previous games, even noting when the player resets a game to save or kill a character. The entire game can be won without killing a character; likewise, every character in the game can be killed in a so-called "genocide run." The quirky dialogue and atmosphere, similar to the Nintendo game *Earthbound* (Ape Inc., 1995), makes you grow to like some of the characters. Further, their acknowledgment of your involvement in their deaths in previous save games can be disconcerting. Not to spoil too much, *Undertale* culminates in a boss battle that manipulates save games and discusses the player's actions throughout the game.

Pony Island

The indie surprise hit *Pony Island* (Daniel Mullins Games, 2016) is an absurdist video game like many of the others mentioned above, but is also a game that traffics in metafiction, trying to upend the relationship between game, developer, and player. As Melissinos noted (Mustich, 2012; Tucker, 2012), video games have three voices split between the player, developer, and the game itself. Metafiction games like *Pony Island* offer a fourth voice that resembles an ouroboros, a snake eating its own tail, between the three. At first, *Pony Island* resembles a facile video game from the late 1980s, based on a Lisa Frank sticker book, from its cutesy fonts to unicorn lead character to explosions of rainbow colors. Quickly the game glitches and breaks down into a jumble of 1s and 0s and mixed-up code, revealing that Satan—THE Satan—is the designer of the game, trying to suck the player's soul out through the video game itself. The role of the player of the game *Pony Island* and the video game *Pony Island* itself and the video game within the video game *Pony Island* is blurred with increasing frequency. Satan takes control of the mouse, changes the powers of the titular pony, and flips the Start Button upside down, to name a few tricks, and a running joke throughout is that, well, Satan is just not that great of a game designer. To escape the game, the player must recode it and break the rules of the game space, angering the devil each time as he cries "foul" to the lack of "fair play." Though *Pony Island* is a linear experience, its various twists and turns are told through this push and pull between the player and designer, all of it based on subverting player expectations of how video games traditionally operate. The game's developer, Daniel Mullins, says:

A big part of what Pony Island was, was about taking the expectations you have about games, particularly the [user interface] of a game, and flipping them upside down…the beginning, you see a start button. First thing you do is try to click it. That expectation of, 'oh, the start button starts the game, obviously'—when that's flipped upside down, it puts [players] off and makes them a little uncomfortable. (Webster, 2016)

There are similarities between these video games about games themselves and so-called "metafiction," many of which revolve around their relationship to play. In a broad sense, metafiction is fictional or narrative art whose existence as a piece of art is part of the artwork itself, a book or movie that self-consciously defines itself as such and uses this to tell its story (Waugh, 2013). A distinguishing feature of metafiction is that its playing with the rules and purpose of fiction, for example, breaking the so-called "fourth wall" between the author and the reader (Waugh, 2013). The use of the word "play" here is purposeful, as it is an important part of metafiction. Many creators of metafiction see the creation process and/or their final works as a play experience, even comparing them to games (Waugh, 2013). In her book *Metafiction*, Patricia Waugh sees play as an essential component to art-making of all types, suggesting that all "art is 'play' in its creation of other symbolic worlds" (2013, p. 34).

This emphasis on symbolic playful art runs similar to the notion of play as fantasy and its necessary make-believe qualities (Caillois & Barash, 1961; Huizinga, 2014; Juul, 2011; Koster, 2013; Rieber, 1996). It seems counterintuitive, but in breaking the rules of literature, metafiction also establishes the rules that must be broken, as most novels or short stories do not begin by listing a set of rules needed to experience their content. Unlike literature, video games do put a more explicit emphasis on rules, but video games about games like *Pony Island*, *The Magic Circle*, and *The Stanley Parable* manipulate and/or push against the tropes of the medium, subverting the game's rules and the boundary between player and developer. In doing so, they acknowledge the importance of rules to a video game, while challenging player expectations. Just as Salen and Zimmerman (2004) feel that rules are a key component to establishing play in a video game, Waugh (2013) feels that setting rules is important to metafiction because then the reader (or player) can know what is being twisted, changed, or subverted. To use a reductive cliché, these rules were made to be broken. This aligns with some video gamers' tendency to explore the boundaries of game play spaces and environments through emergent gameplay.

VIDEO GAMES OF THE ABSURD

Besides their metafictional designs, part of *Undertale* and *Pony Island*'s appeal—and the reverence shown for its kooky forebear *Earthbound* (Ape Inc., 1995)—is its willingness to embrace the fantastical, quirky, absurd, and dadaesque potential of video games. Even one of the earliest and most successful series, *Super Mario Bros.*, exists within a nonsensical universe, wherein Italian plumber brothers explore pipes in the Mushroom Kingdom while hopping on evil sentient mushrooms and flying turtles while eating altogether different mushrooms that imbue them with magical powers and collecting coins and fighting fire-breathing dinosaur men and so on. Video games are "possibility spaces" (Bogost, 2008; Salen, 2008), and that means they are capable of more than just realistic graphics and grim-and-gritty stories. In a sense these video games are similar to the theatre of the absurd of Beckett and Albee, there to explore the boundaries of theater—or, in this case, video games—more than they are to tell traditional stories. There have been surrealistic, absurdist games like *Katamari Damacy* (Namco, 2004) and *Noby Noby Boy* (Namco Bandai, 2009) before in the mainstream game world, to say nothing of the rather insane premise behind the *Mario* games. But these video games, no matter how bizarre, are still games with victory conditions and points. The following video games do little to concern themselves with such matters, instead using game mechanics to explore bizarre possibilities.

Jazzpunk

Perhaps it is no small coincidence that *Jazzpunk* is published by the gaming wing of Adult Swim (Necrophone Games, 2014), the Cartoon Network subsidiary behind *Aqua Teen Hunger Force* (Crofford, Lazzo, Willis, Maiellaro, & Edwards, 2000) and *Squidbillies* (Lazzo, Crofford, Fortier & Willis, 2005). *Jazzpunk* plays like a video game reincarnation of the early joke-a-minute ZAZ (Zucker-Abrams-Zucker) movies like *Airplane!* (Davison, Abrahams, Zucker, & Zucker, 1980), *Kentucky Fried Movie* (Jorgensen, Kostroff, Weiss, & Landis, 1977), and *Top Secret!* (Davison, Lowry, Abrahams, Zucker, & Zucker, 1984). Set in a 1980s Cold War spy world, populated almost exclusively by robots that look like the restroom sign, *Jazzpunk* crams jokes, however corny, into every dialogue choice and nook and cranny of the game world. Turn other robots into flies with a fly swatter, fight pizza monsters when you open the pizza box in the garbage, listen to an endless string of double entendres from a robot prostitute: these are all things you can do in *Jazzpunk*, all without accomplishing any of the game's "goals." Though there is a nominal mission structure and story pushing the game forward, each new level exists more as a carrier wave for joke delivery or an environment within which to stuff jokes rather than an achievement to overcome. Though *Jazzpunk* fans will want to explore and complete everything in the game, this is more in service of uncovering all of the robot puns the game has to offer.

Goat Simulator

Another "joke game" is the game jam product and cult favorite, *Goat Simulator* (Coffee Stain Studios, 2014), which presents playgrounds of pedestrians, plate glass windows, exploding barrels, and more, all for the titular and quite indestructible goat to smash and head-butt. The game is glitchy, goofy, and relatively goal-free, even as it piles on the points and mini-achievements. The points serve no purpose, but there is still a gratification to watching the numbers mount as you send your goat flying from an exploding car onto a trampoline. The silly premise and opportunity for hilarious emergent gaming are what have made *Goat Simulator* popular and inspired plenty of joke "[insert object here] Simulator" retreads, such as *Bear Simulator, Tank Dating Simulator*, and *Shower With Your Dad Simulator* (see Steam, 2016).

Octodad: Dadliest Catch

Octodad: Dadliest Catch (Young Horses, 2014), another video game with an absurdist comical premise, has the opposite goal of *Goat Simulator*; the point of the game is to avoid causing chaos, so you can blend in with humans. You play as Octodad, an octopus stuffed into a suit with a human wife and human (!) children who must blend into "normal" suburban society, despite the fact that you stick to everything and have eight arms. The controls in *Octodad: Dadliest Catch* are purposefully awkward and clumsy in accordance with the non-humanity of the lead character. He flails about, smashes things, and sticks to the walls, all while trying to perform a series of escalating tasks, such as washing the dishes and mowing the lawn, without "other humans" noticing.

Hot Date

An example of this absurdist, experimental spirit is the itch.io game *Hot Date* (Batchelor, 2016), a member of the durable "dating simulator" genre, in which the player goes on a rather awkward candlelit date with an unusual, snarky pug. Even though this is a date with a dog, it is no less awkward than a real date with another human. The player must choose from a random list of strange, often funny, conversation topics and then follow the conversation forward from there. Whether the player succeeds or fails romantically on the date is beside the point, as the game gives little indication as to success or failure other than the reactions of the pug to the conversation. *Hot Date* is more concerned with the player enjoying its quirky premise and wealth of conversation choices then it is with notions of winning or losing or finding the right match, a usual feature of the "dating game" genre. *Hot Date* is not alone in its absurdist romantic. Platforms like itch.io, Steam, and GOG are now full of video games that exist as nothing more than experiments, quick narratives, explorative environments, and art pieces, in contrast to fully-fledged "game games," which feature traditional game-like exercises such as winning, points, and victory.

SERIOUS GAMES AND GAMES FOR EMPATHY

Gone Home, Cibele, and even the Telltale *Walking Dead* game are all examples of games that deal with serious topics, however specific or realistic. Still, you would not usually hear these games called "serious games," at least how we typically understand that term. Serious games is used, primarily in academia and educational discourse, to mean games that can teach about "serious" topics, mostly in reference to so-called "edutainment" or "educational games." Mainstream—or even indie—games that do not explicitly target the educational market are rarely tagged serious games. This is unfortunate because the word, serious, suggests solemnity and dourness, while video games, serious or otherwise, have a great opportunity and ability to tackle serious topics from any number of angles. The *Bioshock* series has lampooned Ayn Rand's Objectivist theories and American Exceptionalism. Bioware games in the *Dragon Age* and *Mass Effect* series push the boundaries of traditional video game romance away from straight-only romance where gay, bisexual, and inter-species relationships are allowed. The *Grand*

Theft Auto series satirizes greed, capitalism, and the media, particularly in its in-game radio stations and advertisements. However, these are smaller aspects of larger games, political or social critiques made on the way to telling bigger stories. The games below—serious, empathy, or whatever one prefers to call them—build their designs and narratives around their heavy, complex themes.

Papers, Please

Papers, Please (Pope, 2013) might be the world's first and only border guard simulator. Developed by Lucas Pope, the central player in *Papers, Please* is a hapless immigration officer, checking identification, work visas, and travel permits in a cold border checkpoint leading into the fictional Arstotzka. Every day, you arrive to find a growing set of ever-changing rules: one day immigrants from the United Federation might need an extra work permit; the next day they might not be allowed at all. As contradictory immigration laws pile up, so do the documents on your work space, as you check birthdays, dates, heights, weights, pictures, and more to try to spot forgeries. When forgeries and contraband are found—sometimes involving invasive full body searches—the violators are sent to the Gulag, sometimes for a monetary bonus. The game has a sly sense of humor embedded in its pixelated graphics and its Soviet-esque oompa music, but as the sad encounters pile up, as you reject sick people for minor infractions, as you send more people to the Gulag, your guilt begins to grow. All the while, the higher-ups are breathing down your neck to do better. *Papers, Please* is not there to make you feel good, but the game is fun to play, as there is no small measure of satisfaction to mastering the rules in one day and gleefully dispatching someone to the Gulag for an expired license. Sending people through pays you a little, but sending people to prison pays more; doing badly at your job pays nothing, and your family needs medicine, heat, and food. At one point, when you are turning away the mother needing to see her sick son, *Papers, Please* makes the player confront the terrible sacrifices we often have to make for survival, as well as the ambiguous and arbitrary ways ordinary citizens are affected by geopolitics.

This War of Mine

This War of Mine (11 bit studios, 2014) is another serious game of recent note and takes place in the same area of the world as *Papers, Please*, with radically different gameplay. In an unnamed Eastern European or Balkan country meant to resemble the breakup of the former Yugoslavia, the player must try to survive the ravages of war in an ad hoc shelter along with a number of other survivors. Instead of the traditional soldier-based combat of most war games, this game focuses on the experiences of the civilians left behind as they hunt for food, materials, and other survivors in terrible conditions. Zombie and post-apocalyptic narratives are often used to tell the story of humans' response to extreme duress, but *This War of Mine* builds on actual events in the Bosnia-Serbian conflicts of the 1990s, however fictionalized, to show the extremes of human behavior when survival is at stake.

That Dragon, Cancer

For most people, gamers and non-gamers alike, words like "video games" and "play" conjure up fun and fantasy, much in the way writer and game designer Raph Koster (2013) emphasizes the fun aspect of them. As discussed earlier, a number of definitions of video games emphasize their capabilities for fantasy, make-believe, and escapism, just as play is defined as having make-believe qualities, satisfying a need for fantasy, and self-improvement (Rieber, 1996). Because of these parallel definitions, the concepts of play and gaming are linked. Fun gets attached to play because the object of so much of our play is fantasy, escapism, and, hopefully, fun. But people watch depressing dramas, listen to sad songs, and read tear-jerker novels because they inspire great emotion within them, not necessarily because they are fun. Games have been marketed almost like toys from the beginning, and there are not many hot-selling toys whose pitch is "makes you super sad." Since the late 2000s, the video game space has found greater virtual shelf space for games that tell more serious, dramatic stories, using the immersion and embodiment aspect of video gaming by placing players in spaces to force them to look at other perspectives and perform tasks they might not otherwise have done (Young, 2015). Along the way, this might educate them, challenge their preconceived beliefs, and even give them empathy for others in different situations. This breed of video games has earned the name "empathy games," games whose primary purpose is not fun or happiness, but inspiring empathy in the player (D'Anastasio, 2015; Young, 2015). Prominent game designer of personal games, Anna Anthropy, pushed back on the notion that these empathy games can give players actual understanding and empathy of another's situation, in her case games she developed about being a transwoman (D'Anastasio, 2015). Despite this criticism, others feel that games have great emotional potential to tell stories that are rarely told, especially those from marginalized voices in the game development community (D'Anastasio, 2015; Shapiro, 2016; Young, 2015).

Possibly one of the most widely discussed empathy games is *That Dragon, Cancer* (Numinous Games, 2016), a game based on the sobering topic of cancer and its repercussions on a family. The game is less about inspiring empathy and more about coming to terms with the impending tragedy and subsequent loss of a child to terminal cancer (Shapiro, 2016). When the creators discoved their son had a terminal form of cancer, they turned to art creation and self-expression to process their feelings, but they chose to use the medium of video games as the means to tell their story, however sad the inevitable ending. The autobiographical game's players take on a series of dreamy and poetic vignettes, mini-games, and narrative diversions, some as mundane and dour as talking to a doctor about pain management, quiet poignant moments between loved ones, and fantastical digressions like riding a horse through the stars and flying away on balloons. There are even a number of side-scrolling video game-themed levels. Included throughout the game are letters sent in to the Greens from other parents who dealt with this sort of grief. While almost everyone who played it noted its emotional resonance, the gameplay was criticized for not being compelling, noting that it felt more like an experience than a game, echoing some of the other "not a game" critiques out there (Sterling, 2016; Stuart, 2016).

Three-Fourths Home

Even though many of these serious and empathy games deal with heavy issues like war, autocracy, and cancer, many of these games are dealing with personal issues that might have lower-stakes, but just as much narrative complexity. In *Three-Fourths Home*, the player portrays Kelly, who is driving home through a blinding rainstorm across lonely rural Nebraska. Kelly receives a phone call from her mother that starts out banal but eventually reveals deeper, hidden family dysfunction as the dialogue plays out. The monochromatic world of barns and cornfields occasionally gives way to fantastical mirages in the white, blinding rainfall, but beyond the surreal images, *Three-Fourths Home* is a grounded, realistic experience. Most of the controls involve pressing the right arrow key to drive and selecting dialogue options, none of which change the onscreen action, per se, but all of which color the story in different shades, as you find out more about your dad's drinking and your brother's accident, which left him with possible brain trauma (Ramsey, 2015; Walker, 2015). The game's resolution and epilogue end in ambiguity and serenity, rather than a big boss fight. While it might push against player expectations of fun and interactivity, the story is rich and highly personal and the dialogue choices, at the very least, make the player a more invested participant in your family's drama (Ramsey, 2015; Walker, 2015).

I Get This Call Every Day

"Oh, that's the video game that got the dude who made it fired." That is how *I Get This Call Every Day* was described to one of the editors. Its reputation is not undeserved, as its creator David Gallant was indeed fired from his job at a Canadian tax office. Gallant is part of the wave of indie developers designing indie games based on personal issues and autobiographical vignettes. Buoyed by easier-to-use and cheaper game development tools and more democratic distribution platforms, such as Steam, itch.io, the iOS store, and Google Play, developers are tackling topics overlooked by mainstream games, which have to maximize sales numbers to justify their large development costs (The Giant Beastcast, 2015). This requires sticking to well-worn narrative paths and game mechanics. Perhaps no game is more anti-conformity than this revealing experience about the drudgery of being a call center "meat popsicle" (Campbell, 2013, para. 1). *I Get This Call Every Day* paints the experience of working the phones at this call center as thankless, exhausting, and demoralizing (Campbell, 2013; Hernandez, 2012). The graphics are amateur, but they remind the player that the game is a work of self-expression, while the mechanics are built around following the tedious protocols for tasks like updating account information. Gallant used game development as an escape from the disillusionment with his own job; his frustration inspired a video game about that frustration (Hernandez, 2012). However, his honesty in the press and the game itself about his experiences angered the Canadian Revenue Agency, which led to his firing (Campbell, 2013; Hernandez, 2012). Though a compelling story, Gallant's firing–and move toward full-time game development–should not overshadow the achievement of *I Get This Call Every Day*; through frustrating, boring, and annoying the player, it paints a dehumanizing picture of this kind of work.

TOWARD A BROADER DEFINITION OF VIDEO GAMES

We have surveyed only a few of the new ways in which video games have come to mean much more than interactive digital challenges, linear narratives, and non-interactive cinematics. From the exploration-based narratives like *Gone Home* to the fantastical random eulogy of *Oases* to the drudgery simulation of *I Get This Call Every Day*, the boundaries of video gaming stretch with each newly introduced mechanic, perspective, point of view, or narrative twist. Video games can entertain, but they can also educate, elicit empathy, and challenge beliefs. While some exist as branching, interactive fiction, others are sandboxes for endless, creative play. Video games continue to forge their own unique path among media, and this chapter does not include boundary-pushing gaming trends: the online streaming of video games, competitive video gaming or e-sports, the janky game-created animations called machinima, and participatory experiments like *Twitch Plays Pokémon* (2016).

After reviewing many definitions of video games, we offer our own modest contribution to the discussion. Our goal is to reintroduce play to the definition and move away from a rules focus, while acknowledging that mechanics, interactivity, social interaction, audio-visual components, and narratives might still be essential parts of the video game experience. Many video games today exist as exploratory play experiences rather than systems bounded by conflicts, victory conditions, and points. This definition focuses on the video game as an interactive experience wherein the player engages overlapping systems, such as mechanics, visuals, and audio:

An interactive digital play experience in which the player explores layered systems of mechanics, visuals, audio, cinematics, narrative, and/or social interaction.

Our definition of "video games" as digital play experiences attempts to shift the focus to the emergent, social, and play-oriented side of the video game experience. This stands in contrast to classical and traditional game definitions that look at rules and competitive exercises, something that must be won (Juul, 2011; Koster, 2013; Salen & Zimmerman, 2004; Schell, 2015). Similar to video games presented in this chapter, our definition is emergent and organic. Its broadness tries to accommodate most video games, but it hopefully provides room to grow and expand with new video games and emerging technologies in the market. Given the discussion of *This War of Mine* and *That Dragon, Cancer* earlier in the chapter, we also eschew the requirement that "fun" be featured, even if it is important to the critical success of so many games. Anyone who has played a competitive sport for a long time or had to play, even lost, a thoroughly dispiriting game of Monopoly can attest to the fact that play does not equal fun.

More importantly, we hope to shift the focus of these definitions away from defining boundaries, resulting in the "not a game" debate that haunts *Gone Home* and *Proteus*. This debate rubs elbows with a few other long-running video game debates: "are games art?" and "story vs. gameplay." All of these debates seem to hang on the putative purpose of video games as well as value expectations from players. What are games supposed to do? What stories are games allowed to tell? The number of disparate definitions of video games—and we touched on only a fraction of them—represents how unresolved these issues are, even though most of us recognize a video game when we experience it. Furthermore, these definitions set boundaries on what a video game can be; our definition, at least as we intended, attempts to shift the focus toward the broad tent that video games are right now and the expanding possibilities of what video games can be.

And perhaps all of these definitions, including our own modest contribution to the fray, will prove inadequate in the protean game landscape of the near-future. Mobile gaming continues to change the landscape of who plays video games, as the democratization of development and delivery put a video game-playing device in nearly everyone's pocket. Virtual reality ended the 1990s as a disappointment, but new systems have arrived with the promise of greater immersion. The social component of gaming has exploded; Twitch, YouTube, and e-sports have turned video games into community events, televised programs, and spectator sports. Online discussions surrounding social and competitive online video games like *Hearthstone: Heroes of Warcraft* (Blizzard Entertainment, 2014), *Destiny* (Bungie, 2014), and *League of Legends* (Riot Games, 2009) often dissect the metagame or "the meta"—meaning the higher level strategies and rules that exist beyond the game itself—wherein a developer's minor tweak to gameplay might unleash howls of anger from players. *League of Legends* even has its own fantasy league a la fantasy football. If watching someone else play a video game is a game itself then what exactly is a video game?

A recent experience with Nintendo's Mario construction set *Super Mario Maker* (Nintendo EAD Group No.4, 2015) illustrates the possible inadequacy of these definitions to handle this new world of social and participatory gaming. One of the editors, being a *Super Mario Maker* fan himself, logged onto Twitch (2016), an online video game streaming site and community, to watch some high-level Super

Mario players show off their skills. He randomly clicked on one of the most popular Twitch streamers playing *Super Mario Maker*, and, upon entering their channel, was taken aback by the amount of onscreen activity. On the right fifth of the screen, a chat window full of onlookers scrolled by, spouting "lol"s, "wtf"s, animated gifs, and emojis, the conversation almost too fast to comprehend. Across the top of the screen, the streamer had a running count of how many followers they had and how much money they were donating on PayPal. Anyone who donated money would be entered into a raffle to win a Mario-themed prize, and each new subscriber to the channel was thanked by the streamer as animations exploded onscreen. The Twitch streamer himself was in the bottom left-hand corner, commenting on the expert Mario levels he played with relative ease. Somewhere, squeezed in the middle, was the actual gameplay of *Super Mario Maker*. And even this was given a set of meta-rules, as the streamer was taking part in an informal *Super Mario Maker* format that involves skipping levels even if you die once. This was played inside *Super Mario Maker's* 100 Mario Mode on the punishing expert setting—a random 16 level trip through the most difficult of the game's user-generated levels. To recap: people pay money to win a raffle while watching someone talk over playing someone else's Mario levels using informal meta-rules on top of formal rules while people spout memes in a chat window. Maybe?

This convoluted, even overwhelming system within a system within a system speaks to the complexity of the current and future games landscape, with a tacit acknowledgement of the different play styles and preferences video games accommodate and satisfy within players. The person who creates the *Super Mario Maker* level might be seeking a creative outlet, while the person watching the Twitch stream might enjoy being part of the community or watching a player better than themselves. The Twitch streamer makes money but also seeks out extra challenge through newer external rule-sets when the game becomes too easy. All of the participants in this experience are seeking out play for different reasons—power, fantasy, self, and progress—yet only one might be said to be the player, the person with the controller. With so many participants, however, this feels inadequate, raising questions about who the players are and what the actual game being played is. The current definitions of video games, ours included, still revolve around the facile "game or not a game" debate, with their emphasis on conflict, rules, and choices. Perhaps redefining video games as digital play experiences will better encompass the complexities and expanding boundaries of these new possibility spaces.

REFERENCES

11 Bit Studios. (2014). *This war of mine* [Microsoft Windows/OS X/Linux video game]. Warsaw, Poland: 11 bit studios.

AcademySoft. (1986). *Tetris* [MS-DOS video game]. AcademySoft.

Adams, E. (2013). *Fundamentals of Game Design*. New Riders.

Alexander, L. (2013, September 20). *The tragedy of Grand Theft Auto V*. Retrieved January 15, 2016, from http://www.gamasutra.com/view/news/200648/Opinion_The_tragedy_of_Grand_Theft_Auto_V.php

Alientrap. (2015). *Apotheon* [PlayStation 4 video game]. Saskatoon, Saskatchewan, Canada: Alientrap.

Ape Inc. (1995). *Earthbound* [Super NES/Game Boy Advance video game]. Kyoto, Japan: Nintendo.

Atari, Inc. (1982a). *Dig dug* [Arcade video game]. Sunnyvale, CA: Atari, Inc.

Atari, Inc. (1982b). *ET* [Atari 2600 video game]. Sunnyvale, CA: Atari, Inc.

Atari, Inc. (1983). *Krull* [Atari 2600 video game]. Sunnyvale, CA: Atari, Inc.

Atlus. (2011). *Catherine* [PlayStation 3/XBox 360 video game]. Setagaya, Tokyo, Japan: Atlus.

Bally Midway. (1982a). *Ms. pac-man* [Arcade video game]. Chicago, IL: Bally Midway.

Bally Midway. (1982b). *Tron* [Arcade video game]. Chicago, IL: Bally Midway.

Barlow, S. (2015). *Her story* [Microsoft Windows/OS X/iOS video game].

Bartle, R. (1996). Hearts, clubs, diamonds, spades: Players who suit MUDs. *Journal of MUD Research*, *1*(1), 19.

Batchelor, G. (2016, March 10). *Hot date*. Retrieved March 30, 2016, from https://georgebatch.itch.io/hot-date

Bateman, C. (2015). Implicit game aesthetics. *Games and Culture*, *10*(4), 389–411. doi:10.1177/1555412014560607

Bethesda Game Studios. (2011). *The elder scrolls V: Skyrim* [Microsoft Windows, PlayStation 3, XBox 360 video game]. Rockville, MD: Bethesda Softworks.

BioWare. (2003). *Star wars: Knights of the old republic* [XBox video game]. San Francisco, CA: LucasArts.

BioWare. (2007). *Mass effect* [Xbox 360 video game]. Redmond, WA: Micorsoft Game Studios.

BioWare. (2014). *Dragon age: Inquisition* [Microsoft Windows/Playstation 3 video game]. Redwood City, CA: Electronic Arts.

Blizzard Entertainment. (2004). *World of warcraft* [Windows, OS X video game]. Irvine, CA: Blizzard Entertainment.

Blizzard Entertainment. (2014). *Hearthstone: Heroes of warcraft* [Microsoft Windows, OS X, iOS, Android video game]. Irvine, CA: Blizzard Entertainment.

Bogost, I. (2008). The rhetoric of video games. *The Ecology of Games: Connecting Youth, Games, and Learning*, 117–140.

2K. Boston. (2007). *Bioshock* [Xbox 360, PlayStation 3 video game]. Oklahoma City, OK: 2K Games.

Bungie. (2014). *Destiny* [PlayStation 3, PlayStation 4, Xbox 360, Xbox One video game]. Santa Monica, CA: Activision.

Caillois, R., & Barash, M. (1961). *Man, play, and games*. Champaign, IL: University of Illinois Press.

Campbell, C. (2013, March 7). *Fired for Making a Game: The Inside Story of I Get This Call Every Day*. Retrieved February 10, 2016, from http://www.polygon.com/features/2013/3/7/4071136/he-got-fired-for-making-a-game-i-get-this-call

Campo Santo. (2016). *Firewatch* [Microsoft Windows, OS X, Linux, PlayStation 4 video game]. Portland, OR: Panic.

CD Projekt RED. (2007). *The witcher* [Microsoft Windows/OS X video game]. New York, NY: Atari, Inc.

Clover Studio. (2006). Okami [PlayStation 2 video game]. Chuo-ku, Osaka, Japan: Capcom.

Clover Studio. (2008). Okami [Wii video game]. Chuo-ku, Osaka, Japan: Capcom.

Coffee Stain Studios. (2014). *Goat simulator* [Microsoft Windows/OS X/Linux/iOS/Android video game]. Skövde, Sweden: Coffee Stain Studios.

Coldwood Interactive. (2016). *Unravel* [Microsoft Windows/PlayStation 4/Xbox One video game]. Redwood City, CA: Electronic Arts.

Cormon, R., Brock, D., & Daniel, D. (Producers), & Brock, D. (Director). (1987). *Slumber party massacre II* [Motion Picture]. United States: New Concorde.

Crofford, K., Lazzo, M., Willis, D., Maiellaro, M., & Edwards, J. W. (Producers). (2000). Aqua teen hunger force [Television series]. Atlanta, GA: Williams Street.

Csikszentmihalyi, M. (2000). *Beyond boredom and anxiety: Experiencing flow in work and play*. San Francisco, CA: Jossey-Bass Publishers.

Csikszentmihalyi, M., & Rathunde, K. (1993). The measurement of flow in everyday life: Toward a theory of emergent motivation. In J. E. Jacobs (Ed.), *Current theory and research in motivation* (Vol. 40, pp. 57–97).

Cyan. (1993). *Myst* [Mac OS video game]. Eugene, OR: Brøderbund Software, Inc.

D'Anastasio, C. (2015, May 15). *Why video games can't teach you empathy*. Retrieved February 10, 2016, from http://motherboard.vice.com/read/empathy-games-dont-exist

Daniel Mullins Games. (2016). *Pony island* [Microsoft Windows, OS X, Linux video game]. Daniel Mullins Games.

Darabont, F., Hurd, G. A., Alpert, D., Kirkman, R., Eglee, C. H., & Mazzara, G. …Luse, T. (Producers). (2010). The walking dead [Television series]. Beverly Hills, CA: AMC Studios.

Davison, J. (Producer), Abrahams, J., Zucker, D., & Zucker, J. (Directors). (1980). *Airplane!* [Motion picture]. United States: Paramount Pictures.

Davison, J., & Lowry, H. (Producers), Abrahams, J., Zucker, D., & Zucker, J. (Directors). (1984). *Top secret!* [Motion picture]. United States: Paramount Pictures.

Dejobaan Games. (2014). *Elegy for a dead world* [Microsoft Windows/OS X/Linux video game]. Dejobaan Games.

Digital Pictures. (1992). Night trap [Sega CD/Sega 32X video game]. Ōta, Tokyo, Japan: Sega.

Dinosaur Polo Club. (2015). *Mini metro* [Windows/OS X/Linux video game]. Tokyo, Japan: Playism.

Double Fine Productions. (2014). *Hack "n" slash* [Microsoft Windows/OS X/Linux video game]. San Francisco, CA: Double Fine.

Ekaputra, G., Lim, C., & Eng, K. I. (2013). Minecraft: A Game as an Education and Scientific Learning Tool. *Information Systems*, *2*, 4.

Eno, B. (1996, June). *Generative music*. Presented at the Imagination Conference, San Francisco, CA.

feministfrequency [Screen name]. (2013). *Damsel in distress: Part 1 - Tropes vs women in video games* [Video file]. Retrieved from https://www.youtube.com/watch?v=X6p5AZp7r_Q

Fullbright. (2013). *Gone home* [Windows, OS, Linux video game]. Portland, OR: Fullbright.

Galactic Cafe. (2013). *The stanley parable* [Windows/OS X video game]. Galactic Cafe.

Gibson, A., & Dziff. (2016). *Oases* [Windows, OS X video game]. itch.io. Retrieved from https://armelgibson.itch.io/oases

Good-Feel. (2010). *Kirby's epic yarn* [Wii video game]. Kyoto, Japan: Nintendo.

Good-Feel. (2015). *Yoshi's woolly world* [Wii U video game]. Kyoto, Japan: Nintendo.

Grant, C. (2014, September 15). *Minecraft's immense popularity, broken down by platform*. Retrieved January 14, 2016, from http://www.polygon.com/2014/9/15/6154437/minecraft-platform-xbox-ps3-ios-android-pc-mac

Harmonix. (2005). *Guitar hero* [PlayStation 2 video game]. Mountain View, CA: RedOctane.

Harmonix. (2007). *Rock band* [Xbox 360/PS3 video game]. Redwood City, CA: Electronic Arts.

Hernandez, P. (2012, December 21). *I'm glad I played this depressing game about working in a call center*. Retrieved February 10, 2016, from http://kotaku.com/5970524/im-glad-i-played-this-depressing-game-about-working-in-a-call-center?tag=i-get-this-call-every-day

Holkins, J. (Writer), & Krahulik, M. (Illustrator). (2008, May 2). *Making an impression* [Cartoon]. Retrieved April 4, 2016, from https://www.penny-arcade.com/comic/2008/05/02/making-an-impression

Huizinga, J. (2014). *Homo ludens Ils 86*. New York, NY: Routledge.

Infocom. (1977). *Zork* [PDP-10 video game]. Cambridge, MA: Infocom.

Intelligent Systems. (2007). *Super paper mario* [Wii video game]. Kyoto, Japan: Nintendo.

Jorgensen, K., Kostroff, L., & Weiss, R. K. (Producers), & Landis, J. (Director). (1977). *Kentucky fried movie* [Motion picture]. United States: KFM Films.

Juul, J. (2007, February 1). *Guitar hero II: Playing vs. performing a tune*. Retrieved March 28, 2016, from http://www.jesperjuul.net/ludologist/guitar-hero-ii-playing-vs-performing-a tune

Juul, J. (2011). *Half-real: Video games between real rules and fictional worlds*. Cambridge, MA: MIT Press.

Karlsen, F. (2007). Emergence, game rules and players. *Nordisk Medieforskerkonference*. Retrieved from http://www.ipd.gu.se/digitalAssets/873/873905_karlsen.pdf

Key, E. (2013, February 1). *What are games* [Blog]. Retrieved from http://www.visitproteus.com/

Key, E., & Kanaga, D. (2013). Proteus.[Linus, OS, Windows, PS3, PSVita video game].

Klepek, P. (2013, August 15). *Gone home review*. Retrieved January 15, 2016, from http://www.giant-bomb.com/reviews/gone-home-review/1900-591/

Klepek, P. (2015, November 13). *Beautiful Game Pays Tribute To Grandfather Lost In a Plane Crash*. Retrieved January 8, 2016, from http://kotaku.com/a-game-that-imagines-a-happy-ending-for-a-tragic-loss-1742203440

Konami. (1986). *Castlevania* [Nintendo Entertainment System video game]. Tokyo, Japan: Konami.

Konami Computer Entertainment Japan. (1998). *Metal gear solid* [PlayStation/Microsoft Windows video game]. Tokyo, Japan: Konami.

Koster, R. (2013). *Theory of fun for game design*. Sebastopol, CA: O'Reilly Media, Inc.

Lazzo, M., Crofford, K., Fortier, J., & Willis, D. (Producers). (2005). Squidbillies [Television series]. Atlanta, GA: Williams Street.

Lee, J. J., & Hoadley, C. M. (2007). Leveraging identity to make learning fun: Possible selves and experiential learning in massively multiplayer online games (MMOGs). *Journal of Online Education, 3*(6).

Martin, G. (2013, September 30). *Grand theft auto V review (Multi-platform)* [Magazine]. Retrieved January 15, 2016, from http://www.pastemagazine.com/articles/2013/09/grand-theft-auto-v-review-multi-platform.html

Maxis. (2008). *Spore* [Microsoft Windows/Mac OS X video game]. Redwood City, CA: Electronic Arts.

McGonigal, J. (2011). *We don't need no stinkin' badges: How to re-invent reality without gamification* [Video file]. Retrieved from http://www. gdcvault. com/play/1014576/We-Don-t-Need-No

Media Molecule. (2013). Tearaway [PlayStation Vita video game]. Minato, Tokyo, Japan: Sony Computer Entertainment Europe.

Meyer, R. (2013, December 16). Facebook Advice: Don't Mistake Anti-Racist Satire for Patriotism. *The Atlantic*. Retrieved from http://www.theatlantic.com/technology/archive/2013/12/facebook-advice-dont-mistake-anti-racist-satire-for-patriotism/282406/

Mojang. (2011). *Minecraft* [Windows, OS, Linux, Android, iOS video game]. Stockholm, Sweden: Mojang.

Mustich, E. (2012, March 10). *Video games as multi-player art projects*. Retrieved March 28, 2016, from http://www.salon.com/2012/03/10/video_games_as_multi_player_art_projects/

Namco. (1980). *Pac-man* [Arcade video game]. Chicago, IL: Midway.

Namco. (2004). *Katamari damacy* [PlayStation 2 video game]. Tokyo, Japan: Namco.

Namco Bandai. (2009). *Noby noby boy* [PlayStation 3 video game]. Tokyo, Japan: Namco Bandai.

Narcisse, E. (2010, June 25). Press "B" to Skip: A Brief History of the Cutscene. *Time*. Retrieved from http://techland.time.com/2010/06/25/press-%E2%80%9Cb%E2%80%9D-to-skip-a-brief-history-of-the-cutscene/

Naughty Dog. (2013). The last of us [PlayStation 3]. Minato, Tokyo, Japan: Sony Computer Entertainment.

Necrophone Games. (2014). *Jazzpunk* [Microsoft Windows/OS X/Linux/PlayStation 4 video game]. Atlanta, GA: Adult Swim Games.

Nintendo, E. A. D. (1991). *Pilotwings* [Super Nintendo Entertainment System video game]. Kyoto, Japan: Nintendo.

Nintendo, E. A. D. (1995). *Super mario world 2: Yoshi's island* [Super Nintendo/Game Boy Advance video game]. Kyoto, Japan: Nintendo.

Nintendo, E. A. D. (1998a). *The legend of zelda: Ocarina of time* [Nintendo 64 video game]. Kyoto, Japan: Nintendo.

Nintendo, E. A. D. (1998b). *Yoshi's story* [Nintendo 64 video game]. Kyoto, Japan: Nintendo.

Nintendo R&D1. (1984). *Excitebike* [Nintendo Entertainment System video game]. Kyoto, Japan: Nintendo.

Nintendo. (1981). *Donkey kong* [Arcade video game]. Kyoto, Japan: Nintendo.

Nintendo. (1985). *Super mario bros.* [NES/Famicom video game]. Kyoto, Japan: Nintendo.

Nintendo. (1986). *Metroid* [NES video game]. Kyoto, Japan: Nintendo.

Nintendo. (2002). *Metroid prime* [Nintendo GameCube video game]. Kyoto, Japan: Nintendo.

Nintendo EAD Group No.4. (2015). *Super mario maker* [Wii U video game]. Kyoto, Japan: Nintendo.

Numinous Games. (2016). *That dragon, cancer* [Microsoft Windows, OS X, Ouya video game]. Numinous Games.

Pellegrini, A. D. (1995). *The future of play theory: A multidisciplinary inquiry into the contributions of Brian Sutton-Smith*. Albany, NY: SUNY Press.

Playdead. (2010). *Limbo* [Xbox Live Arcade video game]. Redmond, WA: Microsoft Studios.

Poe, E. A. (1843). The tell-tale heart. *The Pioneer*, *1*(1), 29–31.

Poe, E. A. (1846). The cask of Amontillado. *Godey's Lady's Book*, *XXXIII*(5), 216–218.

PopCap Games. (2009). *Plants vs. zombies* [IOS video game]. Redwood City, CA: Electronic Arts.

Pope, L. (2013). *Papers, please* [Windows, OS X video game].

Question. (2015). *The magic circle* [Microsoft Windows/OS X/Linux video game]. Question.

Ramsey, C. (2015, August 17). *The stormy world of Three Fourths Home has drama, cornfields*. Retrieved January 14, 2016, from https://killscreen.com/articles/stormy-world-three-fourths-home-has-drama-cornfields/

Rieber, L. P. (1996). Seriously considering play: Designing interactive learning environments based on the blending of microworlds, simulations, and games. *Educational Technology Research and Development*, *44*(2), 43–58. doi:10.1007/BF02300540

Rigby, S., & Ryan, R. M. (2011). *Glued to Games: How Video Games Draw Us In and Hold Us Spellbound: How Video Games Draw Us In and Hold Us Spellbound*. ABC-CLIO.

Riot Games. (2009). *League of legends* [Microsoft Windows, OS X video game]. Los Angeles, CA: Riot Games.

Rockstar North. (2008). *Grand theft auto IV* [PS3, Xbox 360, Windows video game]. New York, NY: Rockstar Games.

Rockstar North. (2013). *Grand theft auto V* [PS 3, Xbox 360 video game]. New York, NY: Rockstar Games.

Rockstar San Diego. (2010). *Red dead redemption* [Playstation 3/XBox 360 video game]. New York, NY: Rockstar Games.

Salen, K. (2008). *The ecology of games: Connecting youth, games, and learning*. Cambridge, MA: MIT Press.

Salen, K., & Zimmerman, E. (2004). *Rules of play: Game design fundamentals*. Cambridge, MA: The MIT Press.

Schell, J. (2015). *The art of game design: A book of lenses* (2nd ed.). Boca Raton, FL: CRC Press.

Schiesel, S. (2008, January 26). Author Faults a Game, and Gamers Flame Back. *The New York Times*. Retrieved from http://www.nytimes.com/2008/01/26/arts/television/26mass.html

Selzer, E. (Producer), & Jones, C. M. (Director). (1953). *Duck amuck*. [Motion picture]. United States: Warner Bros.

Shapiro, A. (Host). (2016, January 15). In "That Dragon, Cancer," "Unshakeable Empathy Gives Game Life" [Radio program]. All Things Considered. National Public Radio.

Sierra Entertainment. (1984). *King's quest* [IBM PC/Apple II video game]. Fresno, CA: Sierra Entertainment.

Silicon Knights. (2002). *Eternal darkness: Sanity's requiem* [Nintendo Game Cube video game]. Kyoto, Japan: Nintendo.

Sinclair, B. (2015, April 22). *Gaming will hit $91.5 billion this year*. Retrieved January 15, 2016, from http://www.gamesindustry.biz/articles/2015-04-22-gaming-will-hit-usd91-5-billion-this-year-newzoo

Star Maid Games. (2015). *Cibele* [Microsoft Windows video game].

Starbreeze Studios. (2013). *Brothers: A tale of two sons* [Xbox 360/Microsoft Windows/PlayStation 3 video game]. Milan, Italy: 505 Games.

Steam. (2016, April 1). *Steam search - simulator*. Retrieved April 2, 2016, from http://store.steampowered.com/search/?snr=1_4_4__12&term=simulator

Sterling, J. (2016, January 12). *That dragon, cancer review – Betwixt "game" and "experience"*. Retrieved from http://www.thejimquisition.com/that-dragon-cancer-review/

Stuart, K. (2016, January 14). That dragon, cancer and the weird complexities of grief. *The Guardian*. Retrieved from http://www.theguardian.com/technology/2016/jan/14/that-dragon-cancer-and-the-weird-complexities-of-grief

Supermassive Games. (2015). Until dawn [PlayStation 4 video game]. Minato, Tokyo, Japan: Sony Computer Entertainment.

Sutton-Smith, B. (2009). *The ambiguity of play*. Cambridge, MA: Harvard University Press.

Team Ico. (2005). Shadow of the colossus [PlayStation 2 video game]. Minato, Tokyo, Japan: Sony Computer Entertainment.

Team Ninja. (2003). *Dead or alive: Extreme volleyball* [Xbox video game]. Tokyo, Japan: Tecmo.

Telltale Games. (2012). *The walking dead* [PlayStation 3/Xbox 360 video game]. San Rafael, CA: Telltale Games.

thatgamecompany. (2009). *Flower* [PlayStation 3 video game]. Minato, Tokyo, Japan: Sony Computer Entertainment.

thatgamecompany. (2012). *Journey* [PlayStation 3 video game]. Minato, Tokyo, Japan: Sony Computer Entertainment.

The Chinese Room. (2012). *Dear Esther* [Windows, OS X video game]. Brighton, United Kingdom: The Chinese Room.

The Giant Beastcast. (2015, August). *The Giant Beastcast - Episode 14*. Retrieved from http://www.giantbomb.com/podcasts/download/1332/ep14_thegiantbeastcast-08-28-2015-3863808300.mp3

Timbre Interactive. (2015). *Sentris* [Linux/Microsoft Windows/OS X/Ouya/PlayStation 4 video game]. Seattle, WA: Timbre Interactive.

tobyfox. (2015). *Undertale* [Microsoft Windows/OS X video game]. tobyfox.

Tucker, A. (2012, March). *The art of video games*. Retrieved March 28, 2016, from http://www.smithsonianmag.com/arts-culture/the-art-of-video-games-101131359/

Twitch. (2016, April 5). *Twitch*. Retrieved April 5, 2016, from https://www.twitch.tv/

TwitchPlaysPokémon. (2016, April 5). *Twitch plays pokémon*. Retrieved April 5, 2016, from http://www.twitch.tv/twitchplayspokemon

Walker, A. (2015, April 3). *Three Fourths Home: Extended Edition Review*. Retrieved January 14, 2016, from http://www.gamespot.com/reviews/three-fourths-home-extended-edition-review/1900-6416087/

Wark, M. (2009). *Gamer theory*. Cambridge, MA: Harvard University Press.

Waugh, P. (2013). *Metafiction*. Routledge.

Webster, A. (2016, February 19). *Video game stories don't have to suck | The Verge*. Retrieved March 5, 2016, from http://www.theverge.com/2016/2/19/11056794/video-game-storytelling-writing-firewatch-the-witcher

Young, N. (2015, January 17). Why empathy is the next big thing in video games. *Spark*. CBC. Retrieved from http://www.cbc.ca/radio/spark/286-empathy-games-intangible-art-and-more-1.3073000/why-empathy-is-the-next-big-thing-in-video-games-1.3074676

Young Horses. (2014). *Octodad: Dadliest catch* [Microsoft Windows/OS X/Linux video game]. Young Horses.

Zimmerman, E. (2012, February 7). *Jerked around by the magic circle - Clearing the air ten years later*. Retrieved March 28, 2016, from http://www.gamasutra.com/view/feature/135063/jerked_around_by_the_magic_circle_.php

KEY TERMS AND DEFINITIONS

AAA Video Game: Video games supported with large design, development, and marketing/distribution budgets. The AAA games are often characterized by higher graphic and audio fidelity, content typically geared towards large groups of gamers, and similar to blockbuster hits in the film industry.

Branching Narrative: A game storytelling device where the story splits into many possible paths, often based on player choices or actions rather than requiring a linear, pre-determined gameplay sequence.

Indie Video Game: Those video games developed without substantial corporate funding. Although not a defining factor, indie games are usually developed by a small team or even a single individual.

Magic Circle: A phrase first used by Johan Huizinga in *Homo Ludens: A Study of the Play-Element in Culture*, signifying the boundary of a play space, such as the arena, the sandbox, the video game world, even the space within which a specific set of rules apply (e.g., Red Rover). Salen and Zimmerman in *Rules of Play* use this phrase to denote the game space or the space created by a game.

Metafiction: A playful fiction device that acknowledges the "rules" of fiction, only to break them. Metafiction sometimes breaks the so called fourth law between the author and the reader. In a game, this might be an overt reference to the fact that the player is playing a game.

Open World (Sandbox) Game: Open world games feature immersive environments where the player is free to move around the game space.

Play: It is a mode of being in which a person engages in activity—often voluntary, intrinsically motivating, pleasurable, make believe, and/or self-fulfilling.

Procedurally Generation: A programming mechanism where algorithms are used to create the game space, mechanics, characters, items, and more.

Serious Games: A game that is designed with a motive other than primarily fun or enjoyment, often to educate on a specific concept or process.

Simulator/Simulation Games: The goal of these games is to replicate complex systems and their interactions, sometimes giving players extra control over environments like a city or a civilization.

Chapter 2
Telling Tales with Technology:
Remediating Folklore and Myth through the Videogame *Alan Wake*

Dawn Catherine Stobbart
Lancaster University, UK

ABSTRACT

This chapter analyses the 2010 videogame Alan Wake, *a narrative based videogame that makes frequent use of intertextuality. As well as using contemporary examples, the game also uses traditional international folklore in its narrative, with the antagonist Barbara Jagger being recognisable as the Russian folk tale character Baba Yaga, for example. Using the concepts proposed and elucidated by Vladimir Propp, Joseph Campbell, the chapter will first establish that the videogame offers a remediation of several traditional mythical narratives in one contemporary videogame, before going on to use the classifications found in* The Morphology of the Folktale *and* The Hero with a Thousand Faces *to place this videogame within the folklore and mythical tradition. It will also serve to establish whether these classifications are suitable for the narratives found in videogames, and if they depart from them, where the scholar needs to establish new concepts and definitions for these traditional classifications.*

INTRODUCTION

As the technology used to create videogames evolves, videogame designers are progressively able to tell more complex stories, constructing narratives that support the perception that "many video games are stories, as well as games" (Egenfeldt-Nielson, Heide Smith, & Pajares Tosca, 2008, p. 204). Whilst these narratives need new methods of analyses to account for the interplay between ludology (the study of games, especially videogames, as a form of play) and narrative in videogames, such as interactivity, physical agency, and narrative involvement, there remains a narrative core that can be interrogated through existing literary methodologies and concepts. Using existing concepts allows a videogame to be situated within narrative studies and makes easier the remediation and inclusion of traditional themes, structures, and narratives in videogames, as they become increasingly adept as narrative carriers, an evolution in gaming and in narrative. This, in turn, enables older narratives to have continued recognition and survival in the 21st century. Contemporary videogames are able to carry explicit political or

DOI: 10.4018/978-1-5225-0261-6.ch002

moral messages, can retell fairy tales, and remediate myths from around the world, entwining traditional narratives into a contemporary setting, whilst retaining a recognizable core that has existed as long as the narratives they are retelling.

The narrative of the 2010 videogame *Alan Wake* (Remedy Entertainment, 2010), released by Microsoft for the Xbox 360 and Windows PC's, is created through an amalgamation of several myths from different cultures around the world that are entwined and updated to create a contemporary narrative. This game focuses on the protagonist, Alan Wake, as he engages with an entity known as "The Darkness" who has abducted his wife, Alice. This chapter will deconstruct the structure of the game, using the concepts proposed and elucidated by Vladimir Propp (who "holds a canonical position within the fields of literary criticism and folklore studies" (Smith & Riley, 2009, p. 184)) and Joseph Campbell (whose influence can be seen in film such as *Star Wars, Escape From New York*, and *The Terminator* amongst others (Palumbo, 2014)). This will be achieved through an analysis of the classifications found in *The Morphology of the Folktale* (Propp, 1968 edition) to show the game as a whole fits this structure, and *The Hero with a Thousand Faces* (Campbell, 2008 edition) to show the character types adhere to his classifications. (All subsequent references to these texts are from these later editions, as opposed to the original publications). This analysis will allow the placement of *Alan Wake* within a folklore and mythical tradition, highlight the remediation of several traditional mythical tales that appear in the videogame, and allow the videogame to be seen as entering into a dialogue that other media are invested in. This will show an historical evolution in videogame design and delivery. The overarching aim of the chapter is twofold. Firstly, it will show that folk tales are being shared by a global community who otherwise might never interact with them. These folklore stories are, in part, being kept alive by their inclusion in a popular contemporary videogame, breathing new life into tales no longer deemed relevant by a 21st century audience. This analysis will establish whether the experimental narrative delivery (at the time of the game's release) is noteworthy enough to be able to transcend the medium it is delivered through, offering an insight into the role of the videogame as part of the evolution of narrative, placing it alongside other media that have enabled narrative to evolve.

BACKGROUND

Remediation, the "re-presentation of one medium in another" (Bolter & Grusin, 2000, p. 45) is not new; in their book *Remediation: Understanding New Media*, Jay David Bolter and Richard Grusin cite examples throughout recorded history, including print remediating oral tales, photography remediating painting, and the novel being remediated by film (*Blade Runner* (Scott, 1982) remediates the novel *Do Androids Dream of Electric Sheep* (Dick, 1968) for example). Recent years have even seen digital texts being remediated by print, and new media, such as computer technology and the internet are "doing exactly what their predecessors have done: presenting themselves as refashioned and improved versions of other media" (Bolter & Grusin, 2000, p. 14-15). Furthermore, film is frequently adapted (rather than remediated) into the videogame form, and there have been numerous attempts to adapt videogames into film, albeit not always to critical or popular acclaim, as the popular Nintendo characters Mario and Luigi highlight. When these characters were exported unsuccessfully, both in critical and economic terms, from game to film and this adaptation is frequently cited as the foundation for rejecting all subsequent filmic adaptations of videogames. Whilst visual media such as film is both remediated—and adapted— to and from the videogame, the reworking of less visual media into the videogame form is not as often undertaken, despite an understanding that "we can still recognise 'the story' even when its medium has been considerably changed" (Brooks, 1992, p. 4). Literature is rarely considered suitable material for videogame adaptation and remediation, although it has been attempted with varying degrees of success in games across multiple media platforms, like *Dante's Inferno* (Electronic Arts, 2010), *The Great Gatsby* (Hoey & Smith, 2011) and *Bioshock* (2K Games, 2007), which Joseph Packer (2010) sees as attempting to remediate the political subtext of the 1957 novel *Atlas Shrugged* (Rand, 2007).

Entering into the growing range of videogames that seek to expand the ability of the medium and forming part of an evolution of both videogames and narrative, *Alan Wake*'s narrative has been constructed using Propp's classifications in *The Morphology of the Folktale* (1968) and those of Campbell's *The Hero with a Thousand Faces* (2008). Whilst it is true that both of these theoretical approaches have been criticised for being too broad and too reductive as an interpretive tool for the study of mythologies across all cultures (Hollwitz, 2001), and some scholars from other disciplines have dismissed their contributions to literary analysis (Jonnes, 1990), both authors' works use easily recognisable concepts. It might appear that these approaches are not relevant to new media, but using historical and analytical methodologies are useful to establish that the structures they propound exist across media, as well as showing the explicit presence of these structures in videogames such as *Alan Wake*, and therefore form part of the ongoing evolution of narrative, and of videogames.

Based on my own primary playing experience of the game and supported by the game guide (Hodgson, 2010), I consider *Alan Wake* to be a psychological horror-thriller in the Gothic style of Stephen King (Lehtinen, 2010) and Dean Koontz, which offers an account of the fight between good and evil, drawing heavily on the familiar symbolisms of light and dark to denote the two, respectively. The player controls the actions of the protagonist, Alan Wake, as he makes his way through the narrative, which can be summarised like this. Wake and his wife, Alice, travel to Bright Springs, where Alice (unbeknownst to him) has arranged for Wake to be treated at the Cauldron Lake Lodge mental health facility by Dr. Emil Hartmann in order to cure his writer's block. However, Alice is kidnapped by an entity called "The Darkness" who takes the form of Barbara Jagger, (a woman who was drowned in Cauldron Lake, and reanimated by her lover Thomas Zane many years previously). Alan awakens a week after the kidnapping with no memory of the events after Alice's kidnapping, but has to recover a manuscript he wrote whilst under Jagger's influence (which would allow The Darkness to infest the real world) in order to save Alice. Whilst looking for the manuscript Alan learns how to defeat Jagger, and aided by Bright Springs resident Cynthia Weaver, and the spirit of Thomas Zane, Wake uses light to destroy Jagger and free Alice. In doing so, Alan must sacrifice himself, leaving a doppelganger, Mr. Scratch, living his life.

Whilst this synopsis appears simple, the game itself takes many hours to play, and a full discovery of this narrative involves revisiting the game several times, as the player discovers information such as pages of manuscript that she can collect, which renders earlier discoveries more relevant, or that complicates previously understood information. Internet media company IGN considers that the game "is a swirling tale of fiction that's endearingly self-aware" (Onyett, 2012) creating a complex narrative that will be clarified as the chapter proceeds and the theoretical structure of the analysis requires. The analysis begins with the characters in the novel, and their relation to the work of Propp and Campbell.

A WRITERS DREAM: *ALAN WAKE* AS MYTH

The boundaries between myth, fairy tale and folktale are blurred according to Marina Warner in *Once Upon a Time: A Short History of Fairy Tale*, noting that "fairy tales are called 'folk tales', and are attributed to oral tradition, and considered anonymous" (2014, p. xvi), and whose building blocks "include certain kinds of characters and certain recurrent motifs" (2014, p. xiv), where

a hero or heroine or sometime both together are faced with ordeals, terrors, and disaster in a world that, while it bears some resemblance to the ordinary conditions of human existence, mostly diverges from it in the way it works, taking the protagonists—and us, to another place where wonders are commonplace and desires are fulfilled. (2014, p. xxii/xxiii)

Jack Zipes also recognises this, and cites a

distinction between wonder folk tales, which originated in oral traditions throughout the world, and still exist, and literary fairy tales, which emanated from the oral traditions through the mediation of manuscripts and print, and continue to be created today in various mediated forms around the world. (2012, p. 2-3)

Joining these definitions, myth is "a traditional story, typically involving supernatural beings or forces" by the *Oxford English Dictionary.* Nordic Mythology, which is the expression of religion of Norse and Germanic peoples before they were converted to Christianity, and which can be seen in *Alan Wake* can be placed in this definition, as can many of the creation myths from other cultures around the world. The *OED* also states that "myth is strictly distinguished from allegory and legend by some scholars, but in general use it is often used interchangeably with these terms" (OED Online, 2015). In this paper, I shall use the term folk tale to refer to a story (generally focusing on an individual) that has emerged from an oral tradition, which may be written, or accessed through an audiovisual media through remediation. Such is the case with *Alan Wake.*

The influence of Campbell's *The Hero with a Thousand Faces* can be seen in videogames as diverse as PlayStation's *Journey* (thatgamecompany, 2012) and the multiple platform game *Deus Ex: Human Revolution* (Eidos Montreal, 2011). Jenova Chen, author of *Journey,* cites Campbell as an influence in its creation (Ohannessian, 2012), with the game consisting of a single character's journey across a landscape (and can be seen as a metaphor for the journey of life). The use of the hero's journey, which Campbell distilled from studying myths across the globe, is recommended by Andrew Rollings and Ernest Adams in their 2003 work *On Game Design* (quoted in (Egenfeldt-Nielson, Heide Smith, & Pajares Tosca, 2008, p. 194)) and is considered as "good way to organise narrative progress in a game" (Egenfeldt-Nielson, Heide Smith, & Pajares Tosca, 2008, p. 194). Added to this recognised videogame design structure, Propp's structuralist classifications in *The Morphology of the Folktale* widens the scope of the videogame to produce a narrative that not only strengthens the use of Campbell's text, but allows designers to explicitly use these to create *Alan Wake.* In doing so, they highlight the ability of the medium to remediate the myths that are the foundation of the theoretical approaches themselves. Here, the videogame becomes part of the evolution of both narrative, and of the mythical tales that are being remediated by the games.

Alan Wake enters into discussions of both narrative structure and remediation through the influence of both *The Morphology of the Folktale* and *The Hero with a Thousand Faces.* As already stated, the use of the hero's journey is accepted as a way to organise narrative progress in a game (as well as other media, such as film), and therefore its structural presence should not be surprising. However, this is supported by inter- and metatextual evidence of Campbell's influence in the fictional blog *This House of Dreams* ("Samantha", 2012), which is set in the same fictional world that Wake occupies, and elaborates on the history of *Alan Wake* characters, Jagger, Zane, and Hartmann in the 1970's. The character creating the blog post transcribes a page from a shoebox she finds with the following information: "Note: as said, this is not a poem, more like a title page for something. The name of the author has been thoroughly and violently scratched out. Written above the title: "Campbell's <u>MONOMYTH!</u> I) Departure II) <u>Initiation!</u> III) Return" " ("Samantha", 2012, p. 2012/07/26). This suggests that Campbell has a bearing on the games narrative structure, and the game design team have not only used this, but draw attention to it explicitly. This then raises the question, "why are they doing so?", and it is this that the rest of this paper is concerned with.

Character Types in *Alan Wake*

Characters, for Propp, are agents of the action, and as such who they are is less important than what they do (Brooks, 1992, p. 15). Designating the characters in a folktale the *dramatis personae*, Propp writes in *The Morphology of the Folktale*, that the actions they undertake are distributed amongst seven character types, defining these seven character types as:

1. The Villain
2. The Donor
3. The Helper
4. The Princess and Her Father
5. The Dispatcher
6. The Hero
7. The False Hero (Propp, 1968, pp. 79-80).

For Propp, these types are important for "their role as vehicles of the action, their placement and appearance in order to make sure that the Hero is dispatched" (Brooks, 1992) to complete his quest. I shall begin, then, by showing that all of these character types appear in *Alan Wake*, thereby foregrounding the evolutionary and experimental nature of the game narrative structure at the time it was released.

Beginning with character type number one, the villain in *Alan Wake* is The Darkness, who manifests as Barbara Jagger—a character who shares many characteristics with the Slavic witch, Baba Yaga, as I argue elsewhere (Stobbart, 2012). In *Alan Wake,* Jagger enters into a "struggle with the hero" (Propp, 1968, p. 79) pursuing him throughout the game, until her defeat at the end. Taking a role in direct opposition to the villain, The Donor is represented by Cynthia Weaver, who also takes the role of The Helper, along with Sheriff Breaker of the local police force, and Barry Wheeler, Wake's literary agent. Weaver is known as The Lamp Lady, carrying an oil lamp with her at all times, and being concerned about the presence of darkness. In her role as The Donor, Weaver hides caches of weaponry and batteries for Wake to find, to aid him in his battle against The Darkness. The role of The Princess and her Father is taken by Alice Wake and the psychologist Dr. Emil Hartmann. Hartmann initially appears to be a minor character, but as the game progresses, it is revealed that he was involved with Thomas Zane and the resurrection of Jagger after her drowning in Cauldron Lake in the 1970s. Furthermore, in episode 4, Wake discovers that Alice has had several conversations with Hartmann about Wake, and that he is responsible for several of the sub-quests that Wake undertakes to save Alice.

The fifth character type to be found in the game is that of The Dispatcher, the spirit of author Thomas Zane, who introduces Wake to his quest, thereby making Wake the hero. Whilst this is not apparent upon first playing the game, replay shows that it is the voice of Thomas Zane that is talking to Wake in the beginning of episode 1 "Nightmare", the introductory section of the game that teaches the player how to control Wake, and how to defeat the Taken. Furthermore, Zane, also a writer, is discovered to have written several pieces that have become reality, including reanimating Barbara Jagger (and thereby triggering all of the events) and also creating the means of her destruction, "The Clicker." His spirit also enables Wake to escape from Jagger's influence, which begins the main body of the game. These two characters share many similarities: they are both writers, and are both able to rewrite reality, and their physical appearance is so similar that the retired rock stars Tor and Odin Anderson mistake Wake for Zane.

Whilst there are similarities between Wake and Zane, there is another character who wears similar features: the False Hero Mr. Scratch, the sixth character type to be found in *Alan Wake*. It is Mr. Scratch who takes over Wake's life when he sacrifices his presence in the world in exchange for his wife's release, and whose presence is central to the narrative of the second game. His role in *Alan Wake* is small, as he is introduced at the very end of the game, when Zane tells Wake that "your friends will meet him when you're gone" (Remedy Entertainment, 2010) as Wake realises he must sacrifice his own presence in the world to save Alice. Mr Scratch is a doppelganger of Wake, and is mistaken for Wake in the second game several times: he is literally a false hero.

Finally, the Hero of *Alan Wake* is Alan Wake. Functioning as the Hero of Propp's morphology, Wake also serves as the hero figure that Joseph Campbell describes in *The Hero with a Thousand Faces*. In this work, Campbell considers that the hero undertakes an adventure that can be split into three parts: "a separation from the world, a penetration to some source of power, and a life enhancing return" (J. Campbell, 2008, p. 27-28). Whilst the functions of the *dramatis personae* in Propp's work encompass all of the characters in a narrative, I shall concentrate on Campbell's analysis of the hero, and the actions that surround that character in his 1949 work, *The Hero with a Thousand Faces* (J. Campbell, 2008) to analyse the hero in *Alan Wake*.

The Hero, Alan Wake

Campbell's *The Hero with a Thousand Faces* (2008) offers a theory of the journey of the hero across the many mythologies of the world, intending to show that different cultures and their mythologies share a fundamental structure, which Campbell designates the monomyth. He considers that "the standard path of the mythological adventure of the hero is a magnification of the formula represented in the rites of passage: *separation—initiation—return:* which might be named the nuclear unit of the monomyth" (J. Campbell, 2008, p. 23) and this structure is one that is adhered to in *Alan Wake* and its sequel, *Alan Wake's American Nightmare*, and is also specifically referenced in the blog *This House of Dreams*, which I referred to earlier. However, I shall limit my discussion to the first game, *Alan Wake*, and the examples that appear therein, to show that the narrative structure Campbell offers is present, and explicitly followed by Remedy Entertainment in their construction of the game.

When writing in *The Hero with a Thousand Faces,* Campbell separates each of his primary three sections of the monomyth into several subsections, which detail the trajectory of the journey the hero makes in its entirety. This begins with the "Call to Adventure," in the section titled Departure, and ends with the hero's "Freedom to Live," in the section entitled Return. *Alan Wake* also begins with the Call to Adventure, although it ends not with the Freedom to Live, but rather with the "Refusal of the Return," that begins the final section of Campbell's classification.

For Wake, the Call to Adventure comes when he meets the villain of the game, Barbara Jagger, and collects keys to the wrong property from her for his stay in Bright Falls. Campbell describes a scenario such as this as "a blunder—apparently the merest chance" (2008, p. 42), which "signifies that destiny has summoned the hero and transferred his spiritual centre of gravity from within the pale of his society to a zone unknown" (J. Campbell, 2008, p. 48). For Wake, collecting keys from the wrong person and going to the wrong place allows Jagger to kidnap his wife, Alice, whom he calls his muse and is his "spiritual centre". His dependence on her is made explicit when he states "Jagger had Alice, and so she had me" (Remedy Entertainment, 2010), after Jagger spirits her away to an unknown place Wake must try to save her from. Jagger is the herald or announcer of the adventure then, "dark, loathy, or terrifying, judged evil by the world" and "a vague mysterious figure—the unknown" (J. Campbell, 2008, p. 44). Campbell's words effectively describe Jagger, an old woman wearing black clothing, a black veil, who is seen only in shadows and in the dark, and whom the local residents consider a mythic figure related to the Slavic witch Baba Yaga.

From this beginning, after Alice is kidnapped, Wake accepts the call to adventure to save her, through the "Crossing of the First Threshold" and entry into the "Belly of the Whale" the fourth and fifth aspects of Campbell's departure section. This is achieved by Wake jumping into Cauldron Lake after Alice, whom he sees sinking into the water. By diving into the lake, Wake enters "the darkness, the unknown and danger" (J. Campbell, 2008, p. 74) that marks such a passage, and it appears that Wake, "the hero, instead of conquering or conciliating the power of the threshold, is swallowed into the unknown, and would appear to have died" (J. Campbell, 2008, p. 74). This is upheld in the game when the narrative is taken up a week later, when Wake regains consciousness in a wrecked car, and takes up his journey to find and to save Alice, and it becomes clear that he has been missing for the last week. In responding to the call to adventure, Wake comes into contact with the "protective figure who provides [him] with amulets against the dragon forces he is about to pass" (J. Campbell, 2008, p. 57). For Wake, these amulets are torches, batteries, and weapons that allow him to remove the Darkness from the Taken with light, which then allows him to kill them in a traditional manner—with a gun. This protective figure is Cynthia Weaver, an old lady considered to be mad, and who leaves caches with these amulets inside for Wake to find all over Bright Falls. In Weaver, the figure of the fairy Godmother is invoked, "a familiar feature of European fairy lore" (J. Campbell, 2008, p. 59), seen in stories such as *Cinderella* and *Sleeping Beauty*, and like these characters, her benevolence is in direct competition with her opposite—Jagger's—evil. Weaver literally provides the light that can fight Jagger's darkness.

Much of the game (outside its introductory section) takes place as the first of Campbell's Initiation section, the "Road of Trials". Wake must travel across Bright Falls, and interact with several characters and many enemies in order to reach the final confrontation with the villain. Campbell describes the Road of Trials as "a dream landscape of curiously fluid, ambiguous figures, where he must survive a succession of trials" (J. Campbell, 2008, p. 81), and when playing *Alan Wake* it is easy to arrive at the conclusion that this has been directly transposed onto the game. The Taken are shadowy figures, seeming to come out of a misty haze in the darkness, and Wake (along with the player) must survive encounters with successively more difficult versions of the Taken to progress to the end of the game. Wake is helped during these trials by Weaver, who has left the caches full of aid for him, and who has provided visual clues for him to follow through the darkness and to reach the final confrontation.

Weaver, whilst being the figure that provides Wake with the most aid, is only one of a series of female figures that appear in the game. Campbell considers that "the goddess … is incarnate in every woman" (J. Campbell, 2008, p. 99), and therefore the female characters in the game all represent different aspects of the "Meeting with the Goddess", also seen in the Arthurian myth as the Lady of the Lake. Jagger, "promise[s] more than he (Wake) is yet capable of comprehending. She lures, she guides" (J. Campbell, 2008, p. 97), and when this does not succeed, she uses a facsimile of the physical persona of Wake's wife to tempt him away from his quest in episode 6, thereby invoking "Woman as the Temptress" the next subsection of Campbell's Monomyth. This figure can be found in several guises in *The Odyssey*: as Circe, Calypso, and as the Sirens, who tempt Odysseus to stay with them, rather than complete his journey.

As well as highlighting the interaction with the female in the form of the goddess, Campbell considers the role of the male, through the "Atonement of the Father", which is evident in the *Star Wars* films through the character of Darth Vader (J. Campbell, 2008, p. 225). In *Alan Wake* the father figure is the psychologist Emil Hartmann, who is employed by Alice to help cure Wake of his writers block. After she is kidnapped, Hartmann uses an employee to pretend that he is the kidnapper of Alice, and that Wake must produce the manuscript to save her, thereby curing his writers block. He also suggests that Wake himself killed her, and that he is suffering delusions in the aftermath. Here then, Hartmann provides "the frightening experiences" (J. Campbell J., 2008, p. 110) that the father figure initiates.

Taking place across all of the trials provided by Jagger and Hartmann, Wake reaches the "Apotheosis" section of the mythic structure of the narrative, where he acquires the knowledge to complete his quest, when he learns HOW to defeat Jagger. This knowledge, and the defeat of the villain results in the "Ultimate Boon" where, just like the Buddha in the Campbell's example of the Bo Tree, Wake "with the sword of his mind…pierced the bubble of the universe—and it shattered into nought" (J. Campbell, 2008, p. 164). Wake defeats Jagger by depressing the switch on the clicker that was written into existence by Zane and guarded by Weaver, illuminating her with light, and destroying both Jagger and the darkness inside her. For Wake, the boon for defeating Jagger is to save Alice, allowing her to return to the world, whilst he invokes the first of the subsections Campbell uses for the Return section of his analysis, the "Refusal of the Return". He realises that to save Alice, and to defeat Jagger, he must sacrifice his own freedom, and remain in the place where Alice has been—the Dark Place—and so refuses to return to the world when Alice does.

It is at this point that *Alan Wake* ends, and although the third section of the monomythic structure appears in the second game *Alan Wake's American Nightmare* (Remedy Entertainment, 2012), the scope of this investigation does not include this second game (my own playing experience supports IGN's hypothesis that "the story is thin and hackneyed" (Neigher, 2012) and cannot withstand more than a superficial analysis), which features Wake returning from his sacrificial place of imprisonment to defeat the false hero, Mr. Scratch. However, it is clear that the game does conform to the structure that Campbell offers, without any deviation and these can easily be mapped onto the narrative's structure. Wake acts as the monomythic hero of the game, and interestingly, Campbell's thesis is referenced in the game, and in the wider mythology of the franchise. *Departure*, as well as being the classification that Campbell uses for the first part of the monomythic journey, is also the name of the novel that Wake is made to write for Jagger, and it is at the point where Wake frees himself from her influence and returns to the real world with a nearly completed manuscript that is then lost, and must be recovered along the Road of Trials, that Campbell's classification moves from Departure to Initiation.

The Functions of the *Dramatis Personae*

Having established that Wake functions as the monomythic hero, and that all of Propp's character types appear in *Alan Wake,* the chapter now turns to the detailed study of the narrative as a reworking of

Propp's *The Morphology of the Folktale*, further supporting the evolutionary and experimental nature of the game as narrative-centric. This work was first published in English in 1958, as a study of the Russian fairy tale and sought to establish that all folktales have the same basic structure, and that a story can be created by instantiating a sequence of plot elements that he describes as the functions of the *dramatis personae*. Whilst Propp's structuralist approach was confined to Russian tales, and does not imply that the functions of the *dramatis personae* occur in tales across the world, it has become apparent in the years since, with the publication of works such as Campbell's *The Hero with a Thousand Faces*, that folk tales and myth on a global level share many similarities, and that Propp's approach can be used for the folktales of many cultures, despite its reductiveness. It is therefore prudent to consider *Alan Wake* using the structuralist approach formulated by Propp to establish whether the game can be viewed as a tale with a folk structure, just as the first section considers the characters in the game in relation to Campbell's monomythic structure.

Propp's seven character types (hero, villain, dispatcher, donor, helper, the princess and her father, and false hero) behave in a set pattern of up to 31 chronological functions. Not all of the 31 functions exist in every folktale, but of the ones that do, they appear in a set pattern, with no deviation. This pattern can be seen in *Alan Wake,* where of the 31 functions, two thirds are present in the game, and the final third occur in the sequel *Alan Wake's American Nightmare* (Remedy Entertainment, 2012), which sees Wake returning to the world to thwart his doppelganger and where he is reunited with his wife. However, it is beyond the scope of this chapter to continue the analysis into the sequel game, so I will limit the analysis to the functions found in *Alan Wake*, using the structure found in the chapter 3 of *The Morphology of the Folktale* (Propp, 1968, pp. 25-66).

The game opens with a tutorial, framed as a nightmare that Alan Wake is having, which introduces the player to the ludic structure of the game, and to Wake himself. In this part of the game the emphasised prosperity of Wake is established. Wake states in the opening monologue of the game that he is a writer (Remedy Entertainment, 2010) and there are pictures and posters in this part of the game that show that Wake is successful, including a poster for Wake's latest novel, *A Sudden Stop.* After the ludic structure of the game is established, the initial situation is discovered: Wake awakens to learn that he has been dreaming, and that he and his wife Alice have arrived at their holiday destination, Bright Springs, where Wake's emphasised prosperity is given further credence when a local radio broadcaster states that he recognises Wake as "a famous writer" and that he is "an avid reader" (Remedy Entertainment, 2010) of Wake's novels. Propp does not consider either of these aspects of the narrative to be a function, but states that they are "nevertheless [are] important morphological element[s]" (Propp, 1968, p. 25) and as such should be included in the analysis.

It is following the arrival of the couple in Bright Springs and the establishment of the initial situation and emphasised prosperity that the functions of the *dramatis personae* come into effect. The seven character types found in Propp's structural analysis represent the foundation upon which the functions of the dramatis personae are created. Propp uses examples from his collection of tales to exemplify the functions, a system I will follow to show that the same occurs in my case study, beginning with establishing the initial situation and the emphasised prosperity that is evident at the beginning of the narrative.

1. **One of the members of a family absents himself from home:** Alice Wake asks Alan to go into the Oh Deer Diner and get the key to the holiday home the couple will be staying in. Alan therefore, absents himself from the family unit.

2. **An interdiction is addressed to the hero:** Local resident Cynthia Weaver tells Wake "Don't go in there, young man. You can hurt yourself in the dark" (Remedy Entertainment, 2010) when he sets off to find Carl Stucky, the key holder who has gone to the restroom.

3. **The interdiction is violated:** Wake disregards the interdiction and goes into the shadowy passageway to get to the restroom.

4. **The villain makes an attempt at reconnaissance:** Wake meets an old woman in the shadows, who establishes that Wake is with his wife, and that the couple will be staying in her cabin on Cauldron Lake.

5. **The villain receives information about his victim:** This function does not occur in *Alan Wake*. Alan is very quiet in the face of the comments being made by the old woman and does not deliver any information that the woman can use.

6. **The villain attempts to deceive his victim in order to take possession of him or of his belongings:** Jagger gives Wake the keys to her cabin instead of the one they should be staying in.

7. **The victim submits to deception and thereby unwittingly helps his enemy:** Alice accepts that the cabin on the lake is the one they are staying in, despite it being different to the one she hired.

8. **The villain causes harm or injury to a member of a family:** Alice goes missing. Propp writes that "the forms of villainy are exceedingly varied" and this is an example of "the villain abducts a person" (Propp, 1968, p. 31) and "the villain imprisons or detains someone" (Propp, 1968, p. 34)

9. **Misfortune or lack is made known; the hero is approached with a request or command; he is allowed to go or he is dispatched:** Wake returns to the cabin, hearing Alice calling for help, to find a broken window and Alice gone. Looking out of the broken window, he sees Alice sinking in the lake.

10. **The seeker agrees to or decides upon counteraction:** Wake dives into Cauldron Lake through the broken window to save Alice.

11. **The hero leaves home:** Wake awakens in a wrecked car, a week after the first ten functions, with no memory past Alice's disappearance. He sets out to find her.

12. **The hero is tested, interrogated, attacked, etc., which prepares the way for his receiving either a magical agent or helper:** Wake must reach the nearest inhabited building, a gas station. Along the way he is attacked by shadowy figures—the Taken. Specifically, this adheres to "a hostile creature attempts to destroy the hero" and "a hostile creature engages the hero in combat" (Propp, 1968, p. 42).

13. **The hero reacts to the actions of the future donor:** Wake reaches the gas station and makes contact with Sheriff Breaker, Cynthia Weaver, and his agent, Barry Wheeler.

14. **The hero acquires the use of a magical agent:** Cynthia Weaver provides Wake with a series of boxes, containing light and weaponry that can defeat the Taken throughout the ludic parts of the game.

15. **The hero is transferred, delivered, or led to the whereabouts of an object of search:** Weaver leads Wake to The Well-Lit Room, where he is given The Clicker, which Weaver has been protecting.

16. **The hero and the villain join in direct combat:** Wake engages Jagger, writing the ending to the novel and she responds by attacking him with darkness.

17. **The hero is branded:** Wake is repeatedly told by his wife's voice that she does not love him and is leaving him, as part of the combat between him and Jagger. This adheres to "the hero receives a wound during the skirmish" (Propp, 1968, p. 52), although this is not a physical wound.

18. **The villain is defeated:** Wake defeats Jagger through using The Clicker to destroy the darkness in her body, thereby destroying her.
19. **The initial misfortune or lack is liquidated:** Alice is returned to the world when Jagger is defeated. Specifically, this relates to "the spell on a person is broken", and "a captive is freed". (Propp, 1968, pp. 54-55)
20. **The hero returns:** The return of Wake and all the subsequent functions occur in the second game, *Alan Wake's American Nightmare.*

Taken in their entirety, these functions comprise the basic narrative of *Alan Wake*, and show the foregrounded and evolutionary narrative structure of the game. Many of the functions are found in the first episode of the game, which ends with Wake meeting Sheriff Breaker, (function 13). Episodes five and six contain functions 15-19, which is where the game ends (the functions continue in the sequel game, which begins with function 20). Much of the ludic body of the game takes place around function 14, in a series of movements across the game's landscape, which serve to fill out the narrative. Clearly then, the narrative of *Alan Wake* fits into the structural functions as laid out by Propp, with even the functions that do not readily correspond to the narrative appearing as an inversion of themselves. Such is the case with function five: delivery. Propp's analysis states that in this function, the villain receives information about his victim. However, in *Alan Wake*, Jagger's attempts to converse with Wake are met with polite silence, and she is not given the information that the function requires. The game as a whole then can be mapped directly onto Propp's morphology, just as the role of the hero can be transposed onto that of Campbell, making clear that the role of myth in the game is an important part of its structure, just as the narrative's mythological content is important to the construction of the game. Many narratives that use this model do not feature all of the functions Propp describes, and it becomes clear when the game is deconstructed in this way that *all* of the functions are present, and that Remedy Entertainment have taken pains to construct the narrative around this structure, and that of Campbell.

Myths in Alan Wake

So far, this chapter has considered the structure of *Alan Wake,* using the theoretical approaches pioneered by Campbell and Propp. However, this game not only uses these mythical structures as a means to create new myth, but it also explicitly includes lore from around the world in its construction, thereby remediating existing mythic tales, even as it tries to creates a contemporary myth for the twenty-first century, again offering an evolutionary structure to the game.

Remedy Entertainment, the Finland-based creators of *Alan Wake*, are known for inserting aspects of their local mythologies into their games. The Max Payne franchise contains many allusions to Norse mythology, with several locations and characters bearing the names of Norse Gods and mythos (GameAxis Unwired, 2008). Remedy revisits this remediative method to similarly insert mythological elements into *Alan Wake*, including the placement of Native American myth via Cauldron Lake, which is based on Crater Lake in Oregon a site held sacred by Native American tribe The Klamath (Lehtinen, 2010). A major source of myth in *Alan Wake* (as well as other Remedy games) is the Norse tradition that Remedy are familiar with, especially in relation to minor characters, The Anderson brothers, who embody this tradition. However, the biggest use of mythology in the game is through the presentation of the antagonist Barbara Jagger as the witch Baba Yaga.

Alan Wake references Baba Yaga throughout, linking Jagger to the witch and signalling her importance as the dominant folk figure of all those referenced in the game. Zipes, in *The Irresistible Fairy Tale,* states that "Baba Yaga has appeared in hundreds, or perhaps thousands, of folk tales [and] is an amalgamation of deities mixed with a dose of sorcery, shamanism, and fairy lore" (Zipes, 2012, p. 61), noting that she is a well-known Slavic and Eastern European witch, and whilst she sometimes wears a different name, her function remains the same across the legends of the different cultures that utilise her lore. Literally translated as Old Woman Hag, Baba is usually described as an ugly, emaciated, old crone who rides a pestle and mortar and uses the broomstick she carries to destroy any evidence of her passage through the mortal world. The laws of nature obey her commands and she has the ability to induce nightmares and hallucinations in people if she is upset – as well as the capability to be benevolent to those she deems worthy. Baba Yaga's relationship with Barbara Jagger is acknowledged by the game's designers, Remedy Entertainment, and characters explicitly refer to Jagger as Baba on a number of occasions in the game, as well as using a variety of other names, such as Granny Claws or the Scratching Hag. The Anderson Brothers explicitly reference her in song lyrics, and the in-game song titled *The Poet and the Muse* is based on the events of Jagger's death and reincarnation in the game's narrative, and the lyrics refer to Jagger as a witch. As well as these explicit references, the game contains more subtle, spatial, references that promote the legend of Baba Yaga in *Alan Wake*: Jagger and Zane lived in Bird Leg Cabin, named for the shape of the island it was located on, before it disappeared in 1970, and it should be noted that Baba Yaga's cottage stands on chickens legs. Diver's Island, on which Bird Leg cabin was situated, was on Cauldron Lake, an obvious reference to witches and witchcraft, and is also the place where Barbara Jagger drowned and was reborn as the Dark Presence, where immersion in the cauldron transformed the young woman into a wicked witch.

In *Alan Wake*, the characters that are remediated from folk lore to the game are made contemporary. The Anderson Brothers remediate aspects of Norse Mythology through a colourful history as part of a Rock group, and Barbara Jagger is a reinvention of Baba Yaga. For the player who has not been exposed to a character such as Baba Yaga, this not only introduces the character, but also invites further exploration of her history. For example, internet forums for the game describe how players have looked into the folklore the game details, including characters names and history. In folk lore, characters such as Baba Yaga function as "ready-made". That is, instantly recognised as a stereotype and one of the functions of a character such as Baba Yaga is to be a teaching mechanism, to provide (in the guise of a tale or anecdote) moral values – just as the more familiar tales of *Red Riding Hood*, or *Hansel and Gretel* do, depending on the particular circumstances of the tale being told. For *Alan Wake*, this means that the player will recognise the character type, even if she does not recognise Baba Yaga herself. Furthermore, it is through the juxtaposition of the formal structure of the game and the folkloric content that Remedy's narrative intent becomes clear.

In 2010, when *Alan Wake* was first released, games with a strong narrative thread were not as common as they are today, and it's designers wanted to "push the envelope in the industry" (G. Campbell, 2010) and create something with a strong story, and that would deliver "a tightly scripted experience" (G. Campbell, 2010). The use of Propp's—and Campbell's—simplistic structure allows the game designers to do this, and to show explicitly that they are following a structure that is itself part of an evolution of storytelling that has taken place over hundreds, if not thousands, of years. This is further supported by the use of characters from the very folklore that the two critics based their theses on, which allows the player to recognise specific character types as they appear, and more than this, introduces the player to the specific examples of character types, (as is the case with Barbara Jagger/Baba Yaga) that they may be unfamiliar with. Videogames such as *Alan Wake* then, do not simply enact the traditions, or the folkloric structure they are remediating, offering the videogame as a new means of accessing these older materials: they literally refashion them, placing them in a contemporary context and setting, and offering the player the chance to be an active part of the games narrative, and therefore, the legend itself. This interactivity allows the player who is unfamiliar with a folkloric tale to interact with it in an environment that facilitates the understanding of allegories, meanings, and symbolism through direct action – while engaging in familiar gameplay. In the case of *Alan Wake,* Barbara Jagger is equipped with a set of morally and emotionally loaded characteristics which explain both Jagger and Baba Yaga; while becoming familiar with Jagger, the unfamiliar player is being exposed to the games interpretation of Baba Yaga. Furthermore, digital media such as the videogame enables designers and players to develop the tools to recognise unfamiliar myths, and presents them with the chance to interfere with the myth's temporal dominion and uses the medium's unique tools to redraft and distribute alternatives to the original mythic characters (Bassett, 2011) whilst presenting an entertaining, contemporary narrative.

CONCLUSION

Whilst the theoretical structures of this chapter are reductive, and have been criticized for their approach, as Hollowitz and Jonnes amongst others suggest, they nevertheless show that *Alan Wake* adheres to a strict narrative structure that is recognizable, long established, and that predates the written text. Analyses such as these, which draw on existing— and even potentially redundant — literary approaches are an important part of establishing the role and functions of the videogame as a narrative carrier. In creating *Alan Wake* with a recognisable narrative structure Remedy Entertainment engage with the evolution of videogames as a narrative carrier. Videogames, in order to make ludic or narrative progress, place the player in a position where she must interact with and navigate the game space, which in *Alan Wake* encompasses the majority of the game, and takes the form of the Road of Trials and function 14 of Propp's structure. Without mastering the trials facing Wake, just as with the mythical hero Campbell writes of, the game cannot progress and neither can the narrative. This interactivity creates a new relationship of narrative consumer to narrative space, a concept that some literary scholars are resistant to. Direct interaction with the narrative, rather than observation also heightens the immersion the player has with the game and the narrative. This is also true of the player's interaction with the folkloric content of the game.

The inclusion of folklore in videogames does not foreground the oral traditions from which they emerge. However, in a world where media such as film and videogames are able to rival and possibly even outstrip traditional tales in the audiences they are capable of interacting with, this remediation allows them to be introduced to a wider demographic. Videogames, therefore, have the potential to keep folklore alive by their very remediation into this interactive media, breathing new life into tales just as has occurred many times throughout history. As well as offering a continuation and remediation of folk lore, including folk characters in the game highlights its narrative structure. Although technological and game design advances in 2015 makes this seems unsophisticated and simple, at the point the game was created, it was a pioneering narrative approach for videogames.

Future studies of videogame analysis need to consider the role that interactivity plays on the narrative and on the folklore that is being remediated in videogames such as *Alan Wake*, and the way the player interprets a narrative when it is delivered in this manner. Remediated texts are appearing in videogames in increasing numbers, and to further understand the unique immersive qualities they contain, the analyst needs to consider the role of player/protagonist identity in videogame narratives and consider how videogames allow the player to take on a specific perspective. Furthermore, understanding the construction of characters and narrative structures in which videogames bring about new ways of presenting information to the player (and viewer) of videogame narratives, alongside the more traditional methods such as film and literature. This requires the designer, and the player to ask questions such as "Does the player take on the role of the monomythic hero when playing this game?" The role of player response to the remediated texts is also something that should be considered, to ascertain whether the information that is being presented, regardless of the intent of the game design team, is being received by the player, and how it is being interpreted at the point of delivery.

REFERENCES

2K Games. (2007). *Bioshock* [Microsoft Windows video game]. New York, NY: Take Two Interactive.

Bassett, N. (2011, November 18). *Literature Review: Remediation of Ideology and Narrative, From Old To New*. Retrieved July 29, 2012, from Academia.edu: http://newschool.academia.edu/NathanaelBassett/Papers/1158418/Lit_Review_Remediation_of_Ideology_and_Narrative_From_Old_To_New

Bolter, J. D., & Grusin, R. (2000). *Remediation: Understanding New Media*. Cambridge, MA: The MIT Press.

Brooks, P. (1992). *Reading for the Plot*. Cambridge, MA: Harvard University Press.

Campbell, G. (2010, May 05). *Alan Wake: We speak with Remedy's Matias Myllyrinne*. Retrieved from Gameplanet.co.nz: http://www.gameplanet.co.nz/xbox-360/features/i134842/Alan-Wake-We-speak-with-Remedys-Matias-Myllyrinne/

Campbell, J. (2008). *Pathways to Bliss: Mythology and Personal Transformation: Easyread Large Edition*. Surry Hills, NSW: Accessible Publishing Systems.

Campbell, J. (2008). *The Hero with a Thousand Faces (Collected Works Edition)*. Novato, CA: New World Library.

Deeley, M. (Producer) & Scott, R. (Director). (1982). *Blade Runner* [Motion picture]. United States: Warner Bros.

Dick, P. K. (1968). *Do Androids Dream of Electric Sheep*. London: Gollancz.

Egenfeldt-Nielson, S., Heide Smith, J., & Pajares Tosca, S. (2008). *Understanding Video Games: The Essential Introduction*. New York: Routledge.

Eidos Montreal. (2011, August 23). *Deus Ex: Human Revolution* [Microsoft Windows video game]. Skinjuku, TKY: Square Enix.

Electronic Arts. (2010). *Dante's Inferno* [Playstation 3 video game]. Redwood City, CA: Vicsceral Games.

GameAxis Unwired. (2008). *Valhalla and Back*. Game Axis Unwired, 69.

Hodgson, D. (2010). *Alan Wake Official Survival Guide*. Roseville: Prima Games.

Hoey, C., & Smith, P. (2011). *The Great Gatsby*. Retrieved July 10, 2012, from http://greatgatsbygame. com/

Hollwitz, J. (2001). The Grail Quest and Field of Dreams. In C. Hauke & I. Alister (Eds.), *Jung and Film: Post-Jungian Takes on the Moving Image* (pp. 83–94). Hove: Brunner-Routledge.

Jonnes, D. (1990). *The Matrix of Narrative: Family Systems and the Semiotics of Story*. New York: Mouton de Gruyter.

Lehtinen, S. (2010). *Alan Wake: Light and Dark Presentation*. Retrieved from GDCvault.com: http:// www.gdcvault.com/play/1013666/Alan-Wake-Light-and

Neigher, E. (2012, May 29). *Alan Wake's American Nightmare Review*. Retrieved from IGN.com: http:// uk.ign.com/articles/2012/05/29/alan-wakes-american-nightmare-review-2

OED Online. (2015, September). *myth,* n. Retrieved from OED Online: http://www.oed.com.ezproxy. lancs.ac.uk/view/Entry/124670?rskey=whPmFn&result=1#eid

Ohannessian, K. (2012). *Game Designer Jenova Chen on the Art Behind His 'Journey'*. Retrieved from fastcocreate.com: http://www.fastcocreate.com/1680062/game-designer-jenova-chen-on-the-art-behind-his-journey

Onyett, C. (2012). *Alan Wake Review*. Retrieved from IGN.com: http://uk.ign.com/articles/2012/02/15/ alan-wake-review

Packer, J. (2010). The Battle for Galt's Gulch: Bioshock as Critique of Objectivism. Journal of Gaming and Virtual Worlds, 209-224.

Palumbo, D. E. (2014). *The Monomyth in American Science Fiction FIlms: 28 Visions of the Hero's Journey*. Jefferson: McFarland & Co.

Propp, V. (1968). *The Morphology of the Folktale*. Austin: University of Texas Press.

Rand, A. (2007). *Atlas Shrugged*. London: Penguin Modern Classics.

Remedy Entertainment. (2010). *Alan Wake* [Xbox 360, Microsoft Windows video game]. Redmond, WA: Microsoft Studios.

Remedy Entertainment. (2012, February 22). *Alan Wake's American Nightmare* [Xbox 360, Xbox One, Microsoft Windows video game]. Redmond, WA: Microsoft Studios.

Samantha. (2012). *This House of Dreams*. Retrieved from blogger.com: http://thishouseofdreams. blogspot.co.uk/

Smith, P., & Riley, A. (2009). *Cultural Theory: An Introduction*. Oxford: Blackwell Publishing.

Stobbart, D. (2012, August). *The Darkness and the Light: Traditional Tales in a Modern Environment*. Retrieved from academia.edu: https://www.academia.edu/3622550/The_Darkness_and_the_Light_Traditional_Tales_in_a_Modern_Environment

thatgamecompany. (2012). *Journey*. Retrieved April 19, 2012, from thatgamecompany.com: http:// thatgamecompany.com/games/journey/

Warner, M. (2014). *Once Upon a Time: A Short History of Fairy Tale.* Oxford: Oxford University Press.

Zipes, J. (2012). *The Irresistable Fairy Tale. Woodstock.* Princeton University Press.

KEY TERMS AND DEFINITIONS

Folklore: The beliefs, custom, and stories, which are passed on to new generations via oral storytelling.

Intertextuality: The relationship between texts, the shaping of a texts meaning using another text.

Monomyth: A quest (frequently cyclical) that is undertaken by a mythical hero.

Myth: A traditional story, belonging to a culture, that typically engages with supernatural beings or events, and that explain historical, social, and natural phenomenon.

Narrative: An account (usually but not always spoken or written) of a series of connected events.

New Media: The products and services that provide entertainment through computers and the internet.

Remediation: The process of changing the media a narrative is told through. E.g. A film that is based on a novel is a remediated text.

Videogame: A game, played via an electronic interface, which allows a player to manipulate an on screen avatar to reach a successful conclusion, and can be story based, or not.

Chapter 3

"There Are No Observers Here":
The Video Game Gaze in *Outlast* (2013) and *Outlast: Whistleblower* (2014)

Hazel E. Monforton
University of Durham, UK

ABSTRACT

As an emergent medium capable of telling complex stories, the video game gives us unique insight and challenges to established critical theory. This chapter will examine the ways 'the gaze' is expressed and utilized in video games, particularly the "survival horror" genre. It will discuss some of the ways 'the gaze' has been shaped by literary and filmic studies before turning to Outlast *(2013) by Red Barrels Games as an example of the way the medium can rearticulate our understanding of watching and being watched. Through its player-driven diegesis, immersion and phenomenologically-situated avatar body, and an ability to stimulate emotional response through game mechanics, the video game gaze might be capable of engendering emotional sympathy rather than constructing hierarchical positions of mastery. With its narratives of state control and institutionalization, journalistic distance, and medical invasiveness,* Outlast *uses critical understandings of 'the gaze' to ask questions about privacy, complicity, and responsibility.*

INTRODUCTION

As the video game has stylistically and narratively grown as a medium, the critical approach to games has shifted to accommodate its unique communicative attributes. Despite the unavoidable instinct in literary studies to use existing theory—e.g., film theory developing out of English departments in the 1960's—there has been a shift towards an appreciation for the medium's unique methods of storytelling. Early critical investigations approaching video games on their own terms, from Espen Aarseth's *Cybertext* (1997), Janet Murray's *Hamlet on The Holodeck* (1997), and Gonzalo Frasca's "Simulation versus Narrative" (2003), agree that the video game is unique for its interactivity, immersion, and narrative structure. Instead of merely investigating their complicity in real-world violence, we have moved towards an appreciation for the medium's unique methods of storytelling. Instead of approaching video games

DOI: 10.4018/978-1-5225-0261-6.ch003

as automatically speaking the language of film or as articulating otherwise liner narratives easily-read with extant critical tools, there is an impetus to approach this emerging media as one that might alter our understanding of those tools.

Doris Rusch, in her paper "Mechanisms of The Soul" (2009), identifies three characteristics of games she defines as "real" and unique to the medium: their "affective nature," their "procedurality" and their "metaphorical potential" (p. 1). Similarly, in Jesper Juul's description of the video game in *Half-Real* (2005), he makes a distinction between real and fictive; games are an interaction with "real rules [...] as well as a fictional world" (2005, p. 8). There is also an encounter with the text not found in other media which engenders emotional responses as part of our subject-position within the text but extant of narrative; this emotional range can be everything from "paranoia" to "caring" (Rusch, 2009). She goes on to describe the lacuna between "cognitive" and "emotional" comprehension that can occur in a video game (p. 7); this is the difficult link, which must be made between game narrative and game design. Though mechanically identical, a maze level is thematically distinct from a prison level. To this effect, Ian Bogost (2007) outlines what he terms "procedural rhetoric," as games produce the inner workings of complex systems, from their methods, techniques, and logics. The video game creates a symbolic structure through which the player must navigate; the medium is a space in which these structures are not only described, but also enacted (p. 107). Experienced independently, cognitive and emotional comprehension of a game world might provide vastly different understandings, but as a gestalt whole they provide meaning and context to affective emotions engendered by the game's complex systems. The way the play-space is specifically constrained rather than interactive is the emergence of narrative and design; the amalgamation of affective design, procedural rhetoric, and subject-position must inform a textual analysis of a video game. Diane Carr (2002) cautions on applying a single model to any player-game interaction, as "[p]lay is experiential and ephemeral yet embodied, and culturally situated" (Carr, 2009, p. 2). In this, video games present a puzzle to the literary theorist, and with rare exception there have been few investigations into the video game's relationship with film and literary theory.

In this chapter I will investigate the potentialities of a distinct 'video game gaze,' and while the long history of critical theory on 'the gaze' has inextricably linked vision to violence, I will turn to understandings drawn from trauma theory in order to articulate a conceptual framework of watching and being watched that involves interpersonal connection and articulation across an experiential gulf rather than oppositional tension over scopic mastery. I will then turn to *Outlast* (Red Barrels, 2013). While undoubtedly a violent game, the position in which the player assumes is one of victim rather than perpetrator of violence; the game is distinct in that the only method of defense is a video camcorder (i.e., a method of enhanced seeing). This is used, in the game, to witness and testify to the abuses of power rather than perpetuate that abuse.

BACKGROUND

As Clive Thompson notes in his 2002 survey of the political discussions of video games, the majority of games have players take on the role of "forces of social order"—typically the police or military—which utilize violence to dominate and eliminate threats encountered throughout the game setting (p. 27). The proliferation of titles such as the *Call of Duty* franchise testify to the prevalence and popularity of these types of games; however, as Carrie Andersen (2014) notes in her examination of the role of the soldier in *Call of Duty: Black Ops II* (Treyarch, 2013), the player's ability to exert power in the video game has been metatextually called into question. While critics such as J.P. Grant (2009) might conclude that games teach us to trivialize death and violence, violence is expressed and experienced in a variety of ways in the video game both narratively and mechanically; the distinct movement from the player committing violence to the player experiencing violence opens up the medium to express subject positions heretofore marginalized, and communicate this through the gaze. As I will show, the 'video game gaze' has the potential not just to place players in the role of the producers of violence, but engage in a sympathetic embodiment as a witness to and victim of violence. In light of this understanding, the video game has begun to explore this unique attribute to its medium.

In *Discipline and Punish* (1975), Foucault uses the gaze to illustrate the functions and consequences of widespread surveillance; it trains the unobserved to act as if they were being observed, instilling a type of self-policing—a docile body, as Foucault describes. The holder of the 'gaze' in this model is never, himself, observed. Laura Mulvey's influential feminist examination "Visual Pleasure and Narrative Cinema" (1989) describes what she coins 'the male gaze,' the assumption of a male subject to whom the object of the gaze is offered up. Similarly, Todd McGowan's *The Real Gaze* (2007) describes the Lacanian gaze—upon which much of film theory's definition is based—as an acknowledgement of the anxiety of being viewed, and the vulnerability that comes with that recognition. 'The Gaze' in the narrative is the space in which the observer is pointedly acknowledged and involved. Similarly, in *It Looks at You* (1995), Wheeler Dixon cites horror films such as *The Silence of the Lambs* (1991), *I Spit On Your Grave* (1997) and *Last House on the Left* (1972) as having "a profound and problematic visual hold on viewers, conversely inciting or desensitizing patrons to acts of violence". These films force identification with victim or tormentor to "transfix and collectivize" the experience of the audience (p. 7). He describes the act of watching a film as "

an act of submission [...] The viewer, it seems to me, is instead the subject/object of the gaze of the cinematic image". Our understanding of its mechanics only gives us "the illusion of control [...] The film looks at us, not we at it (p. 43-44).

All of these theoretical models assume a level of violence implicit in the gaze; there is an immediate hierarchical imbalance between observer and observed. As traditional views of the gaze would have it, "[t]he visual seeks mastery of both self and other. Vision promises — or is heralded as the promise of — complete and definitive knowledge, as if Truth can be revealed through technologies of the eye" (McCormack, 2014, p. 30). However, as I will explore, the video game gaze can communicate trauma rather than simply represent structures of power. As the video game experience is embodied, emergent, and affective, the traditional understanding of the gaze in critical theory must adapt to these multifarious means of both emotive and cognitive understanding within the realm of play. From this understanding we shall move towards a theory of the gaze informed by readings in trauma theory, described as witnessing and testimony.

While 'bearing witness' has long had implications of testifying to the presence of the numinous, it now testifies to another type of inarticulable presence: that which we would rather ignore. Kelly Oliver (2001) defines two meanings to the word; "witnessing in the sense of eye-witness to historical facts [and] witnessing in the sense of bearing witness to a truth about humanity and suffering that transcends those facts" (p. 81). The difficulty in achieving this is palpable, as McCormack writes:

Recognition, thus, comes about not through institutionalized norms, which are often the source of violence, but through an attempt to hear what is unarticulated and, in so doing, to take responsibility for a past that cannot be known in its entirety. It is a bodily encounter in which the self is implicated in the process of bearing witness to unarticulated, embodied memories. To speak with the body is to suggest that silence is not always disempowering and that listening is an embodied event" (p. 35).

There is an insistence on the body within the witnessing gaze that is absent in both Foucault and Lacan's accounts; it is a destabilizing act, which transgresses the rigid boundaries in earlier articulations of the gaze. As Nancy Goodman (2012) succinctly writes in "The Power of Witnessing": "Witnessing is a powerful force that allows massively traumatic experiences to become known and communicated." (p. 3). Only those willing to bear witness to trauma—to be a physical carrier of that trauma—may articulate injustice. Foreclosing ourselves from our vulnerability to violence is a fantasy that undoes our connection to what makes us human. We must recognize, and testify to the fact that bodies are exposed to others are at an inherent risk of violence. To create a space that excludes the possibility of trauma is to exclude the possibility of connection, and the possibility of speaking to the presence of something beyond expression. In essence, communication is one of the cornerstones of a mutually understood humanity, and the gaze may be a space for this communication.

Cultural criticism into the modern-day reliance on the film camera—from surveillance footage to reality television—has often focused on the self-reflective aspect of our culture's obsession. While purporting to bring us security by illuminating these gaps in our own vision, the cameras also affirm our existence. Unobserved, we disappear (Staples, 1997). Unfilmed, the player characters believe they will not be able to articulate their stories or escape the scene. As Slavoj Zizek (2002) has observed, "Today, anxiety seems to arise from the prospect of NOT being exposed to the Other's gaze all the time, so that the subject needs the camera's gaze as a kind of ontological guarantee of his/her being" (p. 225). This is at the heart of witnessing—the assertion of one's being. Donna McCormack (2014) engages with this problem as one intimately connected with the body, for "[w]hen words could not be heard, the body became the only means of communication" (p. 184), explaining how "[t]he senses open up the possibility of sharing stories that cannot be spoken, that are not remembered in coherent form, that have been silenced or that are too overwhelming for words" (p. 192). If a feeling is not experienced by the body, how can we attest to its reality? If a horror cannot be articulated, how can we express it to the world? In the end, it is the avatar's experience and not the recorded film that bears witness to the player. The testimony—whatever form it might take—is key. As Felman and Laub (1992) explain, "[w]hat ultimately matters in all processes of witnessing, spasmodic and continuous, conscious and unconscious, is not simply the information, the establishment of the facts, but the experience itself of living through testimony, of giving testimony" (p. 85). The video game allows a player to inhabit a subject position distinct from their day-to-day lived experience. A film, or book, or even a video game is an inert object without their readers—so as speaking is futile if there is no listener. Witnessing is, ultimately, the ability to peel back layers of meaning to understand the mechanism beneath; so to the video game, with its structural emphasis, comes to critique the structures it represents.

There has been an aim since early video games "to produce a sense of diegetic embodiment" as Bob Rehak, in his work "Playing at Being" (2003), notes. This is attended with the tension in our experience of the world between "participation" and "spectatorship"—the split between "self-as-observer" and "self-as-observed" (p. 123). This is the classic tension of the incarnated subject; as bodies, we are subject to the eyes of others, and as players engaging in a sympathetic connection with an avatar body, players are subject to the eyes of the game and its game-world inhabitants. A video game's avatar is an attempt at this type of incarnated subject, and the subject-position experienced by the player is determined by the game's developers as much as the player's responses; "avatars enable players to think through questions of agency and existence, exploring in fantasy form aspects of their own materiality" (p. 123). The video game may be best expressed through this understanding of the gaze; video games create virtual bodies in order to explore, challenge, or negate that vulnerability to violence that makes us human. Inhabiting a subject-position within the game implicates us in the game world, and allows us to testify to the experience of others as experiencing stories in the way the video game allows us to ultimately change the person experiencing them.

However, Rehak's analysis focuses on games produced in the 90's and earlier, citing arcade games alongside *Wolfenstein 3D* (id Software, 1992) and *Quake* (id Software, 1996). Rehak's subjects involve what I term the "fantastic body"—avatars with powers beyond what an average human is capable of performing. While *Quake*, as is noted in Rehak's analysis, created a "somatic character" with footfalls, physical presence, and guttural sounds, Rehak still focuses on the lofted gun as the main element of the player's embodiment. This "corporeal immersion" comes with a lack of limitation. If the avatar is a "reflection" (p. 118), then in the majority of games this mirror reflects a figure able to accomplish what the player's corporeal body never could.

For decades the video game has been explicitly linked to this type of embodied fantasy, particularly the avatar's use in committing acts of violence. Rusch, citing Ralph Koster's *Theory of Fun for Game Design* (2005), indicts games as "not really work[ing] to extend our understanding of ourselves", noting the "crucial difference between games portraying the human condition and the human condition merely existing within games", as "human behavior—often in its crudest, most primitive form—is put on display" (Koster, 2005, p. 174). The phrase "primitive form" is thinly-veiled code for violence. Rather than a lofted gun, Rusch suggests that instead of creating an avatar that is easily inhabitable by the player due to its lack of limitations, the avatar instead be invested with "independent socio-psychological predispositions" which then, through game design, "bridge the gap to the player by bringing the player closer to the avatar [...] How much deeper insights could be gained from a game that make the player experience life from the point of view of a pathologically shy person, an altruist, or someone wracked with jealousy?" (Rusch, 2009, p. 5) This ability to inhabit other subject-positions is integral to both the video game as a cultural medium and the video game's future as an art form capable of telling other stories.

The presence of the avatar body is ultimately what complicates film and literary theory in analyzing video games. The avatar body is a perceiving thing, with sensory-motor functions used to experience and interpret the world through simulated physical, auditory, and visual perceptions. Almost invariably we experience the game's world through our avatar's interactions with it, and the player experiences a type of sympathy with this digital body, which expands the player's experience of himself or herself to include this new form. Our avatar is, like a body, "a system of possible actions" (Merleau-Ponty, 1981, p. 291). Video games attain a type of embodied experience which traditional film and literature typically do not, complicating traditional understandings of 'the gaze' in critical theory. If we are to apply these to video games, its unique methods both of communication with its "reader" and sympathetic engagement with the player's "body" must be taken into account.

SURVIVAL HORROR

Perhaps no genre of video game represents this immersion and embodiment better than 'survival horror', the category into which *Outlast* falls. In an apt turn of phrase, Andrew Tudor (1997) declares, "no observer would deny" how "horror, literary and audio-visual, has proved attractive throughout the modern era" (p. 444). Horror video games have been no exception, and while, as Tudor explains, there is no universal trait that draws people to horror media or even links fans of horror media to one another, video game designers have quickly adopted and adapted the genre for their chosen medium. There are, as Tudor concludes, both conscious and unconscious appeals in horror as a genre. While the effect of the game mechanics might easily be confined to mazes, puzzles, and hide-and-seek, there is an appeal—and a text to be read—in video games' frequent overlaying of these cognitive puzzles with the emotional puzzles of hospitals, family homes, and prisons. These emotional puzzles have been a key feature of horror for decades: Grixti (1989) asserts that horror helps us make sense of and come to terms with "potentialities of experience" too disturbing and debilitating to navigate in the real world. (p. 164) The horror video game is a clear extension of this principle; its intimate processes are linked with the exercise or loss of power, a theme on which horror video games have a "fundamental dependence" (Krzywinska, 2002, p. 14), one intimately located within the body and the gaze. Rather than inhabiting a fantastical body that can perform feats of unbelievable power and athleticism, the hallmark of survival horror is a character's powerlessness. In both survival horror specifically and video games broadly, this embodiment is a part of a sympathetic engagement on the part of the player; the player occupies this experience-position within the game narrative and, through the game's affective mechanics, the player experiences emotion.

Though games such as *Silent Hill* (Konami, 1999), *Penumbra: Overture* (Frictional Games, 2007), and *Resident Evil* (Capcom, 1996) offer some weapons for the character to use, albeit with ammunition that must be conserved, others such as *Clock Tower* (Human Entertainment, 1995)—arguably the first survival horror of this type—*Amnesia: The Dark Descent* (Frictional Games, 2010) and *Outlast*, do not. In the latter category hiding is difficult and discovery is possible, while darkness offers both safety and danger.[1] Players exist in dark and confusing worlds fraught with dangers, and are provided with little protection and little means to protect themselves beyond sensory perceptions. As with horror films, players of horror games are made to feel fear and threat through a variety of visual tricks—jump scares, darkness—and gruesome or shocking imagery.[2]*Outlast* also does so through embodiment; players can look down and see their character's torso, and running from enemies or climbing over obstructions or into air ducts is frustratingly slow and takes breathless, grunting effort. While hiding from one of the roving enemies, the player can hear the character's stilted breath and heightened heart rate. Fear is represented and experienced as a bodily reaction rather than the cumulative effort of lighting, sound, and music. This is distinct from film's sense of fear or powerlessness, Perron (2004) contends, as the player's agency defines the protagonist more than the protagonist's expressed emotions. Players might make their avatars act, but those actions are constrained by the physical ability of the avatar. How that avatar is specifically constrained engenders the fearful emotions more than a frightful atmosphere; how the avatar is vulnerable is specific to the game design. The aforementioned *Amnesia: The Dark Descent* distorts the game's screen and plays the sound of heavy breathing and a pounding heart if the player spends too much time hiding in darkness or watching the grotesque monsters that patrol the corridors; to counter this, players must balance the use of light as both psychologically stabilizing and dangerously revealing.

This embodied fear has been tentatively taken to an even more intimate level; *Alien: Isolation* (Creative Assembly, 2014) uses an optional microphone which picks up ambient noises in the player's vicinity; if the player gasps, shrieks, or receives a phone call the in-game monster is alerted to their in-game presence. *Nevermind* (Flying Mollusk, 2015), a "biofeedback-enhanced" horror game, uses heart rate monitoring technology to enhance the game's immersion. It purports to read a player's bodily responses and introduce more of whatever element most scares them, and progression is only possible if a baseline "at rest"—unfrightened—heart rate is maintained.[3] While the video game might be a space to exert control, this illusion is tested and complicated by the game responding to player actions even without it reading our hearts.[4]

But the game does indeed look at us; *Five Nights at Freddy's* (Scott Cawthon, 2014) has the player-character take on the role of a night security guard in a Chuck-E-Cheese style family restaurant, complete with unsettling animatronic creatures. Using surveillance cameras in order to ensure progression through the increasingly difficult levels, the continuous goal of the game is to avoid being seen and caught by the malicious robots who roam the restaurant. The player's position is static while the antagonists hide in dark corners, and their bulging eyes often, frighteningly, stare back through the surveillance screen. When the game's "power meter" runs out before time is called, the player watches motionless as a pair of glowing eyes watch from the darkness, signaling a failure state.

While we, the player, see them, they also see us, and our fear comes from the gaps in our vision. While according to Krzywinska (2002) the first-person perspective of many video games renders their engagement with the gaze "less complex" (p. 18), in both *Outlast* and *Five Nights at Freddy's* the most powerful tool is the eye, and while the player might appear to see all, the player's mastery is less complete than they might hope; it is in these gaps the illusion of safety is shattered, and the cultural anxiety surrounding the gaze might be explored. While for many games the avatar's reflection is "of a mapping of [...] control" (Rehak, 2003, p. 107), the power exhibited by the fantastic avatar body is not present in the survival horror genre; indeed, the avatar body in a game like *Outlast* explicitly stresses powerlessness. This feeling is an integral part of the game experience; the game's efficacy as a game is predicated on its ability to inspire this emotion through sympathy with the avatar body. Successful survival horror frightens and terrorizes. On both a mechanical and diegetic level, a video game's greatest strength as a medium is its ability to affect emotion and, by this, engender immersion and sympathy. The player explores their materiality in the game not in terms of committing violence, but in terms of experiencing violence as a victim. The video game does so, invariably, through an engagement with the gaze.

There has been an increasing trend in video games—particularly horror games—to include recording devices integral to their narrative mechanics. Alongside the aforementioned *Five Nights at Freddy's* series, the *Fatal Frame* series (Tecmo & Grasshopper Manufacture, 2001-2014), *Silent Hill: Shattered Memories* (Climax Studios, 2009), *Dead Rising* (Capcom, 2006), *Heavy Rain* (Quantic Dream, 2010), and *Outlast* all heavily feature the player character documenting or being documented in their respective narratives. The use of cameras in video games has been explored before; Deborah Mellamphy's textual examination "Torture Porn in *Dead Rising*" (2013) investigated the voyeuristic use of the camera in zombie survival horror game *Dead Rising* (Capcom, 2006). In this game, photojournalist Frank West's documentation of the horrors he sees is translated by the game into "prestige points" for the player to accumulate for witnessing and photographing grotesque scenes (Mellamphy, 2013, pp. 41-42). The game encourages the player to construct increasingly absurd displays of violence so that it may be documented for posterity. Here, as with *Outlast*, the player character's seemingly-objective stance as a journalist documenting violence is contentious, as is the player's seemingly-objective stance as uninvolved in the production of the game's narrative.

Survival horror is the genre in which this vulnerability to violence becomes the most acute—it rarely takes more than a few strikes from an enemy to reach a fail state. But unlike the majority of survival horror games, *Outlast* and *Five Nights at Freddy's* does not provide the player with any means of defense beyond the camera lens. We are without defense and subject completely to the violence of the non-player characters that inhabit the world, on a mechanical level, to explicitly do us harm. *Five Nights at Freddy's* is survival horror honed to its sharpest thematic point: those who watch are the masters; those who are watched are the victims. The game forces the player to constantly wrest that control back from their pursuers. That tension is the core of the game, and the genre as a whole.

THE GAZE IN *OUTLAST*

Outlast is obsessed with sight, both mechanically and narratively. The passive spectatorship of film studies is abandoned here; players are actively looking, and their looking has consequences, both as a necessary condition of the game's progress and for the character's thematic journey. *Outlast* and its DLC[5] both feature a handheld camcorder as an essential element to the game's narrative structure and gameplay, but in *Outlast* there is a complication over who is the producer of objective truth, and whether truth can truly be objective. The title of this chapter comes from a line of non-player character dialogue: a patient stabbing a doctor pointedly tells the player, "There are no observers here." In most video games—and the focus of the criticism of the late 1990's in which video games were seen as complicit in the proliferation of school shootings—the player character takes up a role as a creator of violence, enacted upon non-player character objects. The position of subject enacting violence on objects has been rightly criticized for feeding into a culture of dehumanization; as Kelly Oliver (2001) writes, "To see oneself as a subject and to see other people as the other or objects not only alienates one from those around him or her but also enables the dehumanization inherent in oppression and domination." (p. 3). When the video game gaze is turned on the player, the player must acknowledge their vulnerability.

Todd McGowan's emphasis on where the film takes the viewer into its purview is recursive; "this theory takes an interest in film for what film can reveal rather than for what film hides" (2007, p. 173). *Outlast* is concerned with sight, the loss of it, and the relative truth and untruth of the sights being witnessed and articulated. The darkness of the corridors is not frightening for what it hides, but for what it reveals about the player's feelings of powerlessness on personal, psycho-sexual, and institutional levels. The film camera, while enhancing the player's vision and creating a one-way mirror between the filmer and the filmed, is easily turned back on the player character, with grotesque consequences. The camera is there to film atrocity, regardless of the victim. It is there to affirm, not observe. Rather than articulating imbalances of power, trauma theory grapples with the difficulty of communication. In my defining of the "video game gaze", I will look to theories of witnessing, which have become inextricably enmeshed with trauma theory in these last decades. In the modern world, haunted by memories of atrocity, the necessity of articulating and effectively communicating this trauma has come to the fore in branches of critical theory. Here there is a radical shift away from equating the gaze with mastery, and imbuing subject-object positions with this power; as Kelly Oliver writes in *Witnessing: Beyond Recognition* (2001),

[I]f we start from the assumption that relations are essentially antagonistic struggles for recognition, then it is no wonder that contemporary theorists spend so much energy trying to imagine how these struggles can lead to compassionate personal relations, ethical social relations, or democratic political

relations. From the presumption that human relations are essentially warlike, how can we imagine them as peaceful? (p. 4).

How can a video game, by all accounts violent, invite the possibility of communication? *Outlast* makes this attempt through the subject-position of a victim of violence. The game presents this struggle between two opposing understandings of 'the gaze': the powerless player inserted into the dangers of the scene being viewed, after Lacan's understanding, and the powerful supplier of security technology, the game's overarching antagonist, which exemplifies Foucault's description of the gaze as a cornerstone of institutional control. But through this tension, between the struggle for power, comes the powerful and distinct call to witness; against these Hegelian and Lacanian descriptions of subjecthood and recognition as one that implicitly asserts control and exerts violence, the call to witness is specifically relational (McCormack, 2014).

The player is, from the outset, complicit in the scene being viewed/filmed, and *Outlast* presents the player with scenes of physical and mental trauma—and then inflicts this trauma on the player. The tension earlier described between self-as-observer and self-as-observed is intimately and self-referentially grappled with in *Outlast*; the video game questions our voyeurism by introducing the element of fear and danger from which we cannot meaningfully escape without removing ourselves entirely from the realm of play, and *Outlast* presents us with traumatic scenes so that the player may understand and articulate the role of violence in the production of trauma.

Outlast has the player take on the role of Miles Upshur, an investigative reporter who is sent to find "the truth" about the sinister Murkoff Corporation. He personally conducts a search into their activities within Mount Massive Asylum, which purports to be a charity for the care and treatment of the mentally ill. An anonymous email from an inside-source 'whistleblower' points Miles, who had previously investigated Murkoff's unethical activities abroad, to the abuses going on inside. Gaining access to the asylum underneath the omnipresent gaze of security cameras, Miles is quickly out of his depth and trapped within the building. The player is forced to navigate the horrific scenes inside Mount Massive, where order has broken down. The patients within the asylum are either harmless and traumatized or lucid and violent. Called 'Variants', these malicious non-player characters seek out and pursue the player, and the methods of survival are plainly explained: "run, hide, or die". The game's DLC, *Whistleblower*, presents the similar journey of Waylon Park—the eponymous whistleblower who sent Miles the original email—as he attempts to escape his institutionalization for speaking out. "Don't believe half the things I saw," it states. This leaves Miles—and the player—to investigate this claim in order to affirm the unbelievable. The antagonists are designed from a technical standpoint to be viewed; players watch them stalk the halls as they sneak by, trying to preserve the privilege of not being seen. Murkoff's goal with their project at Mount Massive is summoning an amorphous, half-myth, half-technological creature called the 'Walrider' through what is called the 'morphogenic engine', which may only activate, according to a film recording found in-game, when a test subject "had witnessed enough horror". The mastery of Murkoff's gaze is not just the ability to see all and choose not to be seen, but to directly control the eyes of others. As the opening of *Whistleblower* tells us, "you don't have to wake up, but open your eyes." To this effect, one must be present and conscious in order to empower one's gaze.

Unlike *Dead Rising*'s use of the camera, Miles uses it to tell his own story of survival. Though he initially comes to Mount Massive in order to expose "the truth" via the mute, seemingly-objective lens of the camera pointed on patients' bodies in a mechanism eerily similar to Murkoff's invasive practice, the camera instead becomes a means to testify. To return briefly to Rehak's insistence on the lofted gun, one of the earliest scenes in-game involves Miles stumbling upon the first shocking image—an impaled security officer who, in his last breath, warns Miles/the player to leave while he can. Immediately the game makes clear that entering the scene by force results in a swift death. While many games, particularly the *Resident Evil* franchise, would place the player in the subject-position of one of the "forces of social order" as previously discussed, *Outlast* explicitly tells us that this is not the narrative being explored, and how that narrative leads to death. Miles is specifically kept alive as a "witness"; *Outlast* explores iterations of the gaze from its position as a horror game, and ultimately settings on the model of bearing witness to trauma as an example of the video game moving forward as a storytelling genre.

Watching is, in effect, worse than performing the act which is being watched; Miles films a patient without their knowledge, and when Miles is noticed, the patient, startled, stumbles away and screams "You like to watch? You're sick!" The camera takes on many meanings depending on who is behind it, but none of them involve passive spectatorship. There is an immediate confrontation with the viewer's complicity in the scene being viewed—because it's true, we do like to watch. The game's appeal lies in its gruesome images, and filming these gruesome displays of atrocity in the game using the camcorder's record function—a impaled security officer, a bowl of severed fingers, a pile of corpses—prompts written documents to be read by the player, and the collection of these notes is encouraged by the game's structure. In *Outlast* the player has no hand in constructing the violence they film, but in filming these events, the player becomes the author of the images which the game has presented, complicating the question of who creates narrative authorship as well as implicating the player.

The game breaks down the barriers between the player character and the non-player character through this institutionalization and loss of power. The collapse of order within Mount Massive only further complicates this distinction; as Branson and Miller (2002) argue in their investigation into the pathologization of deafness, deinstitutionalization "threatens not only [the identity of the non-institutionalized], especially when faced with the everyday presence of those formerly hidden away, but also the disciplined and orderly nature of their environment" (p. 52). As the patients within Mount Massive allege, the player is both "sick" and "no observer". His body exists within the game, and the player exists through his body—he is not merely the film camera's eye.

Through the technology of this artificial eye, the player can see in the dark and zoom in to observe possible danger. It is an asset. One of the most difficult and frightening parts of the game is when, during a cut-scene in which the player has no control, Miles drops his camcorder through a collapsed floor and into the darkness below, forcing the player to navigate the dangerous pitch-black corridors of the asylum to retrieve it. When out of the player's control, the last pretense of distance and safety is stripped from them; there are several points in both games where the character is forcibly restrained and, pointedly, the camera taken and turned on him; the opening of Whistleblower has Waylon, free of his restraints, immediately reach for and use the camera that had been filming him. Later, when restrained and subject to tortured by patient Eddie Gluskin, Waylon clothes himself and retrieves the camera that had been consciously placed by Gluskin to record Waylon. Similarly, when Miles is caught and restrained by a Variant named Trager in a scripted event, Trager takes Miles's film camera and immediately turns it on him, placing it on a nearby shelf so that Miles's torture can be filmed. When Miles manages to free himself, he takes the camera back into his control; however, it is precisely during these moments of powerlessness that the player character is subjected to bodily trauma. Tension is created through the imbalance between subject and object of this gaze, and that relationship and all its power is explored in visceral, emotional moments for the player.

The antagonists we see in-game are victims of the same gaze which that they are now enforcing; the game creates this sympathy by putting the player on the same level as the antagonists. Murkoff's experiments attempt to create the "docile" bodies explicated in *Discipline and Punish*, subject to their regulation and exposed totally to their instruments which not only gaze at their bodies, but also the secrets within. As film and cultural critic Nina Martin (2007) has noted in her work, "the awareness and acknowledgement of surveillance produces pleasures in performance and gives rise to exhibitionism" (p. 136). Ultimately, the patients in Mount Massive demand to be looked at; when in possession of the camera, they turn it on themselves to perform their acts of memetic violence.

Indeed, the whole of the video game is peering into "something he or she is not supposed to look at" (Lacan, 1990, p. 56)—we take on the role of an investigative reporter or escaped patient, moving through spaces to which the character is forbidden. Miles trespasses onto the grounds of Mount Massive, and Waylon escapes from his institutionalization. The player takes on the "ideological interface" described by Rehak (2003): "They work to remove themselves from awareness, seeking transparency—or at least unobtrusiveness—as they channel agency into new forms" (p. 122). The player's agency is forcibly stripped away in order to create sympathy and connection with the other victims of Murkoff's experiments. Despite any effort to passively observe a scene in-game, the player is intrinsically a part of it. There is a level of complicity—of involvement—which we are reluctant to acknowledge; there are no observers here, either.

Outlast makes explicit reference to present-day self-policing in American politics; the word 'whistle-blower' in American discourse is someone who has made public—'blown the whistle on'—on corruption within an institution. The journalist, the investigator, is attempting to turn the eye on the possessor of Foucault's gaze. The game's end, in which Waylon discusses disseminating the information he's gathered with a man with an Australian accent—a clear reference to Julian Assange—contextualizes and casts their look as political. A document found in the game commands its employees "IF YOU'RE SEEING THINGS, SAY SOMETHING." Your own eyes are as dangerous to you as unattended luggage, and must be policed. That the game is set in a privately-controlled mental institution is both an appeal to established horror tropes and a calculated critique of institutional control. Many video game franchises involve the investigation of powerful institutions: the *Resident Evil* (Capcom, 1996-2015) and *Half-Life* (Valve Corporation & Gearbox Software, 1998-2007) series, and earlier in games like *Sanitarium* (Dreamforge & Intertainment, 1998). *Silent Hill 4* (Konami Computer & Entertainment Tokyo, 2004), most notably, even included Bentham's panopticon—the all-seeing prison design that so enchanted Foucault—in its 'Water Prison' level; the only escape is to use this prison's all-seeing gaze from its central tower, forcing the player to take up the ontological position of the abusers in order to survive.

All of these games depict the struggle against excessive corporate and government power. The most frightening aspect of Murkoff's control is its ability to watch and its ability to disempower those watching them; the employee attempting to radio for outside help is not allowed to do so because it will invite the disruptive eyes of outsiders. In the main game we learn of an orderly named David Annapurna who, after questioning what he had seen, was institutionalized by Murkoff. Waylon, similarly treated, hallucinates the disturbing images he was forced to watch under the control of Murkoff, and Miles reports the same kind of hallucinations towards the end of the main game. The experimentation going on in the asylum is explained in physically and mentally violating terms; the patient Gluskin describes it as 'rape' before he is put into a machine that, through tubes and instruments put inside him, takes information from his body, and, as we later see, takes away his sanity. Even our inner workings are subject to Murkoff's panoptic gaze.

But there is a requirement, in journalism, to obtain experiential knowledge of trauma and horror, to traverse the anxiety of watching and being watched that dominates post-9/11 Western culture. There is a confusing mixture of the desire to look and the desire not to be looked at, alongside the desire to be seen and the desire not to see the traumatic. Safety or trauma might be found through identical means. As explored earlier, the whole of the video game is peering into "something he or she is not supposed to look at"—we take on the role of an investigative reporter or escaped patient, moving through spaces forbidden to the character, doing so in a physically present way with physical consequences. Miles trespasses onto the grounds of Mount Massive, and Waylon escapes from his institutionalization. *Outlast* is ultimately a discussion on the production of narrative and the production of knowledge, and it complicates our understanding of the possession of knowledge. For this reason we turn to theories of witnessing and the epistemological difficulties of 'bearing witness' to trauma. Miles as an investigative reporter, Murkoff as a security company performing unethical experiments—they are there to see what is not supposed to be looked at, and the player is there to witness and articulate to the world what has been hidden away.

As Waylon prepares to upload his video footage—containing both others' trauma and his own—he is warned that the process will be difficult but instigate extraordinary change; it becomes "a call," as McCormack (2014) says, "to take on the responsibility for the telling of the story, to willingly repeat the tale even when narration is painful" (p. 192). Miles as a journalist and Waylon as a whistleblower rely on this understanding of physical presence as a necessity for witnessing. Today's journalism has increasingly used nonprofessional film recordings (Mellamphy, 2013, p. 43), from the infamous Zapruder film of JFK's assassination to repeated eyewitness recordings of the 9/11 attacks played on television; we have privileged the accounts of those who were there. *Outlast* interrogates this idea of an eyewitness; as discussed earlier, Waylon and Miles are both complicit as the authors of the gruesome images they have come to passively view. They exist in the game's narrative as witnesses, and they exist as avatars for the player to experience the game in a physically present way. The only character in-game that helps the player move forward, a patient who calls himself Father Martin, describes explicitly how Miles was brought to them to "witness" their actions, to "tell them", and that this would "save them from death". Early in the game he disrupts Miles's attempt to escape, explaining that "there is so much yet for you to witness" and "the only way out of this place is the truth"—it is no accident that this scene takes place under the multitudinous security screens displaying the corridors of the hospital. The player and the characters must experience Mount Massive for themselves; they can't tell its story without the use of their body. The security cameras are not enough to know the horrors of this place.

Returning to Kelly Oliver's texts, she articulates witnessing as having two meanings: as an eyewitness to events in a judicial sense and bearing witness in a religious sense. The latter is recognition of that which is "beyond recognition" (Oliver, 2001, p. 16). John Peters (2001) likewise describes how witnessing has "two faces: the passive one of seeing and the active one of saying", and through this, the witness comes to be the "producer of knowledge" (p. 710-711). The tension, he contends, comes between the seeing and the saying and that this witnessing is located in the body; the truth of a witness's experience is not just in their proximity, but in their suffering and pain—the only way we can truly gauge their authenticity. Against the notion of the witness as a mirror or a mute recording device through which the truth may be discerned unclouded by subjective experience, *Outlast* shows us the deeper meaning of witnessing—one of bodily affect.

Recognition of the survivor, witnessing and testimony restore subjectivity to victims of trauma. Oliver (2001) describes how oppression and objectivity undermine subjectivity specifically by destroying the ability to witness. Witnessing "works to ameliorate the trauma particular to othered subjectivity"

(p. 7). The patients cannot articulate the events that have happened to them, which therefore never took place—only through Miles's or Waylon's recognition of them as an external witness does their ability to self-articulate become possible. Trauma, In Oliver's analysis, "cognitively and perceptually" destroys the patients' ability to witness (p. 89). The victims of Murkoff's experiments are literally dehumaniszed—they are turned into monsters, which eventually come to enact retributive violence on the player character. But in the events of *Outlast* the Variants, as they are named, are not dehumanized. By experiencing the context in which they are created—Murkoff's experiments that harm the mentally ill for private research—we understand their humanity: "It is easier to justify domination, oppression, and torture if one's victims are imagined as inferior, less human, or merely objects who exist to serve subjects" (Oliver, 2003, p. 3). Rather than nameless non-player characters who exist to serve a player's violent impulses, Miles is there to investigate and bring to light the humanity and trauma of the patients' lives. The player character, as an outsider to their trauma, must traverse it bodily in order to understand, and this is a moral responsibility. As Oliver (2001) describes, "If subjectivity is the process of witnessing sustained through response-ability, then we have a responsibility to response-ability, to the ability to respond" (p. 18).

We come to see that Father Martin was right; the truth is something experienced in the body, and Miles and Waylon must both traverse the dangers in order to be a witness. Like the other Variants, Martin, too, is an exhibitionist, asking for his own death to be watched and recorded as he immolates himself before the player's eyes. If his death is filmed, the player is given access to a note written by Miles, which says he'll "tell the whole fucking world" what happened at Mount Massive; and when he descends to the final figurative and literal level in the asylum, Miles writes that he will bury Murkoff with "my mutilated dead body". His witnessing is told through his body.

But he doesn't—he can't. He becomes wholly engulfed by the scene, his camera destroyed, his story too traumatic to be articulated. He tells the story, instead, through his body. The player only comes to understand what has happened to him because they have experienced his story through their avatar body. We only catch a glimpse of Miles in *Whistleblower*; as a phantom haunting Mount Massive, a memory of trauma, his dissipated remains shambling from the building. Only in the DLC, through Waylon's experience, does the player come to testify to his experience and bear witness to the traumas of Mount Massive. Entering into these systems as a journalist and a whistleblower, they, through their listening, are affected rather than given mastery. They are made to listen to and through their body, as McCormack says, through "repeatedly listening and retelling these stories, we forge ties that extend beyond what we might understand as belonging. We […] forge alternative epistemological forms that can listen to what bodies may say." (McCormack, 2014, p. 194). In *Outlast*, the body is the bearer of trauma and testimony—from Miles's severed fingers and eventual possession by the Walrider to Waylon's limping body as he escapes Mount Massive—and the somatic experience of the avatar allows the player to bear witness to this violence as the victim. As McCormack explains, "bearing witness to trauma is an embodied event" (p. 27)—an experience felt and listened to. While the anxiety over control of the gaze, of being watched and of watching, is present throughout the game, ultimately the anxiety comes from not being watched, but the implicit threat of being forgotten. Entering the play-space as a voyeur, the player becomes, through bodily trauma experienced through the avatar, a witness to the events of the game narrative.

There is no single way to observe what is happening in the game; a player has personal control over what is or isn't filmed. By the end of the game Waylon's film camera gaze has been anonymized and dissipated. Similarly, at least two million copies of *Outlast* were sold, with two million players taking up the video game gaze and witnessing the atrocity of Mount Massive for themselves. The experience is mediated by the camera both as a tool for navigating the levels, and as a critique of the myth of objective distance by keeping culpability at a literal arm's length. Both protagonists, at their games' completion, escape the institutional control of the asylum. While *Whistleblower* ends with his experience disseminated by the camera, an attempt to articulate his pain, the main game shows the camera's inherent limitations to conveying experience. Miles' camera, worse for wear and unable to function as a penetrative eye that illuminates the darkness, becomes obsolete. Possessed by the game's final antagonist, the unknown and ephemeral Walrider, Miles becomes fully subsumed by the scene he could not merely passively view, and in the end a Murkoff executive, too, is drawn into the scene from which they thought they could passively extract the truth. There are no observers here—the hierarchy of the filmic gaze is destabilized in the video game context.

Outlast shows us the power of looking: how it can inscribe and circumscribe, empower and disempower, how it is intimately located in the body. *Outlast* makes the point that looking is a political act, and "bearing witness" only has meaning when we are forced to acknowledge the place we have in the scene we are observing, and our responsibility to respond. Both Murkoff and the player character attempt to assert their mastery, to maintain a position of observer and draw knowledge from those being observed. *Outlast* reveals that this is an impossible state; there is always someone watching, and ultimately it is the observer who is willing to step beyond the realm of the purely visual who may take the responsibility of the narrative.

CONCLUSION AND FUTURE RESEARCH

What is, then, the 'video game gaze'? *Outlast* tells us that it is one in which there are no observers. Video games are, at their core, about inhabiting other bodies and exploring the system of actions presented to us by the game world. Rehak remarks how "the magical projections of telephone line, movie screen, and computer-generated battlefield flower before us as spaces into which we can nimbly step—then step back as suddenly, without suffering any consequences save, perhaps, the memories left by a vivid dream." But is this lack of consequence our privilege as a player? *Outlast*'s use of "dreaming" and "dream therapy" as a core theme and the catalyst for the story's events is recursive; as the spectator is pulled into the dreamworld and disturbed by his interaction with what he sees, so too is the player drawn into the dreamworld of the video game, with limited control and linear progression through a structured, unreal environment, and is forced to acknowledge a role as neither that of passive spectator nor active master, but somewhere between. It is a space mediated, in *Outlast*, by eye of the film camera. While the dreamstates in *Outlast* might be merely dreams, the screen is left with impressions of them, disturbing visions that inflict themselves on the "reality" of the game's scopic view. Ultimately, what we have seen affects our reality. *Outlast* might seem dreamlike to someone who has yet to experience trauma, and certainly the events of both games are fictitious, but their message is not: it is there to be read and experienced by the player, and in the case of *Outlast,* inflicted on the avatar body with direct mechanical consequences to the game controls and physiological consequences to the player feeling fear. The average player of *Outlast* might be able to step back from the video game's sense of powerlessness and positionality as a victim and back into their relative safety of the Western world. As Miles or Waylon's handheld camera creates a sense of artificial protection, so does the video game's veneer of player inconsequence. *Outlast* and *Outlast: Whistleblower* bear witness to a truth too traumatic to say aloud: safety is a feeling as frail as the lens of a camera, and as easily broken when dropped into the darkness of the real. *Outlast* not only testifies to the future interrelationality of video games—their ability to engender sympathy, inspire emotion, connect bodily with players in ways traditional media cannot—but testifies to our anxieties, and how we might work through them. They are the "works of art" which, as McGowan (2007) says of film, "translate private fantasies into public ones, which provide an imaginary response to shared forms of dissatisfaction" (p. 24).

This is present in many smaller-scale games: *Gone Home* (Fullbright, 2013), *Everybody's Gone to The Rapture* (The Chinese Room, 2015), and *Journey* (Thatgamecompany, 2012) are all concerned with the difficulty of communicating aspects of who we are and how we relate to others. All are, at their core, about witnessing; we play through these game spaces in order to better understand the game's subject-position. *Gone Home*'s design involves the player exploring closets, crawlspaces, and other hidden-away elements of a family home in order to uncover notes left behind for the player which describes a teenage girl discovering she is in love with her female friend. *Everybody's Gone To The Rapture* encourages players to watch, to the point of granting an achievement to those who do so for long enough. Through exploring, the player witnesses scenes between the villages' inhabitants leading up to their deaths. The villagers—confused, inarticulate, enmeshed in systems they neither perceive nor understand—mirror the player's feelings as they move through the game world and try to piece together the events that lead to these peoples' deaths: the loneliness, the confusion, the inability to connect to one another. Their stories are preserved and remembered through the game's design. *Journey* is in essence a multiplayer game that allows randomly-paired players to work together to solve puzzles and move forward more easily through the levels. But players may also simply sit together in one another's company, or jubilantly sing notes of music, which displays an identifying glyph which players carry on their backs. The relation between players in *Journey* is decided not antagonistic; players are given the space to experience joy, hardship, and triumph together through the shared journey. The video game has the unique potential to create and strengthen these moments of interpersonal connection.

Similarly, Sabine Harrer and Henrik Schoenau-Fog's paper for the Digital Games Research Association's 2015 conference puts forward the process involved in accurately presenting and inhabiting the grief experienced by mothers mourning the loss of a child; the resulting game was named *Jocoi*. This follow's Harrer's previous research in the experience of loss in games (Harrer, 2013). As they describe in their design process, for the mothers they consulted and involved in the game design process, the game was a "tool to foster dialogue", but to the designers it was "an exercise in learning how to listen" (Harrer & Schoenau-Fog, 2015, p. 14). As *Jocoi* portrays, the approach taken to witnessing the grief of a bereft mother is one in which formal expectations or definitions must be set aside to make appropriate space for feeling. Facts, as it were, must be set aside for truth. Loss must be articulated on terms familiar to those who have lost for their story to be told. This witnessing is articulating experience beyond the articulable, and forging ties across this gulf of inexpression. This ability to listen through the game space—to give voice to disempowered or marginalized elements of society—is coming to the fore in game design. As video games diversify and tell new stories from marginalized positions, we might see how video games are, instead, unique mediums through which our cultural anxieties may be brought to light. Janet Murray (1997) once described the multitasking mechanics of the popular game *Tetris* (Pajitnov, 1984) as a "rain dance for the postmodern psyche, meant to allow us to enact control over things outside our power" (p. 144).

Just as *Tetris* grappled with the anxiety of the cascading problems of modern life, *Outlast* bears witness to the powerlessness felt by a generation both heavily surveilled yet unable to meaningfully express their stories and subject-positions to those who watch them. In these games there is a call to witness, a demand to observe and be changed in the observance; complicity can't be ignored, community can't be discounted, and to do so is dishonest to both the observer and the observed.

REFERENCES

Aarseth, E. J. (1997). *Cybertext: Perspectives on ergodic literature*. London: Johns Hopkins University Press.

Andersen, C. (2014). Game of drones: The uneasy future of the soldier-hero in *Call of Duty: Black Ops II*. *Surveillance & Society*, *12*(3), 360–376.

Baird, R. (2000). The startle effect: Implications for the spectator cognition and media theory. *Film Quarterly*, *53*(3), 13–24. doi:10.2307/1213732

Bogost, I. (2007). *Persuasive games: The expressive power of videogames*. Boston: MIT Press.

Branson, J., & Miller, D. (2002). *Damned for their difference: The cultural construction of deaf people as disabled*. Washington: Gallaudet University Press.

Canossa, A. (2014). Reporting from the snooping trenches: Changes in attitudes and perceptions towards behavior tracking in digital games. *Surveillance & Society*, *12*(3), 433–436.

Capcom. (1996). *Resident evil* [PS 1 video game]. Chuo-ku, Osaka, Japan: Capcom.

Capcom. (2006). *Dead rising* [Xbox 360 video game]. Chuo-ku, Osaka, Japan: Capcom.

Carr, D. (2002). Playing with lara. InScreenPlay: cinema/ videogames / interface (pp. 171-180). London: Wallflower Press.

Carr, D. (2009). *Textual analysis, digital games, zombies*. DiGRA digital library.

Cawthon, S. (2013). *Five nights at freddy's* [PC]. Desura.

Climax Studios. (2010). *Silent hill: Shattered memories* [Wii, Playstation 2, Playstation Portable video game]. Minato, Tokyo, Japan: Konami Digital Entertainment.

Creative Assembly. (2014). *Alien: Isolation* [PS 4, Xbox One, PC video game]. Shinagawa, Tokyo, Japan: Sega Games.

Cybulski, A. D. (2014). Enclosures at play: Surveillance in the code and culture of videogames. *Surveillance & Society*, *12*(3), 427–432.

Dixon, W. (1995). *It looks at you: The returned gaze of cinema*. New York: SUNY Press.

Dreamforge Intertainment. (1998). *Sanitarium* [PC video game]. Darien, CN: ASC Games.

Felman, S., & Laub, D. (1992). *Testimony: Crises of witnessing in literature, psychoanalysis, and history*. New York: Routledge.

Flying Mollusk. (2015). *Nevermind* [PC video game]. Glendale, California: Flying Mollusk.

Foucault, M. (1975). *Discipline and punish: The birth of the prison*. New York: Penuin.

Frasca, G. (2003). Simulation versus narrative. In M. J. P Wolf & B. Perron (Eds.), *The video game theory reader* (pp. 221-36). New York: Routledge.

Frictional Games. (2007). *Penumbra: Overture* [PC video game]. Helsingborg, Sweden: Frictional Games.

Frictional Games. (2010). *Amnesia: The dark descent* [PC video game]. Helsingborg, Sweden: Frictional Games.

Goodman, N. R. (2012). The power of witnessing. In N. Goodman & M. Meyers (Eds.), *The power of witnessing: Reflections, reverberations and traces of the holocaust* (pp. 3-26). New York: Routledge.

Grant, J. P. (2011, July 29). Life after death. *Kill Screen Daily*. Retrieved from www.killscreendaily.com/articles/life-after-death

Grixti, J. (1989). *Terrors of uncertainty: The cultural contexts of horror fiction*. London, New York: Routledge.

Grodal, T. (2003). Stories for eye, ear, and muscles: Video games, media, and embodied experiences. In M. Wolf & B. Perron (Eds.), *The video game theory reader* (pp. 129-155). New York: Routledge.

Harrer, S. (2013). From losing to loss: Exploring the expressive capacities of videogames beyond death as failure. *Culture Unbound*, *5*(35), 607–620. doi:10.3384/cu.2000.1525.135607

Harrer, S. & Schoenau-Fog, H. (2015). *Inviting grief into games: The game design process as personal dialogue*. DiGRA digital library.

Entertainment, H. (1995). *Clock tower* [SNES video game]. Tokyo, Japan: Human Entertainment.

id Software. (1992). *Wolfenstein 3D* [DOS video game]. Garland, TX: Apogee Software.

id Software. (1996). *Quake* [DOS video game]. New York, NY: GT Interactive Software.

Juul, J. (2005). *Half-Real*. Cambridge: MIT Press.

Kirkland, E. (2009). *Horror videogames and the uncanny*. DiGRA digital library.

Konami. (1999). *Silent hill* [PS 1 video game]. Minato, Tokyo, Japan: Konami Digital Entertainment.

Konami. (2004). *Silent hill 4: The room*. [PS 2, Xbox, PS 3, PC video game]. Minato, Tokyo, Japan: Konami Digital Entertainment.

Koster, R. (2005). *Theory of fun for game design*. Scottsdale: Paraglyph Press.

Krzywinska, T. (2002). Hands-On horror. In H. Wu (Ed.), *Axes to grind: Re-Imagining the horrific in visual media and culture*. Academic Press.

Lacan, J. (1990). *Televison: A challenge to the psychoanalytical establishment* (J. Copjec, Ed., D. Hollier, R. Krauss, A. Michaelson, & J. Mehlman, Trans.). New York: Norton.

Martin, N. K. (2007). *Sexy thrills: Undressing the erotic thriller*. Chicago: University of Illinois Press.

McCormack, D. (2014). *Queer postcolonial narratives and the ethics of witnessing*. London: Bloomsbury.

McGowan, T. (2007). *The real gaze: Film theory after Lacan*. Albany: State University of New York Press.

Mellamphy, D. (2013). Dead eye: The spectacle of torture porn in *Dead Rising*. In G. Papazian & J. M. Sommers (Eds.), *Game on, Hollywood! Essays on the intersection of video games and cinema* (pp. 35-46). London: McFarland & Company.

Merleau-Ponty, M. (1981). *Phenomenology of perception* (C. Smith, Trans.). Humanities.

Mulvey, L. (1989). *Visual and other pleasures*. London: Palgrave Macmillan. doi:10.1007/978-1-349-19798-9_3

Murray, J. H. (1997). *Hamlet on the holodeck: The future of narrative in cyberspace*. New York: The Free Press.

Oliver, K. (2001). *Witnessing: Beyond recognition*. Minneapolis: University of Minnesota Press.

Oliver, K. (2003). Witnessing and testimony. *Parallax, 10*(1), 79–88.

Pajitnov, A. (1984). *Tetris* [PC, Commodore 64 video game]. Alameda, CA: Spectrum Holobyte, Inc.

Perron, B. (2004). *Sign of a threat: The effects of warning systems in survival horror games. COSIGN 2004*. Croatia: University of Split.

Peters, J. D. (2001). Witnessing. *Media Culture & Society, 23*(6), 707–723. doi:10.1177/016344301023006002

Quantic Dream. (2010). *Heavy Rain* [PS 3 video game]. Minato, Tokyo, Japan: Sony Computer Entertainment.

Red Barrels. (2013). *Outlast* [PC, PS 4, Xbox One video game]. Montreal: Red Barrels.

Red Barrels. (2014). *Outlast: Whistleblower* [PC, PS 4 Xbox One video game]. Montreal: Red Barrels.

Rehak, B. (2003). Playing at being: Psychoanalysis and the avatar. In M. J. P. Wolf & B. Perron (Eds.), *The video game theory reader* (pp. 103-128). Routledge: New York and London.

Rusch, D. (2009). *Mechanisms of the soul: Tackling the human condition*. DiGRA digital library.

Rusch, D. C. (2009). *Mechanisms of the soul: Tackling the human condition in videogames. In Proceedings from DiGRA 2009: Breaking new ground: Innovation in games, play, practice and theory*. London: Brunel University.

Staples, W. G. (1997). *The culture of surveillance: Discipline and social control in the United States*. New York: St. Martin's Press.

Tecmo & Grasshopper Manufacture. (2001-2014). *Fatal Frame* [PS 2 video game series]. Kyoto, Japan: Nintendo.

Thatgamecompany. (2012). *Journey* [PS 3 video game]. Minato, Tokyo, Japan: Sony Computer Entertainment.

The Chinese Room. (2015). *Everybody's Gone to the Rapture* [PS 4 video game]. Minato, Tokyo, Japan: Sony Computer Entertainment.

The Fullbright Company. (2013). *Gone Home* [PC video game]. Portland, Oregon: The Fullbright Company.

Thompson, C. (2002). Violence and the political life of videogames. In L. King (Ed.), *Game on: The history and culture of videogames* (pp. 22-31). London: Laurence King Publishing Ltd.

Treyarch. (2013). *Call of Duty: Black Ops II* [PC, PS3, Xbox 360, Wii U video game]. Santa Monica, CA: Activision.

Tudor, A. (1997). Why horror? The peculiar pleasures of a popular genre. *Cultural Studies*, *11*(3), 443–463. doi:10.1080/095023897335691

Valve, L. L. C. (1998). *Half-Life* [PC video game]. Fresno, CA: Sierra Entertainment.

Vidler, A. (1999). *The architectural uncanny: Essays in the modern unhomely*. London: MIT Press.

Zizek, S. (2002). Big Brother, or, the triumph of the gaze over the eye. In T. Y. Levin, U. Frohne, & P. Weibel (Eds.), *Ctrl space: Rhetorics of surveillance from Bentham to Big Brother* (pp. 224-227). Cambridge, MA: MIT Press.

ENDNOTES

[1] The survival horror genre has always had a penchant for rendering safe spaces fearful; Ewan Kirkland (2009) notes the predominance of domestic spaces in the survival horror genre, from *Sweet Home* (Capcom: 1989), *Haunting Ground* (Capcom, 2005), *Clock Tower 3* (Capcom & Suncoft, 2002) to *Silent Hill: Homecoming* (Double Helix Games, 2008). He cites Anthony Vidler's work on the "architectural uncanny" as an "instrument for [...] narrative" (Vidler, 1999, p. 17). The genre has a long history of exploring our anxieties surrounding the loss of power or protection, and Outlast is no different.

[2] For more on these techniques, see Robert Baird's 'The Startle Effect: Implications for Spectator Cognition and Media Theory' (2000).

[3] For more on this see Torben Grodal's paper 'Stories for Eye, Ear, and Muscles: Video Games, Media, and Embodied Experiences' (2003), which stresses the necessity of "coping" in video game play.

[4] One aspect of the gaze beyond the scope of this paper is the use of game telemetry to gather player data. This idea is explored by Alessandro Canossa in 'Reporting from the Snooping Trenches: Changes in Attitudes and Perceptions Towards Behavior Tracking in Digital Games' and Alex Dean Cybulski in 'Enclosures at Play: Surveillance in the Code and Culture of Videogames.' An obvious example of the game watching the player can be found in the choice-driven, episodic game *Life is Strange* (Square Enix, 2014), as after each episode is completed a page of statistics is displayed comparing the individual player's choices with the choices made by players worldwide.

[5] 'Downloadable Content', an additional story set in the same game-world.

Chapter 4

The Game Space of *Dear Esther* and Beyond:
Perspective Shift and the Subversion of Player Agency

Harrington Weihl
Northwestern University, USA

ABSTRACT

This chapter argues that the spaces created by video games are central to the formulation of player agency in the game. More precisely, this chapter analyzes several recent independent and experimental games—Dear Esther, Menagerie, and the work of games collective Arcane Kids—to argue that the dislocation or alienation of player agency through the formal category of game space has political and aesthetic significance. The dislocation of player agency sees 'agency' taken away from the player and granted instead to the game space itself; players are placed at the mercy of the game space in such a way that their lack of agency is emphasized. The effect of this emphasis is to enable these games to critique the atomized, neoliberal undercurrents of contemporary cultural production.

INTRODUCTION

Game spaces are as diverse (if not more so) than real spaces: the theme-park world of Azeroth,[1] the seemingly boundless landscapes of Skyrim,[2] the home-made, pixelated expanse of *Minecraft* (Mojang, 2009), and even the porous and experimental spaces of *Portal* (Valve, 2007). This paper positions the particular game space of The Chinese Room's 2012 game *Dear Esther* –which grew from a mod alongside other contemporary game experiences in order to examine what is most superficially conventional and at the same time most radical about it: the unity and homogeneity of its space. *Dear Esther* pushes the boundaries of what a video game *is* so far that project member and creative technology professor Dan Pinchbeck calls it an "interactive ghost story" (2008, p. 51) Each of the game spaces referenced above—drawn from some of the century's most popular and innovative games—present the player with means of conceptualizing and interacting with the world that reinforce player agency. For example, in

DOI: 10.4018/978-1-5225-0261-6.ch004

Minecraft and *Portal,* the player is able to alter the landscape or at least the means of moving through the landscape. In *World of Warcraft* and *Skyrim,* maps (along with the cities, dungeons and landmarks that they chart) position the player as an entity for whom the world is sometimes a play-thing at their disposal, and sometimes an adversary. The role of the game world in *Dear Esther*, however, is less predicated on the centrality of player control and agency, and, as a consequence, precipitates shifts in perspective that subvert the dominant logic of the protagonist. The game's invisible player-character is also an invisible narrator; instead of encouraging a multiplicity of protagonists through the random ordering of the narrative, *Dear Esther* erases the protagonist by reallocating the central role to the island itself.

This chapter argues that the heightened unity of *Dear Esther*'s game-world, which consists entirely of a small island whose looming agency displaces the agency of the player-character, encourages a perspective shift in the player by reducing and decentering their agency. This central argument will be supplemented by analysis of other recent games, including the work of the game collective Arcane Kids and oleomingus's "small experiment" (Oleomingus.itch.io, 2015, para. 1) entitled *Menagerie* (2015). Space operates differently in each of these instances; nevertheless, as this chapter will demonstrate, the predominance of game space over narrative (whether total or partial) signifies a significant shift in contemporary video game production. These games use the formal category of space that decenter the player in ways that speak to the particular political moment of their production. The perspective of the protagonist is normally so closely allied to the atomized subject of the (increasingly post) neoliberal[3] present that when it is reduced in these games to little more than a cipher-like frame on which the space of the game exerts itself, a formidable political critique is being made. As we will see, the variety with which this critique is carried out in contemporary games points toward social and political promise from the genre.

GAME SPACE AS A CATEGORY

Game space is used here to talk about what appears to be the physical space that the player character moves through in a video game. This definition, of course, leaves a lot to be desired. What would the game space of *Tetris* (Pajitnov & Pokhiko, 1984) be? Or of *Street Fighter* (Capcom, 1987)? These are potentially illuminating questions, but the preponderance of contemporary games that use first or third-person control of a character in a three-dimensional space impels us to define the category of game space—for our purposes—as content of a video game that is viewable and/or accessible through the movement of the player. More often than not, this content fundamentally resembles the world as human beings normally experience it. Some games, such as *Prey* (Human Head Studios, 2006), defy the laws of gravity, yet nevertheless these deviations still understand the rules of our universe as the norm.

Game space, then, is intentionally created to be analogous to 'real' space; it would be a mistake, however, to simply understand game space as a metaphor for or mirror image of real space, or even as an artistic interpolation of real space. Jesper Juul (2005) has argued for game space as an intersection of restrictive rulemaking and creative worldmaking, and in rejecting game space as an imitation of real life, we can see that game space is like literary space—fictive, generated and malleable—its rules are those of a fictional space that is consciously created for readerly[4] or playerly navigation. What is important for us about game space, however, is that its mimicry of real space allows us to apply our understanding of real space to it—the narrative stroll[5] and strategies and tactics[6] are both real-world spatial concepts that can readily applied to game spaces. The embrace of 'social construction' in contemporary theory paves the way for this; in fact, the analogy between game space and real space is perhaps never more true than it is when we consider the constructedness of both spaces. For our purposes, then, game space will from here on be used to mean not only the viewable and accessible terrain of the game but also as the written terrain of the game—form masquerading as content.[7] Game space's formal quality is equal parts truth and charade, as we see in the case of *Dear Esther*, where the narrative content of the game overshadows (and in turn, sits under the shadow) of its formal elements. To draw on Henri Lefebvre's definition of monumentality, game space is "not text but texture"—a "total experience in a total space" (1974/1991, p. 222) that the player enters and cannot escape. Game space is written but not readable like content is—instead it is experienced as the structuring form of the game.

DEAR ESTHER

Dear Esther is a game that defies easy categorization, and is even more defiant in the face of summarization. Set on an abandoned island in the Hebrides (off the northwest coast of Scotland), the game follows an unnamed protagonist—assumed to also be the narrator—as he traverses the island while simultaneously attempting to navigate his grief over the death of his wife Esther, having been behind the wheel in the car accident that resulted in her death. The game is narrated entirely by the protagonist in letters to Esther (hence the name). There are a few other characters that feature as well: pharmaceutical salesman Paul, who was driving the car with which Esther and the narrator collided; syphilitic eighteenth century traveler and historian Donnelly (who shares a last name with Esther and, perhaps, the narrator), whose writings fascinate the narrator; a shepherd named Jakobson whose life and people Donnelly sought to study. The latter two men died on the island, with the narrator apparently meeting the same fate. Esther aside, the only other person referenced in the narration is the Hermit, an unseen and legendary figure for whom gifts are left at the mouth of a cave on the island. He, like Donnelly, Jakobson and the narrator, went to the island seeking solitude, and the parallels between these characters (along with their notably congruous races, ages and genders) suggest that they could be different avatars of the same person, the narrator. As this tangent suggests, the interpretive possibilities presented by the complex and ambiguous narrative of *Dear Esther* are numerous, and this interpretive richness is one of the keys to the game's success.

The only action that the player can undertake in the game is the action of walking. Walking invisibly triggers randomly selected clips of the narrative, and walking (along with occasional swimming) is the only expression of playerly agency in the game. In oversimple terms, the *Dear Esther* experience is that of listening to random snippets of narrative while trudging around a bleak and deserted island. Its dominant thematic structure, as the synopsis above demonstrates and as our further analysis will show, orbits around the pathos of loss, the complexity and multiplicity of the psychic landscape, and the processing of trauma. The tradition that *Dear Esther* draws upon could be traced back to Twine games or *Myst* (Miller & Miller, 1993), yet it is difficult to locate ancestors of the game; its influence can be traced more readily among its contemporaries: *Gone Home* (Fullbright, 2013) (with its retrospection and psychodrama), *The Stanley Parable* (Wreden, 2011) (an interactive story with narrative flexibility), and *Proteus* (Kaganga & Key, 2013) (where the player freely explores a procedurally generated island) all have various congruities with *Dear Esther*.

Critical response to the game upon its release in early 2012 was, according to Metacritic, "generally favorable" (2015), with major game review sites almost universally giving it an 8/10 and using strikingly similar language: Keza McDonald at IGN called it "that rarest of things: a truly interesting game" (2012, para. 9). while Gamespot's Maxwell McGee emphasized its "intriguing narrative" (2012, para. 1). Nathan Grayson at GameSpy classified it as something "truly different. It's an experiment to be sure... a strong start to a new breed of adventure that asks players to think instead of clicking on items until something arbitrarily happens" (2012, para. 8). Game Informer's Tim Turi recommended *Dear Esther* for those interested in "taking a close look at a piece of art that goes against the grain of the medium... the same way you'd appraise a film... absorbing an intellectual story and gorgeous visuals without having to exert a drop of effort" (2012, para. 5). Each review emphasizes content over form, and even an amateur review by Phill Cameron at Videogamer.com leads by asserting that "The beauty of *Dear Esther* is that it raises questions about content rather than mechanics... Your left mouse button is useless. It's not needed, and neither is your right. *Dear Esther* doesn't require you to interact with these inputs. It merely asks you to walk, to explore, and, most importantly, to listen" (2012, para. 1). The focus on content over form is reflected in the fan community—the Steam Game Discussions forum for *Dear Esther* is devoted almost entirely to interpretational work (see Figure 1).

Such work has its place, but this chapter asserts that no reading of *Dear Esther* is complete without a consideration of form and mechanics, and goes a step further to suggest that form and mechanics are the primary way in which the 'meaning' or cultural significance of the game can be understood. Cameron's review mistakes the absence or dulling of player interaction with space with a lack of significance for those categories. On the contrary, the spatial and formal aspects of *Dear Esther* are present in their apparent absence: a game that so emphasizes its overflow of interpretable content at the same time highlights the significance of those aspects that don't obviously invite interpretation. It is these aspects—the formal use of randomized audio to create the narrative, the confusion of player identity, and the game space

Figure 1. The landscape of Dear Esther was praised for its beauty
(The Chinese Room, 2012)

Dear Esther. The gulls do not land here anymore; I've noticed that this year, they seem to shun the place. Maybe it's the depletion of the fishing stock driving them away. Perhaps it's me. When he first landed here, Donnelly wrote that the herds were sickly and their shepherds the lowest of the miserable classes that populate these Hebridean islands. Three hundred years later, even they have departed.

of the island itself—that are our objects of study in this chapter. They demonstrate how *Dear Esther* subverts the dominant logic of the protagonist and makes a political claim through form that it could never make through content.

RANDOMIZED AUDIO NARRATIVE

The narrative fragments that make up the literary text of the game are activated when the player reaches certain points on the map, but each piece of narration is chosen from a number of possible clips, resulting in a different narrative in each playthrough. This chapter asserts that the unity of space and narrative here, which is divorced from the visual, rends the fabric of the *total experience* that video games are so often meant to produce. This effect repositions the player—typically understood as an agent and instigator—as more than just a reader. T.L. Taylor (2009) argues in *Play Between Worlds* that developer agency is ceded to the player in video games. A more appropriate comparison would pair the developer with an architect and the player with an inhabitant of an architect-designed space. Gameplay and movement within space both occur at the behest of the user with a greater degree of freedom[8] than in the case of a reader of literature or art. The physical (or digital) possibilities for quite literal shifts in perspective and the multiplicity of options for navigating (game)space and negotiating its obstacles are distinct from all but the most experimental and unconventional literature. Chris Melissinos, speaking as curator of the 2012 exhibit at the Smithsonian entitled "The Art of Video Games" claimed in an interview that "video games are the only forms of artistic expression that allow the authoritative voice of the author to remain true while allowing the observer to explore and experiment" (Tucker, 2012, para. 5). This is a fascinating assertion for our purposes, and deserves some closer examination: to call the player an 'observer' is to position them in such a way that exploration and experimentation can only take place on their end. This is accurate, as we understand it—players can only really impose themselves on games by experimenting with their own perspective; space provides players with opportunities to alter their perspectives both tactically and strategically. The fit between gaming and architecture vis-a-vis the agency of the player depends on the style of the game in question, of course. Just as architectural styles can vary in their approaches to the management of the inhabitants of space, games can vary according to the ways that they afford agency and freedom to the player. Even in those games that rest at the more linear, literary end of the spectrum (with the more radical freedom of *Minecraft* resting at the other end)—say in a traditional first-person shooter like *Half-Life* (Valve, 1998)—the degree of player freedom in moving and solving puzzles is distinctly unliterary.

The continuum that I propose here is based around the freedom of player movement and the actualization of player agency; the games analyzed in this chapter are those that, crucially, subvert player agency in non-traditional ways that are literary while still exploring the spatial potentials of the genre. Their spaces are open—or at least unconventional—but their narratives are stifling and frozen. *Dear Esther* introduces the player to both the literary and the spatial immediately: the game begins with the player standing near a lighthouse on the shore of a deserted Hebridean island, and one of four[9] opening monologues begin as the player starts to move around. All begin as letters read aloud or dictated "Dear Esther" and two of them are preoccupied with an ahistorical, synchronic[10] frozenness; that is to say that they approach a singular moment in time, extracted and isolated from the temporal continuum. Conversely, the other two possible openings are diachronic, preoccupied with the passing of time as an organic, unified continuum (see Table 1).

Table 1. Synchronic and diachronic opening monologue options in Dear Esther

Synchronic Options
I sometimes feel as if I've given birth to this island. Somewhere, between the longitude and latitude a split opened up and it beached remotely here. No matter how hard I correlate, it remains a singularity, an alpha point in my life that refuses all hypothesis.
I have lost track of how long I have been here, and how many visits I have made overall. Certainly, landmarks are now so familiar to me that I have to remind myself to actually see the forms and shapes in front of me.
Diachronic Options
The gulls do not land here anymore; I've noticed that this year they seem to have shunned this place... the herds were sickly and their shepherds the lowest of the miserable classes... Three hundred years later, even they have departed.
The morning after I was washed ashore, salt in my ears, sand in my mouth and the waves always at my ankles, I felt as though everything had conspired to this one last shipwreck. I remembered nothing but water, stones in my belly and my shoes threatening to drag me under to where only the most listless of creatures swim.

The sorrowful notes struck in the synchronic passages are similar to those in the diachronic passages, but the methods by which they are presented are quite different. The emphasis on synchrony and diachrony, timelessness and timefulness, in the opening of the game highlights the literary and game-spatial effects of the game. *Dear Esther* is, we are shown from the very beginning, neither an experimental story nor a visual exploration. It is both and more—an artwork that contains and sets at odds the two primary modes of player experience (architectural and literary) in order to subvert them. The unity of narrative and space introduced above is produced by the emphasis on their distinctness; *Dear Esther* is shown to be *nothing more* than narrative and space.

This is not to say, however, that the content of the narrative (the space will be discussed further below) does not merit analysis. As we have seen, the beginning of the game sets the tone for the way in which the game relates to the significance of its own narrative. The central narrative concern of the game is the reliability of the narrator, which is itself a question of perspective. The formal effect of narratorial unreliability established through the randomization of what passages are included in a certain playthrough is mirrored at the level of content. The narrator never definitively links himself to a specific time or place while hinting at only a few details: he was driving on the highway with his (possibly pregnant) wife Esther when they were involved in car accident with Paul—a pharmaceutical worker who may or may not have been drunk—that leaves Esther dead. The narrator visits Paul in his home after the accident and the latter is scarred by his responsibility. It is unclear from here how the narrator made his way to the island or whether the island exists in any real sense.

At the same time, there is a parallel storyline that the narrator relates based on his research of and on the island. In the eighteenth century, a researcher named Donnelly visited the island in search of a legendary religious hermit. Syphilitic and obtuse, Donnelly did not find a hermit; instead, he observed and wrote about the Scandinavian shepherds that inhabited the island. The first among them was Jakobson, who died alone on the island in his first Winter there. Both men serve as ciphers for the narrator, as does the fictional hermit: he remarks that "I find myself increasingly unable to find that point where the Hermit ends and Paul and I begin." The narrator's personal drama is contextualized through a deeply historical set of references. His singular and personal misery is rooted in idiosyncratic historical accounts that are linked to him through the space of the island. This tension between the private present and the subjective historical obscures the scope of the game, and returns the focus of the narrative to the space of the island itself. The convoluted, obscure and intentionally vague backstory is not un-interpretable or meaningless, but rather emphasizes the materiality of the island for the player.[11] The suffusion of reference, allusion (often Biblical), and historical minutiae serves to push the content of the narrative beyond the realm of simple elucidation and establishes it instead as a category that is defined differentially by comparison to the island. When speaking of the Scandinavian former inhabitants of the island, the narrator says that

They were godfearing people those shepherds. There was no love in the relationship. Donnelly tells me that they had one bible that was passed around in strict rotation. It was stolen by a visiting monk in 1776, two years before the island was abandoned altogether. In the interim, I wonder, did they assign chapter and verse to the stones and grasses, marking the geography with a superimposed significance; that they could actually walk the Bible and inhabit its contradictions?

Dear Esther permits the player to 'walk the narrative' and inhabit its very obvious contradictions—the narrative of the game establishes contradictions and confusion so as to make the walking of it that much more essential and effective as an interpretive practice. In fact, the surplus of lore and narrative in the game, and the confusing way in which it is presented, gestures toward the foregrounding of form in the game. This is not to say that *Dear Esther*'s plot is mere window-dressing. Instead, we should understand that plot is secondary to form in the ways that *Dear Esther* encourages a shift in perspective.

PLAYER IDENTITY

Avatar customization and definitive player-appearance are typically presented as laudable strengths in contemporary video games. In *Dear Esther*, however, the randomization of narrative content, the variety of narrative voices, the absence of any traditional Non-Player-Characters (NPCs) and—most crucially—the unresponsive nature of the game-space in the presence of the player all subvert the norms of the player's status within the game. This discord is emphasized by the rare, but notable, appearance of a hooded figure in the distance in certain parts of the game: the antagonist that the protagonist never meets. Additionally, the absolute and unrestricted freedom of exploration that the player is afforded on the island only serves to further highlight the complete impotence of the player in relation to the space—both physical and narrative—that they traverse. The logic of the protagonist is undermined fundamentally in the game so as to affect a dislocation of player agency.

The highly customizable avatars found in contemporary games have not always been the norm: in *Doom* (id, 1993), a seminal first-person shooter, the player was not visible beyond their hand. While the convention of the invisible player-character persists to this day, player customization is even more pronounced—from *Mass Effect* (Bioware, 2007) to *The Sims 4* (Maxis, 2014). Even in *Doom* or *Half-Life*, however, the player's invisibility was supplemented by the visibility of their hands and the weapons that they held; the protagonist of a first-person shooter existed as a weapon and nothing else. The 'nothing else' is all that comprises the player character in *Dear Esther*. The player does not cast a shadow, nor are they reflected in water or glass—lateral movement across the landscape is the only index of the player's physical existence, save for two incidents. The first, at the beginning of the third chapter and the halfway point of the game, provides aural proof of the player-character's corporeality. After falling through a hole in a cave (the player must choose deliberately to descend through the hole, and the narrative space of the game guides the player to this choice), the player is heard to splash in the water below and gasp for air as their vision adjusts to the glowing dark of the cave. A second free-fall, at the conclusion of the game, does not reinforce the materiality that the first descent suggests, and instead unmoors the sense of reality that the game has established.

The player-character, having progressed through the game (and, necessarily, through the island) ascends the blinking radio tower that looms ominously over the island. As the final monologue begins, the player and the player-character are sundered from one another: the player loses control as the player-character approaches the ladder and ascends. The two closing available closing monologues mirror the synchrony/diachrony division of the opening monologues. The longer option is diachronic:

Dear Esther. I have burnt my belongings, my books, this death certificate. Mine will be written all across this island. Who was Jakobson, who remembers him? Donnelly has written of him, but who was Donnelly, who remembers him? I have painted, carved, hewn, scored into this space all that I could draw from him. There will be another to these shores to remember me. I will rise from the ocean like an island without bottom, come together like a stone, become an aerial, a beacon that they will not forget you. We have always been drawn here: one day the gulls will return and nest in our bones and our history. I will look to my left and see Esther Donnelly, flying beside me. I will look to my right and see Paul Jakobson, flying beside me. They will leave white lines carved into the air to reach the mainland, where help will be sent.

It moves from a recounting of the past to a vision of the future; Esther will join the narrator in the sky along with the centuries-dead historian who died on the island while chronicling it. Their salvation will rest in their reunification in death. The future vision is mournful, yet redemptive and contrasts with the more urgent, sorrowful synchronic monologue:

Dear Esther. I have burned the cliffs of Damascus, I have drunk deep of it. My heart is my leg and a black line etched on the paper all along this boat without a bottom. You are all the world like a nest to me, in which eggs unbroken form like fossils, come together, shatter and send small black flowers to the very air. From this infection, hope. From this island, flight. From this grief, love. Come back! Come back...

This passage moves from the past into an absolute present—the vision of Esther as a "nest" is more fantastic than the future vision of the gulls in the first passage, yet it is not a vision of a time to come but a vision of immediacy. The synchronic scope of the passage shifts from the emphasis on movement in the first passage to an emphasis on space, yet both passages emphasize an embodiment of space. The narrator *is* the island; Esther *is* a nest, and as the player's time comes to an end, the space(s) that they are is all that remains.

The concluding monologues persist in the thematic concern with time and space that the game introduces in its opening even after control is wrested from the hands of the player. This heightens the alienating effect of the player losing control, and gestures toward the fact that the player, having navigated and remained always on the island, never had control to begin with. Once the player reaches the top of the tower, they leap into the air in what would amount to a suicide if the logic of the fall into the cave was followed. Instead, as the player-character approaches the ground, they begin to soar low over the beach that the player traversed earlier, back to a collection of candles and paper boats as the camera fades to black. The player-character, who never before cast a shadow, casts a shadow in the moonlight as they fly—the shadow of a gull. The implicit transfiguration here retroactively imbues the physical nature of the player-character with a weight that it never appeared to have, as the player's attention was

Figure 2. Dear Esther concludes with the transfiguration of the player character and the persistence of the island as a space
(The Chinese Room, 2012)

not drawn to it. The avian shadow and the flying movement of the player highlight the assumptions around player-character identity that the literary aspects of the game had called into question all along. Consequently, there is a visual and spatial articulation of the game's literary thematic commitments, and this articulation serves to reinforce, solidify and make clear those commitments (see Figure 2).

After the view of the now flying player fades to black, a view of the island, with the full moon lighting it and waves washing the candlelit beach, is held for a few seconds before the game ends completely. This final return to and focus on the landscape of the island itself instead of the climactic viewpoint of the player is the ultimate gesture toward the game's thematic preoccupation with space: as the narrator's story resolves and recedes, the text of the island remains intact and persistent. This is particularly significant when the way that the narrative is constructed in *Dear Esther* is taken into consideration. The randomization of narrative fragments gives the literary portion of the text a degree of fungibility that the island distinctly lacks. It is the game's constant, and does not change in the slightest compared to other playthroughs. This is not to say that it is more important to the game-text than the game's literary aspects—instead it should be understood that space can be read differently than the literary, as the game's dominant index of meaning.

THE GAME SPACE OF DEAR ESTHER

The overflow and chaotic intermixing of literary text in *Dear Esther* only enhances the clarity of the island's stark, austere landscapes. The third way that perspective-shift for the player is produced is through the total space of the game itself. In what appears to be a dead world, the island, it becomes apparent, lives and breathes. The slow, flashing light of the radio antenna tower takes on an omnipresent, ever visible, panoptic character, complemented by the occasional appearance of the distant, ethereal onlooker. Mysteriously lit candles and folded paper boats never hint at a creator and instead read as manifestations of the island's will. The player's descent into the island is visceral and carnal—flowing waters, glowing caverns and scattered ultrasound printouts evoke an embodied interiority that enhances the corporeality and agency of the game-space of the island while simultaneously stunting the agency of the player. The submission of the player to the total space of the island reduces the player to a powerless observer (for whom even suicide by drowning in the surrounding sea is impossible, as they are returned to the shore at the moment of death) and thus emphasizes the perspective of the player as simply that: the player is nothing more than their floating, camera-like perspective within the space of the island. The island— more than the player or characters who populate the story proper—truly *alive*, with light, water, birds and the sound of the ocean. The inhuman emptiness of the space seems at first to suggest death, yet it is the former human occupants of the island and of the story who are dead and empty mirages.

This is emphasized by the presence of ghost-like shades that stand in the distance in a couple instances on the island. Resembling hooded, cloaked figures, the shades can't be reached conventionally in the game, and can only be viewed from a distance. Their presence is not imposed on the player—they are so distant, small and subtle that one could easily play the entirety of the game without ever noticing them. The narrative purpose of these shades is fairly clear, as they suggest that the story does not take place in 'normal' empirical reality, but perhaps in the interior of someone's psychology or on another plane. Of course, this is revealed to us to be the case at the end of the game, when the player takes flight just before striking the ground, having jumped off of a radio tower. Pages upon pages of internet message board discussions are dedicated to the ontological question of 'where' the game takes place, yet in tangible terms, the 'where' of *Dear Esther* is the easiest question to answer: on the island. The supernatural aspects of the game—always embodied by the (apparently) human player or by ghostly human shapes are never manifested in the body of the island.

This is not to say that the island is entirely natural, either. Indeed, the island is covered with both traditional remnants of human settlement and non-traditional markers specific to the narrative. The first traditional sign of human settlement and activity dominates the opening frame of the game— a small lighthouse and the attached building are the first things that the player sees, as the begin standing on a boat ramp leading up to it, with no boat behind them. The player (though not directly compelled to) then normally explores the structure, finding a couple of photographs and books that hint at the story to come, and is spooked by a gull that flies out of the darkness. With two or three rooms, the lighthouse is the most complex man-made structure that the player can explore on the island. A dilapidated shed (constructed centuries previous), a wrecked, small cargo tanker without an accessible interior, and the radio tower are the only other man-made spaces to be found in the game. That the most formidable man-made space in the game is so conspicuously foregrounded speaks to how the game prioritizes space while resisting conventional modes of representation (see Figure 3).

The interior of the island, lit by candles, bioluminescent organisms and the occasional beam of moonlight is subterranean inversion which contrasts sharply with its bleak, craggy green-grey surface, demonstrates the unique operation of space in *Dear Esther*. Space here suggests its own interiority and in doing so emphasizes the emptiness of the player-position in the game, and it is inside the island that the player sees numerous biological diagrams, biblical quotations and other man-made markings that relate to the narrative made in glowing paint on the cave walls. This captures perhaps the most devastating critique advanced by the form of *Dear Esther*: the interiority of the protagonist/player is suggested differently by the narrative and by the interior of the island itself, but ultimately the island has an interior that the player lacks. Covered by so many converging identities and narratives, the narrator is little more than a procedurally generated absence, an inversion of the hulking, material presence of the island. The

Figure 3. The subterranean depths within the island are vibrantly lit and suggest an organic unity to the island
(The Chinese Room, 2012)

When I was coming round from the operation, I remember the light they shone in my eyes to check for pupil contraction. It was like staring up at a moonlit sky from the bottom of well. People moved at the summit but I could not tell if you were one of them.

link between player-character agency and game-space is an intimate one; as we will see, even in other spatial configurations many contemporary games are carrying out the same sort of reorientation of player perspective through related means that are different in important ways.

SCALE AND SPACE IN THE WORKS OF ARCANE KIDS AND OLEOMINGUS

The melancholy content of *Dear Esther* should not overshadow or be understood as a necessary condition of the formal characteristics that have been identified in it. The pathos of the narrative in *Dear Esther* contrasts sharply with other contemporary games that take up the same questions of space. One independent game development collective, Arcane Kids, make formal innovations through space that pursue some of the same lines of inquiry identified in *Dear Esther*. Arcane Kids describe themselves in their manifesto as "an award winning internet gang from L.A." —their games are referential and comedic works that emphasize their own failure to meet the standards of normal video game play. The manifesto (stylized on their website as a menu list from Valve's Steam video game platform) is as follows:

- Shut up about video games
- The fastest way to the truth is a joke
- Stop listening to advice
- Start your own scene
- Art is about giving people what they want

- Do NOT call us punk
- Communities need spaces to grow
- Fuck formalism
- Fuck puzzles
- Play with structure
- Bad is more interesting than good
- The purpose of gameplay is to hide secrets
- Make games u wish 2 see on the dreamcast (Arcane Kids, n.d.)

This manifesto (and even the existence of such a document) provides us with some guidance on how to read their games: video games can be taken seriously as art only through a refusal to take them seriously as traditional entertainment objects. The three games by Arcane Kids that we will discuss (in open and ongoing defiance of their first commandment) are radically different in size and scope. The most well-known of these is *Zineth* (2012), a proof-of-concept piece from their time at university that received praise and publicity for its unique gameplay and design. The player guides their skier over the colorful and obtuse landscapes of the game in order to reach extreme speeds and execute enormous jumps. The game also features an integrated smartphone-like device on which the player can battle NPCs in mini-games that consist of nothing more than clicking to shoot a small creature three times. The smartphone (manufactured by Catco[12]) also keeps track of the player's missions, which include work for their employer, a zine meant to "save the minds" of the city's inhabitants and "show them what the real world has to offer" (Unity3d.com, 2012, para. 1). The phones also allow the player to engage with NPCs in mobile arcade-like combat (so simplistic and reduced that it appears parodic). The juxtaposition of extreme speeds, visuals and spaces with the technological mundanity and financial precarity of twenty-first century life in the U.S. lends *Zineth* a level of nuance and political critique that it would otherwise lack (see Figure 4).

*Figure 4. The player-character swiftly approaches Zineth's city from a great distance
(Arcane Kids, 2012)*

That said, the unique spatial proportions of the game are what set it apart. Like the island of *Dear Esther*, the landscape of *Zineth* is unified—there are no loading screens or separate levels. Instead, increasing the player's speed is the game's primary aim; outside of skiing quickly around the city and its surroundings in mini-games or interacting with NPCs via games on their mobile phone, the player is meant mostly to traverse the game space as quickly as possible and make ever more ridiculous and audacious jumps off of ramps, which can be found everywhere. In fact, the most extreme and difficult achievement in the game (so much so that it is easy to find chronicled variously on YouTube) is jumping to the Moon. Space in *Zineth* is an index of speed, and as such the vastness of the game space serves a very straightforward, pragmatic function. What is most important about *Zineth*'s game-space is that Arcane Kids attempt to maintain a degree of realism or functionality in a space that is built for high-speed skiing and jumping. The city, though not entirely functional and fleshed out, is a populated space that sets out to be more than a simple skate-park. The player's perspective—as the hyper-fast, cowboy-hat wearing master of space that is nevertheless subjected to the menial tasks required of an overeducated twenty-first century petty-bourgeois clerk while being bombarded by vacuous advertisements and indulging in an inane mobile phone game as an escape from the 'real' (game) world—is dependent on the game-space as something that can be superficially dominated and mastered despite the fact that fast travel does nothing to change the class-position or the socioeconomic conditions of the space the player occupies.

This player-character impotence is familiar to us, having been one of the central concerns of *Dear Esther*. Another game by Arcane Kids, *Room of 1000 Snakes* (2013), takes an approach to space that is an inversion of the approach in *Zineth*. The game is claustrophobic, taking place entirely within the confines of an ancient Egyptian crypt. The game opens with text that sets the stage for the game with a comically direct sparseness: "They told you not to enter. / You, an explorer didn't listen / 'I will find out the mystery of snakes.'" The game itself is remarkably short—the player crosses the room and finds a large button, and the text "Press E to push button" appears. Of course, as a well trained video game player, they push the button without question, and The Verve's "Bitter Sweet Symphony" (1997) begins to play. As the hit song (which was accompanied by a plagiarism controversy) builds toward its first crescendo, the room begins to shake, and sand pours from openings in the walls. When the crescendo hits, static green snake figures begin to spray out of the holes in the walls, and obscure the player's view as the begin to fill the room. Regardless of how quickly the player follows the command to "Press F to shake", the snakes eventually cover them, and the game ends. The browser then redirects to a Tumblr page that offers (non-existent) *Room of 1000 Snakes* merchandise. The comedic angle of the game is what makes it effective as a critique of video games; the vacuous set up, the oversimplified tutorial commands and the arbitrary, inescapable conclusion all highlight the often arbitrary and alienating norms in contemporary video games. Furthermore, in the confined space of the crypt, player movement is rendered meaningless: there is no entrance or exit, and the snakes are inescapable (see Figure 5).

There are spatial implications of understanding *Room of 1000 Snakes* as a critique of the games industry as well. The restricted and overly-simplified space of the game contrasts sharply with the push for ever more expansive games spaces in contemporary titles, both AAA (such as *Fallout 4* (Bethesda, 2015)) and independent (*Minecraft*). To use a commonplace, the cramped space of the titular room is 'a feature, not a bug.' Arcane Kids utilize space to carry out an immanent critique of video games, and the utilization of space as an index of meaning in a game is something that will be familiar to us from *Dear Esther*. The convergence of literary and spatial categories in *Dear Esther* is echoed in the small space (even smaller than the *Room of 1000 Snakes*) in oleomingus's *Menagerie*, which is "[b]ased on a script and performance" by artists Prayas Abhinav, Vidisha Saini and Agat Sharma (Oloemingus.itch.io, 2015,

Figure 5. The pyramid's crypt quickly fills with snakes once the player pushes the button (Arcane Kids, 2013)

para. 4). In *Menagerie,* the player witnesses a monologue by a wooden, human-like figure who repeats cryptic statements: "Will me be as you?" "The machine is a state." "The ability to understand is fixed." The mysterious nature of the text draws the player/reader in through a question of content—'what do these lines mean?'—but quickly shifts the focus to questions of form. Any time that the player moves around the small room, cluttered with grass, plants, plumbing and housewares, a clone of the original speaker is created (see Figure 6).

The clones' monologues are increasingly convoluted and eventually become illegible. This shift from content to form is significant: it is similar to the foundational tension in *Dear Esther*, wherein the overflow of interpretable content shifts the game's hermeneutic center of gravity to the space of the island and the formal randomization of the narrative content itself. Like *Dear Esther*, *Menagerie* challenges interpretation, but takes this one step further and progressively eschews interpretation. What's more, oleomingus links the deterioration of comprehensibility with movement in the game's tiny space—movement is a futile exercise of player agency, which reflexively challenges narrative obtuseness with spatial movement, only to see that backfire and complicates things further. The disjunction of player perspective that is accomplished through an alienation of spatial coordinates and norms extends a political critique to the larger matrix of western culture and globalized capital from which games are produced.

The purposeful peregrination that characterizes typical video game play is undermined and parodied in what is perhaps the most pointed piece by Arcane Kids—*Bubsy 3D: Bubsy Visits the James Turrell Retrospective* (2013). It is billed as an eighteenth birthday celebration of *Bubsy 3D: Furbitten Planet* (1996), a "would-be Mario killer" (1UP, n.d.) that has been listed among the worst games of all time. This new tribute features Bubsy visiting the Los Angeles County Museum of Art's James Turrell exhibition while a hauntingly off-tone and childish soundtrack plays on loop in the background. The controls are clumsy, the obstacles to reaching the museum arbitrary, and the items collected—rainbow colored

Figure 6. The small room of Menagerie fills with wooden figures who speak in increasingly incomprehensible phrases
(oleomingus, 2015)

balls, snakes and hearts (inconsequential items masquerading as health bonuses) are all tallied and so meaningless that the icons marking where they are counted drift around the screen as the player moves.

As Bubsy progresses through a recreation of the LA County Museum of Art, populated by NPCs that are variously abnormally small, cheering, or too tall for the room in which they stand, he makes earnest observations in a text bubble above his head: "Wow. People seem to really be enjoying installation art." Bubsy becomes more sophisticated as he progresses through the exhibit: "These light works are reminiscent of early 3D computer graphics!" "Art's cool ;^)" "Light defines form. But light also has a form of its own. Light has thingness." Despite his ridiculous appearance and the ironic overtones to everything that he says and does, Bubsy has a mimetic relation to the player, who is also experiencing the meticulous recreations of Turrell's art, which uses light to manipulate space and perspective. Upon entering a room full of large crates labelled "ART" Bubsy remarks, "Finally! This is my favorite form of art. So practical and easy to use!" "I forgot that there's so much art outside, right outside your house, to learn from." Reaching the end of the exhibit, Bubsy remarks that, in Turrell's *Key Lime*, "It's like as if light is a form of architecture. Damn, B-) it's shaping our understanding of space." We can see this as complementing the definition we've established for game space—light replicating space as we understand it. Bubsy goes on to quote Turrell: "James Turrell says 'If you use the medium of light to tell a story, you're using the power of a story, not the power of light.'" Turrell, via Bubsy, expands on the form/content relationship here—light is pure form, mobilized by narrative content, yet Turrell emphasizes light in his art—form is always at the forefront (see Figure 7).

The game really takes off when Bubsy steps into the blacklit space of Turrell's *St. Elmo's Breath*, which he has heard is a "spiritual experience"—a coffin comes out of the floor and Bubsy lies down in it. The second chapter of the game features the player controlling a coffin as it slaloms to Hell, eventually landing there in chapter three (entitled "Cat out of Hell") having transformed into a short, balding

Figure 7. Bubsy and fellow museum-goers take in Turrell's St. Elmo's Breath as the icons representing points, snakes and health float aimlessly around the screen
(Arcane Kids, 2013)

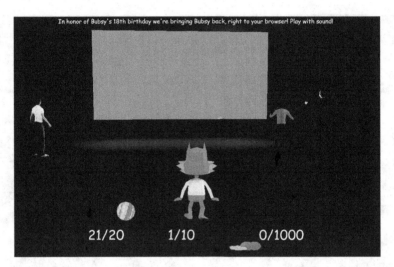

middle-aged man and remarking that "I'm finally an adult." Blue Öyster Cult's "(Don't Fear) The Reaper" (1976) plays and skeletons dance; before Bubsy descends into the flames, a skeletal creature tells him "You have no alternative. The wheels of capitalism will forever grind our bones into dust." Flying into the flames, Bubsy repeats "No Object. No Form. No Relief. No Salvation." The game's final chapter completes the hellish turn of the game's latter half, as an exhausted Bubsy appears in a deserted, endless parking lot and seeks relief at an Applebee's. Any attempt to enter the building causes the building to collapse to reveal the word "ART" glowing as the words "NO RELIEF" flash across the screen.

The darkly comedic and otherwordly finale to a game that begins with some light-hearted (and light-art) weirdness casts the claims about art made by Bubsy at the museum in a different light. Art is not only the serene, manicured light-spaces of Turrell, with clean formal conventions that inspire Bubsy's perceptive quips. Art is also messy, violent and disorienting—a bewildering journey to the center of capitalism's madness (the game 'grinds our bones to dust' as well with its ever-deepening, bewildering horror). Unlike *Dear Esther* or *Menagerie*, where the space and narrative of the game conspire to declaw the protagonist, or *Zineth* and *Room of 1000 Snakes*, where speed and scale shift the player's relation to the game space, in *Bubsy 3D: Bubsy Visits the James Turrell Retrospective*, the protagonist is gleefully and sadistically starved of agency in spaces that are increasingly bizarre and abnormal. Even the recreation of the museum, which mimics a real-life structure is alien: museums are spaces that use movement control to establish temporal and narrative structures that have social and ideological value (Huang, 2001). They are then a mirror-world of the video game, where the subtly controlled movement of the player through space creates a narrative. In *Bubsy*, the progression through the museum and through the game create narratives of diverging alienation—Turrell's work uses form to question materiality and the mediation of externality (Adcock & Turrell, 1990), whereas the game lays bare the machinic quality of capitalism and contemporary life both through the destruction of the protagonist and through the juxtaposition of this process with Turrell's artistic process. That the game, which has sent Bubsy through the air, through an art museum, on a rail through the underworld and finally into hell itself concludes in an endless parking lot, interrupted only by an Applebee's, demonstrates by contrast the way that space can be used to alienate its inhabitants—this alienation is not the transcendent, enlightening alienation of Turrell, but the terrifying, chaotic alienation of the player character that instructs the player on the inexorability of modernity's constitutive structural processes. These processes abuse and mold Bubsy into whatever he needs to be (and, indeed, they alter and abuse him to excess), and render the player helpless. Like Bubsy, the player is a cipher through which these processes express themselves.

CONCLUSION

Ultimately, the new perspectives offered by *Dear Esther* and other contemporary games are not neutral aesthetic ones. Instead, as this chapter demonstrates, through their subversion of player perspective, these games carry out an immanent critique of the formal norms of video game design and, by extension, the contemporary social and cultural landscape that produces them. That this critique is rooted in the game-space is no coincidence: as described above, Fredric Jameson famously writes of the postmodern subversion of the modernist "narrative stroll" in architecture (1992/1997, p. 41). *Dear Esther*, whether a video game or an interactive ghost story, is at its core little more than such a narrative stroll (and has, in fact, been criticized with the pejorative of "walking simulator" (Sweeney, 2015, para. 1)). Indeed, what Jameson calls the "great transformation" of postmodernity—"the spatialization of the temporal" (p. 156) marks space as the dominant and definitive category of the contemporary moment. Space in *Dear Esther* is shown to be dominant in contrast to everything else in the game: while the space of the game remains constant, player identity is confused and the narrative is constantly shifting in ways that redefine that space. For example, the ultrasound images that litter the interior of the island only appear in instances where the selected narrations precipitate them; other photographs appear elsewhere when alternative narrations are generated. This appears to point, of course, to the ultimate agency of the player as reader, but the arbitrary nature of how the narrative is produced subverts the player's predominance.

Similarly, the games of Arcane Kids and oleomingus dislocate player agency through a variety of spatial techniques—from the claustrophobic constrictions of *Room of 1000 Snakes* or *Menagerie* to the dizzying expanses of *Zineth* to *Busby*'s transdimensional and extracorporeal meditation on art. All these spaces differ in shape and scope, but they are united by the fact that they are mobilized to overwhelm and alienate the player by circumscribing them within spaces that do not adhere to the traditional, protagonist-centered logic typically found in video games.

In *Dear Esther*, the individual, immutable protagonist is eschewed in favor of a unified, immutable space that consumes and digests different interlopers on its own terms. The rejection of individual agency by the game, which beyond the space of the game embraces a multiplicity of narrative possibilities, gestures toward a cultural critique that is simultaneously a critique of perspective. The supremacy of individual agents in contemporary late capitalism and its cultural products cannot even be remedied by a collective that is formed of such individuals. Instead, *Dear Esther* suggests that only spaces of reflection and thoughtfulness where the individual subject is dissolved (the most readily discernible narrative strand in the game concerns the death of one speaker's pregnant wife, Esther) present alternatives to the present social, economic and cultural tyranny of the individual. Likewise, the alienation and dislocation of the protagonist in the works of oleomingus and Arcane Kids (along with a number of other excellent and innovative game designers whose works merit attention that was precluded by the scope of this chapter, such as Strangethink and Lilith Zone) serve to critique the atomized, neoliberal subject and suggest possibilities for radically reconfiguring such a subject, whether through language, art, comedy, or space itself.

The social and cultural significance of this subversion of perspective in video games is linked to the video game's potential to serve as an art object that instructs players instead of enabling them to live out their fantasies of individualized power and agency. Rather than rooting the distinction between 'low' cultural products and 'high' art objects in naïve generic divisions, in *Dear Esther* and its compatriots we are able to grasp that the formal critique of their generic contemporaries and the cultural moment that produced them qualifies these games as artworks that mark a significant point in the evolution of the video game via their calls for radical and emancipatory new perspectives through the use of the formal category of game space. The technological and medial aspects of video games endow them with enormous political potential; the radical and unprecedented engagement with space as a category in the games examined above evinces this potential. The fundamental ties that video games have to globalization and the neoliberal capitalist order grant them novel techniques for critiquing and undermining the cultural and economic dominant that gave birth to them. In 1992, Gilles Deleuze christened the postmodern replacement for Foucault's disciplinary societies as "societies of control" —systems more diffuse than their predecessors, exemplified by corporations compared to factories (p. 4). Noting that "[t]ypes of machines are easily matched with each type of society... because they express those social forms capable of generating and using them" (p. 6), Deleuze identifies computers, and their digital networks, as the definitive machines of the societies of control. At the same time, he sees the societies of control as being comprised (like the orders that preceded them) of "different internments or spaces of enclosure" that are made increasingly malleable in postmodernity; this privileging of space complements Jameson's discussion of space that we identify above and points further toward the primacy of space as the key category wherein postmodern cultural products can work through the contradictions of the world from which they spring. While arguing for a new and amorphous society of control, Deleuze refuses to paint an entirely bleak picture, famously asserting that "[t]here is no need to fear or hope, but only to look for new weapons" (p. 4). Ultimately, in these radical and experimental video games that subvert and critique the logic of the protagonist (and by extension the subject) through recourse to space, new weapons have been found.

REFERENCES

1Up. (n.d.). *Beyond the mushroom kingdom*. Retrieved 15 December, 2015, from http://www.1up.com/features/essential-50-tomb-raider

Adcock, C. E., & Turrell, J. (1990). *James Turrell: The art of light and space*. Berkeley: U of California P.

Arcade Kids. (n.d.). *AxK manifesto*. Retrieved December 16, 2015, from http://arcanekids.com/manifesto

Barthes, R. (1977). *Image-music-text* (S. Heath, Trans.). New York: Hill and Wang.

Barthes, R. (2002). *S/Z* (R. Miller, Trans.). Malden, MA: Blackwell. (Original work published 1973)

Blue Öyster Cult. (1976). "(Don't fear) The reaper". On *Agents of Fortune* [Vinyl]. New York: Columbia Records.

Bubsy 3D: Bubsy visits the James Turrell retrospective [Computer Software]. (2013). Los Angeles: Arcane Kids. Available from Bubsy3d.com

Cameron, P. (13 Feb. 2012). *Dear Esther review.* Retrieved 15 December, 2015, from http://www.videogamer.com/pc/dear_esther/review.html

Certeau, M. (1984). *The practice of everyday life* (S. Rendall, Trans.). Berkeley: U of California P.(Original work published 1980)

Dear Esther [Computer Software]. (2012). Portsmouth: The Chinese Room.

Dear Esther script. (18 January 2014). Retrieved 15 December 2015, from http://dearesther.wikia.com/wiki/Dear_Esther_Script

Deleuze, G. (1992). Postscript on the Societies of Control. *October, 59,* 3-7.

Doom [Computer Software]. (1993). Richardson, TX: id Software.

Fallout 4. [Computer Software]. (2011). Rockville, MD: Bethesda.

Gone home [Computer Software]. (2013). Portland, OR: Fullbright.

Grayson, N. (16 Feb. 2012). *Dear Esther review.* Retrieved 15 December, 2015, from http://pc.gamespy.com/pc/dear-esther/1218914p1.html

Half-life [Computer Software]. (1998). Bellevue, WA: Valve.

Harvey, D. (2005). *A brief history of neoliberalism.* Oxford: Oxford U P.

Huang, H. (2001). The spatialization of knowledge and social relationships: A study on the spatial types of the modern museum.*Proceedings of the Third International Space Syntax Symposium.*

Jameson, F. (1997). *Postmodernism, or the cultural logic of late capitalism.* Durham, NC: Duke U P. (Original work published 1992)

Juul, J. (2005). *Half-real: Video games between real rules and fictional worlds.* London: MIT Press.

Kanaga, D., & Key, E. (2013). *Proteus* [Computer Software]. London: Curve Digital.

Lefebvre, H. (1991). *The production of space* (D. Nicholson-Smith, Trans.). Malden, MA: Blackwell. (Original work published 1974)

Lukacs, G. (1974). *The theory of the novel* (A. Bostock, Trans.). Cambridge, MA: MIT Press. (Original work published 1920)

Mass effect [Computer Software]. (2007). Edmonton: Bioware.

McDonald, K. (2012). *Dear Esther review.* Retrieved 15 December, 2015, from http://www.ign.com/articles/2012/02/13/dear-esther-review

McGee, M. (2012). *Dear Esther review.* Retrieved 15 December, 2015, from http://www.gamespot.com/reviews/dear-esther-review/1900-6349936/

Menagerie [Computer Software]. (2014). oleomingus. Available from olelomingus.itch.io/menagerie

Metacritic.com. (n.d.). *Dear Esther for PC*. Retrieved 15 December, 2015, from http://www.metacritic.com/game/pc/dear-esther

Miller, R., & Miller, R. (1993). *Myst* [Computer Software]. Mead, WA: Cyan.

Oleomingus.itch.io. (2015). *Menagerie by Studio Oleomingus*. Retrieved 28 December, 2015, from http://oleomingus.itch.io/menagerie

Pajitnov, A., & Pokhiko, V. (1984). *Tetris* [Computer Software]. Multiple Publishers.

Persson, M. (2009). *Minecraft* [Computer Software]. Stockholm: Mojang.

Pinchbeck, D. (2008). *Dear Esther*: An interactive ghost story built using the source engine. In U. Spierling & N. Szilas (Eds.), *Lecture Notes in Computer Science: Vol. 5443. Interactive storytelling* (pp. 51–54). Berlin: Springer. doi:10.1007/978-3-540-89454-4_9

Portal [Computer Software]. (2007). Bellevue, WA: Valve.

Prey [Computer Software]. (2006). Madison, WI: Human Head Studios.

Room of 1000 snakes [Computer Software]. (2013). Los Angeles: Arcane Kids. Available from http://arcanekids.com/snakes

Roy, D. (2015). Fighting heroic hegemony with *ennui*: The remarkable everyday in *World of Warcraft*. *Journal of Gaming and Virtual Words, 7*(2).

Saussure, F. d. (1959). *Course in general linguistics* (C. Bally, A. Sechehaye, & A. Reidlinger, Trans. & Eds.). New York: Philosophical Library. (Original work published 1916)

Sontag, S. (2013). *Against interpretation and other essays*. New York: Picador. (Original work published 1966)

Steam Game Forums. (n.d.). *Dear Esther Forum*. Retrieved 15 December, 2015, from https://steamcommunity.com/app/203810/discussions/

Street Fighter [Computer Software]. (1987). Osaka: Capcom.

Sweeney, J. (2015). *Indie implosion: Walking simulators*. Retrieved 15 December, 2015, from https://supernerdland.com/indie-implosion-walking-simulators/

Taylor, T. L. (2009). *Play between worlds: Exploring online game culture*. London: MIT Press.

The elder scrolls V: Skyrim [Computer Software]. (2011). Rockville, MD: Bethesda.

The sims 4 [Computer Software]. (2014). Redwood City, CA: Maxis.

Tucker, A. (2012). The art of video games. *Smithsonian Magazine*. Retrieved 15 December, 2015, from http://www.smithsonianmag.com/arts-culture/the-art-of-video-games-101131359/?no-ist]

Turi, T. (13 Feb. 2012). *Dear Esther: A haunting indie story worth listening to*. Retrieved 15 December, 2015, from http://www.gameinformer.com/games/dear_esther/b/pc/ archive/2012/02/13/a-haunting-indie-story-worth-listening-to.aspx

Unity3d.com. (2012). *Zines, screens, and all in betweens.* Retrieved 28 December, 2015, from https://unity3d.com/showcase/case-stories/arcanekids-zineth

Verve. (1997). Bitter sweet symphony. On *Urban Hymns* [CD]. London: Hut Records.

World of Warcraft [Computer Software]. (2004). Irvine, CA: Blizzard Entertainment.

Wreden, D. (2011). *The Stanley parable* [Computer Software]. Austin, TX: Galactic Café.

Zineth [Computer Software]. (2012). Los Angeles: Arcane Kids. Available from http://zinethgame.tumblr.com/

ENDNOTES

1   The fictional 'world' of the *Warcraft* series; here referring to its iteration in Blizzard's *World of Warcraft* (2005).

2   The eponymous region of Tamriel (the continent where *The Elder Scrolls* series is set) in the fifth installment of Bethesda's series, *Skyrim* (2011).

3   In *A Brief History of Neoliberalism* (2005), David Harvey defines neoliberalism as "a theory of political economic practices that proposes that human well-being can best be advanced by liberating individual entrepreneurial freedoms and skills within an institutional framework characterized by strong private property rights, free markets and free trade" (p. 2). This program of privatization and atomization dovetails, of course, with globalization and the broader cultural forms of late capitalism, which have become increasingly dominant and pervasive in the late twentieth and early twenty-first centuries. Video games are obviously one of the most radically new of these cultural forms.

4   I am drawing here from Roland Barthes's conceptions of "readerly" vs. "writerly" texts, and his definition of the latter, though somewhat elusive, boils down to "products (and not productions), they make up the mass of our literature" (1973/2002, p. 5)—the readerly aspect of any text constitutes its solidification as a unified product (such as a book) as opposed to the diffuse and variable field of the writerly text. My use of "playerly" here gestures toward such a unity in conventional games. At the same time, however, the games discussed in this chapter trend, according to Barthes's distinction emphasize their writerly aspects by defying the norms of spatial representation. It bears mentioning here that, in addition to defining the readerly text, Barthes in "The Death of the Author" defines the reader as the point which "holds together in a single field all the traces by which the written text is constituted" (1977, p. 148)—although the depth of analysis such a claim deserves exceeds the scope of this chapter, we could think of the player of a video game as a similar unifying point through which the game is refracted.

5   Fredric Jameson in *Postmodernism* calls elevators and escalators in postmodern architecture "allegorical signifiers" of the "narrative stroll" that they supplant and replace (1992/1997, p. 41). Video games are nothing if not such "narrative strolls"—though they do not necessarily allegorize the stroll, they certainly serve as signifiers of ways of moving that have some sort of conceptual real-world corollary.

6 Michel de Certeau's dual conception of "strategies"—the constitution of a space and way of being instituted by the dominant power—and "tactics," or the "space of the other" that is carved out by the marginalized (1980/1984, pp. 36-37) could be adapted to games studies in order to better theorize the hegemony of game designers within their creations.

7 Gyorgy Lukacs identifies the "refusal of the immanence of being to enter into empirical life" as the novel's central dissonance; this problem is he says a formal one that "looks like a problem of content" (1920/1974, p. 71). We can see in video game space—which is unique in its texturing and not entirely semiotic structure -- something similar to what Lukacs identifies in the novel: the spatial material that the player navigates, made up of images that comprise part of the game's content, are at the same time disguised articulations and enforcements of the game's formal limitations.

8 Freedom is perhaps the wrong word here, or at least it is insufficient. The encounter with visual art or literature is, for the viewer or reader something that is not as simple and straightforward as the input of the information into the recipient. Rather, readers and viewers are informed by a multitude of factors like their reading / viewing practices, their historical / social context and even their gameplay practices. For example, Dibyadyuti Roy has written about the potential for resistance in gameplay styles that challenge the "normative structures of dominant violent hypermasculinity" (2015, p. 174) in *World of Warcraft*.

9 I want to note here my debt to the creators of and contributors to the *Dear Esther* wiki, and in particular the *Dear Esther* script page, wherein the scores of passages that are played in the game are listed and organized by the point in the game at which the player hear them. The collective popular commitment to indexing and interpreting the game dwarfs my work here, which would not be possible without the work done by others who have played the game and engaged with it as an artwork.

10 It is important to note here the distinction between synchrony and diachrony. In using these terms, I am drawing on Ferdinand de Sausseure's (1916/1959) foundational distinction between the two in linguistic terms: the synchronic pertains to the isolation of the linguistic element (or sign) whereas the diachronic is concerned with the arc of linguistic development over time. For our purposes, synchrony and diachrony are here *narrative* terms—the synchronic passages create a sense of atemporal isolation and 'presentness,' whereas the diachronic passages are deeply historical and clearly influenced by the flow of time.

11 This is achieved precisely through the exhausting amount of literary content in the game. Susan Sontag famously argued against the primacy of content (itself the product of a somewhat arbitrarily enforced form / content division): "What the overemphasis on the idea of content entails is the perennial, never consummated project of interpretation" which is itself a totalitarian imposition by "the intellect at the expense of energy and sensual capability" (1966/2013, p. 5). *Dear Esther*'s overflow of literary content demands a sensory response that revolves around the form of the island as the lone certainty in a sea of randomized narrative.

12 Catco is the game's omnipresent corporation, the name of which appears to be a commentary on the dominance and ubiquity of internet culture (and its stereotypical obsession with 'cat videos'), which appears democratic but is co-opted by reactionary and corporate interests (whether for data-mining by Google or for misogynistic and racist gatherings on Reddit).

Chapter 5
Apportioned Commodity Fetishism and the Transformative Power of Game Studies

Ken S. McAllister
University of Arizona, USA

Judd Ethan Ruggill
University of Arizona, USA

Tobias Conradi
ZeM – Brandenburgisches Zentrum für Medienwissenschaften, Germany

Steven Conway
Swinburne University of Technology, Australia

Jennifer deWinter
Worcester Polytechnic Institute, USA

Chris Hanson
Syracuse University, USA

Carly A. Kocurek
Illinois Institute of Technology, USA

Kevin A. Moberly
Old Dominion University, USA

Randy Nichols
University of Washington Tacoma, USA

Rolf F. Nohr
Hochschule für Bildende Künste Braunschweig, Germany

Marc A. Ouellette
Old Dominion University, USA

ABSTRACT

This chapter explores the ways in which the field of Game Studies helps shape popular understandings of player, play, and game, and specifically how the field alters the conceptual, linguistic, and discursive apparatuses that gamers use to contextualize, describe, and make sense of their experiences. The chapter deploys the concept of apportioned commodity fetishism to analyze the phenomena of discourse as practice, persona, the vagaries of game design, recursion, lexical formation, institutionalization, systems of self-effectiveness, theory as anti-theory, and commodification.

DOI: 10.4018/978-1-5225-0261-6.ch005

INTRODUCTION

From its earliest days, the video game industry has capitalized on not only the technology that drives games but also on the people who make them: Will Wright's *Raid on Bungeling Bay* (1984); Chris Crawford's *Balance of Power* (1985); Sid Meier's *Civilization* (1991); and *Roberta Williams' Anthology* (1996) are just a few of the many games in the Learning Games Initiative Research Archive that feature the developer's name—and not infrequently, a head shot—on the packaging.[1] More than for just superstar designers and skilled programmers and artists, however, the game industry is also known by gamers and many in the general public as an enterprise where exploited and harassed so-called "code monkeys" and victims of what is euphemistically termed by globalization pundits "global cost arbitrage" are employed, laborers whose job is to infuse games with cultural and economic value in return for low wages and staggering levels of stress.[2] If ever there were an industry in which the central commodity was commonly recognized as a product of many hands, it would be the video game industry.

Or would it? In this chapter, we propose that as a result of the unique combination of geek cultures, game cultures, and media studies cultures that have emerged since the 1980s, a curious facade has been constructed in and around the game industry that both reveals and masks the inner workings of the video game medium's cultural and political networks of production. As the byline of this chapter makes clear, we make this argument as part of a collective of game studies scholars who have been both independently and collaboratively studying games through the Learning Games Initiative since 1999. Although our respective areas of expertise vary widely, for many years we have together tracked the interactions of academic and gamer discourses as they manifest in popular, subcultural, and trade venues. Like all discourses, the ones that prevail are contradictory: they demand that one work to experience fun, to reframe tyrannical control over player behavior as the auteur's privilege, to cast technical details such as shader values and particle systems as primarily aesthetic considerations, and to define the video game medium itself in ways that are more perambulatory than specific. We accept these contradictions as predictable outcomes of a culture industry that trades in commerce-driven play and the business of fun, and each of the authors has her or his own approach to understanding these industry-culture dynamics.

It was the charge of this volume's editors, however, to examine how video games "cause players to shift perspectives." And this charge brought into focus for us the fact that the enormously complex set of interactions among gamers, producers, industrial processes, cultural adaptations, subjectivity, and identity performance not only produces a perpetually unfurling network of contradictory discourses, but also requires a dense but malleable facade that, like a radiologist's lead apron, shields the most sensitive inner workings even as it enables a seemingly transparent perspective. In effect, the set of relationships that has emerged among game producers, distributors, and consumers is such that a discourse of labor is now a popular commonplace even though a clear understanding of how those relationships function interdependently is almost entirely unknown. We call this phenomenon "apportioned commodity fetishism," by which we mean the perceptual tendency of the social relations involved in commodity production (including games) to be obscured, even as a discursive scaffold is constructed to give these fetishized objects a multi-dimensional cultural-economic topology that includes a characterization of the labor that assembled them. Put simply, we argue that the discourses of the game industry and its cultures operate together to give the appearance that games-as-commodities have not been disassociated from the labor that produced them—i.e., designers, artists, programmers, and so forth—when in fact knowledge about this labor has developed over time to mask a vast array of important labor-related details, from internal management practices, to workplace abuses, to wage-impacting financial decisions.

In this chapter we also argue that apportioned commodity fetishism—now pervasive in the game industry—not only helps drive how games transform players, but also explains how something like an academic discipline such as Game Studies, which lies at the industrial periphery, can simultaneously sharpen and further obscure an object's social relations to the labor that produced it. In what follows, we detail several different ways that apportioned commodity fetishism functions, but in general it substitutes superficial personal information (e.g., age, education, job title) and detailed object metadata (e.g., genre, narrative, agentic capacity, representation) for attention to material relations. In effect, apportioned commodity fetishism is a sort of high-level consumer consciousness that enables sophisticated articulations between objects and their affiliated definitive abstractions, even as it anneals the reified intrinsic value of virtually every product of the game industry. We begin by generally parsing the industry's use of discourse.[3]

DISCOURSE AS PRACTICE

In its 2015 call for papers, the Digital Games Research Association (DiGRA) hailed a multiplicity of gamer/subjects:

Today the popularity of games has increased dramatically, games have become more specialized and gaming is taking place in a number of divergent practices, from e-sport to gamification. In addition, the gamer position includes a number of roles and identities such as: players, learners, time-fillers, users, fans, roleplayers, theory crafters, speed runners, etc. (2015)

The focus on a plethora of possible "gamers"—the term we use most often in this chapter to signify these manifold identities—not only demonstrates academic interest in the formation of gamer subjectivity, but also represents the shifting and altered position(s) of gamer/subjects in Game Studies. Defining "gamer," in other words, necessarily enacts a transformation of subjectivity and reveals an impulse to control the practice of play by nominating it. It also serves to expand how academics think about "the gamer," that is, as more than just the person at the end of a game controller. It is precisely this kind of definitional expansiveness—the utility and insightfulness of which we do not dispute—that opens a door to apportioned commodity fetishism. It does so by pointing out (but not examining the relationships among) the various kinds of people— "players, learners, time-fillers," and the like—who contribute to and comprise the identity "gamer," in effect apportioning types of labor that stand behind the seemingly simple sign "gamer." Thus in a single discursive gesture, DiGRA both expands and controls how academics—and the broader audience of journalists who routinely consult DiGRA—think, write, and speak about what it means to play games.

Inevitably, of course, any critical practice creates discursive effects, and discourse—in the conventional sense of written statements that are construed as knowledge—is only one facet of a broader understanding of discourse as practice.[4] Discourses always involve a multiplicity of statements, texts, actions, or personas, and can never be assigned a single origin point. Discourses as the materialization of socially structured knowledge are never completed or closed; on the contrary, as semioticians such as Charles Sanders Peirce and Ferdinand de Saussure observed, they are continuously changing and are only ever temporarily fixed in meaning, if at all.

In *Versuch über den Normalismus: Wie Normalität produziert wird* (2013), Jürgen Link helpfully distinguishes between "special discourses" and "interdiscourses" (p. 42f). The former are marked by explicit regularity, a predominate unambiguity, and clear consistency, and their ideal can be found in the specialized knowledge of the structurally differentiated sciences. Interdiscourses, in contrast, are less strictly regulated, tend to rely on extensive connotation and polysemy, and allow for the integration of simultaneously competing and incongruent knowledges. The central product of both types of discourses, however, are certain subjectivities that are simultaneously prescribed by specific discursive currents and altered by actions inside discursive boundaries.

Addressing the question of how Game Studies transforms gamers—again, in DiGRA's broad sense—entails reflection on the different perspectives in which this question itself can be understood. Broadly, we see at least three key perspectives, taking into account that the "how" of the question assumes that there is a transformation in the first place.

1. Does Game Studies Affect How Gamers Understand Their Play?

On the one hand, an affirmative answer to this question has to assume that gamers both perceive and reflect on the findings of the special discourse—unambiguous, consistent, and regularized—that is Game Studies. Given the number and diversity of game players in the world and the relative size and newness of Game Studies as a field, such an assumption seems improbable in the aggregate.[5] That said, presuming that academic attention paid to games and gamer subjectivity inevitably makes an impression on at least some gamers—and periodically makes its way into local newspapers and magazines, radio broadcasts, and blogs to influence even more—such an impression might produce a subject position of self-reflexivity and possibly even pride. Gamers might feel that their play and practice is taken seriously, and therefore that play generally is a meaningful cultural practice—with gamer/subjects ennobled as cultural actors—in addition to being a mere pastime.[6]

2. How is the Gamer as an Academic Concept Transformed by Game Studies?

The notion of the gamer/subject here takes a different form than in the previous question, becoming the product of a discursive conceptualization. Just as with the production of subjectivities such as "viewer," "spectator," or "active audience" found in other media formations, the production of a multiplicity of different gamer/subjects influences the way subject positions are anticipated in the production of cultural artifacts, goods for economic and symbolic consumption, and how meaning is understood in analytical models. Here, too, is a paradoxical operation as the gamer/subject in the special discourse of Game Studies is transformed from actor to object, from the fetishizer into the fetishized. It is in this power/knowledge that Game Studies as special discourse operates most effectively: its presuppositions, assumptions, and discursive regularities produce the gamer as an object of knowledge. And it is here where certain powerful conditions of what it means to be a "gamer" are invented, conceptualized, transformed, and disseminated reflectively in a broader cultural and discursive context (e.g., by being addressed in newspapers or academic calls for proposals).

Critical discourse, in this instance, is performing power over the gamer/subject. Game Studies—in a much more complex way than we can account for in this chapter (though we do address it more below) is able to shape the language and self-awareness of gamer/subjects. It provides a grammar and vocabulary for meaningfully talking about games and play within the restricted boundaries of a specialized discourse, a language that may well compete with alternative, interdiscursive articulations of gamer/subjects. While this vocabulary often makes possible the practice of taking gamers into account as gamer/subjects and hence assigns (micropolitical) power to them, it also has a limiting effect, ruling out other, alternative ways of articulating gamer subjectivity. To use a game development analogy, apportioning "gamers" as key components of game production effectively textures them onto the game industry object, giving the appearance of depth where none exists.

3. Is There a Connection That Interrupts the Special Discursive Practice of Game Studies with the Interdiscursive Practices of Gamer/Subjects?

This third question makes games the center of reflection and is perhaps the most productive avenue for considering how Game Studies as a field of inquiry shapes gamers themselves. This is so because it is (generally) games that produce the motivation for gamers to play, as well as the incentive for theoretical reflection by game scholars, and the means of earning a living for game developers. It is games that secure mediated contact between diverse and heterogeneous gamer/subjects on the one hand, and the theoretical and analytical practices of Game Studies discourses on the other. Games are a combination of material interfaces and symbolic artifacts, and the medium of negotiation among the play of gamer/subjects, the reflection of scientific practices, and the creativity, ideologies, and economic interests of developers and their industry.

The notion that discourses produce certain subjectivities, however, does not make it possible to describe with scientific accuracy precisely how Game Studies transforms gamers. Indeed, it would be erroneous (not to mention arrogant) to suggest that one might, for example, write a book chapter that would instantly and radically change the way gamers perceive play and subjectivity. Rather, the question of how Game Studies changes gamers has to imagine a circuitous, mediated relationship wherein a particular discourse both describes a distinct cultural moment and enacts a set of societal practices. It is this protean context—which simultaneously arrests and expands what we might term "gamer delta" (the amount of change a gamer experiences)—that lends a bit of movement to the phenomenon of apportioned commodity fetishism, enhancing its illusion of depth with an illusion of life. Such enactments trigger new comments, descriptions, and analyses (and thus new discursive currents), and because analysis and enactment are interrelated but do not necessarily coincide or collapse into each other, they effectively lend the appearance of a cognition of industrial labor to anyone who does less than scrutinize *who* makes video games possible. In short, Game Studies affects games (qua cultural artifacts) and the practices of playing them, and these effects influence how gamers perceive themselves, the games they play, and the relationship between the two. In the process, a discursive *trompe-l'oeil* or optical illusion emerges that seems to indicate an informed recognition of the labor origins of video games, but that is in fact a relatively controlled animation with little substance or depth.

PERSONA

If discursive processes and practices interweave to create a false (or at least superficial) impression of labor in the game industry, how then is it possible to see more than the *trompe-l'oeil* constructed by apportioned commodity fetishism? One answer might lie in an anecdote Aristotle tells about Heraclitus of Ephesus (535-575 BC). The story goes that a group of tourists, excited to meet the renowned thinker, were taken by surprise when they reached his home and found Heraclitus standing near the oven warming himself. To their chagrin, Aristotle suggests, Heraclitus was neither preparing food fit for a philosopher (whatever that would be), nor was he lost in brilliant contemplation. His surroundings were plain, his demeanor common, his body chilled. Recognizing his visitors' disappointment that neither his abode nor his bearing were in the least impressive, Heraclitus called them into his humble kitchen saying "Don't fret. Even here the gods are present." The same might be said of apportioned commodity fetishism's labor-related *trompe-l'oeil*: even here there are depths to be sounded.

As with painted visual illusions, revealing the trickery of angles and shadows is often as easy as changing one's perspective. Coincidentally, the game industry's own characteristic contradictions—most readily observed in its promotional discourses—point the way to such an alternate view. Consider, for instance, EA Sports' marketing slogan "It's in the game!" More than a pithy tagline, it also serves as a rallying cry for much about the modes of production connected to AAA game development. At the top studios, the design emphasis is constantly directed inward, centered on mechanics, narrative, interface, control schemas, networking, and the code that constitutes and binds them all. For designers, energy and understanding are devoted to a game's constitutive components at the expense of what the game is in, to borrow Garry Crawford's (2015) equally pithy reversal of EA Sports' slogan. In other words, commercial game development is generally unconcerned with the social, cultural, and historical contexts through which a game becomes meaningful to its interlocutors, save when those contexts directly impact game production, distribution, and consumption (e.g., regulatory policy, technological innovation, and so forth). In the context of this chapter, apportioned commodity fetishism directs its audience to see "what's in the game": its play, competition, cool art, realistic rules, and all the incredible people who make such experiences possible to the player. Indeed, "It's in the game!" is arguably a form of rhetorical eclipsis, where the key agents have been both disappeared and emphasized: "[We] put it in the game!" Crawford usefully shifts this perspective, however, asking in effect: "What are the conditions that empower a game studio to put things into a game so that it will be lucrative in particular markets?"

Put another way, while Johan Huizinga's (1955) concept of *the magic circle* has undergone vigorous critique by game scholars in recent years, it remains a vibrant, pervasive, and structuring mythos among game developers. Accordingly, many developers continue to create games as art, entertainment, and escape, effectively accepting Huizinga's proposition that play stands within but closed off from society and culture, occupying a space, as he says, "standing quite consciously outside 'ordinary' life…" (Huizinga, 1938, p. 13). Nathan Grayson's recent interview with *Heroes of the Storm* (Blizzard Entertainment, 2015) game director Dustin Browder for the PC gaming website *Rock, Paper, Shotgun* provides a pointed example of this mindset:

RPS: *MOBAs [Multiplayer Online Battle Arenas] tend to hyper-sexualize female characters to a generally preposterous degree…. How are you planning to approach that in Heroes?*

Browder: *Well, I mean, some of these characters, I would argue, are already hyper-sexualized in a sense. I mean, Kerrigan is wearing heels, right? We're not sending a message to anybody. We're just making characters who look cool…We're not running for President. We're not sending a message. No one should look to our game for that.* (Grayson, 2013, para. 35)

Here is apportioned commodity fetishism being constructed in full view: a developer is being highlighted—readers of *Rock, Paper, Shotgun* now know the name of an actual person who labored over the production of the popular game *Heroes of the Storm*—yet that executive-level employee informs readers that his team (i.e., workers) should not be thought about so intently that they are realized as agents of socio-political work in the world. In one breath, Browder says, in effect: "There are people working hard on making the game...but they are just workers making a game, disconnected from the world in which that game is played." Game industry workers are in the world but apparently not of it.

Shifting the perspective slightly again, it becomes clear that Grayson's important question—how are you planning to deal with the problem of hyper-sexualized female characters in your game—is also incomplete, failing to broach the larger issue of the coordination of vision and interaction. From the perspective of critical scholarship, this is a key and instructive lapse. Not only is the male gaze active in mainstream video games (as the question makes clear), but so too is the male hand that enables the player to indulge in an assumed pleasure of aggressive, even violent, action. In games, as in life, to perceive is to (re)act; this is the heart of Foucault's idea of interpellation. Refusal to see and address this obvious articulation arguably reflects the myopic approach many developers abide within as they do their work, a refusal that only sharpens the effectiveness of apportioned commodity fetishism. Paradoxically, even as the optical illusion of apportioned commodity fetishism is sharpened for consumers, another one is created, signified by what we might term "apportioned gamer fetishism." Here, the imagined gamer is both a kind of transcendent being—an entity floating freely outside of an historical context—and a young, white, heterosexual male. Gamers, then, are encouraged to see games as the products of nerdy-chic, lucky, talented geniuses rather than a small town's worth of employees slogging through life in their workaday jobs, while developers idealize "the gamer" as a human type trying to escape *his* workaday job by playing their games rather than as a single unique member of the human race, each of whom is absorbed in what Martin Heidegger (2013) called "being-in-the-world." From this latter perspective, one's performance of and as a gamer is wrapped up in one's sense of identity, in an understanding of gender, class, nationhood, and the like—all of which are inscribed upon the player's body through the way one talks, walks, stands, eats, exercises, sleeps, and so on. Regardless of developer consciousness and desire, games speak, make demands, and attempt to enforce particular performances of identity. Gamers can certainly resist the performance, subvert it, and modify games through hacks and cheats, but these acts are always already political dialogues. The way the avatar, user interface, narrative, mechanics, and control scheme of a game make sense is through historicity, through the gamer's being-in-the-world.

Subjectivities such as "mother," "friend," or "customer" are, then, preconfigured by society. Each is a specific mask, a suit off the rack, awaiting adornment for the existential self. But they are never creation. Every subject position demands particular performances which draw together expectations of race, gender, age, tone of voice, language (body and textual), dress, behaviour, and so on in line with social convention. To be sure, one is allowed certain latitude in an interpretation of, for example, *Hamlet*, but should one stray too far from audience expectation there is sanction, sometimes relatively inconsequential—boos, stares, guffaws, admonishment, gossip—sometimes dire—being fired, ostracised, or even arrested if the performance is deemed particularly egregious. It is the same in the roles of "office worker," "partner," and "parent." And in "gamer."

There is some precedent for at least trying to refuse apportioned commodity fetishism and apportioned gamer fetishism, that is, games and gamer-developer relationships that recognize that their contexts are invariably situated in discrete and complex networks of meaning, not ideal subjects prognosticated through psychological abstractions, material objects quantifiable and reducible to rules structured by physicochemical processes, or superficial fantasies about life in the industry. Games such as *Cart Life* (Hofmeier, 2011), where one plays a character living hand-to-mouth, or *Papers, Please* (Pope, 2013), where one plays an immigration officer in an authoritarian government, specifically avoid the game industry's more well-worn taxonomical abstractions that catalog gamers as socializers, achievers, team-mates, customizers, discoverers, and so forth. Such abstractions fail to capture or explain the deeply affective experience of games like these that effectively militate against the pursuit of system mastery, customizable characters, undiscovered mechanics, or sensory immersion. Rather, the play in these games is designed to generate a profound sense of anxiety. In the Heideggerian context:

All things, and we along with them, sink into indifference—but not in the sense of disappearing. Rather, as things recede, they turn toward us. It is the receding of the meaning-giving context of things that presses in on us and oppresses us. Without the meaning-giving context there is no hold on things. As things slip away, what remains and overwhelms us is precisely this "no...." Dread reveals the no-thing. (Heidegger, 1929, pp. 111-112)

A pervasive, ineffable apprehensiveness is meant to envelop the player of these games, and the longer one plays, the stronger it is meant to grow. In their articulation of vision and (re)action of the medium and the world within which that medium operates, games such as these give the lie to both kinds of apportioned fetishism.

Importantly, neither *Cart Life* nor *Papers, Please* offer the traditional pleasures intended to gratify the male gaze or male hand. Instead, they reach for a far more vulnerable political, historically-situated sense of self, a broader being-in-the-world. But how does one explain—let alone design a game around—a sense of being-in-the-game (so to speak) without recourse to an infinite array of specific historical, social, and political contexts? How, in other words, might games be designed to be anti-fetishizing?

While we do not have comprehensive answers to such questions, in recent years, game developers have progressed from system-centered design to user-centered design, inaugurating a long overdue recognition that audiences routinely approach games from a set of understandings and biases quite dissimilar from the designers'. Here too, however, there is a risk that the focus on the narrow subjectivity "user" will ultimately disserve the radical potential underwriting this epistemological shift. Like "gamer," "user" is but one dimension of a multidimensional being, and is just as likely to insist that an existential self be rather more narrowly performed, less a self than a *persona*. If truly affective and non-fetishizing games are ever to be had, ones that stay with gamers beyond mere moments and impact their sense of being, such entertainments must speak not just to the player-mask, but to the being beneath.

This was precisely Heraclitus' message to his disappointed visitors: look more closely and the mundane surface will give way to bottomless depth and interconnection. We recognize that such a momentous epistemological reorientation may be easy to document in an academic context but extraordinarily difficult to enact among the all-too-real complexities of the game industry's production schedules, internationally-scoped budgets, and interpersonal dynamics. In the next section, we attempt to reframe this practical context by briefly considering the quotidian demands on an actual designer, always with an eye on the mechanisms enabling—and potentially subverting—apportioned commodity fetishism.

THE VAGARIES OF GAME DESIGN

So far, we have established that the game industry has seen the emergence of apportioned commodity fetishism—a kind of perceptual *trompe-l'oeil* that creates the illusion of visible relations between commodities (specifically, video games) and the labor that produced them—and we have offered several examples of how the game industry perpetuates this illusion by relying on the mask made available through the idea of the magic circle, as well as through the practical reliance on an idealized user during the process of development. It is to some of these practical concerns that we now turn, particularly those of game designers—the people whose job it is to imagine a play scenario and environment, then lead the way in its development toward a deliverable and profitable product (i.e., a commodity).

In many respects, the designer is the shiniest labor fetish that gamers and the public are offered by the game industry. Names such as Cliff Bleszinski, Brenda Braithwaite Romero, Chris Crawford, Richard Garriott, Sid Meier, Peter Molyneux, John Romero, Warren Spector, Kim Swift, and Will Wright are legendary among gamers, and as we noted earlier, for a time in the 1990s and 2000s it was common industry practice to include a "dust jacket" photo of the lead designer on the back of game boxes. It makes sense in an analysis of apportioned commodity fetishism, then, to investigate how the cult of personality that often surrounds game designers contributes to this phenomenon and by ready extension to the ways that it can generate transformations in gamers.

According to Katie Salen and Eric Zimmerman (2003), designers create "meaningful play," the most fundamental element of any game. Meaningful play, they propose,

emerges from the relationship between player action and system outcome; it is the process by which a player takes action within the designed system of a game and the system responds to the action. The meaning of an action in a game resides in the relationship between action and outcome. (p. 34, emphasis in original)

Given the significance of this role in the development process, it is understandable how the designer comes to loom large in popular mappings that connect the game-commodity to the labor that produced it.

Notably, however, this recognition of the designer's work reveals that attention to, for example, a game's aesthetic and technical details—details that are often what differentiate products in the marketplace and that create emotional connections between the system and the player (Reimann & Schilke, 2011; Hseih, 2013)—is not among their primary tasks. For game designers, the production of mediated experiences dominates aesthetic and technical choices; designers lead the process whereby experiences are converted into systems through hardware, software, rules, interfaces, and narrative structures, but they typically do so without a deep understanding of each of these key development arenas. Instead, they depend on the expertise of others to translate their visions into attractive and playable content, and the act of play converts these designed systems into ludic experiences. In this way, the gamer is always in relationship with the designer, but the designer is a metonym for everyone who contributed to the production process.[7] Designers, in other words, are both real and imaginary, actual workers and discursive constructions, and it is through this dual role that they contribute to the illusion that commodity fetishism is relatively absent from the game industry. To know the designer—her background, her accomplishments, perhaps even some of her eccentricities—is to connect at an intimate level with the *work*, done by human minds and hands, that went into the making of a game...or so the metonymic logic goes.

Consider, for example, Shigeru Miyamoto, famed designer of such games as *Super Mario Bros.* (Nintendo, 1985) and *The Legend of Zelda* (Nintendo, 1986). In interviews, Miyamoto often discusses his childhood—specifically playgrounds and exploration—as providing a notable starting point for his design processes. When discussing his ongoing philosophy about making games, Miyamoto states, "I think great video games are like favorite playgrounds, places you become attached to and go back to again and again. Wouldn't it be great to have a whole drawer full of 'playgrounds' right at your fingertips?" (Arakawa, 1991, p. 32). Readers of such anecdotes are readily able to see such personal stories materialized in *Super Mario Bros.*, for instance, where bright colors, jaunty music, and energetic jumping—the stuff of the most delightful playgrounds—predominate. Moreover, Miyamoto's well-known love of exploration—well-known because he and Nintendo's promotional materials about him often tout it—is one of several central play mechanics in Miyamoto's titles, appearing in both the Mario and Zelda series (together comprising more than 100 different titles) as numerous and notable secrets for gamers to discover (deWinter, 2015). And as technologies have evolved over the course of his career, Miyamoto has been vocal about how designers (in the metonymic sense) have been able to increasingly strengthen the emotional attachment between games and players by representing emotional content in games—an advancement made possible by various technical breakthroughs. In one of his earliest reflections on this interconnectedness among the designer, the (implied) team, the technology, and the gamer, Miyamoto commented, "Before, in earlier games, we couldn't show the entire game world in detail and we couldn't convey all the emotions of the characters. Now, we can do that on the Nintendo 64. I've always wanted to create realistic experiences, full experiences such as you or I could have, but in exciting worlds" (*Nintendo Power*, 1996, p. 25). Miyamoto's vision then, presumably like the visions of less famous designers, scaffolds predictable and shared experiences within fantastic worlds and events, and connects them both directly and indirectly to popular conceptions of the relationship between a commodity and the labor that produced it.[8]

In at least two ways, then, the designer—real worker and metonym—transforms players by providing them with impactful experiences and by administrating their understanding of how such experiences are produced and packaged into the game medium. Part of how these conjoined roles evolve is through a duplicative process of fetishization, that is, as the game-commodity is fetishized, so too is the designer; since the two are already linked, the two become one, perceptually speaking, a phenomenon often amplified (as suggested above) by media coverage of designers' extra-ludic peculiarities. In Miyamoto's case, such characteristics include his notorious tendency to "upend the tea table" ("chabudai gaeshi" in Japanese), that is, to scrap or seriously redirect projects. The fetish power of Miyamoto is such that stories like this only add to his (literally) iconic status. Few game designers, however, command such power, and more often than not such behavior results in a decrease rather than increase in fetishizing distance. Famously, *BioShock* (2K Games, 2007) designer Ken Levine has been lambasted rather than praised in the media for his seemingly capricious control of the *BioShock* franchise; stories about his late changes to the art direction, his tendency to yell at production teams, and to demand full participation in abusive crunch time schedules are common among developers and gamers alike.

Significantly, in either version of the game designer myth—demanding genius or tyrannical but productive functionary—the upshot is the same: the designer serves as a kind of two dimensional billboard signifying the labor (as in *people who labor*) involved in any given game's production. Importantly, however, most games do not even have a "cult of the designer" personality attached to them (there are only a handful of designers who are really well-known); all the public has to go on in such mundane instances is common knowledge about game designers drawn from the mass media and (perhaps) Game Studies. For those games that do have access to luxury labor, apportioned commodity fetishism is most powerfully at work shielding the public from seeing beyond the facade of the virtuosic Miyamoto, the autocratic Levine, the compulsive exaggerator Peter Molyneux, and so on.

Such ad hominem details about designers and their egos work to construct superficial mythologies of industrial labor, effacing in the process not only the work of people who work with designers but also of designers themselves. Masking the very real constraints that designers and their teams work under—

rigid production cycles, mercurial hardware standards, severe budget limitations, the crushing pressure of competition in the global marketplace—means that gamers are transformed in ways that buttress their ignorance of how and why the games they play look and feel the way they do. Designers are accorded responsibility for game quality (good or ill)—sometimes studios and publishers as well—even as understandings of such matters as safe and healthy working conditions, gender and racial discrimination, and fair pay are rendered invisible to consumers, disappeared behind technical specifications, promotional hyperbole, and vapid personal interest stories about "the making of…." Here is apportioned commodity fetishism in full bloom. In the next section, we examine one of the key mechanisms of this process, the one that most almost irresistibly ensures that no matter one's level of critical consciousness, moving beyond the habits that attend apportioned commodity fetishism remains remarkably challenging.

RECURSION

As we have described in a number of different ways already, video game developers have long played an active role in the discourses of Game Studies, both directly and indirectly. Books such as Mark Stephen Meadows' *Pause and Effect: The Art of Interactive Narrative* (2003), Noah Wardrip-Fruin and Pat Harrigan's *First Person: New Media as Story, Performance, and Game* (2004), and Katie Salen and Eric Zimmerman's *The Game Design Reader: A Rules of Play Anthology* (2006)—all now common on new media syllabi in higher education—feature essays by and interviews with game developers. Simultaneously, websites such as *Kotaku* and *Rock, Paper, Shotgun* (among many others) have provided venues for specialized game criticism and helped push elements of Game Studies into the mainstream. Moreover, the emergence of digital games—and particularly their movement into mass culture—has been roughly concurrent with the growth of online resources, first in dial-up bulletin board systems, and subsequently into the ubiquitous use of the Internet. For many years now, online forums dedicated to game design—from early usenet newsgroups such as rec.games.design to websites such as *Gamasutra: The Art & Business of Making Games* to the proliferation of podcasts like *Idle Thumbs* and *Designer Notes*—have served as hubs of information exchange about best practices in game production, facilitating an impressive cross-pollination between the disciplines of game design and Game Studies.[9]

Of course, the intersection of game design pragmatics and theory preceded the digital era. Game designers such as Bernie DeKoven and phenomena such as the New Games movement deliberately combined philosophical praxis with the act of game design in the 1970s, creating games to implement and exemplify theoretical beliefs (DeKoven, 1978; The New Games Foundation, 1976). Following upon the advent of video games, mediumic analysis—audience, interface, experience, and so on—became an essential part of game design and development. Critically and commercially successful game creation now virtually always involves prototyping and playtesting, effecting an important and continued feedback loop among designers, gamers, and critics (often the same person). As a result, while the formalized discipline of Game Studies has evolved as an institutionalized field of study in the last couple of decades, the careful study of games—that is, their critical consideration and analysis—is as old as games themselves, and has almost always been undertaken by game players and makers.

Like its object of study, then, Game Studies is fundamentally recursive, and as with other fields of inquiry, it depends on the process of modified return—the feedback loop—to create stasis (i.e., freezing an otherwise working system in order to study it), as well as experiential variety and innovation (i.e., study leads to change). Simply put, knowledge production is inexorably self-perpetuating and self-modifying. Consider, for example, the introductory-level game history course, a common requirement in many university game design programs. Such a course necessarily entails students becoming relatively familiar with the discipline of Game Studies: its ludic and scholarly canon, its research methods, its theoretical trends, and so forth. Just as film production students may become inspired by and mimic a film they see in a film history or theory course, game design students are influenced by and explore the conceptual and theoretical frameworks to which they have been exposed in their coursework. They make what they know plus a little something extra, or as Eileen Meehan (2005) so succinctly puts it: "tried-and-true-with-a-twist" (p. 113).

Designer Jenova Chen's 2006 MFA thesis project, *flOw*, offers a striking instance of the recursiveness of the academy and game design simultaneously. This game, which also became the first official release by Chen's studio thatgamecompany [sic] in 2007, sought to enact the theories of psychologist Mihalyi Csikzentmihalyi, about whom Chen had learned as a USC graduate student (Naone, 2008).[10] Among other things, Csizentmihalyi's work explores the "flow state" which an artist or athlete might achieve while fully focused on her practice. Chen not only makes this state the centerpiece of his game, but of his master's thesis as well, effectively reiterating and refracting the intellectual and aesthetic training he received (Chen, 2006).

Understanding, then, that the game industry, Game Studies, and gamers have from the beginning mutually moulded each other through a sometimes more, sometimes less complex process of modified return, clarifies how it is that Game Studies transforms gamers, and also how apportioned commodity fetishism itself is perpetuated through and among all three highly attentive groups. In other words, it is difficult to call capitalism's bluff (so to speak) when virtually all of its participants have been trained *and have trained each other* to see its illusions as real: games stand outside society, have no readily identifiable origins, and are attached to systems of labor that are so straightforward that the impression of understanding (even down to the level of privities) is commonplace. Working recursively, apportioned commodity fetishism functions to shape common and critical perception alike, and in the process redoubles its own illusory power. Fascinatingly, one of the most easily recognizable sites of this ideological redoubling is also one of the video game complex's most heavily engineered discursive realms: its lexicons.

LEXICAL FORMATION

Conceived of broadly, the field of Game Studies—typically envisioned within an academic context—also includes researchers working in industry, as well as critics publishing in newspapers, magazines, and online outlets. Writers working across this spectrum participate in public discourse around gaming and in turn help define that discourse at fundamental levels. Together, those working in Game Studies both within and outside the academy form a constellation of contributors that has helped cultivate a shared critical language of gaming. This language has shaped not only critical discourse, but also gaming discourse more generally as players articulate their desires and experiences using this recognized vocabulary. For example, players on game company message boards regularly (and, again recursively) discuss products using a technical and critical framing gleaned from a now decades-old set of media analysis discourses. In this way, players learn to speak their desires through a codified vocabulary through which they can legitimate not only their interest in games but themselves as gamers.

Some of the curation and cultivation of gaming's critical vocabulary has been deliberate, as in the case of *Critical Distance*. Launched in 2009, *Critical Distance* curates computer game writing and criticism through features such as "This Week in Videogame Blogging" and "This Month in Let's Plays." Featured content of the website includes pieces from established news and information outlets such as *Kotaku* and *Al Jazeera* alongside independently produced material ranging from comics to blog posts. According to the *Critical Distance* Mission Statement:

Back in 2009, Critical Distance was founded to answer the question: "Where is all the good writing about games?"

Now in our sixth year of operation, we've seen the proliferation of thoughtful, incisive criticism, commentary and analysis across dozens of sites and publications. However, our goal remains the same: to bring together and highlight the most interesting, provocative and robust writing, video and discussion on games from across the web. In addition to providing our readers with a consistent level of quality and critical insight, we want Critical Distance to be as inclusive as possible, to accommodate as many different perspectives and unique voices as we can. It's our belief that a diverse pool of writers and thinkers produces a much more interesting conversation than the alternative.

At our heart, Critical Distance is not here to create a canon of "best" works.

Instead, we want to facilitate dialogue. (Critical Distance, 2015 , para. #1)

While presenting a diversity of content, the site's curatorial efforts still point toward a shared, public understanding of what it means to "keep up" with games writing, and the pieces highlighted in *Critical Distance* often extend ongoing discussions.

For example, in a "Blogs of the Round Table" post from April 2015, Mark Filipowich highlights a series of posts that question the utility or purpose of people in games, linking to Ian Bogost's deliberate provocation, "Your Games Are Better Without Characters" (Bogost, 2015) and presenting John Osborne's "Video Games without Characters" (Osborne, 2015) as a counterpoint. Rather than homing in on this particular debate, however, Filipowich includes a handful of pieces from other writers, both well established and unknown (Filipowich, 2015). While some of these pieces—Bogost's and Osborne's, most notably—were in deliberate conversation, others were related only in that they addressed related issues. By placing them in a shared context, Filipowich invites a cross-publication discussion about shared issues that highlights a diversity of perspectives. In this way, *Critical Distance* is engaged in engineering community discourse, not by controlling it but by making it visible and inviting further discussion.

Discussion of games, of course, takes place across a wide range of venues. Children discuss video games on the playground, co-workers talk about games around the proverbial water cooler, and scholars analyze them in publications and conference talks. Social media, including platforms such as Facebook and Twitter, as well as official channels such as corporation-sponsored message boards, are an important arena for this kind of discourse, and their significance at least in part accounts for the increasing visibility of, for example, community managers in the game industry. The effort to frame discussion in venues such as *Critical Distance* is an extension of a broadly diffuse process that contributes to, among other socio-cultural dynamics, enmeshment in apportioned commodity fetishism. This discussion about games, as diffuse as it is, contributes to a shared vocabulary of games, a mutuality that, as with the mechanism of recursion, reinforces the general perception that commodity fetishism is minimized (rather than amplified) around games.

One particularly impactful instance of this phenomenon was initiated in 2002, when Mark J.P. Wolf carefully laid out a number of game genres in *The Medium of the Video Game*. Today, it is common for gamers—even casual gamers—to demonstrate a fairly subtle knowledge of genre distinctions even in informal settings. In one discussion thread concerning the Big Fish Games release *Antique Road Trip: American Dreamin'* (Boomzap Entertainment, 2013), for instance, players with usernames such as "caseymom" and "sleeplady" pick apart gameplay, praising, for example, the integration of minigames while singling out the game's music as inferior to the audio incorporated into earlier games in the series. This kind of specific, pointed critique is made possible because of a growing shared vocabulary of games criticism that crosses boundaries between professional Game Studies scholars and others who do the critical work of Game Studies as journalists, bloggers, and fans. This shared vocabulary, in turn, has become foundational to the work of Game Studies at every level; it is, to return to Jürgen Link's helpful designation discussed earlier, a special discourse, but one decreasingly rarified as it moves out of the academy and into use by gamers across a broad cultural spectrum and who are interested in engaging in critical discussions about games. Paradoxically, these emergent critical discussions fracture some ideological framings that are operative among games, their makers, and consumers, even as they temper others. Perhaps the most pointed of such fractured framings is the one that most directly shapes the industry's troublesome labor relations.

INSTITUTIONALIZATION

Thus far, we have shown from a variety of perspectives how the phenomenon of apportioned commodity fetishism works within the context of video game production and consumption. We have done this primarily by analyzing the game industry's role in creating and maintaining the fetish aspect of its primary vendible, but we have also gestured toward the fact that the field of Game Studies plays a role in masking the labor relations embedded within games as commodities. In fact, this role is highly significant, routinely elaborating on—typically in modest detail—the work that goes on in the game industry. Like any other academic field, Game Studies embodies a larger sociopolitical desire to describe, measure, quantify, and ultimately discipline its subjects.

As suggested earlier, Game Studies is a lexicographical and ontological project. Working through definitions, genres, canons, discourse, and many other apparatuses (critical and otherwise), it attempts to "fix"—that is, limit—the free play of otherwise fraught terms such as "games," "gamers," "rules," "story," and, of course, "play." Game Studies works to establish the rules and police the boundaries of what is arguably the larger enterprise of making meaning from an otherwise impossible subject: the complicated and increasingly decentralized modes of production that intersect with the broader game ecosystem. In so doing, Game Studies produces and maintains its own magic circle of sorts: a consensual fantasy defined in dialog with a presumably larger, external reality, yet insulated from this reality via an assemblage of rituals, fictions, and other chicaneries that is as complex as it is carnivalesque.

This preoccupation with definition and difference is evident in some of the earliest works of Game Studies—attempts on the part of ludologists such as Espen Aarseth (2004) and Markku Eskelinen (2004) to establish Game Studies as a discipline in its own right. Imaging the field as "virgin soil, ready to be plotted and plowed by the machineries of cultural and textual studies" (Aarseth, 2004, p. 45), they invoked and ritually exorcised the specter of "scholarly tribes" (Eskelinen, 2004, p. 36) of narratologists who, trained in literary and film studies, were eager to colonize video games as the latest front in a grander project of cultural reform. But what the ludologists produced was in some ways more of the same. Working through rigid definitions of terms such as "simulation," "time," and "order," they produced a version of Game Studies that, in its games-as-games emphasis, was unfortunately as hegemonic and institutionalized as that which they had hoped to vanquish. Much of the same can be said of Eric Zimmerman's (2004) aptly titled essay, "Narrative, Interactivity, Play, and Games: Four Naughty Concepts in Need of Discipline." In it, Zimmerman argues that the key to achieving a middle ground between the otherwise binary extremes of narratology and ludology is "some good old-fashioned discipline" (p. 154). "[T]his essay," he writes, "is about identifying a desperate need for discipline and the delivery of that discipline to its well-deserved targets" (p. 154).

Unsurprisingly given its academic welcome (tepid though it may sometimes be), Game Studies scholarship continues to emphasize difference, definition, and discipline. Consider Ian Bogost's (2007) work on procedurality, or Miguel Sicart's (2011) response, "Against Procedurality." In an attempt to formulate ruling principles, both scholars distill games to what Kenneth Burke (1969) would describe as God-terms—either rules or play—around which almost every other aspect of the medium is subordinated. As a result, they diminish what L. S. Vygotsky (1966) understands as the fundamentally dialectical relationship among play, games, and rules. For Vygotsky, the rules of a game are the outward manifestations of an imaginary situation that is constructed around unsatisfied desires (and vice versa). As he explains, "every game with rules contains an imaginary situation in a concealed form. The development from an overt imaginary situation and covert rules to games with overt rules and a covert imaginary situation outlines the evolution of children's play from one pole to the other" (Vygotsky, 1966, np.). More significantly, the antithetical God-terms that Bogost and Sicart privilege function to define the outer limits, the extremes of the arena within which the quotidian discourse of Game Studies plays out. As with the so-called ludology and narratology debates, the result is something like what Bruno Latour (1993) understands as a "Middle Kingdom" (p. 48) in that everything of significance takes place in the middle between binary positions that, no matter their labels, in one way or another emblematize "purification" (p. 11) and "hybridization" (p. 41), respectively.

Importantly, the goal of disciplining Game Studies is to provide gamers, designers, and the scores of other denizens of the game ecosystem with a common framework through and against which to understand and discuss video games—and their attendant cultural and industrial para-phenomena—critically. This is a crucial and to some degree unavoidable undertaking. However, it is also and inevitably mystifying and repressive in the sense that what is at stake is not simply a question of what video games mean, how they make meaning, or even how they work. What is at stake is the question of how people should construct themselves as productive subjects, both in relationship to games themselves, and in relationship to the larger decentralized networks of late-capitalist production within which video games are ensconced.

Whether Game Studies succeeds in this project—and perhaps to the extent to which it does not and cannot succeed—it reinforces a more subtle and pernicious message: that institutionalism is inescapable. It is a prerequisite to and a consequence of any activity, no matter how productive or unproductive, and one must therefore construct oneself accordingly. It does not matter if one is a good gamer, a bad gamer, or a middling one. In order to exist as any or all of these things, gamers (and game scholars for that matter) must imagine (and thereby fantasize and police) themselves in the image of the institution as it is ritualized and disciplined through the spectacle of Game Studies and other political and cultural endeavors through which knowledge and desire are universalized and commodified as critical praxis.

Apportioned commodity fetishism—with its filter tuned to see just enough of the labor machinery driving the game industry that one can perform (but not actually possess) expertise—is thus central to the process by which Game Studies transforms players and scholars alike. As noted earlier, there is a fundamentally recursive quality about this process, a driver that rewards—institutionally and person-ally—such self-policing. We close this chapter with a set of examinations that are now perfectly positioned to extend an analysis of self-policing's transformative role in the gamer/Game Studies configuration, particularly as it establishes how the discursive triangle formed by the academy, industry, and consumer is able to depend so heavily on what seem to be acceptable levels of ignorance.

SYSTEMS OF SELF-EFFECTIVENESS

"Ignorance" is typically not a term used to describe gamers, except perhaps as a way to mark the liminal stage prior to their understanding of how a game's rules, narrative, interface, and so on are working. Such liminal ignorance is usually transitory, and would better be characterized as anabatic awareness rather than ignorance. Indeed, almost everything about video games is designed to advance players from a state of not knowing to knowing, and to function as experiential spaces of self-effectiveness, that is, spaces where players receive direct responses to their actions and thus discern and adapt their performance within the system. This experience requires an appropriation of technical and symbolic systems, to be sure, but it is also a point of entry into a complex discursive system of self-effectiveness moderated by intrinsic and extrinsic rules, protocols, and patterns. In the context of a discussion of apportioned com-modity fetishism, the examination of self-efficacy offers a helpful explanation for why gamers willingly accept their ignorance of industrial labor relations, even as they voraciously consume most other types of game-related information.

The concept of "perceived self-efficacy" can be traced to the work of psychologist Albert Bandura (1977). He describes it as a phenomenon in which the subject looks to itself as the impetus for a solved task or an effected performance rather than to external circumstances, other people, chance, luck, and/or other uncontrollable factors. The concept of self-efficacy or its anticipation is often seen as an anthro-pological constant—humans are always making assessments about whether or not they can accomplish various tasks—but it is relevant beyond anthropological or psychological contexts, particularly when dealing with questions of subjectivity and agency.

In the face of neoliberal (Foucault, 2010), self-control oriented (Deleuze, 1993), or entrepreneurial (Bröckling, 2007) societal structures, self-efficacy may not seem like a meaningful or politically suitable term for clarifying agency. In the context of digital cultures, however, and especially gaming culture, the ambivalence of self-efficacy is very useful.[11] Video games produce a strong concept of rapidly reciprocated *action*: interface inputs are articulated to system outputs with decidedly short couplings. When a gamer clicks at just right the moment using just the right vector, the marauding monster drops dead; mission accomplished (e.g., *Neverwinter Nights* [BioWare, 2002]). Push a button and the avatar jumps. Dance around and your moves are scored (e.g., *Dance Dance Revolution* [Konami, 1998]). Swing a virtual 9-iron and you are on the green (e.g., *Lee Trevino's Fighting Golf* [SNK, 1988]). This is a far cry from less ludic computer usage, wherein a given action is answered by a digital system designed to provide users with an immediate experience of *efficiency*, less "I'm really acing this level" and more "I'm really being productive."[12] In contrast to the gameplay examples above, when one clicks in a Google Spreadsheet, the software simply enters a state in which it can accept a number as part of a perpetually unfolding work task: doing taxes, tracking budgets, monitoring sensor data, and so on. Gilles Deleuze, in his 1993 work on societies of control, observes that "In the disciplinary societies one was always starting again…while in the societies of control one is never finished with anything" (p. 5); games discipline both players and play, to be sure, but almost always within the context of control societies.

It is helpful here to think of Ralf Adelmann and Hartmut Winkler's (2014) extension of Norbert Elias's (1939) civilization theory and imagine the "short chains of action" of the video game as opposed to the infinitely unfolding chains of modernity. They point out that a complex labor environment, marked by specialization and differentiation, distances subjects (through time and space) from moments of fulfillment (i.e., task performance) and the performance of their own efficacy. The video game is a compensational system, where the (post)modern alienated subject reconciles with a world of self-inefficacy. In this way, the experience of self-efficacy in video games ("I can do this") represents a kind of emancipation, a place where gamers can engage a comprehensible and prescribed system and have moderate confidence that they can effect change within it.

Such emancipation can quite feel empowering.[13] Ulrich Bröckling (2007) has examined the close relationship between self-empowerment and the experience of self-efficacy. In both processes, he observes, there is an externally motivated steering effect which is then internalized by the subject. In certain cases, this external governing effect may be rendered invisible when internalized, then confused for intrinsic self-indicated drivers of intention. In the context of video games, for example, this process may well be operative when gamers justify volunteering to test unreleased games with the rationale that their free labor will help produce the kinds of quality games they like to play. The player converts the company's need (external) into a self-benefit (internal), and in the process forges a link that both contributes to the production of—and creates a defensive shield around—a marketable commodity.

A good example of this curious reconciliation can be found in business games and economic development simulations. Such titles are characterized by a "dual control principle": on the one hand, the control requirements of the simulated economic processes and causal relationships are carried out by the regulatory and rule-governed decision action of the game; on the other hand, there is the self-regulation of the playing subject who, by taking over action roles and positioning, is internalizing specific actions and ways of thinking. In this way, the video game becomes a covert learning environment. Similar to other neoliberal control techniques (such as personal empowerment rhetorics and mediation), such environments have to be positioned in an ambivalent (or dialectical) relationship between self-empowerment and self-government.[14] When they are, subjects (e.g., gamers) experience action as autonomously motivated. Seeing self-efficacy as a kind of ideological hub, then, shows how game action simultaneously reconciles the gamer to the industry's labor-related discourse (e.g., that working in the industry is stressful but worth it) and deters gamers from avenues of inquiry that would undermine their own agential power.

In some of the original psychological work on perceived self-efficacy, this sort of efficient circularity—a high perceived self-efficacy leads to high demands on the self, which then motivates seeking out more demanding, difficult challenges—was noted and described as a "high performance cycle" (Locke & Latham, 1990). Such a cycle is not only useful for exploring recent trends like gamification, but also goes a considerable way toward explaining why apportioned commodity fetishism works so well in the context of video games.[15] Between the rapid response systems that drive games themselves, and the highly competitive industry out of which they emerge, the epistemological optimization of the gamer is completely rational. For a gamer to know not just that developers exist but that they work in certain ways—that they deal with certain kinds of technical, workplace, and marketplace constraints—is for that gamer to have inside knowledge of a game, a more *efficient* repertoire of possibilities from which to choose in order to progress. For developers, being able to count on gamers to have certain kinds of industrial knowledge diminishes the onus on them to design systems capable of responding to any kind of input, which is to say, it allows them to design more efficient systems. More efficient systems make for more efficient experiences that make for more efficient players who want more efficient systems in which to play. In this way, apportioned commodity fetishism helps drive the industry (which here includes gamers themselves) into a high performance cycle, first by masking off most details that are unconnected to in-game engagement, and second by carefully selecting extra-ludic details aimed not at producing a more efficient gamer (e.g., tight level design) but rather a more efficient consumer (e.g., brand loyalty).

The limit to these efficiencies precisely demarcates apportioned commodity fetishism. Expose the player to too-comprehensive an understanding of the industry's labor relations and she is bogged down (and potentially repulsed by) such practices; too little and the gamer's affinity for the company, its star developers, and its products are diminished.[16] Critical to identifying how Game Studies transforms gamers, then, is an understanding of how this academic field helps drive—particularly through one-dimensional industrial analyses—the epistemological optimization of gamers by deploying education as a mechanism to increase perceived self-efficacy. In the next section, we document a curious reaction formation to this process, one in which Game Studies produces not just certain kinds of gamers but certain kinds of games.

THEORY AS ANTI-THEORY

It should be clear by now how, in a variety of ways, Game Studies not only changes players' understandings of games, it also precedes and conditions their cognitive and affective responses through a cause-effect reversal. Instead of commentary, analysis, or caution, Game Studies—like most media criticism—often serves to produce its critical subjects and how they are engaged, especially through their depictions of race, class, gender, sex, and violence. From its earliest days (e.g., Provenzo, 1991; Griffiths, 1999), studies have critically (which is not to say correctly) documented popular and academic concern over such representations in video games. Video game genres, for example, serve not only to identify particular productions for the purpose of marketing and sales, they also have become some of the discipline's primary analytical categories. In this way, cultural critique maps onto and shapes expectations about genre and game alike, and the effects of this relationship can be seen most pointedly when the institutional study and criticism of games occasion the very responses they wish to avoid. This reactive phenomenon has grown increasingly common as Game Studies has gained a more robust institutional foothold in the academy and society. From *Grand Theft Auto* (DMA Design, 1997), *Duke Nukem* (Apogee Software, 1991) and *Gears of War* (Epic Games, 2006), to the *Rayman* series (Ubisoft Montpellier, 1995-2013)—especially through its various *Raving Rabbids* spinoffs (Ubisoft Montpellier/Ubisoft Motion Pictures, 2006-2014)—video games now anticipate, include, and respond to the study of games in and through their own visual, auditory, and programming codes.

In the interactive television show/game *Rabbids Invasion* (Ubisoft Motion Pictures, 2013-present), for instance, the show/game's instructions form a series of commentaries and responses aimed at the perceptions and criticisms of the *Rabbids* video games found in the popular press. The game portion of *Rabbids Invasion* is designed to work with either the Microsoft Kinect or the PlayStation Move, requiring players to perform specific corporeal motions and activities since, as the hardware vendors suggest, the player's body is the controller. The *Raving Rabbids* games are rife with running jokes and gags, and the instructions are no different. In them, an octogenarian woman appears on screen, offers an explanation of each level's objective, and demonstrates the necessary moves players must perform. In instances requiring full body movement and not just posing, she comments on the action and the player's involvement. For example, she implores players to "stand up" and to "be fit" (while doing chin-ups as she talks).

Here, the message is twofold: first, both the on-screen activity and the character on the screen relate to the oft repeated notion that in addition to their antisocial content and effects, video games contribute to the obesity of children through a lack of actual exercise (cf. Miller, 2006); second, the presence of the stereotypical "blue haired old lady" presents a comment on the definition of "gamer" insofar as the almost universal presumption is that games attract and affect only young people. Not infrequently, game scholars themselves invoke and (re)inscribe the construction of such stereotypes and cliches about gamers—the categorical diversity of which was discussed earlier—lending an academic heft to them that then accords with pop culture's too often determinist paradigms. When placed in the cartoonish atmosphere of the *Raving Rabbids* world, complete with toilet plunger arrows and assorted slapstick paraphernalia, this phenomena begs the question of how seriously any of these charges—or any of these games—can be taken.

In cases like this, then, Game Studies plays a role in shaping the cultural discourse surrounding games generally, which then leads some developers to respond, not through the press but through the game medium itself. Such a blurred boundary between the fictive game world and the people who created it—blurred because the diegesis is, at least to experienced gamers, clearly tainted by extra-diegetic discursive incursions (i.e., academic research and journalism)—exacerbates the apportioned commodity fetishism of games by using games as a medium for reminding gamers that real people are responsible for the product they are playing with. Yet true to the superficiality of apportioned commodity fetishism's indexical capacity, such diegetic play only serves to further cement the stereotype of developers themselves, namely, as creative apologists for the medium that is their bread and butter. As gamers are tickled with inside jokes and meta-commentary through the course of a game, in other words, they are simultaneously being congratulated for their expertise and being constructed as sufficiently semi-knowledgeable subjects.

Such self-referential work has been undertaken in innumerable games in virtually every genre, from the *The Secret of Monkey Island* (LucasFilm Games, 1990) and *Portal* (Valve, 2007), to *Katamari Damacy* (Namco, 2004), *Psychonauts* (Double Fine Productions, 2005), and *Mass Effect* (BioWare, 2007). Two game series, however, have blurred the diegetic boundaries most instructively: the *Duke Nukem* and *Grand Theft Auto* franchises. The influential *Duke Nukem* series, initiated with *Duke Nukem* (Apogee Software, 1991), routinely mocks itself and its genre (first-person shooter) through its cartoonish style and its famously controversial violent and sexual content. In addition to their animated imagery, the *Duke Nukem* games draw heavily on other popular cultural productions for themes and, most notably, the eponymous character's frequent droll and self-congratulatory remarks. A quick scan of the Wikiquote (Duke Nukem, n.d.) listing of Duke's wellknown lines indicates his—or rather, the games' designers—preference for quoting well known and/or catchy statements from action and cult films. As much as Duke the character is designed to resonate as the ultimate mediated masculine figure—as do the prevailing criticisms of the character—his plethora of catch-phrases and taglines prove him to be a shameless regurgitator. Moreover, the fact that the character borrows so unapologetically from *Die Hard* (Gordon, Silver & McTiernan, 1988), *The Terminator* (Hurd & Cameron, 1984), and other action staples makes Duke part of the joke, adding to the perceived joke on his detractors. The boldest statement the *Duke Nukem* series makes is that film and television now constitute the lingua franca of the generations that produced and consumed Duke.

These various threads come together most prominently in the *Grand Theft Auto* series. Almost from the beginning, the series was designed to include replies to critics both real and imagined. The ingame radio in several installments tells as much: a series of commercials tout the "Degenatron" video game system in which young minds are destroyed by the addictive power of games such as *Defender of the Faith* and *Penetrator*. These messages are reinforced in and through a talk-radio program featuring a reactionary mother who blames the Degenatron for corrupting her children while being oblivious to her own bad, absentee parenting. The *Grand Theft Auto* series is an equal opportunity offender since it also features rightwing conspiracy theorists who suggest that games include subliminal messages to warp children's minds.

No other franchise has received more critical attention, both from scholarly and popular sources, for its content. Yet, as Steven Poole explains in an article for *The Guardian* magazine (2012), this was all part of an orchestrated campaign developed by infamous media strategist Max Clifford, who hoped to increase the games' publicity through their notoriety. Clifford not only responded to criticism, he planned for it and helped the games' designers build their franchise around it. In this regard, the critical commonplaces of violence and sex(ism) become both rationale and outcome: the study of games produces games.

Ultimately, criticizing games, particularly for their violent and/or sexist content, elicits games that offer metacommentary on their role and contribution to the cultural circuit. At the same time, they establish a seemingly intimate link between the sides of labor and consumer—intimate because inside jokes and metacommentary are only recognizable as such by those privy to the industry's secrets. This process essentially interpellates gamers into a pro-industry (rather than pro-labor) subject position: "Hey gamer! Isn't it fun that we're all on the same page about the high strung and reactionary critics of video game violence, racism, and sexism?" This alliance forged, no deeper understanding need be pursued by the gamer; the game exists, not discreet unto itself, but rather conjured by developers who purportedly have gamers' best interests at heart, even as these developers are assailed by so-called knee-jerk media watchdogs and unsophisticated conservative pundits who clearly do not understand the postmodern condition. This is the manufacture and maintenance of apportioned commodity fetishism, humorously packaged, in one of the most influential video game series of the industry's 50-year history. In our concluding section, we wrap up our examination of apportioned commodity fetishism by looking squarely at the process of commodification itself, asking in the process what it is about capitalist modes of material production that so readily facilitate the conjunction of desire and ignorance.

COMMODIFICATION

Like a number of other game scholars (e.g., Kerr, 2006; Zackariasson & Wilson, 2012), in this chapter we have turned our attention specifically to the production of games (including their ideological production) and to the consequences of that production and consumption on gamers, the industry, and cultural trends generally. Thinking of games not just as sites of play or as purveyors of narrative but as actively produced artifacts raises a host of issues: that which is produced consumes resources; that which is produced by others represents the decisions and ideological priorities of others; and most pointedly for this volume, that which is produced changes those who consume it. This material turn moves Game Studies from strictly cultural concerns toward the political and economic arena, from games qua games to media commodities that increasingly rely on the productive power of players for their value. Predictably, as consumers increasingly participate in the production of the very commodities they purchase—for example, gamers volunteering their labor to test pre-releases of forthcoming titles—the necessity for establishing mechanisms that will mask the inner workings of the industry become increasingly necessary, including barriers like apportioned commodity fetishism.

One of the major challenges in understanding any media artifact, therefore, is moving beyond the relatively simplistic notion of perceived use—and as such, use value—to include what was required and ignored in the artifact's production, as well as the ways the artifact functions within wider circles of meaning-making. Often, games are seen primarily in terms of player experience. Considering games from the perspective of production, however, can also be immensely illuminating from a critical standpoint, as can (as we have mainly tried to do here) thinking about the dialectic that exists among producers, consumers, and the political-economic context within which the exchange of goods and experiences alike take place. This latter approach not only yields useful critical concepts such as apportioned commodity fetishism, but also raises questions about, for instance, how it is that video games can facilitate social inclusion even though their production depends on exclusionary practices, or how calculations of value might be developed that offer critical alternatives to conventional pricing methods, cost/benefit (i.e., price/play time) ratios, and the monetization of pleasure. Indeed, discussions of gamification and the rise of the Serious Games movement emphasize an implicit economic value that can be extracted from gameplay, irrespective of questions of pleasure. While all too often gamers—and as we illustrate above, some developers—resort to the old canard that games are "just entertainment," Game Studies has provided considerable complication to how games mean, demonstrating that the focus on pleasure and entertainment is a fiction that masks a wide variety of social and economic relations.

Nonetheless, many of today's games (digital or otherwise) are purchased, rather than passed down through rituals of lore sharing and community building as they once might have been. As such, they emerge from an industrial context as commodities designed to be sold. This is true even for most independent and serious games, which are positioned as distinctly different from mainstream offerings but in fact still carry the same need to be profitable—directly through revenue streams or indirectly through cultural capital of some sort—for the developer. Seen this way, Huizinga's magic circle entails not just a price of admission but also an implicit set of rules related to commerce. And like all commerce, the exchanges involved carry different consequences according to circumstance, a point well illustrated by Nina Huntemann and Ben Aslinger's recent (2013) anthology which documents how gaming varies considerably from one locale to another for players and producers alike. Moreover, as Nick Dyer-Witheford and Greig De Peuter (2006) have pointed out, the resources used to produce games are derived at significant cost and consequence for laborers and the environment, a terrifically important register of industrial comprehension, yet one that most gamers are likely to comfortably situate behind the protective facade of apportioned commodity fetishism: "I know those issues are there, but that's for the studios [i.e., the company's people] to deal with."

Similarly, the interactive stories that games present to players have grown up in the palliative shadow of decades of Hollywood focus groups, television audience ratings systems, and other scientistic measures of manufactured satisfaction. As Robert Alan Brookey (2010) argues, modern game development owes as much to Hollywood production as to the computer and toy industries. For reasons like this, it can hardly be surprising when gamers concurrently complain about a lack of originality among the industry's latest offerings even as they line up to purchase the sequel to the game they bought last year: a blockbuster is a blockbuster, ubiquitous and hard to ignore regardless of the medium. And as noted earlier, like Hollywood films, the artistic nature of games has become less a goal than a defense against unwelcome criticism, even as more direct economic strategies such as region locking and localization have become the norm—strategies that, in part, are designed to curtail bottom-line reducing catastrophes born of globalization's inevitable culture clashes. Here also, phenomena like apportioned commodity fetishism serve as bulwarks against too much information about labor; again, "tried and true with twist" protects producers and consumers alike, not only from the vicissitudes of the 21st century marketplace, but also from the ethical burden of ensuring that the workers who produce the goods that are purchased are fairly treated and compensated.

By foregrounding the industrial and commodity origins of games and articulating them with the ways in which Game Studies has, in a variety of ways, contributed to how gamers (academic and otherwise) increasingly understand the production contexts of their games, we have meant in this chapter to offer a new framing of the production/consumption dialectic. We have aimed to concurrently celebrate the critical advances the discipline has lead and acknowledge the discipline's responsibility for the ways in which Game Studies has contributed to gamer transformations that have been more rather than less patient with the industry's turpitude, from its defense of demeaning imagery to its encouragement of what Kathleen Kuehn and Thomas F. Corrigan (2013) call "hope labor," i.e., free labor given in hopes of someday gaining fairly compensated employment. Through its reliance on desirability—of game production as the latest alluring form of information labor—the industry has long sought to secure not just legitimacy—one of the most common tropes for explaining why the industry is so retrograde in its labor practices—but also help and protection from the State in its efforts to be profitable rather than in-novative, experimental, and inclusive. Apportioned commodity fetishism is but one significant element in this system of interlinked stages and transformations, but it is one that we think warrants continued examination for the good of gamers—players, producers, and scholars alike—everywhere.

REFERENCES

2K Boston and 2K Australia. (2007). *BioShock* [Microsoft Windows (et al.) video game]. Novato, CA: 2K Games.

Aarscth, E. (2001). Computer game studies, year one. *Game Studies*, *1*(1).

Aarseth, E. (2004). Genre trouble: Narrativism and the art of simulation. In N. Wardrip-Fruin & P. Har-rigan (Eds.), *First person: New media as story, performance, and game* (pp. 45–55). Cambridge, MA: MIT Press.

Adelmann, R., & Winkler, H. (2014). Kurze Ketten. Handeln und Subjektkonstitution in Computer-spielen. In S. Böhme, R. F. Nohr, & S. Wiemer (Eds.), Diskurse des strategischen Spiels: Medialität, Gouvernementalität, Topografie (pp. 69–82). Münster, Germany: Lit Verlag.

Apogee Software. (1991). *Duke Nukem* [DOS (et al.) video game]. Garland, TX: Apogee Software.

Arakawa, M. (1991). The man behind Mario. In Mario mania: Nintendo player's strategy guide. Red-mond, WA: Nintendo of America.

Bandura, A. (1977). Self-efficacy: Toward a unifying theory of behavioral change. *Psychological Review*, *84*(2), 191–215. doi:10.1037/0033-295X.84.2.191 PMID:847061

BioWare. (2002). *Neverwinter Nights* [Microsoft Windows video game]. Lyon, France: Infogrames/Atari.

BioWare. (2007). *Mass Effect* [Microsoft Xbox 360 video game]. Redmond, WA: Microsoft Game Studios.

Blizzard Entertainment. (2015). *Heroes of the Storm* [Microsoft Windows video game]. Irvine, CA: Blizzard Entertainment.

Bogost, I. (2007). *Unit operations: An approach to videogame criticism*. Cambridge, MA: MIT Press.

Bogost, I. (2015, March 13). Video games are better without characters. *The Atlantic Monthly*. Retrieved May 4, 2015 from http://www.theatlantic.com/technology/archive/2015/03/video-games-are-better-without-characters/387556/

Bröckling, U. (2007). *Das unternehmerische Selbst. Soziologie einer Subjektivierungsform*. Frankfurt: Suhrkamp Verlag.

Brookey, R. A. (2010). *Hollywood gamers: digital convergence in the film and video game industries*. Bloomington, IN: Indiana University Press.

Burke, K. (1969). *A grammar of motives*. Berkeley, CA: University of California Press. (Original work published 1945)

Chen, J. (2006). Flow in games (Master of Fine Arts Thesis/Game). Los Angeles, CA: University of Southern California; Retrieved from http://www.jenovachen.com/flowingames/introduction.htm

Crawford, C. (1985). *Balance of Power* [Microsoft Windows (et al.) video game]. Northbrook, IL: Mindscape.

Crawford, G. (2015). Is it in the game? Reconsidering play spaces, game definitions, theming, and sports videogames. *Games and Culture*, *10*(6), 571–592. doi:10.1177/1555412014566235

Critical Distance. (2015, January 1). Retrieved May 4, 2015 from http://www.critical-distance.com/about/

de Saussure, F. (1986). *Course in general linguistics* (C. Bally & A. Sechehaye, Eds., R. Harris, Trans.). La Salle, IL: Open Court. (Original work published 1972)

DeKoven, B. (1978). *The well-played game: A player's philosophy*. Garden City, NY: Anchor Books/ Doubleday.

Deleuze, G. (1993). Postscript on the societies of control. *October, 59*(Winter), 3–7.

Design, D. M. A. (1997). *Grand Theft Auto* [DOS (et al.) video game]. Darien, CN: ASC Games.

deWinter, J. (2015). *Shigeru Miyamoto: Super Mario Bros., Donkey Kong, The Legend of Zelda*. New York, NY: Bloomsbury.

Digital Games Research Association. (2015). *Cfp: DIGRA 2015—Diversity of play: Games—Cultures— Identities* (updated). Retrieved from http://www.digra.org/cfp-digra-2015-diversity-of-play-games-cultures-identities/

Double Fine Productions. (2005). *Psychonauts* [Microsoft Windows (et al.) video game]. Edison, NJ: Majesco Entertainment.

Duke Nukem. (n.d.). Retrieved from Wikiquote: http://en.wikiquote.org/wiki/Duke_Nukem

Dyer-Witheford, N., & De Peuter, G. (2006). "EA Spouse" and the crisis of video game labour: Enjoyment, exclusion, exploitation, exodus. *Canadian Journal of Communication, 31*(3), 599–617.

Elias, N. (1978). *The civilizing process: The history of manners* (E. Jephcott, Trans.). Oxford, UK: Blackwell. (Original work published 1939)

Epic Games. (2006). *Gears of War* [Microsoft Xbox 360 (et al.) video game]. Cary, NC: Microsoft Game Studios.

Eskelinen, M. (2004). Towards computer game studies. In N. Wardrip-Fruin & P. Harrigan (Eds.), *First person: New media as story, performance, and game* (pp. 36–44). Cambridge, MA: MIT Press.

Filipowich, M. (2015, May 1). *April roundup: 'Palette swaps' | Critical Distance*. Retrieved May 4, 2015 from http://www.critical-distance.com/2015/05/01/april-roundup-palette-swaps/

Foucault, M. (1972). *The archaeology of knowledge and the discourse on language* (A. M. Sheridan Smith, Trans.). New York, NY: Pantheon Books. (Original work published 1969)

Foucault, M. (2010). *The government of self and others: Lectures at the Collège de France 1982-1983* (A. I. Davidson, Ed.). New York, NY: Palgrave Macmillan. doi:10.1057/9780230274730

Gordon, L., & Silver, J. (Producers) & McTiernan, J. (Director). (1988). *Die Hard* [Motion picture]. United States: 20th Century Fox.

Grayson, N. (2013, November 22). Blizzard on *Heroes of the Storm*, female designs in MOBAs. *Rock, Paper, Shotgun*. Retrieved April 1, 2015 from http://www.rockpapershotgun.com/2013/11/22/blizzard-on-heroes-of-the-storm-female-designs-in-mobas/

Griffiths, M. (1999). Violent video games and aggression: A review of the literature. *Aggression and Violent Behavior, 4*(2), 203–212. doi:10.1016/S1359-1789(97)00055-4

Heidegger, M. (2013). *What is metaphysics? An interpretive translation* (T. Sheehan, Trans.). Stanford University. Retrieved March 29, 2015 from http://religiousstudies.stanford.edu/wp-content/uploads/1929-WHAT-IS-METAPHYSICS-2013-NOV.pdf (Original work published 1929)

Hofmeier, R. (2011). *Cart life* [Microsoft Windows video game]. self-published.

Huizinga, J. (1955). *Homo Ludens: A study of the play element in culture*. Boston, MA: Beacon Press. (Original work published 1938)

Huntemann, N. B., & Aslinger, B. (Eds.). (2012). *Gaming globally: Production, play, and place*. New York, NY: Palgrave Macmillan. doi:10.1057/9781137006332

Hurd, G. A. (Producer) & Cameron, J. (Director). (1984). *The Terminator* [Motion picture]. United States: Orion Pictures.

Kerr, A. (2006). *The business and culture of digital games: Gamework/gameplay*. London: Sage.

Klimmt, C., & Hartmann, T. (2006). Effectance, self-efficacy, and the motivation to play computer games. In P. Vorderer & J. Bryant (Eds.), *Playing video games: Motives, responses, and consequences* (pp. 143–177). Mahwah, NJ: Erlbaum.

Konami. (1998). *Dance Dance Revolution* [Coin-operated video game]. Tokyo, Japan: Konami.

Kuehn, K., & Corrigan, T. F. (2013). Hope labor: The role of employment prospects in online social production. *The Political Economy of Communication, 1*(1), 9–25.

Latour, B. (1993). *We have never been modern* (C. Porter, Trans.). Boston, MA: Harvard University Press. (Original work published 1991)

Link, J. (2013). *Versuch über den Normalismus. Wie Normalität produziert wird* (5th ed.). Göttingen, Germany: Vandenhoeck & Ruprecht. (Original work published 1997)

Locke, E. A., & Latham, G. P. (1990). *A theory of goal setting and task performance.* Englewood Cliffs, NJ: Prentice Hall.

Lucasfilm Games. (1990). *The Secret of Monkey Island* [Amiga (et al.) video game]. San Fransco, CA: LucasArts.

Meadows, M. S. (2003). *Pause & effect: The art of interactive narrative.* Indianapolis, IN: New Riders.

Meehan, E. R. (2005). *Why TV is not our fault: Television programming, viewers, and who's in control.* Lanhan, MD: Rowan & Littlefield.

Meier, S., & Shelley, B. (1991). *Civilization* [DOS video game]. Hunt Valley, MD: MicroProse.

Miller, T. (2006). Gaming for beginners. *Games and Culture, 1*(1), 512. doi:10.1177/1555412005281403

Namco. (2004). *Katamari Damacy* [PlayStation 2 video game]. Tokyo, Japan: Namco.

Naone, E. (2008). Jenova Chen, 26. *MIT's Technology Review, 111*(5), 64.

New Games Foundation. (1976). *New games book.* New York, NY: Doubleday/Dolphin.

Nintendo R & D4. (1985). *Super Mario Bros.* [NES/Famicom video game]. Kyoto, Japan: Nintendo.

Nintendo R & D4. (1986). *The Legend of Zelda* [NES/Famicom video game]. Kyoto, Japan: Nintendo.

Nintendo Power, 80 (January, 1996). The game guys. 24–25.

Osborne, J. (2015, April 7). Video Games without characters. *Medium.* Retrieved May 4, 2015 from https://medium.com/@jmarquiso/video-games-without-characters-3e99856cd0e4

Peirce, C. S. (1932-58). In C. Hartshorne, P. Weiss, & A. W. Burks (Eds.), Collected papers of Charles Sanders Peirce (Vols. 1–8). Cambridge, MA: Harvard University Press.

Poole, S. (2012, March 9). Bang, bang, you're dead: How *Grand Theft Auto* stole Hollywood's thunder. *The Guardian.* Retrieved May 20, 2015 from http://www.theguardian.com/technology/2012/mar/09/grand-theft-auto-bang-bang-youre-dead

Pope, L. (2013). *Papers, Please* [Microsoft Windows video game]. n.c.: self-published.

Provenzo, E. (1991). *Video kids.* Cambridge, MA: Harvard University Press. doi:10.4159/harvard.9780674422483

Reimann, M., & Schilke, O. (2011). Product differentiation by aesthetic and creative design: A psychological and neural framework of design thinking. In H. Plattner, C. Meinel, & L. Leifer (Eds.), *Design thinking: Understand—improve—apply* (pp. 45–60). New York, NY: Springer. doi:10.1007/978-3-642-13757-0_3

Reviews for Antique Road Trip: American Dreamin'. (n.d.). Big Fish Games. Retrieved May 4, 2015 from http://forums.bigfishgames.com/posts/list/257559.page

Salen, K., & Zimmerman, E. (2003). *Rules of play: Game design fundamentals.* Cambridge, MA: The MIT Press.

Salen, K., & Zimmerman, E. (2006). *The game design reader: A rules of play anthology.* Cambridge, MA: MIT Press.

Schwarzer, R., & Jerusalem, M. (1995). Generalized self-efficacy scale. In J. Weinman, S. Wright, & M. Johnston (Eds.), *Measures in health psychology: A user's portfolio. Causal and control beliefs* (pp. 35–37). Windsor, UK: Nfer-Nelson.

Sicart, M. (2011). Against procedurality. *Game Studies, 11*(3). Retrieved June 6, 2015, from http://gamestudies.org/1103/articles/sicart_ap

SNK. (1988). *Lee Trevino's Fighting Golf* [Nintendo Entertainment System video game]. Suita, Japan: SNK.

Ubisoft Montpellier. (1995). *Rayman* [PlayStation (et al.) video game]. Montpellier, France: Ubisoft.

Ubisoft Montpellier. (2006). *Rayman Raving Rabbids* [Nintendo Wii (et al.) video game]. Montpellier, France: Ubisoft.

Ubisoft Motion Pictures. (2013). *Rabbids Invasion* [Television series]. Montreuil, France: Ubisoft.

Valve. (2007). *Portal* [PlayStation 3 (et al.) video game]. Bellevue, WA: Valve Corporation.

Vygotsky, L. S. (1966). *Play and its role in the mental development of the child* (C. Mulholland, Trans.). (Original work published in 1933). Retrieved from the Psychology and Marxism Internet ArchiveWeb site: www.marxists.org/archive/vygotsky/works/1933/play.htm

Wardrip-Fruin, N., & Harrigan, P. (Eds.). (2004). *First person: New media as story, performance, and game.* Cambridge, MA: MIT Press.

Williams, R. (1996). *Roberta Williams' Anthology* [DOS video game]. Fresno, CA: Sierra Online.

Wolf, M. J. P. (2002). *The medium of the video game.* Austin, TX: University of Texas.

Woolgar, S. (1986). On the alleged distinction between discourse and praxis. *Social Studies of Science, 16*(2), 309–317. doi:10.1177/0306312786016002006

Wright, W. (1984). *Raid on Bungeling Bay* [Commodore 64 video game]. Eugene, OR: Brøderbund.

Zackariasson, P., & Wilson, T. L. (2012). Marketing of video games. In P. Zackariasson & T. L. Wilson (Eds.), *The video game industry: Formation, present state, and future* (pp. 57–75). New York, NY: Routledge.

Zimmerman, E. (2004). Narrative, interactivity, play, and games: Four naughty concepts in need of discipline. In N. Wardrip-Fruin & P. Harrigan (Eds.), *First person: New media as story, performance, and game* (pp. 154–164). Cambridge, MA: MIT Press.

KEY TERMS AND DEFINITIONS

Commodification: The process by which by which use value is transformed into exchange value.

Culture: Communally established ways of seeing and doing, as well as the products of this seeing and doing.

Discipline: The subjugation of desire, agency, or ideology.

Discourse: The materialization of socially structured knowledge.

Game Studies: The interdisciplinary scholarly field whose object of study is the video game complex.

Gamer: A person who plays video games.

Recursion: The act of self reference and modification.

ENDNOTES

[1]   For more about the Learning Games Initiative Research Archive, see http://lgira.mesmernet.org/about.

[2]   See, for example, the now legendary post by "EA Spouse": http://ea-spouse.livejournal.com/274.html.

[3]   While our focus in this chapter is principally on the critical political economy of the video game complex, it is important to consider the studio/developer culture side of the equation too. We are very grateful to the anonymous reviewer who reminded us of this analytical opportunity, and though we do not have the space here to conduct such a study, we look forward to doing so in a subsequent project.

[4]   For an authoritative explication of the concept of discourse as practice, see Foucault (1972, p. 46) or (1972, p. 117). For a discussion of this concept and its conflicted relation to discourse as a linguistic concept, see Woolgar (1986).

[5]   In his editorial "Computer Game Studies, Year One," Espen Aarseth proclaims that "2001 can be seen as the **Year One** of *Computer Game Studies* as an emerging, viable, international, academic field" (2001, emphasis in original).

[6]   Gamer/subjects might dismiss such attention as paternalistic infringement, but that is another question.

[7]   This phenomenon is not unique to the game industry. Film directors, music composers, and athletes routinely serve as metonyms for small armies of labor that go largely unrecognized.

[8]   For a detailed study of Miyamoto, see deWinter (2015).

[9]   http://gamasutra.com/; https://www.idlethumbs.net/; http://www.designer-notes.com/.

[10]   http://thatgamecompany.com/.

[11]   For a cogent example of Bandura's work in Game Studies, see Klimmt & Hartmann (2006).

[12] From a media theory perspective, perceived self-efficacy presents a problem in the sense that it suggests that an abstract sensory motor action is also an abstract representation. To be precise, one would need to speak of a "sign-based perceived self-efficacy," because the homogenized acting (e.g., pressing a button) simulates a broad variety of action-representations (e.g., jumping, diving, shooting, building a house, and so forth).

[13] For more examples of perceived self-efficacy, consult virtually any management skills or self-empowerment book, which routinely draw on self-efficacy research to encourage readers to believe in such self-statements as "I always manage to solve difficult problems if I try hard enough"; "If someone opposes me, I can find the means and ways to get what I want"; and so on. See Schwarzer & Jerusalem (1995) for how such self-efficacy assessment instruments are created.

[14] See Bröckling (2007).

[15] By "gamification" we mean the use of features common to games—racing, collecting, score keeping, and so on—in non-game contexts.

[16] Indeed, pushed to its limit, the isolation of the consumer from understandings of the industry describe the conventional sense of commodity fetishism.

Chapter 6
Co–Creation and the Distributed Authorship of Video Games

Stephanie C Jennings
Rensselaer Polytechnic Institute, USA

ABSTRACT

This chapter reconceptualizes the authorship of video games through the development of a theory of distributed authorship. It defines distributed authorship as the interplay of negotiated capacities of a number of actors (including but not limited to developers, publishers, and players) to create the content, structures, form, and affordances of video game works. However, the theory does not assume that these actors always work together collaboratively or that capacities for authorship are shared equally among them. Rather, distributed authorship understands the authorship of video games as a relationship of power—the power to create, shape, and influence video game works.

INTRODUCTION

Who Are the Authors of a Video Game?

Traditional notions of authorship would give a straightforward answer: a game's authors must be its developers, the designers and artists and writers who create its content, rules, and form. But video games have posed incessant challenges to this view; their creation is not restricted to their developers alone. Countless developments in recent years have proven longstanding perceptions of authorship inadequate to explain the processes of video game creation.

Thus, to fully answer the first question, we need to explore a few others: How do video games necessitate transformations in concepts of authorship? What are the qualities of video games that have prompted this shift? How does authorship function for video games in ways that it may not in other media forms? And ultimately—why are questions of authorship significant, meaningful, and in need of answering in the first place?

DOI: 10.4018/978-1-5225-0261-6.ch006

Defining authorship in any manner is a political act. Author is a culturally constructed category, fiercely contested and deeply ideological, fraught with issues of power. The authorship of video games can be a guarded platform for hegemonic, capitalist authority or an empowering channel for marginalized voices. Yet it can also be uncertain and shifting, perpetually fracturing and reforming amid struggles over the power to create. Nevertheless, even as we recognize authorship as a socially formulated concept—and even as we resist an all-controlling authorial intent in our interpretations and analyses—the considerations of who is creating a video game, how they are creating it, and *why* have major implications for how we play, receive, and understand games. Authorship remains a conflicted realm in which battles over meaning-making and the power to create are fought.

For video games, authorship spans across a vast range of spaces, encompasses manifold activities, and is conducted by many diverse actors that occupy different positions at different times. These spaces, activities, and actors are not always mutually supportive of or in cooperation with one another; often they conflict, clash, and compete. The collaborations and the tensions—the dynamics of power—between prospective authors throughout the creation of video games all point to upheavals in ideas of authorial intent and artistic integrity.

However, it is not sufficient to focus on authorship pertaining to games-as-art alone. Embedded within the contested spaces and activities of game authorship are video games' identities as technologies. Games are authored as technologies. And as technologies, they afford and shape authorship in specific ways, in ways much unlike previous media forms. Thus, the authorship of video games cannot be understood without acknowledging that video games are both works of art and technological artifacts.

In this chapter, I reconceptualize the authorship of video games through the development of a theory of distributed authorship. I define distributed authorship as the interplay of negotiated capacities of a number of actors (including but not limited to developers, publishers, and players) to create the content, structures, form, and affordances of video game works. To be clear, though, this theory does not assume that these actors always work together collaboratively or that capacities for authorship are shared equally among them. Rather, distributed authorship understands the authorship of video games as a relationship of power—the power to create, shape, and influence video game works. That power is constantly contested and negotiated among various and differently positioned actors, an intricate and ever-mutating tug-of-war.

Before we go further, however, I have a point of clarification with regard to my method:

As I have done above, I will be using the term works rather than texts in my discussions of the authorship of video games. I am basing this distinction on that in Roland Barthes's 1977 essay "From Work to Text." According to Barthes, the difference between these two terms is the presence, significance, and involvement of the author against the presence, significance, and involvement of the reader. Text implies the act of interpretation, and thus implies the presence of an interpreter. The text is a process, "a methodological field," and it "only exists in the movement of a discourse" (p. 157). A work, on the other hand, is that which has been authored; it is material, tangible, and "can be held in the hand" (p. 157). It is the static container of the authored contents, while the text is the ever-flowing plurality of interpretive potentialities.

I use the term work because my purpose is to expound upon the authorship of games and not necessarily on strategies of interpretation. However, as I will explain more later in the chapter, I also wish to make this distinction in order to ultimately call attention to the ways that video games muddy what might be understood to separate these two terms. Video games have caused the line between authorship and interpretation to grow quite fuzzy. Ultimately, they manage to convert works into processes, transforming the materiality of what we might otherwise conceive as a rigid, unchanging whole.

Moreover, examining the authorship of video game works has significant implications for the interpretation and criticism of game texts. Authors influence the assemblages of works; and the assemblages of works influence the assemblages of texts. Thus, understanding who the authors of video games are and how they conduct their acts of authorship has profound ramifications for how we conduct critical analyses of video games. We may wish to proclaim the death of the author in our interpretations, just as Barthes (1977) set out to do. But the presence of authors in video games is not so easily extracted from our readings of texts or acts of play—though not for the reasons that have traditionally held sway.

WHAT IS AUTHORSHIP?

The Myth of the Individual Author

Authorship is a socially constructed category, a designation reflecting particular cultural values and expectations. As a number of scholars have previously asserted, the dominant, traditional conception of authorship has, in fact, been a fairly recent historical occurrence in Western society. That traditional conception is the myth of the individual author, "a view that is directly related to the Western philosophical tradition of defining the autonomous individual as the source or foundation of all knowledge" (Ede & Lunsford, 1990, p. 73). It is the basis upon which our culture has sanctified the origination of ideas and knowledge, the ownership of works, the notions of authorial intent and artistic integrity. It is also ideological, influencing to whom we attribute the power to create and whose voices we elevate over others.

As Ede and Lunsford (1990) have pointed out, "the history of the concept of authorship cannot be separated from the evolution of authorship as a profession" (p. 80). They note that a significant factor in this evolution was the ability for writers to profit from their work. The myth of the solitary author started to solidify in the eighteenth century as intellectual property rights and copyright laws emerged to protect these opportunities for profit. Thus, authorship and its accompanying cultural valuation has not been a consistent feature of Western culture. Rather, it is, as Foucault (1969) described, "a privileged moment of individualization in the history of ideas, knowledge, and literature, or in the history of philosophy and science" (p. 115). Yet, it is a deeply entrenched cultural belief that has lingered into the present, even as it directly contradicts actual writing and creative practices. And it is also an idea that has witnessed a great deal of legal protection in the form of copyright laws.

The legal construction of authorship has developed hand-in-hand with the myth of the individual author. However, copyright laws have usually been instituted and deployed for the sake of publishers rather than writers. Peter Jaszi (1994) suggested that publishers have perhaps benefited most from the myth and the laws that have sought to enshrine it, as "the interests most directly at stake in disputes over the content of copyright law usually are those of firms and individuals with capital investments in the means by which the productions of creative workers are distributed to consumers" (pp. 32-33). Our cultural understandings of authorship thus cannot be extricated from their origins in and cultivation of capital. We must not overlook the connection between authorship and power in authorship's evolution, in the ways that the myth has become rooted in our culture, and in how the myth has been invoked to protect profit interests.

In the second half of the twentieth century, a number of theorists started to resist what we continue to view as the commonsensical concept of authorship in the present. Two of the most pivotal and widely cited pieces in this regard are Barthes's (1977) "The Death of the Author" and Foucault's (1969) "What is an Author?" Barthes's essay is a call to literary criticism to wrench interpretation away from the ruling grip of authorial intent. In it, he condemned critics' relentless privileging of the power of the author over readers' capacities for meaning-making in questions of interpretation. His now-famous concluding lines firmly declare: "We know that to give writing its future, it is necessary to overthrow the myth: the birth of the reader must be at the cost of the death of the Author" (p. 148).

Foucault (1969) characterized authorship as a function, an overdetermined power that is socially constructed and imposed on texts and discourse. To Foucault, who occupies an authorial role is not a simple question of who wrote a particular piece; nor is it a rigid, unchanging assumption in all discourses. Instead, the author-function

does not operate in a uniform manner in all discourses, at all times, and in any given culture; it is not defined by the spontaneous attribution of a text to its creator, but through a series of precise and complex procedures; it does not refer, purely and simply, to an actual individual. (p. 131)

Foucault's dramatic reconsideration of authorship is "one that would view texts as contested sites in a complex, situated world of political, cultural, economic, ideological, and other forces" (Ede & Lunsford, 1990, p. 88). By reframing authorship in this manner, Foucault pointed to subsequent shifts in understandings of subject positions and in the questions that literary critics would ask of their objects of analysis.

More recently, challenges to the authorial myth—such as those issued by Ede and Lunsford (1990)—have focused on widespread practices of collaborative writing, as well as on the implications that destabilizations of the myth would have on pedagogy and copyright law. These have pitted defenses of the solitary author myth against actual writing practices, the diffuse and uneven production of knowledge, and the collective contributions in processes of creation.

As a part of this uprising, an even more disruptive challenge to the traditional authorship myth erupted in the early 1990s as a result of the emergence of writing practices in digital narratives. The resulting debates have carried on into the present, bleeding into studies of video games and remaining troubled and inconclusive even in the present.

Authorship and Digital Narratives: Debates over Interactivity and the Author-Player Merger

If the construction of authorship has been a politically charged development in recent Western history, so too has been the strongly preserved divide that has separated authors from readers. As Espen Aarseth (1997) wrote:

...the perceived gap between consumer (reader) and producer (author) is one of the most profound ideological divides in the social reality of modern Western society...To elevate a consumer group to producerhood is a bold political statement; and in the production and consumption of symbolic artifacts (texts) the boundary between these positions becomes a highly contested ground. (p. 163)

The technological possibilities and affordances of digital media blurred the boundaries between readers and writers while also triggering a new wave of interest in collaborative writing. As pertains to video games, many early efforts to reconfigure authorship in light of digital media largely focused on questions of interactivity and collaboration: Was interactivity redefining authorship? Were readers of hypertext fiction also becoming authors of the work as they clicked on links and strung together pages of pre-written text? Were players of video games authoring games as they played?

One of the earliest such attempts to reconceptualize authorship was George Landow's (1992)*Hypertext*. In this book, Landow proclaimed that "the figure of the hypertext author approaches, even if it does not entirely merge with, that of the reader; the functions of reader and writer become more deeply entwined with each other than ever before" (p. 71). To Landow, in hypertext environments "all writing becomes collaborative writing" (p. 88) because a reader's engagement with a hypertext is an act of collaboration between that reader and the hypertext's original author.

Later, but along similar lines, Larry Friedlander (2009) argued that the interactivity of digital media did not eliminate authorship, but multiplied it. Much like Landow, he regarded digital narratives as fostering a reciprocal dialogue of authorship between designer-writers and readers. Including video games in his analysis, he suggested that

in a digital story...the reader/user/player takes over some of the functions of the author. In these new forms, it is the user's playful engagement with the digital environment that creates the sense of mastery and commitment that makes for a coherent narrative. (p. 180)

Thus, a video game narrative would only become a cohesive whole through the activated, authorial participation of a player.

And recently, Rachel Meyers (2014) has sought to develop a theory of participatory authorship, which she defines as "the active participation of audience members in the creation, expansion, and adaptation of another's creative work" (p. 9). Meyers's primary goal was to include players into the designation of video game authors. Her theory leaned heavily on assumptions of interactivity, player choices in game narratives, and collaboration, thus strongly resembling the assertions of Landow. Players, she argued, "by their very nature, are participatory authors and co-creators of the games they play, and a game cannot even exist without their input. Video games close the divide between the author and audience, creating a medium that is inherently collaborative" (p. 10).

In opposition to the claims of theorists such as Landow, Friedlander, and Meyers, there has also been a body of games scholarship that has firmly denied that authorship takes place by way of players' interactive choices. For Espen Aarseth (1997), the question of video game authorship was not merely one of who was piecing together fragments of narrative possibilities to form a coherent story. The authors of digital narratives were, rather, those who were responsible for crafting the rule systems. He wrote,

As with most games, the rules are well beyond the player's control, and to suggest the user is able to determine the shape of such as text is the same as to confuse the influence of a city's tourist guide with that of a city planner. (pp. 138-139)

Similarly, Janet Murray (1997) noted that "there is a distinction between playing a creative role within an authored environment and having authorship of the environment itself" (p. 152). As Aarseth did, Murray defined authorship according to who writes the rules: "Authorship in electronic media is procedural. Procedural authorship means writing the rules by which the texts appear as well as writing the texts themselves" (p. 152). To call users' interactivity and choice-making an act of authorship was, according to Murray, a failure to understand the procedural, rule-based nature of digital narratives.

In his essay "Playing with Oneself," Alec Charles (2009) contributed another contention to the interaction-as-authorship debate by drawing on Barthes's (1974) distinction between the lisible text and the scriptible text—that is, the readerly text and the writerly text. The scriptible, Charles explained, "invites, embodies and requires cooperation and co-authorship: it understands that meaning is an act of interpretation rather than of intention or expression" (para. 34). Video games and other participatory media may be understood as creating a related third category, the faux-scriptible. This type of text offers an illusion of interactivity, an illusion of authorship. Charles described the faux-scriptible text as proclaiming "its openness to interactivity, which gives its user the illusion of meaning, power, and active participation, and which, in appearing to satisfy its audience's desire for agency, in fact sublimates and dilutes that desire" (para. 41). He presented this concept with a warning: the faux-scriptible may lure players into the false sense that they have authorial powers, while nullifying critical capacities that would aid players in resisting games' ideological messages.

Marie-Laure Ryan's (2011) analysis of interactivity accounted for the possibility that users may influence rule systems, but denied that the role of player and author would overlap at these points. Ryan established five layers of interactivity, comparing these layers to an onion. The outermost layers of the "Interactive Onion" consist of a player's exploration of a predetermined text; in the middle layers, the player becomes personally involved in the story, but the plot is still predetermined. It is at the innermost layers—presumably the layer of emergent narrative—that "the story is created dynamically through the interaction between the user and the system" (p. 37). Ryan also added a fifth layer: meta-interactivity, a point at which the player is no longer consuming the onion, but "preparing new ways to cook it for other users" (p. 59). At this level, the player creates, develops, and implements new content for other players to utilize in-game, such as player-generated mods. When a player is engaged in meta-interactivity, "the idea of the user as co-author becomes more than a hyperbolic cliché, but the two roles do not merge" (p. 59). According to Ryan, the player can either be a player or the player can be a co-author, but within the confines of a game's narrative, the player cannot be both roles at once.

While I have provided only a small sampling of writings in the debate over whether interactivity can be an act of authorship, what is ultimately clear is that there has been a rigid and inconclusive schism in writing on video game authorship. A number of these works engage with another extant and heated debate in game studies: what *interactivity* actually means and whether it is, in fact, a defining characteristic of video games. Whatever the case, interactivity has been the primary hinge upon which theories of game authorship have revolved. And as long as that remains the case, the questions of game authorship will undoubtedly remain unanswered—unless one is simply willing to pick a side and stick with it. Is interaction a sufficient condition for a player to be an author? Or is influence over rule systems necessary? At what point does authorship occur?

Co-Creative Tools and Player Labor

As the overview above may indicate, most literature on game co-authorship has tended to focus not only on interactivity, but also on the creation of game narratives. However, related but apart from this scholarship has been another body of work that has approached the possibilities of co-creation from another angle: technological tools and player labor. Rather than concerning themselves exclusively with the authorship of game narratives, these pieces have instead sought to examine tools for content creation and the work that players perform when using them. This scholarship offers another way of understanding video games: not just as narratives offering ranges of choices within systems of authored rules, but also as authored technologies with accompanying technological constraints and affordances that may shape, appropriate, and exploit the creative productions of players.

These discussions have brought the power relationships of co-creation to the fore. To scholars conducting such analyses, questions of co-creation are less a matter of collaboration. Instead, they center more on the ways that technological tools allow for or inhibit certain kinds of co-creative production, and on the tensions between players and developers—as well as publishers—regarding how this production is incorporated into games. And more often than not, these examinations highlight the many ways that these negotiations and creative capacities are unequal.

A great concern of many such texts has been the exploitation of player labor. A particular area of player creation that has drawn a great deal of attention in this regard—and which has recently created another firestorm of controversy—is modding. A number of games and game development studios have provided players with toolkits with which to modify (mod) and design their own in-game content, as well as with means by which to distribute this content to other players. At other times, players have generated their own methods for modding, subverting the authority of developers and publishers. Typically, modding activities have been an open, do-it-yourself hobby space, with players creating and sharing their creations amongst themselves. However, while these activities have often clashed with the control of studios and publishers, they have also been frequently appropriated, commodified, and monetized by the games industry. Julian Küklich (2005) thus described modding as an example of a hybrid of leisure activity and work: playbor.

Küklich observed that the problem was that the games industry was channeling a voluntary leisure activity into sources of free labor and capital. As he wrote, modding:

still has to struggle to free itself from the negative connotations of play: idleness, non-productiveness and escapism. And while the digital game industry increasingly acknowledges the contribution of modders, they have no incentive to contest this view: the perception of modding as play is the basis of the exploitative relationship between modders and the games industry. (para. 26)

Building on Küklich's work, Dyer-Witheford and de Peuter (2009) spoke of the "playbor force" that includes not only modding, but also co-creative activities in areas such as massively multiplayer online games (MMOs) and machinima. They caution, "the game industry has increasingly learned to suck up volunteer production as a source of innovation and profit...Commercial game production today culls the prototypes of micro-enterprises, buys back mods, assimilates machinima, and makes MMOs a source of endless subscription" (p. 27).

Casey O'Donnell (2013) took a technological approach to considerations of co-creation and development toolkits, emphasizing the ways that these tools, the know-how to use them, and the cultural spaces surrounding them shape the kinds of games that users may produce. As he wrote, "tools structure the roles in which users and their means of (co)creation are allowed to function" (p. 172). Related to the warnings of Küklich, Dyer-Witheford, and de Peuter, O'Donnell commented that game development companies closely monitor and control toolkit usage. Moreover, they have frequently excluded users from conversations on the design, release, and permissible activation of these tools—although players nevertheless have found ways to assert their desires and decisions against those of the games industry.

A decade after the publication of Küklich's playbor essay, the exploitation of modding erupted into a furious debate as game studio and publisher Valve attempted to introduce paid mods on its gaming platform Steam. Interestingly, the company employed the language of authorship to justify its reasoning as benevolent and empowering for player-creators and not as capital harvesting on Valve's part. As Michael McWhertor (2015) of *Polygon* reported, "Valve says it's 'putting mod authors in business via a new streamlined process for listing, selling and managing their creations'" (para. 3). But Valve would be taking a substantial share; meanwhile, mod creators would see only twenty-five percent of the sale. After a massive, outraged response from mod authors and players, the company decided to reverse its decision, admitting that it "didn't understand exactly what [it] was doing" (Alden, 2015, para. 2).

As this situation implies, and as Banks and Humphreys (2008) suggested, player co-creators are not always unknowingly duped into performing work when they use developer-provided toolkits to contribute to game content, even as those development companies mobilize rhetorics of collaboration to veil their profit-seeking motives. Their own ethnographic study revealed that players have diverse motivations behind their creative practices, are often well aware of how their production may be exploited as work, and may negotiate fiercely for influence and control over their own production decisions and autonomy. Banks and Humphreys note the implications that this would have for markets and business models. However, as we will soon discuss more in depth, it also points towards the negotiated power dynamics behind the capacities to contribute to game authorship.

Such scholarship introduces significant considerations into our efforts to understand what video game authorship is and to understand how video games may demand shifts in concepts of authorship. While authorship may be a socially-constructed category, it involves capacities to create and the ability to be attributed as a legitimate (co-)creator of a work. Thus, when we move outside of narrative considerations, we run into a number of additional questions where the powers of co-creation are concerned: Who controls tools of production? Who has access to and who is able to use these tools? Who controls the creative products resulting from the use of these tools?

So, What is Authorship for Video Games?

Up to this point, we have encountered a number of approaches to and theories of authorship. We have discussed the myth of the solitary author, authorship's roots and evolution in capital and power, and challenges to long-preserved notions of authorial authority. We have also encountered two significant strains of writing on authorship and co-creation in video games literature: a divisive and inconclusive dispute over the abilities of players to be authors within games' interactive systems, and a more technologically-oriented collection of scholarship on co-creative tools and labor. The scholarship on video game co-creation has left us with two outstanding questions: To what extent are players also authors in their engagements with video games? And, to what extent are players authors when they use development toolkits? In order to answer these questions, we must first ensure that we understand what it means to be an author.

As I mentioned at the start, the authorship of video games involves the power to create, shape, and influence the content, structure, form, and affordances of video game works. It involves the power to alter, to write, and to create. It is not, however, an *i*nterpretive power alone.

One of the issues in the interaction-as-authorship debate (and, perhaps, a reason why it has remained so inconclusive) is that many of the theories that equate interactivity with authorship have confused the distinction between work and text; that is, they have confused the creation of a work with the interpretation of a text. For instance, Meyers (2014) connects the actively-interpreting audience of reader-response theory to the active choice-making of players in game narratives as a way of bolstering her theory of participatory authorship. Her theory is grounded in the idea that players are a part of the text and therefore create the text in their acts of play.

The idea that players are a part of game texts has also been widely discussed in games criticism (Fernández-Vara 2014; Keogh 2014; Jennings 2015). However, this claim concerns the interpretation of a text and not the creation of a game work. When players make choices in a game narrative, they actualize and interpret a specific instantiation of circumstances drawn from pre-authored possibilities. Players may construct a playthrough and that playthrough's meanings, but they do not author the game's capacities for supporting the actualization of that playthrough. Even so, who we understand to be the authors of those capacities strongly influences our interpretation—and the carving out of our interpretation is also an endeavor toward the power of meaning-making.

Although this argument may resemble those of Aarseth (1997), Murray (1997), Charles (2009), and Ryan (2011), I wish to ultimately underscore the propensity of players to adopt and maintain authorial roles even while continuing to occupy their roles as players. Further, I also aim to demonstrate how video games have possibly problematized the work-text distinction and have led to this confusion. What, after all, is a video game work?

As mentioned previously, the authorship of video games occurs for a range of components, throughout a number of activities, and in a number of spaces. Video game authorship does not merely pertain to the writing of narratives. It also pertains to a game's art, code, rules, form, genre, technological affordances, and so on.

More and more, these technological affordances are shaping, facilitating, and enabling forms of creation and co-creation that differ from those of other media forms. These changes are directly confronting previous concepts of and expectations for authorship, necessitating new formulations of what authorship might mean and who authors might be. At the same time, however, they are not sweepingly empowering, although they may imply potentials to challenge and disperse authorial control. They are also generating new struggles for power and influence; they may provide new means for surveillance and seizure at the same time that they may allow for protest, reclamation, and subversion. Thus, when analyzing the authorship of video games, we cannot overlook the status of video games as authored technologies.

As such, we also cannot forget the significance of the technological foundations and components of video games, whether these considerations pertain to their coding, software, platforms, creative tools, or otherwise. A particularly striking example in this regard, and one that is central to understanding the authorship of video games, is that of game engines. When creating new games, developers do not always start from scratch, per se. Frequently, they construct games from the basis of a pre-established game engine for which they purchase a license to use. These engines may, for instance, "abstract routines for characters and objects in the world; manage physics routines to keep objects from falling out of the world and to dictate their interaction; and provide sound management, artificial intelligence (AI), network communications, scripting, and tools" (Bogost, 2006, p. 60).

As Ian Bogost further (2006) described in *Unit Operations*, "Game engines are partly responsible for the massive growth of the game industry...they take much of the drudgery out of game development, which should allow developers to focus on innovation instead of mechanics" (p. 60). What this means is that many separate video games from separate studios with separate development teams may share technological bases and coding for their environments, animations, physics, sounds, and so on. While some studios may tweak certain engines to suit the aspirations of a new project, many others simply license available engines such as Epic Games' Unreal Engine. Thus, many games share certain pre-authored elements in common as a crucial foundation for their development.

As we can see, the myth of the solitary author crumbles in the face of game authorship. More often than not, video games are authored by teams of developers: coders, engineers, artists, animators, writers, sound technicians, so on. The creative production of these teams in game studios is often driven by the profit-seeking goals of publishing companies. And increasingly, players are asserting their own input into the publishing process—or they are seeking to modify game content on their own terms after a game has been released.

Nevertheless, the individual author cannot simply be totally tossed aside—nor can authorship itself. Although the solitary author myth is often invoked as a cultural pacifier to safeguard the profits of powerful publishing corporations, I suggest that it be reframed to protect a different group: video game creators from marginalized populations. As we will soon see, members of marginalized communities are increasingly taking up game creation tools as a way of expressing their own experiences and sharing their identities. Even if we acknowledge and accept Foucault's (1969) assertion that authorship is a function of power, those channels of power can be rerouted to benefit and elevate the voices of the oppressed.

For this reason—and others—it would be damaging to entirely dismiss the function of authorship, even in spite of the many challenges to it. As Aarseth noted, "it would be irresponsible to assume that this position has simply gone away, leaving a vacuum to be filled by the audience" (p. 165). Authorship may be a socially constructed category, but the recognition of game creators is still significant and is bound up in our processes of interpretation and meaning-making. Along those lines, Mark Filipowich (2013) admonished:

the consequence of putting the author on the pedestal is that it limits what the reader can get from a text, but ignoring where the author(s) come from entirely gives the reader room to confirm their biases. It exchanges the author's biases for the reader's. (para. 8)

These biases can then lead to a different form of hegemony of meaning.

To address these considerations, we need a theory of authorship that identifies and examines uneven flows of creative power, that recognizes challenges to traditional authorities and attributions of creation processes, and that can contend with the dispersed locations where creation may occur.

THE DISTRIBUTED AUTHORSHIP OF VIDEO GAMES

We have already begun to observe a number of the ways in which authorship is wrapped up in struggles over power. Authorship involves access to and autonomy over the tools of creation. The creation of these tools themselves shape the ways that authors are able to create and what kinds of works they can produce. Due to cultural values like that of the myth of the solitary author, authorship also influences who we recognize as being a creator, whose voices and perspectives we are willing to acknowledge, preserve, and value. Furthermore, while an act of interpretation is not the same as authorship, the specters of a work's authors are present in readers' efforts to decipher and construct meaning from texts.

Distributed authorship is an attempt to respond to these myriad concerns, to treat authorship as a relationship of creative power. To reiterate, I am defining distributed authorship as the interplay of negotiated capacities of a number of actors (including but not limited to developers, publishers, and players) to create the content, structures, form, and affordances of video game works. However, distributed does not mean distributed equally. The power of these actors is not equal, and it is not always collaborative or mutually supportive. It is more often tense, conflicted, and uneven. Moreover, these power relationships are constantly in flux, perpetually negotiated, and are not the same from one game to the next.

Unlike many previous theories of video game authorship, distributed authorship is not fixated exclusively upon narrative. Rather, it understands that the creation of video games is many-faceted and multi-layered—games may have narrative components, but they are not narratives alone. Even the most narrative of game forms—for instance, many hypertext Twine games—still have other features of authorship: their coding and their technological foundations as software, for instance. The fact that video games' identities as authored technologies must be taken into account is one of the primary reasons as to why traditional concepts of authorship cannot be sufficiently applied to them.

If the authorship of video games is distributed, then where can authorship take place? And by whom?

Repositioning the Player-Author

Due to the commercial nature of many video games, a number of attempts to reframe the authorship of video games have focused on the positions of players. Commonsense notions of authorship would focus on the creative role of developers and, perhaps, the possible influences of publishers. However, there has been a great deal of disagreement as to whether or not players can be authors—and if they can, then at what point and in what ways.

Some scholarship that has sought to raise the player to the status of author has done so by fitting players into capitalist relations of power. In this model of analysis, players are understood as consumers fighting against mighty capitalist behemoths for some modicum of creative influence. In these cases, concepts of authorship have been regarded as maintaining hegemonic control of corporations with sanctified cultural values like authorial intent and artistic integrity. Meyers (2014), for instance, suggested "this exclusivity of authorship ensures a linear line of control between the powerful author to powerless audience, or in capitalistic terms, active producer to passive consumer" (p. 8). Nevertheless, many of these theoretical approaches have not comprehensively accounted for the many ways that the authorial positioning of players is shifting—after all, many of these reframings of authorship have gone about their task by claiming that players may become authors through their interactive choices alone.

We have already encountered one realm of activity in which players compete with development studios and publishing companies for co-creative capacities: developer-provided toolkits and modding. Game mods enable players to design their own creative tools, implement their own content changes and rule systems into extant game works, and even originate their own game works. As discussed earlier, players may then distribute these mods to other players, or even pass along toolkits with which other players may author their own mods. Some of these mods become official game content, incorporated into the structure of corporate-sanctioned game products. At other times, they may become separate, distinct game works. Such was the case with the mod to *Half-Life* (Valve, 1998) by modders Mihn Le and Jess Cliffe that ultimately became *Counter-Strike* (1999) (Küklich, 2005). When such mods are embraced by the games industry, their creators may be boosted to celebrity status within modding communities. On the other hand, their work may be appropriated in a relationship of exploitative capital-harvesting.

Although not a direct, concrete contribution to game content in the same manner as a mod, we cannot entirely exclude the extra-textual fan creations and activities of players outside of the game. These activities may take a number of forms: fanfiction, fanart, machinima, and even conversations between players and developers on online forums. While they may not definitively be acts of authorship, their potential to steer the creation process cannot be discounted. In fact, many players have come to expect—if not demand—these extra-textual works and conversations to be regular interactions between developers and player communities throughout authoring processes. Meyers (2014) explained, "video games transgress the author/audience divide by not only inviting the player to help create the text but also by making the author beholden to the demands and desires of the player" (p. 21). We will soon examine an especially noteworthy instance of this interplay between players and developers. It is an example that, in fact, Meyers points to as well: the *Mass Effect 3* ending controversy.

One of the areas of players' authorial authority that has remained undertheorized and even overlooked as an act of co-creation is found in the growth of crowdfunded games. Simply put, crowdfunding is the power of (prospective) players to collectively determine what games are made by providing or withholding monetary support. Many game designers are increasingly taking to sites such as Kickstarter in order to find financial backers who will and can supply funding for their games. These designers create campaigns that offer details of what the game would be, including teasers, artwork, and even early gameplay footage. Prospective players who are interested in the game and that want it to be created can then donate money to the designers. The crowdfunding model is meant to subvert the financial barriers that rule over much of game creation, side-stepping the restrictions of publishing corporations and aiding in the proliferation of independently developed games. In this way, Kickstarter and other such outlets allow games to be made that otherwise might not be. Lest we forget, however, this model is also very much open to being exploited by major corporate publishers and development studios.

Nonetheless, crowdfunding also offers players opportunities to fuel the games that they want to be created, to have a say in what they want to be able to play. A particularly powerful example has been the record-setting *Star Citizen,* which has garnered the most funding ever committed to a Kickstarter campaign—over $65 million from over 700,000 player-backers (Woolf, 2014). Nevertheless, whether these games actually reach fruition—or reach fruition in ways that funders wish them to be—is largely out of the control of funders.

In some cases, designers may use authorship opportunities as a way of attracting substantial donations. For instance, they may offer those that give the most money a chance to determine aspects of the content, or even write their own contributions. These situations provide informative examples of distributed authorship. In particular, a fairly recent controversy exhibits interplays of negotiated authorial capacities: a Kickstarter-funded game, *Pillars of Eternity* (Obsidian, 2015), became a contested site over who had the power to determine game content.

Backers that donated more than $500 to *Pillars of Eternity's* Kickstarter campaign were promised a reward: an in-game memorial stone with a custom message of their choice. At the game's release, one of these custom-created memorials contained a transphobic poem. Once it was discovered, a social media outcry exploded in response that demanded that the game's development studio, Obsidian, remove the hateful content. Charlie Hall's (2015) report on the incident for *Polygon* emphasized the dispersion of responsibility for the poem's authorship:

Yes, it stands to reason that Obsidian could have said no to what the backer put into their game in the first place. They missed that opportunity. But now that it was in the game, it wasn't merely Obsidian's problem. It was also their backer's problem. And therefore, it required a joint solution. Together with that backer, the team at Obsidian discussed their options via email. (para. 10)

The decision at which Obsidian and the backer arrived was to remove the poem. However, another outcry arose in response, consisting of players who accused Obsidian of censorship and acquiescing to the wishes of an angry mob. There was thus another, counter attempt at collective action to preserve the authorial decisions of Obsidian and its backers.

Here, we have a clear example of game authorship as an uneven distribution of influence, a negotiation of authorial capacities. What took place was a struggle over the ability to determine the content of the game. In examining this situation, we also cannot overlook the ways that video games' technological structures have afforded these changes. Their digitization and increasingly prevalent requirements for internet connectivity have facilitated circumstances in which players can demand that changes be made to a game work well after the game's release and expect to see those changes enacted. A cultural milieu has formed around these expectations: players insist that developers be ready and at-hand to hear their pleas, and players are ready to take collective action when they wish to see their desires reflected in game content. At the same time, these same technological characteristics may allow for a very different kind of situation—one in which developers and publishers are not at the whims of players' creative capacities, but may instead exert their own authorial control at players' expense.

Another domain of contested creative power—one that has both facilitated and inhibited players' authorship capacities—lies within massively multiplayer online role-playing games (MMORPGs). The worlds of MMORPGs only exist when they are populated with players and their activities. T. L. Taylor (2009) refers to this element of MMORPGs as an "emergent culture" that players collectively develop and sustain. She argued firmly, "Most radically put, the very product of the game is not constructed simply by the designers or publisher, nor contained within the boxed product, but produced only in conjunction with the players" (p. 126). Moreover, she made a point very similar to the one I wish to highlight: there is "a constant push and pull among these parties around not only the question of what the game is but also whose game it is" (p. 127).

Despite the fact that players may be inhabiting these online worlds as citizens, they can often exercise little self-determination in the governance and status of these spaces. They are often at the mercy of stringent end-user license agreements (EULAs) that regulate their behavior. Should players deviate from mandated rules, the game's moderators can severely punish them—by, for instance, instituting bans on their accounts. Players must also pay monthly subscription fees to maintain access to the game, within ownership models that treat them as renting the service to play, not as enjoying rights as citizens or owners. These various regulatory frameworks do not recognize players as co-creators of these spaces. And, in fact, Taylor has pointed out that the designers and publishers of MMORPGs frequently strive to preserve these models of corporate ownership by employing the rhetoric of the authorship myth.

In response, Taylor asked, "At what point does something shift from being solely the property of an original author to being that of those who not only use it but give it meaning?" (p. 129) The question leaves our study of authorship with new questions of its own: Are players' constructions of a game world an act of authorship or an act of interpretation? We have already discussed that interpretive acts alone are not sufficient to be acts of authorship. But what, then, is the status of players' activities in the worlds of MMOs? Charles (2009) further problematizes this question with the suggestion that "the multiplayer experience does not dissolve authorial authority, it disseminates it. The multiplayer game does not promote the interactivity of co-productive and dialogic readership so much as it proliferates authorship as a set of parallel but solipsistic or monologistic experiences" (para. 43).

Where do we draw the line between interpretation and authorship, between text and work? Is a monologistic experience an actual act of authorship or a privately-narrated interpretation? How would this type of authorship be any different from the construction of a playthrough?

Taylor (2009) perhaps finds a solution in the implication that what players of MMOs are accomplishing is the construction of an entire culture. What exists in these game worlds, then, is not merely a solipsistic experience of events, character interactions, and environments—it is an emergent culture that arises out of the interactions and activities of the many player-characters that populate the world.

Still, we are left with a problem: If emergent culture counts as an act of authorship, what can we say of emergent narrative?

As Henry Jenkins (2004) explained, emergent narratives "are not pre-structured or pre-programmed, taking shape through the game play" (p. 684), and further, "in the case of emergent narratives, game spaces are designed to be rich with narrative potential, enabling the story-constructing activity of players...it makes sense to think of game designers less as storytellers than as narrative architects" (p. 686). Rather than consisting of pre-written events and characters, emergent narratives are assembled and conjured by the actions of players. The structures of the game—its rules and mechanics and fields of possibilities—give rise to these narrative potentials. However, it is ultimately up to players to design characters, to guide their interactions, to color the world in which they engage, and to assign connections and meanings to otherwise disparate events. Emergent narratives are common in sandbox games such as Maxis's famed *The Sims* (2000), games that may appear unstructured and free-form, apparently rich with possibilities from which players may choose. But, though this may appear to grant players authority over the authorship of their gameworlds, Jenkins advised, "let's not underestimate the designers' contributions...designers have made choices about what kinds of actions are and are not possible in this world" (p. 685).

Emergent narrative illustrates another field across which players and designers wage a constant and unresolved tug-of-war. Designers provide the setup, the infrastructure, and the tools that players use to craft—to varying degrees—their own characters, scenarios, and settings. The capacities for the authorship of a narrative are therefore perpetually negotiated over the course of gameplay between the designers' instituted rules, objects, opportunities, and constraints, and the players' assemblages and resulting emergent creations. Complicating this is the fact that players may string together and employ certain tools in ways the designers may not have anticipated. These unexpected forms of play may run up against author-intended functions as players carve out their own play space.

But we again run into the same issue that we saw with MMORPGs: to what extent is the player's conduct authorship, and to what extent is it interpretation? Do players actually have the power to influence or change the game work when they mold and experience emergent narratives?

Can play itself actually be an act of authorship? Miguel Sicart (2011) argued that this is the case. He wrote:

If there is an exceptionalist argument to be made about games, an argument that justifies that games as aesthetic form are different than others, it is that games belong to players—at most, games belong to the designer if she wants to establish dialogue with the player through the game—but play, the performative, expressive act of engaging with a game, contradicts the very meaning of authorship in games. Players don't need the designer—they need a game, an excuse and a frame for play. (para. 81)

Up until now, I have insisted upon a divide between the concretely-constructed work and the interpretive-field of text. While many previous examinations of video game authorship may have fallen into the trap of equating text and interpretation with work and authorship, the examples above have indicated that the divide between authorship and interpretation is very, very hard to maintain where video games are concerned. As video games and their technological affordances have evolved, they have muddled our very understanding of what creation and authorship might mean.

Two persistent and unanswered questions have hovered over this excursion into authorship: What is a video game work? And might the very idea of a work have changed in light of media artifacts such as video games?

While texts are generally understood to be fluid fields of interpretive possibilities, works are perhaps conceived of as static, bounded wholes. What I wish to suggest through this analysis is that the game work is a process. It is an unfinished process, always under negotiation, always in a state of becoming. Its materiality as a work is uncertain and unstable. But this instability gives rise to a realm of possibilities: modifications, restructurings, additions, retractions. Game works become eternal drafts, always inviting revisions, updates, and re-releases.

Distributed authorship recognizes and allows for this reconfiguration of work and text. By conceptualizing the authorship of video games as an interplay of negotiated capacities, it offers necessary flexibility with which to face the ever-metamorphosing challenges that video games pose to authorship. Moreover, it also accounts for the fact that these negotiated capacities are inextricably intertwined in networks of power. However, these networks of power are also not stiff or immutable. These relationships of power—among players, developers, publishers, so on—also fluctuate and shift.

In light of these moving dynamics of power, should we necessarily get rid of the distinction between work and text, between authorship and interpretation altogether? Or might there be a reason why we would wish to preserve authorship according to its more traditional concept? As I mentioned earlier, we cannot completely dismiss the concept of authorship; and one reason for it is that the power implications of an authorial status are not always the same.

Shifting the Power Dynamics

Players are not always underprivileged consumers that must battle against the profit-seeking conquests of powerful corporate entities. And game developers are not always capitalists that try to seize creative control from players for monetary gain. It is, therefore, neither responsible nor correct to always characterize developer-player relationships as such.

While development tools for video games have often been enormously expensive and under tight corporate control, some software—such as the free and open-source program Twine—are opening new opportunities for game design and creation. Twine has few barriers to entry, low technical requirements, and is relatively simple to use, while offering a great degree of malleability for creative expression. These games have become an outlet for marginalized voices, an opportunity for those from oppressed groups to create games on their own terms. As Laura Hudson (2014) has reported:

While roughly 75 percent of developers at traditional video-game companies are male, many of the most prominent Twine developers are women, making games whose purpose is to explore personal perspectives and issues of identity, sexuality and trauma that mainstream games rarely touch on. (para. 4)

She went on to remark that "the very nature of Twine poses a simple but deeply controversial question: Why shouldn't more people get to be a part of games? Why shouldn't everybody?" (para. 5).

In these negotiations for authorial capacities, though, players are not exploited creators struggling for rights over co-creation. Instead, they may be conceived as taking on a different role in a different kind of power relationship: as a hegemonic force infringing on a space that is not their own. In this case, the myth of the solitary author is not a rhetorical strategy to maintain a status quo of capitalist power relations—rather, it can be a moment of empowerment for people whose identities, experiences, and creations often go unheard and unnoticed in mainstream gaming.

In "Death of the Player"—an obvious reference to Barthes—Mattie Brice (2013) argued, "Gamers are trained to expect certain things from games, like explicit rules, goals, visual quality, and of course, agency. To put it frankly, gamers are set up to be colonial forces" (para. 6). Earlier, we discussed these expectations as a way for players to gain authorial authority from corporate powers. But here, we have a much different power dynamic in which players are instead colonizers that may further appropriate power from those that are oppressed.

Thus, when we examine the distributed authorship of video games and the latent power relations implied in negotiated creative capacities, we cannot always assume that players can or should have complete authorial control. Sometimes they may be hegemonic forces; and sometimes we may need to preserve the authority of solitary authors.

The authorship of video games is intricate, messy, and incessantly vacillating. To further understand the complexities of video game creation, the negotiations of creative power, and the nature of video game works as processes, we turn to a case study that represents an especially visible, explosive, and pivotal moment in the evolution of game authorship: the *Mass Effect 3* ending controversy.

CASE STUDY: THE *MASS EFFECT 3* ENDING CONTROVERSY

Within days of the March 6, 2012 release date of *Mass Effect 3* (BioWare), a series of player-generated polls, petitions, and forum posts appeared online that proclaimed a single demand: a change to the game's ending. What at first seemed to be merely scattered and unconnected gripes by a handful of disgruntled players rapidly evolved into an organized and unified protest movement primarily under the banner "Retake Mass Effect" on the "Demand a better ending to Mass Effect 3" Facebook page (Hornshaw, 2012). The Retake movement, its offshoots, and subsequent controversy surrounding the game's ending were unprecedented for video games at the time. While players had certainly asserted their opinions regarding video game creation previously, no such protest had then occurred of its size, scope, and magnitude. The movement expanded as tensions rose between protestors and the game developers, publishers, journalists, and critics that objected to their demands. Against the players' requests, opponents expressed concerns that any capitulation to players' demands would fundamentally compromise, undermine, and possibly destroy the game developers' artistic integrity.

Writing for the website *Destructoid*, video game journalist Jim Sterling (2012) commented during the early stages of the ending protests, "I suppose it's a testament to how engaging *Mass Effect* has been, that it's prompted such a heartfelt reaction from fans" (para. 5). Indeed, that engagement was frequently cited as a major impetus behind the players' insistence on a change to the ending. Above and beyond all other complaints, players noted that the ending made them feel stripped of their capacity for in-game choice-making, as well as their status as co-authors of the *Mass Effect* narrative. In fact, the very name "Retake Mass Effect" suggested that players believed they were reclaiming something that already belonged to them: their role, perhaps, as the game's co-creators.

To many protesters, each of the few possible endings was fundamentally the same, regardless of players' many previous choices throughout all three games or even the final concluding choice of *Mass Effect 3*. The *Mass Effect* trilogy was, perhaps, particularly primed to provoke such expectations—and such a backlash. Starting with the first installment of the trilogy released in November 2007, player choices—their protagonist, their protagonists' relationships, their narrative and plot decisions—were saved and carried over from one game to the next. Players could thus expect to see the consequences of their individual actions played out in each of the subsequent titles. And as a result, many players came to expect that this vast array of choices would also result in a vast array of possible endings.

Although the construction of an individual playthrough may be an interpretative act—and questionable as an authorial one—there is still clearly a power dynamic at work in these moments. Players understand themselves as authors of their experiences. And when they believe that they have been deprived of this power—or that developers or publishers have infringed on it by not including game content that would facilitate these monologistic processes—they may reach out to developers to reassert their authorial status and insist upon changes. These are the negotiated capacities of distributed authorship at work.

Some players were quick to suggest that the endings as given in the game perhaps contradicted developer commentaries prior to the game's release that had promised dramatically different outcomes based on player choices ("Mass Effect 3 Debacle," 2012). Certain protest methods were particularly illustrative of these concerns: for example, players created videos that offered comparisons of the similarities between endings (Crosscade, 2012) and even sent vanilla-flavored cupcakes to the game's developers at BioWare with red, blue, and green frosting to call attention to the fact that no matter what color was chosen, the flavor—the choice—was always the same (Schreier, 2012a). In short, players wanted new endings: most of all, more endings that better reflected the unique narrative constructions that they believed they had contributed to authoring.

But outrage over the ending was not targeted at the game's developers alone; in fact, many players doubted that BioWare had been left to decide the game's conclusion on its own. A number of these players suspected the tyrannical and exploitative involvement of BioWare's publisher, Electronic Arts (EA), as possibly being at fault.

Before the release of *Mass Effect 3*, BioWare announced that it would release a downloadable content (DLC) package entitled *From Ashes* on the same day as the game. Typically released months after a game's release to allow for feedback and for additional time for developers to complete the extra content, DLC has enabled the possibility of games being altered, updated, or expanded upon after their publication. That quality is one that is increasingly found in video games but that is encountered to a significantly less frequent degree in other media forms. As a result of the prevalence of these technological capabilities, players—and critics—have come to regularly anticipate patches or updates in response to their feedback, whether these are for fixes to glitches and bugs, or for substantial rewrites to game events.

On the other hand, DLC has also been blamed for publishers and developers making punishing, exploitative authorial decisions. Many publishers—such as Electronic Arts—are increasingly insisting that developers design DLC prior to a main game's release. These DLC packages may contain crucial information without which players may not be able to understand or complete elements of the game's plot, missions, or other gameplay threads. A current popular model for DLC release is through a season pass: players may pay substantial amounts of money—sometimes as much as the original game—to gain access to a set of pre-planned DLC packages. As a result, many players have grown wary of DLC releases, as more and more, the packaged products that they buy are incomplete, broken, and to be finished with later, expensive DLC.

And indeed, the *From Ashes* DLC contained a number of significant plot points for the main game—but for an additional cost of $10, unless players had already paid extra for the *Mass Effect 3* Collector's Edition (Schreier, 2012b). Many players were left asking: If *From Ashes* was already finished as of the game's release, why wasn't it included in the game itself? Why were BioWare and EA charging players additional costs for plot details that should have already been included in the game? Many players linked the pre-release furor surrounding the so-called Day-1 DLC to the controversy over the ending, accusing EA and BioWare of having intentionally released an incomplete game with the goal of publishing subsequent installments for which players would need to pay additionally if they wished to have the full experience of the game. Some players thus speculated that EA may have been responsible for the game's ending, perhaps even having forced BioWare to write the ending in a particular way that would allow for later DLC. What if, they wondered, the ending as it appeared in the game wasn't the *actual* ending? What if it was yet to be released—and would eventually appear in the form of an expensive DLC add-on? Suspicions of the publisher's ruthless, profit-seeking influence thus added another angle to the protests, fueling players' calls for a free DLC update that would reflect their wishes for changes to the ending.

However, Sterling (2012) continued his article by saying, "Still, to demand a game be rewritten to suit your own opinion of what makes a better ending could definitely be seen as a little arrogant" (para. 5). Such attitudes came to define much of the commentary about the Retake protests, with the concept of entitlement dominating in place of Sterling's arrogant. One of the first and perhaps most visible users of entitlement to describe the Retake protesters was game journalist Colin Moriarty of *IGN*. In an opinion video (2012), Moriarty declared of the ending controversy that "all this culminates in a huge problem which is entitlement." Using entitlement interchangeably with spoiled, Moriarty thereby sought to characterize Retake protesters as unfairly and angrily whining simply because *Mass Effect 3* did not end the way they had wanted.

Moriarty was far from the only critic of the Retake movement to use the language of entitlement to describe protesting players. Charlie Brooker (2012) described protesters as "spoiled little emperors with a mind-boggling sense of entitlement" (para. 9). In light of the controversy, Erik Norris (2012) posted an article that outlined three "Severe Cases of Gamer Entitlement." For an individual to be entitled to something generally indicates that they have a right to it. Yet the language of entitlement that commentators employed against the Retake protests suggested that the players were demanding access to a right that they neither had nor deserved: the right to contribute to the game's authorship.

Other critics built upon the idea of player entitlement, but focused their concerns on the implications that players' demands for a newly written ending would have for authorial integrity. These arguments drew upon the myth of the solitary author to defend BioWare's work and exclude players from the authorship process. Luke Plunkett (2012) expressed the concern that "there's a *very* big line to cross between being disappointed in the creative work of others and actively asking for it to be changed (or added to) to suit your own wishes" (para. 4). Jeff Marchiafava (2012) declared that

BioWare complying with these demands, in some form or another, is also unprecedented, and is a goodwill tactic that I believe will likely backfire. Not just in the sense that BioWare may compromise its artistic integrity to appease a disgruntled section of its fan base. I think it will blow up in the face of gamers. (para. 1)

While these are only a very few condemnations out of many leveled against Retake protesters, they demonstrate a strong sentiment that emerged throughout the *Mass Effect 3* ending controversy—the effort to preserve traditional conceptions of authorial integrity.

However, a number of critics and players observed that player participation in the authorship of video games was by no means an unprecedented notion. Many pointed to the case of *Fallout 3* (Bethesda, 2008), a situation similar to that of *Mass Effect 3*, though on a smaller scale. Players of *Fallout 3* that were dissatisfied with the ending expressed their thoughts to the game's parent studio Bethesda; the developers then put that commentary to use and subsequently released a DLC package that included new possible endings (Alexander, 2009). In fact, the *Mass Effect* series had already been shaped by similar contributions prior to *Mass Effect 3*. For instance, during an interview in 2010 about the making of *Mass Effect 2*, executive producer Casey Hudson indicated that certain romantic options for the game's protagonist Commander Shepard came about as a result of player interest and requests (Hudson, 2010). Thus, of course, player involvement in the authorship of video games was neither novel nor unprecedented at the time of the *Mass Effect 3* ending protests, despite the condemnations of some commentators.

There are, however, dangers to the potentials for these collective actions that cannot be overlooked. Speaking specifically of the protest movement following *Mass Effect 3*, Filipowich warned of the possibility that "a common interpretation gains hegemony and divergent voices are silenced or met with resistance or even outrage. Over time, satisfying those readers in power—whose interpretations are standard—becomes paramount" (para. 6). Filipowich's comments point to the interconnectedness of interpretation and creation in considerations of game authorship. Players may have favored interpretations of what a game can and should mean, but they may wish to see more concrete, material evidence of these interpretations in a game's content. These interpretations may conflict with those of the developers, as well as with those of other players. Again, players are not always underpowered groups. At other times, their efforts to exert authorial control may, in fact, be hegemonic, stamping out and silencing other voices.

Ultimately, on April 5, 2012—almost a month after the initial release of *Mass Effect 3*—BioWare announced its ongoing work on an "Extended Cut" DLC in response to player protests. The game studio denied that the DLC would substantively alter the ending, explaining in a blog post that the company "believes in the team's artistic vision for the end of this arc of the Mass Effect franchise" and therefore did not wish to significantly modify its artistic production ("Mass Effect 3 Extended Cut," 2012, para. 4). Nevertheless, the addition of DLC would serve to "provide a more fleshed out experience" (para. 1) as well as "help answer some questions and give closure to this chapter of the Mass Effect story" (para. 1) for free of charge to players. Despite BioWare's attempt to maintain that it would not fundamentally alter the ending, the Extended Cut nevertheless came about as a reply to the ending protests. The new content explicitly addressed a number of protester concerns, for instance by providing the aforementioned "more fleshed out experience" that included a greater range of alternate outcomes that more closely corresponded to the players' narrative choices. With the release of the Extended Cut, the developers at BioWare attempted to strike a balance: protecting their authorial intent while also answering the efforts of its player base to have the ending reconsidered and rewritten.

The *Mass Effect 3* ending controversy is illustrative of numerous aspects of distributed authorship. Players, developers, and publishers struggled for control of authorial capacities. Amidst the controversy, commentators invoked the myth of the solitary author to defend the artistic integrity of the developers—and, by extension, the decisions of BioWare's publisher, Electronic Arts. Meanwhile, the situation revealed a dismantling of those traditional concepts of authorship, proving that commonplace understandings of authorship cannot fully account for the ways that games are created and constructed. The changes to the ending also demonstrate that game works are a process. As we have seen, negotiations over a game's authorship may continue well after a game's release and may result not only in new interpretations of meaning, but also material changes to what composes the game's content and form.

CONCLUSION

We have faced many sticky, complicated questions throughout this investigation into video game authorship. Many of these questions have not yielded simple, clear-cut answers; in some cases, we have been left with ambiguous insights and boundaries that flicker, morph, or even fade away. What we have come to understand, though, is that the authorship of video games can't always be easily explained or answered with some simplified yes-or-no conclusion. Answering a question like "Who are the authors of a video game?" is not as simple as making a sweeping proclamation that players are or are not authors, as previous literature has suggested. Game authorship is contingent, fluctuating, and negotiated—it is not the same from one game to the next, or even from one moment to the next for a single game.

In response to these challenges, this chapter has provided a theoretical framework with which to conceptualize the intricacies of game authorship. Distributed authorship understands the creation of video games as a relationship of power and a negotiation of creative capacities, enabling more nuanced explorations into the making of video games. Further, its approach to authorship is flexible and dynamic, able to be adapted to circumstances that are always in the process of becoming. It moves beyond the constraints of previous concepts of authorship and allows us to analyze game creation in new ways. As such, it may also challenge longstanding beliefs in originality, creativity, artistic integrity, and authorial intention.

Even so, distributed authorship does not entirely do away with *authorship* as a capacity to influence or determine the content and form of a game work. Although we have witnessed the destabilizing influence of concepts such as emergent narrative and the ways that these may muddle the divide between authorship and interpretation, we cannot make a rash declaration that authorship should be definitively dismissed. One reason for this is the goal of bolstering the work of those in marginalized groups. Even if we agree that authorship is a socially constructed category, there are significant roles that these categories may play, from the societal positioning of particular works to interpretations of them. (And I highly doubt many academics would be willing to entirely forsake authorship, given the crucial importance we tend to place on publications, citations, and attributions).

While many scholars disdain analytical methods that would privilege authorial intention as a source of meaning-making, who we understand as being an author is nevertheless influential in our interpretations of texts. As I mentioned earlier in the chapter, authors influence the assemblages of works, and the assemblages of works influence the assemblages of texts. Even as many of us agree with Barthes (1968) that "the birth of the reader must be at the cost of the death of the Author" (p. 148), many of us nonetheless conduct textual analyses that presuppose particular authors. The most subjective or resistant of interpretive analyses may still draw conclusions that assume—however implicitly—certain sources of authorship, intention, and construction. Our perceptions of a game's authorship still color the ways we play and receive video games. For instance, when conducting ideological critiques, we assume that authors come from particular subject positions that may influence their inclusion of certain ideological viewpoints. To deal with such considerations, distributed authorship is equipped to comprehensively account for the ever-shifting processes that make up a game work.

Moreover, distributed authorship grants vital insights into the uneven, competing flows of power that are constantly in motion. We cannot make blanket statements that assign all players to oppressed status. While it is certainly important to keep in mind the capitalist structures behind much of game creation and publishing, players are not uniformly marginalized or even subversive. Often, they can be hegemonic, destructive, and oppressive. At times, their collective actions may give voice to diverse opinions and perspectives—but their efforts may lead to attempts to silence developers, critics, and scholars as they seek to have their opinions responded to and reflected in game creation. As capacities for game authorship continue to be negotiated and games continue to evolve, game authorship itself will continue to mutate and change. Distributed authorship offers one way of contending with these ongoing changes.

ACKNOWLEDGMENT

The author would like to thank June Deery for generously providing feedback during the writing of this chapter.

REFERENCES

Aarseth, E. (1997). *Cybertext: Perspectives on ergodic literature*. Baltimore, MD: Johns Hopkins University Press.

Alden. (2015, April 27). Removing payment feature from *Skyrim* workshop. [Web log]. *Steam Community*. Retrieved from http://steamcommunity.com/games/SteamWorkshop/announcements/detail/208632365253244218

Alexander, J. (2009, April 21). *Broken Steel* DLC makes *Fallout 3* endless on May 5. *Engaget*. Retrieved from http://www.engadget.com/2009/04/21/broken-steel-dlc-makes-fallout-3-endless-on-may-5/

Banks, J., & Humphreys, S. (2008). The labour of user co-creators. *Convergence*, *14*(4), 401–418.

Barthes, R. (1974). *S/Z* (R. Miller, Trans.). New York: Farrah.

Barthes, R. (1977). *Image, Music, Text* (S. Heath, Trans.). New York: Hill and Wang.

Bethesda Game Studios. (2008). *Fallout 3*. Bethesda Softworks.

BioWare. (2012). *Mass effect 3*. Electronic Arts.

Bogost, I. (2006). *Unit Operations*. Cambridge, MA: MIT Press.

Brice, M. (2013, October 29). The Death of the Player. [Web log]. *Alternate Ending*. Retrieved from http://www.mattiebrice.com/death-of-the-player/

Brooker, C. (2012, April 15). Some people are gay in space. Get over it. *The Guardian*. Retrieved from http://www.theguardian.com/commentisfree/2012/apr/15/charlie-brooker-gay-video-game

Charles, A. (2009). Playing with one's self: Notions of subjectivity and agency in digital games. *Eluda-mos. Journal for Computer Games Culture, 3*(2), 281–294. Retrieved from http://www.eludamos.org/index.php/eludamos/article/viewArticle/vol3no2-10/139

Crosscade. (2012, March 14). *Mass Effect 3*—Ending movie comparison—All the colors. [Online video clip]. *Youtube*. Retrieved from https://www.youtube.com/watch?v=rPelM2hwhJA

Dyer-Witheford, N., & de Peuter, G. (2009). *Games of empire: Global capitalism and video games*. Minneapolis: University of Minnesota Press.

Ede, L., & Lunsford, A. (1990). *Singular texts/Plural authors: Perspectives on collaborative writing*. Carbondale, IL: Southern Illinois University Press.

Obsidian Entertainment. (2015). *Pillars of Eternity*. PC: Paradox Interactive.

Fernández-Vara, C. (2014). *Introduction to game analysis*. New York, NY: Routledge.

Filipowich, M. (2013, November 29). From game to play: Roland Barthes, video games, and criticism. [Web log]. *Bigtallwords*. Retrieved from http://big-tall-words.com/2013/11/29/from-game-to-play/

Foucault, M. (1969/1977). What is an author? In *Language, counter-memory, practice* (D. F. Bouchard & S. Simon, Trans.). Ithaca, NY: Cornell University Press.

Friedlander, L. (2008). Narrative strategies in a digital age. In K. Lundby (Ed.), *Digital storytelling, mediatized stories: Self-representations in new media*. New York, NY: Peter Lang Publishing.

Hall, C. (2015, April 10). Obsidian's CEO on P*illars of Eternity* backer's hateful joke. *Polygon*. Retrieved from http://www.polygon.com/2015/4/10/8383627/pillars-of-eternity-transphobic-kickstarter-hate-feargus-urquhart

Hudson, C. (2010, June 15). Interview: BioWare's Case Hudson on the making of *Mass Effect 2* [Interview conducted by J. McElroy]. *Engaget*. Retrieved from http://www.engadget.com/2010/06/15/interview-bioware-casey-hudson-on-the-making-of-mass-effect-2/

Hudson, L. (2014, November 19). Twine, the video-game technology for all. *The New York Times Magazine*. Retrieved from http://www.nytimes.com/2014/11/23/magazine/twine-the-video-game-technology-for-all.html?_r=0

Jaszi, P. (1994). On the author effect: Contemporary copyright and collective creativity. In M. Wood-mansee & P. Jaszi (Eds.), *The construction of authorship: Textual appropriation in law and literature*. Durham, NC: Duke University Press.

Jenkins, H. (2004/2006). Game design as narrative architecture. In K. Salen & E. Zimmerman (Eds.), *The game design reader: A rules of play anthology*. Cambridge, MA: MIT Press.

Jennings, S. C. (2015). Passion as method: Subjectivity in video games criticism. *Journal of Games Criticism, 2*(1). Retrieved from http://gamescriticism.org/articles/jennings-2-1

Keogh, B. (2014). Across worlds and bodies: Criticism in the age of video games. *Journal of Games Criticism, 1*(1). Retrieved from http://gamescriticism.org/articles/keogh-1-1

Küklich, J. (2005). Precarious playbour: Modders and the digital games industry. *The Fiberculture Journal,* 5. Retrieved from http://five.fibreculturejournal.org/fcj-025-precarious-playbour-modders-and-the-digital-games-industry/

Landow, G. (1992). *Hypertext: The convergence of contemporary critical theory and technology.* Baltimore, MD: Johns Hopkins University Press.

Marchiafava, J. (2012, March 30). Why changing the *Mass Effect 3* ending is a mistake. *Game Informer.* Retrieved from http://www.gameinformer.com/b/features/archive/2012/03/30/why-changing-the-mass-effect-3-ending-is-a-mistake.aspx

Mass Effect 3 Debacle. (2012). *GameFAQs.* [Post by user nospacesinmyname as a repost of an original post by BioWare Social Network user cato_84, which has since been removed].

Mass Effect 3 extended cut. (2012, April 5). [Web log]. *BioWare Blog.* Retrieved from http://blog.bioware.com/2012/04/05/mass-effect-3-extended-cut/

Maxis. (2000). *The Sims.* Electronic Arts.

McWhertor, M. (2015, April 23). Valve now lets modders sell their work through Steam, starting with Skyrim. *Polygon.* Retrieved from http://www.polygon.com/2015/4/23/8484743/steam-mod-sales-workshop-skyrim

Meyers, R. E. (2014). *In search of an author: from participatory culture to participatory authorship* (Masters Thesis). Brigham Young University.

Moriarty, C. (2012, March 12). *Mass Effect 3: Opinion video.* [Online video clip]. IGN. Retrieved from http://www.ign.com/videos/2012/03/13/mass-effect-3-opinion-video

Murray, J. (1997). *Hamlet on the holodeck: The future of narrative in cyberspace.* New York: Free Press.

Norris, E. (2012, March 13). 3 severe cases of gamer entitlement. *CraveOnline.* Retrieved from http://www.craveonline.com/gaming/articles/184645-3-severe-cases-of-gamer-entitlement

O'Donnell, C. (2013). Wither *Mario Factory?:* The role of tools in constructing (co)creative possibilities on video game consoles. *Games and Culture, 8*(3), 161–180. doi:10.1177/1555412013493132

Plunkett, L. (2012, March 14). Charitable donations don't give you the right to ask for changes to *Mass Effect 3. Kotaku.* Retrieved from http://kotaku.com/5893119/charitable-donations-dont-give-you-the-right-to-demand-changes-to-mass-effect-3

Ryan, M. (2011). The interactive onion: Layers of user participation in digital narrative texts. In R. E. Page & B. Thomas (Eds.), *New narratives: Stories and storytelling in the digital age.* Lincoln, NE: University of Nebraska Press.

Schreier, J. (2012a, March 27). Gamers send BioWare 400 cupcakes. *Kotaku.* Retrieved from http://kotaku.com/5896847/gamers-send-bioware-400-cupcakes

Schreier, J. (2012b, February 23). *Mass Effect 3* DLC triggers fan outrage, BioWare response. *Kotaku.* Retrieved from http://kotaku.com/5887626/mass-effect-3-dlc-triggers-fan-outrage-bioware-response

Sicart, M. (2011). Against procedurality. *Game Studies, 11*(3). Retrieved from http://gamestudies. org/1103/articles/sicart_ap

Sterling, J. (2012, March 10). *Mass Effect 3* fans petition BioWare to change the ending. *Destructoid.* Retrieved from http://www.destructoid.com/mass-effect-3-fans-petition-bioware-to-change-the-ending-223615.phtml

Taylor, T. L. (2006). *Play between worlds: Exploring online game culture.* Cambridge, MA: MIT Press.

Valve. (1998). *Half-life.* Sierra Entertainment.

Valve. (1999). *Counter-strike.* Valve Corporation.

Woolf, N. (2014, December 3). *Star Citizen* sets crowdfunding record as players spend $65m on spaceships. *The Guardian.* Retrieved from http://www.theguardian.com/technology/2014/dec/03/star-citizen-crowd-funding-record-65m-game

KEY TERMS AND DEFINITIONS

Author: A socially constructed category, widely understood to be a single person who determines the content of a work.

Distributed Authorship: The interplay of negotiated capacities of a number of actors (including but not limited to developers, publishers, and players) to create the content, structures, form, and affordances of video game works.

Emergent Narrative: Rather than consisting of pre-written events and characters, emergent narratives are assembled and conjured by the actions of players out of the structures of video games.

Interactivity: A term frequently employed to define video games against other media forms by focusing on the involvement of the player; as such, it is a source of debate regarding the extent to which players are also authors of the games that they play.

Mods: Developer-provided or player-generated toolkits that facilitate the modification of video game content.

Video Game Text: Texts are ever-flowing pluralities of interpretive potentialities. Some areas of games criticism consider players to be part of game texts.

Video Game Work: Unlike a text, a work is the static container of the authored contents; a video game work is a negotiated process in a shifting state of becoming.

Chapter 7
She Designs Therefore She Is?
Evolving Understandings of Video Game Design

Carolyn Michelle Cunningham
Gonzaga University, USA

ABSTRACT

Girls and women play video games in equal number to boys, yet they continue to be under-represented in the video game industry. The goal of this chapter is to examine initiatives that encourage gender equality in video game design. This chapter argues that the process of becoming a video game designer may have the potential to shift girls' notions of identity. Drawing on research on girls and video game design, as well as analyses of informal programs that teach girls video game design, this chapter emphasizes the intersection of design and identity. This chapter offers directions and recommendations for future research, including the need for expanded understandings of the cultural and democratic benefits of video game design for girls.

INTRODUCTION

Free and open source software, such as Alice and Scratch, have arguably democratized video game design, making it more accessible to a broader and more diverse group of designers. This shift in the sources of video game design has opened up definitions of what constitutes a video game. Different aesthetics, different types of games, and different character representations are all part of this shift.

Despite the shift in video game design production, there continues to be persistent gender inequalities within the video game industry. Girls and women play video games in equal numbers to boys and men, yet they are under-represented in the video game industry (Entertainment Software Association, 2015). Currently, little more than ten percent of video game designers are women. Contemporary controversies, such as the widespread cyber-harassment of several female game designers collectively called Gamergate, have drawn renewed attention to the importance of increasing diversity in the video game industry (Rosen, 2015).

DOI: 10.4018/978-1-5225-0261-6.ch007

This lack of diversity in the sources of video game production leads to incessant and pervasive racist and sexist representations in games, reinforcing a masculine culture of gaming. Additionally, the under-representation of women in the video game industry stalls the potential for innovation and creativity. There are several explanations for gender inequality in the video game industry, including a perceived disinterest in video game playing by girls, structural inequalities in educational and corporate institutions, lack of female role models and mentors, and a hostile work environment that has led several female game designers to leave the industry.

Despite the many cultural and democratic reasons for women's inclusion in the video game industry, much of the discussion emphasizes economic rationales for gender equality. Economic rationales highlight the importance of gaining technical skills to enter the STEM workforce. For example, policy initiatives stress the growth of STEM fields and the importance of job creation and retention. Educational initiatives stress the importance of preparing girls and women to enter this growing industry.

Women's inclusion in the video game industry can provide new perspectives to the field as well as contribute to building and sustaining a more democratic video game industry. Gender inequality in technology is problematic for society at large. Educators suggest that video game playing can enhance students' 21st century skills (Gee, 2005; Prensky, 2006). Video game playing requires problem-solving, decision-making, simulation, and spatial reasoning, all important aspects of 21st century learning. Video game design can help students develop important computer programming skills that can apply to other science, technology, engineering, and mathematics (STEM) fields. Thus, if girls do not play video games and are not involved in video game design, they are excluded from participating fully in society.

In the 1990s, several informal education programs emerged as a strategy for attracting girls to STEM fields. Despite these efforts, there have been little gains in gender parity in STEM fields in the United States. In fact, recent numbers show the numbers are declining down from 35 percent in the 1980s to 12 percent today (Vermeer, 2014)

One area that may shed light on this stall is the ideologies present in video game design programs for girls. While these programs have similar objectives of improving girls' technical proficiencies, they have different strategies for accomplishing these aims. Each program emphasizes different economic, cultural, and democratic rationales for why girls should be video game designers. Economic rationales, that highlight girls' entrance into the industry, may not resonate with girls, especially since the industry is dominated by male video game designers. Additionally, popular stories of video game designers do not highlight how workers may be able to balance work and family life, a concern that would be useful to communicate to girls. The objective of this chapter, then, is to understand the ideologies present in the development of games marketed toward girls and in informal video game design programs for girls. A common thread in these programs is that beyond learning the technical skills of video game design, video games can shift girls' perspectives, offering them opportunities to express themselves, challenge normative sexist and racist representations, and create social change.

BACKGROUND

Video Games and STEM: From Entertainment to Necessity

Since the 1980s, there has been growing concern that the U.S. is falling behind other industrialized countries in STEM education. Currently, the U.S. ranks 25th in the world for mathematics and 17th in science

(U.S. Department of Education, 2015). This positioning is problematic because STEM occupations are the fastest growing and highest paying in the country. Thus, there is widespread agreement that there will not be a supply of U.S. students to meet the job demands, establishing an economic rationale for encouraging youth to pursue STEM careers.

Beyond the economic importance of youth pursuing STEM careers, many scholars and educators cite the development of 21st century skills as essential to all aspects of social, cultural, and civic life. Twenty-first century skills include problem-solving, decision-making, collaboration, and creativity, in addition to technical proficiency (Prensky, 2006). Video games can help promote twenty-first century skills, especially deduction and hypothesis testing, abstract thinking, and visual and spatial processing, key concepts of computer programming. Video games create a learning environment in which players make connections between activities and tools within the environment (Winn, 2002). Often, video games are valued for promoting constructivist learning (Denner, Werner, & Ortiz, 2012; Dondlinger, 2007). Constructivism is the theory that students construct their own ideas about the world through experience and reflection. Playing video games requires exploration, interaction, and manipulation, all characteristics of active learning. As Denner, Werner, and Ortiz (2012) found, computer game design was useful for developing three key computer science competencies: programming, organizing and documenting code, and designing for usability.

As the category "video games" continues to expand, educators are understanding their learning potentials. For example, McGonigal (2011) lauds the learning that can come from pro-social games, such as attitudinal or behavioral change. Serious games have the potential to teach about health, empathy, and compassion, important elements of a healthy society (Connolly et al., 2012). Finally, there is a trend toward gamification, or introducing game-thinking, in the public and private sectors to solve problems and enhance collaboration (Zicherman & Cunningham, 2011).

Policy efforts to address the STEM gap have included increased funding for K-12 STEM education. In 2013, President Obama announced an initiative to create STEM-focused schools. He framed STEM learning as important for a range of the systems that we depend on, including environment, national security, health, and energy.

The importance of video games and STEM education is reflected in the National STEM Video Game Challenge, started in 2010 and supported by public and private interests. As the website states,

Game design is a promising area of innovation in STEM learning. Research suggests that empowering youth to create their own video games promotes learner independence. Moreover, it encourages youth to take ownership over STEM knowledge, rather than viewing it as belonging to others. Thereby ushering them into STEM communities of practice. (http://www.stemchallenge.org/stem/#/whygames)

The Challenge includes a resource website that explain how video game design teaches computational thinking and fundamentals of computer programming.

Video Games and Informal Learning

While STEM curriculum is becoming a mainstay in K-12 schools, informal education is an important component in bridging the STEM gap (Denner et al., 2008). Informal education can occur in a variety of settings, such as workshops, afterschool programs, or youth groups. In general, informal education is defined as education that occurs outside of the traditional school setting.

Because public schools have limited resources and many demands, informal education programs can offer supplemental education to students. These programs extend learning beyond the confines of the classroom day, offering breadth and depth of knowledge. Students can explore their own interests, while being part of a larger group or community of interest. Through informal education programs, students are exposed to subjects that may not be taught in K-12 classes. Informal education, then, can deepen understanding, spark interest in a new subject, and increase students' confidence.

As several scholars point out, informal education programs are the predominant places in which twenty-first century learning is taught to youth (Schwarz & Stolow, 2006; Wilson, 2006). There continues to be a digital divide where many youth attending these programs do not have access to computers and the Internet in their homes and these programs become important places for them to engage in technological learning. They aim to offer a "third space" where youth can engage with digital technologies, while also form relationships with adult role models and mentors, engage in activities with their peers, and develop some "real-world" skills, such as information about careers (Wilson, 2006).

Informal education can incorporate a youth development framework that engages students in the broader community, especially for low-income and minority youth. It is estimated that 8.4 million children participate in an average of 14.5 hours of afterschool programs a week (Afterschool Alliance, 2012). Students from under-represented populations participate more. Twenty four percent of African American students, 21 percent of Hispanic students, and six percent of Native American students participate in afterschool programs (Afterschool Alliance, 2009). Thus, these programs have the potential to increase diversity in STEM.

Within these programs, there is a range of approaches to address barriers to equality in STEM. While some of these programs are technical and skill-based in nature, others incorporate a youth development model, which aims to raise self-esteem and promote civic engagement. Self-esteem is especially important for minority groups who often need to assimilate or acculturate into a dominant culture. Additionally, minority students often experience stereotype threat, where teachers from dominant groups may treat students a certain way based on stereotypes. Stereotype threat occurs when people feel they may confirm negative stereotypes about their social group. Stereotype threat can undermine girls' and women's interest and performance in STEM-related fields (Shapiro & Williams, 2012). For example, Shapiro and Williams (2012) found that negative cultural stereotypes about girls' math abilities shape girls' attitudes about their own math abilities, impacting their performance.

Girls and STEM Education

Informal education is especially important for increasing gender equality in STEM. Currently, only 12 percent of computer science majors are female. Seventy-four percent of girls say they are interested in STEM, but they do not enroll in those majors (Girl Scouts, 2015). And, the numbers are far worse for Hispanic, African-American, and American Indian women (AAUW, 2015).

Researchers identify a "leaky pipeline" to STEM education and careers that begins in elementary school. This pipeline is rooted in emotional, cultural, and structural explanations. While girls perform equal if not better than boys in math, by middle school, girls become less confident in their abilities. Research shows that girls' negative attitudes about ICTs can limit their ability to achieve their full potential and can be a hindrance to social equality (AAUW, 2000; Barker & Aspray, 2006; Cooper & Weaver, 2003; Fancsali, 2002). Psychologists suggest that in middle school, girls experience a crisis in self-esteem, where they begin to become aware that there are different social roles and expectations for girls and boys (Pipher, 1994). Girls recognize that, in a patriarchal society, their physical attributes are valued more than their intellectual capabilities (Brown & Gilligan, 1992). This crisis of self-esteem can have potential systemic ramifications. If girls do not pursue advanced math and science courses in middle school and high school, they will not enter the pipeline into STEM careers.

In addition to a loss of self-confidence in their abilities, girls recognize that there are different social values attached to different careers and academic subjects. Computer science and engineering, in particular, are associated with masculinity. Although researchers identify several other factors contributing to girls' negative attitudes and beliefs about ICTs, including teachers' expectations, parents' expectations, and stereotypical media representations that portray females as incompetent with digital technologies, research shows that girls continue to adopt these negative stereotypes about gender and computers, influencing their attitudes and beliefs about their own abilities to succeed in these pathways (AAUW, 2000; Furger, 1998; Owens, Smothers, & Love, 2003; Sadker & Sadker, 1995; Steinke, 1999).

According to the AAUW's (2000) report *Tech Savvy: Educating Girls in the New Millennium*, girls have an "I can, but I don't want to" attitude (p. ix). Girls believe they have the ability to perform different computer-related tasks, yet they are uninterested in the ways in which computer classes are taught, associating the curriculum with a masculine culture that does not incorporate their interests.

Finally, there are structural barriers to gender equality in STEM. Shumow and Schmidt (2014) found that science teachers spend 39 percent more class time directly addressing boys. Over the course of a month, this adds up to 40 minutes, or an entire class period. Surprisingly, these behaviors were not related to a teacher's gender. Thus, it cannot be assumed that the identity of a teacher may lead to more equal treatment in the classroom.

Title IX prohibits sex-discrimination in educational programs that receive federal funding, prohibiting a structural change that would include all-girl classrooms that may counteract these emotional, cultural, and structural barriers to STEM. Instead, there has been success with all-girl informal STEM education programs. Evaluation suggests that strategies such as providing girls with adult role models, tailoring curriculum to girls' interests, and emphasizing collaboration, can have a positive effect on girls' learning, especially in relation to STEM subjects (Crowe, 2003; Fancsali, 2002).

When it comes to video games and STEM, the questions to ask are no longer about whether or not video games are useful to education, but instead how to ensure that video games are inclusive. In other words, it is important to ask how female-oriented design encourages constructivist learning environments. How do video game include design elements that engage both male and female participation? And, how do educators and parents communicate to girls the importance of game design?

MAIN FOCUS OF THE CHAPTER

Issues: Gender and Video Games

In general, research on gender and video games suggests that mainstream video games portray female characters in stereotypical ways (Williams et al., 2009). Male characters are over-represented in video games. In their study titled "A Virtual Census," Williams et al. (2009) found that male characters comprised 89 percent of the top 100 selling games. When female characters did appear, their appearance was hypersexualized, represented by overly large breasts, thin waists, and revealing clothing (Down & Smith, 2009). These representations can be discouraging to female players (Walkerdine, 2007).

Not only are female characters physically represented in stereotypical ways, their roles within the games tend to be passive. They are rarely the protagonists. Instead, female characters are often victims of violence, submissive, or "damsels in distress" that need to be rescued by male protagonists. For example, in the controversial video game *Grand Theft Auto: Sin City* players can have sex with a prostitute, then kill her and take their money back. Negative portrayals of female characters in violent video games can reinforce stereotypes of women as submissive and valued for their beauty over their intellect. These representations also can lead to a low self-image among girls and women and discourage them from being video game players.

The limited ways in which females are portrayed in video games has been a subject of concern for female video game players. In 2013, Anita Sarkeesian created a series of YouTube videos discussing gender tropes in video games (Feminist Frequency, 2015). She identified five common stereotypes of female characters in videogames, including damsel in distress, fighting sex toy, sexy sidekick, sexy villainess, and females as background decoration. The reception of her work has been controversial. Sarkeesian is a victim of harassment, and has received rape threats, death threats, and hate mail. This example shows the challenge that is faced by females when they try to shift dominant perspectives about video games (Marcotte, 2012).

In addition to the sexist representations of female characters, researchers have suggested that girls do not like the type of gameplay that is available in most mainstream video games. Most popular video games such as *Call to Duty* center around violence. Instead, research suggests that girls prefer classic board games, card games, quizzes, and puzzles, while boys prefer shooting games, sports, and fantasy role-playing (Jansz, 2005). Of course, not all popular video games include violence. *The Sims* is a good example of a video game that has appeal for both girls and boys (Beavis & Charles, 2005; Gee & Hayes, 2010).

Finally, lack of social interaction and competitiveness are seen as negatively impacting girls' experiences of video games (Hartmann & Klimmt, 2006). Lucas and Sherry (2004) argue that girls prefer games that encourage social interaction and communication. Many mainstream games, such as first-person shooter games, can be played with others but do not encourage communication. Additionally, girls tend to avoid competitive games (Agosto, 2004; Lucas & Sherry, 2004).

The Rise of Girl Games: Broadening Definitions of "Video Games"

The 1990s saw a rise in video games marketed toward girls. In general, girls' games offered an alternative to popular mainstream video games, such as first-person shooter games, that were not appealing to girls. This genre of games includes gameplay that revolves around narrative development (instead of shooting people) and offers a range of female characters that girls can identify with.

There were two main strategies to broaden the definition of video games and capture the girl game market. First, there were a number of traditionally feminine, or "pink" games that were on-boarded. "Pink" games center around gender-specific activities, such as cooking and clothing. *Barbie Fashion Designer* is often cited as one of the most successful girl games. In this PC game, players designed clothing and accessories for their Barbie dolls. *Barbie Fashion Designer* is significant because it does not engage players in pretend play, such as in first-person shooter games, but instead allows girls to create objects and engage in play that they find compelling (Subrahmanyam & Greenfield, 1998). In this way, the software makes the computer "yet another accessory for Barbie play. The computer takes on the role of a tool and, unlike other games, ceases to be an end unto itself" (Subrahmanyam & Greenfield,

1998, p. 59). The computer is no longer a machine, but rather a "tool in the player's imaginative play" (Subrahmanyam & Greenfield, 1998, p. 59).

In the 1990s, several female game designers started their own companies and marketed games directly to girls. These included HerInteractive, started in 1995 whose most notable games centered on Nancy Drew, a mainstay in girls' popular culture. Purple Moon, started by Brenda Laurel, offered games designed around storytelling and exploration, as opposed to competition.

A second strategy to attract a female audience was to introduce stronger female characters into available games. In 1996, the British Company Core Design launched *Tomb Raider*, which featured the female protagonist Lara Croft, an archaeologist who ventures into ancient tombs and ruins. Instead of being submissive, as female characters are often portrayed in mainstream video games, Croft is portrayed as tough, competent and dominant. Croft is also depicted as an athletic woman, and her outfit consists of a sleeveless tank top, shorts, combat boots, a utility belt and a backpack. While Croft's design did challenge dominant representations of femininity, she is still sexualized through her exaggerated breasts and thin waist. Many critics have argued that Croft is conceived in terms of male, rather than female, pleasure (Jansz & Martis, 2007).

Others cite Jill Valentine from *Resident Evil* or Princess Zelda from *The Legend of Zelda* as strong female characters (MacCallum-Stewart, 2008). However, it should be noted that these characters, who play active role in narrative, are few and far between and have been received differently by male and female players.

Controversies: Have Girl Games Shifted Perspectives?

Since the 1990s, technological advances and expanded notions of gender have transformed the ways in which gender is portrayed in video games. Academic researchers and female game designers have argued that there are many differences among girls' interests that should be reflected in the games available for girls. As Kafai et al. (2008) have argued, there is a better understanding within gaming communities that gender is "situated, constructed, and flexible" (p. xvi). Kafai (2008) writes about three different approaches in the genre of girl games: games for girls that promote femininity, games for change that support gender play by challenging stereotypes, and games as design that position girls as creators of their own learning

While "pink" games are still around, there are more diverse offerings that offer a wide array of characters and types of gameplay that are attractive to both male and female players, as can be seen in the popularity of games such as *Second Life*. One game that has been popular among female players is *The Sims* (Gee & Hayes, 2010). The game centers on designing and building material objects, such as houses, furniture, landscape, and clothes. Additionally, players become part of the larger community of *Sims* players on the Internet, and they become co-constructors of meaning (Beavis & Charles, 2005; Jansz, Avis, & Vosmeer, 2010).

Another recent trend is to redefine what gaming for girls is. Since gaming is still perceived as a masculine domain, the idea is to change the construction of the identity of a gamer to allow for a feminine gamer. In 2012, Nintendo launched *Style Savvy: Trendsetters* for the 3DS. In the game, players take on the role of fashion designers, managing their own boutique and helping customers find the perfect outfit. Marketing materials for the game clearly target female players. The website features screenshots of female avatars trying on dresses, hats, and stilettos. A television commercial for *Style Savvy* features Sara Hyland, who plays a teenager on the hit show *Modern Family*. In the commercial, Hyland is in her bedroom, talking about fashion as she selects clothes and hairstyles for the main character on her pink handheld DS. At the end of the commercial, she looks into the camera and states, "My name is Sarah Hyland and I'm not a gamer. With My 3DS, I'm a stylist" (Nintendo, 2012). The overall message is that girls can play the 3DS and still maintain their femininity. The commercial challenges the dominant stereotype of videogame players as both male and nerdy. As Hyland suggests, the 3DS and the game she is playing can offer a different, feminine experience for girls.

Problems: Girls in Flux: Challenging the Category of "Girls"

Several scholars have commented on the limitations of the category of "girl" games (Alison, 2009; Denner et al., 2005; Seiter, 1993). As Flanagan (2005) points out, creating the category of "girl" creates murky territory that can lead to generalizations about the type of games girls like to play. As she writes, if designers want to work toward gender equality, then they need to recognize the diverse needs of girls themselves. Girl games may reinforce stereotypes of femininity and limit possibilities for innovation. She points out that some girls like traditional girl play, such as games focused on fashion, while others like more "masculine" violent games, such as *Call of Duty*.

Dickey (2006) is also critical of the attention to "girl" games. She is critical of how girls' games emphasize gendered interests. As she writes, "existing research into gender and what females want in gameplay is too often predicated on the notion that gender is a static construct" (Dickey, 2006, p. 789). As a result, she writes that its important to ask whose notion of femininity is being portrayed in girl games. Girl games tend to rely on gendered stereotypes which can reinforce, rather than challenge, gender norms.

One way to understand this shift is through design rather than consumption of video games, an emerging study of academic research. Analyses of girls as video game designers show that when girls make games, girls prefer not only less violence, but also different types of characters, types of games, and game environments. Given the chance to design their own games, girls choose to create their own worlds and characters, "compensating for the sexism and violence found in many video games" (Kafai, 1998, p. 109).

SOLUTIONS AND RECOMMENDATIONS

Girl Game Designers

Since the 2000s, there have been a number of informal education programs for girls and video game design. While these programs all aim to expose girls to the mechanics of video game design, they have different strategies for achieving these goals. One common theme is shifting girls' perspectives through using video game design as a medium for exploring identity and self-expression.

Video Games and Identity

Since the culture of technology, and gaming, is perceived as a masculine domain, it is believed that girls need to develop "tech-savvy" identities to see their potential in these domains. This requires challenging stereotypes and moving beyond accepted norms. As Bettie (2003) writes, those who succeed in computer science must negotiate identities that reject negative stereotypes and maintain cultural identity. As Denner et al. (2005) write in describing the *Girls Creating Games* program, "we put girls in the role of designer by teaching them to program an interactive computer game" (p. 90). Game design "puts girls in the role of technology leaders, which can break down personal identity barriers as well as external barriers, such as gender role stereotyping and discrimination" (p. 90). Thus, one of the main goals of many informal education programs is for girls to take on a "tech-savvy self-identity" (p. 95). A tech savvy identity is one in which girls feel confident in their technical abilities and identify as video game designers.

In addition to participating in all-girl environments that encourage girls to take on tech-savvy identities, the medium of game design can offer girls a space to explore identity, especially contradictions of being a woman in U.S. society. In their analyses of girl-created games, Denner, Bean, and Werner (2005) found that themes included personal triumph, like making a sports team, working through fears, such as getting in trouble (detention or being grounded), the threat of violence, negative repercussions for relationships (such as social exclusion). Games also included making moral decisions, such as working hard or having fun. Interestingly, they found that only 53 percent of the games involved the theme of helping other people, even though this is an assumption in research that focuses on girls and video games. Finally, the games allowed flexibility in choosing gender. Denner, Bean, and Werner (2005) write,

Our research suggests that when given the opportunity, girls design games that challenge the current thematic trends in the gaming industry. In particular, they use humor and defiance of authority to play with gender stereotypes and reject the expectation that girls are always well-behaved. Through their games, the girls have shown us new ways to make games and new ways to play. (p. 8)

Thus, game design can be a site for girls to resist and transform traditional stereotypes.

These findings mirror research on other forms of girls' media production (Kearney 2006). For example, Stern (2004) found that the content of online home pages allowed adolescents opportunities for self-expression and self-disclosure, which she argues is a necessary component of adolescent development. Since adolescents often have limited opportunities to express themselves in public fora, online spaces and multimedia tools provide alternatives for adolescents' expression. Web pages allowed girls an outlet where they could explore their unique experiences of being girls, such as physical changes brought on by puberty, experiences with dating, and emotional development. Stern's analysis of girls' home pages showed that girls often used these online spaces for self-disclosure, self-expression, cathartic release, discussions of their emotions and to develop relationships.

Girls' Experiences with Video Game Design

In the section, the researcher offers insight about girls' experiences with video game design through interviews and observations of girls who participated in a Girl Scouts video game design program in Central Texas.[1] This program was offered as both a four-hour workshop for Girl Scout troops, ages 11-15, as well as part of a larger summer camp titled *Groovy Games for Girls,* ages 8-16. This research draw from a situated learning perspective, which sees individual development as influenced by cultural factors (Gee, 2004; Lave & Wenger, 1991). A situated approach looks at the context of girls' technological learning and asks how girls' engagement in cultural practices allow them to take on different types of technological identities, such as video game designers (Hug, 2007). As noted in the previous section, construction of "tech-savvy" identities is especially important for increasing gender equality in video game design, since girls often report that they are disenchanted with the masculine culture of gaming.

Background of the Program

Since its inception in the early 1900s, the Girl Scouts have emphasized the connection between girls' self-development and their involvement in the broader community. The program encourages girls' physical, social, and emotional development. To this end, the program provides girls with activities to pursue their own interests and encourages leadership opportunities. The Girl Scouts Technology Center (GTC)[2] aims to fulfill the mission of the Girl Scouts by increasing girls' 21st century skills, preparing them to pursue their own interests, such as hobbies and leisure activities, opening up new career opportunities, and applying their learning to develop service projects to better their communities.

The GTC aims to bridge the digital divide. While many of the girls who use the GTC have access to home computers, there is a range of the quality of this access. Many of the girls in the program have outdated computers that cannot handle current applications or they have to share computers with other family members. Because of their limited access to computers, they may not be as confident in their technological abilities. As Hargittai (2010) argues, while physical access to computers and the Internet has become more affordable and available, there continue to be significant differences in how youth use computers.

The Animated Game Design Workshop was advertised in the Girl Scouts' quarterly publication *Possibilities* with the following description:

Create an animated game to publish on-line or email to your friends! Use the Flash development environment to create and import artwork into your game. Storyboard your game using action scripting to bring it alive! At the end of the day you'll take a copy of your game home on a CD!

In the Animated Game Design Workshop, which took place over a four-hour period, girls learned how to create their own *Girl Scout Style* game. Using Flash, the girls learned to design their own main character, a Girl Scout, along with clothes and accessories that they could drag and drop onto the character. In the workshop and camps, the girls also learned how to use the drawing tools, group objects together, import objects, and write action script to make their objects move within the program. This game is similar to *Barbie Fashion Designer*, yet rather than choosing from a range of pre-made clothing, girls learned to design their own outfits, choose their own colors, and write computer code to make the objects move.

Why Did Girls Participate?

Eleven girls, ages 11-15, and three parents attended the workshop. In total, six girls were white, four girls were Latina, and there was one African American girl.

In interviews with the girls about why they wanted to participate in the workshop, many of them emphasized that they wanted to learn about different careers. Erin, a 13 year-old Latina in the 7th grade, attended the workshop with her mother. Erin was interested in gaining exposure to a range of career opportunities and learning about what education she needed to pursue those interests.

Jennifer, a 15 year-old white girl, attended the workshop with her father. Jennifer is an artist who brought a sketchbook with her that contained her Japanese anime drawings. Jennifer's father was eager to speak with me about how weekend technology classes were a way for the two of them to spend time together. His work in the biotechnology industry required that he travel extensively during the week.

Weekend technology classes were a way for the two of them to participate in activities they both enjoyed, while also helping Jennifer to become technologically literate.

Abby and Allie also spoke about how they enjoyed attending Girl Scout workshops so that they could spend time together. For them, they stressed the social interaction as the biggest benefit to participating.

Other girls spoke about how the workshop would offer increased access to technology. For example, Diane spoke about how participating in the workshop would allow her to have greater access to computers, since her home computer was outdated and this workshop gave her access to the latest software and fast computers.

Interviews with girls offer some insight into why they may be interested in learning video game design. For some, exploring career options are important. Other girls may be interested in spending time with friends and family. There are also some girls who want access to newer technology to increase their own cultural capital. In other words, video game design is not just about gaining technical skills, but is also situated within larger social and cultural contexts that can be appealing to girls.

What Were Girls' Experiences in the Classroom?

Greg Herman, an instructor at a local community college, was the workshop facilitator. In observations of the classroom, Herman emphasized a skill-based approach to teaching, in which he showed the girls how to master different features of the software program. While some girls easily picked up on this approach to teaching, other girls got lost and confused easily, reflecting different levels of technological literacy. Herman could sense that girls were not following and periodically would ask questions of the girls to gauge their learning. For example, one of the first tasks Herman had the girls complete was to draw shapes in "object drawing mode." Many girls commented that they did not understand how to perform this task and were frustrated that their screen looked differently than the one projected in front of the room. Abby, a 13-year old white girl, raised her hand and said, "I'm confused." Karen, also 14, commented, "I don't get it." When girls were confused, Herman's approach was to help girls individually, rather than explain the steps to the entire classroom several times or to pair the girls up with those who understood the steps.

One of the goals of programs like this one is to increase girls' confidence in their technological abilities. In this case, it is important to ask how the gender of the teacher as well as the instructional strategies helped or hindered the girls' learning. Some of the girls appeared apprehensive about a male teacher. For example, both Abby and Allie were shy and hesitant to ask Herman questions when they did not understand. Throughout the workshop, Abby raised her hand a few times to ask questions of Herman. When she spoke, she tended to whisper her question, indicating her apprehension with the male adult teacher. Too often, accomplishing a task is the main goal in teaching computer programming. However, boys and girls are socialized to communicate differently in the classroom. Boys may express more confidence in their abilities, even though both girls and boys tend to perform the same in math classes at the middle school level (Girl Scouts, 2015). It is during adolescence that girls begin to pick up on cultural stereotypes that emphasize a negative relationship between females and math. Thus, there is a concern that girls may experience stereotype threat, or the feeling that they will live up to that stereotype. In this instance, it may be important for teachers to understand these dynamics so that they can increase girls' confidence in their abilities.

In interviews with both Isabella, a 14-year old Latina girl, and Karen, they spoke about how they did not really understand most of what they learned. This was evident in their final project which was not completed. However, when asked if they enjoyed attending the workshop, they both commented that they were happy to have a completed project and responded that they had fun during the workshop.

While many of the girls had difficulty following along with the instruction, both Angie and Victoria figured out the steps quickly and waited quietly while Herman helped the girls who did not understand. Angie, a 12-year old African American girl, seemed especially confident in her learning. She switched back and forth between the Flash program and a game of Solitaire while she waited for Herman to explain the next steps. However, there was little opportunity in the classroom to offer Angie some more advanced skills because the teacher spent so much time on the girls who did not understand.

Expressions of Identity in Girls' Video Games

In observations in the classroom and analyses of girls' finished projects, girls appeared to be motivated by the design elements of the game, which allowed them to make the main character look more like them. Girls used the game as a medium for self-expression to develop their own ideas about fashion and taste. They were also motivated by the ability to customize the features of the game, such as the color backgrounds, hairstyles, accessories or clothing, to reflect their own sense of style. Erin, for example, chose to draw several different blond and brown hairstyles for her main character doll.

Not all girls chose to design traditionally feminine accessories for their doll. Jennifer, who attended the workshop with her father and did not interact with the other girls, did not identify as traditionally feminine, like the other girls in attendance. Many of the girls' designs emphasized feminine colors, like pink and purple, and feminine clothing, like skirts and high heels. Instead, Jennifer's design reflected her own gender-neutral style. She dressed in all black and baggy clothing. In her project, she used the medium of the video game to reflect this style, with her palate including a main character with long bangs, dyed black hair, skate shoes, and a baggy t-shirt.

In addition to the range of gender performances by girls in the class, it is also important to attend to the racial and ethnic differences among the girls. As Herman was demonstrating how to design the game, he used a white girl as the prototype. This lack of diversity was immediately apparent to Angie, the only African American in the room. As Herman explained how to change the background colors, Angie raised her hand and asked how she could change the color of her doll's skin. It was clear that Herman, who was white, did not anticipate this question. He then demonstrated how to change the skin tone on the main character. Interestingly, the other non-white girls in the classroom began to experiment with different shades for their characters as well.

While the software had the capacity for girls to create different representations, it is important to ask why the program did not account for diversity in the design, given that one of the goals of the program is to increase diversity in STEM. While girls may be able to use video game design for self-expression, it is important to understand how informal education programs see the limits or bounds of this self-expression. In the example of Jennifer, it was clear that she identified as not traditionally feminine in her dress and was able to use video game design to reflect this. However, the demonstration by the teacher used a stereotypical example of a main character with feminine accessories. In the example of Angie, there were assumptions that a white female prototype would be universal and resonate with girls. If girls can use video game design as a medium for self-expression and identity-formation, then it is important to recognize differences among girls. In order to work toward gender equality, this is essential. How can informal education programs work toward inclusivity, especially in terms of race, class, sexual orientation, and able-bodiedness, among other things?

Girls' approaches to their projects suggest the need for informal education programs to better understand how video game design can offer girls increased opportunities to represent their own interests and experiences. Girls seemed motivated to learn computer programming not so that they could master a skill, but instead so they could learn how to better apply their learning to develop projects that reflected their own sense of identity. In order to interest a diverse group of girls in video game design, it is important to understand that there are many differences among girls, which can affect how girls approach video game design.

Beyond the Classroom: Strategies to Attract Girls to Video Game Design

Research suggests that video game design is important for forming girls' tech-savvy identities, yet little research has examined the underlying rationales for encouraging girls to be video game designers. This section includes qualitative content analyses of ten informal video game design programs for girls. Qualitative content analysis is a method for describing the meaning of the qualitative data, in this case images, text, and video on websites (Schrier, 2014). This study adapts Raphael et al.'s (2006) study of portrayals of ICTs on websites that encourage girls in STEM. The present study identifies the extent to which these programs incorporate economic, cultural, and civic (or democratic) rationales of video game design. Economic rationales emphasize the importance of gaining technical skills to enter the STEM workforce and pursue education in STEM pathways. Cultural rationales emphasize the importance of video game design for self-expression, creativity, and communication. Democratic rationales emphasize the importance of video game design for helping girls to participate in the broader society, whether through using video game design to create social change or developing twenty-first century skills that can help girls in other fields.

Like Raphael et al. (2006), this study argues that since not all girls will enter into video game design, informal education programs should not only emphasize economic rationales. There are other justifications for why girls should become familiar with video game design, especially for self-expression and civic engagement. Civic engagement is important because there are decisions made about the technological world, such as network neutrality, privacy and security, and cyber-harassment that citizens need to engage in. Additionally, video games are increasingly used in educational and corporate settings, pointing to the importance of girls' participation.

Sample

It is unlikely that any study could fully identify all of the available programs for girls, especially given the vastness of the web. The sites chosen were ones that were commonly referred to in directories for STEM programs for girls, such as the National Girls Collaborative Project. Additionally, these programs have received national press coverage. This study was limited to the United States, although some of the programs have locations outside of the U.S., such as in Canada. More research could look at the global reach. Table 1 lists the sample.

Research Design

The websites were the unit of analysis. Content, which included testimonials by program staff and participants, "About Us" pages, mission and vision statements, and promotional materials, was evaluated to

Table 1. Video game programs for girls

Program Name	URL	Year Started	Locations
App Camp for girls	http://appcamp4girls.com/	2013	Oregon, Washington, British Columbia
Black Girls Code	https://www.blackgirlscode.org	2012	San Francisco, CA
CompuGirls	https://sst.clas.asu.edu/compugirls	2007	Arizona, Colorado
Geek Girl Camp	http://geekgirlcamp.com/	2006	USA
Girl Game Company	http://www.niost.org/pdf/afterschoolmatters/asm_2009_8_spring/asm_2009_8_spring-3.pdf	2005	California
Girl Scouts	http://www.girlscouts.org/program/basics/science/		USA
Girls Learning Code	http://ladieslearningcode.com/	2011	Canada and USA
Girls Make Games Camp	http://girlsmakegames.how/	2014	San Jose, CA
Girls Who Code	https://girlswhocode.com/	2012	New York
Just for Girls! Video Game Camp	http://dcl.niu.edu/index.php/labs/79-labs/game-development-lab/82-games-camp-just-for-girls	2007	DeKalb, IL

identify the presence or absence of economic, cultural and democratic rationales for encouraging girls to be video game designers.

Drawing on Raphael et al.'s (2006) coding scheme, programs were coded as economic if they emphasized the use of video game design for entering a job or pursuing STEM educational pathways. Programs were coded as cultural if they emphasized the importance of game design for girls' self –expression or participation in popular culture. Programs were coded as democratic if learning video game design was seen as a broader way to participate in the civic world. Democratic is broadly defined in terms of not just traditional institutional politics, but also for forming opinions about technological policy issues, such as ethics.

Economic Rationales

Seven of the ten programs incorporated economic rationales. For example, the *App Camp for Girls*

seeks to address the gender imbalance in technology professions by inspiring middle-school age girls with a broad introduction to the process of app development, from brainstorming and designing ideas to building and pitching their apps. We believe that the experience of creating an app that runs on a device in one week can spark the enthusiasm that will propel girls to pursue further tech education. (App Camp for Girls, 2015).

The mission of *Black Girls Code* is "To increase the number of women of color in the digital space by empowering girls of color ages 7 to 17 to become innovators in STEM fields, leaders in their communities, and builders of their own futures through exposure to computer science and technology" (Black Girls Code, 2014)

The vision of *Girls Who Code* is "to reach gender parity in computing fields. We believe this is paramount to ensure the economic prosperity of women" (Girls who Code, 2015). The website also states that "we believe that more girls exposed to computer science at a young age will lead to more women working in the technology and engineering fields." The model of the program emphasizes paired instruction combined with exposure to female engineers and entrepreneurs. It should be note that much of the material on *Girls Who Code's* website emphasizes economic rationales, without mentioning cultural or democratic dimensions of computer programming.

The Girl Scouts had the most comprehensive economic rationale, offering insight into a range of careers within the video game design industry. "Be the Video Game Developer" is a video and a video game builder that takes audiences inside a design studio and explains what the different jobs are. In the process, girls design their own game and learn coding (http://forgirls.girlscouts.org/makeagame/). This was the most comprehensive integration of economic rationales. In the video, the majority of the women working in the studio are female. There are efforts to have racial and ethnic diversity, with African American, Asian, and Latina women. Throughout the game, girls choose a main character, obstacles, color scheme, and sound design. They try to use accessible language to explain what each role is. For example, they explain that engineering puts ideas into action, "kind of like putting a puzzle together." At the end, girls can test the game, go back for quality assurance to make adjustments to the code, and share the link to the game. While the game was not associated with a particular informal education program, the Girl Scouts of Los Angeles, in conjunction with Women in Games International, recently launched a video game badge for Girl Scouts. As Amy Allison, vice president of Women in Games International, commented,

Our ultimate goal is to create a STEM-aligned video game badge for the Girl Scouts of the United States of America. Creating this badge will get young girls excited in technology and science and let them know that they, too, can have a career in the video game industry. (Women in Games International, 2015)

This badge was launched six months after the Boy Scouts launched its own video game badge.

Economic rationales emphasize the importance of girls taking on tech-savvy identities. However, many of the representations on the websites did not offer a cross-section of possible careers within the industry. Raphael et al. (2006) are critical of the emphasis on elite occupations in STEM fields and not enough on other types of jobs, like writers and technicians. As they write, "social learning theory suggests that realistic role models are the most powerful for media users, who are more likely to imitate a modeled behavior if they perceive the model as similar to themselves and the model's behavior is portrayed as valuable" (p. 779). Thus, there is a need to re-think how occupations are represented. Some girls may not feel like they can achieve the elite occupations and would want to be in other roles.

Cultural Rationales

Six programs were coded as having cultural rationales for video game design. These included emphasis on self-expression and creativity. These also emphasized the importance of creating all-girl spaces to increase girls' self-esteem. For example, a quote from the founder of the Girls Make Games camp stated,

We had a girl that came in and she wasn't even talking the first week. She was just looking at the ground when you would talk to her. By the end of week one we had a programming challenge that she was able to solve. She didn't expect to be able to solve it, and in week two she started talking a little bit more. And by week three... she'd be dancing in front of the camera. (Hall, 2014)

In another example, *Girls Learning Code* programs "are designed to help girls see technology in a whole new light – as a medium for self-expression, and as a means for changing the world." Their website also stated, "We are a not-for-profit organization with the mission to become the leading resource for women and youth to become passionate builders - not just consumers - of technology by learning technical skills in a hands-on, social, and collaborative way." This program emphasizes the research that in all-girl settings, girls are more comfortable exploring tech-savvy identities.

Cultural rationales also emphasized the specific demographic groups. This was true in both *Black Girls Who Code*, that is focused solely on African American girls, and *The Girl Game Company*, whose clientele are Latina girls in rural California. For *The Girl Game Company,* they also tried to address the cultural barriers, such as offering English and Spanish curricula, and having monthly family dinner events that close the gap between home and school culture.

Finally, CompuGirls emphasized the importance of cultural relevance and self- esteem. Their goals are "To enhance girls' techno-social analytical skills using culturally relevant practices" and "To provide girls with a dynamic, fun learning environment that nurtures the development of a positive self-concept" (Center for Gender Equity in Science and Technology, 2015).

Democratic Rationales

Six programs emphasized democratic rationales. For example, *Geek Girls Camp*, which is not just for young girls, was started in 2006 to counteract the masculine culture of computing. As founder Leslie Fishlock explains,

We wanted something for the "average wannabe geek girl." In an environment where no one ever has to feel silly about asking the wrong question and getting laughed at by some 19 year old pimply know it-all World of Warcraft cretin." With braces. And a Marilyn Manson t-shirt. (Geek Girl, 2015)

To that end, Geek Girl offers meet-ups and workshops in several locations throughout the U.S.
In a Huffington Post article that talked about the types of games made at *Girls Who Code*,

There were gaming apps, like Scoop Stacker (a kind of brickbreaker for ice cream); travel apps, like Mood Foods ("find a restaurant that corresponds to [your] craving") and Capture Memory (a travel guide for out-of-towners in New York); and several designed to help users help others. HandiHelp, for example, is made to help disabled individuals navigate public transportation. Say Something is meant to help smartphone owners assist the homeless in finding soup kitchens and shelters. (Bosker, 2012)

Here, there was an emphasis on how girls were designing video games and apps for social change.
The Girl Scouts also emphasized democratic rationales, "STEM experiences are framed within the context of leadership: As girls participate in Girl Scouting, they develop leadership skills to make the world a better place. Research shows girls are more interested in STEM careers when they know how their work can help others" (Girl Scouts, 2015)

Discussion

There are several limitations to this study. First, this is not representative of all informal video game design programs for girls, but instead a small sample. Additionally, a content analysis cannot discern the impacts of the programs on girls who enroll in these programs, or how girls and parents come across and interpret the messages conveyed on the websites. However, it can offer insights into the kinds of materials that girls are introduced to when searching for video game design programs online.

This study differed from Raphael et al.'s (2006) in that there was very little technical information about video game design available on these websites. Raphael et al. (2006) found that websites that encouraged girls to pursue STEM fields also offered some instruction or skill development. While this was a minority of the websites studied, the authors concluded that this is an important component to increasing girls' technical skills. Instead, the websites in the current study were primarily used to promote enrollment into video game design programs. With the exception of the Girl Scouts, these websites offered little information about the video game industry. This may not be a problem, since there are many other sites that provide this kind of information. Future research could examine how girls and parents respond to the information provided on these websites. How do they interpret the importance of video game design? Does this information invite girls to take on tech-savvy identities?

Raphael et al. (2006) found that civic uses of ICTs were a less common rationale for closing the gender gap in computing. They hypothesize that

this may reflect that American public culture tends to be more individualistic and market-driven than collective or civic in nature. In addition, the economics of commercial sites likely militate against a civic focus, as it would be less likely to attract an audience of teen girls to deliver to advertisers. Many of the nonprofit sites depend on grant money from the National Science Foundation and private foundations associated with the ICT industries, which tend to frame the problem of the gender gap as an economic one. (p. 800)

The results of the present study also found an over-emphasis on economic rationales for video game design, which may limit the possibilities for girls to take on identities as video game designers.

These results suggest the need for informal video game design programs to reframe the gender gap to include cultural and democratic rationales. Indeed the video game industry is just one of the main opportunities for girls to take on tech-savvy identities.

FUTURE RESEARCH DIRECTIONS

This chapter offers several opportunities for future research directions. First, much of the research on girls and video games tends to incorporate quantitative, rather than qualitative research methods. Instead, interviews and observations of girls participating in video game design offer insight into some of the dynamics of play. Qualitative research can also provide contexts for what strategies work or not in these settings. This study only focused on one such workshop. Future research could look at comparative studies of different types of informal video game design programs.

This chapter provided some insight into how video game design is communicated to girls, through qualitative analyses of websites of informal education programs. This analysis revealed that girls are presented a narrow view of the importance of video game design. The majority of the programs emphasized the importance of video game design for entering the video game industry. This narrow focus may not resonate with all girls, who might be interested in creatively using the medium to express themselves. Future research could supplement these initial findings with interviews of program directors to better understand how they see the importance of video game design in girls' lives. These interviews might lead to improved messages to girls.

One area for future research would be to examine how to integrate democratic rationales into these educational programs. While some of the programs in this study did emphasize the importance of civic engagement and social change, this is an under-explored area. While girls may be designing games that are about social change, how can these programs and programs like them emphasize this in their program materials as an important aspect of video game design? How can these programs communicate to girls that they are important beyond their economic potential to enter the video game industry.

Finally, little research has explored how girls respond to some of the new game genres, such as serious games, that have challenged the masculine culture of gaming. In the future, it would be important to see how these games shift girls' perspectives of gaming and the larger industry.

CONCLUSION

The goal of this chapter was to examine how informal video game design programs for girls offer shifting perspectives. For girls, one of the main identified barriers is not technical proficiency, but instead emotional, cultural, and structural barriers that get in their way. As shown in this chapter, when girls are video game designers, they tend to design games differently than boys. Rather than a place of competition, game design becomes a place for identity exploration and formation. Girls use video game design to challenge sexist representations, make sense of the world around them, and provide social change.

Indeed, as video game software continues to become more accessible, a diverse group of video game designers will offer broadened definitions of what the medium of a video game can be. That said, both observations of the Girl Scouts video game design program and qualitative content analyses of informal all-girl programs analyzed in this chapter showed that these programs emphasize economic rationales for being a game designer. This is a missed opportunity, since it does not adequately communicate the potential of the medium and what girls can do with it.

Finally, many of the programs used the term "empower" to describe what it is their programs due for girls. However, there is the need to expand this notion of empowerment to also address the structural change that needs to happen in educational and corporate institutions in order for gender equality to truly be possible. As some of the testimonials in the programs conveyed, girls were largely unaware of the discrimination they faced in their classrooms or social settings. Through their participation in these programs, they became aware that it is not only their individual contribution to society that is important, but also that there are cultural and structural barriers they face.

One of the disappointing outcomes of the Gamergate controversy, which was mentioned at the beginning of this chapter, is that some women are leaving the video game industry because they don't see an end to the problems in the industry, such as sexist workplace policies or lack of supportive for innovation and change. This is alarming for an industry that already only has 10 percent of women.

In the end, this chapter shows that much more research is needed to understand the potential cultural and democratic benefits to video game design.

REFERENCES

Afterschool Alliance. (2009). *America after 3pm: Key Findings*. Retrieved from http://www.afterschoolalliance.org/documents/AA3PM_Key_Findings_2009.pdf

Afterschool Alliance. (2012). *Afterschool Essentials: Research and Polling*. Retrieved from http://www.afterschoolalliance.org/documents/2012/Essentials_4_20_12_FINAL.pdf

Agosto, D. (2004). Design vs. content: A study of adolescent girls' website design preferences. *International Journal of Technology and Design Education, 14*(3), 245–260. doi:10.1007/s10798-004-0776-y

Alison. (2009). Calling all gamer girls. *Dance Spirit, 13*(2), 24.

American Association of University Women. (2015). *Solving the equation: The variables for women's success in engineering and computing*. Washington, DC: AAUW.

American Association of University Women. (2000). *Tech-savvy: Educating girls in the computer age*. Washington, DC: AAUW.

App Camp for Girls. (2015). *Home*. Retrieved from http://appcamp4girls.com/

Barker, L. J., & Aspray, W. (2006). The state of research on girls and IT. In J. M. Cohoon & W. Aspray (Eds.), *Women and information technology: Research on underrepresentation* (pp. 3–54). Cambridge: The MIT Press. doi:10.7551/mitpress/9780262033459.003.0001

Beavis, C., & Charles, C. (2005). Challenging notions of gendered game play: Teenagers playing the Sims. *Discourse (Abingdon), 26*(3), 355–367. doi:10.1080/01596300500200151

Bettie, J. (2003). *Women without class: Girls, race, identity*. Berkeley, CA: University of California Press.

Black Girls Code. (2014). *Home*. Retrieved from https://www.blackgirlscode.org

Bosker, B. (2012, October 23). *'Girls Who Code' sets sights on teaching 1 million girls to code*. Retrieved from http://www.huffingtonpost.com/2012/10/23/girls-who-code_n_2005659.html

Brown, L. M., & Gilligan, C. (1992). *Meeting at the crossroads: Women's psychology and girls' development*. Cambridge, MA: Harvard University Press. doi:10.4159/harvard.9780674731837

Cassell, J., & Jenkins, H. (Eds.). (1998). *From Barbie to* Mortal Kombat*: Gender and computer games*. Cambridge, MA: MIT Press.

Center for Gender Equity in Science and Technology. (2015). *CompuGirls*. Retrieved from https://cgest.asu.edu/compugirls

Connolly, T. M., Boyle, E. A., MacArthur, E., Hainey, T., & Boyle, J. M. (2012). A systematic review of empirical evidence on computer games and serious games. *Computers & Education, 59*(2), 661–686. doi:10.1016/j.compedu.2012.03.004

Cooper, J., & Weaver, K. D. (2003). *Gender and computers: Understanding the digital divide*. Mahwah, NJ: Lawrence Erlbaum.

Crowe, M. (2003). Jump for the sun II: Can a monthly program change girls' and women's attitudes about STEM? *Journal of Women and Minorities in Engineering, 9*, 323–332.

Cunningham, C. (2011). Girl game designers. *New Media & Society, 13*(8), 1373–1388. doi:10.1177/1461444811410397

Denner, J., Werner, L., Bean, S., & Campe, S. (2005). The Girls Creating Games Program: Strategies for engaging middle school girls in information technology. *Frontiers: A Journal of Women Studies, 26*(1), 90-98.

Denner, J., Werner, L., & Ortiz, E. (2012). Computer games created by middle school girls; Can they be used to measure understanding of computer science concepts? *Computers & Education, 58*(1), 240–249. doi:10.1016/j.compedu.2011.08.006

Denner, J., Bean, S., & Werner, L. (2005). Girls creating games: Challenging existing assumptions about gender content. *Proceeding of DiGRA 2005 Conference: Changing Views-Worlds in Play.*

Dickey, M. D. (2006). Girl gamers: The controversy of girl games and the relevance of female-oriented game design for instructional design. *British Journal of Educational Technology, 37*(5), 785–793. doi:10.1111/j.1467-8535.2006.00561.x

Dondlinger, M. J. (2007). Educational video game design: A review of the literature. *Journal of Applied Educational Technology, 4*(1), 21–31.

Down, E., & Smith, S. L. (2009). Keeping abreast of hypersexuality: A video game character content analysis. *Sex Roles, 62*(11-12), 721–733. doi:10.1007/s11199-009-9637-1

Entertainment Software Association. (2007). *Game player data.* Entertainment Software Association.

Fancsali, C. (2002). *What we know about girls, STEM, and afterschool programs: A summary.* Washington, DC: Educational Equity Concepts, Inc. Retrieved from http://www.afterschool.org/sga/pubs/whatweknow.pdf

Feminist Frequency. (n.d.). Retrieved November 16, 2015, from http://feministfrequency.com/

Flanagan, M. (2005). Troubling 'games for girls': Notes from the edge of game design. *Proceeding of DiGRA 2005 Conference: Changing Views-Worlds in Play.*

Furger, R. (1998). *Does Jane compute?: Preserving our daughters' place in the cyber revolution.* New York, NY: Warner Books.

Gee, J. P. (2004). *Situated language and learning: A critique of traditional schooling.* New York: Routledge.

Gee, J. P. (2005). *What video games have to teach us about learning and literacy.* New York: Palgrave MacMillan.

Gee, J. P., & Hayes, E. (2010). *Women gaming: The Sims and 21st century learning.* New York, NY: Palgrave. doi:10.1057/9780230106734

Geek Girl. (2015). *About.* Retrieved from http://geekgirlcamp.com/about-geek-girl

Girl Scouts, Girl Scout Research Institute. (2015). *Generation STEM: What girls say about science, technology, engineering, and math.* Retrieved from https://www.girlscouts.org/research/pdf/generation_stem_summary.pdf

Girl Scouts. (2015). *Imagine STEM.* Retrieved from http://www.girlscouts.org/program/basics/science/

Girls Who Code. (2015). *Home.* Retrieved from https://girlswhocode.com

Hall, C. (2014, July 30). What it's like to attend Girls Make Games, the all-girls game dev summer camp. *Polygon.* Retrieved from http://www.polygon.com/2014/7/30/5952139/the-hole-story-girls-make-games-all-girls-game-camp-the-negatives

Hargittai, E. (2010). Digital na(t)ives? variation in internet skills and uses among members of the "Net generation". *Sociological Inquiry, 80*(1), 92–113. doi:10.1111/j.1475-682X.2009.00317.x

Hartmann, T., & Klimmt, C. (2006). Gender and computer games: Exploring females' dislikes. *Journal of Computer-Mediated Communication, 11*(4), 910–931. doi:10.1111/j.1083-6101.2006.00301.x

Hug, S. (2007). *Developing technological fluency in a community of digital storytelling practice: Girls becoming tech-savvy* (Doctoral dissertation). Retrieved from ProQuest. (3256474.)

Jansz, J. (2005). The emotional appeal of violent video games for adolescent males. *Communication Theory, 15*(3), 219–241. doi:10.1111/j.1468-2885.2005.tb00334.x

Jansz, J., Avis, C., & Vosmeer, M. (2010). Playing the *Sims2*: An exploration of gender differences in players' motivations and patterns of play. *New Media & Society, 12*(2), 235–251. doi:10.1177/1461444809342267

Jansz, J., & Martis, R. G. (2007). The Lara phenomenon: Powerful female characters in video games. *Sex Roles, 56*(3), 141–148. doi:10.1007/s11199-006-9158-0

Kafai, Y. B., Heeter, C., Denner, J., & Sun, J. Y. (2008). Preface: Pink, purple, casual, or mainstream games: Moving beyond the gender divide. In Y. B. Kafai, C. Heeter, J. Deener, & J. Y. Sun (Eds.), *Beyond Barbie and* Mortal Kombat*: New perspectives on gender and gaming* (pp. xi–xxv). Cambridge, MA: MIT Press.

Kafai, Y. B. (2008, June). Considering gender in digital games: Implications for serious game designs in the learning sciences. In *Proceedings of the 8th international conference on International conference for the learning sciences-Volume 1* (pp. 422-429). International Society of the Learning Sciences.

Kafai, Y. B. (1998). Video game design by girls and boys: Variability and consistency of gender difference. In J. Cassell & H. Jenkins (Eds.), *From Barbie to Mortal Kombat: Gender and computer games* (pp. 90–114). Cambridge, MA: MIT Press.

Kearney, M. (2006). *Girls make media.* New York: Routledge.

Lave, J., & Wenger, E. (1991). *Situated learning: Legitimate peripheral participation.* Cambridge, UK: Cambridge University Press.

Lucas, K., & Sherry, J. L. (2004). Sex differences in video game play: A communication-based explanation. *Communication Research, 31*(5), 499–523. doi:10.1177/0093650204267930

MacCallum-Stewart, E. (2008). Real boys carry girly epics: Normalising gender bending in online games. *Eudamos. Journal for Computer Game Culture, 2*(1), 27–40.

Marcotte, A. (2012, June 13). *Online misogyny: Can't ignore it, can't not ignore it.* Slate.com.

McGonigal, J. (2011). *Reality is broken: Why games make us better and how they can change the world.* New York: Penguin Press.

Nintendo. (2012). *Style Savvy: Trendsetters Sarah Hyland TV commercial* [Television commercial]. Retrieved from https://www.youtube.com/watch?v=4RU3EuoIl8M

Owens, S. L., Smothers, B. C., & Love, F. E. (2003). Are girls victim of gender bias in our nation's schools? *Journal of Instructional Technology, 30*(2), 131-138.

Pipher, M. (1994). *Reviving Ophelia: Saving the selves of adolescent girls.* New York: Putnam Books.

Prensky, M. (2006). *"Don't bother me mom, I'm learning!": How computer and video games are preparing your kids for twenty-first century learning.* St. Paul, MN: Paragon House.

Raphael, C., Bachen, C., Lynn, K.-M., Baldwin-Philippi, J., & McKee, K. A. (2006). Portrayals of information and communication technology on world wide web sites for girls. *Journal of Computer-Mediated Communication, 11*(3), 771–801. doi:10.1111/j.1083-6101.2006.00035.x

Sadker, M., & Sadker, D. (1995). *Failing at fairness: How our schools cheat girls.* New York: Touchstone.

Schwarz, E., & Stolow, D. (2006). Twenty-first century learning in afterschool. *New Directions for Youth Development, 110*(110), 81–99. doi:10.1002/yd.169 PMID:17017259

Seiter, E. (1993). *Sold separately: Children and parents in consumer culture.* New Brunswick, NJ: Rutgers University Press.

Shapiro, J. R., & Williams, A. M. (2012). The role of stereotype threats in undermining girls' and women's performance and interest in STEM fields. *Sex Roles, 66*(3), 175–183. doi:10.1007/s11199-011-0051-0

Shumow, L., & Schmidt, J. A. (2014). *Enhancing adolescents' motivation for science.* Thousand Oaks, CA: Corwin.

Steinke, J. (1999). Women scientist role models on screen: The case of contact. *Science Communication, 21*(2), 111–136. doi:10.1177/1075547099021002002

Stern, S. (2004). Expressions of identity online: Prominent features and gender differences in adolescents' world wide web home pages. *Broadcast Education Association, 48*(2), 218–243.

Subrahmanyam, K., & Greenfield, P. M. (1998). Computer games for girls: What makes them play? In J. Cassell & H. Jenkins (Eds.), *From Barbie to Mortal Kombat: Gender and computer games* (pp. 46–71). Cambridge, MA: The MIT Press.

Vermeer, D. (2014, October 25). *The decline of women in computer science* [Web log post]. Retrieved from http://daniellelvermeer.com/blog/women-computer-science

Walkerdine, V. (2007). *Children, gender, video games: Toward a relational approach to multimedia.* New York: Palgrave MacMillan. doi:10.1057/9780230235373

Williams, D., Martins, N., Consalvo, M., & Ivory, J. (2009). The virtual census: Representations of gender, race and age in video games. *New Media & Society, 11*(5), 815–834. doi:10.1177/1461444809105354

Wilson, B. (2006). Why America's disadvantaged communities need twenty-first century learning. *New Directions for Youth Development, 110*, 47-54.

Winn, W. (2002). Current trends in educational technology research: The study of learning environments. *Educational Psychology Review, 14*(3), 331–351. doi:10.1023/A:1016068530070

Women in Games International. (2015). *Home*. Retrieved from http://wigigsprogram.org/

United States Department of Education. (2015). *Science, technology, engineering and math: Education for global leadership*. Retrieved from http://www.ed.gov/stem

Zichermann, G., & Cunningham, C. (2011). *Gamification by design: Implementing game mechanics in web and mobile apps*. Sebastopol, CA: O'Reilly Media, Inc.

KEY TERMS AND DEFINITIONS

Constructivism: A learning theory that argues that humans construct their own understandings and meanings of the world through experience and reflection.

Cultural Rationales: An ideology that emphasizes the importance of video game design for self-expression, creativity, and communication.

Democratic Rationales: An ideology that emphasizes the importance of video game design for helping girls to participate in the broader society.

Economic Rationales: An ideology that emphasizes the importance of video game design for gaining technical skills to enter the STEM workforce and pursue education in STEM pathways.

Informal Learning: Learning that occurs outside of the institutional school system. Includes after-school programs and youth organizations.

Stereotype Threat: Refers to a feeling that one is at risk of confirming a negative stereotype about one's social group.

Self-Expression: The expression of one's unique personality, including thoughts, and ideas.

Twenty-First Century Skills: Refers to a set of abilities students need to develop in order to succeed in the information age. Skills include critical thinking, creativity, collaboration, communication, technological fluency, and information and media literacy.

ENDNOTES

[1] Parts of this case study have been previously published in Cunningham, C. (2011). Girl Game Designers. *New Media & Society, 13*(8), 1373-1388.

[2] The name of the actual program has been changed to protect anonymity.

Chapter 8
Gaming before E-Sports:
Playing with Gender in Early Gaming Communities, 1993–2001

Marley-Vincent Lindsey
Brown University, USA

ABSTRACT

Discussions of competitive gaming often begin and end with the development of professional E-Sports. However, competitive gaming has a history that stretches back to the first days of networked play with first generation games like Doom, Warcraft II *and Multi-User Dungeons (Henceforth MUDs). Within these games, digital communities became a prominent means of discourse and discussion, heavily reliant on gender as a habit of thought to describe inequality and disparities between players. Using an archive of Warcraft II histories, and forum threads for the game, this chapter describes a social history of this digital community with specific emphasis on the ways that gender was used.*

INTRODUCTION

February 9, 2001 was an infamous day for a popular *Warcraft II* Forum called the Warcraft Occult. ~Summoner, a notorious trash-talker on the forum, was caught hacking in a game of *Warcraft II*[1]. The game was saved, and then posted on the forum for all other posters to view and download on a thread entitled "SUMMONER IS CAUGHT HACKING" with a description:

Ender-Wiggin: *A dear friend sent me a save game in which it shows Summoner with 3 weapon upgrades, and 1 shield upgrade. Thanks to DK's wonderful program, we should have one less hacker in the "community"* (Ender-Wiggin, 2000, [msg 1]). [2]

Response was fast and furious: in a forum where most threads only garnered three or four responses, this initial thread had four pages in response, filled with anger, frustration, and even threats of physical violence. Over the course of the next week, numerous other threads were created to gleefully discuss the

DOI: 10.4018/978-1-5225-0261-6.ch008

allegations against ~Summoner, many of which took similar tones. Posts on the initial thread included the following:

sfg: *in the names summoner posted as hackers they all do hahah and i know u hacked every single game and not once in a while so stfu fag but u suck anyway so it doesn't matter.* (Ender-Wiggin, 2000 [msg 39])

PCSPEAKER: *[to another poster in the thread] Get a fucking clue you fucking scrub. Justify the rest of your heterosexual allegations before trying to impress with the horseshit you think is insight.* (Ender-Wiggin, 2000, [msg 76])

SloBz: *You faggots who accused paper/cinder/myst/nail are moronic. None of them hack. They love the game and wouldn't cheapen it with Summoner's B.S. and Summoner ur posts are fucking stupid.* (Ender-Wiggin, 2000, [msg 94])

7VIesSiah: *I can't beleive Summoner (aka GenMike, JenMike, GayMike, there are a lot of names for this fag) is still playing this game. It isn't surprising that he cheats. This guy has always sucked.* (Ender-Wiggin, 2000, [msg 97])

Ash-: *Our conflict ends here. I was right about you hacking, and all your bullshit now sees the light. I am the better player and the better man. In the end I will always be the better man. Thank you for the satisfaction of victory.* (Ender-Wiggin, 2001, [msg 41])

Ash-: *[responding to someone asking Summoner if he will attend an offline event, as people could try to hurt him after this] I won't hesitate to deal out punishment as is necessary. Don't worry though sum; you will survive.* (Ender-Wiggin, 2001, [msg 48])

The following was posted on another a thread started by ~summoner, entitled "get a life please":

Ash-: *WS and SLAM [two other players accused of hacking] used to be pretty good on kali. When they came back to war2 on bnet, they got raped. They got raped all the time that I played on bnet.* (~summoner, 2001, [msg 5])

Another thread entitled "SUMMONER IS FUCKING GAY" contained this description:

cancer: *POST HERE ABOUT HOW GAY SUMMONER IS. P.S. SUM UR A FUCKING FAG.. HACKING PIECE OF SHIT.* (cancer, 2001, [msg 1])

One of the most common themes in these threads is also one of the most confusing: What about being a good or honest video game player necessitates a discourse that invokes gender, sexual orientation, and physical violence? Meta-level discussions of trash talking on the same forum, within the same time period yield unsatisfactory answers, such as this post from a thread entitled "Trash talking":

korpo: *It's only fair to say that no one is the greatest trash talker of all time. There are so many people who talk trash (including myself), that they cannot be counted on a calculator. It only adds flavor to the game and it's pretty cool after you talk trash, and then you rape them fairly hard. You get the satisfaction of feeling "I told you so."* (reaverlisk, 2000, [msg 2])

These threads embody a specific habit of thought often amplified by the Internet, that which uses gendered performance to describe social relations. Reading through a popular "Welcome to the Internet" post by blogger redpaw, the amplification of this reactionary tendency is made clear:

redpaw: *3. Do you want a picture of you getting anally raped by Bill Clinton while you're performing oral sex on a cow saved to hundreds of thousands of people's hard drives? No? Then don't put your fucking picture on the Internet. We can, will, and probably already HAVE altered it in awful ways. Expect it to show up on an equally offensive website.* (redpaw, 2000)

The Internet as a space ripe with possibilities was never mutually exclusive from tacitly accepting many of the social and cultural values of the spaces and societies that had come before it. What made the habit of thinking with gender so difficult to break was the way it permeated critical consciousness and was affirmed through communal participation.

In order to explore this idea—and hopefully offer an explanation for these threads—this chapter evaluates a range of posts, histories, writings, and discussions held within the *Warcraft II* community. This evaluation specifically focuses on gender as a habit of thought, often used to insult, brag, and humiliate opposition. What made *Warcraft II* unique was its position as one of the first popular video games designed for online play and whose players could communicate not only in-game and chat channels, but also on these forums. While the chapter will briefly evaluate similar practices of gendered performance in the game Doom, it will focus on *Warcraft II* through two sets of sources: one uses the *Warcraft II* preservation page, accessed through the Internet Archive's WayBack Machine, to evaluate how the top tier of players created a specific memory of their community, one in which trash-talking, hacking, and the everyday life of a forum was largely ignored. In order to evaluate how these forums worked and what role gender played in them, the chapter presents a close reading of threads like the one above to see how gender figured into these discussions and what purpose it served.

BACKGROUND

Thinking through contests of domination and submission with gender was hardly new to forum discussions in 1995. Individuals and societies have been using gender to describe fields of power since at least Homer's *Odyssey*, as Mary Beard reminded readers (Beard, 2014). However, the Internet was often envisioned as a radical challenge to the issues of inequality, and systematic discrimination of non-digital society. In an interview, Sir Tim Berners-Lee himself offered a qualified vision of the Internet as an information space and the good it could do:

It changes the way people live and work. It changes things for good and bad. But I think, in general, it's clear that most bad things come from misunderstanding and communication is generally the way to resolve misunderstandings—and the Web's a form of communication—so it should be good. (developerWorks, 2006)

It was in these early days of the Internet that it seemed the power of communication was the key for liberation. The premise of this liberation underlay many of the first forays into research on what people were doing with the Internet. Some scholars on the early Internet believed control over self-representation would lead to a structure of self-determination for identity (Turkle, 1997). Economists like Edward Castronova saw in synthetic worlds a broad structure of governance dictated by the market, and therefore the "common good." (Castronova, 2005, p. 24, pp. 210-211). Donna Haraway's *Cyborg Manifesto* most famously gave an idea of gender that could transcend the individual, suggesting that the cyborg metaphor allowed for the perception of gender as a structural, rather than personal issue (Haraway, 1991).

As people asked questions further focused on human interaction within the Internet, there was less assurance in this premise. The first pushback was found in the writings of scholars and journalists on Multi-User Dungeons (MUD): text-based environments within which people could engage freely with other users. Julian Dibbell used this example in 1993, telling the story of a rape within the *LambdaMOO* MUD. Dibbell's narrative of *LambdaMOO* told the story of how Bungle, a seemingly normal user, took advantage of a popular voodoo program to enact the violent rape of another user at a public party hosted on the MUD (Paragraph 11-12). This rape gave rise to the first political concerns of the MUD, forcing former self-described libertarians and anarchists to cede the necessity for some basic form of digital government. This libertarian streak is highlighted in an early essay of Lisa Nakamura's on the same MUD, which highlights the optimism of practitioners on Lambda specifically against the more pessimistic predictions of certain theorists (Nakamura, 1995).

Dibbell's narrative is paralleled by Elizabeth Reid's publications on a similar trajectory of events in an MUD centered on sexual assault survivors. For her work, it was the avatar of "Daddy" that operated as a figure of terror, deliberately targeting this MUD in order to make survivors relive the experience of their trauma (Reid, 1998). Once again, this attack led to the centralization of administrative and moderator duties, ruining the earlier utopia in which all users could message other users. The need to prevent such an occurrence from happening again was the impetus for a range of reforms:

The system became far more security conscious. The 'shout' command, which enabled 'Daddy' to send messages to all users connected to the system, was deactivated. The information displayed to all users on connecting to the system was modified to include directions on how to avoid unwanted messages by preventing the MUSH system from relaying messages from a particular user, a facility known as 'gagging.' New users had to be vouched for by an established user before being given a character, and all users were required to provide the administrator of the MUSH with their legal name and telephone number. (Reid, 1998, p. 116)

A more recent pushback recognizes that simply creating digital networks did not alleviate all previous forms of inequality. Lisa Nakamura and Peter Chow-White made this point explicit in the Introduction of their *Race After the Internet* by emphasizing the digital's nature, conducive to nurturing new types of inequality:

The pervasiveness of the digital as a way of thinking and of knowing as well as a format for producing and consuming information forces intellectuals to produce new methodologies and ways of working to reflect current media realities. Equally important but often less discussed is this: the digital is altering our understandings of what race is as well as nurturing new types of inequality along racial lines. (Nakamura & Chow-White, 2012, pp. 1-2)

This "pervasiveness of the digital" and its inability to erase inequality are also highlighted in several recent monographs. Both danah boyd [sic] and Whitney Phillips evaluated how inequality was encoded in the transition between analogue—or physical—reality and digital networks (boyd, 2014; Phillips, 2015). While the idea of digital communities themselves was novel, both authors stress the continuity of analogue inequality in digital spheres. This continuity was the emphasis of one of Phillips' conclusions:

Consequently, if lawmakers and pundits really are serious about combatting the most explicitly racist, misogynist and homophobic iterations of trolling, they should first take active, combative steps against the most explicitly racist, misogynist and homophobic discourses in mainstream media and political circles. (Phillips, 2015, p. 158)

By connecting these pushbacks to game studies, one can conceptualize the Summoner thread as what boyd called a "networked public" for the video game *Warcraft II*. While video game magazines and arcade culture both allowed for community bonding over games, these communities were not yet primarily bound through a forum like Warcraft Occult (Kirkpatrick, 2012; Picard, 2013) and therefore were still largely analogue in their structures. Beginning in the mid-90s, games created for online play began to use online forums as a primary space to connect beyond geopolitical limits. If one had a copy of the game, one could participate in building a community.

The construction of these communities, as with MUDs, soon expressed continuities of analogue inequality. Someone reading through the debate over Lara Croft, for example, can see that issues of representation often reflected a range of academic and activist perspectives on whether sexualization could be reclaimed, or whether the feminism of Croft depended on her body type (Kennedy, 2002; MacCallum-Stewart, 2014).

This discourse, however, also came with political questions about the ways that non-digital communities had politicized femininity, and found within it useful metaphors to think about power in games. Sociologist Natasha Chen Christensen took these metaphors seriously in an analysis of terms like "rape," "fag," and "suck," in *Quake Live* games (Christensen, 2006). Similarly, Kishonna Gray and Wanju Huang recently examined another strategy to cope with this power dynamic: their article highlighted women gamers who chose to abandon femininity, instead preferring to embrace more masculine identities for a normative gaming experience (Gray & Huang, 2015).

If the Internet had remained a relatively marginal space, these structural inequalities would also have remained marginal. Gray and Huang point out, however, that the Internet has moved from a marginal "third place" to a more centralized "place where people socialize, access information, receive education, find entertainment or do business" (Gray & Huang, 2015, p. 135). It is this centralization of the Internet that created "digital space," a region in which people could interact and understand each other not through the norms of how personal relationships and communities ought to work in analogue space, but through the etiquette expected on Internet forums, in-chat during games, and on third party communication programs like Ventrilo and AIM. To quote the redpaw post once again:

Some of you are smart enough to realize that, when you go online, it's like entering a foreign country and you know better than to ignorantly fuck with the locals. You take the time to listen and think before speaking. (redpaw, 2000)

In these early digital game communities, gender, as a useful habit of thought, could often describe the difference between individual players as "superior" or "inferior." Helen Thornham in her ethnography on video game culture in the United Kingdom noted that this habit of thought stretched to video game activities that conceptualized performance, fantasy, and power, saying, "My central argument is that gaming needs to be reconceptualized, not in relation to what the game offers the gamer, but as a gendered corporeal and embodied activity, framed by and deeply contingent on techno-social experiences" (Thornham, 2011, p. 1).

The socialization of players in digital space has also helped normalize this "gendered, corporeal, and embodied activity" to the point that it is now hardly questioned as a facet of video game communities. Scholars like Victoria Gosling and Garry Crawford have argued conceptualizing gamers as an active audience is essential to understanding how games influence players (Gosling & Crawford, 2011, p. 140-141). Like players, community members, and audiences, gamers also build on each other in communities. Xeniya Kondrat applied these questions of active participation using elements of cultivation theory, within which media influences people's views of reality (Kondrat, 2015). Combined with the prominent stereotypes of women portrayal in media and games, she suggests part of the effect of these gaming communities is to create a vicious circle in which developers are successful while not producing strong women characters, and so they associate success with the standard formula. To quote one of her interviews, "it makes young men (in particular) intellectually lazy," at the end of this cultivation process (Kondrat, 2015, p. 187).

As digital space has become a more usual environment in which connections are made, it also became less a novel mode of expression and more a banal method of communication. That *Warcraft II* celebrates its twentieth birthday this year emphasizes the need to think historically about how digital space has influenced social perceptions. One method of evaluating this is through a social history of the Warcraft Occult Forum. Social history is often conceived as the history of institutions: markets, farms, or political structures. It is a history in which any specific individual or any specific event becomes backdrop to what institutions allow in space and time (Hunt, 1986). For the purpose of this chapter, the institution of the forum—an essential area for information exchange for the beginning of the Internet—is the history told by the information exchanged within it.

Given the institution of the forum, and its longevity in how individuals conveyed information through digital space, it is important to ask questions about how such institutions developed and enforced gender as a habit of thought for its players and participants alike. Such an approach sets aside questions about the video game as a text (Consalvo & Dutton, 2006) and rather asks what the relationship between video games and its players were like, and how the structure of the forum contributed to the use of gender. By evaluating the posts and threads within the forum with specific focus on how they use gender or gender roles, the historian is given a brief glimpse into the habit of thought that is gender.

The choice of this *Warcraft II* community is not because *Warcraft II* players were unique in their thinking with gender: a glance at the literature available on gender in fighting game communities is enough to suggest that thinking with gender was an action that transcended any individual gaming community. Rather, it is the banality of these conversations that makes this evaluation useful. Through the perspectives of gamers in a community and through the small history of networked gaming presented here, this chapter will make clear that such thinking with gender was ingrained in digital communities from their inceptions, and that attempts to separate the two will inevitably be frustrated. Its suggestion is that the perspectives of gamers and their communities were guided by what the Marxist Antonio Gramsci called the "historical process" (Gramsci, 1971). Video game communities presented a perfect opportunity for this habit of thought to transcend from the individual and into the structural, by means of a community that accepted and tolerated its use.

GENDER, HISTORY, AND GAMES

Gender in Digital History

Why gender? Why not focus on how women specifically are portrayed and displayed in digital space? In 1986, historian Joan Scott helped steer the conversation about gender as an analytic category between the Marxist and Post-Structuralist readings of gender in order to articulate several clear things about how gender ought to function as a category of historical analysis. First, historians should scrutinize their methods of analysis by thinking about the interconnected processes from which gender gains social meaning rather than looking for a single origin: in context for this chapter, ideas about gender in analogue communities and the participation of players in this digital community influenced each other, they were not unidirectional. Second, in thinking about these interconnected processes, the historian ought not to emphasize a "beginning" or "point of entry" into them, but rather focus on the fluidity of these processes and how they shifted and grew over time. Finally, instead of thinking that the social power brought by gender as unified and centralized, historians should think of it as disparate and a series of case studies. There is no government mandate for how gender works; there are only groups of people whose practices with gender constitute the system.

This intervention allows a scholar concerned with gender to separate the sphere of relations enacted within society from the biological reality of sexual differences. While the latter started the former, the former has gained a life of its own in social and cultural interactions. It is within these elements that people inscribe meaning into relations between genders. Laine Nooney brought this to light by framing her discussion as not only about incorporating women through an "additive move," but also asking how one might read a chronology of game history with critical awareness to the ways that "gender is an infrastructure that profoundly affects who has access to what kinds of historical possibilities" (Nooney, 2013, para. 8). Such a move allows a basic separation between what one might call the reality of history—how things actually happened—and the organization and structure given to the meaning found by historians.

To see this separation function in the context of popular history, one can read David Kushner's *Masters of Doom* (2003), a book published a decade after the release of *Doom* on its history. The history functions to give its fan base an insider's account of how one of the most influential games ever released was made. Kushner's narration therefore accounted not only how things happened, but also how this history was marketed to the imagination of *Doom*'s fan base. It is in this context that Kushner assigns specific identities to many of its protagonists. Such specificity was reflected in gender: the most hardcore of programmers and designers are all young males. Non-masculine identities only appear through two performances of feminine identity: the love interests of Carmack and Romero, and the "mom" figure of the gamers' varying residencies (Butler, 2006). Perhaps there truly were no women involved in the creation, testing, and release of *Doom* worth mentioning between these two identities. Nevertheless, that such a choice went largely unquestioned by publishers, writer, or editors exemplifies Nooney's claim about the role of gender in video game history:

In other words, our sense that videogame history is 'all about the boys' is the consequence of a certain mode of historical writing, preservation, memory, and temporally specific affective attachments, all of which produce the way we tell the history of videogames. (Nooney, 2013, paragraph 1)

If one doubts the positioning of Kushner's narrative in the structure of gender that Nooney articulates, one might look at John Romero after his success with the first person shooter games *Quake* and *Doom*, and his later efforts with *Daikatana*. The game's company, Ion Storms, released a dynamic advertisement on a number of gamer magazines. In black letters on a red background read: "John Romero is about to make you his bitch," followed with the infamous *Doom* tagline: "Suck it down" (Funk, 2010).

In context, "suck it down" referred to the act of blowing one's brains out in *Doom*: placing the gun in one's mouth, and colloquially sucking on the bullets that come out. While suggestive, the connection in a gendered space was not made as explicit as it was in the poster. The connection between "being one's bitch" and "sucking it down" allows for a specific elision between the social roles of being a better gamer and the sexual roles as understood between masculine and feminine subjects. That it was this reading Romero's fan base understood is reflected in an account given by Romero for the campaign in 2010:

I have never called anyone my bitch in my whole life and I never will because that is gay. I would say 'I'm gonna kick your ass' or 'I'm gonna blow your head apart or whatever.' I'm going to do something to you but like, I'm not gonna make you my bitch. I'm not like, going to have sex with you... I should not have done that, I should've said no way in hell are you putting that out because that basically ruined my connection with the fans and the community—calling them bitches, basically and that's not something I wanted to do. (Barton, 2010)

Romero's statement plays with gender by juxtaposing normative sexual actions with their engagement by gamers who are men—hence Romero's declaration that the practice of calling someone "his bitch" is gay. This clarification also helps perceive the problem with the *Daikatana* poster: it was not the implication of how gender was used, but who the target was. While one cannot readily verify how Romero's fans and *Doom*'s community perceived this statement, one can still view it as the aftermath of a longer digital history in which gender played the easily recognizable role of describing skill disparity.

Gender in *Doom* was therefore seen as a way of thinking about social relations between the fans and its creators. However, this was inherently a relationship between producers and consumers: David Kushner, John Romero, and the rest of the *Doom* team made specific decisions about their advertisements, stories, and games they thought would appeal to the *Doom* audience and the *Doom* audience either did or did not buy the products. How might one envision the ways a digital community work with gender, more independently from such producers? Moving from that primary circle of creators and writers, the Warcraft Histories demonstrated how the more dedicated members of the Warcraft community wanted to remember the game.

WarCraft II, as a Real-Time Strategy game, neatly enjoined the growing demand for Internet and networked play with a style of game often compared to chess. Its primary server, Kali, was created in the spring of 1995, envisioned as a way to broaden the horizon of PC gaming. Leagues and ladders sprung up for games like *Warcraft II* and *Duke Nukem 3D*, and Blizzard even sold *Warcraft II* with a copy of the Kali program and specific ports for players, recognizing the potential of Internet play to generate revenue.

The goal in most real-time strategy (RTS) games is to build an army, society or civilization that is capable of beating an opponent in a number of fights through the duration of the game. In *Warcraft II*, this meant the management of natural resources and information to build an army or economy capable of consistently defeating opposition. It is difficult to explain how challenging this management is. The element of "real time" is one way of describing the skill in RTS where players regularly averaged 300 actions per minute in certain games, with an action defined as any keystroke. Beyond that, a player needs to know every element of the game on a deeply intimate level: the map, the race one is playing, the race one's opponent is playing, the positioning of players on specific maps, how certain building designs are most effective, these are all tiny elements in the broader picture that determine who wins and who loses.

This high skill ceiling was essential in producing a demand for a vocabulary of disparity between players. Looking through the Warcraft Histories, a continual trope was the experience of moving from the campaign to the online server, where a player would play against other humans for the first time:

FrielFan: *Having beaten the pc so easily I actually thought I was a good player! Lol, my first game changed all that. It was a 2V2 on Gardon of War, I was at 4.30 [refer to a clock face] and one of my enemies was at 5.30. I started to build units and after no time at all they were getting hit by guard towers. I had been towered at the edge of my base and within a couple of minutes I was totally dead. That was my first game and I probably learnt more from that game than I did from all my games against the pc.* (Friel, 2005)

ArchAngel: *I remember logging into Starlink and Castlenet (Kali servers before Kali went to Kali95) as a brand new player to the on-line environment... ...Eventually I played a few games and wondered how people got so many grunts so fast and then I was hooked.* (Archangel, 2005)

Sypher: *The first game I played actually vs Gokun... I will remember it to this day... I had like 5 lvl 2 grunts and was just upgrading to stronghold when he gaming raling into my base with about 15 lvl 5 grunts... I got completely destroyed and it blew me away. I asked him how the hell he did that and he just said 'you will get the hang of it eventually.'* (Sypher, 2005)

A number of *Warcraft II* forums and leagues developed to satisfy the demand of players wishing to get better, as well as evaluating who the best players were at any given time. Clan websites from the early 2000s also confirmed the ways in which players could play with a range of parameters in order to figure out who was the best at particular styles, maps, and team set-ups (Morpheus, 2005).

This was an open field, in terms of how people negotiated contact with each other, as well as how they dealt with the issue of establishing hierarchy. While ladder rankings still exist from varying seasons, it is often difficult to keep track of which players used what accounts. Despite the lack of assurance of who was where on the ladder, however, these ladders alone were often enough to get players discussing hierarchies of skill. To quote one of the older players looking back on the pre-Battlenet days:

ArchAngel: *I can't really put into words how different this game was during the era of Kali as opposed to now. It was just a completely different environment because nobody was established and there was so much fierce competition out there because of that. I mean, people had choices when it came to leagues. There was IWL, OZWL, a Mac Warcraft League, NWL, Cases Singles and teams, WGL by Gadianton, later there was SGWL and Kpuds and NWL and IWL, rebirths and finally Battlenet's Ladder.* (Archangel, 2005)

Throughout the Archangel's account, these leagues feature prominently in the identification of specific players, alluding to the elision between national and digital identities. The International *Warcraft*

II League (IWL) was acknowledged by a number of guides from 1997 as the space in which top-rank Kali players competed. The Aussie Warcraft League (OZWL) was meant for Australian based players to compete against each other without fear of latency delaying the actions of any one player. The Mac Warcraft League was meant for players whose Macintosh computers required a different set-up from PCs.

The competition between these communities is important to note on the Preservation site. This website was dedicated to preserving the memories of *Warcraft II*, as recorded by players who began in 1996. While the website is now dead, the WayBack Machine on the Internet Archive still provides a workable link to view the page (Rossi, 2013). This practice of writing a Warcraft History was likely inspired by Geoff "Schlonger" Fraizer, whose webpage was one of the most popular in regards to *Warcraft II* news and events. Schlonger's Warcraft Page helped popularize several tendencies, including the practice of "smurfing" where top level players would beat up on lesser players using fake accounts, and "stories" where players would recount everything that had happened in a specific game on ladder (Schlonglor, 1997). Schlonger is cited as one of the main inspirations for Jason "Wicked Al" Chang's Warcraft history:

Wicked Al: Warcraft II *was a huge part of my life over a year. The game has been through some good times (ie: at it's prime) as well as some hard times (ie: the War2 hack came out). And after this big chunk of my life over, it is fun to look back at what happened and how it got all started. And that's what I'm doing in this section. I stole this iea from shaf and shlonglor. My War2 history won't be quite as long or entertaining as theirs, but I'll do my best in remembering what has happened.* (Chang, 2001)

Wicked Al's history, in turn inspired a series of players to write their own memories of the game, giving each the title of "Warcraft History." As these were players who had spent close to nine years with the game, their selective memories inevitably wanted to highlight what was beautiful about the experience. This is most clear in the ways that community could inspire competition, as summarized by Friel:

Frielfan: *I started to get some build orders together. After a week or two I was winning as many as I was losing. One game which was my first really 'good' game was a 2V1 on Garden of War. My ally dropped so I decided to carry on and fight the other two. I don't remember much about the game except I was top left and they had the bottom. I ended up losing, but had managed to fend them both off for quite a while, I actually thought I had it won at one point, but in the end they overran me, however I met up with them in the lobby of the next game and they both praised my play which was pleasing as I still saw myself as a below average player.* (Friel, 2005)

Friel emphasized the affective qualities of the game. This was both a contest and a way of building communities within any given server. Nevertheless, the friendly elements of the game could be set aside for earning a good reputation. As Friel got better, his claims shift. It was not enough to discuss the ways he could make friends or receive compliments from random players. He began to cite authorities both by their levels of play and his records against them:

Frielfan: *I racked up an impressive list of scalps, MindB, BattleTech, and Meathead who was the top player in the [OZWL] league at that point, he was much better than me, I just got lucky on a game of POS where I rushed him before he could finish his wall-in.* (Friel, 2005)

For ArchAngel, friends were also crucial to the development of his gaming community and networks. He further grouped people on the basis of their servers:

ArchAngel: *Anyway, you would see people with the acronym NWL attached to the end of their name and word spread fast that there was a league out. My friend caleb told me to avoid these games because they were too good of players but I wasn't having that so I kept joining and getting stomped on so many times. We had fights between which Kali server would own which other Kali server until finally I played and beat down a guy named HeatWaveNWL. He was so impressed with my playing that he invited me to join his team in the NWL (Burning Blade).* (Archangel, 2005)

Being a strong player gave a player access to more elite communities. By joining such a community, one became invested in the prowess and ability of that space's ability to play the game on a whole. Archangel epitomized this investment in his account of how Battlenet changed the community. In his words:

ArchAngel: *Battlenet came out and suddenly we were all one huge shit talk community. Egos and names like Valkrie got thrown into the mix and it was up to us to beat them the fuck down. Nobody really good wanted to play ladder games on a slower speed than even faster so it wasn't as competitive as Blizzard couldve made it. Egos meshed and people became hostile all while we were struggling to make an impact.* (Archangel, 2005)

Battlenet—Blizzard's official alternative to the Kali program, as part of their attempt to capitalize on the revenue offered by this proto E-Sports community—was responsible for the "huge shit talk community." There are two useful points here: first, ArchAngel's use of "us" as compared to "egos and names like Valkrie" highlight that it is difficult to describe this as one coherent *Warcraft II* community, as sometimes is forgotten in the present, where most games play on a single server. Rather, the range of clients available on which to play the game—Heat, Kali, and Battlenet—had given rise to communities of players who felt protective of the average skill levels these communities represented. It was the combination of these communities in ArchAngel's account that lead to the second point: "one huge shit talk community" is symptomatic of how most of these histories record the everyday chatter of players on servers, in game, and on the forums.

There is not enough evidence to definitively claim this selective memory wanted to forget "the huge shit talk community." Perhaps it was simply an assumption that the Internet operated like this and anyone reading these Histories would know it without mention. As late as 2004, for example, a pseudonymous poster came to reclaim his position, and brought his shit talk with him:

FigureFromThePast: *I am a figure from the past. I have come back to* Warcraft II *as an assassin to take out the figures from the past that I once dominated years ago. My first rendezvous came as an encounter with an old foe. Archangel and I saw each other on bnet and exchanged words before agreeing to the Match for the ages.*

Considering ArchAngel was number 3 on my Prime Target list of War2 players assigned for assassination I was excited to destroy the legend that he is. After asking him to make sure he doesnt hack, we hosted the game.

I dominated in 7:34 seconds beating his s9/9 dual from 4. He said gg and left like a man, for that I admire him. But I can not marvel at a loser for that is not what I am. (FigureFromThePast, 2004, [msg 1])

Such "trash talk" could be seen as central to game discourse, and therefore not worth mentioning. While one cannot determine why this absence appears, it is important either because of its significance (by refusing to record it) or its banality (by forgetting to do so.)

Despite this tendency, the language of force and violence still comes through in some threads and histories; Friel mentioned scalping, and Archangel's account mentioned his getting "raped" once. In some accounts, the language of force is conflated with gender in ways parallel to Romero's poster. Sc~nixon's account (2005), for example, began with the following: "ArchAngel, slut. Didn't even mention old Nixon. Yet us in Azeroth dominated your little Burning Blade clan season after season."

Here, the reader starts to envision what "shit talking" entailed: while "slut" is a gender-neutral term, it is most often used as part of that package of discursive tools used to belittle or demean women in the public sphere. In this space, nixon's casual use of it against ArchAngel asserted his use of "slut" in a traditional sense: power and authority. Nixon's clan, Azeroth, dominated the Burning Blade. And quickly it is contextualized in hostile territory:

sc~nixon: *My 'play everything' approach hurt me a bit on cases, as did my preference for team games on a 1v1 ladder, as I again got spanked by people on their pet settings. This did not bother me nearly as much as fags not reporting their loses:/ Some people just can't stand to see their hot streak broken by some upstart from nowhere.* (nixon, 2005)

Nixon used these terms—devoid of their usual context—to establish differing levels of ability through a metaphor of power. For the first term, "spank" referred to his lower status compared to those who practice intensely on specific settings. "Fag" on the other hand referred to those players who were too weak to admit their losses. This is the first incident of language that explicitly denoted power as a gendered form of field. To "get spanked" or "be a fag" was to indicate some form of weakness.

Sappy's Warcraft history also included a couple allusions, this time in the form of sexual violence:

Sappy: *I decided to try out for the BANG clan, which was quite a popular team at the time. In the tryout, I had to play against a player known as YuckFoO. As noted above, I did the dualing from 6 to 11 strategy and was promptly raped.* (Sappy, 2005)

"Rape" as a term describing "lost badly" has found a home in the common parlance of competition. That such a metaphor has survived transmission from analogue to digital space is indicative of its value as a habit of thought. Yet, these moments are relatively controlled in the Warcraft Histories. If language of rape, sluts, and faggots were so prominent in early game communities, why did they not show up more frequently here? A tentative answer may be found on Schlonglor's page. He was cognizant of this specific distinction between broadly disseminated stories and casual conversation. This is confirmed on a page hosted by nostalgic fans from 1996-1997, which posted the following message:

Warning: the stories below may contain explicit adult language. I have tried to prevent any truly disgusting words from making it on these stories but strong language found in every day life might be found in these stories. If such things offend you, I suggest you probably shouldn't read them. (Schlonglor, 1997)

What follows on that page is a collection of 75 stories, some written by Schlonglor during his smurf days, some written by his friends. The efforts of Schlonglor were a set of respectability politics that eliminated some of the more coarse realness for an aesthetic of professional integrity. In this regard, the logic of how these histories were recorded largely mirrored the ways that Kushner thought about his book as recording the historical value of the *Doom* communities in regards to gender. Schlonglor carefully edited the most offensive elements of the stories for broader dissemination, while Kushner focused on telling the stories of the most compelling individuals for a broader game audience.

Of course, some part of this editing process was envisioning what would be acceptable for readers: that is to say, reading terms like "rape," "fag," or "bitch" is often undesirable, even if they are separable from direct conversations about gender. Nevertheless, these terms, as seen from Romero's poster, were part of an evolving discourse inspired by gender and transformed through daily exchanges about the role of gender in creating power discrepancies. In the case of digital communities, these terms were useful as metaphors for social relations between individuals. Yet hitherto, the chapter has only focused on elements of digital forums and histories that were expected to survive as the memory of their games. What happens when one extends discussion to how people interacted on day-to-day threads and posts that had, on the surface, no real significance?

Forum Discourse

When people discuss digital space today, they consciously separate groups based on certain tendencies or characteristics: "Political Correctness" lives on Tumblr, libertarians live on Reddit, activists on Twitter and so on. For many digital forums at the turn of the century, such distinctions did not exist. Forum-posters learned which individuals espoused what perspectives through repeated engagement. In an era where identity on digital space is more centralized, tactics like "dog piling"—where multiple users message, or Tweet a target—and "doxxing"—where an individual's home address, Amazon orders, and personal information is publically revealed against her consent—have displaced the significance and importance of the "flame war" as another example of an abusive Internet.

Simply put, a flame war was a thread that had deteriorated from exchanging information to attacking and harassing participants on the thread, or derailing the exchange through unnecessary and inflammatory examples. While Phillips accurately described the "flame war" as a passé form of trolling in the second decade of the twenty first century, it was practically avant-garde in the last decade of the twentieth century. An edited volume of essays by scholars honored the centrality of this method of trolling by entitling itself *Flame Wars* (Dery, 1995).

A major methodological problem for future historical research involving early Internet archives and forums is surveying the wreckage after a major flame war. As flame wars often included a range of targeted threats and abusive posts, moderators attempted to keep threads at some baseline level of civility and therefore would delete or erase threads and posts that crossed lines. There is a clear example of this problem in a thread posted by (DC)Draco-Dawgg on September 23, 2000. His thread focused on attempting to recruit players for his new clan, "Dawgg Clan Elite." The first response is Axolotl, a moderator:

Axolotl: *Deleted all replies for obvious reasons.* ((DC)Draco-Dawwg, 2000, [msg 2])

What are "obvious reasons"? Based on a later response from Tarquinn one can imagine what they said:

Tarquinn: *It is obvious that this clan is a group of lesser experienced players however, it seems to me that they are trying. The only way these players are ever going to be known as players and not flamers is if we give them a chance.* ((DC)Draco-Dawwg, 2000, [msg 6])

The rest of his post is dedicated to the separation of elite players from rookies, and attempts to reconcile that difference. Yet his implication was clear: this post was the site of a massive flame war, requiring moderator intervention. Whether a gendered discourse was part of this specific flame war is now impossible to tell, and it is often in such flame wars that the tendency to perpetuate analogue inequalities is at its strongest. Nevertheless, one can look at tamer examples of exchange throughout the forum to fill the gap left in these loud absences. For example, the following happened in a friendly thread titled "Valkrie"—the tag of a player—dated to October 7th, 2000:

Sappy: *what's up*
Valkrie: *someone told me sappy is gay. Wasn't sure whether or not I shoulda believed him >:O*
Sappy: *after the night we just had valk, u should know the answer to that...*
Valkrie*: shh this is a public forum. U don't want ppl to know ur my bitch...*
~Summoner: *I stick my dick in both of you.* (Sappy, 2000, [msgs 1-5])

Read in the context of the threads, one understands that Sappy and Valkrie are friends, and this is the sort of teasing done between friends within the *Warcraft II* community. Nevertheless, it freely borrows from the established metaphor in which penetration reflected dominance. Summoner's offhand comment was probably meant to draw the thread to a close by asserting his position above Valkrie, who established himself over Sappy. The act of penetration still is a metaphor for dominance, and became intimately tied to the notion of "trash talking" for many of these players. On a thread encountered in the Introduction of this chapter, reaverlisk asked the following question:

reaverlisk: *Who is the greatest trash talker of all time?* (reaverlisk, 2000, [msg 1])

The first response, given by Korpo shows the connection:

Korpo: *It's only fair to say that no one is the greatest trash talker of all time. It only adds flavor to the game and it's pretty cool after you trash talk, and then you rape them fairly hard. You get the satisfaction of feeling 'I told you so'.* (reaverlisk, 2000, [msg 2])

What follows in the thread is a collection of eleven players, posting opinions that included two mentions of rape and one request for a poster to shoot themselves. The metaphor of physical and sexual violence within virtual space is tantalizing for these individuals to discuss their own prowess.

Due to the inherent anonymity of usernames on digital space, it is often difficult to evaluate how community members would react to women in their sphere. There are few examples of feminine identity being expressed within this time span. One example comes in a thread titled "parents" from November 11th, 2000:

genocider: *does your parents play war2? Mine doesn't. but itried to learn them tho.* (genocider, 2000, [msg 1])

It is in this thread that a poster who crosses gendered expectations gave a response. The username, Sailor Mini-Moon—who identified himself in his signature as a boy—mentioned that he taught his grandmother to play, which is the title of the last response:

-Buzzbomb-: *Your grandma sounds like a tough bitch, especially for a guy who is a sailor moon fan, wtf?* (genocider, 2000, [msg 28])

His grandmother's "toughness" is juxtaposed by the expectation of women as typically weaker. If this isn't accomplished by her description as a "bitch," it is done so by the mention of Sailor Mini-Moon's professed fandom of a show about girls saving the world. Sailor Mini-Moon only has thirty-six posts registered to the forum, but it is a trope wherever he posts. On another thread, specifically titled for him "haha sailormoon ide own u in chess =/" he is chastised twice for his deviation. First in the opening post:

SaBiQ:*i goto an all boys skewl. Instead of watching girls in between basketball games we play chess =).* (SaBiQ, 2000, [msg 1])

And again:

reaverlisk: *Sailor Moon, change your name and get rid of that long message you keep posting at the end.* (SaBiQ, 2000, [msg 13])

While many of these expectations are not inherently gendered, it is their exchange in social relations that makes them so. It is in exchanges like this one that traits like Sailor Moon become gendered, and then are accessible as a political tool, deployed as a pedagogy of shame against Sailor Mini-Moon's online identity. The point is that it is not simply women who are patrolled, but also displays of femininity, which ties neatly into Gray & Huang's earlier exposition on the Militant Misses as rejecting these displays in order to participate as equals.

These descriptions have been relatively tame, and account for many of the ways a thread could use gendered performance in everyday communication. Nevertheless, not all examples of flame wars were censured, and those that survive provide examples of how hostilities could escalate, as a post in a war over "hacking" showed (sluggo, 2000):

PCSPEAKER: *HAHAHA, that is fucking hilarious. You seem to be implying nex was at a disadvantage because of the circumstance. I let nex pick EVERYTHING. Map, resources, speed, race, and he even picked the fucking watchers, then I proceeded to insert my penis into his anal cavity and fuck him over like a 2 dollar whore. After his ass was bleeding and cum dripping down his leg, both he and the watched accused me of hacking. Ash, let nex make his own excuses as he feels I needed to hack to beat him. Yes, yes I do have bragging rights. Shut the fuck up.* (sluggo, 2000, [msg 75])

While this post was chastised by a number of other posters in the thread, an earlier post written by the same individual in a less explicit manner received little of the same criticism:

PCSPEAKER: *Valk may suck a lot of dick and dodge me all day long, but the reasons I don't think he hacks is because the fags accusing him are dumbfucks.* (sluggo, 2000, [msg 55])

Both of these posts emphasize the same sort of physical manifestation to the action of being bad at a video game. To play poorly is equivalent to being a "fag." The phrasing in "suck a lot of dick" reminds the reader of Romero's poster, in which a previously implicit action—to suck—is made explicit by other elements of the action.

These forum exchanges also give tantalizing hints to another set of communities dedicated to trash talking on the game servers themselves. However, this archive would require access to the chatlogs of *Warcraft II* channels and games themselves. One thread titled "the good thing about 24-7 [a clan channel on the Kali server] being back up" finishes in the first post with:

super radish: *Now there's less 'I Own you fag ass cocksmoking homosexual faglover" in this forum.* (super radish, 2000, [msg 1])

That these sort of characterizations are common throughout trash-talking on the *Warcraft II* forum is implied on the topic of language in *Warcraft,* where a poster named chalupa vented about the ways in which people fail to express their skills in creative manners, wishing they would "use [their] own shit." The second post by a poster named ep on this thread included the following:

ep: *Rather then using ur own things, why not just stop talking trash and get on with ur lives.. 'owned raped rox' all those words are for idiots. Play the game and keep ur mouth shut – its as simple as that.* (chalupa, 2000, [msg 2])

Later on, reaverlisk—mentioned earlier in these examples—also offered his own perspective on this issue:

reaverlisk: *I don't use any of those wrods except for maybe raped, but who cares? People say it to get a point across, not to be OrIgInAl or some crap.* (Chalupa, 2000, [msg 6])

That each of these individuals—even chalupa who deemed the practice "gay"—felt no qualms about using the terminology to describe their victories in the general discourse of trash talking is generally indicative of a sense in which it was natural to project any victory of a particular caliber as a "rape."

Digital History, Community, and Gender

With this context, the thread about ~Summoner's transgression becomes more legible. Hacking was often perceived as the lowest transgression one could commit against a game and its community. Rachel Wagner conceptualized hackers, trolls, and a range of other players not serious about a game as "unearnest" compared to those seeking to expand skills, narratives and the game universe, who were "earnest." (Wagner, 2014) Unearnest behavior contributed to the attrition rate of a game—for example, because if there were too many hackers on a server, no one could find a real game to play—and therefore were often portrayed as placing the well-being of the individual over the game itself.

Despite the limitations of knowledge in regards to who these posters were and what experiences they had in other networks, these exchanges express a deeper side of digital space. Digital space could be conducive to faster ways of exchanging information, especially experiences with hackers, sharing strategies, and getting better. But such information exchange still contained within it the metaphors that reflected gender. The metaphors of "rape" "sluts" and "fags" were about continuing a field of power predicated on the assumptions of gendered roles amongst a fraternal community. It is these metaphors, used to explain the experience, which contributed to the binaries of feminine objects as passive and masculine subjects as active. (Thornham, 2011, p. 3-4) These binaries, despite living in the era of deconstruction, survive as useful habits of thought where disparity between individuals exist and thus continue as representations of how gender could either consciously or subconsciously reflect difference. Such representations are ideas that can be historicized in the context of digital communities.

Part of what made digital communities appear revolutionary was their youth relative to other forms of social communities. These were spaces not born of some history that pre-dated notions of biological and social equality, but after the mid twentieth century and the attempts to restructure analogue society into a more equitable space. And yet, the use of metaphor in all communities often signifies both the depth at which habits of thought operate and the breadth at which people on these digital communities understood them. For even Benedict Anderson slipped into the metaphor of fraternity in his discussion of imagined communities:

Finally, it is imagined as a community, because, regardless of the actual inequality and exploitation that may prevail in each, the nation is always conceived as a deep, horizontal comradeship. Ultimately it is this fraternity that makes it possible, over the past two centuries for so many millions of people, not so much to kill, as willingly die for such limited meanings. (Anderson, 2006, p. 7-8)

The "fraternity" that dissolves the "actual inequality and exploitation" has been subject of considerable scrutiny for scholars in analogue contexts. Gayatri Chakravorty Spivak's "Can the Subaltern Speak?" for example targeted not only the colonial traditions within which gender was imposed, but also how anticolonial historians like the Subaltern Studies Collective engaged in the practice of essentializing specific levels of removal from the Marxist "pure form of consciousness" given by identities of race and gender (Spivak, 1988, p. 284-287). Here, one ought to be careful: the metaphor should not be taken as the root cause of material inequality, but rather a reflection of how specific habits of thought continued to reproduce themselves in many analogue spaces, activist and academic. Gender on this level would require an engagement not specifically in changing the metaphors themselves—although there has been reasonable advancement on this front—but also engaging the epistemological change required to make such metaphors feel less useful.

The failure to engage this epistemological change in analogue communities has led to its reproduction in digital ones. In light of this failure, one cannot see *Warcraft II* players as a community of trolls or a group of irrational people. They embodied a digital community that learned how to use gender to describe power, and continued to develop layers for that description's utility. As more people engaged in the metaphor, it became a more normal tendency. This was seen in several of the forum threads, where discussions of trash talking inevitably became associated with discussions of explaining wins and losses as "rapes," and continually using penetration metaphors to imply dominance. While such tropes and metaphors of gender predate digital communities, their rapid amplification on digital networks, due to their twenty-four-hour accessibility from any place with an Internet connection, implied a fundamental shift on the perspective of players who became more comfortable deploying these tropes.

One way to carry out further research on this topic therefore is to resist the tendency that describes these gendered ways of thinking and the sexist practices that often accompany them as entirely irrational. Listening to Beard, one learns that critical consciousness has often been trained to effectively use this habit of thought in a range of useful ways: "These attitudes, assumptions, and prejudices are hardwired into our culture, our language, and our millennia of our history" (Beard, 2014).

By resisting this tendency, scholars can evaluate whether or not the exchange of information fundamentally shifts the paradigms in which people find themselves discussing race, gender, orientation or class on digital spaces. In other words, they can ask how and where "reason" exists in a space constituted of communal cultivation. Conceptual and empirical studies are coming to the forefront wherein notions of reason in digital space are taken seriously (Campbell & Grieve, 2014; Lindsey, 2015; Zimmerman, 2009). A "big" intellectual history—to use historian David Armitage's term—of the Internet might show sporadic bursts of seeming irrationality are not a surprise; they arise as a result of hundreds of digital networks within which everyday interactions and experiences help normalize the perspectives of individual participants (Armitage, 2012).

Research into forms of communication beyond the forum is necessary as well. For example, Twitter gave new methods and tools by which identity could be centralized, or ephemeral. The ways in which some users centralized their identities have given other people, focused on targeted harassment, new ways of making life difficult for their targets. Twitter's continual engagement with harassment and its implementation of hurried solutions in the aftermath of its worst users echoes the ways that MUDs in the accounts of Dibbell and Reid only retroactively realized their systems could be abused (Sinders, 2015). Whether or not one can envision a digital space free from the violent abuse that sends SWAT teams to an individual's house for expressing an opinion is a pressing design concern for future work (Hern, 2015).

CONCLUSION

There are many unanswered questions presented here that are required to fulfill an analysis according to Scott's use of gender: what sort of people were present on these forums? In what other networks did they participate? How did gender connect these networks in a broader sense? Without answers to these precise questions, one can only echo the traditional academic call to action: more research must be done.

Nevertheless, even without answers to such precise questions, one can look at the events of 2014 and recognize the influence of digital space on pre-existing tensions between social relations and gender. The conspiracy that allegedly existed between game designer Zoe Quinn and game journalists who reviewed her game was the new form of an old trope: women degrade themselves by using sex to get ahead. Without digital space, the story of GamerGate would look depressingly familiar (Hathaway, 2014). Its digital nature, however, runs against many of the optimistic assumptions of the Internet as a revolutionary space. Despite the sheer amount of information available and the ease with which one can figure out the veracity of such information, conspiracies and ambiguities still exist especially as they pertain to a range of marginalized perspectives.

The crux of this chapter has been to suggest that critical consciousness can easily be bound by habits of thought by examining gender as such a habit. On a meta-level of reflection in "A Conspiracy of Fishes," Shira Chess and Adrienne Shaw attempted to reconstitute the logic of GamerGate through the conspiracy of connections between Zoe Quinn, Anita Sarkeesian and members loosely affiliated with DiGRA (Chess & Shaw, 2015). Rather than evaluate the critical scholarship of Game Studies, many GamerGate-affiliated accounts have seen fit to incorporate the academy into a broader conspiracy theory involving feminism designed to stifle free discourse, the sort of discussions in which gender was never a problem until women named it as such. GamerGate preferred to keep the habits of thought that bound its thinking, rather than critically assess what elements of the discussion they may have missed. This chapter accounted for only a small part of this process.

Whatever the results of further work, it is perhaps most clear that research in this field must critically contextualize gender in games by evaluating how gender functioned for communities centered around specific games over time. By thinking historically about digital communities, one gains new insights in how the transition between analogue and digital spheres still build and grow from each other.

Historical work specifically, however, would do well to think through the transformation of the word within the digital turn:

I have come to hear in them an announcement of the final stages of our decades-long passage into the Information Age, a paradigm shift that the classic liberal firewall between word and deed (itself a product of an earlier paradigm shift commonly known as the Enlightenment) is not likely to survive intact. After all, anyone the least bit familiar with the workings of the new era's definitive technology, the computer, knows that it operates on a principle impracticably difficult to distinguish from the pre-Enlightenment principle of the magic word: the commands you type into a computer are a kind of speech that doesn't so much communicate as makes things happen, directly and ineluctably, the same way pulling a trigger does. (Dibbell, 1993)

The loss of the "liberal firewall" between word and deed has become important as digital space builds for itself an increasingly elaborate past. For historians, the problem is clear: how does one write history— a discipline that is framed, thought through, and centered around words in written sources—for an era where words have become visibly powerful in a different way? The spheres of critique presented at the *History Manifesto* help bring this tension to light (Armitage & Guldi, 2014). Published by Cambridge University Press, the book was made available as a free download to encourage a broader range of discussions in mediums beyond the academic journal. Without getting into the full range of debates around the text, one can note its publication has both elevated the status of blogs, tweets, and comments to citable even as their sources remain anonymous. Do such practices ethically elevate the value of well-spoken words? Or does anonymity protect authors from the social repercussion of refusing to temper their arguments? The answer is likely yes, they do.

Regardless, the nature of such conversations, and their unintentional power appear destined to be the backbone of digital space. Yet, scholars must not delude themselves into thinking such practices will impact all participants evenly. With the background of analogue inequalities and their perpetuation through fiction as much as fact, one can only suggest that the digital politics of liberation may yet still be bound by the limits of social imagination.

REFERENCES

Anderson, B. (2006). *Imagined communities: Reflections on the origin and spread of nationalism* (Revised ed.). New York, NY: Verso.

Archangel. (2005, October 10). *Archangel's war2 history*. [Web.Archive.Org] Retrieved December 28, 2015 from http://web.archive.org/web/20060518133918/http://www.winnieinternet.com/games/war2/reports/ArchangelHistory.htm

Armitage, D. (2012). What's the big idea? Intellectual history and the Longue Durée. *History of European Ideas*, *38*(4), 493–507. doi:10.1080/01916599.2012.714635

Armitage, D., & Guldi, J. (2014). *The history manifesto*. Cambridge, UK: Cambridge University Press; doi:10.1017/9781139923880

Barton, M. (2010, March 27). *Matt Chat 55:* Daikatana *with John Romero*. December 28, 2015 from https://www.youtube.com/watch?v=lQMtVbz_JuE

Beard, M. (2014). The public voice of women. *London Review of Books*. Retrieved November 28, 2015 from http://www.lrb.co.uk/v36/n06/mary-beard/the-public-voice-of-women

boyd, d. (2014). *It's complicated: The social lives of networked teens*. New Haven, CT: Yale University Press.

Butler, J. (2006). *Gender trouble: feminism and the subversion of identity*. New York, NY: Routledge Classics.

Campbell, H. A., & Grieve, G. P. (2014). Introduction: what playing with religion offers digital game studies. In H. A. Campbell & G. P. Grieve (Eds.), *Playing with religion in digital games* (pp. 1–24). Bloomington, IN: Indiana University Press.

cancer. (2001, February 14). *Summoner is fucking gay*. [War2.Warcraft.Org] Retrieved December 28, 2015 from http://war2.warcraft.org/forum/viewtopic.php?t=483

Carmack, J., & Romero, J. (1993). *Doom* [PC game]. Mesquite, TX: id Software.

Carmack, J., & van Waveren, J. P. (1999). *Quake III Arena* [PC game]. Mesquite, TX: id Software.

Castronova, E. (2005). *Synthetic worlds: The business of culture and of online games*. Chicago, IL: University of Chicago Press.

chalupa. (2000, October 26). *Warcraft language*. [War2.Warcraft.Org] Retrieved December 28, 2015 from http://war2.warcraft.org/forum/viewtopic.php?t=123

Chang, J. [Wicked Al] (2001, August 6). *Wicked al's war2 history*. [Web.Archive.Org] Retrieved December 28, 2015 from http://web.archive.org/web/20060518133759/http://www.winnieinternet.com/games/war2/reports/WickedAlHistory.htm

Chess, S., & Shaw, A. (2015). A conspiracy of fishes, or, How we learned to stop worrying about #gamergate and embrace hegemonic masculinity. *Journal of Broadcasting & Electronic Media*, *59*(1), 208–220. doi:10.1080/08838151.2014.999917

Christensen, N. C. (2006). Doing masculinity in an online gaming site. *Reconstruction: Studies in Contemporary Culture, 6*(1). Retrieved June 28, 2015 from http://reconstruction.eserver.org/Issues/061/christensen.shtml

Consalvo, M., & Dutton, N. (2006). Game analysis: Developing a methodological toolkit for the qualitative study of games. *The International Journal of Computer Game Research, 6*(1). Retrieved from http://gamestudies.org/0601/articles/consalvo_dutton

(DC)Draco-Dawgg. (2000, September 23). *Dawgg clan elite*. [War2.Warcraft.Org] Retrieved December 28, 2015 from http://war2.warcraft.org/forum/viewtopic.php?t=22

Dery, M. (Ed.). (1994). *Flame wars: The discourse of cyberculture*. Durham, NC: Duke University Press.

developerWorks [Scott Laningham]. (2006, August 22). *developerWorks Interviews: Tim Berners-Lee*. Retrieved November 27, 2015 from http://www.ibm.com/developerworks/podcast/dwi/cm-int082206txt.html

Dibbell, J. (1993, December 23). A rape in cyberspace: How an evil clown, a Haitian trickster spirit, two wizards and a cast of dozens turned a database into a society. *The Village Voice*. Retrieved June 28, 2015 from http://www.juliandibbell.com/texts/bungle_vv.html

Ender-Wiggin. (2001, February 9). *Summoner is caught hacking*. [War2.Warcraft.Org] Retrieved December 28, 2015 from http://war2.warcraft.org/forum/viewtopic.php?t=548

FigureFromThePast. (2004, January 4). *My return.vs arch and more!!!!* [War2.Warcraft.Org] Retrieved December 28, 2015 from http://war2.warcraft.org/forum/viewtopic.php?t=7372

Fraizer, G. [Shlonglor] (1997). *Shlonglor presents: The original war 2 story page*. [Nathandemick.com] Retrieved December 28, 2015 from http://nathandemick.com/warcraft2-stories/story.shtml

FrielFan. (2005, October 10). *My warcraft II history*. [Web.Archive.Org].

Funk, J. (2010, May 18). John Romero apologizes for trying to make you his bitch. *Escapist Magazine*. Retrieved June 28, 2015 from http://www.escapistmagazine.com/news/view/100748-John-Romero-Apologizes-for-Trying-to-Make-You-His-Bitch

genocider. (2000, November 11). *Parents*. [War2.Warcraft.Org] Retrieved December 28, 2015 from http://war2.warcraft.org/forum/viewtopic.php?t=220

Gosling, V. K., & Crawford, G. (2011). Game scenes: Theorizing digital game audiences. *Games and Culture, 6*(2), 135–154. doi:10.1177/1555412010364979

Gramsci, A. (1971). *Selections from the prison notebooks of Antonio Gramsci* (Q. Hoare & G. N. Smith, Trans. & Eds.). London: Lawrence & Wishart. (Original work published 1955)

Gray, K., & Huang, W. (2015). More than addiction: Examining the role of anonymity, endless narrative and socialization in prolonged gaming and instant messaging practices. *Journal of Comparative Research in Anthropology & Sociology, 6*(1), 133–147.

Haraway, D. (1991). A cyborg manifesto: science, technology and Socialist-Feminism in the late twentieth century. In D. Bell & B. M. Kennedy (Eds.), The Cybercultures Reader (pp. 291-324). New York, NY: Routledge.

Hathaway, J. (2014, October 10). What is Gamergate and why? An explainer for non-geeks. *Gawker*. Retrieved June 28, 2015 from http://gawker.com/what-is-gamergate-and-why-an-explainer-for-non-geeks-1642909080

Hern, A. (2015, January 13). Gamergate hits new low with attempts to send SWAT teams to critics. *The Guardian*. Retrieved June 28, 2015 from http://www.theguardian.com

Hunt, L. (1986). French history in the last twenty years: The rise and fall of the Annales paradigm. *Journal of Contemporary History, 21*(2), 209–224. doi:10.1177/002200948602100205

Kennedy, H. W. (2002). Lara Croft: Feminist icon or cyberbimbo? On the limits of textual analysis. *Game Studies, 2*(2). Retrieved from http://www.gamestudies.org/0202/kennedy/

Kirkpatrick, G. (2012). Constitutive tensions of gaming's field: UK gaming magazines and the formation of gaming culture 1981-1995. *Game Studies, 12*(1).

Kondrat, X. (2015). Gender and video games: How is female gender generally represented in various genres of video games? *Journal of Comparative Research in Anthropology & Sociology, 6*(1), 171–193.

Kushner, D. (2003). *Masters of doom: How two guys created an empire and transformed pop culture*. New York, NY: Random House.

Lindsey, M.-V. (2015). The politics of Pokémon: Socialized gaming, religious themes and the construction of communal narratives. *Heidelberg Journal for Religions on the Internet, 7*(1), 107–138. doi:10.11588/rel.2015.0.18510

MacCallum-Stewart, E. (2014). "Take that, bitches!" Refiguring Lara Croft in feminist game narratives. *Game Studies, 14*(2). Retrieved from http://gamestudies.org/1402/articles/maccallumstewart

Millar, R. (1994). *Warcraft II: Tides of Darkness* [PC game]. Irvine, CA: Blizzard Entertainment.

Morpheus. (2005 October 10). *Burning Blade's War2 History*. [Web.Archive.Org] Retrieved December 28, 2015 from http://web.archive.org/web/20060518133933/http://www.winnieinternet.com/games/war2/reports/BurningBladeHistory.htm

Nakamura, L. (1995). Race in/for cyberspace: Identity tourism and racial passing on the Internet. *Work and Days, 13*, 181-193. Retrieved June 28, 2015 from http://www.humanities.uci.edu/mposter/syllabi/readings/nakamura.html

Nakamura, L., & Chow-White, P. A. (2012). Introduction–race and digital technology: code, the color line, and the information society. In L. Nakamura & P. Chow-White (Eds.), *Race after the Internet*. New York, NY: Routledge.

Nooney, L. (2013). A pedestal, a table, and a love letter: Archaeologies of gender in videogame history. *Game Studies, 13*(2). Retrieved from http://gamestudies.org/1302/articles/nooney

Phillips, W. (2015). *This is why we can't have nice things: Mapping the relationship between online trolling and mainstream culture*. Cambridge, MA: The MIT Press.

Picard, M. (2013). The foundation of *Geemu*: A brief history of early Japanese video games. *Game Studies, 13*(2). Retrieved from http://gamestudies.org/1302/articles/picard

reaverlisk. (2000, October 20). *Trash talking*. [War2.Warcraft.Org] Retrieved December 28, 2015 from http://war2.warcraft.org/forum/viewtopic.php?t=112

redpaw. (2000, January 16). *Welcome to the internet*. [Web.Archive.Org] Retrieved December 28, 2015 from http://web.archive.org/web/20001110014700/http://deeplight.net/editorials/redpaw/welcome.shtml

Reid, E. (1999). Hierarchy and power: social control in cyberspace. In P. Kollock & M. Smith (Eds.), *Communities in cyberspace* (pp. 107–134). New York, NY: Routledge.

Romero, J. (2000). *Daikatana* [PC game]. Dallas, TX: Ion Storm.

Rossi, A. (2013, October 10). *Fixing Broken Links on the Internet*. [Blog Post]. Retrieved June 28, 2015 from https://blog.archive.org/2013/10/25/fixing-broken-links/

SaBiQ. (2000, October 11). *haha sailormoon ide own u in chess =/*. [War2.Warcraft.Org] Retrieved December 28, 2015 from http://war2.warcraft.org/forum/viewtopic.php?t=115

Sappy. (2000, October 8). *Valkrie*. [War2.Warcraft.Org] Retrieved December 28, 2015 from http://war2.warcraft.org/forum/viewtopic.php?t=60

Sappy. (2005, October 10). *Sappy's war2 history*. [Web.Archive.Org] Retrieved December 28, 2015 from http://web.archive.org/web/20060518133833/http://www.winnieinternet.com/games/war2/reports/SappyHistory.htm

Sc~Nixon. (2005, October 10). *Nixon's war2 history*. [Web.Archive.Org] Retrieved June 18, 2015 from http://web.archive.org/web/20060518133812/http://www.winnieinternet.com/games/war2/reports/NixonHistory.htm

Scott, J. W. (1986). Gender: A useful category of historical analysis. *The American Historical Review, 91*(5), 1053–1075. doi:10.2307/1864376

Sinders, C. (2015). *Twitter has a UX problem*. Paper Presented at the Fifth Annual Conference on Theorizing the Web, New York, NY.

sLuGGo. (2000, October 14). *Ash = War2 god*. [War2.Warcraft.Org].

Spivak, G. C. (1988). Can the Subaltern speak? In G. Nelson (Ed.), *Marxism and the interpretation of culture* (pp. 271–316). Champaign, IL: University of Illinois Press. doi:10.1007/978-1-349-19059-1_20

~summoner. (2001, February 13). *Get a life please*. [War2.Warcraft.Org] Retrieved November 27th, 2015 from http://war2.warcraft.org/forum/viewtopic.php?t=485

super radish. (2000, December 5). *The good thing about 24-7 being back up*. [Web.Archive.Org] Retrieved December 28, 2015 from http://war2.warcraft.org/forum/viewtopic.php?t=296

Sypher. (2005, October 10). *Sypher's war2 History*. [Web.Archive.Org] Retrieved December 28, 2015 from http://web.archive.org/web/20060518133848/http://www.winnieinternet.com/games/war2/reports/SypherHistory.htm

Thornham, H. (2011). *Ethnographies of the Videogame: Gender, Narrative and Praxis*. New York, NY: Ashgate Press.

Turkle, S. (1997). *Life on the screen: Identity in the age of the Internet*. New York, NY: Simon & Schuster.

Wagner, R. (2014). The importance of playing in earnest. In H. A. Campbell & G. P. Grieve (Eds.), *Playing with Religion in Digital Games* (pp. 192–213). Bloomington, IN: Indiana University Press.

Zimmerman, L. (2009). *2008 U.S. presidential election: Persuasive YouTube interactions about war, health care and the economy*. (Unpublished Master's Thesis). Georgia State University, Atlanta, GA.

KEY TERMS AND DEFINITIONS

2Thread: A conversation, typically begun with a title or lead post, which all other posts follow. The structure of a thread often is predicated on the first post being considered "Original Post" with all following posts being measured by whether they are "On-Topic." Sometimes when threads get too far "Off Topic" or turn into flamewars or trollfests, administrators will delete or "close" them from further discussion.

Doxxing: A process by which individuals search for private and identifying information for a person and seek to publish that information to a broad audience with the intent to further harass that person.

Flaming: A tactic, typically associated with Internet discussion, where one or more parties begins to express anger or frustration at another participant by targeting that participant's existence. On forums, this typically takes the form of ad hominem attacks predicated on racial or gendered slurs.

Ladder: Short for "Ladder tournament," it is a type of competition especially popular with online RTS games where players play each other and record their results to a third party server—or in the case of Battlenet, the result is uploaded automatically after the game—in order to qualify for select events at the end period of time.

Multi-User Dungeons (MUDs): A multiplayer real-time virtual world that is usually text-based. MUDs are less game and more space of interactions for individuals based on some similar set of interests. MUDs are generally seen as an extension of *Dungeon & Dragon* games, although as seen in these examples, they need not correlate with any non-specific intersection of friends.

Troll: A troll is any individual, generally on virtual spaces, who enters a discussion with the intent of disrupting or ending serious conversation on a topic. Trolls deploy a number of strategies to this end, be it outright obscenities, feigning ignorance on the mundane, or perpetually posting tangential thoughts. Trolls are difficult to entirely categorize as it has become immersed in the very fabric of digital life.

ENDNOTES

[1]   The author would like to thank Lindsay Burgess and Marga Kempner, both of who read versions of this article and his mother Celeste-Monique Lindsey for putting up with the author during the writing. He would also like to thank the anonymous reviewers, generous in their time and feedback in organizing this material coherently and keeping the author from mistakes where they could. Any remaining errors are, of course, the author's doing.

[2]   Two liberties are taken in the reproduction of these threads for convenience. First, the username of the poster who wrote the post is given, demarcated with a colon. Second, for ease of checking the references, the original poster of the thread, the year in which the thread was posted, and the message number within the thread are given at the end of the post. Over time, these posts have become disordered, so the number of the message may not correlate to the actual chronology of the post.

Chapter 9
Serious Games Teaching Values:
Discussing Games Dealing with Human Rights Issues

Sonja Gabriel
KPH Vienna/Krems, Austria

ABSTRACT

The number of serious games dealing with human right issues has increased in recent years. All of them want to teach/present certain values and make players think about the contents presented. Therefore, it is interesting to have a closer look at different ways of how these games try to integrate values. After discussing the development of human rights digital games in brief, this chapter is going to have a look at various game elements that can express and embody values. Several examples will illustrate how games might more or less successfully deal with human rights and values. Finally, some research results will be presented discussing what serious games might be able to achieve.

INTRODUCTION

Games for change (often also called games with a purpose or serious games) are designed in order to influence the behaviour or attitude of players. This fact links them to the basic goals of human rights education, which also aim at changing attitudes as well as teaching values and competences (Amnesty International, 2015). Up to now there has not been a lot of evaluative research showing how a digital game might achieve social change. Klimmt (2009) argues that playing serious games might motivate players to elaborate on the content of desired social changes. They might also lead to knowledge acquisition/ comprehension, and attitude change/persuasion in players because of "the unique properties of digital games" (Klimmt, p. 250). These unique properties are multimodality, interactivity, narrative, social use, and the situation of playing a game. In the same paper, Klimmt admits the following: "But this should not be mistaken for the assumption that one, some or all of these mechanisms are operating in any given serious game and that, consequently, serious games are a guaranteed success for communication campaigns" (Klimmt, p. 265). As this chapter will show, there are some mechanisms that might be applied successfully, whereas other examples show that the same mechanisms did not work out as intended.

DOI: 10.4018/978-1-5225-0261-6.ch009

Swain (2010) and Stokes, Seggerman, and Rejeski (2011) examined factors that further social change in people who were playing certain games. These authors argue that video games as a tool "increase capabilities for civic engagement and outreach" (Stokes et al., 2011, p. 4). Moreover, digital games are seen as an environment providing direct experience and immersive learning as well as social actors, meaning that digital games can create relationships, provide feedback, and model behavior. Bogost (2007) sees digital games as an expressive as well as a persuasive medium as they represent how real and imagined systems work. Players are invited to interact with these systems and should judge them. Wagner (2007) claims that transfer from a (digital) game to reality can only take place if there is a strong emotional binding between virtual and real identity, which is important when talking about empathy – a factor that is of increasing importance when talking about games dealing with human rights topics.

Having a look at the topics of human rights and human rights education, one will find various serious games dealing with specific (violations of) human rights by having the player either experience a playable character whose rights are violated or putting the player in the role of someone wanting to help groups of people whose rights are violated. Digital games cover various human right topics including the effects of civil war, such as *This War of Mine* (11 bit studios, 2014); civic rights, such as *People Power: The Game of Civil Resistance* (York Zimmerman, 2010); helping people after natural disasters, such as *Inside the Haiti Earthquake* (PTV Productions, 2010); and (trans)gender issues, such as *Dys4ia* (Anthropy, 2012). Certain topics are quite frequently addressed in games (e.g. poverty); others are rarely dealt with at all (e.g. disability). When talking about poverty for example, one can see how diverse the topic is presented. Game topics range from being homeless, such as *Homeless: It's No Game* (Wetcoast Games, 2006) and refugees, such as *Darfur is Dying* (Ruiz, 2006) or *Against all Odds* (United Nations High Commissioner for Refugees [UNHCR], 2005), to linking the topic of poverty to education, such as *Ayiti – The Cost of Life* (Global Kids & Game Lab, 2006). Games that have been developed in the last four to five years make use of social networks (Facebook games like *WeTopia* (Sojo Studios, 2012)) or are designed for mobile devices, such as *Hobson's Choice* (Harris, 1998) or *My Life as a Refugee* (UNHCR, 2012). Some games are restricted to a certain period of time and a large community playing together, such as *Catalysts for Change* (Institute for the Future, 2012). Additionally, some games are also used by charities to raise awareness and quite often use in-game purchases to collect money for their projects. Apart from the topic dealt with and the form of the game, one will find even more differences when having a look at the underlying game design. Some of the games are very educational, while some of them are also fun to play and resemble commercial entertainment games. This chapter is going to discuss the development of serious games dealing with human right topics and is going to have a closer look at how values are embedded and communicated.

BACKGROUND

Human rights education has been an important issue when talking about traditional approaches and teaching material for many years (cf. Brander et al., 2012). The World Programme for Human Rights Education (United Nations Human Rights [UNHR], 2015) is currently in its third phase, meaning that human rights training should be further implemented and promoted. The first phase concentrated on primary and secondary school systems whereas the second phase targeted higher education and human rights training programs for teachers and educators. In order to address the needs of modern education, lifelong human rights education also has to consider digital media and further, games and mobile apps, in order to ensure broad coverage of topics and audience. Games have become part of everyday life – not only for children and teenagers but also for adults. According to statistics, the average gamer in the United States (US) is 35 years old and 27 percent of gamers are older than 50 years of age (Entertainment Software Association, 2015, p. 3). This means that games can be a means to achieve the lifelong learning goal.

Games with the main purpose of changing attitudes and behavior date back quite a long time. In the late 18th century, the *New Game of Human Life* (Newberry, 1790) was sold with the explicit piece of advice that parents should make their children aware of moral decisions that needed to be taken within the game and discuss them (Ruggiero, 2014). Since then, board games have become an innovative tool to address social and moral issues aimed especially at making children and teenagers think about the topics presented as well as influencing and changing their attitudes. When talking about serious digital games, it is necessary to have a closer look at this term. Serious digital games were developed for non-entertainment purposes. They aim at educating or persuading users (cf. Michael & Chen, 2005; Bogost 2007; Walz & Deterding 2014.) Although they seem to be a recent development, they can be traced back to the beginnings of computer games in the 1950s (Djaouti, Alvarez, Jessel, & Rampnoux, 2011). The authors identify several areas for serious digital games like military training, education, and advertising; however, human rights issues as a central topic of video games can only be found within the last ten to fifteen years.

There has been a huge increase in the number of games dealing with human right issues within the last ten years. Today there are hundreds of digital serious games which focus on topics like poverty, discriminations, refugees, gender issues, or child labor. These games – most of them having been supported or funded by non-governmental organizations (NGOs) – can be divided according to their aims: (1) to inform players about certain problems or human right violations and (2) to raise awareness or criticize certain situations and motivate activity on the part of players. Most of the time games provide a mixture of these aims. Similar to commercial games, these digital games use a variety of game-design strategies to deal with human rights. Some of the games are not oriented towards any particularly fun experiences. This might cause players to quit the game without ever turning to it again. Green (2014) writes that "these types of games have earned the pejorative nickname 'chocolate covered broccoli' in that they are little more than basic and boring drills dressed up in a thin video game shell" (p. 39). Fun, therefore, has to be regarded as a key-element of even serious games. However, one has to bear in mind that fun can be seen in different ways (Lazzaro, 2015). Serious fun, for example, refers to purposeful play in which players would like to make a difference in their real world. Making a serious game fun to play can be difficult for designers as "increasing system realism allows you to communicate a deeper message but typically makes for a less accessible, less fun play experience and thus less people will want to play the game" (C. Swain, 2007, p. 808). Apart from fun, other important factors in games include being very emotional or games using the concept of satire. Video-games can also be regarded as useful tools for fundraising and creating awareness (Stokes et al., 2011).

Serious games are important for tackling problems like poverty, as these problems do not play an important role in commercial video games. For example, some games take poverty (or a poor character) as a starting point for the plot and/or setting the goal. The playable character needs to escape poverty by earning money fast or advance in society. Sometimes poverty only provides the background setting (e.g., slums, poor communities). In both cases, commercial games do not depict reality as it is quite easy within the games to find a way out of poverty (Huberts, 2014).

GAMES TEACHING ABOUT HUMAN RIGHTS ISSUES

The next part of the paper will take a closer look at serious games and their ways of dealing with human rights topics, starting out with a short overview of the history of human rights games. As mentioned before, there is not a long tradition of including the topic human rights into digital games; however, some of them have already had a great impact on different levels. On the one hand, some games are interesting to look at because of the game elements they use in order to express certain values. On the other hand, it is also interesting to examine how the public and/or game providers and platforms react to certain games.

Development of Human Rights Games

Escape from Woomera (Wild, 2004) can be regarded as one of the first wider known serious games dealing with a very controversial issue and causing political as well as public discussions. The game, which was funded by the Australia Council for the Arts, focuses on the inhumane conditions refugees face in Australian detention centers. Based on the well-known ego-shooter *Half Life* (Valve, 1998), this modification puts players in the shoes of a refugee whose application for asylum was declined and who therefore needs to flee from Woomera before being sent back to his country where he would have to face political persecution. The game was criticized for giving wrong impressions about refugees and for simply being tasteless (Swalwell, 2003). The fact that the detention center was rebuilt in 3D makes the game realistic and similar to a documentary so that people playing the game can get a glimpse of the site as Australian and international media were not allowed to take photographs. The game was the first possibility for many Australians to have a look at Woomera (and similar detention centers). However, it is not only the pictures that create a feeling of reality but also the sound and references to real events (Skartveit, 2010).

Katharine Neil, who was leading the game design team, stated in an interview that the game was supposed to criticize the government, raise awareness of what was going on in detention centers, and to show that video games were a proper tool for achieving these objectives (Lien, 2014). The game definitely succeeded in making people aware of the conditions, as media coverage (e.g., newspapers and TV) was high. Australia's immigration minister openly spoke out against the game (Nicholls, 2003). Meanwhile the game is seen more positively as it "still remains one of the only representations of life inside an Australian immigration detention centre in any media form. Silence runs through the history of Australia's immigration detention centres – but once a videogame spoke to the nation" (Golding, 2013, p. 1). Although the game has never been finished, it has proved that digital games can tackle political and social issues. Moreover, *Escape from Woomera* (Wild, 2004) might have inspired other game designers as well.

Since 2003, human right issues have become a popular topic for many digital serious games. Today there are hundreds of games focusing on different groups of people in order to make the public aware of problematic situations and human right violations. Doing a web research of serious games that deal with human rights and civic education topics results in numerous websites offering collections of games as well as ratings (Cobb, 2008; Farber, 2015). Most of the serious games to be found are very simple, developed in a short time with low budget and not very well known, but there are exceptions as well. The following section will take examples of games that have either been very successful or make use of new approaches.

Ayiti – The Cost of Life (Global Kids & Game Lab, 2006) was designed with the help of high school students to teach primary school children in industrialized countries the relationship between poverty and education. The simulation presents the player with the Guinnard family (parents and two children) who live in rural Haiti. The game principles are quite easy – the player has to decide who is going to work, who is allowed to attend school, and who should stay at home (and work at the family farm). Players can check on family members' conditions including wellbeing, happiness, and education. Winning the game means that the family has to survive for 4 years (16 seasons). The game challenges typical Western beliefs as sending all children to school ends the family in poverty, sickness, and death (Ferri & Fusaroli, 2009, p. 36). This way the game mechanics show the complex interaction between the need for education in order to get a better pay and a less dangerous job, but at the same time show that education in these countries is quite expensive. This means working hard (and risking one's health) sometimes is necessary. This vicious circle cannot be broken by simply telling people in less developed countries to send their children to school. What is quite remarkable about the game is that it comes with a lesson plan giving implementation suggestions for school use as well as background information about Haiti and the human right to education. The game is still used by many teachers around the world to teach about poverty in less developed countries.

Another game dealing with less developed countries is *Darfur is Dying* (Take Action Games, 2006) – a browser based game about the crisis in Darfur. The game won the Darfur Digital Activist Contest sponsored by mtvU. It consists of two modes. In the first part, players choose a family member and are sent to forage for water. If the character is captured by a patrol of the Janjaweed militia, the player receives information of what would probably have happened to their character and is asked to select another family member. In the second mode, a refugee camp needs to be managed – the character has to use the water collected before for growing crops and has to build huts. When water runs out, the player returns to the first mode. In less than half a year after having been published, the game had been played by more than 800,000 people (Parkin, 2006).

After the first successful creations of games which aimed at making people aware of problems, game designers (and the organizations financing them) also came up with the idea of using games as means of fund-raising. *Free Rice* (United Nations World Food Programme [UNWFP], 2007) is basically a website providing multiple-choice quizzes for different subject areas (e.g., English, mathematics, foreign languages, geography). For every question the user answers correctly, 10 grains of rice are donated via the World Food Programme. In 2007 more than 12 billion rice grains were donated ("Totals | Freerice. com," 2015). As the website is constantly being updated, it still attracts many users. In the first 10 days of July 2015, nearly 60 million grains were collected by visitors answering questions. Players can sign up and keep track of their collected amounts of rice, as well as create and join groups. Meanwhile, there are more games working according to the motto feel good while playing and donate to charities (Basu, 2010). There are games that even go one step further. *Half the Sky Movement: The Game* (Frima Studio, 2013) was co-produced by Zynga and the Games for Change movement as part of a transmedia project. The game is about the empowerment of women around the world and addresses various problems women have to face in today's society. The player starts out in India playing Radhika, who must decide if she should confront her husband about the necessity of getting medicine for their sick daughter. Decisions taken by the player that empower women are rewarded by the game. This game – as usual for games in social networks – encourages players to invite friends to play as well because sometimes support from other players is needed to complete a quest. To be able to play mini-games or travel within the game you need energy – which you can wait to be filled up after some time or you can buy energy using real money. Most of the money earned by in-app purchases is donated to charities. Additionally, there are some more incentives for players to come back and play the game. For example, when reaching a certain amount of points, books or medicine are donated, giving players the good feeling of being able to help by playing the game regularly. There was a huge media discussion when the game was launched, as the plot follows a book and a film dealing with the same topic (Holpuch, 2013; Wolonick, 2013). The game can be regarded as really successful when it comes to the number of players and donations. By June 2015 the game had 1.3 million players, reported 250,000 book donations, and generated a total of more than US $500,000 in overall donations ("Half The Sky Movement Game," 2015).

Apart from using social networks, recent games also make use of the latest hardware developments. *Outcasted* (Köln International School of Design, 2014) is a stand-alone first-person-simulation making use of Google's Oculus Rift to enable a completely new game experience. Players take the role of a homeless person living on the streets of a western city. The player's task is to draw passing pedestrians' attention to the playable character in order to receive money. The only action players can carry out is moving their heads to try and elicit eye-contact. Some of the passersby will start talking. Some will even give the character money. Still, more of them will ignore, insult, or even get aggressive towards the character. The developers of *Outcasted* intend to make people feel what it is like to depend on other people's goodwill.

As this section has shown, there have been a lot of different attempts of expressing values in digital games, even in this very short time span of a bit more than ten years. However, quite often it is not the game itself that makes people think about human rights. That is why the next section is going to look at public and media reactions to games dealing with human right values.

Reactions to Games

Apart from being discussed in the media (like stated for the above mentioned case of *Escape from Woomera*), many games dealing with human rights issues are taken up positively. However, there are also some serious games that have been censored or have been banned from Apple's AppStore for not being appropriate according to Apple's rules and regulations (Apple, 2015). All of the games mentioned in the following section can still be accessed online or by using Android devices.

Sweatshop (Littleloud, 2011) is a typical tower defense game situated in a clothes and shoes factory somewhere in a less developed country. The player takes the role of a mid-level manager and has to ensure that workers work fast and accurately enough. Workers (among them children) have to be hired and fired according to the needs of the factory. In order to win, the player has to exploit workers and employ children as well. Players thus experience the system from within – if they do not manage successfully they will be threatened and scolded by the owner of the factory (called Boss within the game). Although the game developers stated that they wanted to make young people aware of the fact that many of the clothes they buy have been manufactured in sweatshops (Littleloud, 2011), Apple removed the ioS version "stating that it was uncomfortable selling a game based on the theme of running a sweatshop" (Parkin, 2013). While developing the game, the design-team worked with experts on sweatshops to make the experience as realistic as possible. That means that players have to take care that the non-playable characters drink enough water – otherwise they will dehydrate (and of course not be able to work). The conditions shown in the game are quite accurate – fire might break out, there is a lack of toilets, and workers might get hurt or even die in accidents. Throughout the game, facts on workshops are presented to make players aware of the bad situation the workers are in. Although Littleloud (the developing company) made sure that the game should only be regarded as an educational tool and "is a sympathetic examination of the pressures that all participants in the sweatshop system endure" (ibid.), Apple was not willing to offer the game for sale.

Two games that criticize manufacturing electrical appliances – above all smartphones – have been rejected as well. *Phone Story* (Molleindustria, 2011) wants to provoke critical thoughts on the production of smartphones by providing four mini-games that stand for coltan extraction in Congo, production conditions in China, e-waste problems in Pakistan, and excessive consumerism in the Western world. Molleindustria, the developers, state on the game's website that *Phone Story* is a satirical and educational game to remind smartphone users of their impact on the world (Molleindustria, 2011). Reasons given by Apple were the violations of their rules regarding "violence or abuse of children" as well as "excessively objectionable or crude content" (Dredge, 2011). Dealing with a similar topic, *In a Permanent Save State* (Poynter, 2013) can be described as a surreal interactive narration imagining the spiritual afterlife of seven people who committed suicide because of being overworked. The game refers to the suicides that took place at Foxconn's electronics manufacturing site in 2010. Again, the developer, Benjamin Poynter, claims that the point of the game was to evoke empathy (Kopstein, 2012). Apple did not give any detailed reasons why the game was withdrawn from the App-Store after having been available for only one hour (Kalinchuk, 2012).

Another game rejected by Apple is *Smuggle Truck* (Owlchemy Labs, 2011). It deals with illegal immigration and should be regarded – as per the developers - as a satire. Players have to smuggle passengers across the US border in a truck, avoiding all kind of obstacles like hills, armadillos, and also catch newborn babies. Basically it is a physics game, which only uses the immigration issue as setting. The developers, Owlchemy Labs, state on their website that the game arose out of "frustration our friends have experienced in trying to immigrate to the United States. With such troublesome issue being largely avoided in popular media, especially video games, we felt the best way to criticize it was with an interactive satire" (Owlchemy Labs, 2011, p. 1). After having learned that the game had been rejected by Apple because of its content, the developer team changed the game and used fluffy animals instead of immigrants. The game, now called *Snuggle Truck* (Owlchemy Labs, 2011), was accepted by Apple immediately.

Games dealing with current political topics are also unwelcome. *Endgame Syria* (GameTheNews, 2012), a news game (Bogost, Ferrari, & Schweizer, 2010), deals with the conflict in Syria. It resembles a trading card game showing the options Syrian rebels, as well as the regime, have in order to push the conflict. Apple rejected the game because it included people from a specific government, meaning references to the Assad Regime, Palestinian groups, and militia groups. Although the developing company changed and resubmitted the game several times, it was always rejected due to its political content (Lien, 2013).

Rejected games can be published (and often are) on other platforms like Android, but Apple's share in mobile applications is quite substantial. This means a large group of people cannot be reached via these games (Van Roessel, 2014). Apart from using narrative settings or plots showing human rights violations, values can also be expressed in other game elements as discussed in the next section.

Expressing Values in Games

Serious games dealing with human rights topics follow different approaches in their game-design in order to reach their aims. All in all, there can be 15 different game elements identified that can be used in games to foster particular values (Flanagan & Nissenbaum, 2014, p. 33ff). The following section discusses eight elements, citing examples to show how these elements can be realized. The other seven elements presented by Flanagan and Nissenbaum (2014) include: hardware, interface, game engine and software, game maps, context of play, rules for interaction with the environment, and other players or nonplayable characters. These will not be discussed as there are few games dealing with human rights that include these elements.

Narrative Premises and Goals

Nearly all games tell a story or need narration – at least to set the background of the game. When talking about serious games for teaching human rights issues, narration seems to be of central importance. However, there are differences in how far the story/goal are integrated into game play. Looking at *Maria Sisters – Clean Room* (Global Arcade, 1999), which is based on the game mechanics of *Super Mario Bros.* (Nintendo, 1987), the game does not provide the player with much information about the character or goals. Maria, the playable character, is shown working at the assembly line of a computer manufacturer and smoking a cigarette in the restroom during her short break. After a chart with dangerous chemicals has been presented, the player can take over control of Maria. There are two obstacles in the game, which are the managers of the plant and chemicals. Players have to jump on the non-playable characters representing the managers, whereas they have to avoid the chemicals. Although you get some clues when Maria is hit by the managers or the chemical element (e.g., "You're an immigrant. You're lucky to have a job"), you need to read the information on the website to learn that the game criticizes companies in Silicon Valley for exposing (immigrant) workers to toxic chemicals. Players can (similar to the original *Super Mario Bros.*) easily play the game without attending to the narrative and the goal, thus ignoring all the problems the game would like to tackle.

Frontiers (Gold Extra, 2008) uses narrative premises completely different. This 3D online multiplayer game about refugees trying to cross the borders illegally to come to Europe, provides players with the choice between two roles: refugee or border control. The game immerses the player in realistic surroundings of African landscapes and Spanish border control buildings, trying to depict reality as closely as possible. As you work in teams (refugees or boarder control) there is also much interaction among players. *Frontiers* is basically a modification of the commercial ego-shooter *Half Life* (Valve, 1998) where there are many possibilities for exploring the different maps. However, you are always reminded of who you are in the game and what your aim is. Players cannot ignore the narration, as it is part of the game.

Another example for the importance of narration is *September 12th* (Newsgaming, 2003), a game that wants to show players that violence only causes more violence. This newsgame has very simple instructions, which are stated at the beginning: "The rules are deadly simple. You can shoot. Or not." Two illustrations also show which non-playable characters should be regarded as terrorists and which are civilians. The game's setting is a busy marketplace where terrorists can be seen among civilians. Shooting at a terrorist, however, results in killing civilians as well as there are large explosions. As a consequence, more and more terrorists show up – developing out of mourning civilians. "The only sense in which it [i.e. the game] can be beaten is if the player realizes the futility of the playable character's one-dimensional approach to fighting terrorism" (Flanagan & Nissenbaum, 2014, p. 36). The game intentionally confronts players to question the viewpoint taken by the playable character and also seeks to transfer the experience made in the game to real life.

These examples show that games do not convey what they are intended to if game mechanics and narration are not well connected. If the plot can easily be exchanged by using different characters or settings, values are not expressed in a satisfactory way. Therefore, it is necessary to make narration part of the game-mechanics and part of the rules.

Characters

For many games, it is important that players identify with playable characters or at least empathize with them in order to transfer this empathy into real life. When players are provided with possibilities to select or customize characters, they are more likely to identify. Characters might also develop according to the decisions taken by the player throughout the game. Having a look at serious games dealing with human rights, there are not many that allow a lot of choice for players regarding character customization. *P.I.N.G. – Poverty Is Not a Game* (iMinds, 2010) offers two different playable characters, Jim and Sophia. Players can choose one of these at the beginning of the game. The game deals with poverty in European countries, allowing young people to experience how fast teenagers might end up in poverty. Depending on the choice of character, the story line differs presenting either generational or situational poverty. Similar to *Frontiers* (Gold Extra, 2008), it makes sense to play the game more than once in order to take different points of view. If a game offers character choice which leads to different narrations or different points of view, players might think more deeply about a topic or a situation than if they can only choose between a male or a female character without any change of perspective offered by the game (depending on the choice taken).

Values can also be made explicit when having a look at the relationship between player and playable characters. Sometimes games want players to disagree with their character's actions. In order to win *Sweatshop* (Littleloud, 2011), players need to do things one would normally describe as immoral. One needs to exploit workers, make use of child-labor, and risk health and lives of non-playable characters to succeed in the game. But there is also a direct player-non-playable character connection. During the game, players are confronted with a child (visualized with oversized eyes expressing joy, fear, or sadness) explaining the bad working conditions at the workshop and repeatedly asking for understanding or even pleading for mercy. The reactions of this child relate to the player's actions in the game. Putting the players in the shoes of someone who seems to be forced to abuse workers might result in players trying to work against the game (Dixon, 2015).

Layoff (Tiltfactor, 2009) is based on the game mechanics of games like *Bejeweled* (PopCap Games, 2001). Players are part of the management of a company and need to cut jobs by matching workers who are the same. As soon as there are three or more similar employees put next to each other, they are fired, fall off the bottom end of the screen, and are seen wandering to the counters of an unemployment office. The more employees are selected, the more money that can be saved. When the player moves his/her mouse over the non-playable character, a short biography can be read that includes the name, age, kind of job, and other personal information. Managers – who also appear amongst the staff – cannot be removed (and thus not fired). Players' success is expressed via a counter where they can see how much money has already been saved. According to Flanagan and Nissenbaum, "[i]n *Layoff*, a bond of empathy is created not only between the player and the playable character, representing management, but rather between the player and nonplayable characters, representing the workers being laid off" (2014, p. 40). This identification is made when players read the information about the non-playable characters, seeing parallels to their own lives.

As shown here, characters – playable as well as non-playable ones – can be a very important part of game-design when it comes to embedding values. In order to feel empathy, it is not necessary to create extremely realistic looking characters or to offer numerous possibilities to customize the character, but there also needs to be a connection established with the player. In this way, the player feels empathy with the (non-)playable characters.

Actions

Depending on the genre, games usually allow different actions to be carried out by the player. Actions can include running, jumping, talking to other characters, or shooting, to name a few. Interactivity is a feature of games that makes them distinct from books or films. Players are used to very active playable characters in games: If the player does not act (by pressing a button, for example), the game does not react. These actions are primarily necessary to advance in the game but they can also include certain values by putting them in a new context (i.e., in *September 12th*, which cannot be compared to usual ego-shooter games, the only action players can perform is shooting).

A Closed World (Singapore-MIT GAMBIT Game Lab, 2011) tackles sexuality and identity issues. Players of this JRPG must lead their protagonist through a dark wood in order to find a better way of living. The playable character has been separated from his/her lover because of strict society rules in their hometown and is now confronted with demons representing opinions and attitudes of family and friends. If the demons cannot be defeated, the character is forced to walk around the forest forever. Every time players meet a demon, there are three options to choose from (apart from breathing and walking away): a passionate appeal, a logical argument, and an ethical claim. In order to play the game successfully, players have to remember the following: passion defies logic, logic challenges ethics, and ethics sway passion. This triangle is similar to the popular game *Rock–Paper–Scissors*. The player basically has to find out if the demon insulted the character out of logic, passion, or ethics and has to respond correspondingly to cause maximum damage to the demon's strength. For example, when the character meets the demon of his/her mother who was obsessed with other people's opinion, players can defeat it with logic. When pressing the key, an answer to the demon is presented: "Just because everyone else is ignorant doesn't mean you should be too." The bar showing the demon's strength lowers a bit if the player chooses the right strategy. Then the demon attacks the player's character that loses composure (also represented by a bar which is full at the beginning and lowers a bit after each successful attack). The demons, however, will change their tactics occasionally. Consequently, the player also has to use different approaches. If a demon attacks the character more successfully than the player does, one of the three choices (logic, passion, ethics) might be unavailable as an option for defeating this demon. As composure goes down rather rapidly after each attack, it is possible to regain some composure by taking a deep breath (meaning players are not allowed to choose an attack). As soon as the demon is defeated, there is a cut scene in which the player can learn about the character's story as well as the forest and its mysteries by watching a dialogue between the game character and a non-playable character. The game works with many metaphors so that the player is asked to find his/her own meaning. The game primarily relies on decision taking and pushing the "right" buttons – there is not a large variety of actions possible but nevertheless the game succeeds in showing what people might do in similar situations in real life – one can either walk away or speak out against prejudices.

A very interesting approach is used by *Hush* (Antonisse, 2008), which is a game set in the Rwandan Civil War of 1994. The playable character is a Tutsi mother who has to hide with her baby so that Hutu soldiers will not find and kill them. In order to keep the baby quiet, the player has to type the text of a lullaby in the same rhythm as it appears on the screen. If the keys are pressed too early or too late, the baby will cry louder and alert Hutu soldiers passing by. Players have reported feelings of tension and dread if they failed to calm the child (Flanagan & Nissenbaum, 2014, p. 44). Again, an emotional bond between player and playable character is established because of the actions players can take.

Outcasted (Köln International School of Design, 2014), as already briefly described, uses a completely different way of controlling the character. Players are quite passive, the only thing they can do is look at passersby. The game thus shows how helpless and easily frustrated homeless people can be by putting the player in this passive role. The game has already been tested successfully at various game festivals.

What was notable, according to Zerbe [one of the developers] was how people reacted with such glee to pedestrians that stopped and acknowledged them. Any interaction at all was its own reward. Through this, the players came to realize the monotony and tirelessness of being the person reaching out to people for loose change. It's this that affected them most. (Priestman, 2015, p. 7)

This example clearly shows that sometimes it is the non-action that makes certain values visible.

Another approach is used by *This War of Mine* (11bit studios, 2014), an anti-war game putting players in control of a group of civilians whose only aim is to survive. This game contrasts all the blockbuster ego-shooter games where players are put in the role of soldiers. *This War of Mine*, however, requires the player to control the characters' health, hunger, and mood levels until ceasefire day. Food, tools, and other resources can only be searched for at night; during the days, hostile snipers prevent the characters from leaving their shelter. In the meantime, they can craft tools, cook food, heal wounded and ill characters, and upgrade their shelter. At the beginning, the player controls two to four survivors. Each of them have different traits that might be useful or not useful for carrying out certain actions. The state of the characters and how to satisfy their needs is quite complex. All actions taken by the player will influence the ending of each character as the game provides several different endings. Various events and player's action will also influence how the game ends. For example, helping neighbors or other non-playable characters might be rewarded, whereas stealing and murdering might affect the character negatively. There are many events that can occur (e.g. outbreak of crime, raids) randomly, which will also influence the story line. Moral decisions have to be taken as well – shall neighbors be robbed or shall the player's character keep on starving? The player is quite free in deciding what to do and where to go, but is always accompanied by the feeling of fear and frustration as he/she never knows what might happen next. Compared to the other examples mentioned, *This War of Mine* offers a lot of different actions and thus a lot of choices for the player, which will be discussed in detail in the next section.

Player Choice

Compared to books and films, digital games are interactive and thus provide players with choice. However, not all choices provided can be regarded as meaningful ones. Meaningful here stands for choices that will influence the storyline of the game, the character, or its relationship to other (non-playable) characters. *Immigropoly* (IDResearch, 2012) is a game aimed at teaching young people about legal immigration to Europe. Players can choose between six different characters coming from different countries that have different reasons for leaving their home countries. The game is a mixture of adventure game (players have to complete different missions consisting of various tasks until the character safely reaches Europe), board game (you have to throw a virtual dice to advance in parts of the game), and quiz game (after having read extensive texts on historical or current events and country information, players have to take multiple choice quizzes). Most of the choices that can be taken when the playable character engages in a conversation with a non-playable character are quite obvious and cannot be regarded as meaningful choices, as one does not have to think hard about which option to choose in order to complete the mission. The game follows a linear path – even if players choose a "wrong" option, which leads to mission failure, the game continues the same way as if having completed the mission successfully. This results in players either not reading the choices carefully or even quitting the game. The game is thus unsuccessful in delivering its message.

A game completely based on player's decisions is *Papers, Please* (Pope, 2013). The puzzle video game focuses on the player working as an immigration officer at the border of the fictional country of Arstotzka. Players have to decide if people queuing in front of the counter are allowed to enter the country by carefully checking documents, asking non-playable characters questions, and bearing all (constantly changing) rules and regulations in mind. The player also has to care for the family who relies on the officer's income for medicine, food, and heating. The more arrivals are dealt with correctly, the more money the character earns. However, if any mistakes are made, the player is punished by getting less money, being fired, or being arrested. To make things even more complex, individuals or organizations try to bribe the playable character. Money that is offered can either be taken or burnt. There are also various moral choices integrated. For example, some of the non-playable characters start talking and telling about themselves. It is the player's choice if he/she lets the criminal pass whose documents are complete and valid or if the spouse of an Arstotzkian citizen should be allowed to enter the country even if one paper is missing. All the moral decisions taken are always closely connected to the playable character's family and their growing needs and thus make decisions for the player even more difficult. Consequences of the decisions taken can either be seen at once (i.e., getting a warning or penalty for making mistakes) or later on, for example when reading the newspaper. When players decide to let a human trafficker whose papers are okay into the country – although a woman pleaded before to help her by not allowing him in – players will learn from the newspaper later on that this woman was found murdered at a local strip club. When a reporter who wants to report on the country shows up, the player can decide if she should pass (and thus supports freedom of the press) although her credentials should be rejected according to the state regulations. In this way, "[t]he moral choices are layered on top of the action of the game not as a system of its own, but as a complication to the systems at play" (E. Swain, 2014). The game provides different endings so that players' decisions within the game matter greatly. The choices taken do not necessarily decide if a player wins or loses, but they make players think about their own attitude (i.e., do they want to be a loyal employee), even if that means not caring much for their moral values (i.e., do they want to play in a morally and ethically correct way). *Papers, Please* has been quite successful in the way it places this choice on its players.

Another game relying completely on players' choices is *Spent* (McKinney, 2011), a text-based browser game, challenging the gamer to survive on $1,000 a month. Data presented in the game, like housing prices or costs for commuting, are based on real data taken from Durham, North Carolina. Before the game starts, the provoking question "But you'd never need help, right?" is asked, referring to more than 6,000 people per year who need financial or social help in the area of Durham. After having chosen a job (for the most well-paid one the player even has to take a real typing test), players are faced with typical real life decisions (i.e., choosing a health insurance plan or finding a place to live) but also personal decisions ("You've been experiencing some sharp pains in your chest lately, and your family has a history of heart problems. What do you want to do? – Get it checked out ($45) or Ignore it."). All the questions are connected to financial issues, but many also include a social aspect (i.e., what to do with your daughter who was invited to a birthday party and has to bring a present) or bring up moral issues (i.e., will you pay for an expensive treatment for your family pet, have it put to sleep, or let it suffer?). Between most decisions, the game present players with real data showing how many Americans have to face these decisions in everyday life. *Spent* shows that games need not necessarily provide players with good graphics to make them worth playing. According to Heron and Belford (2014), "[a] game does not require photo realism, but it does require social realism" (p. 38). Some decisions taken will show their consequences rounds later. In this way, the player is not only put in the shoes of somebody who has to tackle financial issues, but also experiences that even small decisions matter.

Point of View

There is a difference in how players experience game-play depending on the perspective they take as the playable character and towards the setting and events in general. Games can make use of first person perspective, which means playing directly from the playable character's perspective. Another possibility, which is quite often used, is the player perspective. The player seems to watch the scene from a certain distance. A third possibility is the view from above, which is also called God-view. Depending on the point of view of a digital game, players will experience the game in a different way. A first-person view, for example, allows players to identify with the character more easily:

Since we can't see the character (just like we can't see ourselves in the real world) and since we are seeing the game world through its eyes, this kind of point of view drives the player into accepting more easily a new identity: there aren't obstacles between the player and the character, nothing to separate them, the symbiosis is nearly absolute. (Papale, 2014, p. 2)

Homeland Guantanamo (Free Range Studios, 2008) uses this first perspective. The game deals with inhumane conditions at detention centers in the US. The playable character is an undercover journalist searching for information regarding the case of a 52-year-old immigrant who died in Immigration Customs Enforcement. The player can walk around the detention center, look at various objects, and start dialogues with detainees. Although there is not much interaction, players experience the feeling of walking through the building. They are forced to see everything through the playable character's eyes and therefore can feel more like the person they are playing. Another example of this first person perspective can be seen in *Sweatshop* (Littleloud, 2011) where both non-playable characters (child and boss) talk to the player who has to manipulate the workers at the assembly line and try to influence players' decisions. As the player is directly addressed by these two non-playable characters, she can decide whom to help or please and whom to ignore. The conflict of the mid-level manager is directly transferred to the player. Other games take a third person perspective such as in *Frontiers* (Gold Extra, 2010), where players are nevertheless experiencing everything from the point of view of their characters as the game follows every step the character takes (similar to a film camera following the main character). This special point of view enables players to see their character (or at least the back of their character) and everything the playable character sees. It is not possible to look the character in the face. An interesting mixture of perspective emerges related to being near to the character but at the same time, a sense of distance is created. There are also games that make use of a top-down view like in *Ayiti – The Cost of Life* (Global

Kids & Game Lab, 2006), where players see the figures and the map from a bird's eye view. This point of view matches the values embedded. The player is made to feel responsible for the Guinnard family and thus builds an emotional bond. The scenario presented triggers the players' protection instinct, which makes them want the family happy and healthy (Dillon, 2013).

It can be stated that the point of view chosen by the game designer might influence the way the player experiences her game-play. Similar to books and films, a closer or more distant relationship towards the main (playable) character can be established.

Rewards

It is quite interesting to investigate the reward system of a game, as this can reveal which accomplishments are truly valued (Flanagan & Nissenbaum, 2014, p. 63). Some games reward completely different actions than the game intends. *Immigropoly* (IDResearch, 2012), for example, provides game-currency for answering quiz questions correctly. Players accumulate money for reading texts carefully and memorizing all facts correctly but not for showing respect to or understanding immigrants and their motifs. Rewards that align with the values presented in the game are evident in *Frontiers* (Gold Extra, 2010). When playing as the border control, players get points when they arrest refugees. However, if the refugees are hurt or even killed, points are deducted. Additionally, the country the player stands for is punished according to the Human Rights Index. Points are also deducted when police officers accept bribes. This example shows that players have to accept and play by moral and ethical rules if they want to win the game. But it is still their own decision if they keep to the ethics standards set by the game. *This War of Mine* (11 bit studios, 2014) provides quite a complex reward/punishment system. Helping a non-playable character, for example, will raise the morale of the player's group of characters, whereas ignoring non-playable characters' plea will lower it. Behaving morally correct within the game supports a positive ending for a character, whereas behaving immorally/refusing to help accumulates points towards a bad ending. In some instances, helping/being good is only likely to lead to a positive ending. In this way, the player is never sure what kind of consequence an action will have later on in the game. "A good deed may be rewarded or it may be punished. Maybe nothing will happen. The meaning of your choices is down to you and your circumstances" (Zacny, 2014, p. 8). This way rewards within a game are seen is an important element, although most game designers do not seem to pay that much attention to reward systems as the majority of games contain rewards in form of points, up-leveling, or receiving in-game currency.

Strategies

Games quite often allow various ways of mastering them – especially more complex ones that allow players to think of their own strategies in order to win the game. *Sweatshop* challenges players to forget about ethically correct behavior and, being a satire, allows winning only if players exploit non-playable characters. This involves making use of child labor and trying to save as much money as possible, even if that means putting non-playable characters under constant threats of being injured or killed (Dixon, 2015). By using a strategy that most people would regard as totally immoral in real world scenarios, the game succeeds in showing players that the topic pertaining to sweatshops is much more complex. The situation cannot be changed with only one person refusing to exploit workers. It also depends on wholesalers, retailers, and finally consumers saying "no."

Ayiti – The Cost of Life (Global Kids & Game Lab, 2006) asks players before starting the game which strategy they would like to use. They can choose between health, happiness, education, and money. The strategy that is chosen by the players does not influence the course of the game, as this decision at the beginning should only make players think what they themselves regard as most important. As the game is quite hard to beat, it takes most players several attempts to find a successful strategy – described as a mixture of paying attention to health, education, buying books for homeschooling, and doing community service. This of course supports certain ideologies (Ferri & Fusaroli, 2009) as it is, for example, not clear why home-schooling is more effective than schools are. To contemplate this further, the game subliminally teaches you that it is enough to supply books to even uneducated people to solve the problem of lacking education. This example shows that games might impose values by accepting only a certain strategy to win. *Papers, Please* (Pope, 2013) does not impose a strategy on the player in order to win the game. The players can accept the rules of the game – meaning that they will work for a totalitarian state – or they can decide against this structure and play the game in a moral way. Additionally, they can even decide to help bring down the government. It is in the player's hand to decide their strategy – it does not influence the end state of the game (winning or losing).

Aesthetics

The last game element this paper looks at is aesthetics, as they can also support the values the game would like to express or work against them. Many serious games dealing with human rights issues make use of cartoonish figures. *Half the Sky* (Frima Studio, 2012), for example, addresses a serious topic by presenting stories of women who are oppressed by their husbands, are poor, or are infected with AIDS. However, in playing the game, players will come across nicely dressed, clean, and pretty playable and non-playable characters, often smiling and above all having really big eyes reminding players of manga drawings. When playing the game in the very clean and nice village, players most likely do not think of serious problems. The game thus can be played as an enjoyable casual game, ignoring the cruel and sad reality it basically depicts.

Bad Paper (Fusion, 2014) seeks to show players what might happen once people are in debt. The game is based on the book by Jake Halpern, who followed several debt collectors. Players can choose between two roles – debtor or debt collector. The game is quite simple to play, as it consists of dialogues between the two characters. Depending on the role players have taken, they can choose between two to four different possibilities of what to say or do. The website for the game, as well as the game itself, presents drawings of the acting characters which might remind players of the black and white crime films of the 1930s. In addition, the font of the text resembles text typed with an old typewriter. All in all, the game gives you a dark depressing feeling, conveying the mood debtors might be in.

Papers, Please (Pope, 2013) draws a similar dark and somewhat old-fashioned picture of the scenario depicted in the game due to the 8-bits-graphics. The colors appear to be washed out and are quite dark. This has the ability to lead to a bleak and threatening atmosphere, suitable for the setting of a totalitarian regime. The player can experience what it must be like to work in such an environment. So the aesthetics support the topic well.

Obviously this [the graphics] goes well with the overall theme that the game is set in post-war era (their war with Kolechia) and even the colour palette will instantly reminds [sic!] you that you're working for an authoritative and communist government. (Margathe, 2013)

Bad Paper as well as *Papers, Please* use visual clues that support the topic and the setting of the game, making it easier for the player to empathize with the playable characters.

RESEARCH ON THE IMPACT OF SERIOUS GAMES

After explicating various game elements that might help to integrate values, it makes sense to contemplate the power of games when it comes to teaching about human rights. There is no doubt that learning takes place when a video game is being played. Well-designed games manage to teach players quite complex structures without overtly teaching. Games can be successful at providing places and situations, offering meaningful experiences to players which would not be possible otherwise (Gee, 2007). The advantage of virtual places allows learners to experiment with, as well as to test, abstract concepts (Shaffer, Halverson, Squire, & Gee, 2005; Dunwell, de Freitas, & Jarvis, 2011). Measuring the impact of serious games is not something that can be done easily. It is easy to ascertain the number of people playing/downloading a game within a certain period of time. However, that does not mean that everyone is somehow influenced by the contents of the game. Nor is it known if players acquire additional knowledge or change their attitude towards the topic dealt with in the game or if their behavior changes in any way. In order to find answers to these questions, some more studies need to be carried out. Regarding serious games, however, there are only a few researchers who have dealt with the impact of these games in the way mentioned before. Research results presented in the following section give a clue of what digital games have been shown to achieve related to empathy, knowledge, and attitude.

Digital games are good at simulating situations and enabling players to consider other people's points of view. Many serious games dealing with human rights topics seek to elicit player empathy with the people depicted in the game, thus understanding their situation in real life as well. Taking the role of another person can be a factor that produces empathy (as defined by Davis, 1996). Peng, Lee, & Heeter (2010) used *Darfur is Dying* (Take Action Games, 2006) and a text about the Darfurian conflict as stimuli for their experiment. In this game the players can choose their character out of eight characters representing a family (parents and six children aged between 10 to 14 years) and send them to forage for water, trying to avoid the patrols of the Janjaweed militia. If the character is captured, the player is informed what is likely to happen to their selected character. Then the player is asked to choose another family member to try it again. Results of the study show that people who have played the game were more willing to help the Darfurian people than those who only read the text giving similar information (ibid p. 731f).

Another case study was done using *Homeless: It's No Game* (Wetcoast Games, 2006), which was developed to find out if people could become more empathetic by taking the role of a homeless person. This topic was chosen as it attracts extreme views and is becoming more and more relevant in today's society (Lavender, 2011). The protagonist of the game is a homeless woman who tries to survive in a city, which provides quite a hostile environment for her. The game can be won if 24 hours of game-time are played without self-esteem dropping to zero. The study was set up using three groups (game-players, a group reading a short story about the homeless character, and a control group). Playing the game seems to increase sympathy for homeless people (ibid. p. 22). Another interesting finding was that players who did not regard the game as very realistic felt less sympathetic than those who thought the game showed a realistic picture of homelessness (ibid. p. 24).

Food Force (World Food Programme, 2005) asks players to distribute food in a country affected by a famine caused by drought and war. Six missions set different tasks, for example, locating hungry citizens, producing a balanced diet, or dropping food supplies from a plane. A study carried out with Greek primary school students aged 10 to 11 years sought to find out if playing this game could result in knowledge gains regarding the understanding of procedures that are needed for humanitarian aid in emergency cases. Both groups (game players and control group) were given 15 questions before and after the instructional intervention. There were no significant differences in results between both groups (Provelengios & Fesakis, 2011, p. 480). Regarding attitudes, however, the study showed that Food Force was able to sensitize students about the problem of hunger as well as changing their views and attitudes. After playing the game students were more empathetic with people living in affected countries and were also more likely to help people facing food problems (ibid. p. 480ff).

These three studies show that games might influence attitudes and empathy as long as the contents presented are regarded as realistic. Although these two studies have not been carried out on a large-scale and thus the results cannot be generalized, the results provide valuable proof that games can express values and might be a useful media for making people feel empathetic.

In addition to creating empathy, games might also be good at teaching knowledge. A large-scale, quantitative study was used to investigate affective learning when playing the game *Spent* (McKinney, 2011). In Ruggiero's study (2014), 5,139 US Midwestern students aged 12 to 18 years were divided into three groups (game, reading, and control group) in which they were randomly assigned. The reading group used a text similar to the study regarding *Homeless – It's No Game*, an account of the first night as a homeless person (written in first person view). The results show that students in both groups, reading and game, "increased their affective learning score immediately after treatment and both factors were statistically significant in their difference from the control group" (Ruggiero, 2014, p. 3429). Data from the posttest game group scored higher than the reading group, showing that playing the game led to a higher level of affective learning. This might be due to the fact that students could actually experience what it means to be poor or homeless.

This shows that games can affect players' attitudes; however, at the current time, evidence does not show that video games are better than other instructional media.

CONCLUSION

As this chapter has shown, there are numerous serious games attempting to teach players about human rights issues by addressing certain topics and embodying human values. Their approaches to do so vary extensively as values can be integrated in different game elements. There are examples where these elements were designed deliberately to achieve certain effects but there are also games that might aim at completely different outcomes than the designers' original intentions. Games can provoke – like films and texts – and sometimes their influence is more via media coverage and public reactions than in the gameplay itself. This is especially apparent when discussing Apple's App Store policy or considering the public outcry after *Escape from Woomera* (Wild, 2004) was released. The examples discussed, show that it is not only the game itself which expresses values. The impact of games on society can also be seen from news reports, forum discussions, and games being banned from App Store. When having a look at the example of *Smuggle Truck*, which was accepted by Apple only after the "story" and the characters were slightly altered, one can see that there are some topics which seem to be more offensive than others.

There are different game elements used in order to express values. Although narration is the obvious choice to teach players, examples like *Layoff* (Tiltfactor, 2009) or *A Closed World* (Singapore-MIT GAM-

BIT Game Lab, 2011) prove that there are many possibilities to convey values. A very important factor when wanting to teach players is player choice. As *Papers, Please* (Pope, 2013) shows it is neither the latest graphics nor open world settings that make players think carefully. Being able to take meaningful decisions, which are not obvious but really challenge your own morality, make players think. If the game then takes real life examples as done in *Spent* (McKinney, 2011), transfer into players' lives seems easier. When it comes to empathy, the point of view a game represents, is of importance. Slipping into the role of a playable character and seeing everything through his/her eyes, makes players feel with them. Games like *This War of Mine* (11 bit studios, 2014), on the other hand, use a clever reward system to integrate values into game mechanics. This game makes it hard for players to find the "right" decision but allows at the same time that different strategies and ways (acting morally appropriate or not) can be tried out.

As digital games are regarded more and more a part of our culture and as works of art, there will be possibly be more developers dealing with content apart from mainstream topics. There is little doubt that many human rights issues will be integrated into games in the near future. However, it is necessary to do more intensive and large-scale research related to the different ways game elements influence players in order to find out what works best for these games whose primary goal is to make players empathize with other groups of people, develop understanding, or change their attitudes (and possibly their behavior).

In conclusion, it can be said that games can be regarded as very influential on society and culture by addressing serious topics like human rights issues. These games might not be the most well-known ones or blockbuster games everybody has heard about. But similar to books and films that criticize certain situations in society or political conditions, they are a way of expressing values and thus influencing their players.

REFERENCES

Amnesty International. (2015). *Human rights education*. Retrieved July 12, 2015, from https://www. amnesty.org/en/human-rights-education

Anthropy, A. (2012). *Dys4ia* [Flash game]. Newgrounds. Retrieved 3 August 2015 from http://www. newgrounds.com/portal/view/591565

Antonisse, J. (2008). *Hush* [Flash game]. Southern California: USC.

Apple. (2015). *App store review guidelines - Apple developer*. Retrieved July 7, 2015, from https:// developer.apple.com/app-store/review/guidelines/#objectionable-content

Basu, S. (2010). *5 cool edutainment games you can play and also donate to charitable causes*. Retrieved July 10, 2015, from http://www.makeuseof.com/tag/5-cool-edutainment-games-play-donate-charitable/

11. Bit Studios. (2014). *This War of Mine*. [PC game].Warsaw: 11 bit studios.

Bogost, I. (2007). *Persuasive games: The expressive power of videogames*. Cambridge, MA: MIT Pr.

Bogost, I., Ferrari, S., & Schweizer, B. (2010). *Newsgames: Journalism at play*. Cambridge, MA: MIT Pr.

Brander, P., De Witte, L., Ghanea, N., Gomes, R., Keen, E., Nikitina, A., & Pinkeviciute, J. (2012). *Compass. Manual for human rights education with young people*. Strasbourg: Council of Europe Publishing.

Cobb, J. (2008). *Learning games - 26 serious games to change the world*. Retrieved July 10, 2015, from http://www.missiontolearn.com/2008/04/learning-games-for-change/

Davis, M. H. (1996). *Empathy: A social psychological approach (Revised.)*. Boulder, CO: Westview Press.

Dillon, R. (2013, May). Serious games and fun: An analysis. *International Journal of Innovative Research & Development*, 2(5), 1046–1063.

Dixon, D. (2015). *Human dignity and the bottom line: Sweatshop*. Retrieved July 8, 2015, from http://gamechurch.com/human-dignity-and-the-bottom-line-sweatshop/

Djaouti, D., Alvarez, J., Jessel, J.-P., & Rampnoux, O. (2011). *Origins of serious games*. Retrieved July 6, 2015, from http://www.ludoscience.com/files/ressources/origins_of_serious_games.pdf

Dredge, S. (2011). *Apple bans satirical iPhone game* Phone Story *from its App Store*. Retrieved July 7, 2015, from http://www.theguardian.com/technology/appsblog/2011/sep/14/apple-phone-story-rejection

Dunwell, I., de Freiatas, S., & Jarvis, S. (2011). Four-dimensional consideration of feedback in serious games. In *Digital Games and Learning* (pp. 42–62). London: Continuum.

Entertainment Software Association. (2015). *Essential facts about the computer and video game industry*. Retrieved July 6, 2015, from http://www.theesa.com/wp-content/uploads/2015/04/ESA-Essential-Facts-2015.pdf

Farber, M. (2015). *10 educational games that teach kids about social issues*. Retrieved from http://content.easybib.com/10-educational-games-that-teach-kids-about-social-issues/

Ferri, G., & Fusaroli, R. (2009). *Which narrations for persuasive technologies? Habits and procedures in Ayiti: The Cost of Life*. Retrieved July 6, 2015, from http://www.aaai.org/Papers/Symposia/Spring/2009/SS-09-06/SS09-06-007.pdf

Flanagan, M., & Nissenbaum, H. (2014). *Values at play in digital games* (1st ed.). Cambridge, Massachusetts: Mit Press.

Free Range Studios. (2008). *Homeland Guantanamo* [Flash game]. Washington D.C.: Free Range Studios. Retrieved August 12, 2015 from http://www.homelandgitmo.com/

Frima Studio. (2012). *Half The Sky Movement: The Game* [Facebook app]. Quebec: Frima Studio. Retrieved September 23, 2015 from https://www.facebook.com/HalftheGame

Fusion. (2015). *Bad Paper* [Browser game]. Doral, FL: Fusion. Retrieved September 3, 2015 from http://static.fusion.net/badpaper/

GameTheNews. (2012). *Endgame: Syria* [HTLML5, Android].:GameTheNews. Retrieved August 10, 2015 from http://gamethenews.net/wp-content/games/endgamesyria/

Gee, J. P. (2007). *Good video games and good learning: Collected essays on video games, learning and literacy* (1st ed.). New York: Lang, Peter New York.

Global Arcade. (1999). *Maria Sisters - Clean Room* [Flash game]. San Francisco, CA: Global Arcade. Retrieved September 10, 2015 from http://www.globalarcade.org/sv/

Global Kids & Game Lab. (2006). *Ayiti: The Cost of Life* [Flash game]. Global Kids. Retrieved September 23, 2015 from https://ayiti.globalkids.org/game/

Gold Extra. (2010). *Frontiers* [PC game]. Salzburg: Gold Extra.

Golding, D. (2013). *Videogames and politics: Why was Escape from Woomera so divisive?* [text]. Retrieved July 9, 2015, from http://www.abc.net.au/arts/blog/Daniel-Golding/videogames-politics-Escape-From-Woomera-130901/

Green, S. C. (2014). The perceptual and cognitive effects of action experience. In F. C. Blumberg (Ed.), Learning by playing: Video gaming in education (pp. 29–41). New York: OUP.

Half The Sky *movement game: From oppression to opportunity – raising awareness and funding.* (2015). Retrieved July 10, 2015, from http://designtoimprovelife.dk/half-the-sky-movement-game-from-oppression-to-opportunity-raising-awareness-and-funding/

Harris, T. (1998). *Hobson's Choice* [Browser game].

Heron, M., & Belford, P. (2014). 'It's only a game' - ethics, empathy and identification in game morality systems. *The Computer Games Journal, 3*(1), 34–52.

Holpuch, A. (2013). Half the Sky *Facebook game launches with women's empowerment at core*. Retrieved July 10, 2015, from http://www.theguardian.com/technology/2013/mar/04/facebook-game-half-the-sky

Huberts, C. (2014). Insufficient funds. Prekäre Leben im Computerspiel. *WASD Bookazine Für Gameskultur*, (5), 76–83.

IDResearch. (2012). *Immigropoly* [Flash game]. Hungary: IDResearch. Retrieved August 20, 2015, from http://en.immigropoly2.ittvagyunk.eu/auth

iMinds. (2010). *P.I.N.G. Poverty Is Not a Game* [PC game]. Gent-Ledeberg: iMinds.

Institute for the Future. (2012). *Catalysts for Change*. Palo Alto, CA: Institute for the Future.

Kalinchuk, A. (2012). *Apple bans artistic game based on Foxconn suicides from App Store*. Retrieved July 7, 2015, from http://www.digitaltrends.com/mobile/apple-bans-game-based-on-foxconn-suicides/

Klimmt, C. (2009). Serious games and social change. Why they (should) work. In U. Ritterfeld, M. Cody, & P. Vorderer (Eds.), *Serious games. Mechanisms and effects*. New York: Routledge. Retrieved from https://books.google.at/books/about/Serious_Games.html?hl=de&id=eGORAgAAQBAJ

Köln International School of Design. (2014). *Outcasted*. Köln: Köln International School of Design.

Kopstein, J. (2012). *Apple removes iPhone game based on Foxconn suicides from App Store*. Retrieved July 7, 2015, from http://www.theverge.com/2012/10/12/3495466/apple-bans-another-objectionable-iphone-game-about-foxconn-workers

Lavender, T. J. (2011). *Video games as change agents -- the case of Homeless: It's No Game - viewcontent.pdf*. Retrieved July 8, 2015, from http://s3.amazonaws.com/academia.edu.documents/30989963/viewcontent.pdf?AWSAccessKeyId=AKIAJ56TQJRTWSMTNPEA&Expires=1436335381&Signature=7jOataOgmbFnnFdUKP%2BpXQhKylo%3D&response-content-disposition=inline

Lazzaro. (2015). *The 4 keys 2 fun | Nicole Lazzaro's Blog.* Retrieved from http://www.nicolelazzaro. com/the4-keys-to-fun/

Lien, T. (2013). *The Apple obstacle for serious games.* Retrieved July 7, 2015, from http://www.polygon. com/2013/6/21/4449770/the-apple-obstacle-for-serious-games

Lien, T. (2014, May 16). Escape from Woomera *still highlights Australia's shame 11 years on.* Retrieved July 6, 2015, from http://www.polygon.com/2014/5/16/5717520/escape-from-woomera-immigration-australia

Littleloud. (2011). *Sweatshop.* [Flash game]. Retrieved July 12, 2015, from http://www.playsweatshop.com/

Margathe, J. (2013, August 16). *Review:* Papers, Please. Retrieved from http://blog.jovinomargathe. com/2013/08/16/review-papers-please/

Michael, D., & Chen, S. (2005). *Serious games: Games that educate, train, and inform.* Mason: Course Technology PTR. Retrieved from http://www.amazon.de/Serious-Games-That-Educate-Train/ dp/1592006221

Molleindustria. (2011). *Phone Story.* [Flash game]. Retrieved July 12, 2015, from http://phonestory.org/

Newberry, E. (1790). *The New Game of Human Life* [Board game]. England: J. Wallis & E. Newberry.

Newsgaming. (2003). *September 12th: A Toy World* [Macromedia Shockwave]. Uruguy: Newsgaming. Retrieved July 12, 2015, from http://www.newsgaming.com/ newsgames.htm

Nicholls, S. (2003). Escape game wires the minister. *Sydney Morning Herald.* Retrieved from http:// www.smh.com.au/articles/2003/04/29/1051381951157.html

Nintendo. (1987). *Super Mario Bros.* [NES]. Kyoto: Nintendo.

Owlchemy Labs. (2011). *Snuggle Truck* [Android, iOS]. Austin, TX: Owlchemy Labs. Retrieved July 12, 2015, from http://snuggletruck.com/

Papale, L. (2014, June 22). *Beyond identification: Defining the relationships between player and avatar.* Retrieved July 8, 2015, from http://gamescriticism.org/articles/papale-1-2/

Parkin, S. (2006). Darfur is Dying. *When videogames discovered ethics.* Retrieved July 10, 2015, from http://www.eurogamer.net/articles/i_darfurisdying_pc

Parkin, S. (2013). *A serious game about sweatshops ... you won't find it in Apple's App Store.* Retrieved July 7, 2015, from http://www.theguardian.com/commentisfree/2013/mar/22/sweatshop-game-apple-app-store

Peng, W., Lee, M., & Heeter, C. (2010). The effects of a serious game on role-taking and willingness to help. *Journal of Communication, 60*(4), 723–742. doi:10.1111/j.1460-2466.2010.01511.x

PopCap Games. (2001). *Bejeweled* [PC game]. Seattle: PopCap Games.

Pope, L. (2013). *Papers, Please* [PC game]. Lucas Pope.

Poynter, B. (2013). *In a permanent save state* [Android]. Reno: Benjamin Poynter.

Priestman, C. (2015). *The videogame trying to change how we treat the homeless*. Retrieved July 10, 2015, from http://killscreendaily.com/articles/outcasted/

Productions, P. T. V. (2010). *Inside the Haiti Earthquake* [Flash game]. PTV Productions. Retrieved 20 August 2015 from http://www.insidedisaster.com/experience/Main.html

Provelengios, P., & Fesakis, G. (2011). Educational applications of serious games: The case of the game *Food Force* in primary education students. In *Proceedings of the 5th European conference on games based learning* (pp. 476–485). Retrieved from https://books.google.at/books/about/Proceedings_of_the_5th_European_Conferen.html?hl=de&id=5CoJBAAAQBAJ

Ruggiero, D. N. (2014). *Spent: Changing students' affective learning toward homelessness through persuasive video game play*. ACM Press; doi:10.1145/2556288.2557390

Ruiz, S. (2006). *Darfur is Dying* [Flash game]. Take Action Games. Retrieved 23 September 2015 from http://www.darfurisdying.com/index.html

Shaffer, D. W., Halverson, R., Squire, K. R., & Gee, J. P. (2005, April). *Video games and the future of learning*. Retrieved July 7, 2015, from http://files.eric.ed.gov/fulltext/ED497016.pdf

Skartveit, H.-L. (2010). *Changes in museum practice*. Berghahn Books. Retrieved from https://books.google.at/books/about/Changes_in_Museum_Practice.html?hl=de&id=4OoBXAMKZJsC

Sojo Studios. (2012). *WeTopia* [Facebook App]. Sojo Studios. Retrieved April 23, 2014 from https://www.facebook.com/WeTopiaOfficial

Stokes, B., Seggerman, S., & Rejeski, D. (2011). *For a better world: Digital games and the social change sector*. Retrieved July 7, 2015, from http://www.gamesforchange.org/g4cwp/wp-content/uploads/2011/06/g4cwhitepaper.pdf

Swain, C. (2007). *Designing games to effect social change*. Retrieved September 18, 2015, from http://www.digra.org/wp-content/uploads/digital-library/07311.09363.pdf

Swain, C. (2010). *The mechanic is the message: How to communicate values in games through the mechanics of user action and system response*. Retrieved July 12, 2015, from http://www.irma-international.org/viewtitle/41321/

Swain, E. (2014). *Choice and consequence in "Papers, Please"*. Retrieved July 8, 2015, from http://www.popmatters.com/post/183289-papers-please-morality/

Swalwell, M. (2003). *The meme game:* Escape from Woomera. Retrieved July 6, 2015, from http://www.realtimearts.net/article/issue55/7103

Tiltfactor. (2009). *Layoff* [Flash game]. Hanover, NH: Tiltfactor. Retrieved July 8, 2015, from http://tiltfactor.org/play-layoff

Totals | Freerice.com. (2015). Retrieved July 10, 2015, from http://freerice.com/frmisc/totals

United Nations. Human Rights. (2015). *World programme for human rights education*. Retrieved December 18, 2015, from http://www.ohchr.org/EN/Issues/Education/Training/Pages/Programme.aspx

United Nations High Commission on Refugees. (2005). *Against All Odds* [Flash game]. UNHCR. Retrieved 10 August 2015 from http://www.playagainstallodds.ca/ game_us.html

United Nations High Commission on Refugees. (2012). *My Life As a Refugee* [iOS, Android]. Genève: UNHCR.

United Nations World Food Programme. (2007). *Free Rice* [Browser game]. UNWFP. Retrieved September 20, 2015 from http://freerice.com

Valve. (1998). *Half Life* [PC game]. Bellevue: Valve.

Van Roessel, L. (2014). *Do Apple's policies impede the growth of serious games?* Retrieved July 7, 2015, from http://policyreview.info/articles/news/do-apples-policies-impede-growth-serious-games/305

Wagner, M. (2007). Identitätsrückprojektion in aktiven Medien. Wann können Computerspiele unser reales Verhalten beeinflussen? *E-Beratungsjournal.net*, *3*(2). Retrieved from http://www.e-beratungsjournal.net/ausgabe_0207/wagner.pdf

Walz, S. P., & Deterding, S. (2014). *The gameful world. Approaches, issues, applications*. Cambridge, MA: MIT Press.

Wetcoast Games. (2006). *Homeless: It's No Game* [Flash game]. Wetcoast Games. Retrieved 10 February 2014 from http://www.wetcoastgames.ca/homeless/homeless.swf

Wild, K. et al. (2004). *Escape from Woomera* [PC game].

Wolonick, J. (2013). *The* Half the Sky *movement: Is a Facebook game the next step toward global social justice?* Retrieved July 10, 2015, from http://www.minyanville.com/sectors/media/articles/Half-the-Sky-Movement253A-Improving-Foreign/3/12/2013/id/48644?refresh=1

World Food Programme. (2005). *Food Force* [PC game].

York Zimmerman Inc. (2010). *People Power: The Game of Civil Resistance*. Washington, DC: York Zimmerman Inc.

Zacny, R. (2014). *The uneasy brilliance of "This War of Mine"*. Retrieved July 9, 2015, from http://www.pcgamesn.com/this-war-of-mine/the-uneasy-brilliance-of-this-war-of-mine

KEY TERMS AND DEFINITIONS

Empathy: The ability to understand and share the feelings of another person.

Games for Change: Often used instead of serious games. Digital games that want players to change their behavior or attitude.

Human Rights Education: It summarizes all learning developing knowledge, skills as well as values of human rights.

Non-Playable Character: Any character in a digital game that cannot be controlled by a player.

Serious Games: (Digital) games whose priority goes beyond entertainment.

Values: These are important ideals or beliefs which are common among members of a culture. They define which behavior is desirable or undesirable.

Video Game Design: Designing contents and rules of a video game means dealing with gameplay, environment, story and characters.

Chapter 10
Affordances and Constraints of Analog Games for Ethics Education:
Dilemmas and Dragons

Spencer P. Greenhalgh
Michigan State University, USA

ABSTRACT

Today's students face a wide range of complex moral dilemmas, and games have the potential to represent these dilemmas, thereby supporting formal ethics education. The potential of digital games to contribute in this way is being increasingly recognized, but the author argues that those interested in the convergence of games, ethics, and education should more fully consider analog games (i.e., games without a digital component). This argument draws from a qualitative study that focused on the use of an analog roleplaying game in an undergraduate activity that explored ethical issues related to politics, society, and culture. The results of this study are examined through an educational technology lens, which suggests that games (like other educational resources) afford and constrain learning and teaching in certain ways. These results demonstrate that this game afforded and constrained ethics education in both ways similar to digital games and ways unique to analog games.

INTRODUCTION

Whether they are children, teenagers, or adults, today's students live in a world facing innumerable and seemingly insurmountable challenges. For example, contemporary environmental issues such as climate change are defined both by stakeholders' sharp disagreements over the proper response and by the disadvantage that any proposed response will inevitably impose on at least some of those stakeholders (Ferkany & Whyte, 2011). Likewise, the decades since the Second World War have seen not only continued war but also a widening gap between the world's rich and poor (McWilliams & Piotrowski, 2009). Furthermore, these challenges are not limited to issues of worldwide consequence: Sandel (2009) suggests that students and citizens should be asking questions about how much CEOs should earn, whether psychological injuries merit military decorations, and where the limits of supply and demand are found.

DOI: 10.4018/978-1-5225-0261-6.ch010

Formal education has a role to play in preparing students to deal with these challenges. Roseth (2016) asserts that *morality*—the distinction between right and wrong—and *ethics*—socially-constructed standards for making that distinction—are generally recognized as an essential part of what students need to learn as part of their schooling. However, teaching ethics goes beyond addressing right and wrong to supporting students as they experience new moral perspectives. Gibbs (2014) argues that "[i]maginatively putting oneself in the place of another, or social perspective-taking, is central to moral development and behavior" (p. 1), and these temporary shifts are accompanied by the more permanent changes in perspective that can result from genuine moral reflection and argument (Sandel, 2009). Ferkany and Whyte (2011) suggest that some sort of formal education is necessary to help students develop the traits needed for effective perspective-taking and ethical deliberation. That is not to say that *ethics education* is restricted to philosophy classes; in the case of climate change, it is not inconceivable that classes as diverse as biology, history, and composition would all ask students to distinguish right from wrong within and adopt new perspectives on this topic, thereby incorporating ethics into their curriculum.

Over the past few decades, games and games scholarship have shown increasing awareness of ethics and morality. For example, games scholars have directed their attention to popular titles that explicitly address issues of moral or philosophical importance (Poels & Malliet, 2011a), impose ethical standards on their players (Bogost, 2007), or otherwise offer players a space for moral deliberation (Jansz, 2011). In response to the increasingly ethical nature of these games, Sicart (2009) has argued for the treatment of computer game players as moral agents, a position that other games researchers have since adopted (Poels & Malliet, 2011a). Scholars are also increasingly arguing that all video games represent ethical values in some form or another (Bogost, 2007; Flanagan & Nissenbaum, 2014; Sicart, 2009). Just as any curriculum that touches on distinguishing right from wrong and changing moral perspectives can be said to fall under the category of ethics education, any game that invites its players to make ethical decisions and adopt new perspectives becomes a potential tool for these ethics educators.

The purpose of this chapter is to use one classroom experience to highlight the particular potential of an often-overlooked category of games in ethics education. Although much attention has been paid to the ethical relevance of digital games—consider titles such as *The Ethics of Computer Games* (Sicart, 2009), *Moral Issues in Digital Game Play* (Poels & Malliet, 2011b), and *Values at Play in Digital Games* (Flanagan & Nissenbaum, 2014)—little games scholarship acknowledges the ethical potential of analog, or nondigital, games. In the fields of education and libraries, some have called for continued—and expanded—attention to analog games despite the overwhelming popularity of digital games (Levine, 2008; Mayer & Harris, 2010). In a similar vein, I use this chapter to report on the use of an analog roleplaying game to help students adopt new perspectives and think about questions of right and wrong, thereby inviting games scholars and ethics educators to look beyond digital games. In advocating a shift of the conversation on games and ethics, I set out in particular to demonstrate the affordances that analog games share with digital games, to explain what affordances analog games can offer that digital games cannot, and to acknowledge constraints associated with analog games.

BACKGROUND

The interview data presented in this chapter builds on and responds to an existing body of research on games and formal education. Although I focus particularly on the use of games in teaching and learning ethics, this chapter draws on—and may have implications for—teaching and learning in all formal contexts. In this section, I provide a brief overview of the use of analog and digital games in ethics education (as well as in formal education broadly) and situate games as educational technologies.

Games and Ethics Education

Analog and digital games have both made inroads into formal education. Analog games represent a broad category of games, with examples as diverse as tag, folk games, or "giggly teenage party games" (Salen & Zimmerman, 2003, p. 1); however, advocates for analog games in education may be more likely to focus on "board, card, and roleplaying games that are played on tables instead of on screens" (Copeland, Henderson, Mayer, & Nicholson, 2013, p. 825). Screens serve as a useful distinction between analog and digital games, but advocates for games in education actually predate the era of the video game console: Abt (1970) began discussing so-called *serious games* before the analog/digital distinction was ever necessary. However, the explosive popularity of video games as an entertainment medium has led to increased calls for their use in educational contexts. In fact, Gee (2003) became an advocate for games in education when he found that he could describe the learning he experienced in his first video games in the same way he had long been describing the acquisition of literacy in his scholarly work. Ever since Gee and others began their advocacy, there has been increasing interest in and acceptance of the idea that games have something to contribute to the classroom (Van Eck, 2006).

Ethics educators are among those instructors who have responded to invitations to implement games into their teaching. As befits the broad nature of ethics education, these games invite students to take on new perspectives in a number of contexts. Over the course of his career as an elementary school teacher, Hunter (2013) used his analog *World Peace Game* to invite fourth-grade students to adopt a perspective that was both aware of the complex problems existing in international relations and eager to find peaceful solutions amidst that complexity. The *Reacting to the Past* series of university classroom simulations ask students to distinguish between right and wrong in science courses, freshman seminars, and political science lectures as they wrestle with such events as the French Revolution, Galileo's trial, and debates on slavery (Carnes, 2014). The existence of these analog ethics games and their active use in formal education reinforce the need to expand the discussion of ethics and games to include them.

Of course, digital games have also contributed to ethics education. For example, one series of games simulates problems of environmental ethics (Sadowski, Seager, Selinger, Spierre, & Whyte, 2013; Seager et al., 2010): In *The Externalities Game*, students adopt the perspectives of different members of a community, each of whom must weigh both profit and sustainability when determining how much to produce. After discussion and negotiation, students make final decisions, and the teacher uses a spreadsheet to calculate individual financial profit and collective environmental damage as well as the resulting winners and losers. These games may be played several times in a row to allow students to try different decisions and better understand "winning" and "losing" strategies. There are also ethics games with a digital platform more sophisticated than a spreadsheet. At the time this chapter was being written, designers were preparing to release *Eco*, a game that adds an ethical layer to the visuals and mechanics of games like *Minecraft* (Shapiro, 2015).

Games as Educational Technologies

When they are used to support teaching and learning, both digital and analog games can be thought of as technologies, even if they are not often conceived of as such. Nickerson (2005) defines technologies generally as "tools [that] help people accomplish their goals" or "amplifiers of human capabilities" (p. 3) before focusing in on technologies that "amply cognition either by facilitating reasoning directly or by reducing the demand that the solution of a problem makes on one's cognitive resources" (p. 6). For example, Nickerson (2005) considered both number systems and computers to be cognitive (and by extension, educational) technologies: number systems because they facilitate students' understanding and manipulation of mathematical concepts and computers because they save students the cognitive effort of producing results themselves. These technologies amplify math students' relevant abilities and help them accomplish relevant goals; games may similarly act as technologies for ethics students by helping them more easily conceive of all the factors contributing to a decision regarding right and wrong and thereby reducing the effort needed to step into a new ethical perspective.

However, those who consider games to be educational technologies must recognize that not all technologies are created equal. Borko, Whitcomb, and Liston (2009) asserted that technologies are not neutral artifacts; rather, they have affordances—features which complement a goal (Gibson, 2015)—and constraints—features that impede progress towards a goal (Greeno, 1998). Affordances and constraints can be used to evaluate the utility of an educational technology for a particular learning goal (Kennewell, 2001), and teachers should consider these features in conjunction with their subject matter knowledge and pedagogical experience in order to effectively integrate that technology into their teaching (Mishra & Koehler, 2006). Dickey (2005; 2011) used this framework of affordances and constraints to evaluate the educational utility of game-like virtual worlds such as *Second Life*. Following Dickey's example— that is, assessing games' affordances and constraints—will allow educators to determine whether these games are truly useful instead of integrating them into their classrooms just as an act of faith (Kennewell, 2001). Indeed, one of the key advantages of this perspective is that it invites researchers and practitioners to consider games as individual artifacts rather than a monolithic whole.

METHOD

In this chapter, I use data from qualitative interviews to demonstrate the affordances and constraints of analog games for ethics education.

Setting

These interview data were obtained in the context of an Integrated Language Option (ILO). ILOs are project-based language immersion experiences based in the Residential College of the Arts and Humanities (RCAH) at Michigan State University. They supplement traditional language study and integrate language learning with the study of a topic related to the core values of the RCAH, which include world history, art and culture, ethics, and engaged learning (Plough, 2014). I was the instructor for this ILO, which focused on the French language and drew from Francophone culture. Working with input from the students who enrolled in the French ILO, I focused our activities and conversations on the topics of government, society, and culture and on questions of right and wrong within those topics.

During our discussions to set up the ILO, participants agreed to try a game-based approach—one that was designed to change their perspectives in two ways. First, students would change their perspective by thinking of themselves differently. At the beginning of the semester, students imagined themselves fifteen years in the future and described their ideal family at that time. They then used that information to begin the game, which had the following premise: Fifteen years in the future, they and their families were on the same cruise ship, which suffered an accident at sea, forcing them to take refuge on a desert island. With little hope for rescue, it was up to them to establish the ethical standards underpinning their new government, society, and culture. This premise provided the foundation for the second kind of change in perspective; by asking them to reinvent institutions that they took for granted, I invited them to challenge their own ethical views and emerge with a new perspective on right and wrong.

Two different sources informed the development of this ethics game, which I will refer to as "the desert island game." First, the premise of this game was based partly on *The Daedalus Project*, a class held a number of times at Brigham Young University in which students were tasked with escaping from an uncharted island (Cronin, 2004; Heimburger, 1994; Tripp, 1998). Heimburger (1994) explained that during his experience in this class, he was forced to actively confront "classical debates" and "modern crises" (p. 3) that he had previously only learned about passively; I borrowed the premise of *The Daedalus Project* with the intention of providing these same experiences to the ILO students. Second, I used some of the rules from the analog roleplaying game *Tribes* (Brin & Jackson, 1998) to prompt decisions and represent dilemmas within the simulation. *Tribes* puts its players in the roles of early humans whose every decision impacts not only their own survival but that of their entire community. I felt that these rules would be useful for representing the similar situation associated with the desert island game.

Participants and Data

Nine students initially signed up for this ILO, but two stopped attending during the semester. The remaining seven students—five females and two males—were all undergraduates, ranging from freshmen to seniors. Furthermore, they were all enrolled in the RCAH major, which implies an interest in and exposure to questions of language, culture, ethics, and politics. All seven students agreed to participate in this research. In the ten weeks following the conclusion of the ILO, I met with each of them individually and in-person to conduct 30- to 45-minute long semi-structured interviews in English to ask them about their experience and decision-making in the desert island game.

After transcribing these interviews, I identified the affordances and constraints of the desert island game that were evident in their accounts. I used open coding to look for themes in student responses and then compared these open codes to themes in the literature related to the educational affordances and constraints of games; I looked both in the literature for discussion of the codes emerging from the interviews and in the interviews for examples of affordances and constraints argued in the literature. Furthermore, I supplemented these interview data with excerpts from the lesson plans, handouts, and other materials associated with this ILO, including personal teaching reflections that I had recorded throughout the semester. The affordances and constraints discussed in the following two sections emerged from this repeated cross-referencing between my coded interviews, my other materials, and the existing games scholarship.

AFFORDANCES OF ANALOG GAMES FOR ETHICS EDUCATION

Advocates for using games in education necessarily focus on the features of games that support teaching and learning. Even if these advocates are not discussing games in terms of educational technology, these features can be considered *affordances* in that they complement educational goals (Gibson, 2015). Although contemporary arguments for the educational affordances of games are usually focused on digital games, I will show in the following sections how analog games share these affordances or even demonstrate affordances that digital games do not have.

Affordances Shared with Digital Games

Throughout the ILO, the desert island game demonstrated affordances for ethical perspective-taking that are often attributed to digital games. In this section, I highlight four examples of such affordances and show how they connect to common claims related to digital games. These examples do not represent a conclusive, all-encompassing list of affordances shared by digital and analog games but rather initial evidence that analog games can fulfill the educational promise attributed by advocates to digital games. Likewise, the literature referenced in the following examples is not broadly representative of the entire field of theoretical and empirical games research; rather, since my goal is to call for greater inclusion of analog games in the conversation on ethics, education, and games, I have focused on a selection of thinkers and scholars whose ideas frequently appear in the current conversation.

Games Situate Their Players

The desert island game helped change players' ethical perspectives by directing them to new questions and issues. Indeed, players recognized that the desert island game provided them with a context that was distinct from "real life" and that there was moral value to this context. Two students, Polly and Betty, each described the desert island game as representing something that would never happen to them. This is hardly surprising; it is not unreasonable to predict that none of the participants in this ILO will ever be actually stranded on a desert island. What is significant, though, is how this new context created a space for—or even challenged—their moral thinking. Betty saw the game as an opportunity to practice her ethical reasoning and felt that it was interesting to do so in situations "that aren't really, exactly, that possible... with [her] kind of lifestyle and how [she was] raised." Polly's reaction was even more striking: Considering this new context with its particular situations and dilemmas caused her to call into question the moral perspective that she had developed in "the real world." A third student, Chad, also commented on this value of the game, suggesting that the desert island game helped him "think more about things that [he] probably wouldn't have thought of unless it was brought towards [him]."

This corresponds with a common view of digital games as virtual environments that situate their players in new contexts. For example, Juul (2005) argued that most digital games present a fictional world of some kind; he even went so far as to write that this is one of the things that distinguishes digital games from "traditional non-electronic games" (p. 1). However, Polly and Betty appear to have recognized such a fictional world in the form of the desert island game, suggesting that this phenomenon is not, as Juul argued, unique to digital games. When considered in the context of ethics education, these fictional worlds can be seen as moral thought experiments (Schulzke, 2011) or as spaces for testing one's moral deliberation (Jansz, 2011). Broadly speaking, the desert island game allowed players to bring their existing perspectives to bear in experiences that may not have otherwise been possible. This is especially important in a moral context; while the dilemmas posed by being actually stranded on a desert island would undoubtedly be an educational experience, Schulzke (2011) argued that is not always practical, desirable, or even possible to recreate the circumstances of ethical dilemmas (like those resulting from a shipwreck) in reality.

Other teachers have also used analog games' ability to situate players and their ethical perspectives in fictional scenarios. In some cases, these fictional worlds add context to a moral question. Schofield's (2013)*Superpower Confrontation* and *Multipolar AsianSimulation* are simulations of nuclear war that place students in contexts that are otherwise—and thankfully—inaccessible to teachers. Rather than discuss the history and tactics of nuclear war in an abstract sense, students in Schofield's class faced simulated-but-authentic dilemmas and put their knowledge to the test to work through those dilemmas. On the other hand, fictional worlds may also strip the context from an ethical dilemma. Hunter (2013) saw value in having his students practice international relations in a fictional world where countries and cultures have no strict real-world counterpart. He argued that doing so allowed players of his *World Peace Game* to deal with real issues without the emotional baggage that would exist if his students were playing as real countries. In either case, though, the new situation created by the game is more amenable to the kind of ethical reflection the teacher has in mind.

Games Allow for Different Identities

Because the desert island game took place in an imagined future, the choice of in-game "future" identities—and therefore perspectives—was an important part of ILO participants' experience within their new fictional world. Chad and Quincy made only slight changes to their perspectives, modeling their game identities after the "selves" they wanted to be in the future rather than how they currently saw themselves. As Chad put it,

One part I did like was, you know, actually figuring out how we would expect to see ourselves in the future. That was nice because then it also helps, like, with making ourselves remember what our goals are and remember that we are striving toward it; so, you know, some of us had certain occupations, like a teacher or a babysitter, and maybe that's what that person wants to be, so, I mean, it's just reiterating it in their mind to continue to strive towards that.

Quincy noted that the opportunity to choose her desired potential identity—in her case, the island chef and a mother of four—changed the way she approached certain issues. Because she had chosen her identity and her family, for example, she held them "in consideration maybe above some of the other people in the community." Chad and Quincy's experiences have a precedent in the literature: Sicart (2009) argued that players adopt identities that—like these students'—are partially distinct but not totally separate from their true selves. Furthermore, Konijn, Walma van der Molen, and Hoorn (2011) suggested that playing games may make important contributions to players' identity development, especially as they adopt and experiment with new moral roles.

Other students, though, felt that there was more value in adopting ethical perspectives that were more explicitly different than their own. Samantha described the desert island game as an "opportunity to, say, take on a new persona, or... take on a new point of view" and acknowledged purposefully making decisions that she wouldn't make in real life. However, she didn't see this as a flippant decision; rather, she thought that "it was more interesting to have different points of views from people." She and Jared, another student, felt that it was sometimes too easy to come to a decision as a group and that the game was more valuable when the players had disagreements to work through. In other words, Samantha felt that it was her duty to adopt a game identity that would lead to more discussion, even if it seemed like being a devil's advocate. Jared went one step further, suggesting that the game could require players to adopt identities that were in tension with each other.

Samantha and Jared's experiences are more in line with Gee's (2005) view that players may be required to adopt a new identity to be successful in a game. This is actually an intentional design choice in the *Reacting to the Past* series of games, which—unlike the desert island game—requires players to take certain roles rather than letting them choose their own. Students who have played these games report that they sincerely try to defend the ethical, political, or other stances of their assigned role, even if that stance initially seemed ridiculous (Carnes, 2014). This is perhaps no more striking than in the examples Carnes (2014) gave of one Muslim student and one Jewish student—each active in their respective faith and culture—who were surprised to find themselves deeply respecting and genuinely defending the perspective of "the other side" as they played roles in a game simulating the 1948 Arab-Israeli War. *Train*, a museum exhibit centered on an analog game, goes even further; designed to provoke feelings of complicity, it subtly imposes identities on players that they would—hopefully—never choose for themselves (Logas, 2011). What people don't realize when they begin playing *Train* is that they have assumed the roles of individuals complicit in the Holocaust; part of the game experience is discovering that identity and choosing what to do about it.

Games Provide a Safe Space

Although the players of the desert island game were invested in it as a space for testing and changing ethical perspectives, they also felt that it was just detached enough from the real world to also be a safe space. One student, Barbara, suggested that knowing that the game was not real helped her and her classmates avoid emotional attachment to the game, which allowed them to have serious ethical discussions without ever resorting to the kind of outright conflict which would have interrupted the learning process. This isn't to say that Barbara didn't take the game seriously; rather, she seems to have seen the game as a valuable opportunity to present and *discuss*—but not *argue*—opposing ethical views:

For me, arguments usually come from a place of anger ... there is a disagreement to the extent where you are more than just talking, it's emotional. For us, we weren't – it wasn't quite emotional. We were just discussing, we were talking about different things and – and not becoming super emotional, maybe because it wasn't real ... I'm sure if it was where we were talking about something that was real life, actually happening, we probably would have had arguments and not just talking because we would have been emotional, more, like, involved in it, or attached to what we were talking about.

Barbara also suggested that the safe space of the desert island game helped avoid feelings of regret. She admitted that she might have made mistakes in what side of a debate she chose to support or what decision she made, especially because her ability to follow a conversation in French was not as high as some of the other students. However, she also said that she was not overly worried about that because she "couldn't really regret something when it wasn't going to fully impact anybody's life poorly."

Barbara is far from the first to appreciate the safety afforded by games; Crawford (1984) described games as allowing players to have risky or dangerous experiences while avoiding the consequences that might accompany those experiences in real life. In fact, he saw this affordance of games as being so important that he described it as one of four fundamental elements of games. Wilson et al. (2009), inspired by Crawford, would later identify *safety* as a game attribute with potential to affect learning outcomes. Furthermore, Schulzke (2011) believed that safety extended into the moral sphere, arguing that in games—like in traditional thought experiments—players may explore different courses of action without worrying that they are guilty of immoral behavior.

Hunter (2013) described this same phenomenon in his *World Peace Game* but used very different language. While Crawford's (1984) emphasis was on *safety*, Hunter preferred to talk about *failure*, describing it as a fundamental part of learning that allows students to go beyond what they already know and thereby discover new answers and solutions. Although he never explicitly talks about safety, Hunter's emphasis on failure can perhaps be interpreted as his confidence in the *World Peace Game* to provide a secure environment for what he sees as a crucial lesson. Carnes (2014) seemed to have similar confidence when he suggested that failure is such a critical part of the *Reacting to the Past* games that they are actually designed to ensure that at least some of the players fail. This confidence is also shared by Gee (2003), who described games as having "a relatively low cost of failure and a high reward for success" (p. 63).

Games Persuade Their Players

Although the desert island game provided a safe place for players to *test* existing perspectives and *try* new ones, it was problematic in that it never *imposed* new perspectives. That is, its mechanics only lightly influenced player behavior. The structure and progression of the ILO were such that very few of the rules borrowed from *Tribes* came into play, and the result was a game that focused much more on discussion and interpersonal interaction than on rules and mechanics. While this came with certain advantages, there were also drawbacks. Barbara seemed to identify one such drawback in her end-of-semester interview. At one point, I asked her what she thought might have happened if I had given them a situation where there was not enough food for everyone in the community. She answered that "more than likely, there would (laughter) — we probably would have found a way for there to — to be enough or to find a way to get more." While it is possible that Barbara misunderstood my question (or was extremely confident in her peers' tenacity and creativity), her belief that solving such a problem would not actually be that difficult may suggest that the game did not change players' perspectives to more fully appreciate how difficult ethical dilemmas can be.

This is initially problematic because of the way that recent scholarship has described the rules and mechanics of games as being "persuasive." In fact, a number of scholars have suggested that video games teach their players implicitly by rewarding certain kinds of behavior. Koster (2010) asserted that games are essentially composed of patterns and that successful players are those that best master the patterns. Bogost (2007) took this same idea one step further, advancing a theory of *procedural rhetoric* that sees any game's rules as an embodiment of values and an argument for how the world works. That is, every game designer—whether or not she realizes it—is essentially persuading players to take on a certain perspective. While Bogost suggested a number of ways that this theory might play out, Sicart (2009) specifically focused on how games embody morals and ethics and thereby persuade players to adopt them. "Games force behaviors by rules," argued Sicart, and "the meaning of those behaviors, as communicated through the game world to the player, constitutes the ethics of computer games as designed objects" (2009, pp. 22-23).

Given the failure of the desert island game in this regard, it is striking that some players seemed to recognize what was missing. As previously noted, Jared believed that the game worked best when there were tensions between the players and went so far as to suggest changes to the game's mechanics that would encourage this. At a few points during his interview, he suggested that including more tangible benefits—whether inside or outside the game—might lead to deeper discussions about the ethics of rebuilding society on a desert island. His suggestions ranged from having players compete over a "special crayon [i.e., some kind of gamified reward] for the… day" to designing the game so that there would be a winner at the end, either of which would presumably persuade the players to adopt a selfish perspective and thereby struggle more to act ethically.

Although it seems counter-intuitive, Jared and the other players of the desert island game appeared to believe that the persuasive power of an ethics game's rules should be used to discourage ethical behavior. In other words, they didn't see the desert island game as a Skinner box that gives points for good behavior but as a space where they could put their moral perspectives to the test by pitting them against incentives to act immorally. One of the activities that students completed throughout the ILO was to write a constitution for their new society, and as new situations came up within the desert island game, they proposed laws and rights to cover similar situations in the future. Both Jared and Barbara suggested that it may have been more helpful to have the players write a constitution at the beginning; then, the scenarios in the game would help them fine-tune their perspective by testing their commitment to the values and laws they had previously established. Continuing in this vein, Jared suggested that in-game crises (e.g., "tidal wave destroys half the village … What do we do now?") would help him to better recognize and work through ethical dilemmas. Polly seemed to validate this idea with her own experience. She noted that she had come into the game with certain moral doctrines in mind but that some of the situations in the game had forced her to test and ultimately reconsider them; she even expressed her wish that the game had included more such challenges.

This approach to ethics games is also espoused by Hunter (2013). Although most of his students were only in the fourth grade, he designed a *World Peace Game* that "plunges [them] into complexity—and then gives them the chance to find their own way back to the surface" (p. 3). In other words, this game persuades the player that the world is a difficult place. According to Hunter, making this argument isn't just a question of being faithful to the "starker realities of being human" (p. 25)—it is also a necessary step for preparing his students to solve ethical problems in the real world and helping them unlock their creativity. Schofield (2013) likewise implies that one of the goals of his nuclear war simulations is to demonstrate how easy it is for a conflict between nuclear powers to "escalate out of control" (p. 78). Since his simulation is—like all ethics games—a safe space, he explicitly tries to convince his students of the complexity, difficulty, and confusion that would accompany such an event in the real world.

AFFORDANCES UNIQUE TO ANALOG GAMES

As previously mentioned, not all technologies are created equal; it is therefore not surprising that analog games may have affordances for ethics education and perspective-taking that digital games do not (or have to a lesser extent). Two such affordances became evident as ILO students played the desert island game: analog games are open, and analog games are flexible. Both affordances—while distinct—stem from the fact that analog games are not "hard coded" (as video games are) and that gameplay can therefore be changed on the fly. The *openness* of analog games in ethics education refers to the wide range of choices available to students, and their *flexibility* refers to the ability to modify the mechanics, structure, and content of the game as it is being played in order to change the teaching and learning that is taking place. This section, like the last one, does not represent a conclusive list of affordances unique to analog games or include all of the relevant theoretical and empirical claims about games; however, it represents and includes enough to make a case for an expanded consideration of analog games.

Analog Games Are Open

As students used the desert island game to test and change perspectives, they drew from a wide range of options to make choices. In fact, this range was wide enough that I was sometimes surprised by their decisions. For example, the students' choosing of their ideal families was intended to focus on identifying partners and children; however, some students also decided that pets would be part of their ideal families. Later, as students discussed the "careers" they wanted to have during their stay on the island, I offered each student the chance to have one of the three professions accounted for in the rules for *Tribes*: hunters, gatherers, or crafters. However, prior to this discussion, I had also, as a French vocabulary lesson, introduced several other careers and asked students whether each career would be useful or necessary on the island. Despite my attempts to steer students towards the "default" careers I had imported from *Tribes*, several took inspiration from the discussion and decided that they (or their family members) would play roles as farmers, doctors, or even architects.

The games literature recognizes that this openness is typical of analog games. Salen and Zimmerman (2003) note that although a video game "responds seamlessly to a player's input" (p. 87), that input is more limited than in many analog games. Salen and Zimmerman are chiefly commenting on literal input—on the "anemic activities of clicking, dragging, and typing" (p. 87)—but this observation holds when input is considered in a different light. For example, although many digital roleplaying games offer a stunning amount of customizability, players are still limited to those choices that have been coded into the software. On the other hand, analog roleplaying games like *FATE* (Evil Hat Productions, 2013) or *GURPS* (Steve Jackson Games, 2008) are set up in such a way that players can choose to inhabit any conceivable world, adopt any conceivable identity, and take any conceivable action with the consent of a gamemaster and their fellow players. Although an ethics educator may not wish to allow students to take *any* conceivable action, there are advantages to this level of openness. In the case of the desert island game, it would certainly have been easier from a mechanical point of view to restrict students to a limited set of options. Nonetheless, embracing the openness of analog games created opportunities for students to change moral perspectives that would not have existed otherwise.

Indeed, unanticipated developments in the desert island game often set the stage for important ethical discussions. Although it required some on-the-spot thinking, adding pets to the population of the island created new considerations for students during activities that involved distributing food among members of the community. They were quick to agree that the community should guarantee every family the food it needed to survive, but there was considerable debate as to their moral responsibility toward animals. Likewise, although *Tribes* does not take shelter into consideration, one student's choice to be an architect rather than a hunter or gatherer allowed students to discuss whether the community should guarantee housing for its members and which members of the community should be the first to receive shelter. Allowing students to choose from a wide range of options created the opportunity for a broader range of ethical discussions.

Furthermore, giving students access to a wide range of choices within the desert island game seems to have increased their investment in the game's decisions. During Jared's interview, I asked him how the game might have been different if I had assigned him a family and a career rather than allowing him to choose his own. He responded that he probably would have paid less attention to the scenarios, which would then have had lower stakes for him. In a similar vein, Quincy—who expressed significant allegiance to her game family—explained that her commitment to these simulated people was largely because she had been allowed to choose who they were and that she might have been more flippant if I had arbitrarily assigned her a family.

Teachers using other ethical games have also seen benefits in keeping the game open for players to act how they wish. Hunter (2013) described the criticism that he received from parents who were distraught that their children were being allowed to wage war in a so-called *Peace Game*. Aware of the irony, he nonetheless responded with his conviction that it was only by keeping possibilities like war open that students could learn to adopt peace without being forced to do so. Other ethics games are open enough that they do not even declare an end state or a winner. The rules to *Train* state that the game "ends when it ends" (Logas, 2011), leaving the resolution of the moral challenge it presents entirely in the hands of the players. While Schofield's (2013) simulations do impose an end, they do not declare a winner; rather, players reflect on their game experience and collectively reach a decision on what it means to "win" a nuclear war. The openness of all of these games actually gives their players additional ethical responsibility, expanding the learning experience.

Analog Games Are Flexible

As previously mentioned, the desert island game largely refrained from imposing perspectives on its players. One resulting issue was that the students were often too optimistic about the choices that they made; that is, they were quick to assume that their island would become a utopia where people would donate their goods and labor to the community without reserve and without complaint. There were exceptions to this rule—Samantha, a hunter without any children, complained that she was risking life and limb to help feed child care providers who had nothing to offer her in return—but the majority of the students saw no need to challenge their idealistic assumptions. This presented the possibility that players were not exposed to the moral arguments or engaged in the kinds of moral reflection needed for them to truly change (or defend) their ethical perspectives. Hunter (2013) faced a similar problem in his *World Peace Game*. Although peace is the goal of the game, he expressed frustration at some students' tendencies to "simply 'declare peace,'" (p. 36) rather than work through the implications and complexity of the crises that Hunter had given them.

Fortunately, the desert island game was flexible enough to be adjusted in response to this problem. Near the end of the semester, for example, I invited players to reconsider their optimistic perspectives by inserting a new, previously-unmentioned situation into the game: I informed the players that an animal had attacked Quincy's daughter while Betty—one of the island's child care providers—had been look-ing after her. With some prompting, the students eventually turned this into an opportunity to examine questions of responsibility and guilt and explore what a justice system for their community might look like. During her interview at the end of the semester, Polly acknowledged that she couldn't "remember the specifics, but [this situation] made [her] start to think about, like — like, truly, what the ideal way to solve certain bigger issues would be." Barbara suggested that more of this kind of intervention may have been useful for the ILO. She recognized that the desert island game had the potential to deal with important ethical dilemmas but believed that players would often have trouble recognizing the dilemmas themselves, leaving it up to the instructor to force issues that wouldn't come up otherwise.

A number of authors and game designers have acknowledged this flexibility of analog games. Sicart (2009) notes that computer games, generally speaking, "cannot be adapted or corrected by their users"

(p. 15) while the rules and other features of analog games can be easily changed in order to create a certain atmosphere or accomplish a particular goal. Analog roleplaying games, such as *FATE* (Evil Hat Productions, 2013) or the *Mistborn Adventure Game* (Crafty Games, 2012), encourage gamemasters to be flexible, not only to accommodate unexpected decisions by players but also to decide on the consequences of those decisions and to provide a constant level of challenge for the players. Ethics educators can use the flexibility of analog games to ensure that their students are continuing to engage in moral reflection either when the game did not go as planned or when students are not adequately challenging their perspectives.

Other ethics educators have also taken advantage of this flexibility. Carnes (2014) described how the *Reacting to the Past* community constantly collaborates to make changes to how the games work. Because they are analog, these games are flexible enough that changes are made simply by letting fellow instructors or current students know what is now different. Hunter (2013) has made more impromptu interventions: Although many of his students struggle to resolve all the crises they are faced with before the end of the game, he keeps certain crises in reserve so that he can continue to challenge them in case they solve all of the usual problems with time to spare. Digital games can certainly be modified in similar ways, but these educators were able to make their changes more quickly and more easily than programmers could.

CONSTRAINTS OF ANALOG GAMES FOR ETHICS EDUCATION

This chapter tends to emphasize what analog games have to offer rather than their limitations. This approach is to be expected; since many people are quick to discount the possibility of learning from games (Carnes, 2014; Koster, 2010; McGonigal, 2011), it is not surprising that advocates would try to change that view rather than inadvertently perpetuate it by acknowledging where games sometimes fall short. Likewise, my purpose in this chapter is to demonstrate the suitability of analog games for formal ethics education, and it would seem contrary to that purpose to suggest that this is not always the case. However, not "*all* games are good for *all* learners and for *all* learning outcomes" (Van Eck, 2006, p. 18), and this is just as true of analog games as of digital ones. Indeed, it may be dangerous to speak about any kind of educational game without acknowledging how it might actually complicate learning and teaching.

Therefore, in this brief section, I outline some constraints of analog games that became evident as we played the desert island game. The length of this section should not be interpreted as an argument that analog games have more affordances than constraints. Rather, the affordances and constraints of games are often intertwined, so much of what is said here has already been discussed or at least hinted at. In fact, this section is not focused uniquely on constraints so much as on how constraints are often closely connected to affordances. In discussing this relationship, I give examples that apply equally to digital and analog games and then concentrate on a case unique to analog games.

Constraints Shared with Digital Games

Simply put, for all the desert island game's power to change ethical perspectives, it was, ultimately, "just a game." Schulzke (2011) argues that even though it is possible to have morally meaningful experiences while playing, games remain amoral artifacts as long as players keep them that way. That is, games that—like the desert island game—are distinct from "real life" and do not require players' complete emotional investment might help students apply their moral reasoning to new situations without unnecessary conflict, but they may instead impede the actual shifting of perspectives or the transfer of new perspectives to actual ethical dilemmas. During his interview, Jared seemed to wrestle with this conflict. Although he generally felt ethically invested in the simulation, he found himself asking why he should feel invested in the first place. In other words, he recognized that the game didn't always demand his moral attention; there was more going on, then, than just game design.

This is ultimately an important recognition that the affordances and constraints of analog games—like those of any technology—depend heavily on other factors. Many of those same features of games that can enhance ethical learning may also detract from it. This is in keeping with educational technology theory, which suggests that not all of a technology's affordances and constraints in a particular educational situation are attributable to the technology itself; rather, personal and contextual factors can also impose affordances and constraints on tools (Borko et al., 2009; Koehler & Mishra, 2008). Previously in this chapter, I described how games situate their players, allow for different identities, create safe spaces, and persuade their players. While these features may have tremendous potential for ethics education, Jared's experience suggests that these features could also be detrimental to ethical reflection and learning.

If features such as these have the power to both support and undermine ethics education, instructors should pay attention to what else is affecting this relationship. For example, Jared felt that his classmates played a large role in whether or not he found a decision to be ethically significant. If a particular decision—for example, what his in-game family was like—would have little effect on others, he saw the decision as being of little consequence: "[The simulation] is not the life I have to live, you know, like, so I don't have to, kind of, be weighed with that." On the other hand, he explained that he was more likely to take the issue seriously when a decision stood to affect the entire community. In either case, there was a clear separation between the game world and reality, but it was this issue that determined whether this separation constrained or afforded Jared's ethical reflection.

A Constraint Unique to Analog Games

As previously mentioned, rules and mechanics ultimately played a small role in the desert island game. Part of this was because its inspiration, *Tribes*, was designed as a fairly simple analog game, so there weren't many rules to begin with. However, when it came time to present the mechanics of the desert island game to the students in the ILO, it was immediately clear that the students felt overwhelmed. It became necessary for me to take care of all of the mechanical aspects of the game "behind the scenes" while leaving decisions in the students' hands. Even with these modifications, though, the mechanics of the desert island game largely faded to the background, keeping the focus on debate and discussion. In this instance, analog games fall short of Nickerson's (2005) assertion that an appropriate technology can reduce cognitive demand on its users.

This finding is in keeping with some scholars' explanation that although analog games are more open and flexible than digital games, they are also less automated. Salen and Zimmerman (2003) argue that "the most pervasive trait of digital games is that they can automate complicated procedures and in so doing, facilitate the play of games that would be too complicated in a non-computerized context" (p. 88). Even if a game is not too complicated to be played without the help of a computer, there is no denying that a digital game can automate most of the minutiae of a game, reserving for the players only the most critical decisions and actions. Ethics educators who choose to implement analog games instead of digital ones will face important decisions in how to structure and pace their teaching of the rules to the students (Mayer & Harris, 2010).

Although automation was not strictly necessary to play the desert island game, it may have made its mechanics more important for its players. Mechanics and rules play a large role in embodying the ethical arguments and assumptions of a game (Bogost, 2007; Sicart, 2009), and their weak presence in the desert island game meant that there was sometimes little reason for players to change their decisions. As previously mentioned, some of the players of the desert island game actually craved pushback from the game, and others took advantage of the lack of resistance to make idealistic decisions without considering whether they would actually work. Although the flexibility of analog games made it possible to respond to some of these concerns, automated game mechanics could have played that same role. For example, *The Externalities Game* (Sadowski et al., 2013; Seager et al., 2010)—previously mentioned in this chapter—is an ethics game that uses a spreadsheet to calculate the results of the game and the corresponding winners. Students are expected to act morally, but because the models in the spreadsheet are strictly imposed and non-negotiable, they must weigh morals against the mechanics of the game when making their decisions.

FUTURE RESEARCH DIRECTIONS

This chapter's purpose is focused on demonstrating that analog games deserve continued (and expanded) attention in discussions about games, ethics, and education; however, it also highlights some potential areas for future research. For example, students like Jared perceived the desert island game as both a sort of thought experiment and "just a game," depending on how parts of the game were presented and what else was going on during play. Since educators presumably have an interest in helping students approach ethics games as thought experiments, they would benefit from further exploration of when students adjust their moral perspectives and when they just have fun. Furthermore, although the desert island game was not as persuasive as it could have been, the students generally recognized its potential to impose new perspectives and test their ethical thinking. This potential has tremendous implications for the use of games in ethics education; future research needs to explore just how games can effectively convince players to change their perspectives.

In pursuing other veins of research, scholars should move beyond the game, participants, and methods featured in this chapter. Analog games represent a broad category, and the desert island game is likely unique enough to not be representative of other analog games that could be used in ethics education. The same is true of the desert island games' players; these students were enrolled in an undergraduate program that put a heavy emphasis on questions of politics, civics, and ethics. Three of them even drew explicit connections with the program when discussing their experiences with the desert island game, raising the possibility that other students may not be as interested in changing their moral perspectives. Furthermore, the fact that these students played the desert island game in a foreign language may have had an impact on their perspectives and experiences. Although this chapter may serve to draw practitioners' and scholars' attention to analog games, examination of other such games, other groups of students, and other settings is necessary to fully understand their affordances and constraints for ethics education.

Furthermore, exploring other qualitative and quantitative methods for assessing the effects of a game on ethics education would help create a clearer and richer picture of these effects. For example, researchers could supplement interview or focus group data with observational data, reducing a study's dependence on self-reported information. Alternatively, by developing or repurposing an instrument to measure ethical beliefs or reasoning, researchers could examine whether and how these attributes change throughout a class that uses analog ethics games. In both of these cases, affordances and constraints would shift from being a central focus of the study to playing a more peripheral role; researchers could then concentrate on the educational effects of analog games rather than just their features.

CONCLUSION

Whatever their age, background, or field of study, today's students are all being shaped by their education to think about questions of ethics and morality in certain ways (or not at all). Formal ethics education provides students with the training and experience necessary to actively respond to contemporary dilemmas. As gaming continues to grow in popularity, the conversation about how games intersect with ethical issues and ethics education will likely grow as well. This conversation will undoubtedly continue to be dominated by discussion of computer and video games, but, as this chapter has shown, there is room in this conversation to consider what analog games contribute to the field. The desert island game demonstrates some of the same affordances and constraints as digital games and also interacts with ethical education in unique ways, suggesting that instructors engaged in helping students evaluate and change their ethical perspectives ought to consider them alongside digital games. Indeed, if scholars and educators are genuinely interested in how games affect players' ethical perspectives, to fail to make room for analog games in their work and correspondence would be to miss a valuable opportunity.

REFERENCES

Abt, C. C. (1970). *Serious games*. New York, NY: The Viking Press, Inc.

Bogost, I. (2007). *Procedural rhetoric: The expressive power of video games* [Amazon Kindle version]. Retrieved from http://www.amazon.com

Borko, H., Whitcomb, J., & Liston, D. (2009). Wicked problems and other thoughts on issues of technology and teacher learning. *Journal of Teacher Education*, *60*(3), 3–7. doi:10.1177/0022487108328488

Brin, D., & Jackson, S. (1998). *Tribes* [roleplaying game]. Austin, TX: Steve Jackson Games.

Carnes, M. C. (2014). *Minds on fire: How role-immersion games transform college*. [Amazon Kindle edition]. Retrieved from http://www.amazon.com

Copeland, T., Henderson, B., Mayer, B., & Nicholson, S. (2013). Three different paths for tabletop gaming in school libraries. *Library Trends*, *61*, 825–835. doi:10.1353/lib.2013.0018

Crafty Games. (2012). *Mistborn adventure game* [roleplaying game]. Author.

Crawford, C. (1984). *The art of computer game design*. Berkeley, CA: Osborne/McGraw-Hill.

Cronin, M. (2004, December 7). BYU students play Survivor for credit. *The Salt Lake Tribune*. Retrieved from http://sltrib.com

Dickey, M. D. (2005). Brave new (interactive) worlds: A review of the design affordances and constraints of two 3D virtual worlds as interactive learning environments. *Interactive Learning Environments*, *13*(1-2), 121–137. doi:10.1080/10494820500173714

Dickey, M. D. (2011). The pragmatics of virtual worlds for K-12 educators: Investigating the affordances and constraints of *Active Worlds* and *Second Life* with K-12 in-service teachers. *Educational Technology Research and Development, 59*(1), 1–20. doi:10.1007/s11423-010-9163-4

Evil Hat Productions. (2013). *FATE Core System* [roleplaying game]. Author.

Ferkany, M., & Whyte, K. P. (2011). Environmental education, wicked problems, and virtue. *Philosophy of Education, 16*, 331-339. Retrieved from http://ojs.ed.uiuc.edu/

Flanagan, M., & Nissenbaum, H. (2014). *Values at play in digital games.* Cambridge, MA: The MIT Press.

Gee, J. P. (2003). *What video games have to teach us about learning and literacy.* New York, NY: Palgrave Macmillan.

Gee, J. P. (2005). *Why video games are good for your soul: Pleasure and learning.* Champaign, IL: Common Ground Publishing.

Gibbs, J. C. (2014). *Moral development & reality: Beyond the theories of Kohlberg, Hoffman, and Haidt* (3rd ed.). New York, NY: Oxford University Press.

Gibson, J. J. (2015). The ecological approach to visual perception (Classic ed.). New York, NY: Psychology Press

Greeno, J. (1998). The situativity of knowing, learning, and research. *The American Psychologist, 53*(1), 5–26. doi:10.1037/0003-066X.53.1.5

Heimburger, M. Y. (1994). *No university is an island: Implications of the Daedalus Project for BYU and American higher educational philosophy at large.* (Unpublished undergraduate honors thesis). Brigham Young University, Provo, UT.

Hunter, J. (2013). *World peace and other 4th-grade achievements* [Amazon Kindle edition]. Retrieved from http://www.amazon.com

Jansz, J. (2011). Preface. In K. Poels & S. Malliet (Eds.), *Vice city virtue: Moral issues in digital game play* [EPUB version]. Retrieved from http://acco.be

Juul, J. (2005). *Half-real: Video games between real rules and fictional worlds.* Cambridge, MA: The MIT Press.

Kennewell, S. (2001). Using affordances and constraints to evaluate the use of information and communications technology in teaching and learning. *Journal of Information Technology for Teacher Education, 10*(1-2), 101–116. doi:10.1080/14759390100200105

Koehler, M. J., & Mishra, P. (2008). Introducing TPACK. In American Association of Colleges for Teacher Education Committee on Innovation and Technology (Ed.), *Handbook of Technological Pedagogical Content Knowledge* (TPACK) for Educators (pp. 3-29). New York: Routledge.

Konijn, E. A., Walma van der Molen, J. H., & Hoorn, J. F. (2011). Babies versus bogeys: In-game manipulation of empathy in violent video games. In K. Poels & S. Malliet (Eds.), *Vice city virtue: Moral issues in digital game play* [EPUB version]. Retrieved from http://acco.be

Koster, R. (2010). *A theory of fun for game design* [Amazon Kindle version]. Retrieved from http://www.amazon.com

Levine, J. (2008). Broadening our definition of gaming: Tabletop games. *Library Technology Reports*, *44*(3), 7–11.

Logas, H. L. (2011). *Meta-rules and complicity in Brenda Brathwaite's* Train. Paper presented at Think Design Play: The fifth international conference of the Digital Games Research Association (DIGRA), Utrecht, Netherlands.

Mayer, B., & Harris, C. (2010). *Libraries got game: Aligned learning through modern board games* [Amazon Kindle version]. Retrieved from http://amazon.com

McGonigal, J. (2011). *Reality is broken* [Amazon Kindle version]. Retrieved from http://amazon.com

McWilliams, W. C., & Piotrowski, H. (2009). *The world since 1945: A history of international relations* (7th ed.). Boulder, CO: Lynne Rienner Publishers, Inc.

Mishra, P., & Koehler, M. J. (2006). Technological Pedagogical Content Knowledge: A framework for teacher knowledge. *Teachers College Record*, *108*(6), 1017–1054. doi:10.1111/j.1467-9620.2006.00684.x

Nickerson, R. S. (2005). Technology and cognition amplification. In R. J. Sternberg & D. D. Preiss (Eds.), *Intelligence and technology: The impact of tools on the nature and development of human abilities*. Mahwah, NJ: Lawrence Erlbaum Associates.

Plough, I. (2014). Development of a test of speaking proficiency in multiple languages. *Papers in Language Testing and Assessment, 3*(2), 27-52. Retrieved from http://www.altaanz.org

Poels, K., & Malliet, S. (2011a). Moral issues in digital game play: A multi-disciplinary view. In K. Poels & S. Malliet (Eds.), *Vice city virtue: Moral issues in digital game play* [EPUB version]. Retrieved from http://acco.be

Poels, K., & Malliet, S. (2011b). *Vice city virtue: Moral issues in digital game play* [EPUB version]. Retrieved from http://acco.be

Sadowski, J., Seager, T. P., Selinger, E., Spierre, S. G., & Whyte, K. P. (2013). An experiential game-theoretic pedagogy for sustainability ethics. *Science and Engineering Ethics*, *19*(3), 1323–1339. doi:10.1007/s11948-012-9385-4 PMID:22895636

Salen, K., & Zimmerman, E. (2003). *Rules of play: Game design fundamentals*. Cambridge, MA: MIT Press.

Sandel, M. J. (2009). *Justice: What's the right thing to do?* New York, NY: Farrar, Straus and Giroux.

Schofield, J. (2013). Modeling choices in nuclear warfighting: Two classroom simulations on escalation and retaliation. *Simulation & Gaming*, *44*(1), 73–93. doi:10.1177/1046878112455488

Schulzke, M. (2011). Reflective play and morality: Video games as thought experiments. In K. Poels & S. Malliet (Eds.), *Vice city virtue: Moral issues in digital game play* [EPUB version]. Retrieved from http://acco.be

Seager, T. P., Selinger, E., Whiddon, D., Schwartz, D., Spierre, S., & Berady, A. (2010). Debunking the fallacy of the individual decision-maker: An experiential pedagogy for sustainability ethics. In *Proceedings of the 2010 IEEE International Symposium on Sustainable Systems & Technology (ISSST)*. doi:10.1109/ISSST.2010.5507679

Shapiro, J. (2015, August 16). Something is wrong with '*Minecraft.*' This game has a solution. *Forbes*. Retrieved from http://www.forbes.com/sites/jordanshapiro/2015/08/16/something-is-wrong-with-minecraft-this-game-has-a-solution/

Sicart, M. (2009). *The ethics of computer games* [Amazon Kindle version]. Retrieved from http://www.amazon.com

Steve Jackson Games. (2008). GURPS (4th ed.) [roleplaying game]. Author.

Tripp, S. (1998, Spring). On a wing and a prayer. *BYU Magazine*. Retrieved from magazine.byu.edu

Van Eck, R. (2006). Digital game based learning: It's not just the digital natives who are restless. *EDUCAUSE Review*, *41*, 16–30. Retrieved from http://net.educause.edu/ir/library/pdf/erm0620.pdf

Wilson, K. A., Bedwell, W. L., Lazzara, E. H., Salas, E., Burke, C. S., Estock, J. L., & Conkey, C. et al. (2009). Relationships between game attributes and learning outcomes: Review and research proposals. *Simulation & Gaming*, *40*(2), 217–266. doi:10.1177/1046878108321866

KEY TERMS AND DEFINITIONS

Affordance: A feature of a technology (or a technology within a particular context) that supports learning and teaching in certain ways.

Analog Game: A game that can be played without any kind of digital technology; this includes board, card, and pen-and-paper roleplaying games.

Constraint: A feature of a technology (or a technology in a particular context) that impedes learning and teaching in certain ways.

Digital Game: A game that requires some kind of digital technology to be played; this includes computer, console, and other electronic games.

Educational Technology: Any tool that is used to support processes of teaching and learning.

Ethics: Socially-constructed standards for making moral distinctions.

Ethics Education: Any teaching or learning that includes studying and reflecting on issues of right and wrong or good and evil.

Ethics Game: Any game that is designed or repurposed in order to address, explore, or teach ethics.

Formal Education: Teaching and learning that takes place in association with a school or other institution in contrast to teaching and learning that takes place as part of personal, cultural, or other routines.

Morality: The distinction between right and wrong.

Roleplaying Game: A game in which people adopt and play in accordance with a certain role or identity.

Chapter 11
Knowledge Production
in E-Sports Culture:
Learning with and from the Masters

Robert James Hein
The Pennsylvania State University, USA

Jason A. Engerman
The Pennsylvania State University, USA

ABSTRACT

Competitive video games, commonly referred to as "e-sports," are becoming increasingly popular among young adults (van Ditmarsch, 2013). However, unlike more traditional, physical sports, these video games blur the lines between their participants and spectators (Cheung & Huang, 2011), encouraging veterans and newcomers alike to become contributing members evolving, digital affinity spaces. Bolstered by the affordances of live-streaming technology, e-sports culture constantly gathers its experts and novices together to play, compete, and discuss in real time. These inclusive practices help to facilitate the rapid knowledge and skill acquisition of all of its community members. Consequently, this chapter will explore how and why e-sports culture successfully champions participation and mastery learning. Likewise, the authors will discuss what teachers can learn and apply from this culture's values.

INTRODUCTION

In describing the ever-evolving digital world, Squire (2011) insists that, "to understand how games operate, we need to look beyond the game itself toward the broader cultural contexts in which it is situated. In many game communities, players themselves become the content, making them emblematic of *participatory* media culture" (p. 12). We argue that, via the calculated use of live-streaming technology, the "e-sports" community has risen to become the standard-bearer of that participatory culture—showcasing its aims, methods, and values for increasingly larger and wider audiences. This new era of hypercompetitive gaming is now filling major sports arenas, like Madison Square Garden; e-sports has catapulted gaming into the public eye. Thus, through the mere exposure to e-sports, people are finally

DOI: 10.4018/978-1-5225-0261-6.ch011

coming to see that video games are no longer the "trivial pursuits" of the 80s and 90s arcades (Prensky, 2006). Rather, the likes of *Counter-Strike*, *StarCraft*, and *League of Legends* are solidifying gaming's place as a serious, complex, and social activity that requires the strategic-thinking of chess in addition to the lightning-fast reflexes of mixed martial-arts.

More importantly, the online broadcasts of e-sporting events successfully blur the lines between participants and spectators (Cheung & Huang, 2011), a distinct characteristic that encourages veterans and newcomers alike to become contributing members of an evolving, digital affinity-space (Gee, 2005). With the popular live-streaming website Twitch.tv as its central hub, the e-sports community constantly gathers expert and novice gamers together to play, compete, and discuss in real-time. The immediacy of these decidedly 21st century interactions not only facilitates the rapid knowledge and skills acquisition of Twitch.tv users, but it also separates e-sports spectatorship from other more traditional forms of media consumption. E-sports broadcasts are not as impersonal as televised sporting events nor are they as static as content on video sharing websites like YouTube.com. E-sports are thus revolutionizing how we think about video games, peer production, and knowledge sharing.

As we will explore, e-sports culture maximizes the affordances of its affinity space, provides agency to its members, and champions mastery-learning in striking ways that our classrooms can and should attempt to emulate. By shedding light on the learning practices of this emerging gaming subculture, we hope to provide educators with valuable insights and suggestions to enhance their own pedagogy. Anchored by Gee's (2005) conception of affinity spaces and Brown, Collins, and Duguid's (1989) notion of "cognitive apprenticeships," we will distill the best that this culture has to offer and thereby propose a unifying e-sports learning principle. Consequently, this chapter represents our attempt to take up Squire's (2011) challenge and to "look beyond" the games – to understand why and how e-sports culture harnesses Twitch.tv to simultaneously entertain, include, and, ultimately, instruct its members.

Exploring E-Sports

At their core, electronic-sports (e-sports) are video games that have been either designed or appropriated for head-to-head competition. Given this simple definition, e-sports might not seem like they inject anything new or special into mainstream gaming culture. After all, Taylor (2012) reminds us that video games have always kept score. As early as the 1970s, players competed asynchronously in arcade games like *Asteroids* and *Star Fire*, which could record and display a player's point-total. Although one could certainly feel a sense of pride and accomplishment by having his initials appear on a machine's "high-score list," Taylor (2012) notes that geographic barriers necessarily stunted the growth and development of a more formal and robust competitive scene. The best players in small towns and at local arcades had virtually no way of measuring themselves against other players from around the world. However, the majority of modern e-sports circumvent these spatial constraints by giving players the opportunity to participate in online "ladders," automatically updating rankings of top players and teams that are published on gaming websites. This not only intensifies competition, but it also places participation and recognition under a global spotlight.

In addition to simply being competitive, e-sports have regularly scheduled tournaments and leagues, draw legions of passionate fans, and feature an emerging caste of professional players. This elevated level of organization, via both grassroots movements and corporate sponsorships, separates e-sports from other video games and gaming communities. From the heyday of *Quake* and its "Red Annihilation" tournament in the late 90s to the modern spectacle of Valve's "The International," from the launch of the

Korean e-Sports Association (KeSPA) to the rise, fall, and rebirth of Major League Gaming (MLG) in the United States, e-sports has certainly experienced its growing pains. However, although the business partners, the governing bodies, and even the e-sports themselves have changed over the years, several constants remain—the prize pools keep increasing and fans keep multiplying. With pots as large as ten million dollars, a small group of elite gamers have even gone professional. Likewise, e-sports' economic success has allowed other community members to pursue careers as tournament directors, play-by-play announcers, and color commentators. While it is impossible for us to recount and detail e-sports' complete evolution from hobby to industry in this chapter, it is important to remember that e-sports competitions are highly organized events. There are strict rules to follow and, potentially, large payouts for winners. As we will discuss, this structure and support encourages players to come together in ways that *Asteroids* and *Star Fire* never could. For more information on and discussion of e-sports' formalization, Taylor's (2012) study provides an excellent historical account.

Although many video games now have the support of online competitions, national and global rankings, tournament organizations, and corporate sponsors, there is still debate both outside and within gaming circles regarding which of these games truly deserve the "e-sport" designation (Shaw, 2014; Taylor, 2012; Wagner, 2006). For example, few players would argue that *Counter-Strike*, a team-based "first-person shooter" (FPS), qualifies as an e-sport. Not only does the game have a storied competitive history with a finely-tuned set of rules, but *Counter-Strike* also requires its players to "see while moving" and to maintain "balanced bodies" in their efforts to keep up with the blistering action (Witkowski, 2012). Conversely, *Hearthstone*, a digital card-game and relative newcomer on the e-sports scene, is often mocked by the community for being slow-paced and having inherent elements of chance. While high-stakes *Hearthstone* tournaments are regularly among the most popular events broadcast on Twitch. tv, often drawing well over 100,000 viewers, many feel that its poker-like randomness is antithetical to e-sports culture. Ironic chants of "Skillstone!" are known to erupt from the crowd when wins and losses are determined by improbable—and often cruel—strokes of luck.

Others have questioned whether the term "e-sports" is even an appropriate label for any of these games in the first place. After all, the "sport" in e-sports begs comparisons to more traditional and physical athletic competitions like football and basketball. Some researchers have even attempted to map the qualities, mechanics, and demands of these games to traditional definitions of "sport" (Lee & Schoenstedt, 2011; Shaw, 2014). In 2014, social media exploded into similar, albeit far more heated and contentious, debates when *ESPN*—"the world-wide leader in sports"—televised a major *Dota 2* tournament on one of their subsidiary stations. Taylor (2012) admits that, because of these conversations, "gaming now finds itself sitting, often uneasily, between digital play and sport" (p. 36). Hutchins (2008) elaborates, suggesting that "no one existing category of social perception—sport, media or computer gaming – can account adequately for the totality of [e-sports;]" it is an entirely "new social form" (p. 861-5). Ultimately, we believe that it is helpful to adopt Taylor's and Hutchins's perspectives—to view e-sports as its own unique form of digital engagement. Therefore, by focusing on what the culture does and on what it values differently, we can better understand why and how e-sports' aims and methods appeal to 21st century learners.

Winning and, more specifically, being considered among "the best" is nearly every competitor's goal. However, unlike other types of competitive sports and games, e-sports are far more accessible. First, they require minimal start-up capital; some of the most popular titles, like the aforementioned *Dota 2* and *Hearthstone*, are even free to download and play. Second, although some games can be mentally and physically draining, e-sport players do not need to be in Olympic condition or to have a bodybuilder's physique to succeed. Finally, e-sport gaming servers almost never sleep. Whether it is three o'clock in the morning or in the afternoon, thousands of people are playing online; there are hundreds of matches that are ready and waiting to launch. This "always on" aspect of e-sports culture allows players to practice or compete at their own pace and on their own terms. Furthermore, while climbing the "ladder" and becoming a professional is a goal many players share, it is not the only measure of success in e-sports culture. As we will examine, community members also relish the opportunity to share gaming tips, secrets, and strategies with fellow players via message boards and Twitch.tv. Many of the e-sports' community's most valued members are former players that use their knowledge and experiences to welcome and teach newcomers.

"E-sports" is a difficult term to describe and define. It refers both to a particular set of skill-intensive video games and to a larger cultural movement that values expertise, competition, and participation in digital arenas. Its history, evolution, and ideals have captivated gamers from around the world and, as we will now examine, are bringing them all together on Twitch.tv to share their interests, experiences, and knowledge.

A New Digital Affinity Space

Today's video game players are no strangers to "affinity spaces" —virtual or physical locations where informal learning occurs (Gee, 2005). As games rapidly increased in complexity during the mid-90s, players began to realize that neither pre-packaged instruction manuals nor third-party "code-books" could give them the guidance and support they truly needed to overcome challenges and improve their skills. However, instead of lamenting their situation, the players chose "to participate in—and even *create*—their own self-organizing learning communities" on the internet (Squire, 2011). These sites, like SmashBoards.com and TeamLiquid.net, featured a variety of player-produced content ranging from interviews to polls, from walkthroughs to forums, from reviews to download links (Gee, 2005). While some of these sites still remain active and receive updates to this day, many of their contributors have since migrated to live-streaming websites that amplify the traditional affordances of affinity spaces for a new generation of gamers.

Since 2011, Twitch.tv, the most popular video game live-streaming website, has been a central hub for the growing e-sports community. Over 100 millions unique visitors log onto this affinity space each day to socialize, to be entertained (Twtich.tv, 2015), and to acquire and distribute the knowledge necessary to, as the popular streamer Sean "Day[9]" Plott advertises, "become a better gamer." To facilitate these aims, Twitch.tv allows users to create their own "channels" where they can broadcast themselves playing their favorite video games in real-time. These channels come equipped with chat windows that allow viewers to communicate with one another and with the channel's host. Some users choose to stream casual or classic games like *The Sims* or *The Legend of Zelda*; some users are known for broadcasting "speed-runs" or other attempts to break gaming records; some users play recently released titles for viewers to vicariously experience. However, for all of Twitch.tv's channel diversity, certain users and games are simply more popular than others. By default, Twitch.tv ranks and lists these channels by viewer count—the number of users and guests watching at any particular time. Consequently, e-sports have historically dominated Twitch.tv's main page. Throughout 2015, *League of Legends*, *Dota 2*, *Counter-Strike*, *Hearthstone*, and *StarCraft* have consistently claimed the top positions. Other e-sports, including 2D fighting-games like *Marvel vs. Capcom* and *Super Smash Brothers: Melee*, occasionally make appearances as well.

So what makes Twitch.tv so attractive to e-sports enthusiasts? Quite simply, it possesses nearly all of the eleven features that Gee (2005) insists comprise a "paradigmatic" affinity space (p. 225), the most essential of which we will detail throughout this chapter. Not only do these features promote effective learning in and of themselves, but they also are consistent with the goals and values of e-sports culture at large. For one, in affinity spaces, people form and build relationships based on "common endeavors" instead of along particular socio-cultural lines (p. 255). Since Twitch.tv users are free to make up names and information for their accounts, their real identities often remain a mystery and, ultimately, become secondary to the content they produce and discuss. While many streamers do decide to broadcast their game-play using webcams and microphones, Kaytoue, Silva, Cerf, Meira, and Raïssi (2012) found that, with rare exceptions, the top-level professional players tended to draw the most viewers. Given the emphasis that e-sports culture places on winning and achieving mastery, this should come as no surprise; Twitch.tv users want to watch and learn from the best. A streamer's race, age, and class have little influence on a viewer's decision to tune in. This is not to say that Twitch.tv and, through it, e-sports culture are utopian. As we will explore in a subsequent section, female gamers often struggle to earn the respect of their male counterparts. However, where e-sports live-streaming and competitions are concerned, a player's experience, insight, and raw skill can quickly shatter preconceptions and stereotypes.

In addition, Twitch.tv "encourages and enables [users] to gain and spread both intensive and extensive knowledge" (Gee, 2005, p. 226). Gee (2005) defines "intensive knowledge" as a highly specialized understanding in a single content area. "Extensive knowledge," by contrast, refers to broader types of information. Since e-sports veterans and newcomers alike visit Twitch.tv to improve their gaming skills, both types of knowledge have their place and value. Veterans, looking to gain even small competitive advantages, tend to seek out specific and cutting-edge strategies. Newcomers, often overwhelmed by the speed and complexity of e-sports, generally look for universal tips and suggestions to help familiarize themselves with a game's rules or mechanics. For example, longtime *World of Warcraft* players might only be interested in learning how they can defeat a "mage," a spell-casting character, in one-on-one duels. Conversely, new or prospective players might just want to learn where they can find someone to duel in the first place.

Fortunately, Twitch.tv streamers have figured out creative ways to appeal to both types of learners. Although e-sports streams have certainly drawn inspiration from, and even model themselves after, professional sports broadcasts, van Ditmarsch (2013) insists that e-sports streams add "new dimensions" to the viewing experience (p. 2). To accomplish this, e-sports on Twitch.tv are typically streamed in a one of two distinct ways. First, for major or sponsored events, streams tend to adopt the "traditional" approach. Mirroring the format and structure of telecasts like *ESPN*'s "Monday Night Football," e-sport tournament broadcasts feature pre-game, halftime, and post-game shows hosted by community insiders, commonly referred to as "casters." Serving as liaisons between the tournament participants and stream viewers, casters welcome newcomers and provide just-in-time explanations of and commentary on the action. Since they are generally versed in all aspects of the e-sport, its community, and its history, casters are particularly well suited to supply viewers with extensive knowledge. Likewise, former and current professional players often join casters in the broadcast booths to inject a measure of in-depth and critical analysis. This allows viewers simultaneous access to the extensive knowledge of the caster and the intensive knowledge of the professional, an experience often denied to students in the traditional classroom where information is dispensed from a single authority (Freire, 1994).

Recently, however, e-sport tournament broadcasts are taking additional precautions to ensure that their content is being delivered at appropriate levels of understanding. Some tournaments now boast secondary and tertiary streams designed to appeal to different audiences—viewers with various skill-levels, experiences, and goals. For instance, *League of Legends* and *Dota 2* tournaments regularly broadcast "newbie" or beginner streams alongside of their standard coverage. These newcomer-friendly streams forgo jargon-heavy discussion and "meta-game" analysis in favor of basic explanations designed to help viewers make sense of the chaos and to spark a general interest in the e-sport itself. We believe these types of beginner streams truly highlight the inclusive and participatory nature of e-sports culture. After all, these video game tournaments did not always have the large platforms, corporate support, and scores of devoted fans that they do today. Many e-sports come from humble beginnings – tiny tournaments hosted by passionate players in their own garages and apartments. In the past, it was not unheard of for players to pack their CRT televisions or desktop computers into their cars and to drive hundreds of miles for the crack at a forty-dollar prize pool. For example, Twitch.tv's 2013 broadcast of "The Evolution Championship Series" (EVO) revived the struggling *Super Smash Brothers: Melee* community and inspired numerous gamers to join its ranks. E-sports culture thus thrives on growth; the more fans and players an e-sport community gains, the more money, tournaments, and fun it produces. Twitch.tv exposure, especially through beginner streams, provides newcomers with much of the extensive knowledge they need to start gaming competitively.

As we have alluded to, when they are not competing in tournaments, many professional players stream casual matches and practices straight from their home computers. This method differs from tournament broadcasts in several key ways. Most notably, these personal streams tend to privilege intensive knowledge. While these professional players undoubtedly know their games inside and out, they typically specialize in a few particular roles and modes. Jeffrey "Trump" Shih, for instance, is a *Hearthstone* player known for his intensive knowledge of the "paladin" class, one of the game's nine playable roles. Similarly, he spends a majority of his game-time playing "arena," an alternate game-mode that is rarely showcased at major tournaments. Not surprisingly, Trump's stream appeals to very specific viewers. However, van Ditmarsch (2013) reminds us that the threshold to become a streamer is very low—Twitch.tv does not charge its streamers or viewers and, instead, earns its revenue via advertisements. Therefore, at any given time, multiple professional and high-level players can always be found streaming their game-play; viewers can simply channel surf until they find the content that matches their individual needs.

In addition to providing easy and constant access to intensive knowledge, these personal streams also feature unique delivery methods that simultaneously push the boundaries of spectatorship and foreground their educational purpose. While the sponsored tournament streams, in the tradition of sports telecasts, attempt to provide a panoramic view of the action, personal streams offer a far more intimate viewing experience. For example, when Blizzard Entertainment streams major *World of Warcraft* tournaments, the camera quickly changes angles and positions. At one moment, spectators might have an aerial view showing the teams' relative locations; in the next moment, the camera might zoom in on and follow a particular player through an especially intense skirmish. This omniscient perspective may even lead spectators to see and learn things about a match that are denied to the players themselves. Cheung & Huang (2011) refer to this concept as "informational asymmetry," a form of dramatic irony that heightens the audience's suspense. Since these tournaments tend to draw larger and more diverse audiences, their streams employ such techniques to prioritize entertainment value while supplying more extensive forms of knowledge. However, the personal streams of top-level players, like Elliot "Venruki" Venczel, instead utilize a singular and fixed perspective. After all, without access to more sophisticated technology, a player can only broadcast what appears on his computer screen. Consequently, when viewers tune in to Venruki's stream, they see precisely what he sees. Likewise, they hear his corresponding explanations as the action unfolds. Thus watching a professional player's personal stream becomes the ultimate behind-the-scenes learning-experience. In this space, streamers not only model best practices, but they also engage in metacognitive self-talk that demystifies their problem-solving processes. Interestingly, mainstream sports have attempted—and largely failed—to give their fans similar experiences. Although certain networks are beginning to "mic" players and to experiment with "GoPro" technology, these practices are primarily designed to immerse viewers in the action, not to teach them the sport's fundamental principles or strategies. However, as we will continue to discuss throughout this chapter, e-sports streamers are intrinsically and extrinsically motivated to step into the role of educator.

We previously described Twitch.tv as an e-sports hub. While the tournament and player live-streams are certainly its main attractions, Twitch.tv also recognizes its place in the long line of e-sports websites and actively "encourages people to use dispersed knowledge" (Gee, 2005, p. 227). According to Gee (2005), "dispersed knowledge" is information housed not on the website itself but in other virtual or physical locations. Once again, the Twitch.tv affinity space and e-sports culture reject the notion that knowledge need come from a single authority. In fact, when users first create their channels, they're given the opportunity to add "panels" on their homepages. While these panels can provide viewers with basic information about the streamer and his schedule, they typically feature links to a variety of e-sports resources. Professional players often direct visitors to their sponsors' websites, YouTube.com videos of their latest victories, or guides they have posted on external message boards. Although it might seem odd that an organization would allow traffic to come and go so freely, Twitch.tv is, in many ways, the digital embodiment of e-sports culture. As we have illustrated, this is an evolving culture that values competition, improvement, and participation above all else. If there is relevant knowledge somewhere beyond its boundaries, Twitch.tv certainly arms its users with the tools to find it.

The Participating Spectator

Although "learning by watching" is a timeless learning strategy (Taylor, 2012), Twitch.tv puts a decidedly 21st-century spin on spectatorship that showcases the values and instructional power of e-sports culture. Mediated by Twitch.tv's Web 2.0 affordances, spectators not only watch their favorite players and teams practice and compete, but they are also actively encouraged to participate in broadcasts. Specifically, e-sports spectators build relationships, ask questions, make suggestions, and provide feedback via a channel's text-based chat room (van Ditmarsch, 2013; Hamilton, Garretson, & Kerne, 2014). However, just as the two types of e-sports streams—tournament and personal—privilege different types of knowledge and content-delivery methods, so too do they afford unique avenues to participation. As Gee (2005) reminds us, traditional classrooms often constrain the students, limiting the ways in which they engage with the teacher, the material, and one another. By providing "multiple routes" to participation, and even status, Twitch.tv and e-sports culture are able to highlight their inherently democratic natures (Cheung & Huang, 2011; van Ditmarsch, 2013).

Tournament streams typically invite viewers to participate in various types of "one-way" communication (van Ditmarsch, 2013; Kaytoue et al., 2012). As we have mentioned, e-sports tournaments are becoming increasingly high-stakes affairs, often with thousands of dollars on the line. Consequently, at these events, the competitors are too preoccupied with their own preparation and game-play to interact with stream viewers. While that responsibility can occasionally fall to the casters, who will field questions and conduct polls, the viewers are generally left to interact with one another. Together, they bond over the favorite e-sports, teams, and players, often producing thoughtful discussions and heated debates along the way. Viewers are also known to share "battle-tags" or "gamer-tags" with one another so that they might continue their conversations, or even play together online, after the tournament ends. Of course, as these streams continue to grow in popularity, their chat rooms can certainly become chaotic (van Ditmarsch, 2013). During the largest tournaments, which attract as many as 200,000 viewers, keeping pace with the flurry of messages can be challenging. Nevertheless, tournament spectators still find creative ways to make their voices heard. Collectively, viewers will often "copy-and-paste" complaints, requests, or suggestions in an attempt to get the streamer's attention. For example, Twitch.tv spectators will famously spam the word "RIOT" to signal their disapproval. In response, event organizers and casters will often modify their stream's coverage to appease spectators.

Personal streams, on the other hand, are better suited to facilitate the types of "two-way" communication that, ultimately, allow viewers to become co-creators and co-owners of a channel's content (van Ditmarsch, 2013; Kaytoue et al., 2012). Cheung & Huang (2011) identify nine "personas," ranging from the "uninvested bystander" to the "curious," that comprise e-sports spectatorship. While all nine of these personas regularly tune in to tournament coverage, personal streams are especially attractive to "pupils," viewers seeking to "translate knowledge into practice" (p. 767). Fortunately, streamers are keenly aware of their audiences' goals and needs. After all, many of today's most popular streamers were once passionate fans and motivated pupils themselves. In addition, as we have described, viewers can make their interests and expectations transparent via the channel's text-based chat room. The streamer can easily glance over to read his viewers' comments and adjust his broadcast accordingly. Therefore, unlike writers, streamers do not need to imagine their audiences; in fact, Twitch.tv viewers are present and integral parts of a stream's production. Thus, e-sports spectatorship, like the e-sports themselves, must be seen as a new form of digital engagement. When compared to more traditional and static video-sharing websites, Twitch.tv's affordances necessarily stand apart and align with the overarching aims and values of e-sports culture.

So what does this spectator participation look like on Twitch.tv? In most cases, viewers will simply ask the streamers game-related questions. For example, users visiting Day[9]'s *StarCraft* channel might want to learn the best strategies for countering a "rush" attack. Similarly, those watching Trump's *Hearthstone* channel might ask which cards they should be adding to their Paladin decks. In these cases, users simply type their queries into the chat window and wait for the streamer to notice it and verbally respond. Some of the most popular questions are related to computer hardware and peripherals: "What keyboard would you recommend?" or "What kind of mouse are you using?" These are not trivial questions. In e-sports culture, where even the tiniest competitive advantage is valuable, a player's equipment can be the deciding factor in a close match. Taylor (2012) explains that mice, for instance, can have different sensitivity settings that allow players to manipulate their screens at different speeds (p. 42). For the budding e-sports competitors, purchasing the rights tools is an important first step in their pursuit of mastery.

However, just as tournament streams are becoming more popular, so too are the top- player's personal streams. Although streamers can easily interact with and respond to a handful of viewers, participation becomes more complicated as a stream crowds. If they feel that their chat room is becoming too "noisy," streamers will often temporarily enable a "subscriber-only" mode (Hamilton et al., 2014). While activated, the stream's chatting services—which are free by default—become limited to users that pay a five-dollar monthly subscription fee. Messages in this mode remain visible and public, but only subscribers may contribute to the ongoing conversation. As Hamilton et al. (2014) note, this represents a quick, but often imperfect, solution to improving chat quality, arguing that the mode "fundamentally undermines accessible participation" (p. 1322). Fortunately, many e-sports streamers recognize the dangers of "subscriber-only" mode and only choose to employ it sparingly. Of course, since Twitch.tv splits subscription profits with the channel's host, streamers nevertheless try to offer alternative incentives for their paying viewers. For example, subscribers receive free entry in raffles and have special icons appear next to their usernames in the chat room. The latter feature helps streamers to prioritize their subscribers' questions and comments even when the chat room is open to public discussion. While subscription benefits might seem suspiciously out-of-place in e-sports culture, we would simply remind readers that they do serve a larger purpose. Many e-sport communities are still in their infancy; although *Counter-Strike* and *StarCraft* professionals might be able to make a living from their tournament winnings and sponsorships alone, other games' top-players rely on Twitch.tv for income. Subscribers are actually fueling e-sports' rapid growth. Their constant donations have allowed more players to stream and, consequently, to share knowledge with the community at large.

Even if viewers do not wish to subscribe to a channel, they have the option to "follow" it for free. Borrowing the term from social media outlets like Twitter.com, followers receive automatic e-mail and mobile updates about a channel's schedule. For instance, as soon as a streamer "goes live," his followers are notified and invited to tune in. Since, as we have mentioned, viewers act as co-creators and co-owners of these channels, it is critical for streamers to quickly populate their chat rooms. Likewise, Twitch.tv's Android and iOS applications further embrace the inclusive and "always on" aspects of e-sports culture. Strengthened by the affordances of mobile technology, the Twitch.tv affinity space is becoming increasingly unbound.

Similarly, the e-sports streamers themselves are exploring the edges and limits of spectator participation. While "question and answer" sessions remain channel staples, some streamers have started to experiment with increasingly interactive and hands-on approaches. For example, an emerging trend in the competitive *Hearthstone* community is for streamers to relinquish some of their strategic-thinking duties to the viewers. Although they still control the action that appears on screen, the streamers allow their viewers to plan and decide moves—sometimes via text-based deliberation and other times via polling. This is particularly popular when *Hearthstone* streamers enter "arena-mode," a game-type that focuses on deck construction. Thus hosts, like Trump, often let their viewers design and build the decks that will be featured on stream. Typically, viewers will rise to the challenge and take their responsibilities seriously—seizing the opportunity to apply their knowledge and to practice what they have learned. However, on occasion, viewers will do the exact opposite; they will deliberately choose weaker or "gimmicky" cards, delighting in the streamer's struggle to win despite being hamstrung. While it may seem like the viewers, in this case, are taking advantage of the host's inclusive broadcast, the resulting unpredictable and impromptu moments often provide the stream with a much needed change of pace. Similarly, these types of decidedly democratic activities push back against the encroaching specter of subscriber-only modes.

We suspect that, in the coming months and years, personal streamers will continue to innovate new and compelling routes to participation. As we have alluded to, these particular live-streams foster two-way communication, creating a climate where hosts and spectators can readily exchange information and ideas. For example, it is not unusual for a streamer and his "pupils" to temporarily switch roles—a phenomenon that empowers viewers to disseminate their own intensive knowledge and experiences. Although these conversations generally revolve around issues within the game-space, some streamers are beginning to adopt more holistic approaches to spectator participation. In these models, streamers will often ask their viewers for food or music recommendations as well as for exercising or dating advice. One such streamer has even allowed his viewers to vote on pizza toppings for a dinner he was planning to order. We simply mention this trend because we believe it is representative—not just of e-sport culture—but of gaming culture at large. As Squire (2011) points out, a generation of young people have grown up with video games and their inherently interactive nature. Today, those same young people are starting to make the transition, via technologies like Twitch.tv, from player to "designer" and "community organizer" (p. 44). By watching their streams and carefully studying their design choices, we—as educators—have a golden opportunity to understand how this particular culture prefers to learn.

From Novice to Expert

Traditional schooling often makes it difficult for students to organize information in meaningful ways and to experience the transition from a novice learner to an expert practitioner (Bransford, Brown, & Cocking, 2000). Likewise, superficial coverage of material fails to adequately prepare students for "future learning and work" (Bransford et al., 2000). However, e-sports culture privileges a mastery learning that quickly and efficiently teaches novice players to become expert problem-solvers within and beyond the game-space. After all, its masters—the top-level and professional players—are constantly available to all community members via Twitch.tv streams and through their participation in both public online and live tournaments (Taylor, 2012). This unprecedented accessibility promotes the types of "cognitive apprenticeships" that have the potential to bolster and de-contextualize learning gains (Brown et al., 1989). As Brown et al.(1989) explain, "cognitive apprenticeship methods try to enculturate students into authentic practices through activity and social interaction" (p. 37). Interestingly, these are the very same strategies and goals of many of today's most popular e-sports live-streamers. Fueled by the "always on" and participatory values of its culture, e-sports, especially when compared to more casual gaming communities, stands apart in its desire and ability to foster meaningful novice-expert interactions.

Schwartz, Lin, Brophy, and Bransford (1999) note that learners can more easily grasp the "significance of new information and understand its relevance" when confronted with "expert" perspectives (p. 198). As we have already explored, Twitch.tv users certainly have access to these types of perspectives through tournament and personal streams. However, e-sports culture does more than simply invite its spectators to watch, listen, and peripherally interact. Games are meant to be played. In our modern era of vast and connected networks, it has never been easier for distant gamers to come together online for practices and matches. This is a fact not lost on professional players, casters, and community insiders, many of whom are always looking to support and teach newcomers. For instance, a number of high-level *World of Warcraft* streamers have actually started playing "battlegrounds" with their viewers. This particular game-mode, which challenges two opposing teams to capture flags or command points, allows many players to compete together at once. As the streamer plays along and collaborates with his viewers, he often supplies personalized tips and advice. Since "experts recognize features and patterns that are not noticed by novices," these suggestions could help to reveal previously hidden weaknesses or flaws (Bransford et al., 2000, p. 36). Thus the participatory values of e-sports culture have the power to invert spectatorship. While viewers traditionally watch and analyze the movements of the professional players, certain interactive stream-activities (like the one described here) can trigger role reversals. When the expert eye of the streamer is thus cast on the novice, unique learning opportunities necessarily emerge.

This is not a wholly new phenomenon. Perhaps its most striking example can be found in archives of Day[9]'s long-running *StarCraft* webcast. Although this decidedly educational show was primarily known for featuring in-depth analysis of tournament-level *StarCraft* matches, its host – a former top-rated player and current caster – would also occasionally broadcast and analyze user-submitted replays.

Known as "Newbie Tuesday," this popular weekly segment would discuss various ways for newcomers to begin making the transition to higher levels of play. At the start of each installment, Day[9] would introduce an important game concept that novices tend to overlook, misunderstand, or even completely ignore. For example, like many other real-time strategy games, *StarCraft* requires players to harvest and manage several different "resources." While it might be tempting for new players to quickly spend those resources on additional structures, those shiny new buildings might become worthless if the player is not generating the resource-income necessary to sustain them. Since *StarCraft* novices historically struggle with selecting the optimal units and structures to match their in-game economies, Day[9] has dedicated several shows to teaching players how to make efficient use of their resources. However, instead of relying on matches from top-level players to illustrate his points, Day[9] would feature clips from relative "newbies." Since a majority of his viewers were also novices, Day[9] was thus able to tailor instruction to their needs, presenting material at appropriate levels of understanding. Of course, those viewers that had their own matches critiqued gained the added benefit of personalized coaching from one of *StarCraft*'s finest players. While Day[9] rarely hosts shows in the tradition of "Newbie Tuesday" today, the success of his original webcast cannot be understated; since its last episodes in 2013, "Newbie Tuesday" has inspired many other top streamers to turn their own expert eyes on the work and play of their fans.

For many gamers, their interest and participation in e-sports culture begins on affinity spaces like Twitch.tv. Invariably, as these novices continue to hone their skills, many of them seek out live tournaments in an effort to truly test their learning. While some high-profile tournaments are "invite-only," many e-sports competitions—especially those for fighting games—are open to the public. Even certain events with significant prize pools, like EVO, can feature open registrations. Thus these tournaments regularly provide a physical space where novices and experts can interact with and learn from one another. However, for the first-time attendee, making sense of an e-sports tournament can be overwhelming and confusing. Taylor (2012) describes her own first experience, recalling that she found herself "attending a sort of hybrid event. Half mini-LAN party, half tournament" (p. 12). She continues, noting that "some [players] brought machines to set up in the LAN area for the duration of the event, others just milled around talking with friends, going out for a cigarette, or looking over the shoulder of someone sitting at a machine playing" (p. 12). Although she describes a specific tournament, the 2003 World Cyber Games Danish Finals (WCG), her account is nevertheless representative of and helpful for understanding today's local and regional e-sports competitions. Specifically, as we will discuss, the "hybrid" nature of such tournaments is an essential characteristic of what makes them powerful learning spaces.

Just as Twitch.tv streams offer multiple avenues for viewers to participate and learn, so too do e-sports tournaments. At most events—like the one Taylor describes—the play area is split in two, with one section reserved for official tournament matches and another open for more casual games, sometimes referred to as "friendlies." This latter, lounge-like section is especially important for newcomers because it provides them with a safe place to practice their skills on other competitors. Not surprisingly, the consequences for losing matches in these "friendly" environments are limited. For example, at *Super Smash Brothers: Melee* events, players often congregate together in groups of four. Players will take turns competing against one another, forming a rotation in which the winner keeps playing and the loser moves to the back of the line. Since games only last a few minutes, nobody is forced to wait long for another turn. Interestingly, players often try to seek out strangers when formulating these peer groups. Although many competitors travel to tournaments with their close friends and family members, e-sports players recognize the inherent benefits of playing with and against new opponents. As we have already illustrated, introducing players to multiple perspectives can help them to learn things about themselves that they could not discover on their own. However, in order to truly accelerate their progression from novice to expert, competitors must eventually square off with the masters themselves.

Fortunately, these safe learning spaces are not just for the newcomers. Veteran and even top-level, sponsored and professional players enjoy "milling around," chatting, and practicing during a tournament's down time. E-sports are still fun—even for those who have turned these video games into careers. Furthermore, although the industry itself is now booming, it is important to remember that many e-sports communities were founded and built on grassroots participation (Taylor, 2012). Veterans and experts—many of whom competed before the days of Twitch.tv—often find themselves emotionally invested in the very e-sports communities that they helped to create and grow. As such, these players go out of their ways to interact with the fans now that support them. It is not unusual for lines of novices to form at certain "friendly" machines where masters are playing. One by one, these newcomers not only have the opportunity to meet their e-sports heroes face-to-face, but they can actually compete with and against them. Consequently, these interactions often produce short-term or long-term cognitive apprenticeships in which the expert players directly model for and coach novices. This is a unique affordance of e-sports culture. Conversely, where traditional and professional sports are concerned, novices and experts are generally segregated—high school players compete against other high school players; college players compete against other college players; professional players compete against other professional players. Generally, crossover only occurs when a particular up-and-coming player demonstrates extraordinary promise and potential. In the overwhelming majority of other situations, a novice basketball player, for instance, will never have the opportunity to compete with or against the likes of LeBron James.

As e-sports culture continues to develop, however, we fear that the live and personal interactions between novices and experts may become a thing of the past. Quite simply, e-sports' growing fandom is a double-edged sword. Novices are coming to e-sports faster than its communities can produce the experts and masters to guide them. In other words, the culture's student-to-teacher ratio is widening; the lines to play "friendlies" with the masters are lengthening. Nevertheless, we suspect that e-sports' long history and tradition of fostering meaningful novice-expert interactions and cognitive apprenticeships will endure. As we have discussed, Twitch.tv streamers are already devising creative new ways to rekindle and re-imagine these apprenticeships for their own digital moment. Reflecting on the early days of competitive gaming, Taylor (2012) notes that "playing against others was the real draw" (p. 7). However—in a modern e-sports culture that privileges mastery-learning—player motivations have necessarily evolved. Competing with and against *the masters* is now the "real draw." As we have alluded to, e-sports culture is about more than simply winning. Instead, it is about constantly challenging oneself to improve. This ongoing process, ultimately, takes priority over any individual outcome. Although e-sports culture cannot transform all of its members into tournament champions, its values encourage them to set out on their own, personal journeys—to explore interesting topics in tremendous depth.

Unfortunately, too often, our school systems do the exact opposite. Bransford et al. (2000) note that "curricula that emphasize breath of knowledge may prevent effective organization of knowledge because there is not enough time to learn anything in depth," and thus deny mastery-learning (p. 49). Although, throughout our chapter, we have described and analyzed a number of techniques that e-sports competitors rely on to help improve their play, the actual process of transitioning from a "newbie" to a "pro" is far more complicated than we can adequately express here. In addition to logging dozens of hours watching and learning from high-level streamers, e-sports enthusiasts will undoubtedly spend hundreds more practicing online and with their friends in their unwavering quest to "climb the ladder." While most of these players will never quite reach their lofty competitive goal—to be the best—their exposure to and participation in e-sports culture will nevertheless have a lasting impact on how they view "expertise" and conceive of "learning." After all, e-sports competitors are learning more than just how to become better gamers; they are experiencing first-hand what it takes to become masters. These are revelations that have the power to extend beyond the game-space and into their future lives.

Barriers in E-Sports

In the wake of recent and increasingly mainstream conversations regarding misogyny and sexism in video games and their communities, we feel that it is necessary to address how e-sports culture reacts to and treats its female player-base. Despite evidence suggesting that women are playing video games as frequently as men, Taylor (2012) laments that female competitors are nevertheless the rare "exceptions" at e-sports tournaments (p. 16). Perhaps even more disheartening, e-sports culture's traditionally open and inclusive values often seemingly dissolve in the face of female gamers. Taylor (2012) points out that "contemporary e-sports is deeply segregated, with women and men generally playing on different teams and in separate tournaments" (p. 125). Furthermore, she explains that female competitors that practice online are often "denigrated" and "taunted" to the point where they feel forced to actively conceal their identities, often turning off their headsets or going by gender-neutral usernames (p. 122). However, as video game live-streaming sites like Twitch.tv become increasingly popular, female competitors are starting to step out of the shadows. Today, with their increased visibility, these women are publicizing their e-sport accomplishments and contributions—their male counterparts are beginning to take note. This, of course, does not mean that women are suddenly immune to the overt and latent misogyny that has historically plagued e-sports and gamer culture. We simply use the rise of the female streamer to illustrate how her plight has and will continue to evolve in the coming years—sometimes for better, sometimes for worse.

In 2015, many of Twitch.tv's most popular channels are now hosted by female e-sports competitors. For example, as of September, Rumay "Hafu" Wang's personal *Hearthstone* channel has been viewed over 43 million times. Sponsored by e-sports juggernaut "Cloud9," Hafu consistently places among—and even above—the top male players on *Hearthstone*'s online ladder. Thus Hafu's success subverts the expectations of many male viewers who, as Taylor (2012) claims, often think female players are "not good enough" (p. 126). Interestingly, although e-sports culture has, at times, turned its back on women, today's female streamers regularly exemplify a number of its more inclusive and educational values. Their streams, often more so than those of their male counterparts, foreground the participatory aspects of e-sports culture. They constantly invite their viewers to ask questions, to play games, and to request songs—thus transforming their shows into more lively and social affairs.

However, as we have previously mentioned, these larger and more popular streams, like Hafu's, can easily get "noisy." Sometimes it only takes one "troll," a person that hides behind their online anonymity and attempts to sow discord, to thrust a chat room into chaos. Female streamers often have to ban these users for typing inflammatory and sexist remarks. This was especially common in the early days of Twitch.tv when female streamers, perhaps attempting to "reassure others of their gender identity" (Taylor, 2012, p. 123), would wear decidedly feminine—even provocative—outfits. Male viewers would often join their channels simply to cry, "ATTENTION WHORE!" before promptly leaving. Recently, however, Twitch.tv has amended its terms of service and use to specifically address these issues. Asking users to "keep it about the games," the website now prohibits streamers with webcams, regardless of gender, from wearing "suggestive clothing" or from going shirtless (Twitch.tv, 2015). We think this message is an important one. While enforcing a dress-code is not going to eliminate the many socio-cultural challenges facing female streamers, it may at least help to refocus attention on what really matters in e-sports culture: a player's skill, insight, and competitive drive.

In addition, the e-sports community's lexicon is slowly beginning to change. Throughout the late 1990s and early 2000s, traditional online message boards and gaming communities were rife with sexist and homophobic language. Competitors casually used the word "rape" in reference to lopsided matches. Likewise, players would not hesitate to label and denounce particularly defensive tactics as "gay." In those days, the e-sports communities were far more isolated, insular, and homogeneous. The predominately male player-base sorely lacked perspective; many were oblivious to the fact that their usage was exclusionary and downright offensive. It was not until the Twitch.tv affinity space began connecting disparate gaming communities together that those players started to mature. After all, on Twitch.tv, streamers become more than simply names on a leaderboard. Not only do their split-second decision-making processes become visible, but their raw emotions and humanity go on full display as well. Twitch.tv thus holds up a mirror to the e-sports community. By giving a face and voice to all of its members, it allows gamers to see the psychological impact of their words and actions. While slurs are still thrown around at today's e-sports tournaments, their frequency and vulgarity pale in comparison to those that were commonplace in the past. Furthermore, many players have become quick to reprimand their peers for using such insensitive language. As we see it, Twitch.tv's real power is in its ability to showcase new ideas and perspectives while simultaneously allowing spectators to engage with those thoughts as well.

It is difficult to talk about the treatment of women in e-sports without making some sweeping—and often damning—statements and claims about gamer culture. Make no mistake, e-sport's relationship with its female competitors is complicated. Although Twitch.tv is helping female gamers to increase their visibility and to leave their marks on e-sports culture, it is simultaneously reopening old wounds. Those looking to make the transition from novice to expert certainly have difficult roads before them. Fortunately, the recent success of many female streamers gives us hope that longstanding barriers are poised to fall.

Towards Classroom Application: Rendering the Invisible Visible

With the rise of e-sports culture and the establishment of Twitch.tv as its digital affinity space, our students—boys and, increasingly, girls—are currently in a position to "compare and contrast how learning works in such spaces and how it works [or does not work] in schools" (Gee, 2005, pp. 231-2). They have experienced rapid and successful learning through their participation in e-sports broadcasts and events, and, consequently, they are expecting similar methods and results from our classrooms. Unfortunately, not many teachers are gamers—even fewer appreciate the e-sports phenomenon and how it empowers its members. Therefore, we aim to use this final section to extract and distill a specific learning principle from e-sports culture that educators would do well to harness and foster in their classrooms.

Just as Brown et al. (1989) characterize the affordances of cognitive apprenticeships, e-sports culture similarly has the power to render the invisible visible. From the metacognitive self-talk that streamers so often employ during their broadcasts to the personalized coaching that novices regularly receive at tournaments, e-sports culture encourages newcomers to peer behind the curtain and to learn the games' secrets. While it may be our goal—as teachers—to do likewise in our classrooms, students still have a tendency to find certain disciplines and topics opaque, despite our best efforts. We believe that high school writing instruction, in particular, could benefit from channeling this e-sports learning-principle.

After all, composition theorists have long noted that writing is too often incorrectly studied, taught, and evaluated as a *product* instead of as a *process* (Murray, 1972; Flower & Hayes, 1981; Elbow, 1998). Thus when teachers "use [final written products] as their reference point, they offer an inadequate account of the more intimate, moment-by-moment intellectual process of composing" (Flower & Hayes, 1981, p. 367). While students might have a sense of what good writing looks like, they are not necessarily familiar enough with the composing process to recreate it on their own. Fortunately, as we have explored, e-sports culture excels at revealing and unpacking the details of those "moment-by-moment processes." Consequently, it is helpful to return to the affordances of the Twitch.tv affinity space for inspiration.

We, therefore, propose that writing instructors appropriate screen-capturing technology and tools—not unlike the ones used by Twitch.tv streamers—in an attempt to render the composing process visible for their students. Just as e-sports streamers describe why and how they make complex decisions in their games, teachers could use similar strategies to walk students through the composing processes of brainstorming, researching, crafting sentences, editing, and revising in real-time. Instead of streaming video-game play, teachers would essentially be "streaming" the writing process. Of course, we use the term "stream" more liberally here. We do not expect teachers to actually broadcast their lessons online and to the masses; rather, we simply encourage writing instructors to draw upon the traditions of e-sports spectatorship and to adapt those methods for their own classrooms. For instance, teachers could share their computer screens via projectors and work through particularly challenging portions of a writing project. Students would thus have the opportunity to see and hear precisely how expert writers encounter and navigate various problems. Moreover, students, like Twitch.tv viewers, could ask specific questions and even make their own suggestions as they actively participate in their instructors' composing processes.

Computer technology plays a vital role in this example. While a teacher could simply workshop sentences on a chalkboard, we feel that that approach lacks authenticity—especially where high school and college students are concerned. In 2015, the writing process involves far more than the pen and the paper. Today's students can access online databases and journals; they can instantly look up definitions and synonyms; they can easily rearrange, repurpose, and revise content. "Streaming" the writing process directly from a computer accommodates for these evolving, 21st-century writing practices in ways that a chalkboard never could. It injects the much needed authenticity that Brown et al. (1989) claim is so critical for successful cognitive apprenticeships—"it is the only way [learners] gain access to the standpoint that enables practitioners to act meaningfully and purposefully" (p. 36). By modeling authentic practices with authentic tools, the instructor can ground student-learning in real-world contexts.

As we have discussed, however, e-sports culture values input from all of its community members—regardless of their proficiency and experience levels. While expert perspectives are certainly privileged and promoted, novices have similar opportunities to share and distribute knowledge. Writing instructors should not hesitate to allow students to "stream" their writing processes as well. Students could thus model for one another as their teachers check for understanding. Obviously, the suggestions we describe here are not the only ways to channel e-sports culture in formal, educational settings. Other disciplines and topics could similarly benefit; we simply chose to focus on writing instruction because we think it is particularly well suited to quickly adopt and modify live-streaming practices to render the invisible visible.

Throughout this chapter, we have attempted to explain why and how the e-sports cultural movement values and produces knowledge. Perhaps we have been going about it in the wrong way. After all, we, like our students, have the potential to learn from participation in e-sports culture—not necessarily about the games, but about the young people who play them. E-sports streamers do not simply model bullet-time reflexes and clever gamesmanship, they are modeling the very types of instructional techniques that they wish we would employ in schools. They value intensive, extensive and dispersed knowledge. They encourage and provide multiple routes to participation. They ease in and out of mentoring roles. They lend expert eyes to their novice peers. All the while, they are rendering their invisible cognitive process visible. Do not take it from us—take it from them.

In preparation for writing this chapter, we personally experimented with this affinity space. We watched, we participated, and we learned. We even attempted to host our own Twitch.tv streams, cast tournament matches, and interact with the unlucky viewers who happened to stumble into our admittedly amateur channels. Those experiences confirmed our suspicions—that video game live-streaming is a complicated and authentic 21st century task. It involves careful planning, improvisation, multi-tasking, technological knowhow, public-speaking skills, and sound educational methods. Many of our students, perhaps at this very moment, are logged into this affinity space and are participating in—even hosting— such broadcasts. This, we think, is a good thing. As Prensky (2006) explains, "the true secret of why kids spend so much time on their games is that they're learning things they need for their twenty-first century lives" (p. 5). E-sports and Twitch.tv herald not just a new generation of video games, but a new generation of learners. With the affordances of an affinity space, the constant input from its participating spectators, and an emphasis on mastery learning, e-sports are a force that educators need to respect and understand. These games represent new forms of digital engagement—our classrooms must now transform to accommodate their players.

REFERENCES

Bransford, J., Brown, A., & Cocking, R. (Eds.). (2000). *How people learn: Brain, mind, experience, and school*. Washington, DC: National Academy Press.

Brown, J. S., Collins, A., & Duguid, P. (1989). Situated cognition and the culture of learning. *Educational Researcher, 18*(1), 32–42. doi:10.3102/0013189X018001032

Cheung, G., & Huang, J. (2011). *Starcraft* from the stands: understanding the game spectator. In *Proceedings of the SIGCHI Conference on Human Factors in Computing Systems* (pp. 763–772). doi:10.1145/1978942.1979053

Elbow, P. (1998). *Writing with power: Techniques for mastering the writing process*. Oxford University Press.

Flower, L., & Hayes, J. R. (1981). A cognitive process theory of writing. *College Composition and Communication, 32*(4), 365–387. doi:10.2307/356600

Freire, P. (1994). The "banking" concept of education. In D. H. Richter (Ed.), *Falling into theory: Conflicting views on reading literature* (pp. 68–84). Boston: Bedford Books of St. Martin's Press.

Gee, J. P. (2005). Semiotic social spaces and affinity spaces: From *The Age of Mythology* to today's schools. In D. Barton & K. Tusting (Eds.), *Beyond communities of practice: Language, power and social context* (pp. 214–232). Cambridge: Cambridge University Press. doi:10.1017/CBO9780511610554.012

Hamilton, W. A., Garretson, O., & Kerne, A. (2014, April). Streaming on Twitch: Fostering participatory communities of play within live mixed media. In *Proceedings of the SIGCHI Conference on Human Factors in Computing Systems* (pp. 1315-1324). ACM. doi:10.1145/2556288.2557048

Hutchins, B. (2008). Signs of meta-change in second modernity: The growth of e-sport and the world cyber games. *New Media & Society, 10*(6), 851–869. doi:10.1177/1461444808096248

Jakobsson, M. (2007). Playing with the rules: Social and cultural aspects of game rules in a console game club. In *Situated Play, Proceedings of the Digital Games Research Association (DiGRA) Conference*.

Kaytoue, M., Silva, A., Cerf, L., Meira, W., & Raïssi, C. (2012). Watch me playing, I am a professional: A first study on video game live streaming. In *Proceedings of the 21st international conference companion on World Wide Web* (pp. 1181–1188). doi:10.1145/2187980.2188259

Lee, D., & Schoenstedt, L. J. (2011). Comparison of eSports and traditional sports consumption motives. *ICHPER-SD Journal of Research, 6*(2), 39–44.

Murray, D. (1972). Teach writing as a process not product. *The Leaflet, 71*(3), 11–14.

Prensky, M. (2006). *Don't bother me mom – I'm learning*. Saint Paul: Paragon House.

Schwartz, D. L., Lin, X., Brophy, S., & Bransford, J. D. (1999). Toward the development of flexibly adaptive instructional designs. In C. Reigeluth (Ed.), *Instructional-design theories and models: A new paradigm of instructional theory* (pp. 183–213). Mahwah, NJ: Erlbaum.

Shaw, A. (2014). *E-sport Spectator Motivation* (Doctoral dissertation).

Squire, K. (2011). *Video games and learning: Teaching and participatory culture in the digital age*. New York: Teacher's College Press.

Tassi, P. (2014, January 27). Riot's '*league of legends*' reveals astonishing 27 million daily players, 67 million monthly. *Forbes*. Retrieved October 12, 2015, from http://www.forbes.com

Taylor, T. L. (2012). *Raising the stakes: E-sports and the professionalization of computer gaming*. Cambridge: The MIT Press.

Twitch.tv. (2015). Retrieved July 15, 2015, from http://www.twitch.tv/

Van Ditmarsch, J. (2013). *Video games as a spectator sport*. Thesis.

Wagner, M. G. (2006, January). On the scientific relevance of eSports. In *Proceedings of the 2006 International Conference on Internet Computing & Conference on Computer Games Development, ICOMP 2006,* (pp. 437-442).

Witkowski, E. (2012). On the digital playing field: How we "do sport" with networked computer games. *Games and Culture, 7*(5), 349–374. doi:10.1177/1555412012454222

KEY TERMS AND DEFINITIONS

Affinity Space: Gee's (2005) term to describe virtual or physical locations where people of common interests come together to engage in informal learning.

Cognitive Apprenticeship: An apprenticeship model in which learning occurs through guided cognitive – not physical – processes.

E-Sports: Hypercompetitive video games that allow players to participate in organized tournaments with strict rules. E-sports also refers to a cultural movement within gaming that values expertise.

Message Boards: An older type of affinity space that serves as a searchable database and communication forum. Conversations on message boards often take place over days or weeks as opposed to the instant communication that occurs on Twitch.tv.

Twitch.tv: A popular video game live-streaming website that caters to e-sports competitors and fans. Twitch.tv uses can participate in event broadcasts via text-based communication and in real-time. The authors see Twitch.tv as the next evolution of the affinity space.

APPENDIX

An Overview of Popular E-Sport Games

Throughout our chapter, we reference a number of popular e-sport games. While our focus is primarily on culture, it is nevertheless important for educators to have a passing familiarity with the games themselves.

StarCraft (1998) : Currently in its second iteration, the *StarCraft* series has been a cornerstone of the e-sports community for nearly two decades. A real-time strategy game in which competitors create and control futuristic armies, *StarCraft* initially gained tremendous popularity in South Korea during the early 2000s. There, the game was not only featured on multiple professional circuits, but its top players were also celebrated as rock stars and pop-culture icons (Taylor, 2012). Although it has taken far longer for e-sports to garner mainstream attention in the United States, *StarCraft*'s success in South Korea nevertheless provided the blueprint. Like *World of Warcraft* and *Hearthstone*, *StarCraft* is a product of Blizzard Entertainment – a developer that specializes in online, multiplayer games.

Super Smash Brothers: Melee (2001) : Originally marketed as a light-hearted and low-stakes party game, *Super Smash Brothers: Melee* gives players the opportunity to battle one another using classic *Nintendo* characters. Competitors take the roles of Mario, Kirby, Link, Pikachu, and other fan-favorites as they attempt to knock their opponents off of floating stages. However, despite its cartoony visuals and equally silly premise, players immediately recognized the inherent depth and complexity of its game-play. Over the years, they modified the pre-existing rules to create a more competitive and standardized format for tournament play (Jakobsson, 2007). While it is certainly not the prototypical 2D-fighting game, *Super Smash Brothers: Melee* nevertheless shares many common features with the likes of *Street Fighter* and *Marvel vs. Capcom.*

World of Warcraft (2003) : Although *World of Warcraft* is primarily thought of as a cooperative role-playing game in the tradition of *Dungeons & Dragons*, a number of its players prefer to engage in more competitive interactions. Since the game's launch, Blizzard Entertainment has "patched" in numerous different game modes and arenas in which players can test their skills head-to-head. Working in teams of either three, five, or ten, players must coordinate their offensive and defensive abilities with incredible speed and precision. While more viewer-friendly games like *League of Legends* and *Hearthstone* are beginning to overshadow it, the *World of Warcraft* "three-on-three" competition remains one of *BlizzCon*'s marquee events.

League of Legends (2009) : An evolution of the real-time strategy game, *League of Legends* blends the chess-like gameplay of *StarCraft* with the collaboration of *World of Warcraft* to create a compelling viewer experience. In teams of five, players take the roles of fantasy-inspired "champions" as they race to complete various objectives. Throughout the course of a match, teams will inevitably find themselves in heated skirmishes – the players with better synergy and communication will typically triumph. Like its spiritual counterpart, *Dota 2*, *League of Legends* is free to download and play. As of 2014, an estimated 67 million people play the game every month, making it the world's most popular e-sport (Tassi, 2014).

Hearthstone (2014) : Developed as one of Blizzard Entertainment's side-projects, *Hearthstone* is a digital card-game that draws upon and simplifies many elements from the paper-based *Magic: The Gathering*. In *Hearthstone,* players use cards to summon vicious monsters and to cast powerful spells; they then use these newfound tools and abilities in an attempt to outwit their opponents. Unlike some of the other chaotic and fast-paced e-sports that we highlight, *Hearthstone* translates especially well to the Twitch.tv screen. Not only are players' actions deliberate and clear, but the game's interface is also easy to read and to interpret. Consequently, spectators feel as if they can play along with the competitors, vicariously making decisions and sharing in the thrill of victory.

Chapter 12
Gaming to Increase Reading Skills:
A Case Study

Laura Kieran
Drake University, USA

Christine Anderson
Western Illinois University, USA

ABSTRACT

When considering instructional supports for struggling adolescent readers, Fisher and Ivey (2006) suggested that the interventions be comprehensive, include a variety of authentic reading and writing opportunities, and be based on varied assessment data. The researchers developed a schedule for Maya, an 8th grade student to work on vocabulary and reading comprehension via games that reviewed discreet skills as well as social media per Maya's preferences. The use of technology interventions for Maya allowed her to read, listen to, and think about meaningful texts, while maintaining balance with instruction in skills related to reading for a variety of purposes.

MAYA: STUDY INTRODUCTION

This chapter reviews a case study on 'Maya,' an 8th grade student attending a Midwestern middle school. She has a history of deficits in reading and vocabulary comprehension since elementary school. This case study had exploratory purpose (Yin, 1994) with the function to explore this question: Would encouraging a young girl to use games on mobile devices as an intervention strategy improve her language arts skills? Maya is a talented young artist who would like to be an art teacher. She prefers to use mobile devices for social purposes. Because of Maya's learner profile, it was proposed that selected games and mobile connections might engage Maya, thereby increasing her learning opportunities. Self-evaluation was used to develop habits that would authentically translate to future academic behavior necessary for the transition to high school.

DOI: 10.4018/978-1-5225-0261-6.ch012

Maya was enrolled in an intensive 1:1 reading program previous to this research, in the summer between 3rd and 4th grade. At that time, she caught up with her peers on reading-related tasks including word recognition and reading comprehension. However, since that time, Maya has again fallen behind her peers in both vocabulary and reading comprehension. Recently, Maya's math teacher also expressed concern that an achievement gap existed between Maya and her peers in math application skills; this would potentially result in Maya's registration in remedial classes at the high school level. Maya expressed concern to her parents and the researchers about her current academic levels, questioning her readiness for high school. She has a goal of attending college to become an art teacher and does not want to enter high school behind her peers.

As a result of participation in a language arts workshop presented by the researchers, Maya and her parents contacted the researchers for further assistance with her learning. The agreement was made that tools and strategies introduced in the workshop would be practiced with Maya, and that the information gained could explore the effectiveness of the Language Arts interventions on mobile devices. The Institutional Review Board (IRB) approved the study, which lasted approximately four months. In order to support Maya, the researchers applied behavioral and academic interventions, which included tutoring with game-based and social media-based reading and vocabulary activities and positive reinforcement. These decisions reflected Maya's strengths and preferences as a learner. These strategies were part of the initial workshop, and mobile learning was selected because Maya also has demonstrated a strong interest in handheld devices, common in her age group. Individualized learning pathways should be based on actual student needs, therefore explicit language arts instruction was delivered through Maya's interest in and preference for mobile devices (Melhuish & Falloon, 2010).

Maya frequently expressed frustration with learning, saying she felt dumb. Although Maya's mother recently became a citizen of the United States, her mother was born in the Dominican Republic. Therefore, Spanish is her mother's first language. Maya has dark skin and hair; she appears to have a multi-racial heritage. In addition to her academic frustrations, her ethnic background may impact her learning challenges, self-image, and level of school motivation. Initially, she was not capable of successfully completing tasks that involved reading comprehension, learning new vocabulary, and written expression.

Students who struggle academically frequently avoid the work that is challenging. Such assignments reinforce negative self-concepts and after struggling for years they can withdraw or shut down when presented with difficult academic tasks (Lavoie, 2002). Teachers and parents typically view this behavior as the student being either lazy or defiant. Maya routinely avoided schoolwork that involved her specific areas of challenge: reading comprehension and written expression. Consequently, her parents reported that homework completion was a nightly battle, which Maya frequently won, an obvious manifestation of escape behavior. Another issue was Maya's use of technology for socializing rather than schoolwork, specifically with handheld devices such as her cell phone and tablet. When she was required to use technology for school, she would often lose focus and subsequently use the tablet or cell phone for more desired tasks such as Facebook, Twitter, Snapchat, or Instagram. Her parents were frustrated because they felt that if Maya better applied herself to her schoolwork her grades would improve. Parents and teachers often lament that if students would only try harder they would perform better in school. However, for students that are struggling readers the converse is often true; if they experienced academic success then they would try harder (Lavoie, 2002). Maya did not know how games and social media could be used to support her learning; the researchers decided to leverage Maya's interest in social media and technology to enhance her reading and vocabulary comprehension rather than as a means to disrupt or escape learning.

Traditionally literacy has focused on reading and writing, yet as communication methods evolve the definition has expanded to include multiple forms of print, symbols, graphs and a variety of modalities (Gee, 2007; Hsu & Wang, 2010). Current learning strategies should address both instructional methods for individuals as well as collaborative groups by integrating evidence-based practice, modern technology, and social relationships (Gee, 2007). New literacies have emerged, generally using information and communication technology (ICT) to gather information and communicate answers (Hsu & Wang, 2010). This study examined digital tools and games that effect learning, specifically interventions related to language arts and literacy for adolescent learners. Games were selected based on a mutual agreement between the researchers and Maya. The extent literature provided fundamentals on adolescent interests, academic achievement, language arts interventions, and the needs of specific populations associated with digital resources and gaming.

GAMING AND DIGITAL TOOLS

Researchers reported that adolescents spend an average of 53 hours a week interacting with digital tools, 97% play videogames regularly, and one-third play daily (Beach, 2012; Bowers & Berland, 2013; Gee, 2007; Gerber & Price, 2013). In addition to social communication and gaming, 12% of adolescents participated in online courses (Beach, 2012). Such familiarity with mobile devices indicated a potentially major development of instructional technology (Beach, 2012; Gee, 2007; Vogel, Greenwood-Ericksen, Cannon-Bowers, & Bowers, 2006; Warren, Stein, Dondlinger, & Barab, 2009). The use of mobile technologies has become ubiquitous for today's learners; however, many students such as Maya automatically use mobile technologies for games and social connectivity without also realizing the potential learning benefits of their mobile devices. To further compound this problem, teachers may not have received training in how to use mobile devices as tools for learning. Many school districts have policies that ban the use of mobile devices in the classroom. Cell phones then become a distraction used covertly by students under the desk. Instead, this technology should be used to increase learning and engagement with class content on top of the desk.

Participation in games, social media, simulations, and virtual worlds has increased among all ages in the past decade primarily due to characteristics such as interactivity, 'gamification' (motivation), reward, and challenge (Vogel et al., 2006; Warren et al., 2009). Researchers have validated that effective game-based learning integrates evidence-based instructional strategies without violating the pleasure components of gaming (Ke & Abras, 2013; Warren et al., 2009). Games increased audience interest through good narratives, authentic problems to solve, and balanced scaffolds (Warren et al., 2009). Scaffolds include immediate feedback, sequence of skills, in-game hints, and varied levels of challenge. In the United States, Bowers and Berland (2013) published that moderate levels of gaming positively influenced academic achievement. This is due in no small part to the learning benefits of games with engage students in problem solving, the ability to master skills in sequence and to receive immediate feedback; these are valuable to learning any new skill. Unfortunately, in an assembly-line style or 'one-size-fits-all' approach to education, students too often do not have the ability to solve problems collaboratively in the classroom. Additionally, in overcrowded, diverse classrooms teachers often do not have the opportunity to provide students with varied levels of challenge or immediate feedback.

Previously, patterns of Internet use had been connected to middle school students' achievement primarily due to increased student engagement (Ke & Abras, 2013; Vogel et al., 2006; Warren et al., 2009).

Technology extended educational opportunities, allowing for fluidity across space and time (Gerber & Price, 2013); many positive learning outcomes resulted from online communities (Tobatabai & Shore, 2005). Levels of use influence the results: "Moderate levels of video gaming may provide an additional avenue to improve student achievement in addition to other school activities such as homework, extracurricular activities, and recreational reading" (Bowers & Berland, 2013, p. 64). Examples of such education-based games or 'serious games' include the *Lightspan* curriculum and *Anytown*. These were designed to increase problem solving, reading comprehension, and word study as measured by national norm-referenced tests as well as to provide a digital environment with evidence-based gaming and instructional strategies such as scaffolds, paired learning, thematic mini-games, narrative context, explicit rules and writing (Blanchard, Stock, & Marshall, 1999; Bowers & Berland, 2013; Warren et al., 2009).

As education-based games have evolved we have moved away from problem solving with little academic content or games, which simply drill skills. Anyone who ever played *Oregon Trail* in the 1980's can tell you about the joys of making it to Oregon without being bitten by a snake, starving, or contracting a disease along the way. While the game was engaging and at times the choices you made as a player impacted your chances for success, the skills learned did not readily transfer beyond the early American History class or into real life. Other early educational games that were developed in the 1980's by the Minnesota Educational Computing Corporation were *Number Munchers* and *Spelling Munchers*. These games were designed to build students' fluency in math and spelling, but there were no opportunities for problem solving or collaboration built into the programs. Early game designers and educators typically did not collaborate on the kinds of games that would be pedagogically sound for their curriculum. To further compound the problem, teachers typically did not receive training in how to use technology to further their students' learning. Therefore, early games were based on lower level thinking skills; students who needed skill remediation often had their instruction supplemented with technology-based review. The result was an emphasis on basic skills with technology in the classroom. This led many early critics to question if technology implementations added sufficient value to education given the expense schools incurred in an attempt to update networks and computer systems, as well as expand computer access for all students.

In response to this criticism, educational games began to shift to incorporate problem-solving skills or opportunities for collaboration. Anytown is a multi-user virtual environment (MUVE) designed to enhance learning of social studies content and featured problem solving and collaboration between students in different parts of the world. The Lightspan curriculum was part of an early movement in the 1990's to introduce serious gaming in the classroom; it was a Sony PlayStation-based gaming system for students in elementary and middle school grades. The benefit of this game system was that gaming could be used to both review in-class content and skills, as well as to individualize for students who needed review of previous skills or as a means to enrich learning for students who needed more challenge. One of the researchers had two elementary-aged children enrolled in a district that used the *Lightspan* curriculum on home-based Sony PlayStations (provided by the school district) for homework, and reported that her children would frequently argue over who got to do their homework first. With the especially engaging stories and problems to solve, both sons would spend many hours more on homework in a week than they were assigned. Other attributes of these games included specific quests or challenges that students needed to solve in order to increase levels (and their skills). Players received immediate positive or corrective feedback, and felt a sense of achievement when they 'leveled-up.' Increased engagement and repetition with problem-solving and content area skills improved their performance on the game and in the classroom. Blanchard et al. (1999) conducted a meta-analysis of research to evaluate the efficacy of the *Lightspan* curriculum and found that students who were taught with the *Lightspan* curriculum performed better than control group students on national, norm-referenced district assessments despite inconsistency in how programs were implemented across participating districts.

Recent assessments of digital learning overall have been positive: such as studies that showed no difference in reading and comprehension between digital versus printed texts (Taylor, 2012 in Beach, 2012), enriched self-evaluations and increased motivation on e-portfolios (Beach, 2012). Computer assisted instruction (CAI) also improved spelling via explicit instruction, multiple practice sessions, and immediate corrective feedback (Wanzek, et al., 2006). Transformational play developed collaborative problem-solving reflections and critical evaluations of games (Beach, 2012). Chen and Fu (2009) showed that when the Internet was used for information the yields were positive; however, too much recreation and social use may have a negative impact on academic performance. Specifically, excessive gaming for males and excessive social media use for females have had adversely impacted academic performance. Thus validating the concern of many parents that students were distracted from homework by the Internet. Again, just as in school, students' use of games and social media needs to be harnessed and focused on learning.

Digital literacies provided a connection for social practices among diverse groups (Gerber & Price, 2013). Ke and Abras (2013) affirmed that "educational gaming as a learning tool may be less effective for certain groups of learners" (p. 225). Conversely spatial-based learning strategies were more effective across diverse learners than traditional instruction in reading and writing (Ponce, Mayer, & Lopez, 2013). Foreign language learners also benefitted with improved language skills (listening, reading, vocabulary) and increased motivation with adventure games (Chen & Yang, 2013). Many at-risk populations have developed academic achievement, for example middle school boys and reluctant readers increased reading, improved reading abilities, and self-concept with e-readers (Beach, 2012). Additionally, digital storytelling encouraged people with little confidence in writing (Xu, Park, & Baek, 2011).

Increased student achievement outcomes have historically been based on the quality of technology integration. Key components of educational technology include: purposeful design (Mayrath, Traphagan, Heikes, & Trivedi, 2011), student engagement (Warren et al., 2009), ongoing assessment (Hickey, McWilliams, & Honeyford, 2011), professional development (Beach, 2012; Gerber & Price, 2013), and alignment with standards (Blanchard, Stock, & Marshall et al., 1999; Ke & Abras, 2003). Hutchison and Woodward (2014) added that specific requirements were necessary for successful integration of technology in literacy, such as understanding Technological, Pedagogical and Content Knowledge (TPACK); assessing available technology, and evaluating best tools for learners. Additional benefits resulted from the inclusion of student choice (Gerber & Price, 2013), reflections of group interactions (Hickey et al., 2011), and authentic tasks (Xu et al., 2011). Participatory assessments for authentic school-based engagement sought to improve communal interactions, increase individual understanding and gain aggregated achievement (Hickey et al., 2011). Furthermore, the dichotomy between home and school technology use must be removed in order to enhance academic outcomes (Beach, 2012; Gerber & Price, 2013). When students communicate through social media they are often unaware that they are using the necessary skills for many language arts tasks. For example, as part of a pre-assessment, in an interview Maya was asked in which conditions did she enjoy language arts tasks. As only a typical 14-year-old young lady can respond, she snorted, and replied, "none!" She completely discounted her use of language skills when she communicated with peers or conducted recreational research on the Internet, two tasks in which she regularly engaged. Struggling learners often compartmentalize their types of reading and writing activities without acknowledging that they are participating in and developing their language arts skills, particularly when communicating via technology.

Mobile devices afford the opportunity to develop literacy: Educators must acknowledge and embrace the intersection of virtual worlds, popular culture, and literacy instruction (Gerber & Price, 2013). Apperley and Walsh (2012) write that "Digital games have significant educational value, particularly in the area of literacy" (p. 121). School literacy practices and digital games share many commonalities (Apperley & Walsh, 2012). Teachers use "play, performance, simulation, appropriate multitasking, distributed cognition, collective intelligences, judgment, transmedia navigation, and awareness afforded by uses of digital tools" (Jenkins, 2009 in Beach, 2012, p. 46). Games must be read as well as played (Gerber & Price, 2013). Students must be able to find meaning through multiple sources: images, words, and sounds (Gerber & Price, 2013; Hutchison & Woodward, 2014), as stated in Anchor Standard Five: "Make strategic use of digital media and digital displays of data to express information and enhance understanding of presentations" (NGA Center and CCSSO, 2010, p. 48). Videogames have been used as an instructional tool that offered multiple literacy experiences, enhanced practices, and differentiated learning tasks (Gerber & Price, 2013; Hutchison & Woodward, 2014). Digital literacies included multimodal communications with digital storytelling (Beach, 2012) and writing (Xu, et al., 2011). Digital storytelling was more effective in virtual learning environments than offline because of the flexibility, interactivity and community formation (Xu et al., 2011). Based on this research it is apparent that using social media for literature instruction would be effective with adolescents and the purpose of this research was to examine the impact of serious gaming and purposeful social media on Maya's reading comprehension, vocabulary comprehension, and attitude toward Language Arts tasks.

PROCEDURE

At the time of this study, Maya was an 8th grade student enrolled in a Midwestern middle school. She had a history of struggling with language arts tasks, and her difficulty with reading was beginning to impact her self-esteem and her performance across all academic areas. On the Iowa Tests of Basic Skills administered in the spring of her 8th grade year, Maya's scores were just below the proficient range in Reading, Mathematics, and Science. Within the area of math, Maya scored stronger in Computations that she did on Mathematics; indicating that reading and math application skills found in word problems was more difficult for Maya than was math calculation.

At least one of the researchers worked with Maya twice a week over a period of 14 weeks using language arts games and social media to increase Maya's language arts skills. The iPad and cell phone were selected as the digital tools to be used for the games because of Maya's interest in using the mobile devices. Personal control and dignity have been linked to the variables of choice and preference (Dunlap et al., 1993) as well as to an increase of predictability in the environment (Jolivette, Wehby, Canale, & Massey, 2001; Morgan, 2006), each advantageous to the development of strong interpersonal relationships, which the researchers hoped to develop throughout the study. Games selected by Maya with researcher supervision included four iPad apps: *The Opposites*, *Tools 4 Students*, *Reading High School*, and *iTooch Language Arts*. Maya also selected a web-based vocabulary-building activity, Free Rice. Maya was encouraged to keep a journal of her academic and recreational reading activities both with and without technology in order to further expand strengthen language arts skills and habits and to allow the researchers to track how often she worked on her reading skills over the 14-week period. The researchers worked with Maya on the selected games, talked about the leisure books she was reading (either face to face or via FaceTime) and answered homework questions during the biweekly sessions. Sessions lasted from one to two hours. In addition, Maya was required to log her time spent on homework and gaming; homework was to take precedence over games. Log data was supervised by her parents, who also participated in game playing with Maya as a show of support.

APPS

The Opposites app by Mindshapes Limited is available for Apple devices. With this game a pair of seemingly 'bickering' siblings take turns saying words to each other. As the words stack up, it is the goal for the player to eliminate pairs of antonyms before the screen fills with words and all of the word bubbles pop ending the round. Players have the autonomy to select their beginning level. As the player advances through the game, the pace increases, and the immediacy of matches decreases. At each level players receive immediate feedback regarding the accuracy of their matches, they can earn a 'snack break' to temporarily slow the pace of the game, and ribbons are earned to signify level mastery. Players can also hear the words pronounced through game play, there is an in-game dictionary, and a word list to show players what words they have mastered at each level, so it is very good to increase vocabulary development especially with repetition. The game is recommended for players ages 5-12, but the researchers have also gotten college students addicted to the game, as the pace and words at the higher game levels are appropriate for older students as well. The drawback of this game is that there is not a storyline that will engage and motivate players who enjoy gaming for problem solving or collaboration.

Tools 4 Students from Mobile Learning Services is an app that provides a variety of graphic organizers to support students in comprehension skills such as main idea and detail. For example, this app was used for Maya to develop a 5-minute talk for class. Using the main idea and detail template, she developed an essay on the positive characteristics of her mother, grandmother, and great grandmother for a Mother's Day project. She initially outlined the essay on the app and then transferred the information using Microsoft Word, writing a script for her presentation. The assignment was completed when she read her essay to an audience of over a hundred people.

Reading High School app by TegoSoft Inc. is an app for practicing reading comprehension at the high school level. Students choose the number of articles, 1-5, to read and respond to a series of questions following the read. Questions are multiple choice, and immediate feedback is provided. The app displays your mistakes and recognizes the correct response. The articles represent a variety of types of reading such as prose, poetry, etc. This was Maya's favorite app. The content was more mature than other apps and many good conversations were initiated based on the articles. In fact, on several occasions Maya explored the Internet following up on the topics discussed both with and without the researcher. However, homework took precedence, which meant that Maya rarely interacted with this app alone.

The iTooch 7th grade Language Arts app by eduPad Inc. stresses the following Common Core Standards: editing skills, analyzing the language in written form and developing skills for reference materials. These fundamentals are reviewed in exercises that allow the students options to either take a test or practice for the test. Incentive is created through badges and grades for each test. Each chapter has a lesson summary that details the main ideas. Again, no storyline runs consistently through each chapter. Additional motivation of competition was used with Maya as the researcher would complete a test 'cold' without reading the preliminary information and frequently make errors resulting in a lower grade on the test than Maya. Maya laughed and enjoyed this activity; however, she self-reported that she did not like to use this app independently.

Free Rice is a web-based vocabulary game owned by the United Nations World Food Programme. Players can select from a variety of vocabulary game topics: the humanities, basic math facts, SAT vocabulary, and even learning a foreign language. As players increase in levels, the words become more difficult. Corporate sponsors donate 10 grains of rice to the World Food Programme for each correct answer. When a player gives an incorrect answer, the game provides corrective feedback and the question is administered again within that round of play. *Free Rice* has evolved over the last five years to also include competitive or independent play options, as well as social media groups on the *Free Rice* site and on Facebook. Group options on *Free Rice* are eclectic to say the least; there are hundreds of special interest groups including Christians Fighting World Hunger, Dr. Who Fans Unite, high school and graduating class groups, and Art Lovers Fighting Hunger. *Free Rice* tracks the number of group members, the number of grains earned per day, as well as the total number of rice grains earned since the group's inception. As with *The Opposite*s, there is autonomy in the vocabulary reviewed, different levels of challenge, and immediate feedback. Additional benefits include options for collaborative and competitive play, social media options, and the overall benefit to society by feeding the hungry while learning. As with *The Opposites* though, there is not a story to this game, and higher order thinking skills are not developed.

RESULTS

Maya was administered reading comprehension, writing, word recognition, and listening comprehension portions of the Kaufmann Tests of Educational Achievement (KTEA) as a pre and post measure of her Language Arts skills. She was also given the Survey of Adolescent Reading Attitudes (SARA) (Conradi, Jang, Bryant, Craft, & McKenna, 2013). Weekly logs were kept to monitor how often she read for school and recreationally. With her parents' assistance, Maya's grades in school were also monitored. Multiple types of data were considered to evaluate the impact of purposeful gaming and social media use on Maya's performance, habits, and attitudes toward language arts tasks. Maya's KTEA scores were compared using a paired samples *t* test to evaluate the change in scores for statistical significance. Maya's journals, her grades, and SARA scores were also evaluated for changes in attitude and school performance over the time of the study.

Academically, Maya showed improvement in school and on the KTEA; over a 14-week time span, it is expected that Maya would improve in skills, by at least 3-months grade equivalence (G. E.). As shown on Table 1, however, Maya improved on language-based tasks manifested in the smallest gain of 5 months in Letter and Word Identification to the largest gain of 4 years, 7 months gained in Written Expression. The researchers specifically targeted vocabulary and reading comprehension with Maya and she gained 2 years in this area. She continues to perform behind her peers in letter and word recognition and reading comprehension. For the preassessment, the only area in which Maya was on target compared to her peers was Listening Comprehension; however, on the post-assessment both listening comprehension and written expression had improved to beyond that of a typical student at the end of 8th grade. These scores were compared using a paired samples *t*-test; the two-tailed *p*-value was $p = .0564$, not quite a statistically significant difference in Maya's scores. However, the results for Maya were significant as Maya's grades in school showed a similar improvement; she made the 3.0 honor roll for the first time in her school career for her spring trimester grades.

Table 1. Kaufmann tests of educational achievement

Area	G. E., March	G.E., June
Letter and Word Recognition	4.8	5.3
Reading Comprehension	6.2	8.2
Written Expression	6.8	11.3
Listening Comprehension	8.8	12

Maya's habits and attitude also changed. She began working on homework with less resistance. Over the 14-week period of the study, Maya's logs reflected at least an hour of homework for at least 6 days a week, and an average of 3 days a week playing language arts games. Once school was out of session for the summer, Maya continued to read daily for at least an hour a day. Maya's parents confirmed the accuracy of her logs. Prior to the study, Maya's mother had indicated that Maya would often start books but failed to finish them; however, over the period of the study, Maya read and completed 3 different books for leisure, which she discussed with the researchers, either face to face or with FaceTime. In the course of reading books and exploring reading apps with Maya, the researchers discussed different reading comprehension strategies and supports built into Kindle and other e-books. She indicated that knowing how to use the built-in dictionary and other Kindle book supports including story synopses, character descriptions, and important quotes was also important to help her with reading the books. In a follow up interview 8 weeks after the 1:1 sessions had ceased, Maya reported completing two more books and that she was almost finished with a third, with four in her queue.

The researchers also reviewed Maya's attitudes toward reading use the Survey of Adolescent Reading Attitudes. The SARA considers 4 areas of reading: Leisure Reading with Print, Digital Leisure Reading, Academic Reading with Print, and Digital Academic Reading. The researchers anticipated that Maya's scores would be highest in Digital Leisure Reading, and while she did have a high raw score compared to other 8th grade girls, Maya's scores were in the 26th percentile. Maya's scores were the highest in the area of recreational reading in print, with results in the 70th percentile. Her scores for academic reading in print and digital formats were the 25th and 20th percentiles respectively. Maya's attitudes and habits with reading improved over the course of the study. We feel these results for Maya reinforce the paradigm described by Lavoie (2002): "If they would only do better, they would try harder."

DISCUSSION OF FINDINGS

For Maya, even though she professed that she is not a gamer, the immediate reinforcement she received from the games and the ability to replay until she achieved mastery were key elements of her success. It was undeniable that her eyes would light up whenever she received a positive indicator to a correct response on an app. She was motivated by the successes she earned in the games, especially when she was shown how the skills she was learning connected to the skills she needed in the classroom. The mobile devices also allowed Maya and the researcher versatility in the settings, moving to different rooms or even outside. The lead researcher was able to work with Maya to help her generalize skills from the games to her assignments, by working with her on both the games and language arts assignments.

To further support Maya, the researchers suggested that she capitalize on her interests in art while also developing her language arts skills. For example, Maya expressed interest and enthusiasm when reading the story of Norman Rockwell in the R*eading High School* app. The intent was to read the article and then answer questions to assess comprehension. However, her Maya initiated an online search of Rockwell to gather more information and then continued the conversation with her parents. There are several games in which Maya could continue to work on figurative language, such as *FunBrain* games: *Word Confusion*, *Rooting out Words*, and *Paint by Idiom*. Even though Maya reported, "I'm not much of a gamer girl; I definitely like social media better," the immediate feedback and opportunity to practice language skills without fear of consequences for incorrect errors is valuable in her learning process.

To expand on Maya's social media interests, she should be encouraged to follow her favorite artists and authors on a variety of social media outlets including Twitter, Facebook, and Pinterest. She has previously posted 'how to' images and directions on Snapguide to show others how to complete different art projects. This would be a good continuing outlet for her to blend her art interests with language arts skills. Since she wants to be an art teacher, she will need skills in reading about different kinds of art and understanding the content-area vocabulary of different art genres and then convey directions to others both orally and in writing. Any social media that Maya can use to increase her reading, writing, listening, and speaking skills will be of benefit to her in school and beyond school.

There were limitations to this study; as this intervention was developed with just one student, the generalizability of the study results were restricted. The researchers also worked with Maya one-on-one to assist her with gaining and generalizing her reading skills. Therefore, it is impossible to tell whether Maya's improvements in reading tasks and her classwork were a direct result of her gaming interventions, or if it was the combination of gaming with additional instruction and one-on-one time. Regardless, this is important information for educators; teachers should not expect that struggling learners can simply be 'plugged in' to computer games and that the skills will be learned *and* generalized. Teachers must provide explicit instruction for students to understand the connection between what they learn on the computer and what they are learning in the classroom. Given that struggling learners tend to compartmentalize learning and not see the 'big picture' or connections, it is especially important that teachers help students develop that level of gestalt thinking to really get the greatest benefit from gaming.

FUTURE IMPLICATIONS

There are several other important implications for teachers and students. First, there is not a 'one-game-fits-all' approach that will assist students with gaining requisite skills to reduce the achievement gap between them and their peers. Teachers and students should also realize that an ongoing approach is needed to support the student. Once the achievement gap has been reduced, the student is going to continue to benefit from continued practice of those skills, or risk falling behind their peers again. Teachers must select high-quality and engaging games with adapting levels of support and challenge to assist students in gaining new skills and maintaining their level of motivation. Teachers should also consider social media outlets because not every student is motivated by game formats or competition in games. For those students some aspects of gaming are more motivating than others; for example, students that prefer social media to gaming seek the social engagement, collaboration, and autonomy over competition and the status of leaderboards. Fortunately, online there is no shortage of communities for reading and writing, with various levels of security for classroom access.

Teachers have a multitude of Web 2.0 tools available to develop reading, writing, and collaboration skills with their students. Class wikis and blogs can be created to widen the students' audience thereby increasing both assignment authenticity and collaboration. Students can create video and audio discussions for podcasts and vlogs using GarageBand, VoiceThread, and other apps on their cell phones, and literature can be collaboratively analyzed using social bookmarking sites such as LitGenius, or Delicious. The standard 'letter to the author' can now involve discussions with FaceTime or Skype, and through communication on authors' social media sites such as Twitter or Facebook.

Early critics of technology use in the classroom indicated that skill and drill uses of technology did not lead to deep authentic learning or development of higher order thinking skills. Current critics have stated that the research base is not solid enough to show that students improve academically with technology use, that simply engaging students does not lead to higher scores academically. An additional issue raised is students' lack of communication skills as a result of increased computer screen time versus face-to-face communication.

At the university level, one attempt to engage students in learning and increase students' collaboration, problem solving, and communication skills is a game-based approach to learning called Reacting to the Past (RTTP). There are several dozen games RTTP games spanning different time periods, from Ancient Athens, to the trial of Anne Hutchinson in Puritan New England to human rights debates in 1994 Rwanda. In each of these games students are assigned a role and must assume this persona for class discussions and debates (Carnes, 2014). Participants in RTTP courses must research their assigned person's point of view through a variety of primary and secondary resources. They need to develop strategies to solve the given problem with their like-minded peers, and prepare to defend their position against peers assigned personas with opposing viewpoints. Students must research, collaborate, participate and debate in class. Students who enjoy the competition aspects of gaming enjoy the competition and debates of RTTP classes. Students who prefer social media and collaboration for engagement also benefit for the collaborative aspects of RTTP. RTTP contains all of the attributes that are attributed to gamification: They are interactive, there are clear goals and a clear way to win, there is conflict and competition, and there is a clear story with authentic problems to solve. RTTP has gained interest at universities in the US and abroad since these games were released in 2001. The immersive experience of RTTP is one way that gaming could be brought into the classroom in which students would be clearly active and collaborative participants in their learning.

Virtual worlds are another learning option making its way into the classroom. Here students can also interact with others, navigate through the world, and learn by doing. Teachers facilitate learning while students solve problems while interacting and collaborating with others. *Second Life* was an early virtual option for educators, but newcomers such as *Open Sim* and *Open Wonderland* are free/open source virtual worlds that hold appeal for teachers on a budget.

FURTHERING THE RESEARCH

There are several suggestions for additional research from this study. Additional information is needed on how teachers are incorporating game-based learning, social media and collaborative learning opportunities into their classrooms. Digital resources used by teachers should be appropriate to students' age and grade levels and be pedagogically sound for their content areas. Technology alone is not enough to increase students' learning. Additional study on how teachers are bridging the game to classroom practice for students who struggle with learning. The interventions and use of mobile devices was based on Maya's predetermined instructional needs (Larabee, Burns, & McComas, 2014).

Additional research is needed on the impact of purposefully selected serious games for students who are struggling readers. Follow-up data should be gathered to see if Maya continues to make progress with language arts tasks, and to evaluate if the changes in habits and attitudes toward reading are maintained as she enters high school. The most recent update with Maya showed that she was routinely using her mobile device to read books; her first novel was actually read during the study. She is also monitoring her own study skills. The exploratory question posed was answered in the affirmative that for Maya the self-evaluation and interventions practiced in the study improved both her language arts and general study skills.

As mentioned, technology advances encourage the 21st century students to be familiar with the new literacy. Mobile devices introduce new supports as well as challenges that can positively and negatively impact education. Coiro (2003) has outlined the positive impact that reading on the web has had on "at-risk" learners. The iPad offers a variety of language arts application in addition to the gaming aspect (Harmon, 2011; Melhuish & Falloon, 2010; Shah, 2011). As insights for future language arts strategies can be gained through action research such as this case study and formal qualitative research, the authors encourage others to continue the exploration of gaming, digital tools in connection to language arts instruction.

REFERENCES

Apperley, T., & Walsh, C. (2012). What digital games and literacy have in common: A heuristic for understanding pupils' gaming literacy. *Literacy*, *46*(3), 115–122. doi:10.1111/j.1741-4369.2012.00668.x

Beach, R. (2012). Uses of digital tools and literacies in the English language arts classroom. *Research in the Schools*, *19*(1), 45–59.

Blanchard, J., Stock, W., & Marshall, J. (1999). Meta-analysis of research on a multimedia elementary school curriculum using personal and video game computers. *Perceptual and Motor Skills*, *88*(1), 329–336. doi:10.2466/pms.1999.88.1.329

Bowers, A. J., & Berland, M. (2013). Does recreational computer use affect high school achievement? *Educational Technology Research and Development*, *61*(1), 51–69. doi:10.1007/s11423-012-9274-1

Carnes, M. C. (2014). *Minds on fire: How role-immersion games transform college*. Cambridge, MA: Harvard University Press. doi:10.4159/harvard.9780674735606

Chen, H.-J. H., & Yang, T.-Y. C. (2013). The impact of adventure video games on foreign language learning and the perceptions of learners. *Interactive Learning Environments*, *21*(2), 129–141. doi:10.1 080/10494820.2012.705851

Chen, S.-Y., & Fu, Y.-C. (2009). Internet use and academic achievement: Gender differences in early adolescence. *Adolescence*, *44*(176). PMID:20432601

Coiro, J. (2003). Reading comprehension on the internet: Expanding our understanding of reading comprehension to encompass new literacies. *The Reading Teacher*, *56*(5), 458–464.

Conradi, K., Jang, B. G., Bryant, C., Craft, A., & McKenna, M. C. (2013). Measuring adolescents' attitudes toward reading: A classroom survey. *Journal of Adolescent & Adult Literacy*, *56*(7), 565–576. doi:10.1002/JAAL.183

Dunlap, G., Kern, L., dePerczel, M., Clark, S., Wilson, D., & Childs, K. E. (1993). Functional analysis of classroom variables for students with emotional and behavioral disorders. *Behavioral Disorders*, *18*, 275–291.

Gee, J. P. (2007). *What video games have to teach us about learning and literacy* (2nd ed.). New York: MacMillan.

Gerber, H. R., & Price, D. P. (2013). Fighting baddies and collecting bananas: Teachers' perceptions of games-based literacy learning. *Educational Media International*, *50*(1), 51–62. doi:10.1080/09523 987.2013.777182

Harmon, J. (2011). *Unlocking literacy with iPad*. Retrieved from http://www.throughstudentseyes.ort/ ipads.Unlocking_Literacy_with_iPads/iPads_files/Unlocking_Literacy_iPad.pdf

Hickey, D. T., McWilliams, J., & Honeyford, M. A. (2011). Reading *Moby Dick* in a participatory culture: Organizing assessment for engagement in a new media era. *Journal of Educational Computing Research*, *45*(2), 247–263. doi:10.2190/EC.45.2.g

Hsu, H., & Wang, S. (2010). Using gaming literacies to cultivate new literacies. *Simulation & Gaming*, *41*(3), 400–417. doi:10.1177/1046878109355361

Hutchison, A., & Woodward, L. (2014). A planning cycle for integrating digital technology into literacy instruction. *The Reading Teacher*, *67*(6), 455–464. doi:10.1002/trtr.1225

Jolivette, K., Wehby, J. H., Canale, J., & Massey, N. G. (2001). Effect of choicemaking opportunities on the behavior of students with emotional and behavioral disorders. *Behavioral Disorders*, *26*, 131–145.

Ke, F., & Abras, T. (2013). Games for engaged learning of middle school children with special learning needs. *British Journal of Educational Technology*, *44*(2), 225–242. doi:10.1111/j.1467-8535.2012.01326.x

Larabee, K., Burns, M., & McComas, J. (2014). Effects of an iPad-supported phonics intervention on decoding performance and time on-task. *Journal of Behavioral Education*, *23*(4), 449–469. doi:10.1007/ s10864-014-9214-8

Lavoie, R. (2002). *Self-esteem: The cause and effect of success for the child with learning differences*. Retrieved from http://www.ricklavoie.com/Self-esteem.pdf

Mayrath, M. C., Traphagan, T., Heikes, E. J., & Trivedi, A. (2011). Instructional design best practices for Second Life: A case study from a college-level English course. *Interactive Learning Environments*, *19*(2), 125–142. doi:10.1080/10494820802602568

Melhuish, K., & Falloon, G. (2010). Looking to the future: M-learning with the iPad. *Computers in New Zealand Schools: Learning, Leading. Technology (Elmsford, N.Y.)*, *22*(3).

Morgan, P. L. (2006). Increasing task engagement using preference or choicemaking: Some behavioral and methodological factors affecting their efficacy as classroom interventions. *Remedial and Special Education*, *27*(3), 176–187. doi:10.1177/07419325060270030601

Ponce, H. R., Mayer, R. E., & Lopez, M. J. (2013). A computer-based spatial learning strategy approach that improves reading comprehension and writing. *Educational Technology Research and Development*, *61*(5), 819–840. doi:10.1007/s11423-013-9310-9

Shah, N. (2011). Special education pupils find learning tools in iPad applications. *Education Week*, *30*(1), 16–17.

Tobatabai, D., & Shore, B. M. (2005). How experts and novices search the Web. *Library & Information Science Research*, *27*(2), 222–248. doi:10.1016/j.lisr.2005.01.005

Vogel, J. J., Greenwood-Ericksen, A., Cannon-Bowers, J., & Bowers, C. A. (2006). Using virtual reality with and without gaming attributes for academic achievement. *Journal of Research on Technology in Education*, *39*(1), 105–118. doi:10.1080/15391523.2006.10782475

Wanzek, J., Vaughn, S., Wexler, J., Swanson, E. A., Edmonds, M., & Kim, A.-H. (2006). A synthesis of spelling and reading interventions and their effects on the spelling outcomes of students with LD. *Journal of Learning Disabilities*, *39*(6), 528–543. doi:10.1177/00222194060390060501 PMID:17165620

Warren, S. J., Stein, R. A., Dondlinger, M. J., & Barab, S. A. (2009). A look inside a MUVE design process: Blending instructional design and game principles to target writing skills. *Journal of Educational Computing Research*, *40*(3), 295–321. doi:10.2190/EC.40.3.c

Xu, Y., Park, H., & Baek, Y. (2011). A new approach toward digital storytelling: An activity focused on writing self-efficacy in a virtual learning environment. *Journal of Educational Technology & Society*, *14*(4), 181–191.

Yin, R. (1994). *Case study research: Design and methods* (2nd ed.). Thousand Oaks, CA: Sage Publications.

KEY TERMS AND DEFINITIONS

Digital Learning: Using technology for effective instructional practice.

Reacting to the Past: Game-based instruction used to engage students in reacting to historical events in which students are assigned active roles for in and out of class participation.

Social Media: Sharing information and communicating via technology devices.

Student-Centered Learning: Instruction designed to increase students' engagement through the use of students' learning preferences, needs, and interests.

Universal Design for Learning: A framework to guide teachers' instructional planning to reduce barriers in instruction, materials, and assessment.

Chapter 13

Game/Write:
Gameplay as a Factor in College-Level Literacy and Writing Ability

Sandy Baldwin
Rochester Institute of Technology, USA

Nicholas D. Bowman
West Virginia University, USA

John Jones
West Virginia University, USA

ABSTRACT

This chapter explores the potential correlation between college students' leisurely video game experience and their narrative composition writing ability in a first-semester university writing course. This exploratory survey data report moderate correlations between students' aggregated video game experience (years spent playing) and their ability to articulate tension and turn, and use proper organization in composition assignments, notably a diagnostic essay assigned on the first day of class, prior to formal instruction. Findings suggest that leisure gameplay might help develop competency with the same cognitive and creative skills related to written narrative ability by exposing players – in particular, adolescents – to elements of narrative through the gameplay process, facilitating the learning of these skills in the classroom. In conclusion, the authors suggest areas for future research on this topic.

INTRODUCTION

This chapter explores correlations between college students' video gaming diets, or time playing video games, and their writing ability in order to answer the question: Does time playing games translate into effective navigation of the narrative features of written literacy? Our research looked at the intersection of entertainment computing qua video gaming and compositional writing ability qua scholastic performance on written assignments. Such a question is particularly germane to understanding the impact of

DOI: 10.4018/978-1-5225-0261-6.ch013

video gaming on larger socio-cultural change. How so? Video gaming is among the most popular leisure pastimes across several target demographics for STEM (Science, Technology, Engineering, and Math) learners in middle school, high school and college. Related to this, compositional writing ability has been identified as a key component of STEM education. Our study attempts to begin fusing two rather disparate activities, leisurely video game play and composition education, to suggest the potential for non-directed and leisurely gaming habits to have the potential to impact composition ability, which in turn might both foster an appreciation for composition while also suggesting games to be more than simple and mindless diversions. As detailed below, video game research has suggested that narrative is an important feature of video game play and it is also a key component of written composition. Given this connection, and the lack of directed research on narrative in games and composition, we are prompted to ask if there may be a connection between video game play and student success with the written features of narrative, which might in turn foster a renewed appreciation for narrative concepts and constructs. Specifically, our core research question asks (**RQ1**): Is there a statistically significant correlation between gaming diet and observed compositional abilities?

In our concluding section, we propose future directions for research to examine additional research questions that follow from these results. Our project was unique in combining quantitative approaches to game play with research in literacy and composition, and arose from an interdisciplinary team with scholars from the disciplines of literature, composition, and communications. A review of the literature provides evidence to propose the falsifiable hypothesis that there may be meta-cognitive aspects of narrative composition that apply across media forms. Put simply, while we often think of composition in terms of the specific act of writing essays, the essential elements of good composition—tension and turn, resolution and conclusion, description and detail, and organization—are not necessarily specific to a textual medium; indeed, they are the same elements of good narrative found in film, television, video games, and other media. Such a correlation might prove useful as educators continue to emphasize narrative communication skills in various speaking, writing, and STEM curriculum, as it suggests that students' regular video game play might be an unexpected source of narrative and composition skill.

In the following, we briefly summarize research on the centrality of narrative to video game play and the importance of narrative to written literacy, including emerging scholarship on the nature of videogame play as an act of composition (Alberti, 2008; Robison, 2008). We then connect this literature review to our research question, describing the preliminary study carried out at West Virginia University in the fall of 2014. Finally, we speculate on future directions for our research and offer hypotheses towards understanding what elements of narrative in video game, if any, transfer to other writing contexts.

BACKGROUND

Narrative, Defined

As formulated by Labov and Waletzky (1967), a narrative of personal experience is defined with three elements: an orientation, which focuses the reader on the background of characters involved; a complicating action, or a chain of events that results in the climax or "most reportable event" of a narrative (cf. Ouyang & McKeown, 2014); and the narrator's evaluation, in which the reader learns the narrator's dispositions towards the characters. Labov (2013) later considered the abstract as well as a resolution and coda, or the elements to end the narrative. In simpler form, Labov (1972) defined narratives as "a sequence of two clauses which are temporally ordered [such that] a change in their order will result in a change in the temporal sequence of the original semantic interpretation" (p. 360)—a perspective referred to as a minimal definition of narrative (Howald, 2009), suggesting that any given text need only these elements to be considered a narrative. The most dramatic example of this might be found in American essayist and novelist Ernest Hemingway's infamously short narrative: "for sale: baby shoes, never worn." The temporal sequence here is assumed to be the death of a baby, for reasons unknown to the narrator or reader.

Mills and Exley (2014) provided a detailed account of the myriad reasons why fostering an appreciation for narrative is an important skill for learners. Their work cites research suggesting that early experience with narrative aid in narrative appreciation in a variety of textual forms, such as written and visual media (Painter, Martin, & Unsworth, 2013). This might be at least one reason that narrative and composition lessons, where composition is loosely understood as the act of executing narrative in written form, are enmeshed in the curriculum of most Western nations (Arnold, Lonigan, Whitehurst, & Epstein, 1994). Indeed, some have argued that narrative is an essential element of cultural transmission in general, or at least culturally derived mores (cf. Shweder & Haidt, 1993). As Mills and Exley (2014) have explained: "Research over the last quarter of a century demonstrates that in many homes and communities, the authority of oral storytelling, narrative books, and book-related activities in the lives of young learners is significant" (citing Heath, 1982; p. 136).

Moreover, while it might seem that narrative—understood often in terms of composition—is a skill restricted to textual media such as essay writing, there is little reason to adopt such a myopic view of narrative. Selfe (2009) used the term modalities of expression to describe the many ways in which one might express a Labovian narrative, including, but not limited to, literature, film, and photography (George, 2012). Expanding further, George (2012) suggested that the cognitive processes necessary for narrative appreciation were in no way medium-specific, and certainly not unique to the written form, and advocated for the use of multiple modalities of expression, a key element in preparing students for college writing.

While a Labovian minimalist definition of narrative has been useful for broad discussions of literature and sense-making, the concept can be operationalized in academic instruction on at least four specific dimensions:

- **Tension and Turn:** In which the story suggests a building or anticipation of dramatic progression toward an event, where the event can consist of actions, character development, or narrative details;
- **Resolution and Conclusion:** In which the story leads somewhere, and there are consequences that result from the turn;
- **Description and Detail:** The process of describing the settings, characters, and events of the story, and the use of specific and appropriate language; and
- **Organization:** A recognition that the sequence of events or structure of the piece is logical and appropriate to the story.

Notably, while the definitions above were culled from curriculum on written narrative composition, they are intentionally medium-independent; that is, they should apply to any given modality of expression (indeed, an assumption open to empirical scrutiny in its own right).

These specific operational criteria for narrative were derived from the assessment rubrics used in freshman writing classes at West Virginia University. As part of the West Virginia University General Education Curriculum, all students are required to take a two-semester sequence of writing courses, ENGL 101 and ENGL 102. According to the objectives of this requirement, all students will learn to

- Practice writing as a form of inquiry to discover and create new knowledge.
- Learn to write in response to appropriate audiences, purposes, and genres.
- Learn to read, write, and do research as acts of critical thinking.
- Practice writing simultaneously as a process and as a rhetorical response.
- Foster an appreciation of writing as a communicative art. ("GEC Objective 1")

Although in practice, not all West Virginia University students take this sequence—some transfer from other institutions, some test out of the courses—the objectives remain fundamental to the understanding of general education at West Virginia University. Moreover, as indicated below, these objectives and this sequence are largely similar to those advocated by scholars of college composition (cf. Harrington et al., 2001).

Within this sequence, the purpose of ENGL 101 is to help students "to learn strategies to use in the writing they will do in college" ("GEC Objective 1"). As the first encounter with college level composition for most West Virginia University students, ENGL 101 provided the ideal setting for purposes the present study. The research described below was carried out in collaboration with the administrators and instructors of the ENGL 101 sequence.

Video Games as (Interactive) Narratives

The emergence of video games as a popular entertainment medium has brought with it a level of uncertainty and suspicion about the impact of these games on the thoughts, actions, and behaviors of players. Common debates in the media psychology and human communication literature, for example, centered around the potential for video game violence to encourage similar behavior among players—with some scholars having claimed this to be a rather robust and replicable direct effect (Anderson & Bushman, 2001) and others who argued that the effects were more idiosyncratic and possibly too distal to have an appreciable effect on human aggression (Ferguson et al, 2008).

Of course, not all gaming effects are considered negative. Popular "off the shelf" video games such as *Heavy Rain*, a dark and dramatic murder mystery, and *Spec Ops: The Line*, an action-type shooting game with an interwoven critical war commentary, have the potential to foster feelings of interpersonal relatedness and intrapersonal insight and appreciation (Oliver et al., 2015). Given their ability to simulate realities not readily accessible to the average person, such as the life of a single-cell organism, the human circulatory system, or the center of the nascent star, many have argued that video games and virtual environments were a prime technology with which to foster learning (both in general, and specific to literacy; cf. Gee, 2003). Directed educational games, or games designed with a specific educational end goal, have been commercially available since at least the late 1970s—such as Atari's *Basic Math* (1977) and the earliest iterations of the experiential American history simulator *Oregon Trail*, which was first released in 1971—in part as an effort to encourage learning in non-traditional spaces and in part as an effort to legitimize the medium. However, such games are usually criticized for being less entertaining and thus, students lack any real motivation to play them – simply put, they are not fun (Peters, 2007).

However, research has consistently shown a positive effect of video game play broadly on a variety of target learning outcomes (reviewed extensively in Gee, 2003; 2005). In fact, Gee argued that video game play was inherently educational, as it required players to commit to understanding novel characters, worlds, and mental models associated with their interaction. Bowman, Kowert, and Ferguson (2016) argued similarly that entertainment-focused video games were inextricably linked to creativity, a key feature of literacy and narrative, given the many cognitive, affective, behavioral and even social demands that the medium placed on the gamer (Bowman, 2016).

There are at least three attributes of video game play that make it an activity well-suited to foster an appreciation of and ability to craft narrative. First, video games are an interactive and demanding experience that involves the player with several different levels, no pun intended, of the experience (Gentile & Anderson, 2003). On-screen action does not progress without the player's active input (cf. Bowman, 2016), hence video games have been described as a lean-forward medium (Jansz, 2005).

Second, video games are inherently unfinished texts that require the player's active input, from simple reaction to complex strategizing, in order to be realized as complete narrative experiences (Bowman & Banks, in press; Collins, 2013). Video games often require players to navigate what noted designer Sid Meier called a "series of interesting decisions" (2012, para. 1), which—to borrow from Selfe (2009)— seem to make them potentially fruitful modalities of expression. On this point, Nakamura (1995) and later Grodal (2000) have discussed at length the notion of video game play as an act of identity tourism, the former, and personality exploration, the latter. Moreover, while the earliest video games were more designed to address eye-hand coordination ("twitch") than players' narrative capacity, recent developments have entangled gamers within emotionally and morally unfolding narratives in which they must make increasingly sophisticated moral decisions, the outcomes of which having a significant impact on the interactive narrative they experienced (Boyan, et al., 2015; Lange, 2014).

Third, and somewhat related to the first two, video games have often been defined, at least in part, by their ability to involve the gamers in the on-screen narrative world (Green, Brock, & Kaufman, 2006). While most narratives can be understood in terms of their ability to cognitively and emotionally transport the audience member or user into the narrative world (ibid), the interactive and unwritten elements of video games have been thought to facilitate this process to a greater degree than with other media. Tamborini and Skalski (2006) have made the case for video games' special ability to induce feelings of spatial, social, and self-presence in the on-screen narrative world: feeling physically located, connected with on-screen others, and personally involved, respectively. Notably, while technology has been thought to facilitate these feelings of non-mediation (Steuer, 1992), it was the psychological rather than physical experience of gaming that has been considered most important. Players who feel present are more involved in crafting the on-screen narrative—and in fact, this narrative crafting often represents itself as a headcanon, or held narrative, in the player's mind that might or might not be parallel to the narrative of the digital world (cf. Banks, 2013). For example, players of *World of Warcraft* are tasked with siding with either the Horde or Alliance faction while fighting for control over the realm of Azeroth. Players are motivated to take up this challenge if they want to play through the game's pre-crafted narrative, but they are not required to. Indeed, the open-ended nature of the digital gameworld provides players with all of the necessary components of narrative (Burke, 1969) – act, range of possible behaviors, such as dialogue and batter; scene, the gameworld itself; agent, the player's avatar; agency, the range of possible player-enacted decisions; and purpose, the player's own motivations to engage – so that they could draft their own in-world narrative, completely independent of that told by the programmers. One example of this can be found with the play style of grief gamers, or those gamers who intentionally engage others in a hostile manner in order to show their dominance and game skill (Paul, Bowman, & Banks, 2015). These players often and purposefully choose to bypass or sidestep the canon of the digital world as intended by the game's developers in order to create their own style of gameplay – even at the detriment of other gamers. Similarly, many gamers engage the same gameworld not in an effort to engage aggression towards enemy factions or other gamers, but to simply explore their own emerging identities and sense of self in a socially real environment (Bessiere, Seay, & Kiesler, 2007).

Correlations between Gaming and Narrative and Composition Ability

In their "WPA Outcomes Statement for First-Year Composition," Harrington et al. (2001) noted that after taking a first year composition course, students should be able to effectively "use writing and reading for inquiry, learning, thinking, and communicating" (p. 324), and, as reflected in the objectives for freshman writing courses at West Virginia University, narrative has been generally identified as one writing strategy for achieving persuasive communication (Jackson, 2002). Further, Perrachio and Escalas (2008) have argued for the importance of narrative to research writing, claiming that the difference between published research and rejected research is the author's ability to tell a story using data. Any good research writing, they argued, includes narrative elements such as focus, plot, characters, goals, and outcomes (p. 198).

At present, however, there is little extant research connecting video game play and narrative literacy in college-level composition. Jackson (2002) suggested that assigning game play within the first year composition course enabled students to better understand narrative. Moberly (2008) offered a protracted case for the integral role of narrative as a form of play in video games—making a special case for the inherently compositional elements of how players interacted with characters, both human and non-human, in massive multiplayer online games. As the author explains:

games like WoW *evaluate players on their ability to compose themselves in relationship to these highly symbolic environments—to write and ultimately revise their actions in relationship to the reality that is manufactured on the screen. This activity, which is often constructed as play rather than writing or composition (and which often occurs simultaneously on many discrete levels), is significant in that although its effects appear to be limited to the immediate context of the screen, its focus is ultimately on how players read and write (compose) themselves in relationship to the game. (ibid, p. 291)*

A number of works have made connections between play in games and writing practices. Research by Aarseth (1997) and Ensslin (2014) has suggested that video games can be understood as literary devices, with the former having identified video games as inherently ergodic, a term borrowed from physics to describe an open, or incomplete, system, and the latter conceptualizing video game play as an exercise in literary-ludic text crafting, highlighting the complementary relationship between reading and writing a literary text. Bogost (2006) similarly referred to video games as a technology well-suited for emphasizing more elaborate systems thinking, as they required players to take in numerous amounts of textual and ludic information in order to weave a purposeful and meaningful experience. Alberti (2008) suggested that video games likewise helped composition students reimagine the narrative writing experience as an act of play, trying on different roles and perspectives both of on-screen characters and the meta-roles of player and writer/producer, and Robison (2008) offered similar sentiments.

Although these studies established the connections between gaming and narrative at a conceptual level, they did not account for students' existing gaming habits, nor did they account for students' actual experience of acquiring college-level literacy skills. As a result, they have not provided the grounds for correlating gaming and literacy. This was despite the fact that video games have been an integral part of the socialization of today's youth (Durkin, 2006) and have been among the most popular forms of (entertainment) technology that they use (Entertainment Software Association, 2014).

Another exigence for this study was the evidence that students themselves have not connected their college composition experience with others domains of media practice. For example, Shepherd (2015) suggested that students had a difficult time connecting their writing and communication practices on Social Network Sites to the learning goals of their first year composition courses, a result that may apply more generally to students' media consumption habits outside of the classroom. By establishing a link between students' understanding of their communication practices and the literacy skills associated with those practices, this study can help students and instructors to capitalize on those literacies to improve their writing both within and outside of the classroom.

Research Question

Thus, it is reasonable to pose the question as to whether students' experience playing video games shares some relationship with their ability to compose narratives in the first-year college classroom. Such a relationship would suggest that gamers are better-prepared for narrative writing, having had more experience with narrative broadly. Towards this, the core research question of the current study was *(RQ1)*: Is there a statistically significant correlation between gaming diet and observed compositional abilities?

METHOD

Participants

This exploratory study consisted of a sample of 72 students enrolled in first-year English courses (English 101) at West Virginia University. Students responded to an email inviting them to complete a survey about their media usage, including video game use, but also including other measures to mask the intentions of the study and some basic demographic questions. This survey invitation was sent to them at the immediate start of the semester. At the conclusion of the online survey—which took about 10 minutes to complete—students were invited to register for our study. Study registration allowed us to receive copies of two of their in-class assignments completed at later times during the same semester: an early-semester diagnostic essay, assigned during first the class meetings, the same day or within a day or two of having completed the initial survey, and a narrative essay, revised at the end of the semester as part of a class portfolio. No students were enrolled in any of the researchers' courses, and all study procedures were registered with and approved by West Virginia University Institutional Review Board. Students were entered into a raffle drawing to receive one $25 Amazon.com gift card for volunteering in the study.

Sample Demographics

Of our 72 students, 72 percent ($n = 51$) self-reported as male to an open-ended item, one reporting no gender, and participants had an average age of 18.65 ($SD = 1.26$), in-line with their enrollment in a first-year university writing course. About 77 percent of the sample self-identified as White or Caucasian to an open-ended item assessing ethnicity ($n = 55$) with no other racial group represented by more than five students (Asian and African-American). Participants self-reported an average high school grade point average (converted to a 4.0 scale) of 3.54 ($SD = .342$) and an average ACT score (self-reported SAT scores were converted to ACT scores) of 23.74 ($SD = 4.59$); ACT scores were used rather than SAT scores due to the difficulty in translating ACT scores (which are on a smaller score range) into a precise SAT score.

Survey Measures

Video Game Experience

Participants' experience playing video games was measured using two metrics. First, an adapted version of the social media diet scale developed by Bowman, Westerman, and Claus (2012), replacing "social media" with video games in the question text regarding how many (a) minutes per day (amount), (b) days per week (frequency), and (c) years this pattern of consumption has been stable (duration). Combining (a) and (b), participants reported playing video games an average of 5.68 hours during any given week ($SD = 7.63$), and have sustained this pattern of play for an average of 3.59 years ($SD = 1.97$). Notably, $n = 21$ participants reported scores of "0" on both metrics ($M = 0$, $SD = .00$), suggesting that they have no prior video game experience; these participants are included in all analyses of the continuous measure of gaming experience so as to include what might be considered "gamers" and "non-gamers." Second, participants self-reported perceptions of their video game self-efficacy using a scale developed by Bracken & Skalski (2006). This 10-item, six-point Likert scaled measure assesses participants' reporting of their success playing games, learning game controls, and learning new game mechanics, $M = 4.80$, $SD = 1.65$, $\alpha = .953$. These two scales shared a significant, moderate, and positive correlation, p (72) $= .364$, $p = .002$. Importantly, our study did not assess "gamers" but rather used all participants responses to a continuous measure of their gaming experience and self-efficacy.

Video Game Preferences

Participants were asked to rate on a scale from "1" (least favorite) to "10" (most favorite) one of 10 different video game genres: action, action-adventure, adventure, role-playing games, simulations, strategy games, sports, puzzle, and casual games – these are the most common broad game genres used by industry magazines such as IGN.com and Gamespot.com when discussing and reviewing video games. Compared against the scale midpoint of "5" (neutral), action ($M = 6.81$, $SD = 2.97$, $t(66) = 4.98$, $p \sim .000$, Cohen's $d = 1.69$) and sports ($M = 6.87$, $SD = 3.25$, $t(62) = 4.75$, $p \sim .000$, Cohen's $d = 1.16$ were rated significantly higher; all other categories were rated at or lower than the mid-point, with casual games ($M = 2.98$, $SD = 2.56$, $t(61) = 6.19$, $p \sim .000$, Cohen's $d = 1.59$) rated as the least popular among our sample. Due to a smaller-than-expected sample, statistical analyses examining game preference data were not conducted for the current study, but the data is included here so as to properly represent the gaming experience of the same.

Essay Evaluation

In total, 54 diagnostic essays and 68 narrative essays were retained for analysis (some essays were incomplete or missing from students' registration files). Essays were evaluated for four dimensions of compositional writing (drawn from the West Virginia University curriculum, defined above): tension and turn, resolution and conclusion, description and detail, and organization. Four upper-level undergraduate students blind to the study's central researchers were provided a simplified grading rubric, and asked to assess each of these four categories on a scale from "1" (not at all present) to "4" (clearly present and developed). The appendix contains complete category descriptions and rubric assessment criteria. To further assist in these evaluations, the seven core concepts from each of the coding categories were also provided to the panel of undergraduate evaluators. External evaluators were used to protect against potential biasing factors associated with instructors assessing the surveys of their own students, as well as to protect the identity of students involved in the study: course instructors were never told which students were participating in the study. Notably, coder reliability scores were meager due to the interval-level coding of this data (percent agreement was about 70% across all codes), and this limitation of the current study is discussed in detail in the discussion section of the chapter.

For all four categories, diagnostic essays ($M = 2.97, SD = .617$) were rated lower than narrative essays ($M = 3.46, SD = .523$), and each of these effects fell in the moderate-to-strong effect size, unsurprisingly, suggesting that students' composition writing ability improved substantially during the semester as a function of course instruction. Table 1 displays the average evaluation score for both essay sets, as well as paired-samples t-test results. Moreover, given that the four individual evaluation categories had an acceptable internal reliability when considered as an overall evaluation of essay quality (Cronbach's α =.826 for the diagnostic essay, α =.748 for the narrative essay), a composite score was also calculated (also reported in Table 1).

Table 1. Average assessment of each essay evaluation category, by essay type

	Diagnostic Essay (First Assignment)	Narrative Essay (Final Assignment)	Paired-Samples T-Test
Tension and Turn	2.57 (.742)	3.02 (.855)	$t(49) = 4.19, p \sim .000$ Cohen's $d = 1.20$
Resolution and Conclusion	3.13 (.778)	3.47 (.610)	$t(49) = 3.20, p = .002$ Cohen's $d = .914$
Description and Detail	2.96 (.823)	3.43 (.798)	$t(49) = 5.44, p \sim .000$ Cohen's $d = 1.55$
Organization	3.13 (.754)	3.52 (.702)	$t(49) = 2.04, p = .047$ Cohen's $d = .582$
Overall Evaluation	2.97 (.617)	3.46 (.523)	$t(49) = 4.55, p \sim .000$ Cohen's $d = 1.30$

Note: Pairwise comparisons are only possible for those n = 50 participants who had a complete study registration file (containing both a diagnostic and narrative essay).

PRELIMINARY RESULTS

To assess the potential impact of video game experience on compositional writing ability, partial bivariate correlations were calculated between our metrics of video game experience and the essay evaluation categories, see Table 2. All correlations were calculated controlling for participant age, gender, ethnicity, and prior academic performance – while not an exhaustive list of the potential influences on one's composition ability, a necessary first step in what we see as a more robust line of research into these variables and relationships. Note that the small sample sizes obtained in this analysis did not allow for a robust test of the stability of these correlations or for the inclusion of additional covariates such as preferred games (Schoenbrodt, 2013; Schoenbrodt & Perugini, 2013), but they did provide an assessment of the observed valence/direction (ibid.) and strength of relationship between video game experience and elements of compositional writing ability as reported in our sample (Wong, 2010). Notably, so as not to underestimate potentially meaningful effects, we chose to interpret correlations with a p-value that exceeded a more liberal $p < .01$ threshold; in each case, effect sizes approached or exceeded Cohen's (1988) criteria for a moderate effect size ($r > .30$). As a final statement, we should explain that while some might see correlations in the range of .30 as being less meaningful, it is important to accept that it would be untenable to expect a statistically robust relationship between one's leisurely video game behavior and their observed composition ability in a college classroom. That is, our study is not aimed at developing video game interventions per se; that is, carefully administered gaming treatments that result in immediate composition gains. Rather, this exploratory work is aimed at the establishment and understanding of a distal-yet-statistically meaningful association between video game play, a leisure activity, that might have trace narrative elements inherent to it. Such an approach has a rich history in the study of media effects, wherein distal media impacts on proximal human thoughts, feelings, and behaviors are often not statistically robust (explaining 100 percent of the variance in an observed outcome) but serve as prominent and compelling correlates of behaviors (Valkenberg & Peter, 2013). Put another way, establishing a statistically significant association between leisure activity and directed scholastic experience offers a platform for the further study of the relationship between one's narrative-qua-gaming and their ability to comprehend and execute composition and narrative in a variety of pursuits, such as a school assignment as in this study. The fact that a such a distal-yet-commonplace behavior as video game play could have any appreciable influence – be it causal or, as established in this paper, correlational – on one's ability to compose narrative warrants attention, or at least recognition of video games as more than "just games" but also places of active composition, however leisurely they may be.

Overall, there were positive and significant relationships between aggregate video game play experience, or years spent gaming, and increased quality of students' diagnostic essays—in particular, the use of proper tension and turn as well as the general organization of the essay. Students weekly hours spent gaming also had a positive association with the organizational quality of their diagnostic essay. Both of these findings are compelling, given that the diagnostic essay is among the very earliest university-level writing assignments given to first-semester students, assigned in the first few hours of their compositional writing course as a general assessment of their writing ability in the absence of any course instruction. The narrative essay, assigned as the final composition for the first semester course, showed a smaller positive effect of aggregate video game experience on organization, and player's self-reported video game skill had an unsurprisingly strong negative effect on the same. However, overall evaluations of the narrative

Table 2. Bivariate partial correlations between video game experience and observed compositional essay writing quality (non-partial correlations in parentheses); partial correlations control for the self-report variables: participant age, gender, ethnicity, and prior academic performance

	Video Game Self-Efficacy	Weekly Video Game Experience	Years of Video Game Experience
Diagnostic Essay (n = 54)			
Tension and Turn	.074 (-.001)	.213 (.133)	.394* (.146)
Resolution and Conclusion	.145 (.114)	.195 (.127)	.159 (-.019)
Description and Detail	.133 (.104)	.158 (.182)	.158 (-.023)
Organization	.135 (-.198)	.295+ (.219)	.350* (.159)
Overall Evaluation	.140 (.009)	.243 (.204)	.297+ (.077)
Narrative Essay (n = 68)			
Tension and Turn	-.195 (-.019)	-.021 (-.068)	.191 (.031)
Resolution and Conclusion	-.039 (-.053)	.058 (-.133)	.128 (.068)
Description and Detail	.096 (-.097)	.143 (-.131)	.114 (.106)
Organization	-.313+ (-.213)+	.095 (.022)	.297+ (.217)+
Overall Evaluation	-.163 (-.122)	079 (-.101)	.236 (.135)

Note: Correlations in parentheses represent bivariate correlations without covariates entered into the calculation (simple Pearson moment bivariate correlations). Correlations marked * were significant at the p <.05 or greater; + indicated significance at the.10 level or greater.

essay were not influenced by video game experience – which suggests that enrollment in the class was the most robust predictor of one's end-of-semester composition ability; this is as to be expected, and as supported by the repeated-measures t-tests reported earlier in the chapter.

DISCUSSION

Analysis

This study was an early examination of the potential for a college student's experience with video games—a medium at once lambasted for its negative impact on academic performance (Gentile, Lynch, Linder, & Walsh, 2004) and celebrated for sparking creativity (cf. Gee, 2003, 2005)—to have impact on their performance in the first-year writing course. In general, and controlling for demographic and self-reported academic performance measures, experienced gamers showed a slightly greater mastery of tension and turn in their writing, as well as a better understanding of proper organization, at the start of their course in their diagnostic essay. This result would seem to confirm the importance of player input in progressing video game narratives (Bowman & Banks, in press; Collins, 2013) and making moral decisions (Boyan, et al., 2015; Lange, 2014) on their ability to create narrative in other modalities of expression (Selfe 2009).

Notably, global experience scores, the number of years spent gaming, had the strongest positive association with tension and turn, organization, and overall quality of the diagnostic survey, although there was a moderate, significant, and positive correlation between weekly gaming hours and organizational quality of the essay. Theoretically, it makes sense that the global video game experience would have the strongest impact given that this metric (albeit bluntly) captures players' aggregate video game experience; whereas weekly hours spent playing measures might fluctuate with the start of university. The fact that these correlations were strongest for the diagnostic assignment also made sense, given that this assignment was given in advance of any formal class instruction. Such a finding suggests that experienced video game players may have brought a slightly more refined understanding of narrative principles, at least, those associated with tension and turn, and organization, to the onset of their first-year writing course. Further, this result could also confirm analyses of games that emphasize their literary features (Aarseth, 1997; Ensslin, 2014) and the creative input of gamers (Ensslin, 2014; Jackson, 2002; Tamborini & Skalski, 2006) by demonstrating the ability of gamers to respond to narrative features in their writing. Although these effects seemed to diminish as the semester advanced, this is potentially explainable by the fact that all students in the study would have received the same semester-long narrative composition curriculum. By demonstrating the link between gaming and narrative ability, this research could then help to connect gaming to written narrative for students (Shepherd, 2015), thus enabling more conscious application of narrative knowledge developed through gaming experience to student writing. To emphasize, the current study was not an experimental intervention of a video game task but rather, looked at students gaming diets pre-college and assessed their association with their in-class composition ability. The establishment of this distal-yet-statistically significant association might help inform the more directed use of video games, and importantly, "off the shelf" games not designed with narrative or learning in mind, in the composition classroom.

Limitations of the Study

This study had three primary limitations, two related to the specific analyses presented here and one related to the central concept being studied: the distal nature of video game play to the target dependent variable.

Although often used as a trite limitation in social science research, it was clear that the current study should be replicated with a much larger sampling frame to test the stability of the correlation patterns reported in the current study. Schoenbrodt and Perugini (2013) suggested that correlations often do not enter their corridor of stability, that is, the non-random range around their "true" estimated population size, until a sample of at least n = 161 is achieved, although in practice many accept thresholds as small as n = 80 (Schoenbrodt, 2013). Data collection should be continued and replicated to achieve a larger and more representative sample of students. Related to this second point, our sample was nearly three-quarters White/Caucasian and male—on the one hand, such a population does represent sections of the video gamer population, but on the other hand, games are an increasingly diverse medium (ESA, 2014) and recruitment methods would need to be considered that encourage a broader swath of respondents.

However, we caution against rejection of our current study, and suggest that the early arguments and analyses reported here indicate a need to further explore emerging data trends.

The use of a panel of undergraduate essay evaluators might have also posed problems in the current study, as the panel was only able to achieve agreement on the presence or absence of a given evaluation category between 60% and 70% of the time, and the interval-level nature of the rubric made it difficult to get precise-point agreement at all levels of all categories, although the four coders never deviated more than one point on any given category when said category was present. While all four undergraduate coders were upper-level students (seniors at a four-year university), replication and extension of this study would benefit from using either more advanced-level evaluators or using other faculty trained in composition writing, or a more exhaustive coder training sequence in-line with more rigorous content analysis procedures (cf. Neuendorf, 2001). Access to resources limited our ability to engage these strategies, although we did not want the content coding to be influenced by experimenter bias; hence, the use of students ignorant to the study hypotheses and having no relationship to the student participants in the actual study itself.

Finally, a conceptual limitation to the current study concerns the distal nature of our measures to the observed in-class composition assignments. It is unlikely that one's global video game experience would have been expected to have a direct, powerful and universal impact on their ability to articulate on two discrete essay assignments for a basic-level university course; in some respects, effect sizes were expected to be rather small in nature from the onset. Notably, this study was designed to explore the potential for such broad associations to exist not as a definitive statement of their effects but, rather, as a point of departure for future research.

A natural extension of this work might be – along with a larger and more representative sample – to get a more precise sense of the types of games participants are playing in their experiences, and to analyze the impact of this specific content on their compositional writing ability. For example, not all video game genres might be expected to have a positive association with composition ability. A surface analysis of the association between action and sports game preferences, a bivariate correlation, interpreted with caution to statistical power concerns, showed an overall negative impact on composition quality. The negative impact of action and sports gaming might support Gentile et al. (2004), who found violent video gameplay to negatively impact scholastic performance. Many action games, and to a lesser extent, sports games, often fall into this category. Moreover, and perhaps more specific to our research aims, action and sports games might not feature the same sort of narrative elements found in adventure and role-playing games—the former of which are often focused on more hedonic pleasure and enjoyment (a "pleasure of control") while the latter more associated with eudaimonic appreciation and meaningfulness (a "pleasure of cognition," cf. Oliver et al., 2015). These differences might suggest genre-specific qualities of certain video games that might be more aligned with writing and narrative abilities, and these differences should be explored with more rigor. As mentioned in the literature review, some games such a *World of Warcraft* might be far better suited for fostering an appreciation of composition as the player is more actively involved in both the absorption and composition of the gameworld, and future work should more specifically, and more robustly, investigate these differences. Unfortunately, our study is not equipped to offer insight here.

Study Implications and Future Research

Our study has a number of implications and directions for future research, suggesting additional research questions, namely:

- Is this correlation moderated as a function of the discrete types of gaming experiences, such as genre-specific effects?
- Can these correlations be used to develop games designed to improve compositional writing ability?

The correlations reported here suggest the possibility that students who were experienced video game players were adept with basic narrative principles in ways that their formal university education might not assume. By recognizing this existing skill set on the part of gamers, instructors could tailor pedagogical practices to build upon these existing literacies. Moreover, the fact that some of these skills were being developed in a non-academic setting, as a by-product of students' video game play, reflected their engagement with highly effective non-directed and autotelic learning practices (cf. Gee, 2003; 2005).

Data from this study might also suggest an opportunity for instructors to use video games as markers of narrative quality and complexity (Moberly, 2008; Robison, 2008), and to encourage students to consider video games as modalities of expression (Selfe, 2009). Given the head-start that the study suggests video gaming provided composition students in applying principles of narrative, a thoughtful introduction of video game narratives to the writing classroom may assist all students in the acquisition of narrative-writing skill. Further, these results indicated that writing instructors should purposefully incorporate video gaming into their pedagogical practices to bring that pedagogy in line with students' leisure habits. With this in mind, composition instructors could develop a wider repertoire of teaching strategies that recognize and values learning that occurs in non-academic settings.

At the same time, we do not suggest that players uncritically engage in video game narratives; in fact, Moberly (2008) and Nakamura (1995) argued that narrative elements of video games made them particularly ripe spaces in which to engage and critically analyze on-screen content. Such arguments are echoed by Bogost (2011) and Limperos, Downs, Ivory, and Bowman (2013), who suggested that the antisocial content of many popular video games might provide vehicles for social criticism along with devices for hedonic enjoyment. In this way, understanding the narrative headcanons (cf. Banks, 2013) that players construct around their play experiences might shed light on both the player's ability to craft quality narrative but also their processing of on-screen content, the former being a focal and desired academic and professional skill and the latter being core to understanding media effects (Ferguson et al., 2008).

Future areas of research could include asking players to recall discrete gaming experiences that might have particular narrative elements, and examining the extent to which these elements might be conceptually similar to the key components of compositional skill—in particular, the narrative elements of games related to contemplation and introspection (cf. Oliver et al., 2015) that have greatly increased in popular demand and production (cf. Benedetti, 2007). As alluded to in the Literature Review of the current manuscript, we are unaware of any content analysis or other empirical analysis of the prevalence of the four properties of narrative from this study being present or absent in video games.

Yet another direction for future research might be to adopt a more robust panel design, perhaps identifying children at younger ages and tracking both their video game consumption and composition abilities over a period of time, as compared to a population with no video game play; however, we note that the ubiquity of video games for children today (Durkin, 2006) would make such a study incredibly difficult to conduct.

Finally, an additional area of future research would be to consider the impact of in situ video game play on composition ability, such as having individuals playing a set of video games and assessing the impact of those experiences on their ability to articulate on a composition task; a related study might consider the extent to which players are able to recognize the element of narrative coded in this study as being present or absent in the game played.

CONCLUSION

This study was an early exploration into the correlation between university students' video game play experience and their compositional writing ability in a first-semester writing course. Our data—while based on a small sample of students—highlighted a rather strong broad correlation between students' aggregated video game experience, understood as years spent playing games, and their ability to articulate tension and turn and organize composition assignments, particularly for an early-semester essay assignment assigned on the first day of class, in advance of any formal university-level composition instruction. These data suggested that video games, one of the most popular, and most controversial, forms of entertainment media, might help students develop an appreciation for at least some of the same cognitive and creative proficiencies that seem to foster writing ability. On this point, instructors and researchers alike are encouraged to consider video game play as non-traditional, autotelic, creative, entertaining, and unexpected medium with which to practice composition ability—indeed, many of their students may well have already been engaging in this writing-qua-gaming practice as part of their natural entertainment media usage. While a video game controller bears little resemblance to a quill pen, carbon-lead pencil, or laptop keyboard—our study offers preliminary evidence that there are associations between gaming and writing that are not trivial. Such evidence, however exploratory and preliminary, is of particular importance to understanding how leisurely video game play might influence our appreciation of composition and narrative, which might better allow us to engage the narrative that both involve and surround us on daily basis. For those who content that games are a powerful tool for both academic and social lessons, our paper suggests that one of the mechanisms that could underlie this process is the series of "interesting decisions" that gamers make, each time they press start, flip a lever, or save a digital society from its own impending doom.

REFERENCES

Aarseth, E. (1997). *Cybertext: Perspectives on ergodic literature*. Baltimore: Johns Hopkins University Press.

Alberti, J. (2008). The game of reading and writing: How video games reframe our understanding of literacy. *Computers and Composition*, 25(3), 258–269. doi:10.1016/j.compcom.2008.04.004

Anderson, C., & Bushman, B. (2001). Effects of violent video games on aggressive behavior, aggressive cognition, aggressive affect, physiological arousal, and prosocial behavior: A meta-analytic review of the scientific literature. *Psychological Science, 12*(5), 353–359. doi:10.1111/1467-9280.00366 PMID:11554666

Arnold, D. S., Lonigan, C. J., Whitehurst, G. J., & Epstein, J. N. (1994). Accelerating language development through picture-book reading: Replication and extension to a videotape training format. *Journal of Educational Psychology, 86*(2), 235–243. doi:10.1037/0022-0663.86.2.235

Banks, J. (2013). *Human-technology relationality and self-network organization: Players and avatars in World of Warcraft.* (Unpublished doctoral dissertation). Colorado State University.

Benedetti, W. (2007, April 20). Were video games to blame for massacre? *MSNBC.* Retrieved from: http://www.nbcnews.com/id/18220228/#.U-HgNfmSzSY

Bessiere, K., Seay, F., & Kiesler, S. (2007). The ideal Elf: Identity exploration in *World of Warcraft. Cyberpsychology & Behavior, 10*(4), 530–535. doi:10.1089/cpb.2007.9994 PMID:17711361

Bogost, I. (2006). *Unit operations: An approach to videogame criticism.* Cambridge, MA: MIT Press.

Bogost, I. (2011). *How to do things with videogames.* Minneapolis: University of Minnesota Press. doi:10.5749/minnesota/9780816676460.001.0001

Bowman, N. D. (2016). Video Gaming as Co-Production. In R. Lind (Ed.), *Produsing 2.0: The intersection of audiences and production in a digital world* (Vol. 2, pp. 107–123). New York: Peter Lang Publishing.

Bowman, N. D., & Banks, J. (in press). Playing the zombie author: Machinima through the lens of Barthes. In K. Kenney (Ed.), *Philosophy for multisensory communication.* New York: Peter Lang.

Bowman, N. D., Kowert, R., & Ferguson, C. (2016). The impact of video game play on human (and orc) creativity. In G. Green & J. Kaufman (Eds.), *Video games and creativity* (pp. 41–62). Waltham, Mass: Academic Press.

Bowman, N. D., Westerman, D. K., & Claus, C. J. (2012). How demanding is social media? Understanding social media diets as a function of perceived costs and benefits-A Rational Actor Perspective. *Computers in Human Behavior, 28*(6), 2298–2305. doi:10.1016/j.chb.2012.06.037

Boyan, A., Grizzard, M., & Bowman, N. D. (2015). A massively moral game? *Mass Effect* a case study to understand the influence of players' moral intuitions on adherence to hero or antihero play styles. *Journal of Gaming and Virtual Worlds, 7*(1), 41–57. doi:10.1386/jgvw.7.1.41_1

Bracken, C. C., & Skalski, P. (2006), 'Presence and video games: The impact of image quality and skill level', *Proceedings of the Annual International Meeting of the PresenceWorkshop.* Cleveland, OH: Cleveland State University.

Burke, K. (1945). *A grammar of motives.* Los Angeles: University of California Press.

Cohen, J. (1988). *Statistical power analysis for the behavioral sciences* (2nd ed.). Hillsdale, NJ: LEA.

Collins, K. (2013). *Playing with sound: A theory of interacting with sound and music in video games.* Cambridge, MA: MIT Press.

Durkin, K. (2006). Game playing and adolescents' development. In P. Vorderer & J. Bryant (Eds.), *Playing computer games: Motives, responses, and consequences* (pp. 415–428). Mahwah, NJ: Erlbaum.

Ensslin, A. (2014). *Literary Gaming*. Cambridge, MA: MIT Press.

ESA. (2014, October). *Essential facts about the computer and video game industry*. Retrieved from: http://www.theesa.com/wp-content/uploads/2014/10/ESA_EF_2014.pdf

Ferguson, C. J., Rueda, S. M., Cruz, A. M., Ferguson, D. E., Fritz, S., & Smith, S. M. (2008). Violent video games and aggression: Causal relationship or byproduct of family violence and intrinsic violence motivation? *Criminal Justice and Behavior, 35*(3), 311–332. doi:10.1177/0093854807311719

Gee, J. P. (2003). *What video games have to teach us about learning and literacy*. New York: Palgrave Macmillan.

Gee, J. P. (2005). Pleasure, learning, video games, and life: The projective stance. *E-Learning and Digital Media, 2*(3), 211–223.

Gentile, D., & Anderson, C. (2003). Violent video games: The newest media violence hazard. In D. Gentile (Ed.), *Media Violence and Children*. Westport, CT: Praeger.

Gentile, D. A., Lynch, P. J., Linder, P. J., & Walsh, D. A. (2004). The effects of violent video game habits on adolescent hostility, aggressive behaviors, and school performance. *Journal of Adolescence, 27*(1), 5–22. doi:10.1016/j.adolescence.2003.10.002 PMID:15013257

George, S. (2012). The Performed Self in College Writing: From Personal Narratives to Analytic and Research Essays. *Pedagogy, 12*(2), 319–341. doi:10.1215/15314200-1503613

Green, M. C., Brock, T. C., & Kaufman, G. F. (2006). Understanding media enjoyment: The role of transportation into narrative worlds. *Communication Theory, 14*(4), 311–327. doi:10.1111/j.1468-2885.2004.tb00317.x

Grodal, T. (2000). Video games and the pleasures of control. In D. Zillmann & P. Vorderer (Eds.), *Media entertainment: The psychology of its appeal* (pp. 197–214). Mahwah, NJ: Lawrence Erlbaum Associates.

Harrington, S., Malencyzk, R., Peckham, I., Rhodes, K., & Yancey, K. B. (2001). WPA outcomes statement for first-year composition. *College English, 63*(3), 321–325. doi:10.2307/378996

Howald, B. S. (2009). A quantitative perspective on the minimal definition of narrative. *Text & Talk, 29*(6), 705–727. doi:10.1515/TEXT.2009.036

Jackson, Z. A. (2002). Connecting video games and storytelling to teach narratives in first-year composition. *Kairos: A Journal of Rhetoric, Technology, and Pedagogy, 7*(3). Retrieved from: http://kairos.technorhetoric.net/7.3/coverweb/jackson/index.htm

Jansz, J. (2005). The emotional appeal of violent video games for adolescent males. *Journal of Communication, 15*(3), 219–241. doi:10.1111/j.1468-2885.2005.tb00334.x

Labov, W. (1972). The transformation of experience in narrative syntax. In *Language in the Inner City* (pp. 354–396). Philadelphia: University of Pennsylvania Press.

Labov, W. (2013). *The language of life and death*. Cambridge, UK: Cambridge University Press. doi:10.1017/CBO9781139519632

Labov, W., & Waletzky, J. (1967). Narrative analysis: Oral versions of personal experience. In J. Helm (Ed.), *Essays on the Verbal and Visual Arts*, (pp. 12-44). Seattle: University of Washington Press.

Lange, A. (2014). "You're just gonna be nice": How players engage with moral choice systems. *Journal of Games Criticism*, *1*(1).

Limperos, A. M., Downs, E., Ivory, J. D., & Bowman, N. D. (2013). Leveling up: A review of emerging trends and suggestions for the next generation of communication research investigating video games' effects. *Communication Yearbook*, *37*, 348–377.

Meier, S. (2012. March). *Interesting decisions*. Presentation and the Game Developers Conference, San Francisco, CA.

Mills, K. A., & Exley, B. (2014). Narrative and multimodality in English language arts curricula: A tale of two nations. *Language Arts*, *92*(2), 136–143.

Moberly, K. (2008). Composition, computer games, and the absence of writing. *Computers and Composition*, *25*(3), 284–299. doi:10.1016/j.compcom.2008.04.007

Nakamura, L. (1995). Race in/for cyberspace: Identity tourism and racial passing on the Internet. *Works and Days*, *25*(26), 13.

Neuendorf, K. A. (2001). *The content analysis handbook*. Thousand Oaks, CA: SAGE.

Oliver, M. B., Bowman, N. D., Woolley, J. K., Rogers, R., Sherrick, B., & Chung, M.-Y. (2015). Video games as meaningful entertainment experiences. *Psychology of Popular Media Culture*. doi:10.1037/ppm0000066

Ouyang, J., & McKeown, K. (2014, May). Towards automatic detection of narrative structure.*Proceedings of the 9th International Conference on Language Resources and Evaluation*, Reykjavik.

Painter, C., Martin, J. R., & Unsworth, L. (2013). *Reading visual narratives: Image analysis of children's picture books*. London: Equinox.

Paul, H., Bowman, N. D., & Banks, J. D. (2015). The enjoyment of griefing in online games. *Journal of Gaming and Virtual Worlds*, *7*(3), 243–258. doi:10.1386/jgvw.7.3.243_1

Peracchio, L. A., & Escalas, J. E. (2008). "Tell me a story": Crafting and publishing research in consumer psychology. *Journal of Consumer Psychology*, *18*(3), 197–204. doi:10.1016/j.jcps.2008.04.008

Peters, J. (2007, June 27). World of Borecraft. *Slate.com*. Retrieved November 11, 2015 from: http://www.slate.com/articles/technology/gaming/2007/06/world_of_borecraft.html

Robison, A. J. (2008). The design is the game: Writing games, teaching writing. *Computers and Composition*, *25*(3), 359–370. doi:10.1016/j.compcom.2008.04.006

Schoenbrodt, F. D. (2013, June 6). At what sample size do correlations stabilize? *Nicebread.de* [personal blog]. Retrieved from: http://www.nicebread.de/at-what-sample-size-do-correlations-stabilize/

Schoenbrodt, F. D., & Perugini, M. (2013). At what size do correlations stabilize? *Journal of Research in Personality*, *47*(5), 609–612. doi:10.1016/j.jrp.2013.05.009

Selfe, C. (2009). The movement of air, the breath of meaning: Aurality and multimodal composing. *College Composition and Communication*, *60*(4). Retrieved from http://www.ncte.org/cccc/ccc/issues/v60-4

Shepherd, R. P. (2015). FB in FYC: Facebook use among first-year composition students. *Computers and Composition*, *35*, 86–107. doi:10.1016/j.compcom.2014.12.001

Shweder, R. A., & Haidt, J. (1993). The future of moral psychology: Truth, intuition, and the pluralist way. *Psychological Science*, *4*(6), 360–365. doi:10.1111/j.1467-9280.1993.tb00582.x

Steuer, J. (1992). Defining virtual reality: Dimensions determining telepresence. *Journal of Communication*, *42*(4), 73–93. doi:10.1111/j.1460-2466.1992.tb00812.x

Tamborini, R., & Skalski, P. (2006). The role of presence in the experience of electronic games. In P. Vorderer & J. Bryant (Eds.), *Playing video game: Motives, responses, and consequences* (pp. 225–240). Mahwah, NJ: LEA.

Valkenberg, P. M., & Peter, J. (2013). Five challenges for the future of media-effects research. *International Journal of Communication, 7*, 197-215. doi: 1932-8036/2013FEA0002

Wong, K. C. (2010). Interpretation of correlation coefficients. *Hong Kong Medical Journal*, *16*(3), 237. PMID:20519766

KEY TERMS AND DEFINITIONS

Conclusion: The ending of a narrative.

Description: The process of describing the settings, characters, and events of a narrative.

Detail: The use of specific and appropriate language--i.e., specific nouns and verbs--to support the description in a narrative.

Narrative: An ordered series of events where a change in order would result in a change of the events' meaning.

Organization: The sequence of events or structure of a narrative.

Resolution: In a narrative, the sense of the reader that there are consequences that result from the turn and that these consequences lead the narrative somewhere.

Tension: A building or anticipation of dramatic progression toward an event in an narrative, where the event can consist of actions, character development, or narrative details.

Turn: The climax of a narrative, in which events come to a head; typically the turn is precipitated by a particular event, occurrence, or action.

APPENDIX: COMPOSITION CODING BOOK

Student Name: _____

Table 3. Project (1= diagnostic, 2 = narrative)

4	3	2	1
Tension and Turn			
The tension is developed clearly, creatively, and realistically, and the turn is effectively described.	The tension is sufficiently developed and there is a clearly identifiable turn.	The tension is insufficiently developed and the turn is hard to find.	The tension is not developed and the narrative lacks a turn.
Resolution and Conclusion			
The resolution is clear and creative, and the conclusion effectively reinforces and reflects on the main purpose of the essay.	The resolution is sufficiently clear, and the conclusion adequately reinforces and reflects the purpose or focus of the essay.	The resolution is insufficiently clear, and the conclusion is underdeveloped or inadequately reflects on the purpose of the essay.	The essay ends abruptly, and the conclusion does not reinforce or reflect on the purpose of the essay.
Description and Detail			
The use of sensory description, setting, and character is both clear and creative and adds depth and detail to the essay.	The use of sensory description, setting, and character is sufficient but the essay does not excel in all areas.	The use of sensory description, setting, and character is insufficient, or the essay only uses of a few of these devices.	The essay does not use sensory description. setting, and character.
Organization			
The organization is appropriate for the genre, and the arrangement of the essay helps the reader to understand and remain engaged with the essay.	The organization is sufficient but does not always use appropriate genre conventions, and at times the reader can lose engagement.	The organization only fits the genre sporadically or tangentially, or the arrangement needs tweaking in order to engage readers.	The organization does not fit the genre, or the essay is so disorganized that it confuses the reader.

Chapter 14
Implementing a Game-Based Instructional Design Strategy in the Eighth Grade Science Classroom:
Teaching Science the *Chutes and Ladders* Way!

Angela Dowling
Suncrest Middle School, USA

Terence C. Ahern
West Virginia University, USA

ABSTRACT

This chapter examines the effects of a game-like environment on instructional activity design and learning outcomes in a middle school general science class. The authors investigated if science content can be designed and successfully delivered instructionally using a game-like learning environment. The authors also wanted to investigate if by utilizing a game-design method could class and student engagement be increased. The results indicated that the instructional design of the unit using a game-like environment was successful and students exhibited learning. The authors also address the challenges inherent in utilizing this instructional strategy.

INTRODUCTION

Knowledge is being created at a rapid rate for a myriad of mediums (Schilling, 2013). Adapting to change is a crucial skill for the 21st century because the transition from a linear to an exponential growth of human knowledge requires flexible learners who can cope with this explosion of new information. However, the typical teaching paradigm operating in today's classrooms is *tell and practice* where the teacher first tells or demonstrates a concept and then asks the students to respond to a series of ques-

DOI: 10.4018/978-1-5225-0261-6.ch014

tions (Schwartz, Chase, Oppezzo & Chin, 2011). Heibert and Stigler (2004) describe a typical routine of a classroom teacher:

Lessons are planned (sometimes quickly, by identifying a sequence of activities), then implemented, then assessed (sometimes by watching students' reactions during the lesson, listening to students and questioning them informally, and collecting student work), and then reflected on (sometimes quickly, by making mental notes of what worked well and what didn't, who acted up, and so on). (p. 13)

This form of instructional delivery, however, according to some researchers, limits a deeper and more flexible understanding of the content. Catrambone (1998) notes, "Students tend to memorize the details of how the equations are filled out rather than learning the deeper, conceptual knowledge that is implicit in the details" (p. 335). Further, according to Heibert and Stigler (2004) most practice problems focus on skill development rather than conceptual understanding.

What we need is a shift in the delivery of instruction. Dewey (1963) suggests that we shift delivery from a top-down approach to one that is more personal and individualized to where "change is the rule and not the exception" (p. 19). Dewey also argued that the type of instruction that is disseminated from textbooks or authorities as though it is "a finished product..." is too rigid (p. 19).

Numerous attempts over the past 40 years have seen explicit instruction increasingly supplanted by approaches more closely aligned with constructivist concepts of exploration, discovery, and invention such as discovery learning, problem based inquiry and the like (Alfieri, Brooks, Aldrich & Tannebaum, 2011). As early as 1992, Brown was noticing that the implementation of the discovery types of instructional delivery was somewhat ineffectual. Alfieri, et al. (2011) in a recent meta-analysis found two major drawbacks in the discovery type of implementation strategies. First, students are often unequipped to access the to-be-learned material because they lack the prerequisite content skills or knowledge. Second, the ability to make sense of the instructional experience requires "considerable metacognitive skills, and it is unlikely that all learners, in particular children, would have such skills" (p. 3.) Nonetheless, Brown (1992) noted that the "motivational benefits of generating knowledge cannot be overestimated and the sense of ownership that this creates is a powerful reward" (p. 168).

The problem for teachers and instructional designers is how to design personalized and individualized experiences that are truly effective. Below (1990) suggests that learning is a recursive process that is dependent on prior experiences. Dewey (1963) concurs and notes, that even though "all genuine education comes about through experience does not mean that all experiences are genuinely or equally educative" (p. 25). He further points that out "every experience affects for better or worse the quality of future experiences" (p. 27). Consequently, experiences need to be properly engineered and sequenced so that each experience contributes to the whole.

BACKGROUND

Engineering Experience

The correct experience has to come at the most appropriate time for the experience to be meaningful to a student. In large part, instruction leads students through an appropriate sequence of content and activities, which allows them to "grasp, transform and transfer" (Bruner, 1966, p. 49) what is being taught.

Ahern (2002) notes, "By anticipating what a learner needs to know, instruction synthetically sequences requisite learned states in order to reach the necessary outcome... Instruction is a process that designs not only the specific content but also creates the situation in which that content is experienced" (p. 3).

Engineering appropriate experiences requires that the designer be aware of the needs of the target audience. The designer needs to understand what types or kinds of experiences would be most effective for different types of students. For example, students in the lower grades may find a concrete experience more effective whereas for an adult audience an abstract approach would be appropriate. Secondly, the designer must sequence the content such that the progression is concrete to abstract or abstract to concrete.

The designer analyzes the instructional goal and deconstructs it into its constituent skills and knowledge. This analysis creates a hierarchical sequence that a designer uses to present the instruction. The idea is to make sure that what the learner experiences is in the correct order so that subordinate steps are experienced prior to superordinate steps, as in a process such as addition. Games create an immersive experience as an arc of emotions, decisions and thought within the mind of the player (Sylvester, 2013). From the tactile experience of a board game to the dynamic visual representations of a video game the player is immersed within a defined space of possibility governed by rules and events (Salen & Zimmerman, 2003). This bounded space of possibility allows not only a rich experience, but an emergent path through the space each time the game is played. This makes games uniquely suited as an instructional delivery strategy.

All games have a similar structure. Salen and Zimmerman (2003) define a game as "a system in which players engage in an artificial conflict, defined by rules, that results in a quantifiable outcome" (p. 96). As we have seen, the system is the space of possibility. The game defines an artificial goal—conquer the ogre and save the princess. Accomplishing this goal is constrained by rules. For all games, there are three basic rules. These rules govern the environment (the space of possibility), each player's behavior, and finally what constitutes winning the game.

The first set of rules governs the initial set up of the environment such as in the game of *RISK* (Lamorisse, 1995) where the game board is a stylized map of the world. How to setup a game is defined by the rules concerning where each player's pieces are placed intially. The next set of rules governs game play and defines player behavior not only with other players but also with the game's environment. Game play is further controlled by the game's mechanics, which structure and constrain players' interactions in the game space. Consider the bishop in chess. The player can only move along a particular diagonal based on color in order to capture another player's piece. Or the knight, which moves in a very well defined pattern.

The rules also indirectly govern pacing, which to a large extent is controlled by player movement. For example *RISK* is defined as a "turn-based" game which means that each player gets a turn. Durng a player's turn in *RISK* they receive additional armies, engage in combat with other players and, if successful, receive a game card that is useful later in the game. Consequently, pacing, as defined by Venturelli (2009), is a concept related to the overall rhythm of the game, the relative speed at which the different moving parts of the system are put in motion" (p. 2). Davies (2009) further defines pacing as consisting of a) movement impetus, b) threat, c) tension and d) tempo.

Movement impetus is the requirement that a player has to "literally" make a move. As in *RISK* each player, by rule, is given the opportunity to make a move that involves engaging in combat with other players. The real impetus in *RISK* is the necessity to capture at least one army during a player's move because the reward is a game card, which can be redeemed on a later turn for additional armies. The environment also typically defines threat, such as in *RISK*, where each player is massing his or her armies to attack. Tempo describes the intensity of action. Low tempo games allow for reflection and thinking and such, as with trying to solve puzzles. High tempo is usually in real-time based games for example in basketball or soccer where the action is constant.

Games and Instructional Design

The state that a player is in while playing a game is what Huizinga (1955) called the magic circle. Huizinga (1955) noted that the magic circle is where everyday objects can take on magical properties and where anything is possible. The magic circle is an immersive experience—where you enter a world and play creates the possible. Within the magic circle, a player can risk, can explore and can think without consequence.

Ahern (2009) notes that games and models make abstract concepts more accessible and simplify the complex. In playing a game, students are immediately able to see the results of their play. They can see the effects of their move and respond to the challenge. This notion of recursion is a very powerful idea.

Finally, games are able to engage players to overcome self-imposed challenges by means of their own intrinsic motivations. Players often have no other reason to tackle these challenges beyond their own motivation to put their skills to the test (Tondello, 2015). This is because of the iterative and recursive nature of the games and game play. The game has a finite number of moves; there is a beginning, middle and an end. Given that we fail more often than we succeed, the great thing about playing a game is we can always get another chance.

Games have unique characteristics from other planned activities that are easily adaptable to the classroom (Klopfer, Osterweil & Salen, 2009). When these characteristics are taken into account during the process of designing curricular units the potential for increasing achievement and motivation are greatly increased. Consider the following:

- The requirement to try
  - Games require the player to make a move. Further, each player makes decisions based on the current state of the game and in relation to previous moves of the various pieces on the board. Consequently, based on the player's decisions, a path is created through the content to achieve the goal.
- The opportunity to plan
  - Players weigh the consequences of any given move in order to achieve a possible future outcome. They use prior experience in juxtaposition with the current state of the gameboard. The player decides not only how fast or slow they will proceed through the game but also chooses the path through the game.
- The opportunity to experiment
  - Experimentation is an essential element in game play. Computer-based simulations and games allow students the opportunity to experiment with the "what if" problems.
- The possibility of failure
  - The ultimate beauty of a game is that it is okay to fail.
- Games are iterative
  - Given that we fail in a game more often than we succeed, the great thing about playing a game is we always get another chance. The gameboard is always changing and as Yogi Berra observed "the game ain't over till it's over".

- Games are recursive
  - Games are self-contained. They are sequential and recursive in that every action is built upon prior action. Every output of an action becomes the input for a subsequent action in relationship to what each player "does" in the game.

Further, games foster a playful attitude and produce a state of flow, therefore increasing learning and fostering motivation. According to Malone and Lepper (1987), games introduce a challenge, create learner curiosity, and provide the learner with a sense of intrinsic control. Games can use fantasy to reinforce the instructional goals as well as to simulate prior interest in the learner. Finally, games foster play and in turn produce a state of flow, which increases motivation, and in turn supports the learning process. This makes game-based design an excellent strategy for instruction. Game experiences are structured and sequential while the pacing is self-determinate.

IMPLEMENTING A GAME-BASED DESIGN STRATEGY IN THE CLASSROOM

Study

The study used the design-based methodology based on Brown (1992) which Sandoval and Bell (2004) describe as an in situ methodology "to develop theories of learning (and teaching) that accounted for multiple interactions of people acting in a complex social setting" (p. 199). This study was conducted in a middle school science classroom as a design experiment.

The instructional intervention created a world narrative loosely based on the game *Chutes and Ladders* (2005). The world narrative defined the classroom space so that it carried "emotional and informational charges" (Sylvester, 2003) and offered personal challenges, gave the students a sense of control over both the process and the product, and maintained the students' interest over time (Ames 2002). We were interested in discovering if the game-based design encouraged better-sustained engagement for the students. Engagement is the notion that both participation as well as the cognitive investment is necessary for successful instructional outcomes (Beesley, Clark, Barker, Germeroth & Apthorp, 2010). You cannot have one without the other and still achieve true learning.

We implemented an introductory biology unit that was designed as a game. The different areas within the content were arranged as levels:

- Level 1 dealt with the cell,
- Level 2 dealt with body systems,
- Level 3 involved collaborative presentations of Levels 1 and 2, and
- Level 4 was the programming of a simulation of an epidemic using StarLogo software.

The unit of study was covered in relation to the West Virginia Content Standards and Objectives for 8th Grade Biology (West Virginia Department of Education, 2015). A pretest on the material was given to ascertain the prior knowledge of the students. Any questions that were on the pretest but not the posttest were not included in the scores used for data analysis.

Participants

The participants of the study were learners 13-14 years of age and enrolled in 8th grade at a mid-Atlantic middle school. The study involved 165 students. The learners were able to apply skills from the STEM disciplines (science, technology, engineering and math) to solve a real world problem. Classes at this middle school were divided into 45-50 minute class periods. For convenience, participants involved in the study consisted of the entire 8th grade enrolled at the school. All data gathered from participant resources was collected with explicit permission from the participants and in full compliance with Institutional Review Board (IRB) guidelines. As per current inclusionary practices, the teacher had all enrolled 8th grade students as members of the classroom. The range of student ability levels included mentally impaired (very low level autistic), identified behavior disorder, and academically gifted.

Instruments

The Game

The game was designed to loosely mimic *Chutes and Ladders*. It was immersive, self-contained, and incorporated real-world elements such as quizzes and tests, student presentations and the like. Each student in a team would traverse each level of the unit using a ladder or a chute as depicted in Figure 1.

Figure 1. Gameboard

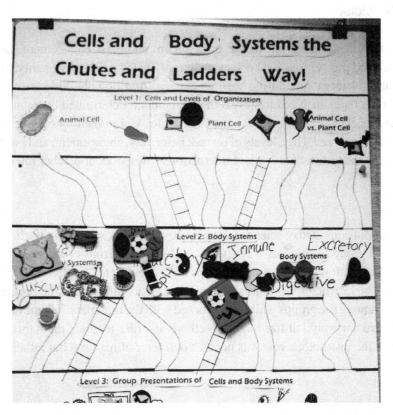

Each student had to master a particular level by "scoring" a minimum percentage on a non-graded exit quiz for that level in order to progress to the next level. The students were able to make their own token, which they could place and move on the gameboard. The gameboard was hung on the classroom wall so everyone could keep track of his or her place in the game.

Pretest and Posttest

Prior to beginning the game a pretest was given to determine current level of knowledge, and the results were used to inform the design of each level of instruction. Questions that were on the pre-test but not the post-test were not included in the scores used for data analysis. The pretest also did not count towards the students' grades and was only used to gauge current levels of knowledge. Scores on exit quizzes were also not used to determine student grades on the unit but were only used to determine advancement to the next level. Subsequently, a post-test was given after reaching the final level dealing with epidemics. The scores were analyzed and compared to the pretests in order to determine the success of instructional intervention based on the game-based design strategy.

Content Material

All students were provided with a folder containing materials necessary to complete the levels within the unit of study. These materials included important vocabulary, resources and ideas for where to complete the research, and ideas to help the students decide how to present what they had learned during the unit.

Observation Checklist

Checklists were used to examine both student engagement and class engagement. Outside observers, including in-service and pre-service teachers, as well as affiliated university faculty, volunteered to use the checklist to make observations during various classes. Additionally, video was taken at different times during the project and analyzed for levels of engagement, determined by counting the number of student-student and teacher-student interactions. Field notes were taken by outside observers and the classroom teacher and analyzed. High levels of on task behaviors, engagement, and peer interaction were observed as well as increased student-student interactions (over student-teacher interactions).

Procedure

Seating in the classroom consisted of science tables in groups of two, which lent itself naturally to groups of 3-4 students. Each group of students was given a packet of materials covering what all of the levels consisted of and a description of the "game." Groups had access to textbooks and a laptop for the duration of the project. The instructor was available for the students throughout the progression of the unit and would circulate among the groups while they worked with the materials. Whenever students required clarification the instructor would utilize inquiry methods in order to guide them through the materials. Throughout the unit the instructor's role was not as a deliverer of material but rather as a guide.

Level 1

The students worked together to research and depict in a way of their own choosing terms related to cell biology and the parts of the cell. The team was required to become familiar with photosynthesis, respiration and fermentation. As an additional aspect of the level, students also needed to demonstrate an understanding of how the parts of the cell worked together. They were also to discuss, compare, or contrast what they had learned in the level. The group could choose whatever method for accomplishing this that they thought was sufficient. Once all members of the group felt ready they were to take a short online quiz to exit the level via the course management web site that the school uses. When students were done with the exit quiz they would come to the teacher and check their grade (immediate feedback) and if they had not attained an 80% they were to retake the exit quiz until they attained at least an 80%. Students could prepare for the retake as they saw fit. Some students would review their group's materials for that level or just review and discuss with members of their group. The stipulation was also made that the group could not progress to the next level in the game until all the members had passed with a minimum score of 80% on the exit quiz. Once all members of the group attained at least an 80% on the exit quiz for that level, the group could progress onto the next level.

Level 2

The students familiarized themselves with the body systems. This level was conducted using the same organization as the first level. Once the students became familiar with the basics of the body systems they were to demonstrate their understanding of the interactions of the body systems by selecting a way to present that information (PowerPoint, diagrams, etc.) to the whole class.

When the group members felt they had mastered the material in Level 2 they could take the online exit quiz. Once all members of the group "passed" with at least an 80% the group could move on to Level 3. If all members of the group did not attain an 80% they could go back to their tables and help each other to review the material and retake the exit quiz until the 80% was reached by all.

Level 3

Level 3 of the game involved a group summary presentation of materials covered in both level 1 and 2. The groups could take everything they had produced in Levels 1 and 2 and combine them into one presentation to present to the rest of the class. Level 3 presentations acted as a review for the students before they could progress to Level 4.

Level 4

Level 4 was conducted as a whole class experience where every student had his or her own laptop with which to work. The teacher used the desktop computer in the classroom that was connected to the virtual whiteboard while leading the students through the steps of constructing a simulation of an epidemic in StarLogo. While programming the model/simulation whole class discussions were held concerning how epidemics work, ways that the program could be altered to better approximate "real life," etc. Classes also were able to construct dynamic bar graphs within the program that changed as the model ran. After completion of Level 4, all students took a post-test, which consisted of questions taken from Level 1 and Level 2 exit quizzes.

Individual student and class engagement checklists were analyzed and compared. Non-biased observers were chosen from the school faculty, student teachers and an affiliated university faculty member for completion of checklists. Additionally, video was taken at different times during the project and analyzed for levels of engagement. Field notes were taken by outside observers and the classroom teacher and analyzed. The pretest was given at the beginning of the unit to determine current knowledge and the results were used to inform the design of each level of instruction. Periodically throughout the study, exit quizzes were administered in order to track learning over time throughout the project.

The post-test was given after the final level dealing with epidemics in order to determine the success of the intervention. Pretest/posttest scores and exit quizzes were compared and analyzed in order to determine if using this type of curriculum delivery had helped students to deepen their understanding of the content.

Results

According to the findings, learning outcomes increased across the participants with most students increasing their scores significantly. A paired sample t-test showed a significant result ($p < .05$) indicating that the intervention was successful with all learners showing improvement from the pre-test to the post-test (Table 1).

Many students commented how surprised they were at the amount of improvement from pretest to posttest. One student in particular, who always scored significantly low, increased his score by almost 40 percentage points. His excitement was evident and he commented on how he thought that this mode of delivery kept the material interesting for him and kept him engaged when he usually would not be. The instructor also made this same observation concerning students who generally were not actively engaged in class becoming more actively engaged with the material and significantly increasing their scores.

Table 1. Pre-test vs. post-test scores paired-samples t-test for all learners

Paired Samples Statistics					
		Mean	N	Std. Deviation	Std. Error Mean
Pair 1	Post Test Scores	73.78	159	20.05	1.59
	Pre Test Scores	34.60	159	19.05	1.51

Paired Samples Correlations				
		N	Correlation	Sig.
Pair 1	Post Test Scores & Pre Test Scores	159	.665	.000

Paired Samples Test									
		Paired Differences					t	df	Sig. (2-tailed)
		Mean	Std. Deviation	Std. Error Mean	95% Confidence Interval of the Difference				
					Lower	Upper			
Pair 1	Post Test Scores - Pre Test Scores	39.19	16.03	1.27	36.68	41.70	30.82	158	.000

High levels of on task behaviors, engagement, and peer interaction were observed as well as increased student-student interactions (over student-teacher interactions). Checklists were used to examine both student engagement and class engagement. The following criteria were used for the checklist with options for levels of Very High, High, Medium, Low, Very Low and N/A (not applicable):

- Positive Body Language.
- Consistent Focus/Time On task/Engagement.
- Verbal Participation.
- Individual Attention.
- Student Interaction.
- Fun and Excitement.
- Meaningfulness of Work.
- Overall Level of Class Engagement.

As can be seen from Table 2 overall class engagement levels were Medium (39) to Very High (30) with marks falling predominantly into the High (62) range. For example, Positive Body Language was noticed 10 instances overall by all observers while Student Interaction with Peers was observed 9 times.

Individual Students Engagement Checklists also showed a predominance of marks in Medium to Very High ranges with the largest number falling into the High range. Overall Student Engagement was observed as High 143 times by observers (Table 3).

The game design allowed the students the opportunity to engage with content from the most basic form of life (the cell), to cell processes and on to how cells became tissues, tissues became organs and organs became part of body systems. Levels 1 and 2 of the unit required students to engage with the

Table 2. Overall class engagement checklist

Observations	Very High	High	Medium	Low	Very Low	N/A
Positive Body Language- Students in the classroom generally exhibit body postures that indicate they are paying attention to the teacher and/or other students (actively listening, questioning, etc.)	4	10	6	1	0	0
Consistent Focus/Time On Task/Engagement- The class is focused on the learning activity with minimal disruptions. Student is engaged with the current task.	2	7	11	0	0	0
Verbal Participation- Students are expressing thoughtful ideas, volunteering reflective answers, and their questions are relevant and appropriate to learning.	3	11	11	0	0	0
Individual Attention – Students in the class feel comfortable seeking help and asking questions	6	10	4	0	0	0
Student Interaction with Peers- Student interacts with and offers assistance to other students instead of asking questions.	8	9	3	0	0	0
Fun and Excitement- Students in the class are exhibiting interest and enthusiasm and using positive humor.	1	7	10	1	0	0
Meaninfulness of Work- The class finds the work interesting, challenging, and connected to learning.	1	8	9	1	0	0
Overall Level of Class Engagement	30	62	39	3	0	0

Table 3. Overall student engagement checklist

Observations	Very High	High	Medium	Low	Very Low	N/A
Positive Body Language- Students exhibits body postures that indicate he/she is paying attention to the teacher and/or other students	13	24	19	3	1	0
Consistent Focus/Time On Task/Engagement- Student is focused on the learning activity with minimal disruptions. Student is engaged with the current task	14	23	15	5	2	1
Verbal Participation- Student expresses thoughtful ideas, volunteering reflective answers, and questions are relevant and appropriate to learning.	15	20	14	7	3	1
Individual Attention – Student feels comfortable seeking help and asking questions	12	30	11	3	1	4
Student Interaction with Peers- Student interacts with and offers assistance to other students instead of asking questions.	19	20	10	6	2	1
Fun and Excitement- Student exhibits interest and enthusiasm and using positive humor.	15	16	22	9	1	0
Meaninfulness of Work- Student finds the work interesting, challenging, and connected to learning.	16	10	22	9	1	2
Overall Level of Student Engagement	104	143	110	42	11	9

material on the lower levels of Bloom's Taxonomy (knowledge, comprehension and analysis). Level 3 of the unit led students through analysis, synthesis and evaluation (upper levels of Bloom's Taxonomy) in order to present what they had learned during the first two levels to the rest of the class. Level 4 required the students to utilize everything that they had learned throughout the Cells and Body Systems unit in order to understand the dynamics of an epidemic.

The students determined the pacing of the unit. All groups were given the same instructions, and resources. Groups could progress at their own pace throughout the levels. When each member of a group was ready to take a level quiz, they could be observed as helping each other study. When, for instance, all members of a group but one would "pass" the members who passed would help the remaining member study for the quiz again before that member would retake the quiz. In this way, as groups progressed from level to level they could move their group token through the levels at different rates. The movement of the tokens by various groups was cause for excitement among group members and also among the other groups in each class. Often times the groups could be seen competing with other groups and making sure that other groups could not see how they were organizing their own materials. A healthy competitiveness and excitement emerged.

Discussion

Results of the study indicate that the delivery of content designed using a game-based design strategy was successful as evidenced by gains in learning outcomes and sustained engagement. Students were on task the majority of the time and were focused on the content.

Anecdotal data showed that the students were very excited and interested during the project and eager to help one another through the material. In general, the students were more likely to interact among themselves than to interact with the teacher. Students were also less concerned about being in a hurry to engage with the content since they knew that there were generous time constraints on their progression through the levels. The pressure to "keep up" was removed and the students were able to relax and fully engage with the content. By using the game-based design strategy as the instructional delivery method, the content had a single organizing structure, which provided a simple objective for the content. This organizing structure was conceptual, procedural and theoretical. The content also had a simple-to-complex organization (Wilson & Cole, 1992).

Reigeluth & Stein (1983) noticed that when implementing the elaboration theory, instruction was more effective if the learner had control over both content and instructional strategy. Because the students had control over the pace of the instruction in this study they took more ownership in their own learning.

Overall class engagement levels were Medium to Very High with scores falling predominantly into the High range. Individual Student Engagement Checklists scored by outside observers also showed a predominance of scores in the Medium to Very High range with the largest number falling into the high range. From the student checklists it was also observed that there were scores in the Low to Very Low ranges. Individual student observations involved students in individual classes, examining data from different students increased the possibility of a student being observed that typically would not demonstrate on task behavior in class. Outside observers noted in field notes attached to the checklists instances of various types of off task behavior that were typical classroom behaviors for those students (as per the author's observations throughout the year). Frequency reports of coded behaviors in the videos demonstrated increased levels of on task behavior, engagement and peer interaction for all classes. The results for each class period were consistent with outside observer field notes and the behavior the instructor was familiar with for those classes also. Videos were also qualitatively analyzed noting student-student versus student-teacher interactions. Student-student interactions greatly outnumbered student-teacher interactions in these video portions that also agreed with the field notes of outside observers.

The design of this study possessed a balance between challenge and frustration and induced a flow state in the learners (Csikszentmihalyi, 1990). The end goal was clear and learners were able to focus on the end products as well as deal with the hindrances. The learners became completely involved in the activity because they were presented with a challenge, were able to set goals, had structured control and were provided with clear feedback. The learners were in a "flow state" and became clearly motivated. The game fostered play and produced a state of flow, therefore increasing learning and fostering motivation. The magic circle (Huizinga, 1955) was instrumental in the students' learning during this study.

Many of today's learners tend to feel the pressure to succeed and become very concerned with whatever grade they might attain on a particular activity. During the study, one of the students became very concerned about whether or not there would be a test at the culmination of the unit and even requested that he be given a test anyway. In contrast the bulk of the study participants seemed to be relieved that there was no "grade" for the various levels and to know that they were free to play.

The learners were in the magic circle while playing within the levels of the game and thus realized that it was permissible to risk with the possibility of failure easily overcome. Conequently, the *Chutes and Ladders* game design was modified so that "failure" would not, as Sylvester (2013) points out, "punish the player " (p. 78). Instead we wanted to encourage the students to collectively succeed at each level no matter how long it took. Within the magic circle of this particular game ("Cells and Body Systems the *Chutes and Ladders* Way") the players could try again and experiment with the results in each level as much as they wanted to. It was all right to fail. We designed the game so that it would foster collaboration within the team members. The learners were able to escape the fear of risk and failure while greatly increasing the opportunities for learning.

SOLUTIONS AND RECOMMENDATIONS

Implications

Wilson and Cole (1992) describe eight basic strategies for the use of elaboration theory in designing instruction: single organizing structure, simple-to-complex organization, within lesson sequencing, summarizers, synthesizers, analogies, cognitive strategy activators, and learner control. These are generally the strategies used by K-12 educators in design of instruction, even if many educators may not be willing to give up control to the learner. Recently this trend is beginning to reverse with the advent of problem-based learning scenarios integrated into instructional delivery. When learner control of instruction is coupled with serious games and simulations in the classroom, learning outcomes can be increased.

The game design strategy used for this unit worked very well within the sphere of elaboration theory. Content for this unit (cells and body systems) had a *single organizing structure* that demonstrated the objectives for the content. Content to be covered had a *simple –to-complex organization*. Content was covered with the sequence beginning at the most basic concepts (cells and cellular processes) and progressed through the students developing understandings of the most complex systems (unique body systems and epidemics). There should also be a specific sequencing within lessons.

Quizzes and group presentations acted as *summarizers* for each of the levels. Student generated *synthesizers* were used as content organizers and were usually in diagram form so that learners could aid each other in visualizing the content. Students often used analogies to relate their own prior knowledge to the new content. *Cognitive strategy activators* (diagrams, flow charts, etc.) were also generated by the learners when they were visualizing a concept. Instruction involved *learner control* so that all learning was personalized. Reigeluth and Stein (1983) state that instruction is more effective if the learner has control over both content and instructional strategy.

This game-like design strategy also met the seven basic requirements for a learning environment (Houser & Deloach, 1998):

1. **High Intensity of Interaction and Feedback:** Learners were able to work in cooperative groups and interact with each other in completion of levels. During the activity, outside observers as well as the researcher noted that the students would help other members of their group to study and review content in order to pass the exit quizzes.
2. **Specific Goals and Established Procedures:** The game-like environment had a set structure and rules that provided guidelines within which to 'play' the game.
3. **Motivation:** It was also noted in field notes that students were quite excited when they were able to advance from one level to the next, which in turn provided motivation.
4. **Continual Feeling of Challenge That Was Not Too Frustrating or Too Boring:** Students felt challenge in that they thought it necessary to review with each other before taking an exit quiz but they also were not bored. Observers noted on checklists that the students were highly engaged with and interested in the material.
5. **Provides Direct Engagement So That the Learner Is Always on Task and Interacting with the Environment:** Checklists indicated high to very high levels related to engagement and student-student interaction. Video that was coded for student-student and student-teacher interaction showed almost twice as many student-student interactions as student-teacher.

6. **Provides Tools and Tasks to Fit the User and Not Distract:** The activity was designed using a game-like design strategy resembling something the students were familiar with (*Chutes and Ladders*). The activity did not distract because the students were familiar with the rules of that particular game.
7. **Distractions and Disruptions Are Avoided in Order Not to Disrupt the Subjective Experience:** Students did not become unnecessarily distracted during the game, which in turn lessened the disruptions and enabled them to focus on the activity.

Because these seven requirements for creating a learning environment were met by the 'game' play it was so much fun for the students that the learning in the play was effectively masked.

FUTURE RESEARCH DIRECTIONS

Results of this research demonstrated the value of using games and simulations in the classroom. Games can increase motivation and content engagement. When instructional delivery is centered on a game-based design strategy an increase in learning outcomes can be observed.

The study results provide substantiation as to why there is a need for this type of innovative instructional design. However, educators need to be willing to give more control over the learning process to the learner so that motivation, engagement, and learning outcomes can increase. Because the use of game-like design and simulations can aid in the acquisition of science content and increase learning outcomes, a new direction can be added to current professional development practices for K-12 educators. Including this type of professional development in the K-12 arena can only add to the repertoire teachers currently have at their disposal for motivating students and increasing learning outcomes. Once teachers understand how to implement this type of game-like design for the classroom (no matter the content area), they can adapt it to their own teaching style and classroom environment.

It should be noted that there is a tradeoff between sequence and pacing. Using a game-based design strategy centers the curriculum on the learner who determines the pace. Nonetheless, implementing this type of curriculum design increases gains in student performance. Students are able to interact with the content given their own unique learning styles and at their own pace. However, because the acquisition of the content is learner-centered this type of instructional design strategy can take more time within the traditional classroom environment. Educators must be willing to give up some control over the timeline for instruction in order to increase learning outcomes. During the school year following this implementation the instructor designed an additional game-based unit. This second unit became very time intensive and required revision and restructuring in order to work well within the time constraints of the school year.

CONCLUSION

In order to advance 21st century skills in today's learners, designing instruction by using a game-based design strategy aids in achieving learning outcomes. Games teach higher order thinking skills whether the game is computer-based or not. Using a game-based instructional design strategy gives the learner control over the instructional process while engaging them with content. The result is a higher degree of focus and engagement, which increases motivation. When motivation is increased, learning outcomes also increase. We have had experience with the deployment of the game-based design strategy not only in STEM based content such as biology, chemistry, and geology but also West Virginia History.

However, this chapter also deals with some of the concerns we experienced with implementing a game-based design strategy in the classroom. There were two issues with the game design approach to instruction.

First, game mechanics can be difficult to design (Sylvester, 2013). The approach we took was rather simple, in that the major game mechanic was for the students to move between levels by passing a goal requirement. They fulfilled this requirement by taking a quiz. Upon reaching a pre-determined level the group would be allowed to move forward. This "real-world" activity was crucial to the design of the game in contrast to a gamification strategy, which uses game elements (badges, points, scores) within a "non-game situation" such as earning points every time you shop at the grocery store. Because "Cells and Body Systems the *Chutes and Ladders* Way" was delivered as a game, this real-world element was not viewed as a "test" by the students but as an obstacle for the team to overcome. This understanding created a space for the students to experiment, to try and even to fail. Given different learning objectives or a more sophisticated world narrative the game mechanics would require a greater design commitment. For example, you might have a richer game world narrative such as the Hero's journey where the Hero would have to perform certain tasks along the way in order to advance through the game.

The second major issue is with the delivery time. Because the game was "self-paced" it took more time to implement the game in the classroom. The students and their groups were responsible to move the teams forward, which took much more time than the normal didactic approach. However as the data indicates the tradeoff was well worth it. The classes maintained participation and were cognitively engaged. Consequently, this design strategy has a tremendous potential to change how we teach science and other content areas in the modern classroom.

REFERENCES

Ahern, T. C. (2002). Learning by design: Engineering the learned state. In N. Callaos & W. Lesso (Eds.), *6th World Multiconference in Systemics, Cybernetics and Informatics* (pp. 308-313). Orlando, FL: International Institute of Informatics and Systemics.

Ahern, T. C. (2009, October). Bridging the gap: Cognitive scaffolding to improve computer programming for middle school teachers. In *Frontiers in Education Conference, 2009. FIE'09. 39th IEEE* (pp. 1-5). IEEE.

Alfieri, L., Brooks, P. J., Aldrich, N. J., & Tenenbaum, H. R. (2011). Does discovery-based instruction enhance learning? *Journal of Educational Psychology, 103*(1).

Ames, C. (1992). Classrooms: Goals, structures, and student motivation. *Journal of Educational Psychology, 84*(3), 261–271.

Beesley, A., Clark, T., Barker, J., Germeroth, C., & Apthorp, H. (2010). Expeditionary learning schools: Theory of action and literature review of motivation, character, and engagement. *Mid-continent Research for Education and Learning (McREL).*

Belew, R. K. (1990). Evolution, learning, and culture: Computational metaphors for adaptive algorithms. *Complex Systems*, *4*(1), 11–49.

Brown, A. L. (1992). Design experiments: Theoretical and methodological challenges in creating complex interventions in classroom settings. *Journal of the Learning Sciences*, *2*(2), 141–178. doi:10.1207/s15327809jls0202_2

Bruner, J. S. (1966). *Toward a theory of instruction* (Vol. 59). Harvard University Press.

Catrambone, R. (1998). The subgoal learning model: Creating better examples so that students can solve novel problems. *Journal of Experimental Psychology. General*, *127*(4), 355–376. doi:10.1037/0096-3445.127.4.355

Chutes and Ladders [board game]. (2005). New York: Hasbro Toy Co.

Csikszentmihalyi, M. (1990). *Flow*. New York: Harper and Row.

Davies, M. (2009). *Examining game pace: How single player levels tick* [online] Gamasutra article. Retrieved from http://www.gamasutra.com/view/feature/4024/examining_game_pace_how_.php

Dewey, J. (1963). *Experience and Education*. Collier Books.

Heibert, J., & Stigler, J. W. (2004). A world of difference: Classrooms abroad provide lesson in teaching math and science. *Journal of Staff Development*, *24*(4), 10–15.

Houser, R., & Deloach, S. (1998). Learning from games: Seven principles of effective Design. *Technical Communication: Journal of the Society for Technical Communication*, *45*(3), 319–329.

Huizinga, J. (1955). *Homo Ludens: A Study of the Play-elememt in Culture*. Beacon Press.

Klopfer, E., Osterweil, S., & Salen, K. (2009). *Moving learning games forward*. Academic Press.

Lamorisse, A. (1995). *RISK: The game of global domination*. Pawtucket, RI: Hasbro Brands.

Malone, T. W., & Lepper, M. R. (1987). Making learning fun: A taxonomy of intrinsic motivations for learning. *Aptitude, Learning, and Instruction*, *3*(1987), 223-253.

Reigeluth, C., & Stein, R. (1983). Elaboration theory. *Instructional-design theories and models: An overview of their current status*, 335-381.

Salen, K., & Zimmerman, E. (2003). *Rules of play: Game design fundamentals*. Cambridge, MA: MIT press.

Sandoval, W. A., & Bell, P. (2004). Design-based research methods for studying learning in context: Introduction. *Educational Psychologist*, *39*(4), 199–201. doi:10.1207/s15326985ep3904_1

Schilling, D. R. (2013). *Knowledge doubling every 12 months, Soon to be every 12 hours. Industry tap into news*. Retrieved from http://www.industrytap.com/knowledge-doubling-every-12-months-soon-to-be-every-12-hours/3950

Schwartz, D. L., Chase, C. C., Oppezzo, M. A., & Chin, D. B. (2011). Practicing versus inventing with contrasting cases: The effects of telling first on learning and transfer. *Journal of Educational Psychology*, *103*(4), 759–775. doi:10.1037/a0025140

StarLogo [computer program]. (2005). *MIT Scheller Teacher Education Program*. Cambridge, MA: MIT University. Available at http://education.mit.edu/portfolio_page/starlogo-tng/

Sylvester, T. (2013). *Designing games: A guide to engineering experiences*. Sebastopol, CA: O'Reilly Media, Inc.

Tondello, G. (2015). *The use of games and play to achieve real-world goals*. Gamification Research Network. Retrieved from http://gamification-research.org/2015/06/the-use-of-games-and-play-to-achieve-real-world-goals/#sthash.7IZaAkdn.dpuf/

Venturelli, M., & Studio, K. (2009). *Space of possibility and pacing in casual game design–A Pop Cap case study*. Paper presented at VII Brazilian Symposium on Games and Digital Entertainment, Rio de Janeriro. Retrieved from http://www.sbgames.org/papers/sbgames09/artanddesign/60345.pdf

West Virginia Department of Education. (2015). *Eighth grade science objectives*. Retrieved from http://wveis.k12.wv.us/Teach21/public/cso/popUp.cfm

Wilson, B., & Cole, P. (1992). A critical review of elaboration theory. *Educational Technology Research and Development*, *40*(3), 63–79. doi:10.1007/BF02296843

KEY TERMS AND DEFINITIONS

Curriculum: Instructional activities and content within a course.

Design Model: Within instructional design, helps to visualize a design problem by breaking it down into smaller manageable parts.

Game Mechanics: Rules or methods designed for interaction while playing a game.

Pacing: The rate at which instructional activities occur.

Sequencing: Designing instruction so that the material is in the proper order for the learner.

Chapter 15
Jamming Econo:
The Phenomenon of Perspectival Shifts in Indie Video Games

Keri Duncan Valentine
West Virginia University, USA

Lucas John Jensen
Georgia Southern University, USA

ABSTRACT

By their nature, video games create perspectival relationships between the game space, with its mechanics, characters, etc. and their players. Perspectival mechanics in games like Monument Valley *and* Fez *require one to simultaneously transform the environment, the objects in the environment, and one's egocentric reference frames, illustrating the complex nature intrinsic to video game spaces. The authors seek to investigate the ways perspectival mechanics in video games are both created and experienced using postphenomenological inquiry. This investigation is situated within the indie genre of games in particular, a context where these mechanics are intentionally being explored. In addition, this chapter draws parallels between indie games and indie music, contexts where boundary pushing is the norm. In addition to explicating the phenomenon of perspectival shifts in indie games, the authors review research related to spatial thinking, conjecturing affordances of indie games as geometric gifts, possibly well positioned to support spatial thinking.*

INTRODUCTION

However humble their origins in *Tennis for Two* (Higinbotham, 1958) and *Pong* (Atari Inc., 1972), video games have always offered a diverse range of player experiences, ranging from simple motor coordination games like *Pong* or *Asteroids* (Atari Inc., 1979) to text adventures like *Zork* (Infocom, 1977) and social online multi-user dungeons (MUDs), ASCII dungeon-crawling "rogues," and protean polygonal flight simulators. Over time, the diversity of genre under the rubric of "video games" has expanded. These old models – many of which endure – have been supplanted or modified into a whole host of genres and

DOI: 10.4018/978-1-5225-0261-6.ch015

subgenres, from massive multiplayer online (MMO) games like *World of Warcraft* (Blizzard Entertainment, 2004) to open-world exploration role-playing games like *The Elder Scrolls V: Skyrim* (Bethesda Game Studios, 2011). Simulated first person games like the *Bard's Tale* (Interplay Productions, 1985) and the Wizardry series begat current high fidelity first person shooters (FPSs) like *Far Cry 4* (Ubisoft Montreal, 2014) and *Call of Duty* (Infinity Ward, 2003). Two-dimensional (2D) side-scrolling platformer series, such as *Super Mario Bros.* (Nintendo, 1985), now exist in three-dimensional (3D) games like the planet-hopping, gravity-defying *Super Mario Galaxy* (Nintendo, 2007). Each one of these newer games might have features that were difficult in the early years of gaming: multiple game mechanics, varied challenges and goals, accommodation of flexible play styles, higher-resolution graphics, branching storylines, and mutable perspectives, to name a few. The convergence of these features of newer, complex games form the player's experience, wherein early games this was often from a mechanical perspective, featuring limited movement, actions, and player goals. For example, an early dungeon crawling shooter like *Berserk* (Yuke's Media Creations, 2004) might feature movement in eight directions and a limitation of one bullet at a time. This is quite simple compared to a supposedly simple, newer dungeon-crawler like *Diablo III* (Blizzard Entertainment, 2012), which features multiple menus and uses an entire keyboard or game controller to play. Obviously this comparison is stilted; this tiny list only scratches the surface of game genres available to current players, but it should serve to demonstrate the varied experiences one might encounter in the video game play space.

In this chapter, we explore perspectival shift in video games as both cultural signifier and video game mechanic, with a particular focus on current experimental and non-dogmatic use within the *indie,* short for independent, game development space. According to postphenomenologist Don Ihde, a perspectival shift is an ""extension" of perceptual and bodily intentionality into the smaller and larger "worlds" which were revealed through science and its instruments" (1993, p. 3). These traditional instruments and tools might be a microscope, telescope, compass, or a high-speed camera affording viewers alternate glimpses of time. Ihde notes that our perceptions are mediated by these instruments, referring to them as mediating technologies (1993). An example includes looking through a telescope to view the surface of the moon. Although we view the same moon we might see with the naked eye, the telescope shifts both our access to detail and the moon's size relative to the vast sky. With these technologies, our world becomes embodied differently, affording perspectival shifts.

Video games might possess the ability to be such a mediating technology, allowing players to engage with spatial relationships through the shifting and exploration of unique perspectives. Shifting and controlling player perspectives is a huge concern in the development of video games, which often changes as game design and development progresses. The Halo series started as a third-person game before settling on the first-person point-of-view (POV) for which it is known. The aforementioned "AAA" games – referring to games supported by large budgets and wide mainstream publicity and promotion – feature perspectival game mechanics, usually centered on the level of player camera movement and control, as well as what the player sees in the environment. Within each one of these game experiences lies a unique perspective or POV – whether technical, narrative, or spatial. Throughout time, most AAA developers might include a few compelling or unique game mechanics in larger games that involve the manipulation of perspective, but, besides the rare example of a perspective-shifting game like *Portal* (Valve Corporation, 2007) from popular game developer, publisher, and retailer Valve, most major perspective shifts happen incrementally. However, a major jump in video games happened during the transition from the Super Nintendo and Genesis generation to the era of CD-Roms, the Playstation, the Nintendo 64, and early 3D games, requiring a reworking of controllers and an expansion of game mechanics into the brave new world of the third dimension, which had mostly been simulated before in the isometric perspectives of 2.5D real time strategy games or the flat first-person dungeon-crawling of the *Wizardry* series and *The Bard's Tale* (Interplay Productions, 1985).

A good example of this kind of radical shift in video game perspectives can be traced through the history of Nintendo's venerated Mario series of platformers, mentioned above. This series has seen radical player perspectival shifts over time, such that one glimpse at an old game might bear little resemblance to a newer game, however similar the ultimate goal of saving poor Princess Peach by bonking turtles and sentient mushrooms on the head. The transformation has evolved from the always-move-right 2D world of *Super Mario Bros.* (Nintendo, 1985) to the trail-blazing 3D world of *Super Mario 64* (Nintendo, 1996); from the mini-planets of *Super Mario Galaxy* (Nintendo, 2007) to the mixed 2D/3D papercraft of the Paper Mario series. Nintendo took chances with the perspectives of their top-selling Mario series, and these experiments in perspective and POV, however slowly they happened over decades, gave the series a reputation for uniqueness and innovation, especially where perspective is concerned. Rather than be a liability, this perspective manipulation remains a commercial commodity for the series; however, Mario's *raison d'etre* is not its unique perspectives, but exploring new possibilities for its platforming mechanics around these. Even while central to the player experience, these perspectival shifting mechanics are still smaller parts of the larger whole of block-busting, traveling through pipes, and collecting coins.

Recently, the indie video game arena, bolstered by less expensive design and development tools and the democratization of gaming platforms, has emerged as a place where video games can challenge and shift typical video game perspectives, whether "perspective" means narrative, point-of-view, camera angle, or some combination of the three. Often this shifting of perspective becomes the central mechanic of the game itself, rather than a mere part of the whole. In this chapter, we trace the similarity of the recent phase of indie video game design and development to the rise of punk rock, indie rock, and the DIY movement. Three indie video games – *Fez, Proteus,* and *Monument Valley* – will be the focus of this chapter, but many other games in the indie video game sphere, such as *Portal* (Valve Corporation, 2007), *Antichamber* (Bruce, 2013), and *Shadowmatic* (Triada Studio Games, 2015), also play with perspective in ways that could not exist outside of video games. By connecting this subset of perspective-shifting games to indie music movements, we attempt to find parallels in how these games shift perspectives to the ways in which indie culture, musically, shifted perspectives by challenging the sounds and business practices of the so-called "major labels," which were seen as profit-driven corporate exercises. Just like fanzines and indie labels challenged print media and music industry orthodoxy, indie games have the commercial and artistic freedom to challenge the dominant perspectival paradigms of mainstream AAA games.

We end by examining the affordances of these perspectival-shifting mechanics in educational settings. Video games, with their unique and challenging perspectives and perspectival mechanics, may be viewed as "geometrical gifts for our day" (Banchoff, 1990, p. 14). *Fez* (Polytron Corporation, 2012) and *Super Paper Mario* (Intelligent Systems, 2007), for example, might *teach* players about navigating between the second and third dimensions. Similarly, a game like *Monument Valley* (Ustwo, 2014) may become a manipulative to consider ways to conceptualize higher dimensions, like the fourth. Throughout, we highlight experiences and observations accrued over years of working with video game design and development youth programs as well as mathematics education. One particular example highlighted in the chapter is the experience of Alistar, a student who used video games as a way to mediate new understandings about dimensionality. Video games were the first media to which he turned when he needed to further understand the story of *Flatland: A Romance of Many Dimensions* (Abbott, 1884/1991), which introduced these concepts to him. These interactions with young learners have opened our eyes, so to speak, to video games' unique ability to engage with visual perspectives.

POSTPHENOMENOLOGY

Before delving deeper into these issues, here is a note on the authors' theoretical and methodological perspectives. This chapter approaches data via postphenomenological inquiry, seeking to open up the phenomenon of perspectival shifts related to unique visual affordances of video games (allowing gamers to uniquely take on and shift various points of view and visual perspectives). Postphenomenology refers to a form of phenomenological inquiry which involves investigating embodied and cultural/historical ways of experiencing phenomena in the world. Rather than describe or even interpret in a finalizing way, all is brought forth in an attempt to understand and make meaning of the phenomenon in the variety of ways it manifests. This includes explicating the contexts where phenomena occur, in this case, the social, cultural, and historical contexts of indie movements generally and indie game movements specifically. The unit of analysis is the variant manifestations of the phenomenon revealed through intentionalit(ies) – plural to indicate the inherent partialities, variants, and multiplicities of post inquiry. Intentionality in phenomenology is not to be confused with the English meaning of the term, such as an action on the part of humans (e.g., intending to mow the lawn on Sunday). Rather, intentionality is akin to a connective tissue in and among contexts, humans, non-humans, etc. In this sense, it is more analogous to the Chinese term *Chi*, an invisible force connecting the universe.

According to phenomenologist van Manen (1990), "the aim of phenomenology" is to create, similar to the act of a painter, an action on the part of the reader (or viewer) whereby "the effect of the text is at once a reflexive re-living and a reflective appropriation of something meaningful: a notion by which a reader is powerfully animated in his or her own lived experience" (p. 36). The presentation of phenomenological data can take many forms, as there is not a singular, accepted technique. Rather, the researcher, according to Vagle (2010), "should feel free to play with form, bringing all that you have (from the data, the [reflexive] journal, other readings, other theories, other philosophies) to bear" (p. 22). For this chapter, phenomenological data include, but are not limited to, players' experiences, descriptions of game play related to perspectival mechanics, documentaries portraying the designer and developers' perspectives on designing indie games, connections to educational perspectives on spatial learning, and social/cultural/historical insights into the broader indie context.

PERSPECTIVAL VARIATIONS IN VIDEO GAMES

Video games feature a wealth of unique player perspectives and points of view. These include two-dimensional games, often seen in top-down and side-scrolling (view from the side) games. The time-honored side-scrolling *Super Mario Bros* (Nintendo, 1985) game exists in what is commonly known as the 2D perspective, wherein a fixed camera follows Mario and scrolls right, with back and forth movement added in later iterations of the series. The graphics are flat sprite art, so the illusion of depth is given by placing objects behind one another in layers. Most early video games employed this perspective, and it remains popular today, even though many 2D games, such as the New Super Mario Bros series, use 3D art assets. Even though most films are technically "2D" we can perceive the third dimension in them, as opposed to most 2D games, which flatten this depth of field

Three-dimensional perspective categories include the first-person, which takes place from the viewpoint of the character, and third-person, behind or angled above the character. First person games are popular with so-called "shooters," like the Call of Duty or Bioshock series. The first person perspective is now employed whenever an immersive perspective is needed, so it also shows up in more experimental narrative games like *Dear Esther* (The Chinese Room, 2012), *Everybody's Gone to the Rapture* (The Chinese Room & SCE Santa Monica Studio, 2015), and *Gone Home* (Fullbright, 2013). Third person perspectives are dominant in games where the player's appearance is a part of the story or when the player needs to grasp the character's relationship in space to play properly.

Video games offer a number of other unique perspectives, such as that of 2.5-dimensional (2.5D), often called a *three-quarters* or *isometric perspective* and are prevalent in a genre of PC games called real-time strategy games (RTSs) like *Command & Conquer* (Westwood Studios, 1995) and RPGs like the Diablo series. In 2.5D game environments, the character's point of view is fixed in conjunction with techniques such as isometric projection and billboarding, revealing aspects of the environment not possible with top-down or side views. This 2.5D perspective was born of early game developer's attempts to create three-dimensional space without the graphical technological prowess at the time.

These attempts to create unique perspectives by game designers go well back to video games' 2D roots. Even in their infancy, 2D games employed a variety of player perspectives in an attempt to escape the flatness and X and Y limitations of the perspective. These included top-down perspectives like *Frogger* (Konami, 1981) and *Dig Dug II* (Namco, 1985), to fixed two-dimensional games like *Space Invaders* (Taito, 1978), to side-scrollers, like *Donkey Kong* (Nintendo, 1981) and *Pac-Man* (Namco, 1980), to wrapped two-dimensional play spaces like *Asteroids* (Atari Inc., 1979). Quickly, innovative arcade games like *Star Wars Arcade* (Sega Interactive, 1993) and *Battlezone* (Atari Inc., 1980) featured first person perspectives, and Sega's *Zaxxon* (Sega, 1982) used an isometric perspective to simulate battling through three-dimensional space. These attempts, however rudimentary they might have been, showed that video game designers, who often came from large developers and publishers like Atari, Sega, and Nintendo, were willing to push the boundaries of perspective in their games.

In today's video game world, informed by years of progress in game design, development tools, and technological capability, video games offer a pantheon of perspectives, many of which cannot be replicated in other media. Even though 2D games remain quite in vogue, exemplified in indie successes such as *Braid* (Number None, Inc., 2008), *Shovel Knight* (Yacht Club Games, 2014), and *Risk of Rain* (Hopoo Games, 2013), video games now offer the full breadth of perspectives available to players, and designers and developers must choose the perspective carefully to affect player immersion. The control of the camera, and with it the perspective itself, has developed as game mechanic and a means of understanding the game world. In today's complex games, players can shoot, roll, jump, solve mysteries, fall in love, play mixtapes, and build giant castles, even in the first person perspective, which used to be limited to simplistic tile-based movements. In the first person game *Far Cry 4* (Ubisoft Montreal, 2014), one might choose to look straight forward the entire time, or use the manipulation of the first person camera – in a sense *looking around* – and use it to stargaze, watch the nights turn to days, and watch out for danger on the horizon. Looking around helps the player discover enemies to avoid, plants to collect, and animals to hunt.

This is not to say that similar feats cannot be accomplished in the third person perspective, popular with 3D action-adventure games, where manipulations of the player's view and perspective of the game world is an essential part of understanding and exploring them. The amount of player control over the camera depends on the game, ranging from an omniscient to over-shoulder perspective. Camera control gives players agency over their perspective for smoother gameplay. In the Super Mario Galaxy series, the Batman: Arkham series, or the recent entries in Grand Theft Auto, the player is in charge of the camera, centering it behind the character or swooping it around them to see chasing enemies. *Grand Theft Auto IV* and *V* (Rockstar North, 2008, 2013) even include a *cinematic* view for use when driving vehicles in which the camera films the player's car (or helicopter, blimp, motorcycle, etc.) from a variety of prescribed angles, quickly edited in the vein of a Hollywood action movie. The camera can be presented as a character or participant in the game, such as the gloating Lakitu cloud that holds the camera in *Super Mario 64* (Nintendo, 1996), who is presented as filming the action, possibly there to cover up the rudimentary camera control in this early 3D game.

Camera control can be used as a puzzle itself, notably employed in the Batman: Arkham series, where the player must manipulate the camera around Batman to complete anamorphic question marks left by supervillain The Riddler. These green question marks are painted across buildings and, like the warped skull in Hans Holbein's *The Ambassadors* (1533) or 3D sidewalk chalk drawings, appear skewed and distended when viewed from the wrong perspective. They come together when the player both stands in the correct position and manipulates the camera correctly. Anamorphosis, relevant to *Monument Valley,* which will be discussed later, is a unique perspective more easily offered by video games than painting and drawing.

Perspective control, by both the designers and players, can have an effect on the game narrative and how the player perceives their own character. A good example is *Metroid Prime* (Nintendo, 2002), a first-person exploration adventure game from Retro Studios in Nintendo's long-running and venerated series. The player, as bounty hunter Samus Aran, feels the humanity of the character through occasional flashes of her face in the glass, lighting up her eyes to remind the character that she is still a human. This is also a call back to an earlier "shocking" moment in the Metroid series, when Samus Aran was revealed to be a woman at the end of *Metroid* (Nintendo, 1986), challenging player's assumptions that a robot-suited bounty hunter in space would automatically be male. *Metroid Prime* also limits the camera movement within the first person perspective, constraining the POV – in contrast to the wild contortionists of most first-person shooter (FPS) lead characters – to remind the player that she is in a suit to which she is dependent and attached, removing some of her humanity. This use of perspective in *Metroid Prime* actually reflects some of the thematic undercurrent of the game, as well as the entire series, that Samus Aran is torn between being an empathetic human – albeit one raised by ancient bird people! – and a solitary robotic killer (Totilo, 2015).

The use of the first person is a good example of the difference in perspective uses between video games and other media, in particular its absence from movies. Movies rarely feature sequences in the first person through the eyes of a character – with Alfonso Cuarón's *Gravity* (2013) being a notable recent exception, and even then for a few minutes of the running time. Until the boom in found footage horror movies in the post-*Blair Witch Project* (Hale, Cowie, Myrick, & Sánchez, 1999) movie landscape (e.g. *Chronicle* (Davis, Schroeder, & Trank, 2012), *[Rec]* (Fernández, Balagueró & Plaza, 2007), and *Cloverfield* (Abrams, Burk, & Reeves, 2008)), the first person perspective had failed at the box office, with Robert Montgomery's infamous flop Phillip Marlowe adaptation, *Lady in the Lake* (1947), being one of the only attempts at an entirely first person movie.

This is quite the contrast with video games, where the first person is not only employed, but is one of the most popular perspectives deployed in video games, across a wide spectrum of game development.

Even indie studios are making use of it, often in decidedly noncommercial ways. The aforementioned *Gone Home* (Fullbright, 2013), a completely violence-free game, employs the first person perspective to tell the story of a troubled time in the player's family through the exploration of a deserted house and an examination of the objects wherein. Were it not developed by Fullbright, an indie studio, the chances of this game getting made would be slim. With the rise of independent (indie) game developers, comes a range of experimentation with innovative game mechanics attending to perspectival concerns. Rather than continue to propagate the AAA game space's reliance on the latest technological innovations (e.g., graphic processors, horsepower) and complex mechanics and sprawling worlds, indie games, sometimes by virtue of fiscal, time, and technological constraints, focus on refining and exploring central ideas, stories, or game mechanics. The three games discussed in more detail later – *Fez* (Polytron Corporation, 2012), *Proteus* (Key & Kanaga, 2013), and *Monument Valley* (Ustwo, 2014) – all attempt to innovate and challenge ideas of perspective while employing relatively simple mechanics and aesthetics, if not simple designs.

JAMMING ECONO: THE INDIE PHENOMENON

In order to properly contextualize why so many indie games challenge current video game design and development paradigms, it is important to examine the indie movement as a whole. The origins of indie as a cultural movement are phenomena in and of themselves and more of a reaction to cultural boundaries and norms, particularly with relation to traditional corporate capitalism. Moving away from monetary concerns meant greater freedom of expression. In the 1950s and 1960s, for example, some artists, writers, musicians, and film-makers sought to work outside mainstream distribution practices, elitist/educational barriers, and/or monetary foci. Oakes (2009) writes:

In both the fifties and sixties, being an artist no longer meant that you needed training, education, or patronage. As Frank O'Hara described his own impulse to write, "going on your nerve" meant making art because you wanted to, and making it in your own way. By creating and following that dictum, the independent artists of that time created the blueprint for indie culture today. (p. 21)

"Jamming econo" is a phrase used by Minutemen band member Mike Watt to describe the do-it-yourself (DIY) culture of early independent punk rock music in the United States. Departing from extravagant arena venues and massive tour vans/airplanes, the Minutemen handled their own "recording, touring, promoting, and making music" on the cheap (Oakes, 2009, p. 46), econo being both a reference to Ford Econoline vans that were popular with punk bands as well as adhering to tight economic constraints. Hardcore and punk bands such as Black Flag, Minutemen, the Descendents, and Minor Threat, played all manner of venues, often to violent crowds, selling merchandise out of the back of their van, barely breaking even on the balance sheets (Azerrad, 2012; Dunn, 2012; Rollins, 2004). However begrudgingly these artists operated within a capitalist system to sustain their recording and touring, profit was not the primary motive for these bands, whose songs and images spoke to anti-consumer and anti-capitalist ideals (Azerrad, 2012; Duncombe, 2014; Moore, 2004; Rollins, 2004). These bands were often challenging authority, but in a way a bit grittier and rawer than the original "punks" like the Ramones, Suicide, and The Clash, whose music appeared on major labels with fairly high fidelity production values (Azerrad, 2012, 2014; Duncombe, 2014). These punks took the more tuneful proto-punk of their forebears and sped it up, filtering it through increasingly grinding, shredding heavy metal; these records were often recorded in "lo-fi" or low fidelity, noisy recordings borne of monetary necessity, an attempt to capture the raw energy of the live show, or some combination of both (Azerrad, 2012; Duncombe, 2014; Triggs, 2006). All of this stood in stark reaction to what they perceived as the slick, produced sounds of disco, synth pop, funk, and modern country, analogous to the homogeneity of consumerism and corporate culture (Azerrad, 2012; Dunn, 2012; Moore, 2004; Triggs, 2006).

It must be noted that for all of their association with left-wing and radical politics, the punk and DIY movements were largely made up of white, disaffected middle class youth (Duncombe, 2014). Some of this opposition to music like disco and funk made for diverse audiences, often by African-Americans, bringing forth some occasional, uncomfortable elbow-rubbing with sexism and white supremacy (Azerrad, 2012; Duncombe, 2014; Dunn, 2012; Moore, 2004; Raha, 2005). Even so, out of this movement featured acts like Bad Brains, Sonic Youth, X-Ray Spex, The Slits, and more who challenged this racial and gender paradigm (Azerrad, 2012; Duncombe, 2014; Marcus, 2010; Moore, 2004; Raha, 2005).

The rise of DIY and punk culture, however, was more than just hardcore punk bands criss-crossing the country in vans, though certainly the music was a major impetus behind the movement. Many of these bands founded independent record labels, like members of Minor Threat and Dischord Records or The Dead Kennedys and Alternative Tentacles (Azerrad, 2012; Duncombe, 2014). Independent labels – typically meaning labels not owned by major media conglomerates – have existed for decades. Early independent labels like Motown, Stax, Atlantic, Kama Sutra Records, and Chess, many of them responsible for decades of legendary music, were still chasing much of the same audiences as the major labels (Azerrad, 2012; George, 2003; Gulla, 2008). By the 1970s, many of these had been subsumed as imprints of major labels or gone out of business, though a number of independent funk, R&B, disco, and dance labels soldiered on, and regional labels like Twin/Tone, dB, and 99 appeared by the late 70s (Azerrad, 2012; George, 2003; Gulla, 2008).

What distinguished punk labels like SST and Dischord – and later Kill Rock Stars, K, and Touch and Go – was that they were founded, ostensibly, on a ethos of doing things differently than major labels, with the profit motive secondary to ethical and political concerns, as well as building a community (Azerrad, 2012, 2014; Duncombe, 2014; Triggs, 2006). Punk rock labels, and punk rock culture in general, embraced notions of authenticity in the face of corporate slickness, and "selling out," whether taking corporate money from a major label or even a nod toward musical accessibility, was frowned upon (Duncombe, 2014; Moore, 2004). Krist Novelic of the hyper-popular rock band Nirvana, itself a product of indie label Sub Pop Records, was influenced by early punk rock (Azerrad, 2014). He notes that, despite some punk conformists, the idea of punk rock was built around a diversity of sounds and no musical orthodoxy was more important, as evidenced by the punk Neil Young-esque hybrid Meat Puppets on Black Flag's label SST (Azerrad, 2012, 2014).

This diversification of indie sounds continued throughout the 1980s and 1990, when an explosion of indie labels such as Matador, Beggars Banquet, Merge, Touch and Go, Drag City, Thrill Jockey, and Sub Pop Records, to name a very few, broadened the definition of indie beyond punk rock and subgenres like underground dance and hip-hop into experimental music, free jazz, lo-fi garage rock, and more. By the end of the 70s, however, "indie rock," for better or worse, became associated with a sound, usually guitar-driven and white male-lead (Wilson, 2015). Still, many of these bands refused to play by the rules of tradition, as prototypical indie rock bands like Pavement, Sebadoh, the Grifters, Archers of Loaf, and Guided by Voices eschewed slick music videos and hi-fi production.

The Indie Video Game Movement

There are a number of parallels between the development of DIY, punk, and indie culture and the recent ascendance of indie video games. Similar to jamming econo, is the idea of going at it alone and designing a video game as part of a small team or even as one person, such as with Jonathan Blow's design of *Braid* (Number None, Inc., 2008), one of the more popular early games in the recent indie game resurgence. This kind of freedom to create with limited resources was difficult, to say nothing of the lack of distribution channels, but cheaper and more open technological tools, much like the lo-fi recording tools preferred by so many punk and indie artists, have made it a possibility. According to Ron Carmel, developer of the *World of Goo* (2D Boy, 2008), the increase of indie games is related to "the rise of digital distribution" (Pajot & Swirsky, 2012). He recounts this shift in distribution practices for video games instigated by the company Valve:

It used to be that retailers had a lot of power over every game creation company because that was the only avenue available to sell games and so nobody was willing to start distributing games digitally because Wal-Mart would get upset at them and they wouldn't take their products off the shelf and nothing would happen. But Valve changed that when they came out with Steam. They had no loyalties to retail and so they just did it and then after that everybody else said, 'well, we have to compete with them' and there was kind of this whole flood of Xbox Live Arcade, and Playstation Network, and WiiWare that kind of followed suit with that. (Pajot & Swirsky, 2012)

Valve was not the first company to distribute games digitally. However, the confluence of increasing Internet speeds paired with this alternative way of distributing digital video games meant individuals and small teams could distribute their games without the backing of major corporations.

The distinctions between indie and so-called larger AAA development houses can be hard to define at times (Keogh, 2015). AAA development houses are usually published by large corporations such as Nintendo, though some of these distinctions are arbitrary. Much like the music industry has trouble defining indie labels versus corporate labels, the lines between publisher, developer, indie and AAA, first party and third party, and so on, are blurred. For the purposes of this chapter, the focus is on very small development teams that are a hallmark of indie video game development, with relatively low development costs compared to large, full-priced, big studio titles. This might help distinguish between indie and the larger publishers and developers that fall under the aegis of Sony, Nintendo, and Microsoft. As Boluk and LeMieux (2012) put it:

Amidst the production of Final Fantasy XIVs and the annual Madden NFL, however, a transformation has begun to occur. The increased power of home computers, availability of open-source game engines, and prevalence of digital distribution services has catalyzed the development of smaller-scale projects like maphacks and modified engines, social and networked games, augmented and alternate realities, and mobile and web applications. The diffusion of the modes of production, the accessibility of design technologies, number of digital distribution platforms, and the formation of a broader audience has permitted experimental game designers to challenge the representational hegemony of traditional genres to develop alternative forms of artgames, antigames, countergames, overgames, notgames, and metagames. (p.1)

A complicating factor in this discussion is the blurring of the lines between AAA publishers and indie developers. The big publishers and console makers have jumped on the indie game bandwagon, seeing a few notable indie successes like *Braid* (Number None, Inc., 2008), *Super Meat Boy* (Team Meat, 2010), and *Terraria* (Re-Logic, 2011), and are now showcasing indie games at their product evaluations. Much like major studios opened up "indie" divisions like Miramax and major labels like Warner Bros. bought into indie labels like Matador in the 1990s, big publishers like Microsoft are now publishing "small" games like Ori and the Blind Forest while Sony has indie game developers onstage at its big product unveilings.

In the film, *Indie Game: The Movie* (Pajot & Swirsky, 2012), Blow talks about his resistance to designing traditional games and rather designing something personal and innovative. *Indie Game: The Movie* features several such games, including *Fez* (Polytron Corporation, 2012), *Braid* (Number None, Inc., 2008), and *Super Meat Boy* (Team Meat, 2010), but those are just a few of the examples of the resurgence of indie games in recent years. The indie video game movement is often characterized by simulations or permutations of the 8 and 16-bit graphics seen on the Atari, Nintendo Entertainment System, and Sega Genesis (Lipkin, 2012). Though it might seem mired in nostalgia, this focus on simpler graphic styles and mechanics could be interpreted as a rebellious act against mainstream AAA game slickness, homogeneity, and poor playability (Lipkin, 2012). Games like *Nidhogg* (Messhof, 2014), *Super Meat Boy* (Team Meat, 2010), *Shovel Knight* (Yacht Club Games, 2014), and *Proteus* (Key & Kanaga, 2013) aggressively push back against today's AAA standards with bright, clashing colors and resolutely lo-fi or "retro" graphics (Golding, 2013; Key, 2013; Rose, 2013). Much like designing indie games around explorations of simple mechanics, these styles are something of a reaction against today's AAA norms.

We are entering an era of video game design, development, and publishing that mirrors much of the early days of video gaming, as well as various waves of punk, DIY, and indie music and movie scenes. Though sites like *Newgrounds* have been active for years, a massive growth of options in inexpensive development tools and places to publish have allowed a surge in game development (Keogh, 2015; Lipkin, 2012). For example, Twine is free, open source, and HTML-based, so its games work on most browsers and operating systems. Just like tools in the music industry, such as Bandcamp and Soundcloud, newer digital distribution platforms like itch.io, Steam, and the iOS App Store offer indie developers an opportunity to reach consumers and publish their games.

Indies, "Zines," and "Zine" Games

Perhaps there is no better place to illustrate the analogues between DIY indie culture and indie video games then in the ascendancy of "zine" games made with Twine. As mentioned above, punk rock – and later indie – was a subculture of more than just music and record labels. The *punk bible* fanzine, the ongoing *Maximum Rocknroll,* got its humble origins as a 1982 Alternative Tentacles LP compilation insert, arriving along with a wave of zines, the publishing side of DIY and punk culture. An important component of DIY and indie culture was the rise of "zines," short for magazines. These homegrown magazines were often handmade, stapled, glued, photocopied, and distributed in person, at alternative bookstores and record stores, or via mail-order (Oakes, 2009). This democratization of publication mirrored the DIY aesthetic of punk rock, allowing for communication of a subculture that was both suspicious of and rejected by the mainstream media. Though zines and punk rock remained primarily the province of white young middle class men, zines, especially in the 1990s, provided access to publishing for marginalized voices, as evidenced by the Riot Grrrl movement, which gave birth to feminist zines such as *Jigsaw*, *Girl Germs*, and *Bikini Kill*, whose editors would go on to found the fearsome feminist punk band of the same name (Duncombe, 2014; Marcus, 2010; Raha, 2005). The Riot Grrrl movement was unafraid to embrace radical politics and confront issues of sexism, gay rights, feminism, and racism and involved bands, record labels, zines, art, and political activism, informed by their DIY ethos (Comstock, 2001; Duncombe, 2014; Marcus, 2010; Raha, 2005; Triggs, 2006). Zines with queer, BDSM, and anything at the edge of sexual and gender norms of the day found a home in zines, which were often hyper-specific to topics and mission statements (Duncombe, 2014; Moore, 2004; Raha, 2005).

This emergence of zines and DIY culture out of the punk and indie music from the 1970s-1990s has parallels in the late 00s surge of indie game development. This is evident in the vibrant community surrounding the open-source programming language Twine, an easy-to-use tool for creating branching narratives, referred to by Anna Anthropy as "indie zines" (Anthropy, 2012; Ellison, 2013; Keogh, 2015). Twine sits somewhere between the long-standing tradition of text adventures like *Zork* (Infocom, 1977) and the Choose Your Own Adventure book, but that description simplifies the impact of Twine, which makes it extremely easy to create (Anthropy, 2012; Ellison, 2013; Keogh, 2015). Because of this, Twine has become quite popular in a variety of settings with a diverse audience, including LGBTQ and people of color, who often do not see themselves or topics of particular interest to them represented in AAA games (Anthropy, 2012; Ellison, 2013; Keogh, 2015). Perhaps the most popular of Twine games, *Depression Quest*, simulates the feeling of suffering from depression, an unusual topic for a video game, to say the least, but in line with the Twine game community and the broad range of hyper-focused topics covered by zines in their heyday (Anthropy, 2012; Duncombe, 2014; Ellison, 2013; Keogh, 2015).

Perhaps it all comes back to the notion of ethos and the perceived drive toward independence, however that is perceived. Christopher Floyd curates the Indie MEGABOOTH, a collection of interesting and innovative indie games that was created as a co-op between 16 indie developers competing for space at 2012 video game convention PAX Prime (Indie MEGABOOTH, 2015). A few years later, the Indie MEGABOOTH is now a major attraction at the PAX conventions, featuring over 75 developers showing off their games in development. For Christopher Floyd, who reviews hundreds of video game entries for each exhibition, indie is a "state of mind" more than anything else, an independent-mind ethos that understands that making games in the indie space will most likely not lead to riches, but will be more artistically satisfying, echoing what many indie game developers say (Harvey & Fisher, 2013; Keogh, 2015; Kerr, Whitson, Harvey, Shepherd, & O'Donnell, 2013; Lipkin, 2012; Phillips, 2015; The Giant Beastcast, 2015).

As AAA game development costs increase, so does the amount of labor needed to deliver the games, but this environment has lead to layoffs, often right after a game is delivered to retail. Many successful indie games, like Fullbright Studio's first person narrative *Gone Home* (2013) or the political border patrol simulator *Papers, Please* (Pope, 2013), were created by small indie teams who had worked on larger games like *Bioshock 2* (2K Marin, 2010) and the *Uncharted* series (Naughty Dog, SCE Bend Studio, & One Loop Games, 2007), respectively. Even seasoned developers working on indie titles as part of teams, like Nina Freeman, as of press time working on Fullbright's *Tacoma*, find time to make "small," experimental games like Freeman's *Freshman Year* (2015), in which a character texts with a friend. In a sense, there are indies for the indies.

Jonathan Blow, designer/developer of the time-shifting 2D puzzle-platforner *Braid*, opens the film, *Indie Game: The Movie* (Pajot & Swirsky, 2012), with his experience of being an independent game designer as "making something personal," something not always allowed in the AAA game development space of large teams and commercial concerns. For Blow, this personal relationship with making games allows a space for him to "put [his] deepest flaws and vulnerabilities in the game" in order to "see what happens." In the same documentary, Phil Fish, designer of *Fez* (Polytron Corporation, 2012), discusses creating a player experience and environment of discovery:

I wanted to create like a nice place, like a pleasant place to be in. I want people to feel like a sense of openness and adventure, but in a really simple, almost child-like way. And I really just want people to enter that world and enjoy their time in it. That's what the game is - it's a nice place to spend time in...I'm trying to recreate that experience of playing games as a kid before the internet existed and hearing these kind of urban legends like, 'hey, if you go and sit in that corner for 5 seconds and you press down and then you jump two times, it warps you somewhere.' Yeah, that's kind of what the game is about. (Pajot & Swirsky, 2012)

Indie game creators Edmund McMillen and Tommy Refenes worked as a team of two to implement their vision for *Super Meat Boy* (Team Meat, 2010), a 2D platformer game. According to McMillen, they were pushing boundaries:

My whole life has been trying to see where the boundaries are and see how far I can push them before I get in trouble and that's what I'm doing now and that's what's exciting to me. I just feel like if I'm not doing that, I'm bored. And if I'm bored, I'm not going to be creative. I make games that center around my life. Things that I like and the things that I think and say and do. I make games to express myself I guess. (Pajot & Swirsky, 2012)

This boundary-pushing is in stark contrast to the design and development cycle of AAA games such as the *Call of Duty* series, where hundreds of people contribute to the design, development, and marketing/distribution of the game, all iterating in small amounts from each year to the next. Brandon Boyer remarks about "a tendency" in mainstream, AAA games to "make everything bigger, and make everything more realistic" (Pajot & Swirsky, 2012). For indie game designers, however, the goals are different and more personal. According to Gus Mastrapa: "it's like frequently one person who says, 'I want a game to be like this' – 'I want a game to be about this special thing'" (Pajot & Swirsky, 2012).

Innovative mechanics are often a byproduct of the differing – and more personal – design and development goals of the indie spaces. *Braid* (Number None, Inc., 2008) is a puzzle platformer game designed and developed by Jonathan Blow. Blow designed a time changing/rewinding mechanic giving Tim, the main character, the ability to manipulate time. Blow describes his idea for the game as stemming from a conversation with friends about the AAA game *Prince of Persia: Sands of Time* (Ubisoft Montreal, 2003). In *Prince of Persia*, the character could also manipulate time with a rewind mechanic, but the power was intermittent. Blow articulates:

So one of my friends said, 'well why not just do it like a VCR, where you can rewind anytime you want?' But nobody in that discussion actually tried it, right. So I said okay, I'm feeling inspired...I spent about a week working on it. And I had a prototype which is really kind of amazing in that – if you look at the prototype and you look at the final game, a lot of the ideas from the final game are actually in that prototype that were done in the first week...the game mechanics were there for rewinding and then rewinding with things that were in view to rewind and then about time and space being tied together so that time changes as you move...It started as a process of experimentation, but then it very quickly became a process of discovery...that was an amazing design experience. (Pajot & Swirsky, 2012)

The manipulation of time changes in each level. At first, the player can rewind time and carry out alternative actions. Next, objects are incorporated into the game that do not react to the time change mechanic. As the game progresses, several other mechanics are introduced, such as an ability to pause, speed, and slow time based on the character's position, an ability to perform simultaneous actions with the appearance of a shadow character, an ability to warp time based on distance from objects, and a level where time is reversed throughout. In addition to this indie game's innovation of a perspectival, time-shifting mechanic, *Braid* is also a game that experiments with a love story in intriguing ways.

Fez (Polytron Corporation, 2012) is a video game that centers on innovating a perspectival mechanic. Gomez, the main 2D character, is able to move through the four-sided 2D world with a rotation mechanic. For Phil Fish, this perspectival mechanic that makes the game unique came out of a reflection of himself and his own personal goals to make a "stop and smell the flowers kind of game":

I started noticing a few things that kind of reflect my experience of working on the game. It's a game about games and the world is very much a computer world. It's a world within a computer and there's a lot of computer logic to it. And every now and then the universe becomes unstable and has to kind of defragment itself and reboot. That's the goal of the game in Fez. You kind of - you're putting these pieces of the universe back together to try and make it stable again. I basically always feel like the entire world is falling apart around me these days...If this fails, I'm done. Like, I don't think I'll work in games again. And it's not just a game, like I'm so closely attached to it. It's me. It's my ego, my perception of myself is at risk. This is my identity. It's Fez. I'm guy making Fez. (Pajot & Swirsky, 2012)

Fish articulates the underlying concept for the perspective-shifting mechanic as "a reflection" of himself. In this sense, making something personal, both for Blow and Fish, led to their innovative mechanics. Fish not only sees his identity wrapped up in *Fez*, but actually used the game as a place to convey his view of an "unstable" world that needs to be reassembled. This is apparent both in the rotation of the world mechanic and in the narrative of the game.

THREE INDIE GAMES THAT CHALLENGE THE DOMINANT USE OF PERSPECTIVE

As exemplified with *Braid* and *Fez,* Indie games can lead to unique perspectives, such as the first-person puzzle game *Antichamber* (Bruce, 2013), the MC Escher-esque mobile game *Monument Valley* (Ustwo, 2014), and the dimension-switching *Fez* (Polytron Corporation, 2012). In the following sections, we illustrate the perspectival shift phenomenon by describing the game play in *Proteus* (Key & Kanaga, 2013), *Fez*, and *Monument Valley*, as well as the experience of Alistar, a novice game designer who used video games to mediate new information about dimensionality he encountered.

Proteus: 3D Atari Music

Proteus is a very unusual video game. The player is presented with the most remarkable island, randomly generated by the game's rules and imagined in strokes of hard, ungradiented colour. The world is a blanket of greens, browns, pinks, blues, whites, oranges. It looks like Kandinsky with a copy of MS Paint. (Golding, 2013, para. 1).

That is how Daniel Golding (2013) described *Proteus* (Key & Kanaga, 2013), a rather indescribable, meditative first-person experimental 3D exploration game with a unique aesthetic that one of the our video game campers described as "if Atari did 3D." The three-dimensional 8-bit graphics incorporate an Atari-like, low-resolution look, while taking advantage of the technological affordances of high-definition graphics and ability to create a 3D game world. For example, the trees appear to be dropping flat 8-bit pixelated leaves. Even in this 3D space, objects are flat no matter which way they are viewed. Walking around a tree in *Proteus's* three dimensions reveals two-dimensional leaves and branches, regardless of the character's position. This is similar to a diorama perspective, typically seen in elementary learners' shoebox projects. The game space harkens Roy Lichtenstein's *House I* (1996/1998) sculpture. No matter where the viewer is in relation to the house, the front door always appears convex. In this way, games like *Proteus* are pushing the boundaries on unique and quite interesting perspectival mechanics in video games. In Figure 1 below, a screenshot from the summer season shows the mesh of 2D objects in a 3D landscape.

Proteus' island is procedurally generated, meaning players experience a remixed version during each playthrough. Although *Proteus* contains the same generated elements, including 8-bit trees, animals, fog, these elements are shuffled. *Proteus* uses few controls, only a mouse to view the environment and the WASD keys to move in the three-dimensional landscape. Objects, such as chickens, frogs, gravestones, and leaves all emit a variant sound as the player approaches them. Although there isn't a typical gaming goal in *Proteus*, such as defeating an enemy or solving a puzzle, a unique space is created that is interactive and playful. *Proteus* takes you through a semblance of a story as the seasons change from spring to summer to fall and finally to winter. During the nighttime phase of each season, 8-bit wisps come out beneath the starry sky creating a sense of beauty and peace. The game grows more sinister when gravestones and idols start to appear.

The enigmatic ambient music island simulator *Proteus* is part of a burgeoning subgenre of video games formally known as "first person exploration games." These games are controversial with a vocal minority of more traditionally-minded gamers, gaining the pejorative "walking simulators" amid cries

Figure 1. Summer valley in Proteus by Ed Key via Wikimedia Commons

of "not a game." Though developers have somewhat embraced the walking simulator tag, narrative, experimental, and/or atmospheric games with little or no mechanics other than movement and looking and light single-button interactions, they often get attacked in comment sections and message boards for their not a game-ness (Keogh, 2015; Key, 2013; Rose, 2013). The developer Ed Key even had to take to his blog to defend the game from accusations of small pockets of gamers arguing that it was not a video game, (Key, 2013; Rose, 2013). Key (2013) decried the absurdity of the debate, while still calling *Proteus* a video game:

Proteus was certainly made by a game developer (and a musician), working in the context of videogames, using game design and development techniques to express a particular set of things. None of that is really important, because the proof is in the playing.

We would argue that what the detractors of *Proteus* (Key & Kanaga, 2013), in particular, and other games miss, is that action, winning, and victory are not the explicit goals of these walking simulators. These games, which include *Dear Esther* (The Chinese Room, 2012), *The Vanishing of Ethan Carter* (The Astronauts, 2014), *Gone Home* (Fullbright, 2013), and *Everybody's Gone to the Rapture* (The Chinese Room & SCE Santa Monica Studio, 2015), are more concerned with narrative and atmosphere, not dissimilar to the narrative-driven 80s games from Sierra Online (*Kings' Quest I* (1983), *Space Quest I* (1986), or Infocom (*Zork* (1977)). However, the negative reaction to *Proteus* demonstrates just how *indie* it is, as it could only have been developed in a sphere with less commercial concerns by a small team, as most AAA developers and publishers would not take a chance on a game that is as much generative music creator (Eno, 1996) as it is traditional video game.

As discussed in the preface of this book, we observed an entire classroom of children engrossed in the exploration of Proteus' strange island, in part because the unique perspective was unlike any they had seen before. They called out to the player to chase flat pixelated frogs and climb icy polygonal mountains, in part because the exploration of this beautiful, impossible world was its own reward. What makes *Proteus* unusual and compelling is also the key to its success, the melding of its wordless, implicit narrative, and its generative ambient music, wrapped in an environment only possible in video games.

Fez, Flatland, and Alistar

Fez (Polytron Corporation, 2012) was conceived as a game that sought to innovate perspectival mechanics. *Fez* is a perspective-shifting puzzle platformer, allowing the player to control not only the character's movement in the seemingly two-dimensional game space, but to also control the rotation of the platforms. In this sense, the 2D platform game allows the character access to four faces of a cube, or four worlds to explore in tandem, approaching access to three-dimensional space. This is comparable to the Nintendo game, *Super Paper Mario* (Intelligent Systems, 2007), where the character, 2-dimensional Mario, is able to access a 3-dimensional world for short periods of time. *Fez* took years to program and the graphics are all relatively "simple" in the 16-bit format. Still, this indie game masks a complexity of design and the term simple doesn't quite capture this hidden quality. In Figure 2 below, a series of 4 screenshots illustrate the 4 sides of the world with Gomez, the main character, in the same position. The bottom-left screenshot in particular captures the world in rotation.

Alistar, a ninth grader, is an avid gamer and part of Valentine's (2014) project, *Space and Perspective*. *Space and Perspective* was a two month supplement to an existing eighth grade mathematics learning

Figure 2. Four screenshots from Fez, showing four sides of the world with Gomez in the same position

environment where learners were asked to consider space and perspective using real world "cases as alternative perspective" (Jonassen, 2011). The cases sought to productively problematize geometric space and dimension and incorporated themes such as art, film, light, and video games. Concerning video games, learners were asked to engage in conversations about the perspectives inherent in games including *Pong* (Atari Inc., 1972), *Asteroids* (Atari Inc., 1979), *Super Mario Bros.* (Nintendo, 1985), and *Portal* (Valve Corporation, 2007). Several students in the class were self-identified gamers and chose to participate in the study following class meetings. Alistar is an admirer of *Fez* (Polytron Corporation, 2012) and credits it with changing his own perspectives on dimensionality. When presented with new perspectives during the course of this project, he turned to video games, specifically *Fez*, to wrangle with the concepts he encountered. In preparation for this interview, Alistar chose to write about *Fez* (Polytron Corporation, 2012) in his lived-experience description and the impact of this game in helping him consider dimensionality, perspective, and point of view as it relates to video games. He wrote:

Because of the class, I look at movies, and mainly video games differently. A 2D world versus a 3D world is now a totally different idea for me because I understand how the dimensions work. It actually inspired me to learn animation in programs like Blender and start making my own projects. I have been making modifications for a game called Fez. The game deals with a 2D world that can be manipulated to change the 2D space inside and make it 3D. It is a very cool concept, and a very good game.

Alistar connects *Fez* to the *Space and Perspective* investigations from class:

I had a feeling of eureka in that class. I never actually knew that dimensions could go beyond what we can perceive. During the time we were reading Flatland: A Romance of Many Dimensions, I started to realize that parts of the book that were not explained might not have been possible. If everything was flat, would laws like gravity and density actually apply? The comprehension of questions like these compelled me to read the book. Going back to Fez, that game is so much more interesting after learning about different dimensions. I would highly recommend giving it a try.

In addition, Alistar shares his own goals for designing a modified version of *Fez,* drawing on the reading, *Flatland: A Romance of Many Dimensions* (Abbott, 1884/1991), and the film, *Flatland: The Movie* (Caplan, Wallace, Travis, & Johnson, 2007):

So when I first bought Fez - this was right after the Space and Perspective class cause I was interested and I had heard of this game before and I bought it. I played through the entire game and I thought it was great. Then I came across this guy on YouTube who had taken another game – like a space fighting game and made a modification where he actually converted the entire game and redesigned all the skins for everything – made all the different weapons for everything. And he made it a Star Wars game, which was kind of interesting. So what I've been trying to do is redesign Fez to kind of pretty much be Flatland. That was my plan.

Flatland: A Romance of Many Dimensions is a fictional satire told by A. Square, a two-dimensional square living among a planar, *flat* land with other male polygons and female line segments. A. Square describes his world of seeing, moving, and generally *being* a two-dimensional polygon. In the story, he articulates a dream where he visits other dimensional worlds (Pointland and Lineland) and his realization that 0-dimensional and one-dimensional beings are more limited in their seeing and movement, unable to conceptualize dimensions higher than themselves. Eventually he is visited by a sphere that shows him the three-dimensional Spaceland. Here he learns that there are dimensions higher than Flatland and uses analogy to conjecture arithmetically and geometrically about dimensions beyond space (e.g., the fourth dimension to infinity). Although there are many more subplots developed in the story, the three-dimensional reader is left wondering about the existence of higher dimensions and given a way, analogously, to conceptualize seeing and perceiving among the dimensions.

For Alistar, *Flatland* and *Fez* have favorable comparisons, and he used *Fez* to try to understand the world of Flatland. Alistar continues talking about his attempts to try and figure out the mechanic for switching the sides of the world – the boundary pushing that *Fez* accomplishes in the perspective-shifting mechanic:

Alistar: *What I'm trying to do now is figure out the tricks they use to make Fez. In that way I can try and convert it. There's no source code anymore so I can't directly take what they made and use it. I have to try and figure it out kind of in reverse by playing the game. I figured out the animation –*

that's fine. Still, I have to figure out the mechanics and how they coded switching the sides of the world. I need to figure that out.

Keri: *Well I mean, wouldn't it be four? Since it's really – its really only four sides, right?*

Alistar: *Right, but when you – but I have to figure out how they coded that, so with one button it would input so that the way the world would flip and then the animations would change. I'm trying to reverse-engineer that pretty much...So I made it into Flatland and it's a big office area and you talk to people there – that's kind of the hub world you go back and forth from.*

Keri: *To the office?*

Alistar: *Yes*

Keri: *With the squaricles?*

Alistar: *Yes, that is the first level. So, that's what I've been doing with the characters.*

Keri: *That is great! So what's your big concept, like you said you're making it like – like the skin of Flatland in a way. It's still Fez, so what is the Flatland part of it?*

Alistar: *So the Flatland part of it is each, so you know how in Fez every level connects to more levels and you go and you can kind of choose your path? So everything is connected to the main office and that's where you choose your path. And so every level, I have some of the dialog from like the book and the movie and the characters saying it – and it kind of – it's not linear, but it tells the story and you kind of have to figure it out yourself. It doesn't give you any set path, but it does tell the story if you go the right way. So I've been looking at other games that have ideas of dimensions and space and I've been trying to figure out or maybe some that I could also try and mod with that have modding capability. Before you discover the Fez hat, it's...the Fez hat's kind of the same thing as the Master Sphere – it's kind of pretty much the same idea. Like, you think it's a 2D world but it's actually more and more and more. So I didn't change that concept because it's kind of the same thing. But um, so yeah, you start out not really knowing the whole mechanic with the way you can switch the worlds and then once you kind of find out, that's when you're given the hat. And the Master Sphere character is in there, but it's mostly – he doesn't actually give the hat to you – you just kind of find the hat. The animations, all the characters in the town are different shapes – triangles, squares – all different shapes. And um, so yeah, I've just been putting a lot of time into that and it's been very time consuming but I think it'll pay off.*

In *Flatland*, the sphere (a.k.a. Master Sphere) gives A. Square the ability to temporarily access three-dimensions just as the Fez hat, a powerful artifact in the game *Fez*, gives Gomez the power to access a three-dimensional play space. In this sense, Alistar's idea to mod *Fez* with the skin of the *Flatland* story complement each other.

Not only is Alistar carrying out his goals to design, he finds himself shifting as a gamer. Alistar articulates his recent transition to indie games like *Fez*. When interviewed, he was asked if he identified himself as a gamer. Not only did he respond emphatically "yes," he continued to talk about the types of games he likes and how this has changed over time, echoing the changes in the indie game sphere itself:

So when I was little, since I was about 8, I only played shooters. I just played loud, obnoxious, over the top shooters. Like before then, I played - you know Quake, that series or Wolfenstein, or Doom? Wolfenstein is like a World War 2 shooter but it's really over the top and crazy and awesome. I would only play Wolfenstein or any games like that. And then, I'm going to say when I was like 10-13, I got into more adventure/RPG [role-playing] games. And then after this class, it's all been indie games for me, like I don't care what they're about. There are so many indie games that have to do with perspective. There's um, well there's another one I haven't told you about – it's called Window Sil: W-i-n-d-o-w-S-i-l. And there's another one called Lume: L-u-m-e. So these are both games by one developer, where they've experimented with putting real life objects into a game, so like some of the objects are real things, like they're not animated. They've filmed things with a camera and put it in the game. These are all 2D games but have real 3D objects in them.

During the interview, Alistar was asked the follow up question, "So you say that after investigating *Space and Perspective* you are more drawn to indie games. Do you think that would have happened anyways or is there something about it that made you look at games differently?" Alistar responds:

No I think that this happened actually because of this class. Because before then, I just liked games that were big, you know were fun, interesting – I didn't really care if they did anything new. And with indie games, a lot of them with their art styles and their mechanics, like Fez, kind of feel like they're almost taken from different perspectives in space where it feels like every game feels different in that regard. I feel like I would not have picked up indie games had I not taken this class. Because before, I was like eew, what? – these indie games look really stupid – they're just like really colorful and short and dumb. And then I played one and it was actually really fun.

According to Alistar, his newfound fondness for indie games is related to a series of investigations into space and perspective, part of his eighth-grade math class. This is most likely why he focused on perspectival aspects he finds innovative in indie games. It is interesting, however, that he is not only shifting his gaming preferences as a player, but is also focusing on the possibility of designing his own games.

The Democratization of 3D and Monument Valley

Video game 3D simulation has been around since its inception in the wireframes and vectors of *Battle-Zone* (Atari Inc., 1980) and the flight simulator, *Star Wars* (Atari Inc., 1983), but it made significant leaps during the 90s, hoisted on the backs of console games such as *Crash Bandicoot* (Naughty Dog, 1996), *Jumping Flash!* (Exact Co., Ltd., 1995), *Super Mario 64* (Nintendo, 1996), and a number of PC games like *Doom* (id Software, 1993) and *Quake* (id Software, 1996). With games like *Grand Theft Auto III* (DMA Design, 2001) and *Deus Ex* (Ion Storm, 2000), the "open world" game was truly born.

Monument Valley (Ustwo, 2014) captivated both of us, from beginning to end, with its perspective-shifting ladders and curious, Spider-man-like qualities when walking on walls, defying gravity. It does not hurt that the game's art style supersedes any technical limitations of the mobile platforms, adhering to a vague, but serene narrative traversing monuments to geometric marvels. The puzzle platformer, similar to *Fez,*, allows the player to move both the character and rotate platforms that are actually impossible, Escher-like shapes that the character navigates. Figure 3 below show the similarities between the Penrose triangle in Escher's (1953)*Relativity* sketch and a screenshot from Chapter IV in *Monument Valley*.

In the sequel/downloadable content to *Monument Valley*, *Forgotten Shores*, the impossible shapes reappear, with even more layers (see Figure 4). In the image below from *Appendix VI: The Citadel of Deceit*, the character, Ida, can be seen walking upside down. In fact, as the game progresses, the player learns that Ida can walk sideways, upside down, etc., which is also depicted in Escher's *Relativity* sketch.

Figure 3. Images comparing M. C. Escher's(1953) Relativity sketch with a screenshot from Monument Valley, Chapter IV, showing the Penrose triangle

Escher's Relativity (1953)

Monument Valley, Chapter IV: Water Palace in which Ida Discovers New Ways to Walk

Figure 4. Screen shot from Forgotten Shore's section, Appendix VI: The Citadel of Deceit. The character, Ida, can be seen walking upside down.

In *Monument Valley*, the goal is to reach an octagram, an eight-sided star polygon by navigating a complex series of connected platforms. These platforms are movable in some cases (by translating in all directions and through performing a series of rotations). Your character, Ida, is a princess walking through the game space. As the game play progresses, you are given clues about the purpose for the journey, such as the words at the end of chapter X, "Those who stole our sacred geometry have forgotten their true selves" amid the image of a Penrose triangle. The isometric view and the increasing addition of mechanics (transforming platforms, moving the friendly pillar totem, and rotating levers to create bridges) throughout the levels engage the player to solve more complex puzzles. Similar to the mechanics of *Fez*, you are able to rotate the entire game space at times to see all six sides of the imaginary cube net consisting of the game space. Each level, or rather chapter, ends with Ida removing her princess shaped cap over the octagram, revealing a complex geometric solid (e.g., hypercube, octahedron, hollow tetrahedron, and even stellated polyhedra), allowing her to enter the next chapter.

From the authors' perspective as educators, *Monument Valley* reveals itself as a geometrical gift – a pedagogical tool to support learners' mathematization of space. Being able to manipulate transformations such as rotations, reflections, and translations to move the character Ida, is not only an engaging way to consider the complexity of dimensions and their relationships, but also seems like a viable gift for learners to conjecture, problem solve, and even consider design constraints. Although *Monument Valley* is one case to explore, the recent design attention to perspectives in video games, causes us to seriously consider Jonathan Blow's question, "if [video games] are going to be one of the foundations of human thought, we need to think about what those games are teaching. Games by definition teach, the only question is - what?" (Boyer & Alexander, 2007). Rather than view educational games as flash cards skinned with video game elements, what if we viewed all games as educational, as thought tools - gifts to better understand our geometric world and our orientation with it?

DANCING ABOUT ARCHITECTURE: EDUCATING LEARNERS ABOUT SPACE AND PERSPECTIVE

There is an apocryphal story that Frank Zappa – also attributed to Elvis Costello, Laurie Anderson, and similar musical iconoclasts – described, writing or talking about music as being similar to "dancing about architecture," (Klein, 2005; Mottier, 2009), which – ignoring the fact that dancing is a form of communication itself – accurately depicts efforts to describe in written form the unusual and unique perspectives, points-of-view, and spatial contortions offered by many of the video games described in this chapter, indie or otherwise. Describing circumventing the crow people by shifting the pylons in *Monument Valley*, projecting the shadows on the wall in *Echochrome* (Game Yarouze, Japan Studio, 2008), *Fez's* cubic 2D shifts, or *Proteus's* Atari 3D, is much like "dancing about architecture."

Our attempts to describe the play, perspectives, POVs, even the game space of these games is difficult. Terms like perspective shifting puzzle platformer, even the fourth dimension, only partially captures the complex nature of discussing space and perspective. Video games, like *Monument Valley, Braid, and Fez*, offer a space where players can "dance" around innovative architecture. This stands in stark contrast to the teaching of perspective in traditional mathematics education. In K-12 learning environments, engaging students in the mathematization of space is often reductive, drawing on Euclidean terms, symbols, and structures that mask or simply do not consider the variety of spaces we may find ourselves – a curved planet, an expanding universe, and in this case, video games that push the boundaries of what space, and our relationship with it, can be. The *Space and Perspective* project described earlier was an attempt to engage leaners in activities of problematizing space and perspective. During the project, middle school learners like Alistar read the book *Flatland: A Romance of Many Dimensions* (Abbott, 1884/1991) and conjectured with classmates about higher dimensions (e.g., 4th and 5th), partial dimensions (e.g., ½, 1.75), and even negative dimensions. The invitation to consider the invisible and the complex may not immediately contribute to students' ability to define a term or solve an equation, but it engages students in spatial thinking, reasoning about dimensions, and considering how limited human seeing/perceiving is in varied, real world phenomena.

In puzzle games like *Tetris* (AcademySoft, 1986), *Monument Valley* (Ustwo, 2014), *Braid* (Number None, Inc., 2008), and *Fez* (Polytron Corporation, 2012), solving problems or reaching the goal of the game requires spatial thinking (sometimes called spatial reasoning, spatial skills, and spatial ability). There is not definitional agreement in the field concerning these terms and how best to measure them (Hegarty, 2010; Uttal et al., 2013). To further complicate the matter, researchers distinguish between spatial visualization (transformations such as rotating and reflecting) and spatial orientation (perspective taking) (Hegarty & Waller, 2004), analytic forms of spatial thinking, such as decomposition and rule-based reasoning (Hegarty, 2010), meta-representational competence (diSessa, 2004), and even create further distinctions such as intrinsic/extrinsic and static/dynamic spatial skills (Uttal, Meadow, et al., 2013). Rather than position our conversation concerning spatial thinking as one of these constructs in favor of another, we see value in considering the range of spatial thinking, be it mentally rotating objects, perspective taking, using analytic forms of thinking, choosing appropriate representations (meta-representational competence), or a combination of these activities.

The authors chose to use the term *spatial thinking* to avoid the common misconception that one's current spatial "ability" is a fixed and non-mutable state. In a recent meta-analysis, Uttal et al. (2013) found that "spatial skills are highly malleable and that training in spatial thinking is effective, durable, and transferable" (p. 365). These findings are quite remarkable, providing support for "spatial training," a phrase used frequently in the spatial thinking literature. Uttal et al. (2013) further note "although males tend to have an advantage in spatial ability, both genders improve equally well with training" (p. 364). Concerning the type of training, the authors conclude that all training types reviewed [video game, spatial task, and course training] support growth in spatial thinking. However, they highlight the affordances of video game training, specifically improving working memory as shown by Green and Bevalier (2003, 2007). Reacting to previous studies that did not find transfer, the authors explicate, "our results clearly show that transfer is possible if sufficient training or experience is provided" (p. 366).

Using Hegarty and Waller's (2004) definition of spatial orientation and spatial visualization is useful for considering the types of spatial thinking video games might support. Perspective taking (spatial orientation) involves "the ability to make egocentric spatial transformations in which one's egocentric reference frame changes with respect to the environment, but the relations between object-based and environmental frames of reference does not change" (p. 176). Spatial visualization, on the other hand, is "the ability to make object-based spatial transformations in which the positions of the objects are moved with respect to an environmental frame of reference, but one's egocentric reference frame does not change" (p. 176). Although this distinction may be important for research measurement purposes, games like *Monument Valley* and *Fez* do not sit squarely on one side or the other, but rather require one to transform the environment, the objects in the environment, and the egocentric reference frames simultaneously. Rather than more realistic 3D graphics as the goal of advancing modern video games, indie games are innovating possible perspectives through rotation mechanics (*Fez*), translation and reflection mechanics (*Monument Valley*), time switching mechanics (*Braid*), and many more wayfinding/navigational mechanics. The concern for game space realism (e.g., *Call of Duty* series) is not primary and is even de-emphasized with the art style of 8-bit and 16-bit graphics.

Benefits of Spatial Learning

The National Research Council argues that not only is spatial thinking "integral to everyday life," but also is " a missing link" across K-12 curriculum (NRC, 2006, p. 7). There is a growing body of literature linking strengths in spatial thinking with success in science, technology, engineering, and mathematics (STEM) academics and careers. Wai, Lubinski, and Benbow's (2009) longitudinal study suggests, "spatial ability is a salient psychological characteristic among adolescents who subsequently go on to achieve advanced educational and occupational credentials in STEM" (p. 827). They demonstrated that spatial ability predicts which students would pursue STEM occupations and degrees. Uttal et al. (2013) found "a causal relationship between spatial training and improvement in STEM learning or attainment" in their meta-analysis, however, they admit, "this assumption has rarely been tested" (p. 369). In addition they conjecture the possibility of spatial thinking "acting as a gatekeeper for students interested in STEM" (p. 369). Uttal, Miller, and Newcombe (2013) review research relating spatial thinking and STEM learning, asking the question, "can spatial training improve STEM learning?" (p. 370). They found that although few studies address this question, "those that have found encouraging results" (p. 370). They, along with Newcombe and Frick (2010), recommend that, in addition to the efforts extended to investigating support for math and other disciplines, we should also investigate supports for spatial thinking. Women's underrepresentation in STEM fields is well documented (e.g., National Center for Education Statistics, 2013). Although the research links between spatial thinking and success in STEM are burgeoning, the fact that women typically test lower than men on spatial measures (Terlecki, Newcombe, & Little, 2008) indicates a need for learning opportunities to address this disparity in spatial thinking.

As mentioned earlier, spatial thinking is mutable. Recent studies indicate several promising findings regarding spatial visualization. Terlecki et al. (2008) conducted a study investigating the growth trajectory, transfer, and durability of mental rotation performance using the video game *Tetris*, comparing men and women and accounting for pre-existing spatial experience. Their study indicates the malleability of spatial ability "regardless of gender or previous spatial experience" (p. 1010). Feng, Spence, and Pratt's (2007) research study investigating spatial attention and mental rotation ability shows "that playing an action video game can virtually eliminate this gender difference in spatial attention and simultaneously decrease the gender disparity in mental rotation ability, a higher-level process in spatial cognition" (p. 850). Regarding connections to STEM, Uttal et al. write:

Using a nationally representative sample, Wai et al. (2009) found that the spatial skills of individuals who obtained at least a bachelor's degree in engineering were 1.58 standard deviations greater than the general population (D. Lubinski, personal communication, August 14, 2011; J. Wai, personal communication, August 17, 2011). The very high level of spatial skills that seems to be required for success in engineering (and other STEM fields) is one important factor that limits the number of Americans who are able to become engineers (Wai et al., 2009, 2010) and thus contributes to the severe shortage of STEM workers in the United States. (2013, p. 368)

If we are interested in closing the gender gap in STEM, or even just increasing the number of people entering STEM fields like engineering, then addressing this spatial thinking gap is a promising place to focus.

Ways to Foster Spatial Learning

There are several ways to foster spatial learning as mentioned in Uttal et al.'s (2013) meta-analysis. These include interventions such as training on spatial tasks and video game interventions. Feng et al.'s (2007) research study investigating spatial attention and mental rotation ability shows an advantage of action video games over non-action games. They conjecture that this may be because non-action games "do not sufficiently exercise spatial attentional capacities" (p. 853). They recommend training with action video games as a "larger strategy designed to interest women in science and engineering careers" (p. 854). Terlecki et al.'s (2008) study using *Tetris* as an intervention, showed that the effects of "videogame training transferred to other spatial tasks exceeding the effects of repeated testing, and this transfer advantage was still evident after several months" (p. 996). Spence and Feng (2010) review many studies concerning video games and their ability to strengthen spatial cognition. Spence and Feng created a table, *Sensory, Perceptual, and Cognitive Functions Exercised by Different Genres of Video Games*, where they compare action, driving, and maze/puzzle games (p. 93). Assigning very high to very low regarding the use of these functions by players (e.g., sensory detection, working memory, etc.), it appears that action games require more of almost all sensory, perceptual, and cognitive functions, whereas maze and puzzle games require less. The authors admit that this table is "intended only as a rough comparative guide," however, depending on the type of maze/puzzle game, this assignment of cognitive capacity might be questioned (p. 93). Their argument for prioritizing first person shooter action games is that even though there are spatial demands inherent in maze/puzzle games, it is rare that they require time sensitive actions and reactions. The authors write:

[A]ction video games seem to have a unique advantage in improving low-level functions such as spatial selective attention (Feng et al., 2007; Green & Bavelier, 2003), spatial perceptual resolution (Green & Bavelier, 2007), and contrast sensitivity (Li et al., 2009), in addition to more complex spatial skills such as mental rotation (Feng et al., 2007). Because fundamental sensory, perceptual, and cognitive skills serve as the building blocks for higher level cognition, the ability of action games to improve basic processes has made them attractive candidates for further experimentation. (p. 95)

We are weary of using the term "training" and more inclined to view learning as a compilation of informal and formal experiences, such as those frequently engaged in informal maker spaces (in our case, game design camps). Still, we are encouraged by the findings – especially the recent connections being articulated among spatial thinking and "STEM learning or attainment" (Uttal et al., 2013). Related to perspectival-shift mechanics in games like *Fez* and *Monument Valley*, we wonder if Spence and Feng's (2010) "Sensory, Perceptual, and Cognitive Functions Exercised by Different Genres of Video Games" might be scrutinized in light of these more experimental, indie genres of games and the potential to use these as exemplars with adolescent game designers. As mentioned earlier, these are not simply puzzles and mazes, but games that require the player to rotate, reflect, translate, and even dilate the game world while at the same time moving objects within this world and their game character. This seems to draw on both perspective taking and visualizing aspects of spatial thinking. Although we admit action games also require a quick response time and danger of death, their tentative classification system may not fully recognize the potential viability of indie perspective-shifting games to support spatial thinking.

We argue that there is potential in both playing and designing games with innovative perspectival mechanics, such as the ones emerging in the indie game sphere. Games that play with perspectival mechanics in particular create opportunities to talk with learners about perspectives in video games, such as in the case with Alistar. Related to Blow's assertion that games "impact the patterns of human thought" (Boyer & Alexander, 2007), it seems likely that patterns related to spatial thinking are brought to the fore for players in the indie games explored in this chapter.

CONCLUSION

This chapter sought to open up the phenomenon of perspectival shifts related to unique visual affordances of video games. We discussed how the phenomenon of perspectival shifts in video games emerges as an innovative mechanic constructed by the game designer and embodied by players as they navigate these play spaces. We highlighted games within the indie genre, as this is a place where perspectival possibilities are intentionally being explored, similar to the sounds, images, and writings of indie artists across genres. As indie video games increasingly attend to perspectival mechanics in an attempt to push games to do what has not been done previously, opportunities are created for players to juxtapose points of view, navigate game spaces in new ways, and deeply consider two-dimensional, three-dimensional, and even four- and partial-dimensional representations of space.

After some online debate over whether or not video games function as art (see Ebert, 2010), gaming has been increasingly taken seriously by the artistic community and the intelligentsia, with gallery shows and academic journals springing up to highlight the relative artistic merit of video games. Jonathan Blow, developer of indie game *Braid* (Number None, Inc., 2008), articulates one reason we may want to consider games more seriously by stating that they "impact the patterns of human thought, and help define what it means to be human" (Boyer & Alexander, 2007). As with books and film, Blow sees games as a thought tool, similar to Fröebel's conceptualization of objects young learners might manipulate to learn about their inherently geometric world. According to mathematician Banchoff:

Fröebel and his colleagues created geometrical gifts from materials available to them, primarily wood, paper, and clay. Today we have the means to improve on the many gifts in many ways – with plastic and Velcro, with tape and magnets, not to mention with the powerful computer graphics. The educator's term "manipulatives" – classroom materials – takes on new meaning when we can put in front of a young student a tool to manipulate not only simple forms but also the very geometry of higher dimensional space. If we care about educating our children toward the perception of space, we should create truly stimulating manipulatives – geometrical gifts for our day. (1990, p. 14)

Although we remain aware of the potential for books and film to teach concepts and classroom manipulatives to support young learners' exploration, we are less likely to view video games as central to human growth and culture in the way that we view other visual art. Video games comprise a set of geometrical gifts, in a sense, made possible by their interactive nature and quality as a tool for thought. In the authors' current work with adolescent game designers, focusing their attention towards the design of games is strongly tied to considering perspective, dimension, interaction, and movement (transformation) among the character and the game world. We have many discussions, rather debates, about the most appropriate perspective based on their game idea. Many times their implemented designs are constrained by their limited knowledge to code complex perspectives and points of view. Even a seemingly simple game such as *Asteroids* (Atari Inc., 1979) integrates a complex, one-sided manifold play space like the Klein bottle and Möbius strip, where asteroids appear to float off the screen and come back into play at the opposite side. During the idea generating stage of campers' designs, we discuss in depth our perspectival experiences playing games and draw heavily on spatial language relevant to art, film, navigation, computer science, and mathematics.

We live in an era where video games are increasingly filling the informal learning spaces of students and adults alike. Statistics show that 97 percent of young learners play video games (Lenhart et al., 2008). Although there is much research being done in games that teach concepts, or educational games, the authors feel there is currently an untapped potential to use games as investigative starting points, as gifts and thought tools to contemplate our place in the world spatially. A more innovative notion than just playing unique perspectival games might lie in giving children (and learners of all ages) the tools to explore space. Nascent game developers could – not to be too corny – "jam econo" on their own, constructing, crafting, and using the burgeoning world of free and inexpensive tool sets like GameMaker and Unity and distribution platforms, like Steam, GOG, and itch.io.

After all, one of the most popular games in the world, by any number of measures, *is* an indie game – *Minecraft* (Mojang, 2011) – where millions of players are stacking, crafting, creating, and destroying randomly generated universes (Ekaputra, Lim, & Eng, 2013; Lang, 2015). In case you are curious as to the game's appeal, one of our campers described it this succinctly: "It's unlimited Legos…what's not to like?" Indeed. Intrinsic to a lot of *Minecraft* gamers' experience is the social aspect of it, and the community built around modding the core game itself. Speaking of making it big, selling out, or getting co-opted by the establishment, whatever your politics, Microsoft paid $2.5B in 2014 for the once-tiny studio Mojang, responsible for the blocky, cube-based game (Lang, 2015). That the notoriously stodgy Microsoft would pay that much money for something that so heavily relied on a community being allowed to manipulate the code of the game shows you how far both hacking and indie gaming has come in mainstream acceptance.

The most illustrative anecdote for the authors' case for using indie games and game development tools to educate is the case of Alistar, so engrossed and challenged by what he read and saw in *Flatland*, that he had to create something himself. Alistar, a fan of indie games of all stripes, wrangled with these advanced notions of dimensionality and spatial reasoning through his preferred medium, modding video games, not books, movies, music, or painting. Not to mythologize it, but this kind of exploration feels similar to the DIY ethos' origins in cut-and-paste art and engaging fringe thoughts. However, in the case of video games, the radicalism comes packaged in visual novels, Minecraft mods, itch.io and Twine games, machinima, and impossible universes and perspectives, rather than the stapled zines and radical politics of punk rock. This new climate of indie games, a state of mind similar to the punk rock and DIY ethos of the past, offers a chance for learners, designers, and players to use an expanse of new tools and existing games to jam econo and challenge dominate AAA perspectives, spatial or otherwise.

REFERENCES

2D Boy. (2008). *World of goo* [Wii, Windows, OS X video game]. San Francisco, CA: 2D Boy.

2K Marin. (2010). *Bioshock 2* [Windows, PS3, Xbox 360 video game]. Novato, CA: 2K Games.

Abbott, E. A. (1991). *Flatland: A romance of many dimensions.* Princeton, NJ: Princeton University Press.

Abrams, J. J., & Burk, B. (Producers), & Reeves, M. (Director). (2008). Cloverfield. United States: Paramount Pictures.

AcademySoft. (1986). *Tetris* [MS-DOS video game]. AcademySoft.

Anthropy, A. (2012). *Rise of the videogame zinesters: How freaks, normals, amateurs, artists, dreamers, drop-outs, queers, housewives, and people like you are taking back an art form.* New York, NY: Seven Stories Press.

Atari Inc. (1972). *Pong* [Arcade video game]. Sunnyvale, CA: Atari Inc.

Atari Inc. (1979). *Asteroids* [Arcade video game]. Sunnyvale, CA: Atari Inc.

Atari Inc. (1980). *Battlezone* [Arcade video game]. Sunnyvale, CA: Atari Inc.

Atari Inc. (1983). *Star wars* [Arcade video game]. Sunnyvale, CA: Atari Inc.

Azerrad, M. (2012). *Our band could be your life: Scenes from the American indie underground, 1981-1991.* New York, NY: Little, Brown, and Company.

Azerrad, M. (2014). Krist Novoselic: '*Meat Puppets II*' inspired me because 'there were no barriers'. *Billboard.* Retrieved from http://www.billboard.com/articles/news/6296973/1984-krist-novoselic-on-meat-puppets-II-influence

Banchoff, T. F. (1990). Dimension. In L. Steen (Ed.), *On the shoulders of giants: New approaches to numeracy* (pp. 11–59). Washington, DC: National Academy Press.

Bethesda Game Studios. (2011). *The elder scrolls V: Skyrim* [Microsoft Windows, PlayStation 3, XBox 360 video game]. Rockville, MD: Bethesda Softworks.

Blizzard Entertainment,. (2004). *World of warcraft* [Windows, OS X video game]. Irvine, CA: Blizzard Entertainment.

Blizzard Entertainment. , (2012). *Diablo III* [Microsoft Windows, OS X video game]. Irvine, CA: Blizzard Entertainment.

Boluk, S., & LeMieux, P. (2012). Stretched skulls: Anamorphic games and the memento mortem mortis. *Digital Humanities Quarterly, 6*(2).

Boyer, B., & Alexander, L. (2007). *MIGS 2007: Jonathan Blow on the WoW drug, meaningful games.* Retrieved from http://www.gamasutra.com/view/news/107343/MIGS_2007_Jonathan_Blow_On_The_WoW_Drug_Meaningful_Games.php

Bruce, A. (2013). *Antichamber* [Windows video game].

Caplan, S., & Wallace, W. (Producers), Travis, J., & Johnson, D. (Directors). (2007). *Flatland: The movie* [DVD]. United States: Flat World Productions.

Comstock, M. (2001). Grrrl zine networks: Re-composing spaces of authority, gender, and culture. *Jac*, *21*(2), 383–409.

Cuarón, A. (2013). *Gravity* [Motion picture]. United States: Warner Bros. Pictures.

Davis, J., Schroeder, A. (Producers), & Trank, J. (Director). (2012). *Chronicle*. United States: 20th Century Fox.

Design, D. M. A. (2001). *Grand theft auto III* [PS2 video game]. New York, NY: Rockstar Games.

diSessa, A. (2004). Metareprentational competence: Native competence and targets for instruction. *Cognition and Instruction*, *22*(3), 293–331. doi:10.1207/s1532690xci2203_2

Dog, N. (1996). *Crash bandicoot* [PS video game]. Minato, Tokyo, Japan: Sony Computer Entertainment.

Dog, N. SCE Bend Studio, & One Loop Games. (2007). Uncharted [PS3, PS4, PSVita, PSNow video game]. Minato, Tokyo, Japan: Sony Computer Entertainment.

Duncombe, S. (2014). *Notes from underground: Zines and the politics of alternative culture*. Portland, OR: Microcosm Publishing.

Dunn, K. (2012). "If it ain't cheap, it ain't punk": Walter Benjamin's progressive cultural production and DIY punk record labels. *Journal of Popular Music Studies*, *24*(2), 217–237. doi:10.1111/j.1533-1598.2012.01326.x

Ebert, R. (2010, April 16). *Video games can never be art* [Web log post]. Retrieved from http://www.rogerebert.com/rogers-journal/video-games-can-never-be-art

Ekaputra, G., Lim, C., & Eng, K. I. (2013). Minecraft: A game as an education and scientific learning tool. *Information Systems*, *2*(4), 237–242.

Ellison, C. (2013). Anna Anthropy and the Twine revolution. *The Guardian*. Retrieved from http://www.theguardian.com/technology/gamesblog/2013/apr/10/anna-anthropy-twine-revolution

Eno, B. (1996, June). *Generative music*. Presented at the Imagination Conference, San Francisco, CA.

Escher, M. C. (1953). *Relativity* [Lithograph print]. Retrieved from https://en.wikipedia.org/wiki/Relativity_(M._C._Escher)

Exact Co. Ltd. (1995). *Jumping flash!* [PS video game]. Minato, Tokyo, Japan: Sony Computer Entertainment.

Feng, J., Spence, I., & Pratt, J. (2007). Playing an action video game reduces gender differences in spatial cognition. *Psychological Science*, *18*(10), 850–855. doi:10.1111/j.1467-9280.2007.01990.x PMID:17894600

Fernández, J. (Producer), Balagueró, J., & Plaza, P. (Directors). (2007). *[REC]* [Motion picture]. Spain: Filmax International.

Freeman, N. (2015). *Freshman year* [Windows, OS X video game].

Fullbright. (2013). *Gone home* [Windows, OS, Linux video game]. Portland, OR: Fullbright.

Games, H. (2013). *Risk of rain* [Windows video game]. London: Chucklefish Games.

George, N. (2003). *The death of rhythm and blues*. New York, NY: Penguin.

Golding, D. (2013). Listening to *Proteus. Meanjin Quarterly, 72*(2). Retrieved from http://meanjin.com.au/essays/listening-to-proteus/

Green, C. S., & Bavelier, D. (2003). Action video game modifies visual selective attention. *Nature, 423*(6939), 534–537. doi:10.1038/nature01647 PMID:12774121

Green, C. S., & Bavelier, D. (2007). Action-video-game experience alters the spatial resolution of vision. *Psychological Science, 18*(1), 88–94. doi:10.1111/j.1467-9280.2007.01853.x PMID:17362383

Gulla, B. (2008). *Icons of R & B and soul: An encyclopedia of the artists who revolutionized rhythm* (Vol. 1). Westport, CT: Greenwood Press.

Haight, G. (Producer), & Montgomery, R. (Director). (1947). *Lady in the lake* [Motion picture]. United States: Metro-Goldwyn-Mayer.

Hale, G., & Cowie, R. (Producers), Myrick, D., & Sánchez, E. (Directors). (1999). *The Blair Witch Project* [motion picture]. United States: Artisan Entertainment.

Harvey, A., & Fisher, S. (2013). Making a name in games: Immaterial labour, indie game design, and gendered social network markets. *Information Communication and Society, 16*(3), 362–380. doi:10.1080/1369118X.2012.756048

Hegarty, M. (2010). Components of spatial intelligence. *Psychology of Learning and Motivation, 52*, 265–297. doi:10.1016/S0079-7421(10)52007-3

Hegarty, M., & Waller, D. (2004). A dissociation between mental rotation and perspective-taking spatial abilities. *Intelligence, 32*(2), 175–191. doi:10.1016/j.intell.2003.12.001

Higinbotham, W. (1958). *Tennis for two* [Analog computer/Oscilloscope video game]. Upton, NY.

Holbein, H. (1533). *The ambassadors* [Painting]. Retrieved from https://en.wikipedia.org/wiki/The_Ambassadors_(Holbein)

id Software. (1993). *Doom* [MS-DOS, Mac video game]. New York, NY: GT Interactive.

id Software. (1996). *Quake* [MS-DOS video game]. New York, NY: GT Interactive.

Ihde, D. (1993). *Postphenomenology: Essays in the postmodern context*. Evanston, IL: Northwestern University Press.

Indie MEGABOOTH. (2015). *Indie MEGABOOTH* [Company website]. Retrieved from http://indiemegabooth.com/

Infinity Ward,. (2003). *Call of duty* [Windows video game]. Santa Monica, CA: Activision.

Infocom. (1977). *Zork* [PDP-10 video game]. Cambridge, MA: Infocom.

Interactive, S. (1993). *Star wars arcade* [Arcade video game]. Ōta, Tokyo, Japan: Sega.

Interplay Productions,. (1985). *The bard's tale (Version Apple Macintosh, Atari ST, Commodore 64 video game)*. Redwood City, CA: Electronic Arts.

Jonassen, D. H. (2011). *Learning to solve problems: A handbook for designing problem-solving learning environments*. New York, NY: Routledge.

Keogh, B. (2015). Between tripleA, indie, casual, and DIY. In K. Oakley & J. O'Connor (Eds.), The Routledge Companion to the Cultural Industries (pp. 152-162). New York, NY: Routledge.

Kerr, A., Whitson, J. R., Harvey, A., Shepherd, T., & O'Donnell, C. (2013). Strategies and tactics for promoting indie game design. *Selected Papers of Internet Research*. Retrieved from http://spir.aoir.org/index.php/spir/article/view/874

Key, E. (2013, February 1). *What are games* [Web log post]. Retrieved from http://www.visitproteus.com/

Key, E., & Kanaga, D. (2013). *Proteus*.[Linus, OS, Windows, PS3, PSVita video game].

Klein, B. (2005). Dancing about architecture: Popular music criticism and the negotiation of authority. *Popular Communication, 3*(1), 1–20. doi:10.1207/s15405710pc0301_1

Konami. (1981). *Frogger* [Arcade video game]. Minato, Tokyo, Japan: Konami.

Lang, D. J. (2015, May 13). "*Minecraft*" most streamed video game in YouTube's history. *Associated Press*. Retrieved from https://www.yahoo.com/tech/s/minecraft-most-streamed-video-game-youtubes-history-140023346.html

Lenhart, A., Kahne, J., Middaugh, E., Macgill, A. R., Evans, C., & Vitak, J. (2008). Teens, video games, and civics: Teens' gaming experiences are diverse and include significant social interaction and civic engagement. *Pew Internet & American Life Project*. Retrieved from http://eric.ed.gov/?id=ED525058

Lipkin, N. (2012). Examining indie's independence: The meaning of "indie" games, the politics of production, and mainstream cooptation. *The Journal of the Canadian Game Studies Association, 7*(11), 8–24. Retrieved from http://journals.sfu.ca/loading/index.php/loading/article/viewArticle/122

Marcus, S. (2010). *Girls to the front: The true story of the riot grrrl revolution*. New York, NY: HarperCollins.

Messhof. (2014). *Nidhogg* [Windows, OS X, PS4, PSVita video game]. Messhof.

Mojang. (2011). *Minecraft* [Windows, OS, Linux, Android, iOS video game]. Stockholm, Sweden: Mojang.

Moore, R. (2004). Postmodernism and punk subculture: Cultures of authenticity and deconstruction. *The Communication Review, 7*(3), 305–327. doi:10.1080/10714420490492238

Mottier, V. (2009). "Talking about music is like dancing about architecture": Artspeak and pop music. *Language & Communication, 29*(2), 127–132. doi:10.1016/j.langcom.2009.01.003

Namco. (1980). *Pac-man* [Arcade video game]. Chicago, IL: Midway.

Namco. (1985). *Dig dug II* [Arcade video game]. Minato, Tokyo, Japan: Namco.

National Center for Education Statistics. (2013). *Digest of educational statistics 2013*. Washington, DC: U.S. Department of Education.

National Research Council. (2006). *Learning to think spatially: GIS as a support system in the K-12 curriculum*. Washington, DC: National Academies Press.

Newcombe, N. S., & Frick, A. (2010). Early education for spatial intelligence: Why, what, and how. *Mind, Brain, and Education, 4*(3), 102–111. doi:10.1111/j.1751-228X.2010.01089.x

Nintendo. (1981). *Donkey kong* [Arcade video game]. Kyoto, Japan: Nintendo.

Nintendo. (1985). *Super mario bros.* [NES/Famicom video game]. Kyoto, Japan: Nintendo.

Nintendo. (1986). *Metroid* [NES video game]. Kyoto, Japan: Nintendo.

Nintendo. (1996). *Super mario 64* [Nintendo 64, iQue Player video game]. Kyoto, Japan: Nintendo.

Nintendo. (2002). *Metroid prime* [Nintendo GameCube video game]. Kyoto, Japan: Nintendo.

Nintendo. (2007). *Super mario galaxy* [Wii video game]. Kyoto, Japan: Nintendo.

North, R. (2008). *Grand theft auto IV* [PS3, Xbox 360, Windows video game]. New York, NY: Rockstar Games.

North, R. (2013). *Grand theft auto V* [PS 3, Xbox 360 video game]. New York, NY: Rockstar Games.

Number None, Inc. (2008). *Braid* [Xbox Live Arcade video game]. Number None, Inc.

Oakes, K. (2009). *Slanted and enchanted: The evolution of indie culture*. New York, NY: Macmillan.

Online, S. (1986). *Space quest*: Chapter 1 - The Sarien encounter [DOS, Macintosh, Apple II, Apple IIGS, Amiga, Atari ST video game]. Fresno, CA: Sierra Online.

Pajot, L., & Swirsky, J. (Directors) (2012). *Indie game: The movie*. Canada: BlinkWorks Media.

Phillips, T. (2015). "Don't clone my indie game, bro": Informal cultures of videogame regulation in the independent sector. *Cultural Trends, 24*(2), 143–153. doi:10.1080/09548963.2015.1031480

Polytron Corporation. (2012). *Fez* [Xbox 360 video game]. Montreal, Canada: Trapdoor.

Pope, L. (2013). *Papers, please* [Windows, OS X video game].

Raha, M. (2005). *Cinderella's big score: Women of the punk and indie underground*. New York, NY: Seal Press.

Re-Logic. (2011). *Terraria* [Windows video game]. Indiana: Re-Logic.

Rollins, H. (2004). *Get in the van*. New York, NY: 2.13. 61 Publications.

Rose, M. (2013, February 1). *Opinion: It's totally OK to not like "anti-games"* [Web log post]. Retrieved from http://www.gamasutra.com/view/news/185885/Opinion_Its_totally_OK_to_not_like_antigames. php#.UQ0vR0pERpY

Sega. (1982). *Zaxxon* [Arcade video game]. Ōta, Tokyo, Japan: Sega.

Sierra On-Line. (1983). *King's quest I* [IBM PCjr video game]. Armonk, NY: IBM.

Spence, I., & Feng, J. (2010). Video games and spatial cognition. *Review of General Psychology, 14*(2), 92–104. doi:10.1037/a0019491

Storm, I. (2000). *Deus ex* [Windows, OS video game]. Wimbledon, London, United Kingdom: Eidos Interactive.

Studios, W. (1995). *Command & Conquer* [DOS, Microsoft Windows, Mac OS video game]. Las Vegas, NV: Virgin Interactive.

Systems, I. (2007). *Super paper mario* [Wii video game]. Kyoto, Japan: Nintendo.

Taito. (1978). *Space invaders* [Arcade video game]. Shinjuku, Tokyo, Japan: Taito.

Team Meat. (2010). *Super meat boy* [Xbox 360, Windows video game]. Team Meat.

Terlecki, M. S., Newcombe, N. S., & Little, M. (2008). Durable and generalized effects of spatial experience on mental rotation: Gender differences in growth patterns. *Applied Cognitive Psychology, 22*(7), 996–1013. doi:10.1002/acp.1420

The Astronauts. (2014). *The vanishing of Ethan Carter* [Windows video game]. The Astronauts.

The Chinese Room. (2012). *Dear Esther* [Windows, OS X video game]. Brighton, United Kingdom: The Chinese Room.

The Chinese Room, & SCE Santa Monica Studio. (2015). *Everybody's gone to the rapture* [PlayStation 4 video game]. Minato, Tokyo, Japan: Sony Computer Entertainment.

The Giant Beastcast. (2015, August 28). *The giant beastcast: Episode 14* [Audio podcast]. Retrieved from http://www.giantbomb.com/podcasts/download/1332/ep14_thegiantbeastcast-08-28-2015-3863808300.mp3

Totilo, S. (2015, March 3). *He saw her face - Why we still love metroid prime* [Web log post]. Retrieved from http://kotaku.com/he-saw-her-face-why-we-still-love-metroid-prime-1691270398

Triada Studio Games. (2015). *Shadowmatic* [IOS video game]. Triada Studio Games.

Triggs, T. (2006). Scissors and glue: Punk fanzines and the creation of a DIY aesthetic. *Journal of Design History, 19*(1), 69–83. doi:10.1093/jdh/epk006

Ubisoft Montreal. , (2003). *Prince of Persia: The sands of time* [Playstation 2, Xbox, GameCube video game]. Montral, Canada: Ubisoft.

Ubisoft Montreal,. (2014). *Far cry 4* [Windows, PS3, PS4, XBox 360, XBox One video game]. Montreuil, France: Ubisoft.

Ustwo. (2014). *Monument valley* [IOS, Android video game]. Ustwo.

Uttal, D. H., Meadow, N. G., Tipton, E., Hand, L. L., Alden, A. R., Warren, C., & Newcombe, N. S. (2013). The malleability of spatial skills: A meta-analysis of training studies. *Psychological Bulletin, 139*(2), 352–402. doi:10.1037/a0028446 PMID:22663761

Uttal, D. H., Miller, D. I., & Newcombe, N. S. (2013). Exploring and enhancing spatial thinking links to achievement in science, technology, engineering, and mathematics? *Current Directions in Psychological Science*, 22(5), 367–373. doi:10.1177/0963721413484756

Vagle, M. D. (2010, May). *A post-intentional phenomenological research approach*. Paper presented at the American Educational Research Association, Denver, CO.

Valentine, K. D. (2014). *Problematizing space and perspective: A middle school mathematics experience* (Doctoral dissertation, The University of Georgia). Retrieved from The University of Georgia Library Electronic Theses and Dissertations. (Record No. 13472).

Valve Corporation. (2007). *Portal* [Windows, PS3, Xbox 360 video game]. Bellevue, WA: Valve Corporation.

van Manen, M. (1990). *Researching lived experience: Human science for an action sensitive pedagogy*. Albany, NY: State University of New York Press.

Wai, J., Lubinski, D., & Benbow, C. P. (2009). Spatial ability for STEM domains: Aligning over 50 years of cumulative psychological knowledge solidifies its importance. *Journal of Educational Psychology*, 101(4), 817–835. doi:10.1037/a0016127

Wilson, C. (2015, April 9). *Against "indie": New albums from Modest Mouse, Sufjan Stevens, and more show it's time to eliminate the racist term for good*. Retrieved from http://www.slate.com/articles/arts/music_box/2015/04/against_indie_new_albums_from_modest_mouse_sufjan_stevens_and_more_show.html

Yacht Club Games. (2014). *Shovel knight* [Windows, Nintendo 3DS, Nintendo Wii U, OS X, Linux video game]. Valencia, CA: Yacht Club Games.

Yarouze, G., & Studio, J. (2008). *Echochrome* [PS3, PSPortable, PSStore video game]. Minato, Tokyo, Japan: Sony Computer Entertainment.

Yuke's Media Creations. (2004). *Berserk* [PlayStation 2 video game]. Minato, Tokyo: Sammy Corporation.

KEY TERMS AND DEFINITIONS

AAA Video Games: Video games supported with large design, development, and marketing/distribution budgets. The AAA signifier indicates a high-quality, mass-produced, popular game in a similar manner to Blockbuster hits in the film industry.

Game Mechanic: Refers to the rules and structures governing the game space and how the player interacts with it (e.g., victory conditions, movement styles, combat, resource management).

Geometric Transformations: Changing a shape by movement on a coordinate plane by rotating, reflecting, translating, or dilating.

Indie Video Games: Those video games developed without corporate funding. Although not a defining factor, indie games are usually developed by a small team or even a single individual motivated by an idea, not primarily monetary concerns.

Jamming Econo: The do-it-yourself (DIY) culture of early independent punk rock music in the United States. This phrase was coined by Minutemen band member Mike Watt.

Lived-Experience: In phenomenological research, a narrative from those experiencing a phenomenon of interest.

Mathematization: Investigating a situation mathematically and/or expressing the phenomenon in mathematical terms.

Perspectival Shift: A shift in visual perspective, usually mediated by technologies that change a viewer's relationship with an object.

Postphenomenology: A modified form of phenomenological investigation that seeks to account for the embodied nature inherent in phenomena as experienced while recognizing phenomena as occurring in cultural/historical contexts. Don Ihde coined the term and makes pragmatism and variational theory (verses a focus on invariant experience) central to his explication of postphenomenology.

Spatial Thinking: Knowing, representing, and reasoning about space. This involves orienting and visualizing as activities.

Chapter 16
Playful Experiments:
Conditions of "An Experience" in Touchscreen Games by a Non-Hermeneutic Perspective

Felippe Calazans Thomaz
Federal University of Bahia, Brazil

Jorge Cardoso Filho
Federal University from Recôncavo of Bahia, Brazil

ABSTRACT

This study investigates the conditions to aesthetic experience in games for touchscreen devices from a non-hermeneutic perspective. For that reason, the body and the technical devices are taken as fundamental dimensions in the process of having "an experience", in which their material aspects are not indifferent. In other words, what is of interest is to analyze game situations and the mutual influence between player and game, in the sense of identifying elements that could lead to "an experience", taking as objects the games Mountain *and* Monument Valley. *Moreover, concerns to understand how such titles contribute to the broadening of the technoludic experience. The article is sustained in the induction that from the moment in which characteristics of traditional games are tensioned, it seems that they assume an air of experimentation in their ways of calling to action. We argue that "an experience" can emerge from the articulation between "effects of presence" and "effects of meaning", so that the material constitution of the medium is not indifferent.*

INTRODUCTION

Contemporary times present us with a very particular scenery of the human condition. Gradually the ways in which the world is felt and experimented seem to orbit in a limbo between the digital and the organic, between the mechanical and the physical. In such a context, perceiving and conjecturing about human manifestations presents itself as a demanding task for interdisciplinary efforts, given the complexity of the phenomena that arise.

DOI: 10.4018/978-1-5225-0261-6.ch016

The objective of this article is grounded in the scenery of hybridization between computing devices and human faculties. Specifically, entertainment is situated as a gear of crucial importance in structuring contemporary times: in a particular way, electronic games stand out as a most salient expression of that very cultural industry[1]. Games are considered as powerful media, especially in regards to its forms of reception. Simply put, the act of playing consists of an interaction between the player and the game through a physical device. This dialogical process is the subject of this article.

The conditions of aesthetic experience in games with touchscreen interfaces are hereby inquired, from a non-hermeneutic standpoint (Gumbrecht, 2004), placing material devices and its relationships with bodily functions as fundamental dimensions of this process. In other words, we intend to analyze game situations and mutual influence between players and the game, in the sense of identifying elements that could lead to "an experience" (Dewey, 1980), examining games as *Mountain* (O'Reilly, 2014) and *Monument Valley* (ustwo, 2014). We sustain that experiential aspects are involved in the performance of playing, departing from the moment when traditional characteristics of games are tensioned – largely due to the digital creative possibilities. We argue that an experience can emerge from the articulation between effects of presence and effects of meaning (Gumbrecht, 2004), in such a way that makes impossible to disregard the material constitution of the game media devices.

AESTHETIC EXPERIENCE AND PERFORMANCE

On a flat surface, the most effective way of joining two separate points is through a straight line. The connection between the poles assumes a connecting element, which, in turn, results in a new spatial configuration. This same line draw itself in a progressive and orderly manner, leaving a place and heading to another, continuously. This illustration is taken as a way to examine some delineations of the concepts of *experience* and *game* and the resulting transposition of the latter to the digital landscape, placing what is in between as a guiding thread of the argument.

Thus, pragmatism addresses the issue of experience as an active movement between the living creature and the surrounding environment (Dewey, 1980). Among past experiences - constructs of socio-historical order - and the situation at hand, the subject captures and is captured, affects and allows to be affected by what is revealed to the senses. It is an everyday game by which subjects constantly sense the surroundings while being inserted in it, in a rather conscious manner. So, to conceive experience in pragmatism one must imply a special attention to the "in-between" space of one and another instance: past and present, with respect to time; body and environment, in relation to space. It is worth noting, however, that this duality is not presented as a separation, but as a continuous sharing that ultimately characterizes the flow of life itself.

In this sense, experience arises primarily from interactive situations. That is, the planning activity aimed at a particular accomplishment is what gives the status of experience to a conscious movement. Through successive phases, the seemingly dichotomic aspect of interactions is integrated in a mutual equilibrium that results in affectations. Just as the line that connects two separate points, it is a cumulative process that aims a specific purpose, as described by John Dewey (1980):

Every experience is the result of interaction between a live creature and some aspect of the world in which he lives. A man does something; he lifts, let us say, a stone. In consequence he undergoes, suffers, something: the weight, strain, texture of the surface of the thing lifted. The properties thus undergone determine further doing. The stone is too heavy or too angular, not solid enough; or else, the properties undergone show it is fit for the use for which it intended. The process continues until a mutual adaptation of the self and the object emerges and that particular experience comes to a close. (p. 44. Emphasis added)

The consummation of experience – the adaptation between subject and environment - derives from a series of mutual affectations, which requires bodily functions and capacities in a particular way through the rational, mnemonic and sensorimotor structures. It is worth mentioning that Dewey (1980) comprehends perception as an indivisible interaction between sensory and rational dimensions of experience. The body, in this perspective, is the medium that concatenates brain and senses as a way of being in the world, leaving and incorporating marks that will generate, in turn, new configurations of both subject and surrounding environment[2].

However, there are situations marked in a special way. At such times, there seems to be an intensification of perception, an interruption of the continuum of ordinary life, a different attraction of attention (Seel, 2014). Such events provide distinctive quality to the experience, figuring in as an experience (Dewey, 2010).

The aesthetic experience, thus, presupposes an involvement intensified with sensual presence of phenomena or situations. Thus, it is not restricted to any particular spheres of objects, but can - and should, as claims Dewey - be likely to occur in everyday life.

Hans Ulrich Gumbrecht (2004) shares a similar understanding of the above presented approach, proposing that aesthetic experience derives from the articulation between effects of presence and effects of meaning. The non-hermeneutic perspective holds that meaning results from pacts between subject and object, considering the influences of socio-historical and particular dimensions. This standpoint suggests that the meaning is constituted in the interaction between the person and the environment, instead of being present on each one, separately. The generative route of the meaning happens, therefore, in context of a subjective sharing of the creature with his environment (Picado & Araújo, 2012).

Similarly, *presence* alludes to the tangibility of a given object in space, to its substance - in Aristotelian terms. In other words, Gumbrecht (2004) clarifies this issue while presenting his own understanding of "production of presence", a central key to his undertaken investigation. According to him, the act of bringing forward or bring forth – from Latin *pro- ducere*, production – a tangible object in space – Latin-entry *prae-esse*, presence – carries with it a sense of mobility, since it involves, as the author says, "movement of greater or lesser closeness and greater or lesser intensity" (Gumbrecht, 2004, p. 39).

Two main aspects stand out here, as emerging in the author's argument: the presence and the body. Both point to the practical, somatic aspects that compose the experience. Therefore, from the standpoint of performance studies[3] it is possible to access non-hermeneutical components constituting these sensitive experiences. The performances are restored behaviors (Schechner, 2006) through which the creature acts (and reacts) to material and symbolic environments – revealing conventional bodily skills and singular gestures of aesthetic emergence. The players' performative activity at moments of interaction with games becomes, thus, the primary research object of this study.

PLAYFULNESS AND DIGITAL MEDIA

As regards to the game elements, in general, the play activity occurs in the context of intermediation. In a game situation, a redefinition of the ordinary space and time can be noticed. This condition puts the subject in a particular dome of activity in which the mutual cooperation between the players is required. So, to play is also to construct a "magic circle", a possible world with specific rules and forms of action (Huizinga, 1980; Salen & Zimmerman, 2003).

Thus, it is not for nothing that the word delude comes from the same root of playful: *ludus*. To play, in Huizinga's (1980) classical perspective, implies the temporary suspension of the ordinary flow of life. Each game type or extension displays to the player several forms of action to be contemplated, so that the game can go on. Rules, fictional universes, dexterity and skills are some examples of the constituent elements of the game. Anyway, in this context, the subject agrees to show itself as a kind of puppet (McLuhan, 1994) for a specified period, acting as the system of rules for fun and excitement purposes, taking advantage of motor and intellectual abilities in order to sustain the illusion of playful activity[4]. Therefore, between player and game, there is a functional and aesthetic system that requires certain physical and intellectual engagement of its participants as living conditions. Such consideration is also present on the contributions of Roger Caillois (1990), especially in the relationship between elements of fun and functional dynamics. The French author presents his concept of play on two oppositions: *paidia* and *ludus*. In his own words,

at one end, reigns, almost absolutely, a common principle of fun, turbulence, improvisation and carefree expansion, through which it manifests a certain restrained fantasy which may be called paidia. At the opposite end, this cheerful and thoughtless exuberance is almost absorbed, or at least disciplined, by [...] a growing need to subordinate the conventional, compelling and troublesome rules, [...] in order to hinder the achievement of the desired goal [...]. Designate as ludus this second component. (Caillois, 1990, pp. 32-33)

From this first classification—dualistic—Caillois (1990) features six fundamental characteristics of the nature of the game, figured in *paidia* or *ludus*:

1. **Free:** From the moment there is an obligation to fulfill such activity, the game immediately loses the characteristic of playfulness.
2. **Delimited:** It is inserted in limits of previously set space and time.
3. **Uncertain:** The result is not given beforehand and its development is relegated to the player's initiative.
4. **Unproductive:** It does not generate goods or wealth beyond the game's own circle.
5. **Regulated:** Insofar as it is subject to conventions introduced briefly, the ones that count for such activity.
6. **Fictional:** There is the awareness that this can become another reality, in opposition to the ordinary life.

Such observations help us in defining what is comprehended as a game. The marking of this concept is the basis for the observations of research subjects in this study—*Monument Valley* (ustwo, 2014) and *Mountain* (O'Reilly, 2014)—especially concerning the experimental basis that both seem to have. Etymologically, the *peri* Latin root corresponds to *peira* (πείρα), from the Greek, and indicates something like obstacle, limitation. With prefix *ex-*, the idea behind this word is the disruption of boundaries, opening new perspectives. Therefore, affirming that a certain video game has an air of experimentalism requires contemplating a basic definition of what is traditionally comprehended as a game, watching what and how certain features are problematized by the tittles in question.

It is thus clear that electronic and non-electronic games invite players to engage in action in different ways. Accordingly, one can say that there are specificities in performances that develop these two broad categories of games. In addition, within each category, it is clear that there are specific behaviors that are stimulated by developers and expected by players. In general, digital products combine audiovisual features to the ability of receiving commands from the player through special devices, providing the player screen responses and continually demanding new actions. The bodily effort of the creature is presupposed by the conduct of technoludic activity, so that, if nothing is done, the cybertext (Aarseth, 1997) cannot be read—at least not in its entirety.

Again, what is in between one and another dimension emerges as a discussion point: in this case, player and screen. This setting is based on the very idea of "ergodic literature" (Aarseth, 1997), a concept widely discussed by many researchers of Game Studies and yet demanding reflections. Thereby in consideration of the constant transformation of the contemporary technological scenario, this need is updated.

In the last decade, the advances of entertainment industry enabled the public to have access to new control devices. Motion sensors, augmented reality, modern and sophisticated joysticks and touch screens are examples of innovations that have achieved great market acceptance, especially in their applications in electronic games. This also implies a set of changes in performance: motor and cognitive stimuli require specific skills of users and vice versa. Previous studies have already taken account of some aspects of the mutual influence relationship between the technical and the human (Crary, 1999; Kittler, 1999; Singer, 2001; Ferraz, 2010), which allows us to state that media—conceived in their materialities—are fundamental items for the development of experience (McLuhan, 1994; Pereira, 2008). Thus, considering that there is a mediating element between player and screen, becoming unviable to ignore that the device not only mediates, but also is the gameplay process agent.

For example, *Monument Valley* (ustwo, 2014) and *Mountain* (O'Reilly, 2014) are two independent games available on mobile devices and can be experienced from a set of touches and gestures on the screen, easily assimilated even by the most inexperienced players. For not having a dense narrative, thus not requiring large investments of time and resources or complex skills from the players, the titles fit as casual games (Juul, 2010). This indicates that the game does not require neither a focused attitude, nor a higher level of concentration and extensive experience in electronic games; on the contrary, the demands of the game to the player are very flexible and easily assimilated.

Considering that mobile devices are intrinsic parts on the constitution of the contemporary world, the "casual revolution" (Juul, 2010) inserts a vast number of people in recreational activities mediated by digital technologies. For example, from 2012 to 2013 ESA[5] detected a 55% increase in the number of casual game players on mobile devices, which makes them the most popular genre in its class. Due to the widespread use of mobile technology, it seems to be an extension of the magic circle. Namely, casual games allow asynchronous remote play, are also imbued in the common life flow and do not require full attention of the players, which reflects the *Zeitgeist* of a society marked by technologies. Finally, in contemporary life, the communication practices are sustained in lexicons of various orders—human and computational—as forms of expression, making it possible to act in the inner layers of the text, interpreting it, modifying it, and experiencing their structures.

TECHNOLUDIC EXPERIENCES IN NON-HERMENEUTIC PERSPECTIVE

In response to the current material and cultural scene, the non-hermeneutic field appears as an epistemological alternative that concerns itself with the extra-literary elements in the various processes and the act of reading extensions, nowadays[6]. Such as Gumbrecht (2004) says, "Materialities of communication [...] are all those phenomena and conditions that contribute to the production of meaning, without being meaning themselves" (p. 28). This approach contains the idea that meaning is established by the articulation of historical and cultural processes with the materialities of the medium when interacting with the body. That is, to apprehend a work is not only to be equipped with instruments that will enable users to extract the meaning of the text that is presented, but understand that this same sense derives from the articulation of multiple instances, especially those of a material nature in its historical and cultural dimensions.

Therefore, some authors suggest that in a non-hermeneutic perspective, "communication is seen less as an exchange of meanings and ideas about something, and more as a performance put in motion through multiple materialized significance"[7] (Pfeiffer cited in Felinto, 2001, p. 6). In the case of touchscreen games, the condition to the gaming experience passes necessarily through an apparatus that is simultaneously the mediation to the player's presence in the simulated environment and the audiovisual response that provides this same sense of ambiance. In other words, the interpretation of what is presented to the senses is invariably imbricated in the very material dimension of that same object.

However, the materialities of digital game should not be limited to the physical structure of the medium, but should include the software as a dimension which is also part of the object. As Felinto (2001) proposes, "the interaction between body and machine, between human thought systems and binary systems, between the real and the virtual is a particularly interesting problem for the tools of the Theory of Materialities"[8] (p. 14). Between the player and the game it sets up a partition of signification that covers hardware, software, senses and intellect; the link between these poles also gather tools, features, rules, ambiences and possible performances.

Thus, the Materialities must not be exclusively understood as something physical and concrete, but as a complex system that also gathers historical and cultural dimensions. For this reason it presents itself as a transdisciplinary subject, placing the description as the main methodological stance. In a more refined manner, in thoroughly reading the work of the Danish linguist Louis Hjemslev, Gumbrecht (2004) presents four poles of the sign concept that in continuous coordination, enable the emergence of meaning. On one hand, there is the structuralist polarization between "signifier" and "signified"—the "signifier" being treated as "expression" and "signified" as "content". On the other hand the distinction is based on Aristotelian thought, between "substance" and "form." Four concepts are configured of the articulation between these poles: "substance of content," "form of content," "substance of expression," and "form of expression" (Gumbrecht, 2004). A reflection on such concepts is valid as a way to introduce what is the Theory of Materialities with propriety, as it is the methodological stance that substantiates the analysis of the research object of this article.

Therefore, Gumbrecht (2004) affirms that the "substance of content" corresponds to what is commonly referred to as "imaginary", i.e., human thought content without any structural intervention. "Form of content" indicates content of human thought in well-structured forms and should not be confused with any spatial manifestation thereof. "Substance of expression" indicates the materials through which the contents may be manifested in space, before any structural definition (a computing device in hardware level or a game engine, for example). Finally, the "form of expression", would be a set of possible formats from the substance of expression (the software, the app, the sounds and images on the screen, according to the previous example).

The non-hermeneutic field turns to the emergence of meaning as an articulation among the aforementioned concepts, presenting an alternative method to any purely interpretive approach or focused exclusively on the subject. Gumbrecht (2004) outlines a methodology from a sequence based on three issues:

1. The emergence of forms of content out of substance of content.
2. The emergence of forms of expression out of substance of expression.
3. The coupling of forms of content and forms of expression into signs or into larger signifying structures – for example, into a written text, a speech, or a pictogram (p. 15).

When the subject of the investigation is an electronic game, some technical peculiarities should be considered, mainly because the engagement of the reader/player is the key for the text to present its layers. Unlike a static picture which is presented in its entirety to the human senses, the game should be played so it can be read. The behavioral factor is central to the ergodic literature (Aarseth, 1997) and is the premise to the experience of digital games. Therefore, it is worth examining the forms of content evoked by the game, with special attention to the ways in which such fictional universe is built and the dialogue it establishes with other works. Moreover, it is necessary to analyze how the forms of expression make use of the ambiance material resources—physical and digital—of the medium, observing potential appropriations and the ways in which the subject's behavior is summoned by the game.

In this case, the Theory of Materialities is valid because it considers the attribution of meaning and the aesthetic experience itself as resulting from complex articulations between subjective and material dimensions, either historical or cultural ones. Departing from this context, the method adopted cannot be any other but a transdisciplinary one – and this because the nature of electronic games articulates aesthetic, sensorial and behavioral dimensions, constructed from computer languages—code and programming—for playfulness purposes.

So if the intention is to discuss the players' performances in touchscreen games in a non-hermeneutic perspective, it is necessary to walk through fields of knowledge related to the making and enjoyment of digital game passive to experimentation by the sense of touch. In this case, it is possible to perceive that the basis of computer language is organized in a coherent order, offering audiovisual stimuli and gaps to be filled by the action of the player[9]. Thus, in touchscreen games, the creature must understand what is presented on screen and use a repertoire of gestures so the textual machinery can work properly. The player's actions are read by the device that provides audio and video responses, perpetuating an interactional cycle between player and game.

HUMAN-COMPUTER INTERACTION

Although distinct in material aspects, the human-computer interaction (HCI) is constantly compared to a conversation among social actors. Crawford (2003), for example, makes an analogy to a reciprocal listening, thinking and speech cycle as a demonstration of the basic conditions to a mutual action process:

the need for cohesion between the three stages, namely, input, process, and output. Such stages, defends the author, should be integrated as links in a chain, otherwise the whole process is compromised.

Although the human and computational lexicons belong to different natures, they can be integrated on a particular communication process through the interface. Crawford (2003) states that the computer "speaks" through the screen and audio, "thinks" algorithmically—language operations in commands and scripts to be followed by software—and "listens" for input devices (keyboard and mouse, joystick and more recently, touch screens). The human, on the other hand, perceives reality transposed by the machine through his senses, understands the presented signs and responds with motor actions, supporting the interactive process. Obviously, as new offerings of interaction appear, new cognitive and motor demands are required. Regarding this, the author states that "the input device determines the size of the vocabulary available to the user. Clearly, we want to use input devices that give our user maximal vocabulary" (Crawford, 2003, p. 51). The player makes of his actions, its words, and with them builds its own text to the medium as it reads, interprets and assimilate the signs that are presented.

In case of mobile devices, the screen is the main way of communication between user and system. Haptic interfaces (Hayward, Astley, Cruz-Hernandes, Grant, Robles-De-La-Torre, 2004) turn the display into a kind of joystick, making use of other peripherals in their manipulation possibilities such as the accelerometer, the gyroscope, the camera and the microphone. The convergence of these media on a device allows us to think of true media arrangements (Pereira, 2008), holders of its own grammars and demanding private interaction forms—like a set of gestures performed on the screen, for example. Obviously, the consolidation of new interfaces and consequent forms of interaction require user training—after all, one cannot lose sight of the marketing context of these products—because they present possibilities of redefinitions in the use of certain tools.

It is essential in this regard, to consider that the interaction between user and system requires a mutual understanding of the possibilities and means of expression. As stated,

having a meaningful, efficient, and productive interaction, just like creating a language or a code, requires that both parties agree on the meaning of the symbol and the meaning of the order in which actions occur. Those particular understandings are going to be quite different depending on the interface and type of interaction that the user undertakes. (Noble, 2009, p. 10)

Besides that, when the media are electronic games, the particularities of the playful activity itself come into the picture. The interactive digital product should entertain the users by calling up their participation and evoking emotions. The first moments of the game industry are characterized by the centrality on the programmer, who performed various functions: code, art, sound and game design. The games were built as unique pieces of software with exclusive source codes and with little or no possibility of reuse. Currently, the development scenario has changed. Technical advances have enabled specific specialization—for example, character movement, physics, artificial intelligence etc. —as well as greater creation resources. It is in this context that the engines are fixed as important tools for the production of digital games.

In that sense, Gregory (2009) suggests that "we should probably reserve the term 'game engine' for software that is extensible and can be used as the foundation for many different games without major modification" (p. 11). This means that the developer relies on software nuclear components (collision system, audio or render, for example) and art assets (characters, environments, objects, etc.), in a logic in which the aspect of modularity (Manovich, 2001) reigns. The engines, as well as Software Development

Kits (SDKs) facilitate the creation, implementation and trials of games. According to McShaffry and Graham (2013), these tools are used to optimize the creative process and provide security to developers since they have already gone through trials and have been implemented by other programmers.

At the software level, the observation of this creation scenario, in accordance with the non-hermeneutic field (Gumbrecht, 2004), enables to point out the "substance of expression" as a set of programs that affords for the development of digital objects, algorithms and operations to constitute a particular "form of expression": an electronic game. By agreeing to the proposal that the Theory of Materialities is not restricted to the physical environment, but also covers the forms of interaction between body and machine (Felinto, 2001), it becomes possible to point out to the substance through which the game is shaped as something of a digital nature. Thus, among the endless creative possibilities, developers elect a set of signs to be experienced by the player. Using the proper terms (Gumbrecht, 2004), it is possible to say that the imagination—"substance of content"—is structured in an internal coherence—"form of content"—presenting environments, objects, motivations and rewards to the individual who accepts entering the magic circle of ludic activity.

In this way, if the fusion between forms of content and forms of expression allows the emergence of broader significant structures, it is necessary to distinguish characteristics from the experience of *Monument Valley* and *Mountain* to other electronic games. Such need is presented from the moment the process of attribution of meaning and aesthetic experience are comprehended as a result of the articulation between subject and work—player and game—not as something inherent to any of the poles alone.

General Aspects of the Objects

Released in 2014 by independent companies, both titles arouse attention from players and critics due to their visual characteristics and gameplay. Immediately it appears to break or at least to put tension on some traditional electronic game brands as the development of specific skills, competition and set of rules and well-defined objectives. While one plays with the geometry of the digital environments in a puzzle (where the rearrangement of the scenery elements hold much of the experience), the other invites players to become a mountain, with little or no interference in the course of in-game activities.

Therefore, it is necessary to analyze these objects carefully, presenting and discussing game situations in accordance with methods suggested by the Theory of Materialities. Once some intervening elements of the act of playing the titles in question are highlighted, it is easier to list the conditions to "an experience" (Dewey, 1980) in touchscreen games. In this sense, one should not forget the Deweyan stance about the experience as a sharing of the subject with the object that gets its attention. It is from this interaction between player and game that the aesthetic experience can emerge.

It has been stated, however, that in electronic games this interactive process is crucial to the uncovering of the cybertext, according to Aarseth's (1997) terms. It is in gameplay situations that the viewer becomes the interactor, player. It is from this set of mutual actions - between human and computational device - that a game can be experienced. In more detailed manner,

the term gameplay refers to the action that takes place in the game, the rules that govern the virtual world in which the game takes place, the abilities of the player character(s) (known as player mechanics) and of the other characters and objects in the world, and the goals and objectives of the player(s). (Gregory, 2009, p. 45)

Therefore, gameplay, audio-visual and narrative elements, the materialities of the medium—hardware and software—and creative processes and authoring should not be considered an analysis that aims to understand the conditions of *an experience* in electronic touchscreen games. So, after analyzing each game a discussion is proposed about the general objective of this study as a way of outlining a methodological approach that connects the non-hermeneutical field to electronic games as research objects.

Monument Valley

Until mid-2011 ustwo studios acted most notably on developing applications and interfaces for large companies like Sony, Google, Nokia and others. The first step to greater notoriety in video games happened with the release of *Whale Trail*, an endless runner game *à la Tiny Wings* (Illiger, 2011), with a pleasant design and easy handleability. Although well accepted by players and critics, the game was based on a widespread genre among mobile casual games, offering few innovations in terms of its mechanics.

However, in 2014 *Monument Valley* was released for iOS, receiving immediate acceptance from the public. Based on the drawings of one of the workers of the studio Ken Wong, the game got an artistry status in several reviews[10]. Much of this immediate success was due to references with which the game dialogues: minimalist sculptures, Japanese paintings, indie games like *Fez* (Polytron, 2012) and *Sword & Sworcery* (Superbrothers, 2011) and, more evidently, the drawings of M.C. Escher, as is evident in Figure 1. The beauty of the in-game environments and their adaptation of puzzles resulted in the award for best 2014 iPad game by Apple Design award.

Figure 1. Similarity between image MC Escher and Monument Valley

The universe of *Monument Valley* consists of the pursuit of Princess Ida for the redemption of something done in the past—which the game does not make clear. The player must guide the character by optical illusion mazes and impossible constructions—which, in the story of the game are referred to as "sacred geometry"—playing with perspective as a way to move forward on the puzzle solving tasks. In addition, during her journey the princess faces an antagonist species, the Crow People, avoiding or using these beings to recover parts of the sacred geometry. Defying physics is the premise for experiencing *Monument Valley*.

The narrative intake is rather vague and allows for several interpretations. It is not known exactly what motivates the main character's actions or who the Crow People are, for example. This characteristic seems to allow for projections of the subject-players in attaching themselves more easily to the object-game. In other words, rather than an exact symbolic representation, developers play with the possibilities of coming-to-be. The *can be* seems to be more important than the *is/is not*, and this dimension of possibility is the basis to puzzles of *Monument Valley*, operating on semantic and narrative levels, architectural and graphics of gameplay.

The player in the first level of the game is presented to a simple resolution challenge in which he receives instructions that will base a good part of his experience. The initial information "tap the path to move Ida" shows how to move the princess around the environment, since the following information—"hold and rotate"—shows how to manipulate elements of the scenario. To perform the required command, the player needs to turn a hand crank so that the path takes shape and the character may reach the end of the path, where it is presented to the game title. All these actions are done due to the characteristic tactility of touchscreen interfaces. Curiously, by crossing the platform that was rotated, the hand crank hides its bars making it impossible for the player to interact with this object until the avatar comes out from the same surface. Figure 2 expresses this sequence of actions, quite emblematic for the future challenges.

As the player also exerts control over the scenery, developers have provided visual clues of how to interact with certain objects in order to solve the puzzles proposed. In this sense, the concept of affordance emerges.

Figure 2. Resolution of the first level of Monument Valley

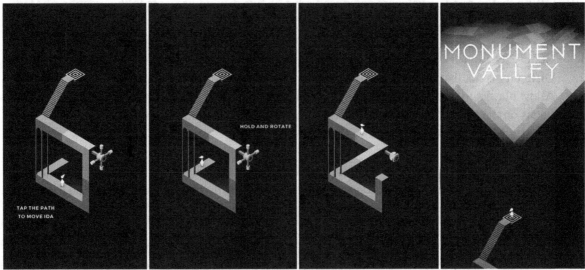

Affordances, as Gibson (1979) presents, result from the interaction between creature and environment, that is, they refer to a complementarity between these two. As the agent perceives his surroundings, he also becomes aware of how to use it in certain ways. For that reason, the concept of affordance does consider the uniqueness of this very process, since different creatures have different perceptions, physical constitutions and abilities. As Gibson (1979) states, "The affordances of the environment are what it offers to the animal, what it provides or furnishes, either for good or ill. [...] It implies the complementarity of the animal and the environment" (p. 127). Also, according to Norman (2002), "an affordance is a relationship between the properties of an object and the capabilities of the agent that determine just how the object could possibly be used" (p. 11).

That is, in providing a hand crank or buttons, developers invite the player to act on such objects. Obviously such use is based on memory and mental processes of representation, so that "the experiences and cultural factors, or the agent's repertoire can influence the way one understands the possibilities of action"[11] (Maia, 2013, p. 6). In this sense, the tapping or sliding of a finger on the screen of an iPhone or iPad on an object like a hand crank, for example, already affords the player with a prior notion of the result of his gesture. Around this phenomenon there is a dimension of reiteration of a behavior, of a quest for past experiences—more or less consciously—that provides meaning to what, in game situation, updates itself. Therefore, the materialities of objects in the digital environment summon a gestural repertoire of the player who relies on the physical apparatus as the mediator device *in game* action. In other words, affordances, past experiences of the player and the very constitution of the medium in which the game is emulated seem to exert direct influence on the gaming experience.

Moreover, there is a curious factor about the game being restricted to mobile devices: *Monument Valley* can only be experienced vertically. The privilege of height is manifested at level design at all times, especially because the structures in which the character moves are remodeled by the player, breaking the habitual conventions of perspective. In general, the princess rises to higher surfaces to advance in the game. Anyway, this feature points directly to the influence of the physical aspect of the medium, either smartphones or tablets. Should it be ported to a computer or console, and the game would suffer changes on level design so it could suit monitors arranged horizontally.

These factors reinforce the positioning of the designer Ken Wong when he says that the game should be considered more as a "premium experience" than a hard challenge, long and repetitive (Sheffield, 2014). With that in mind, developers composed a list of five driving precepts to the creation of *Monument Valley*:

1. Quality over quantity (make each level unique).
2. Difficulty is not that important to the user's experience.
3. Allow players to discover for themselves (don't tell them what to do or how to feel).
4. Focus on the things that make the game special, rather than adding content.
5. The ending is important to the story (Sheffield, 2014).

These points seem to converge to Wong's proposal when he declares in an interview: "We hope players will stay engaged for the same reasons they might enjoy a walk through a museum or an art gallery. [...] We know that are mobile gamers out there looking for this kind of thoughtful, aesthetic experience" (Wong cited in Stinson, 2013, para. 9).

Relating such assertion to the Deweyan stance on the aesthetic experience as something capable of existence by interaction of the living creature with its environment (in which the perception is intensified by setting a particular event where there is a conscious movement towards a particular purpose), it is clear that the digital object in question enables affectations and different interpretations from those ones common to puzzle games. A dialogue is established between player and game that seems to require a more contemplative and less frivolous attitude. There are no records to beat, nor points to win. At each level, the player needs nothing but the character at the final destination, under the promise of recovering one of the parts of the sacred geometry. However, the tone seems to focus much more on the act of experiencing possible paths—often getting lost among the mazes — instead of immediately meeting the proposed objectives. Nevertheless, completing the game is important as the story has a symbolic conclusion to the saga of Ida. In the final animation, there is a sense of accomplishment — under Dewey (1980) —to the *Monument Valley*'s experience as a whole.

Obviously, in accordance with the aesthetic proposed for the work, the end is vague and allows different interpretations. The player must put the pieces together on its own narrative, thus configuring a unique experience. What is presented to the senses — through fingers on screen —is not pointed with clarity; it is only allusions, of possibilities of sense. This deliberate opening of the object invites the player to a mutual constructing pact, in terms of gameplay and meaning, as defends the developer himself: "I like to think that video games can be a bit more open to interpretation, like music" (Wong cited in Stinson, 2013, para. 7).

This trait of abstraction can result in very interesting experiences, bringing video games to other areas of the arts, such as poetry, for example. Titles such as *Journey* (thatgamecompany, 2012) and *Flower* (thatgamecompany, 2009) represent well the possibility of creating interactive pieces which break with the traditional marks of such media, providing a sort of an "elasticization" of what is understood as video game playing.

In this sense, the developers propose innovations to the scenery when using the same tools of production and the final product is presented in a different or unusual way. In this case, *Monument Valley* was created from the Unity 3D engine[12], currently one of the most used for developing games and applications. The creating possibilities with such software are virtually endless. A set of enablers to the development process and implementation of games can be altered and reused, resulting in new products. So it is with the other object of this study, *Mountain*. Although it was created with the same engine, the result is quite another. Under the non-hermeneutic field (Gumbrecht, 2004), it is possible to say that the same "substance of expression" was ordered in a way to produce a distinct "form of expression", which, again, indicates the influence of materialities in the creation of interactive digital objects. Thus, the merger of "form of content" and "form of expression" generates new demands on the player, which will play an appropriate performance — in somatic and intellectual order — as to enable an effective connection with the work — considering therefore the experience as interaction, while connection between poles.

Mountain

Mountain is the first work of the Irish filmmaker David O'Reilly[13] in the field of electronic games. Known for a very distinctive style, the artist explores polygonal shapes, glitch effects and software elements in his creations. Thus, in a context in which the commercial aesthetic prizes for detailed renders, with models, textures and complex lighting, O'Reilly bases his creations on experimentation, presenting unusual applications of the 3D softwares.

Before the creation of *Mountain*, however, the artist worked as animation director on the film *Her*, directed by the American filmmaker Spike Jonze. O'Reilly conceived sequences in which the main character plays a video game in a somewhat unusual manner. Using a kind of thimble as controllers, the game is designed holographically in the living room of Theodore, who is played by actor Joaquin Phoenix. What is interesting in these sequences is the way the avatar responds to the out-game stimuli, interacting with the protagonist and his 'interlocutor spontaneously, beyond the interface and gameplay proposed by the artist, in science fiction context. Although being a creation in audiovisual, some characteristic elements of the creative process O'Reilly can be seen from this example. Among these, perhaps the most vigorous is the fascination with an unusual aesthetic.

This clue is most striking when a game like *Mountain* is experienced. The highlight to the term "experienced" rather than "played" is here justified due to the possibilities of performance of that object. Not surprisingly, the game was first presented in June 2014 at a conference at the Museum of Contemporary Art in Los Angeles, California. The announcement generated great expectations in the public, as it was the O'Reilly game—he was already known for his work in other areas.

Thus, on its official website[14], *Mountain* is described as "the Mountain simulator", belonging to the genres "relax 'em up" and "horror art". The novelty in the use of these terms in the arcades opens the way to the perception of distinctive elements of the game in question before others. Among these definitions, it is remarkable the reference to the games "beat 'em up"—widespread in the industry—by offering relaxation, over speed and struggles, as a defining element. By comparison, in "beat 'em ups" compete to the player the responsibility of fighting multiple waves of enemies, as in the series *Final Fight*, *Double Dragon* and *Battletoads*, for example. On the other hand, on the "relax 'em up"—in the singular because of the uniqueness of the term—the player is summoned much more as eyes and ears than muscles.

This trait is also reinforced in the description: "no controls; time moves forward; things grow and things die; nature expresses itself" (http://mountain-game.com/). Thus, each mountain is unique, generated from the player's drawings corresponding to three keywords. The author himself states that are "questions designed to be far more psychologically invasive than anything Facebook wants to know about you" (O'Reilly cited in Kollar, 2014, para. 5). In interpreting the player's answers, the loading screen simply displays the message "patience", escaping the usual "loading". The mountain is generated and the player can read the following information in capital letters: "Welcome to Mountain. You are Mountain. You are God." Figure 3 expresses this initial sequence:

Figure 3. Process of creation of the mountain in Mountain

Already in the early stages the player is challenged, not for puzzles or complex commands, but more by the rupture to the habitual references of the electronic game. In general, many attempts of interaction are made until it is realized that the mountain is there, impassive of direct controls. To the player, it is possible to change viewpoints: *zoom in* to perceive details and *zoom out* to the galaxy, but there is no way of changing what happens in-game. The first hours in *Mountain* seem to justify the claim the game poses as it is being loaded: patience really seems to be the first step towards the *Mountain* experience.

In this way, the gestural repertoire that *Mountain* evokes is characteristic to tactility, inherent to the touchscreen devices (Palacios & Cunha, 2012). Thus, "to pinch" the screen, moving the fingers in and out, the camera zooms in and out. The "swipe" on the sensitive surface rotates the camera, revealing different perspectives. The "tap" triggers a kind of piano—which will be discussed later—in addition to the main menu. In short, the degree of ease on the use of the controlling device and the responses of the software to gestures on the screen indicate that in this work, a contemplative attitude matters much more than, in fact, participation.

Therefore, to break with traditional brands of simulation games (characters handling or factors towards a certain goal, for example), a new performance is required. Simply put, the covenant that the mountain offers the player can go from an initial strangeness to a contemplative attitude, with resignation and understanding of the mechanics in the process. To the restless player who tries insistently to act upon the simulated environment, the game can seem tedious and boring. To the one who accepts the internal logic of *Mountain*, however, the experience can be almost hypnotic.

As the player/game boundary is settled, the interaction begins to take the contours of a particular experience. This is because, according to Dewey (1980), there is an ordering of a flow of energy for a determined purpose. This movement is integrated and self-sufficient, is cumulative with respect to their constituent stages. Referencing to the gameplay, the assimilation of non-action possibilities in *Mountain* can be understood as the fundamental condition to its fruition When the player acquiesces to the developer's proposal, that is, agrees to enter the *magic circle* he proposes, his/her experience can present traits of "an experience" *per se*. In this way, "that which distinguishes an experience as aesthetic is the conversion of resistance and tensions, of excitations that in themselves are temptations to diversion, into a movement toward an inclusive and fulfilling close" (Dewey, 1980, p. 139).

As the game goes on, the player realizes that certain events happen in the digital environment. The mountain, from time to time, "communicates" through short phrases written on the top of the screen and announced by the sound of a musical note. "This is really, really strange," it says in one moment. After a while, it asks: "What is beauty?" Further on, it states, "Being a thing is not so bad." The mountain, in response to the in-game moment, reports, "I'm deeply connected with this brilliant morning" and later, "I can't get enough of this melancholy night." This strange playful context seems to be contemplated by the mountain itself at some point of the game: "What is the mountain, exactly?"

The insertion of external elements to the surface of the mountain adds to the peculiarities of this game. At times, some objects collide and adhere to the mountain, becoming part of the scenery that uninterruptedly, rotates on its own axis. Among these, there is a fire extinguisher, an airplane, a skull, an egg and a variety of objects without any necessary reference to each other. At first, the entrance into orbit and subsequent crash is a surprise. Such events call the attention of the player into identifying the cause of the crash, which is the object and the why of this phenomenon. Both stand-alone events, messages and collisions, can be seen as a *Mountain* attraction to the user. In this sense, the proposal of Ian Bogost (2014) about such mechanisms is appropriate: "Think of them as little exercises, invitations the game extends to you to help you think through the impassible valley between your own experience and the unknowable experience of an entity like a mountain" (Bogost, 2014). From this perspective, it is clear the concern of the creative process to provide resources to facilitate the interaction between mountain and player.

Similarly, the relationship between doing and fruition is also observed by Dewey (1980), when maintaining that during the creative process, it is up to the artist to determine the oscillation between the producer and spectator stances. In this way, he/she becomes able to sort materials that will result in a specified work, assessing, along the creative action, the course of his/her work. So,

the eye attends and reports the consequence of what is done. Because of this intimate connection, subsequent doing is cumulative and not a matter of caprice nor yet of routine. In an emphatic artistic-aesthetic experience, the relation is so close that it controls simultaneously both the doing and the perception. [...] Hand and eye, when the experience is aesthetic, are but instruments through which the entire live creature, moved and active throughout, operates. (Dewey, 1980, pp. 49-50)

No wonder the trial phase is essential to the creation of a game. It is at this stage that the developer will evaluate whether the "substance of expression" that he calls in question results in a satisfactory "form of expression", in Gumbrecht's (2004) terms. Technically *Mountain* is not a game of great complexity. As the player's presence is evoked in a more appreciative way, it is possible to think of a lower level of interaction than, for example, in *Monument Valley*.

In this sense, the game offers a kind of piano which the player can play while watching the topographical structure that, in some way, represents the gamer in the digital environment. Depending on the platform where it is played, commands vary to the musical notes. On the computer the keyboard is used, in touchscreen devices, the bottom of the screen. Importantly, the mountain reacts to the resulting music from the user interaction. By quickly manipulating this kind of piano, pressing its keys, even randomly, the small planet has its orbit accelerated. In addition to spinning faster, the mountain is temporarily wrapped in a kind of illuminated aura, if observed from the universe. It seems that music cheers this digital entity up.

Such reactions seem to work in a seductive logic of the player. Its "thoughts", the manifestations of nature, the "atmospheric smile" to hearing a song played by the player are behavioral nuances outlined by *Mountain*. Metaphorically, it is as if it reached out waiting for a greeting from the player. Ian Bogost (2014) shares a similar perception:

The 'you' in 'you are mountain' doesn't refer to the terraformed 3D game object, at all. Instead, it describes the game itself. You are not mountain; rather, you are Mountain. You play as the abyss between the human and the alpine. [...] Mountain invites you to experience the chasm between your own subjectivity and the unfathomable experience of something else, something whose 'experience' is so unfamiliar as to be unimaginable. (para. 23)

These aspects seem to open more promising routes to an effective player-game pact. When the subject understands and accepts the vagueness of this work and its performance suits the expectations that the system proposes, it is possible to have *an experience*. In a complementary manner when the object is presented as a game, and at the same time, tightens the usual elements of playful activity, emerges the need to rethink the boundaries that separate the game from other human manifestations. In this perspective, it does not seem unfounded to perceive a trial basis—to the etymological root of the term—in the game in question. Therefore the *Mountain* experience seems to favor the understanding of play in a representation and interpretation bias, rather than its significance as rhythm, speed, manual skill or competition.

FUTURE PROSPECTS

Although the understanding of experience in Dewey (1980) and Gumbrecht (2004) are similar in several points, it is crucial to consider the distinctions of contexts in which the authors write. This exception is justified when the contemporary is observed as a largely mediated scenario, in which a myriad of communicational devices is increasingly incorporated into ordinary life. If the interaction between creature and environment is central to Dewey's pragmatism, we are driven to believe that the changes in both parties derive from their mutual and continuous affectations and that, accordingly, the growing influence of technical means can generate dispositions and particular sensory demands on the organic. It is precisely this perspective that Gumbrecht (2004) justifies the adoption of non-hermeneutic as an epistemological alternative, much due to the cultural and material contemporary environment.

From this perspective, the study of the performances of the players becomes a feasible possibility of identifying the emergence of aesthetic experiences with digital games, from a non-hermeneutic approach. This is because the concept of performance encompasses both a regular dimension—of restored behavior—as the creative force in relation to the uniqueness of that particular game situation. It allows dealing with somatic and material dimension, simultaneously.

In *Monument Valley* one can identify that specificity of performance implies experiencing the beautiful surroundings by manipulating the character and environment—through the affordances of in-game objects—it is possible to relate it to the conventions adopted in the puzzle genre games. In this sense, the gameplay does not approach the competitive dome—quicker resolution or greater accumulation of points—which indicates that, in fact, *Monument Valley* invites the player to appreciate its visual aspects at a more leisurely pace and with less focus on the fulfillment of the objectives themselves.

In *Mountain*, one identifies a performance in which the player is virtually reduced to eyes and ears. The player's actions do not directly influence the course of game events, but are called as the enablers of a pact between subject and software, between the player and the mountain. By providing a context in which the actions of the player do nothing more than cause minimal reactions from the digital object, a key feature of technoludic activity—the effective interaction between player and system—goes to checkmate. As a result, the very idea of digital game seems to expand in order to include such phenomena.

From that follows the observation that objects like *Monument Valley* and *Mountain*, assume an air of experimentation, once they promote tensions to conventions already socially established. The performance of the player emerges then as the pivot of these rearrangements, as it is in the act of playing that the technoludic experience occurs. The search for balance in the interaction between the poles moves the player's actions while in reverse perspective, presents the gamer new contexts of activity. In this sense, the materialities of the medium—physical and digital—are not indifferent. When a conscious and orderly pact between player and game is established, the ideal condition for the aesthetic experience emerges. That is, when the interaction results in the temporary suspension of the division between finger and sensitive screen, integrating them into a self-sufficient equilibrium situation, *an experience* is more than possible, it is expected.

REFERENCES

Aarseth, E. (1997). *Cybertext: Perspectives on ergodic literature*. Baltimore, MD and London: The John Hopkins Univ. Press.

Bogost, I. (2014, July 17). You are Mountain. *The Atlantic*. Retrieved from http://www.theatlantic.com/entertainment/archive/2014/07/you-are-mountain/374543/

Caillois, R. (1990). *Os jogos e os homens: a máscara e a vertigem*. Lisboa: Cotovia.

Carlson, M. (2009). *Performance: um introdução crítica*. Belo Horizonte: Editora da UFMG.

Crary, J. (1999). Suspensions of perception: attention, spetacle, and modern culture. Cambridge, MA, and London: MIT Press.

Crawford, C. (2003). *The art of interactive design: a euphonious and illuminating guide to building successful software*. San Francisco, CA: No Starch Press.

Dewey, J. (1980). *Art as experience*. New York, NY: Perigee Books.

Entertainment Software Association. (2014). *2014 Sales, demographic and usage data: essential facts about the computer and video game industry*. Retrieved in March 8, 2015, from http://www.theesa.com/wp-content/uploads/2014/10/ESA_EF_2014.pdf

Entertainment Software Association. (2015). *2015 Sales, demographic and usage data: essential facts about the computer and video game industry*. Retrieved in April 27, 2015, from http://www.theesa.com/wp-content/uploads/2015/04/ESA-Essential-Facts-2015.pdf

Felinto, E. (2001). "Materialidades da Comunicação": por um novo lugar da matéria na Teoria da Comunicação. In *Revista Ciberlegenda*, Niterói, n. 5. Retrieved from http://www.uff.br/ciberlegenda/ojs/index.php/revista/article/view/308

Ferraz, M. C. F. (2010). *Homo deletabilis: corpo, percepção, esquecimento: do século XIX ao XXI*. Rio de Janeiro: Garamond/FAPERJ.

Gibson, J. J. (1979). *The ecological approach to visual perception*. Boston, MA: Houghton Mifflin.

Gregory, J. (2009). *Game engine architecture*. Wellesley, MA: AK Peters Ltd.

Gumbrecht, H. U. (2004). *Production of Presence: what meaning cannot convey*. Stanford, CA: Stanford University Press.

Hayward, V., Astley, O., Cruz-Hernandes, M., Grant, D., & Robles-De-La-Torre, G. (2004). Haptic interfaces and devices. *Sensor Review*, 24(1), 16–29. doi:10.1108/02602280410515770

Heidegger, M. (1996). *Being and Time*. New York, NY: State University of New York Press.

Huizinga, J. (1980). *Homo ludens: a study of the play-element in culture*. London: Routledge & Kegan Paul.

Illiger, A. (2011). *Tiny Wings* [iOS game]. Kiel, Germany: Andreas Illiger.

Juul, J. (2010). *A casual revolution*. Cambridge, London: The MIT Press.

Kittler, F. (1999). *Gramophone, film, typewriter*. Stanford, CA: Stanford University Press.

Kollar, P. (2014, June 12). '*Her*' game creator releasing a mountain simulator. *Polygon*. Retrieved from http://www.polygon.com/2014/6/12/5804478/mountain-simulator-david-oreilly

Maia, A. (2013). *A materialidade de jogar no Kinect: o terror ganha outras proporções. Anais do XXII Encontro Anual da Compós*. Salvador: Universidade Federal da Bahia.

Manovich, L. (2001). *The language of new media*. London: The MIT Press.

McLuhan, M. (1994). *Understanding media: the extensions of man*. London: The MIT Press.

McShaffry, M., & Graham, D. (2013). *Gaming coding complete* (4th ed.). Boston, MA: Cengage Learning.

Merleau-Ponty, M. (2013). *Phenomenology of Perception*. New York, NY: Routledge.

Noble, J. (2009). *Programming interactivity*. Sebastopol: OReilly Media.

Norman, D. (2013). *The design of everyday things*. New York, NY: Basic Books.

OReilly, D. (2014). *Mountain* [iOS and PC game]. Los Angeles, CA: Double Fine.

Palacios, M., & Cunha, R. (2012). A tactilidade em dispositivos móveis: Primeiras reflexões e ensaio de tipologias. *Contemporânea, Salvador, 10*(3), 668–685.

Pereira, V. A. (2008). *G.A.M.E.S. 2.0: Gêneros e Gramáticas de Arranjos e Ambientes Midiáticos Mediadores de Experências de Entretenimento, Sociabilidades e Sensorialidades. Anais do XVII Encontro Anual da Compós*. São Paulo: UNIP.

Picado, B., & Araújo, J. (2013). *A performatividade da experiência estética: modulações rítmicas e tensivas da sensibilidade. Anais do XXII Encontro Anual da Compós*. Salvador: UFBA.

Polytron Corporation. (2012). *Fez* [PC, PS3, PS4, PSVita, XBOX 360 game]. Nashville, TN: Trapdoor.

Salen, K., & Zimmerman, E. (2004). *Rules of play: game design fundamentals*. Cambridge, London: The MIT Press.

Schechner, R. (2006). *Performance Studies: an introduction* (2nd ed.). New York, NY: Rouledge.

Seel, M. (2014). No escopo da experiência estética. In B. Picado, C. M. C. Mendonça, & J. Cardoso Filho (Eds.), *In Experiência estética e performance*. Salvador: EDUFBA.

Sheffield, B. (2014, October 19). When quality comes before making money: developing Monument Valley. *Gamasutra*. Retrieved from http://gamasutra.com/view/news/228094/When_quality_comes_before_making_money_Developing_Monument_Valley.php

Singer, B. (2001). Modernidade, hiperestímulo e o início do sensacionalismo popular. In L. Charney & V. Schwartz (Eds.), *O cinema e a invenção da vida moderna*. São Paulo: Cosac Naify.

Superbrothers & Capybara Games. (2011). *Sword & Sworcery EP* [iOS, Android, PC game]. Quebec, Canada: Capybara Games.

Thatgamecompany. (2009). *Flower* [PS3, PS4, PSVita game]. Los Angeles, CA: Sony Computer Entertainment.

Thatgamecompany. (2012). *Journey* [PS3, PS4 game]. Los Angeles, CA: Sony Computer Entertainment.

Unity Technologies. (2015). *Unity Manual.* Retrieved from http://docs.unity3d.com/Manual/index.html

Ustwo. (2014). *Monument Valley* [iOS game]. New York, NY: Ustwo.

Webster, A. (2014, April 3). Explore the impossible architecture of '*Monument Valley*'. *The Verge.* Retrieved from http://www.theverge.com/2014/4/3/5573812/monument-valley-mc-escher-ipad-game

ENDNOTES

[1] According to the Entertainment Software Association, USA the games industry moved more than $ 22 billion in 2014. Available at <http://www.theesa.com/wp-content/uploads/2015/04/ESA-Essential-Facts-2015.pdf>.

[2] This phenomenon – the characteristics and effects of the interaction between the creature and environment – is also largely discussed in the phenomenological tradition. Philosophers like Heidegger (1996) and Merleau-Ponty (2013) had worked upon these questions in a similar manner to Dewey's perspective. Specifically, they agreed about the mutual influence that takes place in this kind of interaction. In that sense, further on, this paper takes in consideration some aspects of the ecological approach to visual perception (Gibson, 1979) in order to offer more resources to sustain the discussion presented here.

[3] Whose main reference is the perspective of Performance Studies (Schechner, 2006; Carlson, 2009), in which human actions can be studied while broader gestures, endowed with conventionality and uniqueness. In this study, the focus is to demonstrate the revealing power of aesthetic experience by observing the performances of the players not do a detailed review of studies on performance.

[4] Obviously that the games are not aimed only at entertainment and can assume serious applications, as in law, religion and the arts in general terms. Such thinking is the central point of Huizinga's argument (1980), when proposing that *Homo sapiens* would be better defined as *Homo ludens*, given its deliberate representation nature for its own purposes.

[5] Entertainment Software Association. (2014). *2014 Sales, demographic and usage data: essential facts about the computer and video game industry.* Retrieved in March 8, 2015, from http://www.theesa.com/wp-content/uploads/2014/10/ESA_EF_2014.pdf.

[6] Since the term is constantly criticized, it is good to argue that the *non-hermeneutic*, in its very essence, does not mean a denial of the hermeneutic tradition. Instead, it is an epistemological alternative to comprehend the media context in a broader way. Probably the concept would be less questioned if it took the prefix *post-* instead of *non-* in its composition. Nevertheless, this discussion requires a much deeper effort, which, for the purpose of the present text, will not be held.

[7] Free translation: "A comunicação é encarada menos como uma troca de significados e ideias sobre algo, e mais como uma performance posta em movimento por meio de vários significantes materializados".

[8]   Free translation: "A interação entre corpo e máquina, entre sistemas de pensamento humanos e sistemas binários, entre o real e o virtual constitui um problema particularmente interessante para os instrumentos da teoria das materialidades".

[9]   The fundamental principles to digital media are described by Manovich (2001). According to him, any product of new media is based on five basic aspects: numerical representation, modularity, automation, variability and transcoding.

[10]   See, for example: Stinson, L. (2013, December 13). This might be the most beautiful iPad game of 2014. *Wired*. Retrieved from http://www.wired.com/2013/12/monument-valley-a-gorgeous-game-thats-like-an-m-c-escher-come-to-life/. Webster, A. (2014, April 3). Explore the impossible architecture of '*Monument Valley*'. *The Verge*. Retrieved from http://www.theverge.com/2014/4/3/5573812/monument-valley-mc-escher-ipad-game.

[11]   Free translation: "As experiências vividas e os fatores culturais, ou o repertório do agente podem influenciar o modo como se entende as possibilidades de ação".

[12]   Available at <http://unity3d.com>.

[13]   His works can be seen at <www.davidoreilly.com>.

[14]   Available at <http://mountain-game.com/>.

Chapter 17
Games People Play:
A Trilateral Collaboration Researching Computer Gaming across Cultures

Sandy Baldwin
Rochester Institute of Technology, USA

Kwabena Opoku-Agyemang
West Virginia University, USA

Dibyadyuti Roy
West Virginia University, USA

ABSTRACT

The study of various choices made while producing and playing games allows little opportunity for interrogating video games as a transcultural convergence of multiple subjectivities and institutions. This chapter speaks to this topic by presenting the Computer Games Across Cultures (CGAC) project. CGAC involved humanities researchers from West Virginia University (USA), Bangor University (Wales), and Jawaharlal Nehru University (India) who over a two-year period sought to understand creative and cultural aspects of gaming. CGAC's researchers employed both qualitative and quantitative methodologies to bridge the gap between the academic explorations of gaming in tandem with industry-specific practices within such spaces. This chapter provides an overview of the resultant work through its analysis of a cross-section of games. Examining both Western mainstream games and lesser known games from places like India and Ghana helped interrogate representational politics in videogames and provide a broader view of the relationship between gaming and game making, in a socio-cultural context.

INTRODUCTION

In the days before the 2014 Indian elections, voters played *Modi Run*, a mobile action game where candidate Narendra Modi runs through all the Indian states and wins the election to become Prime Minister of India. In Ghana, teenagers play *Ananse: The Origin*, a 2-D adventure game adapted from traditional African folktales. The game features Ananse, a trickster figure, as the hero, capturing enemies and villains in order to become a master-storyteller. In the USA, over 27 million people play the fantasy game

DOI: 10.4018/978-1-5225-0261-6.ch017

League of Legends daily, with many millions more playing in other countries. The annual *LoL* World Championship professional competition draws over 32 million online viewers and a prize of over one million dollars.

Games are a shared global experience and activity. They can be seen as an overarching cultural identifier. That is, games are a way of life that directly reflect the culture in which they are played. This is true for the most traditional of games, from croquet and *Monopoly*, to games such as *Mancala*, the board game common throughout the Middle East and northern Africa. It is also true today for video and computer games.

Games are simultaneously global and local. Mainstream video and computer games are often designed by multinational corporations with enormous budgets, high production values, voice talents from famous celebrities, and technical requirements limited to state-of-the-art devices and connectivity. At the same time, cultures outside of the West often negotiate a variety of challenges in regard to access and bandwidth. Does this mean they are not playing games? To the contrary, games are everywhere, and this fact means that games must be understood across cultures and for the ways they provide insight into both the local and the global.

The global game industry is projected to generate 86 billion dollars annually by 2016. In India alone, the industry is already close to 890 million dollars (Nasscom.in, 2015). Video and computer games are often studied for their technological construction and aesthetics, but not enough attention is given to games as cultural artifacts. Even more pressing is the need to consider games in a cross-cultural perspective that recognizes both the global phenomenon of gaming and cultural differences as performed and represented in gaming.

CULTURE AND PLAY

In his seminal study *Keywords,* Raymond Williams (1976) argued that the term *culture* involves an "intricate historical development," with the many connotations of this word existing in the twilight zone between "material production" and "signifying or symbolic systems" (p. 91). While acknowledging the varied manifestations of the same term, Johan Huizinga (1949) argued for the integral role of "play" within cultures, since "all play means something," acting as material and non-material signifiers within the larger "scheme of life" (p. 1). Any effort therefore to understand culture must consider play. Efforts to understand how games work must emphasize both the act of playing and the games being played, all as vital clues towards decoding the cultures within which these acts are performed *and* the ways in which games perform cultures. Unfortunately, most attempts at enumerating a history of gaming have been contextually limited, focusing mostly on American games and gaming practices as symptomatic of global conventions. The generalization from the American or Western market to global gaming is easy but deceptive. Computer Gaming Across Cultures (CGAC), a two-year project funded by the British Council, emerged to address this scholarly gap, with the goal of accounting for the various spaces and the multiple mediums in which gamers and gaming practices emerge.

With the proliferation of game studies and the resultant scholarship, studying the aesthetic as well as technological choices made while producing and playing games have become increasingly common. However, such processes allow little opportunity for interrogating video games as a transcultural space where multiple subjectivities and institutions converge, making video games both the subject and tool for study. The scale of the trilateral collaboration at the core of the CGAC research project combined critical tools of humanities researchers from US, UK, and India to understand the creative and cultural aspects of gaming. CGAC's researchers employed both qualitative and quantitative methodologies to bridge the gap between the academic exploration of gaming aesthetics in these three locations in tandem with the industry-specific practices within those spaces. Looking at gaming worlds as transcultural spaces involves acknowledging that such electronic environments, while based on a "logic of simulation" (Gottschalk, 1995, p. 1), are fundamentally cultural spaces and therefore signify the movement from a modern society to a postmodern moment, one that is characterized by a fragmented sense of consciousness, identity and multiple versions of the self. Scholars expounding on the influence of visual cultures in contemporary society are of the opinion that that our "sense of place" is constantly disturbed by the visual blurring of "once clear social boundaries and categories" (Gottschalk, 1995, p. 2). CGAC therefore provided the opportunity of not only understanding of how game-environments allow our digital selves to transgress physical boundaries and explore other cultures within game environments, but also how visual cultures like video games often repeat and reify the dominant Eurocentric assumptions about non-western spaces.

COMPUTER GAMING ACROSS CULTURES: PROJECT DESCRIPTION

CGAC was a two-year project, from 2012 to 2014, funded by United Kingdom-India Education and Research Initiative (UKIERI) program. The following section of this chapter provides a narrative account of the project goals, outcomes, and challenges. The unique interdisciplinary and collaborative aspects of the project presented challenges but also made possible discoveries about games and culture that would not otherwise have been possible. In the largest sense, the project showed that gaming, along with "games" and "play" and similar terms, can only be understood within a thick and contested space of cultural differences.

The UKIERI was started in 2006, with support from multiple agencies within the UK and India, notably the British Council, and various government offices in both countries. The initiative's goal was enhancing educational links between the UK and India. CGAC was funded by the UKIERI program "Trilateral Research in Partnership" (TRIP), announced in 2011. The scope of the program was interdisciplinary, with an open call for research areas, and with an emphasis on graduate student mobility and partnership building. The program's long-term goals emphasized partnerships in the form of faculty exchanges or shared academic programs. The primary requirement for applications to the program was that the project teams include partners from the UK, USA, and India.

In the background, and articulating the program's goals, are assumptions that such partnerships will lead to synergies within and without academic settings. The UKIERI "Programme Background" describes its aim as "driv[ing] value through strategic and system driven projects" (Ukieri 2015). The language is as much economic and industrial as it is scholarly and academic. As such, the background points to the interdisciplinary scope of the initiative and to the multiple agencies providing support. Why is this important? In the context of the USA, funding for research projects in the humanities continues to be driven by agencies such as the National Endowment for the Humanities (NEH), which describes its mission primarily in terms of national ideologies and humanistic values: "Because democracy demands wisdom, NEH serves and strengthens our republic by promoting excellence in the humanities and conveying the lessons of history to all Americans" (NEH, 2015, para. 2). Indeed, the selection, assessment, and outcomes of NEH-funded project continue to be framed in this way: in terms of contributions to the humanities in the USA. While the NEH is certainly not the only funding body in the USA, it remains dominant for humanities scholars.

The situation differs in other settings. With the case of the UKIERI-TRIP project, individual national ideologies are displaced, though not entirely out of the picture, while a neoliberal language of development is in the foreground. The connecting mission of the funding does not foreground any shared sense of nation but rather leverages the "academic sector" in relation to other sectors across the three countries, with economy as the common concept at the source of this articulation. In short, not a national view nor a humanistic view, but a global and post-national theory of industries, systems, and sectors, where the academic is one sector among others, leading to "substantial, long term prosperity benefits" (UKIERI, "Achievements at a Glance").

A clear advantage of such a framework is openness to assembling teams and research areas that can cut across institutional and national constraints. In the case of CGAC, the project was a partnership between West Virginia University (WVU) in Morgantown, West Virginia, USA; Bangor University (BU) in Bangor, Wales; and Jawaharlal Nehru University (JNU) in New Delhi, India. Each team consisted of a cohort of graduate students led by a faculty member. The WVU team was led by Professor Sandy Baldwin of the Department of English and Center for Literary Computing. The BU team was led by Professor Astrid Ensslin of the School of Creative Media. The JNU team was led by Professor Saugata Bhaduri of the Centre for English Studies. CGAC was selected as one of eighteen recipients of the TRIP awards, with others noted in areas such as "solar physics, influenza virus research, [...] and Indian and Pakistani foreign policy endeavours in Afghanistan (UKIERI 2015). In fact, the UKIERI featured CGAC on its announcement of the awards, by including the following description taken from the original project proposal:

Our project develops a critical view of computer gaming, especially massive multiplayer online roleplaying games. How do we recognize and analyze the deep and significant differences in computer gaming across cultures? This is where our project is really unique: our insistence on culture and cultural differences appearing in and through the "world" of games. Such games are a truly global world of "role play" where international teams can meet for shared research and analysis. Our project will really set the future agenda for PhD study in this area.

Whatever this front-page feature may say about the quality of the CGAC project—i.e. in comparison to other UKIERI-TRIP projects from physics, influence, or foreign policy—it suggests that the formulation "computer gaming across cultures" is particularly appropriate or exemplary of the trilateral grant's objectives. To be clear: this exemplarity may be deceptive and may have nothing to do with the project as such. For example, it may simply be that computer games feel particularly exciting and popularist, and are selected and displayed here as a signifier of cross-disciplinary impact. In this case, games become a stand-in for inter-disciplinarity in general, and do not necessarily relate to the CGAC project. Nevertheless, one outcome of the CGAC project was to unpack "computer gaming across cultures"—not to explain it but to extend and intensify this formula's range as a signifier.

The primary project activities included:

1. Mobility between universities, leading to meetings and symposia at each location,
2. Ongoing collaboration and research by the teams at the individual locations,
3. A range of outcomes, including co-authored publications, syllabuses or module descriptions, and proposed a MOOC.

The specific activities of the project were benchmarked by three comprehensive meetings between all the research teams, held at each of the partner institutions: in May 2013 (Bangor), January 2014 (New Delhi), and May 2014 (Morgantown). The meetings were dedicated to discussing and developing pedagogical models for teaching intercultural, media, critical, and other competencies, using games both as a medium and object of study. The format of the meetings included group brainstorming sessions, small group work, and presentations on research and academic culture at the partner institutions.

Each meeting was followed by a public, one-day symposia revolving around different aspects of "Computer Gaming Across Cultures." The symposia featured presentations from research students and staff of all three teams and their host institutions, as well as keynotes given by external speakers.

The meetings allowed the team to develop an ongoing dialogue and to arrive at a shared working relationship. The public symposia, which were intended to showcase graduate student research, gave evidence of an evolving and interwoven discourse. Graduate student presentations across the three meetings often emerged from individual PhD projects—i.e. students necessarily presented work from their thesis in progress – but nonetheless showed a growth and exchange of concepts and contexts through relation to the CGAC project.

To prepare for meetings and discuss research and dissemination activities, the three project leaders regularly met via Skype. Some of these remote meetings involved student team members as well. Locally, each research team met at regular intervals to discuss specific responsibilities such as symposium preparation, literature reviews, and gaming experiences.

The project set specific team activities for the six-month intervals between the group meetings. As it turned out, in the process of the project, these activities were carried out more unevenly than intended. The reasons are various, as will be discussed, but certainly emerge from the different contexts of the partner institutions. The following provides a brief description of the team activities.

The activity for first stage of the project, up until the meeting in Bangor, included a literature review of scholarship on computer gaming and pedagogy, with a specific focus on massive multiplayer games. The teams collected over two hundred items.

In the second stage, up until the meeting in New Delhi, the intention was for the teams to engage in actual gameplay. Initially the participants would be organized into teams at each location, but eventually all the partner teams would meet up in-game. The game *World of Warcraft* (*WoW*) was chosen as a platform, based on its international popularity and wide demographic. In practice, this activity was only partially successful. Time demands prevented full participation at the sites, and issues of access and hardware also limited the effectiveness of this activity. This was notably the case at JNU, where bandwidth considerations prevented any sustained engagement with *WoW*. In the end, project participants self-selected games to play. The results were less homogeneous, reducing possibilities for comparison, but indeed reflected the specifics of cultural differences in gaming at each site.

The activity up until the final stage (the meeting in Morgantown) involved creating and gathering syllabi or module plans for use by the different partners. This also proved challenging, since the nature of a course and accompanying syllabus varied greatly from institution to institution. It proved extremely difficult to propose any single syllabus that could be taught at all three institutions. Some reasons for this are described below. The teams arrived at several solutions, including designing activities, projects, and readings that could be selected for inclusion within a syllabus at any one of the partners; designing best practices or proposals for curricula that could adapted at any one of the partners; and designing separate syllabuses that shared common goals or themes.

The resulting collection of syllabi, shared and discussed at the WVU meeting, reflected all three of these solutions. These syllabi are a major outcome of the project. Thematic foci include games as objects of critical analysis, introduction to games studies, and playable fiction (among others). Ideally, they form the flexible core of an MA or PhD-level curriculum that can be adapted to any of the three partners, and to other institutions as well. The syllabi include practical training, theoretical and historical readings, and carefully crafted sequences of learning objectives. They are purposefully modular, so that teachers can select and modify them to fit their existing courses and existing institutional requirements. In principle, each partner proposes to implement and offer pilot courses based on the syllabi. In practice, since there is no administrative impetus for this to occur beyond the project scope, it remains unclear whether this will be carried out.

Several other outcomes followed the final CGAC meeting. Reflecting the project's emphasis on graduate student development, one significant outcome was a special issue of the *Journal of Gaming and Virtual Worlds*, guest-edited by a group of selected PhD students from the project teams, and supervised by the journal's Principal Editor, Astrid Ensslin. This special issue became the summer 2015 edition, with a focus on "Gaming, Culture and Hegemony." Several other publications are forthcoming based on the project.

The team made plans for a collaborative MOOC (Massive Open Online Course) on intercultural games studies ("Transcultural Games Studies"), hosted by WVU through the Coursera platform yet integrating contributions from each partner organisation. This emerged from discussions beginning in the JNU meeting and taken up again at the WVU meeting. There were several reasons to create a MOOC.

The primary goal of this stage of the collaboration was to create curriculum and MOOCs are at the cutting edge of current curricular offerings. In addition, the project's stated goal was to develop curriculum at the MA and PhD level. MOOCs are in many ways ideal for curriculum at these levels, especially for PhD students. Such students are often not on-site at the university campus in a regular way. In fact, there may not even be courses specifically for them, depending on the university program and curriculum. At the same time, they clearly need ongoing training and engagement with learning. MOOC provide a way for PhD students to gain customized and pertinent training at the pace they need. The collective, distributed, and modular nature of MOOCs accommodate specialized knowledge in short pedagogical units, and can be tailored for larger courses as well.

Furthermore, and perhaps most importantly, MOOCs suit the cross-cultural and cross-institutional nature of the project collaboration. "Cross-cultural" does not only mean different nations, histories, and languages, but also very different institutional/academic cultures, with different sense of the goal of teaching and research, and different roles for practice.

In short, the MOOC offered an ideal way of addressing the different educational and cultural landscapes of the partners. In practice, this outcome is only partly begun. The WVU team created a proposal and sample video for the MOOC. On the basis of this, the project received funding, which was in turn deferred as the PI (Baldwin) began moving to another institution. The longer-term goal is that the MOOC will be re-proposed for funding at the new institution (Rochester Institute of Technology).[1]

Another follow-up project is now in its initial stage. Entitled "Game/Write," and based on the questions raised by the team, it studies potential correlations between game play and university-level writing skills. During the 2014-15 academic year, the project gathered preliminary data from WVU students. The very small sample showed a positive correlation between game play and a number of assessable qualities of writing in academic settings. A second, larger study is intended to be conducted at the other partner institutions. In the long run, the project will have implications for understanding the impact of gaming on literacy, and should be scalable to examine cultural differences in gameplay and literacy.

Several other potential collaborations emerged from the project. All the partners are in the process of signing institutional MOUs as the basis for future collaborations. The WVU team made a second trip to JNU specifically for this purposes, along with a side trip to Presidency University in Kolkata to learn about gaming research at that location. The partners are also engaged in discussion of other forms of collaboration, such as faculty exchanges or team taught-workshops. It remains to be seen how these play out in the long run.

All these outcomes led the project team to insights in collaboration across disciplines, universities, and cultures. A fundamental insight was into the driving forces in such collaborations. Once the grant period ends, there is no incentive to counteract agendas and pressures set by the project member's own institutions. It becomes very difficult to sustain project initiatives. It is important to note that the CGAC partnership was unique and came about precisely for the project – Professors Baldwin and Ensslin had some prior acquaintance but had never worked together, and the collaboration with JNU was entirely new. The team leaders learned of the funding program and constituted the project precisely for the purpose of the program. As soon as the project commenced, cultural differences became evident in collaboration and communication, which ultimately become part of the research process of the project itself. As a result, CGAC was as much about research into "form" of the partnership as it was about the "content" of the research. This fact follows logically from the goals and scope of the project itself. Video and computer games must be understood as cultural objects. The production, distribution, consumption, and critique of these games are all subject to cultural frameworks and are differentiated by these frameworks. What we mean by a "game" or "play" turns out to be very different in the USA, UK, and India. Even more, the seemingly straightforward task of academic study and curriculum focused on video and computer games turns out to be highly contingent and varied depending on cultural differences. In short, the cultural differences in the form of the partnership were in fact part of the content of the research program.

The most obvious difference was technical infrastructure. Conditions for game play in India are far different from those in the UK, and different again in the rural USA of West Virginia. To some degree, the relative affluence of JNU balanced out this difference—the participants in the project did have computers and access to the Internet—but the more significant difference was cultural variation in choice of game and platforms. The Indian emphasis on mobile games and additionally on shared software made for a very different repertoire of games to play and teach. While it was possible to norm the different teams, to insist on playing a single game—as in the attempt to all play *World of Warcraft*—the facts reflected the varied contexts and frames of references the team members brought with them.

In a way, the notion of technical infrastructure as cultural difference is too easy; it simply reflects what is already known about differences between the three locations. In particular, re-emphasizing infrastructural differences in India reinforces a perceived dichotomy between Western and Indian culture. As a result, it was important to shift the project—and the resulting understanding of the form of the collaboration—away from a concern with technical infrastructure. More significant for the project, though not as immediately obvious, were institutional differences between the partners. These proved to be the most palpable cultural differences in the form of the collaboration.

The WVU English Department is situated in a state land grant flagship university, providing the only PhD granting university in the state of West Virginia. As a land grant university, it has a duty to the economy and population of the West Virginia, one of the poorest and most underdeveloped states in America. As a flagship university, it is the most prestigious and research-intensive university in the state. The department's mission is broad, in principle covering the entire range of English language literary and cultural studies. In practice, the department includes a growing emphasis and strength in the field of writing, composition, and rhetoric. This growth is increased because of the department's service function, where it provides composition instruction for virtually all of WVU undergraduate population of approximately 22,000 students across all majors and disciplines. As a result, and similar to other state land grant flagship universities (e.g. University of Kentucky), much of the department's teaching involves composition instruction primarily taught by graduate-level instructors. While there are significant issues around this system—i.e. the cheap and readily available labor for the university cloaked in a valuable apprenticeship in teaching for the graduate students—the interests of this essay lie in the form and focus of the department.

Bangor University is one of the top universities in the UK. While WVU defines its primary mission as to the students of its state, BU foregrounds the impact of its research. This is not to say that teaching is not a priority BU, but rather to characterize basic institutional orientations. Within BU, the School of Creative Studies and Media offers research and instruction in the following areas: Creative Studies, Film, Journalism, Media and New Media, Theatre, and Writing. The school's activities are framed in terms of the "creative industries," with the implication of overlapping academic and other sectors, facilitating production and distribution of knowledge and skills. As a result, research and instruction at the school are built on practice as research. WVU's growing Professional Writing and Editing program is beginning to leverage similar approach—for example, matching students with industry internships—but it remains separate from more teaching and research-focused areas in the WVU English Department. "Research" on computer games would not be a concern of the PWE program, at least at least in its current form. At BU, such research is central, intensive, and productive in terms of partnerships within and beyond academia.

JNU is one of the leading Indian universities, with a reputation for research. It is almost entirely a graduate institution, offering post-undergraduate degrees with only selected undergraduate instruction in languages and linguistics. Within JNU, the Centre for English Studies presents itself as "one of the foremost sites for postgraduate work and research in English Studies in India" (http://www.jnu.ac.in/SLLCS/CES/). The Centre's emphasis is centrally on MPhil and PhD instruction and research. The university maintains a reputation for political activism, both within its research and on the part of its student body. The faculty and students in the Centre for English Studies reflect this, adopting a theoretically-inflected and critical approach. The model of the scholar as activist, intellectual, and critic is primary at JNU.

The point here is the difference in institutional cultures:

- WVU is a regional, flagship university, oriented towards the citizens of its state, with a departmental focus on comprehensive literary and cultural studies, and a common concern with writing instruction.
- BU is a major national university, with a departmental focus on practice as research, and an orientation to the overlap between academia and industry through knowledge/information transfer.
- JNU is an elite graduate institution, with a departmental focus on literary and cultural research, charged with theoretical and political concerns.

From the first, such differences structured the nature of the project and partnership. These institutional differences meant that the practice and product of research and teaching were fundamentally different between the partners. The simplest example emerged in the symposia presentations, which ranged from the theoretical and politically charged to the very practical. The result made it difficult to agree on what constituted a shared research question or an academic curriculum on gaming. Certainly the teams could meet and exchange viewpoints, but arriving at commonalities was a different matter.

It is important to underline that this insight into differences in institutional form is vital to the cross-cultural understanding of gaming. The fact that these are departments of literature or creative arts, and not gaming, and the fact that these differences do not directly involve gaming, are in fact the pertinent institutional frameworks for understanding gaming from cultural perspective. Simply put, to research or study games did not mean the same thing in each setting.

Looking back and reflecting on the project as a whole, it is clear that these differences made the project more complex and contributed to cross-cultural insights. The danger was that such challenges would become impediments to the original goal of studying games, or even that the project would purely become "about" these challenges.

FROM GAMING ACROSS CULTURES TO CULTURES OF GAMING

In the long run, the challenges enriched the project. Rather than become the focus, they pointed to more complex outcomes. The purpose of the project was to interrogate and inform an understanding of the cultural spaces afforded by gaming. The form of the collaboration made cultural spaces a primary concern both in terms of research and university identity. The resulting knowledge production can be understood through discussions of the research presented at the three-project meeting. The following focuses on a broad summary of the presentations given at each symposium, with closer analysis of selected case studies.

Each symposium was organized around the overarching theme "Computer Gaming Across Cultures: Perspectives." The first conference was held in Bangor in May 2013 and the second in New Delhi in January 2014, with Morgantown closing out the meetings in May 2014. The papers touched on thematic concerns such as labor, exoticism, violence, empire, pedagogy, gender, and spaces. Participants spoke from their area of expertise, as would be expected. More broadly, the papers can be categorized under two main research headings: research on computer games as cultural spaces; and research on the cultural contexts that inform computer gaming.

The first conference at the University of Bangor included a keynote talk by Esther MacCallum-Stewart on gender in video games in and the fan culture around games. Presentations on cultural spaces at the first meeting included

- "My Project is Sexy and You Better Know It: The Politics of Video Game Research in Ivy League Institutions" by Dibyadyuti Roy, which critiqued the dichotomy that exists between well-funded and lesser-funded higher learning institutions in America with respect to gaming, drawing conclusions about the resulting research;
- Kayla McKinney's "Frontier Conflicts: Boundless Exploration and Gender Limits in World of Warcraft," an exploration of gender relations and museological drives in the popular game *World of Warcraft*;
- "Playing by the Noose: Understanding Popular Response to Terror through Video Games" by Debaditya Bhattacharya, which analyzed the construction of terror in selected Indian games.

Presentations on the cultural contexts that inform games included

- Isamar Carrillo Masso's "Map & Track: Using Applied Mathematics to Track the Development of the Use of MMORPGs as Educational Tools," proposing math-driven approaches to gathering data on MMORPGs;
- Lyle Skains's "Reading, Writing, Arithmetic...and Programming? Game-coding as Educational Platform," and "Virtual Worlds and Cognitive Science: Implications for Learning," presentations which linked understanding games to the process of writing and learning;
- "Virtual Worlds and Cognitive Science: Implications for Learning" by Xavier Laurent, which suggested ways games could lead to understanding of cognitive processes and vice versa.

Papers in this second category explored the relationship between gaming and specific aspects of education formation including psychology, mathematics, and reading.

A similar pattern followed in the next meeting, in New Delhi. The keynote panel "Where in the World is Indian Gaming?" was jointly presented by Souvik Mukherjee and Padmini Ray Murray. It added a transnational bent to the academic conversations by positioning gaming in India within a larger globalized context. Other presentations included

- Sandy Baldwin's "'We're not beginning to... to... mean something?' or Beckett Spams *Counter-Strike*," which dealt with questions of absurdity and audience in relation to artistic interventions in the game *Counter-Strike*;
- "From the Margins of the Centre towards Tesseraction: Digital Gaming, Virtual Reality and Postcolonialism" by Siddhartha Chakraborti, which paired and problematized political issues in India with politic issues in video games.
- In the second category, of presentations dealing with the cultural context of gaming included:
- Astrid Ensslin's "Alternative models of teaching MMOGs in higher education: the LOTRO MOOC," which surveyed the use of MOOCs to teach about video games;
- "Coding Creativity: Creative Writing in Code Environments" by Lyle Skains, which continued to explore the use of games as part of the creative writing classroom.

Ensslin connected computer games to pedagogy by positioning MOOCs as complementing conventional methods of teaching, while Skains looked at the potential of video games to improve creative writing skills.

More diverse ways of using computer games to inform teaching were further explored in the final meeting, indicating the growth in exchange and concepts across the space of the meetings: Lyle Skains's "Reformation of Culture through Storytelling: Can Game-Oriented Hardware Affect Human Connection?" and Xavier Laurent's "Cognitive and Writing Skills: The Impact of Video Game Play on Writing Ability" were examples of papers that argued differently for closer analyses of the connections between gaming skills and composition and rhetoric skills—one in a creative writing context, and the other in a more psychoanalytical environment.

The Morgantown conference also had "Knowledge, Truth, and the Political Limits of Possibility in MMOs" by Harrington Weihl, which was an argument that certain games reproduce late capitalism ideology; "Ananse in a Box: A Cultural Overview of Ghanaian Video Games" by Kwabena Opoku-Agyemang, a presentation of the relationship between African oral tradition and mobile video games;

and Dibyadyuti Roy's "Gaming Under Post-Colonial Eyes: Narrativizing Performances of Anxious Indian Masculinity," an examination of the construction of gender in relation to audience considerations. These last three were examples of papers that extended the conversation to relate gaming to capitalism, African contexts, and gender in an Indian context.

The diversity of these findings and complexity of the material mean not all of the presentations can be examined in detail within this essay. As such, we look at the last three essays as examples of material and analysis developed in the projects on the use of games in diverse cultural contexts.

Weihl's "Knowledge, Truth, and the Political Limits" focused on ethical dilemmas in MMOs as a content-level manifestation of the ways in which such games (and their contexts) fit within late capitalism. Weihl argued that the relationship between the genre and late capitalism stages an interplay between freedom of choice and action within a certain structure that restricts notions of autonomy. The notions of restricted autonomy were looked at differently in "Ananse in a Box," which presented two Ghanaian mobile video games as case studies. These games, according to the paper, "translated" traditional sources of leisure into an electronic space in divergent ways. The differing methodologies in these papers benefited from the sources of tradition (ethical theory and African folktales) that provided direction without being overly restrictive. "Gaming Under Post-Colonial Eyes" also viewed tradition but through the lens of gender. Analyzing the ideologies behind the production, circulation, and the game-play strategies of a set of popular online games, Roy argued that sections of the Indian video gaming industry facilitate performances of sexism while simultaneously providing evidence of the gender anxiety embedded in postcolonial Indian masculinity. While Weihl looked at a Western (American) milieu, Opoku-Agyemang and Roy were interested in postcolonial spaces – Ghana and India respectively. The relationship between traditional African culture and contemporary re-imaginations in an electronic context related to the ways in which Indian gamers negotiate traditional and contemporary gender roles and expectations while playing video games.

The organization and analysis of the material emerging in the CGAC project changed and reflected a shift from disparate positions to overlapping directions. Over time, the research interests of the project teams and their projects became increasingly intertwined. This move from separation to intersecting dialogues, in other words, spoke to the strength of the project as a collaboration designed to speak to the specificities of three universities. The coalescing of the ideological spaces, in other words, illuminated the importance of culture as a malleable tool in connection with gaming.

THE SPACES OF GAMING

Scholars of gaming unequivocally agree that analyzing and interpreting the spatiality of games, i.e. the two dimensional spaces in which game content is rendered playable, functions as one of the most crucial aspects of the gaming experience. Celia Pearce (2008) pointed out that while all other media forms have specific conventions, which audiences must be well versed in to enjoy as an "immersive" experience, the language of video games is intrinsically tied to analyzing the "two-dimensional, albeit dynamic, plane of the screen…[as the] mode of conventions for 'reading' game space" (p. 1). Pearce is not alone in claiming that spatiality is a key aspect of understanding game play and her assertion is well supported by numerous scholars (Aarseth, 2000; Jenkins, 1998; Nitsche & Thomas, 2003). These scholars let us know that the strategies through which gamers negotiate their in-game avatars often reflect the social spaces that games are physically located in: actions cross such spaces, since "our identities cannot be said to exist outside of these little actions, these minute by minute performances" (Dickinson, 2002, p. 5). Therefore, it must be stressed that any analysis of two dimension gaming spaces acknowledges the three dimensional social spaces in which gamers are located.

Perceiving gaming spaces as social spaces therefore, became an important contention of CGAC, since in-game activities across cultures are not only influenced by the two dimensional playing environment but also the social, economic and cultural capital embodied within the players in a certain three dimensional location. One of the vital components of CGAC was the exchange that took place between project participants from the three different continents at the academic workshops and conferences at each participating institution. Besides allowing researchers to address diverse audiences through their presentation, it allowed them to perceive a cross section of the material conditions that influence gaming culture in each continent. Contextually, the importance of internet connectivity as a vital aspect of gaming came to the fore in when game choices were analyzed across these different locations. Underlining Pierre Bourdieu's (1989) contention that "agents are distributed in the overall social space [...] according to the overall volume of capital they possess" (p. 17), participants chose a wide variety of games ranging from MMORPG's to flash-based mobile games. Importantly, therefore, the idea of looking at the global gaming space as inhabited by agents with different forms of social capital became a key component in studying both the materiality of gaming spaces as well as the cultures within which they are located.

CGAC participants and their research not only questioned the oft-claimed assumption that game worlds "typically aren't so different from our own" but also examined the ideologies that lead to the production of game world spaces. The project examined a broad cross-section of games, using multiple games emerging from the Western canon, and showed that representations of non-Eurocentric cultures were biased and reflected colonialist assumptions. As the journalist Rheingold (1991) posited, videogames are an integral part of the "reality-industrial" complex where virtual environments in mimicking the real spaces, often lay a claim on being "the real." In other words the necessity for CGAC researchers to interrogate the representational politics in videogames arose from the premise that game worlds are created in tune with hegemonic Western conceptualizations about non-western physical, social and human characteristics. Such representations then run the risk of becoming the sole referent of information for game players who have never physically experienced or interacted with these spaces or their inhabitants. While analyzing both the cultures that influence gaming as well as diverse gaming cultures, the CGAC project has taken a vital step toward identifying video-games not only as technological or cultural artifacts but rather as sites of inquiry, which help us interrogate the ideologies governing our daily existence.

REFERENCES

Aarseth, E. (2000). Allegories of space: The question of spatiality in computer games. In M. Eskelinen & R. Koskimaa (Eds.), *Cybertext Yearbook 2000*. University of Jyväskylä.

Baggaley, J. (2014). MOOC postscript. *Distance Education*, *35*(1), 126–132. doi:10.1080/01587919.2 013.876142

Bourdieu, P. (1989). Social space and symbolic power. *Sociological Theory*, *7*(1), 14–25. http://www. soc.ucsb.edu/ct/pages/JWM/Syllabi/Bourdieu/SocSpaceSPowr.pdf doi:10.2307/202060

Gottschalk, S. (1995). *Videology: Video-games as postmodern sites/sights of ideological reproduction.* Academic Press.

Huizinga, J. (1949). *Homo ludens A study of the play-element in culture.* London: Routledge & Kegan Paul.

Jenkins, H. (1998). "Complete freedom of movement": Video games as gendered play spaces. In J. Cassell & H. Jenkins (Eds.), *From Barbie to* Mortal Kombat*: Gender and computer games.* Cambridge, MA: The MIT Press.

Nasscom.in. (2015). *Exciting times ahead for the Indian gaming industry. NASSCOM.* Retrieved 30 March 2015, from http://www.nasscom.in/exciting-times-ahead-indian-gaming-industry?fg=159176

Neh.gov. (2015). *About The National Endowment For The Humanities | National Endowment For The Humanities.* Retrieved from http://www.neh.gov/about

Nitsche, M., & Thomas, M. (2003). In O. Balet, G. Subsol, & P. Torquet (Eds.), *Stories in space: The concept of the story map* (pp. 85–94). Graz, Austria: Springer Verlag.

Pearce, C. (2008). Spatial literacy: Reading (and writing) game space. In *Proceedings, Future and Reality of Gaming (FROG).* Retrieved from http://lmc.gatech.edu/~cpearce3/PearcePubs/Pearce_FROG_FINAL.pdf

Rheingold, H. (1991). *Virtual reality: Exploring the brave new technologies of artificial experience and interactive worlds from cyberspace.* London: Seeker and Warburg.

Ukieri.org. (2015). *UKIERI: UK-India Education and Research Initiative.* Retrieved 1 November 2015, from http://www.ukieri.org/program-background.html

Williams, R. (1976). *Keywords: A vocabulary of culture and society.* London: Fontana.

KEY TERMS AND DEFINITIONS

Cultural Contexts: The circumstances and situations that inform an event under discussion.

Gaming: The act of playing a game through interaction and/or participation.

Gaming Spaces: The socio-cultural milieu – both physical and theoretical – within which gaming takes place.

Trilateral Collaboration: The partnerships and associations that existed between the West Virginia University, Bangor University and Jawaharlal Nehru University.

ENDNOTE

[1]   See Jon Baggaley (2014) for more information on MOOCs.

Chapter 18
Games Beyond the Screen:
Festivals of Play Across the Western World

William Zachary Wood
Stanford University, USA

ABSTRACT

This chapter introduces a phenomenon that has gone largely unaddressed in research since its emergence in western countries in the last decade: festivals of games and play. The bulk of the chapter is drawn from interviews with people involved in these festivals, including founders, current organizers and game designers, using this data to build on the work of researchers on play and playfulness. Taking an auto-ethnographic stance, the author speaks from personal experience as a participant and game designer in order to convey these festivals' unique qualities and potential as sites for public play.

INTRODUCTION

In the past ten years—and especially the last five—festivals presenting games and play to the public have spread across North America and Europe, beginning mainly with Come Out & Play in New York City in 2006. The emergence of these festivals has gone largely unnoticed within both the independent video game development community and research on games, yet the scope and number of these events continue to increase each year.

Because there has been little research on these festivals to date, there is no established terminology with which to discuss them. I will refer to them broadly as "festivals of games and play" to highlight the fact that while diverse in structure they all present to the public a broad range of physical and digital games.

The longest running of these festivals include GameCity in the United Kingdom, Freeplay in Australia, and IndieCade and Come Out & Play in the United States. More recently there have been festivals like Playpublik in Germany, w00t in Denmark, Playful Arts Festival in the Netherlands, and Plaython in Greece. Meanwhile, Come Out & Play expanded from New York to San Francisco in 2010, as did IndieCade from Los Angeles to New York in 2013.

These festivals' explicit themes range from "indie games" to "urban games" to "playful culture," and the stories behind their establishment are similarly diverse. What they all have in common, however, is

DOI: 10.4018/978-1-5225-0261-6.ch018

that the games they feature utilize technology to varying degrees and sometimes not all; they embrace "games" and "play" in a broader sense than sitting in front of a screen using a controller or keyboard. Rather, screens and controllers are just a few potential tools for play. These games exist along a spectrum from digital to physical, exploring the space in between that has yet to be clearly demarcated.

As a physical game designer whose work has been featured at these festivals, a creator of a commercial video game, and someone who has written articles about video games for websites like Gamasutra, I have been following these trends closely. In order to learn more, I conducted twenty-two interviews primarily with founders and organizers of these festivals as well as with game designers whose work is featured there. I also spoke with people working in the more broadly defined fields of games and play.

In the first section of this chapter, I describe in detail six of the festivals—IndieCade, Playpublik, Come Out & Play, Come Out & Play SF, w00t and Plaython—to give a sense of their content and the differences among them. This section is based both on my experiences as an attendee and game designer, and on founders' own words about their intentions and experiences.

In the second section, I consider the festivals' position in the context of broader trends, sharing and analyzing comments from organizers and designers with whom I spoke. Drawing on scholarship about the transformative power of play, I open up space for research on these festivals in terms of their social and political significance.

In the last section I draw conclusions about changes in the conceptualization of "games," "video games," and "play" for developers, players and the general public.

METHODOLOGY

From September 2014 to May 2015, I spoke with twenty-two people involved professionally with games and play. Interview subjects were primarily selected based on their involvement either in long-running festivals such as Come Out & Play that have exerted considerable influence on other festivals, or in particularly unique festivals such as Plaython that reflect the diversity and potential of these events. With the exception of three interviews conducted in person in Germany, Denmark and Finland, the interviews were all conducted through Skype. They generally lasted one to one-and-a-half hours, during the course of which I sought to answer the following questions: What accounts for the sudden appearance and rapid spread of these festivals across the western world in the past ten years? Leading up to and through these festivals, how if at all have attitudes towards games and play changed, both among the general public and among those professionally involved with games and play?

In more concrete terms, I asked about the events and decisions leading up to the founding of each festival and how each festival has evolved since its inception. This also involved discussions of funding and institutional support, which were often closely tied to changes to the location and size of festivals. In cases where I had not personally attended a festival, I sought to understand its setting and the types of games shown there. Even in cases where I had attended, I asked for details about other years the festival had been held in order to better understand its development.

I took notes during the interviews and later used coding to analyze and establish common themes. These are presented both in the first section where I describe the festivals in detail and in the following section about related trends. I confirmed quotes and paraphrased comments with each interviewee afterwards by email, sometimes also asking follow-up questions.

This chapter takes the form of an autoethnography, embracing my involvement in the fields of games and play in order to offer the reader a practical understanding of events that could not be offered by someone who has not attended the festivals or designed and played games there. Jaakko Stenros (2015) argues that, as a form of analytic autoethnography, playing games is "the best way to access some of the data, and to contextualize data," while noting that evocative ethnography on the other hand is better suited for "uncovering a culture or even describing a group within or around the game" (p. 43). He concludes that "through participation in games, researchers gain more in insight than they lose in critical distance" (p. 43). Thus, my chapter will fall somewhere between evocative and analytic ethnography, taking advantage of my position and experiences to access unique data, while also embracing the subjectivity of both my experiences and the stories of those I interviewed in order to paint a clear picture of each festival and the communities that have formed around them.

Stenros also encourages researchers to engage with games more playfully, recognizing that while it is "possible to use games without playfulness, to approach them earnestly and seriously, like a research experiment... it does not capture all the modes of interacting in a ludic context" (p. 42). I would take Stenros' assertion one step further, adding that not only is playing games a valuable form of research, but so is designing games. Familiarity with the design process can contribute to researchers' work by enabling them to better understand game design decisions and their effects on players' experiences.

THE FESTIVALS

IndieCade: Los Angeles, USA, 2005 to Present

In 2013, I attended IndieCade in Los Angeles to promote a mobile game I had been working on called *Cafe Murder* (Beavertoad Software, 2015). Because the event is sponsored by industry giants like Sony and Nintendo and has an explicit focus on independent video games, I expected most games to take place on screens, whether those of televisions, computers, or mobile devices. However, I was surprised to find many games without screens that incorporated instead varying degrees of technology. There were also games that had screens but that also required players to physically interact with one another or their surroundings.

One game, for example, mixed the concepts of the children's games "Capture the Flag" and "Tag" (Hyde, 2013). Players formed teams to chase each other within a prescribed area of the city while attempting to steal a box containing a mobile device that measured how long it had been possessed by each team. Doug Wilson's *Johann Sebastian Joust* (Wilson, 2011), now published on PlayStation as part of *Sportsfriends* (Die Gute Fabrik, 2014), was also there, played at night to take advantage of its performative nature and use of light with PlayStation Move controllers. There was also a performance of physical games resembling those found in theater and improvisational comedy (Rafinski, 2013). My personal favorite was Shawn Pierre's *These Hot Dogs Make Terrible French Fries* (Pierre, 2013), a card game focused on persuasive speeches and creative connections between dissimilar objects. Even among the console games, there were those like *Spin the Bottle: Bumpie's Party* (KnapNok Games, 2013), a collection of party games using Wiimotes that involved players hugging each other while jumping up and down, among other things. All of this took place across several locations in Downtown Culver City in Los Angeles alongside more typical digital games played in tents or inside the city's fire station.

The festival also featured a networking event called IndieXchange where developers could sign up to meet with representatives from Sony and Nintendo to discuss how to make their games available on the companies' platforms and hardware, reflecting these companies' increased interest in indie games. I personally met with a representative from Nintendo who explained how the game I had worked on could be made available for the Nintendo DS—how much it would cost, what changes would need to be made, and so on.

Celia Pearce, one of IndieCade's founders and current Festival Chair, told me that since its inception IndieCade has come to embrace all forms of games, whether they are considered "art games," "serious games," "indie games," or otherwise. Pearce explained that while the first IndieCade in 2008 featured only digital games, after attending Come Out & Play in New York City she and other organizers realized that the kinds of physical games seen there should be included at IndieCade, too.

She and co-founders Stephanie Barish and Sam Roberts also wanted to change an organizational trend they had noticed to separate games by category. For example, indie, serious, casual, and mobile games were in separate sections at the Game Developers Conference, and at E3 the serious and indie game showcases were in two separate booths. This led Pearce and her partners to decide to offer a single space to present these kinds of games together, also discarding distinctions such as "student games" and "art games."

When selecting games for IndieCade, Pearce told me that the most important factor is innovation. Above all else, she said IndieCade values new forms of gameplay and interactivity; judges are not allowed to reject an entry simply because they don't think it is a "real game." According to her, defining games in strict terms has been used in the past to exclude certain people and genres. She cited the example of *The Sims*, a game popular with women that was often critiqued for not being a "real game."

Pearce, who is also a Professor of Game Design at Northeastern University's Games Program, emphasized the role that academia has played in supporting independent video games, noting that many of the games featured at IndieCade, especially in the event's early years, began as Master's projects. Recognizing that her own position in academia gives her the freedom to be involved in organizing IndieCade and citing their "armies of student volunteers," she said that IndieCade wouldn't be possible without academic support.

In terms of attendees, all those I met were either game designers themselves, game journalists, or students interested in game development—that is, people with a strong prior interest in games. Some came from quite far away, including one developer from Venezuela who saw the festival as a valuable opportunity to promote his game (Fernandez, 2014). Pearce said that organizers aim to make IndieCade as accessible as possible to international designers and those within the US who cannot easily travel to Los Angeles by offering travel grants for which they can apply. Established developers often contribute as well, sending organizers personal checks for a few thousand dollars for the sole purpose of travel funding.

At the time of writing, IndieCade Europe was planned to launch in Paris in November of 2016.

Playpublik: Berlin, Germany in 2012 and Krakow, Poland in 2014

In October of 2014 I attended Playpublik, a festival organized by Invisible Playground, a Berlin-based group of game designers, and held that year in Krakow, Poland. Unlike IndieCade, Playpublik focused on site-specific games; designers made proposals for one of more than ten designated sites throughout the city, and Invisible Playground acted as curator to select those that would be featured.

Because games at Playpublik took place at locations throughout the city rather than being gathered in a few large areas like at IndieCade, attendees were asked to come to one central location and from there were led by volunteers to each site when a game was about to begin. Polish translators sometimes accompanied groups to better enable participation by local people.

Some of the games had a clear beginning and end while others were open-ended without clear win conditions. For example, *The Brief and Frightening Reign* (Fono, 2013) involved players gathering in an office meeting room to make decisions about the development of an imaginary island, with the results of their decisions being displayed on a large screen and continuing until the game was clearly finished. The mobile game *Kling Klang Klong* (Straeubig, 2014), on the other hand, was more open-ended; it involved players' collaboratively creating sounds based on their location while walking around the city. In *Hidden Krakow* (Baranowski, Reiche, & Wood, 2014), another mobile game, players unlocked chapters of an illustrated story by visiting different areas of the city. Roughly half of the games at Playpublik had some type of digital element, though as seen in the examples above, they often prominently featured physical movement and real-world interaction. Personally, I led a performance of physical games that took place across two days of the festival in a courtyard and kindergarten playground (Wood, 2014).

The site-specific nature of the games was made possible by holding a two-day "Game Camp" before the festival where designers worked on their games, either creating them from scratch or tweaking a previous game to suit its location in Krakow. In some cases designers who had met for the first time at the Game Camp collaborated on games or on certain aspects of their games.

Playpublik was organized around the theme of "Momentary States," which was further broken down into "Landscape & Bodies," "Attention & Economies," and "Belief & Chaos." Unlike IndieCade, where games were presented broadly by genre ("Big Games," "Night Games," etc.), Playpublik's games were meant to provide attendees with new perspectives on specific topics. There were also question and answer sessions with designers about how their games related to each theme.

Christiane Hütter, a core member of Invisible Playground, mentioned that though games can be funny, they don't have to be; games can be all kinds of things and even handle serious issues. She summarized Invisible Playground's general goal simply as "creating new games that encourage you to do cool things."

Invisible Playground was founded in 2009 after Quack visited New York City's Come Out & Play and was inspired by the American design ethics of collaboration, playtesting, and iteration. There he saw that participants could be players and designers at the same time, as opposed to the model of artistic perfection with a sharp distinction between creator and audience with which he had been familiar given his background in music and theater. This experience led to Invisible Playground's first festival in Germany, "You Are GO!" in 2011, and then the first Playpublik in 2012 in Berlin. The group has also co-curated "72 Hour Interactions," an event where game designers and architects form teams to design and construct new "gameful architecture" over the course of 72 hours.

Playpublik was able to pay for on-site translators, offer artist fees and accommodation to designers and cover other costs thanks to support from cultural organizations including the Goethe Institute, a German governmental organization dedicated to promoting German culture abroad. In Germany, and to varying degrees in other European countries, artists and organizers can find support from major organizations for games and game-related events due to an interest in funding experimental art and cultural projects. Invisible Playground founder Sebastian Quack told me that this requires framing games in just the right way, such as an artistic innovation from the US or as a cultural form that can address political issues in a new way. The Goethe Institute's presence in countries throughout Europe also gives Invisible Playground a potential partner in many cities where they might plan a project.

Come Out and Play: New York City, USA, 2006 to Present

Though I have not attended Come Out & Play, I spoke with founders Nick Fortugno and Greg Trefry about its creation and how the festival has changed over the years. They told me that in the mid-2000s, many people were creating games and game-like experiences in New York City. However, because these designers worked in separate fields—whether performance art, academia, or game development—and showed their work in separate venues, they were not always aware of what others were doing. Fortugno and Trefry created Come Out & Play so that these artists and designers could come together in a single space, form a community, and share and discuss their work. By bringing their work together in one festival they also hoped to reach a larger audience than any one designer or game could reach alone.

The two organizers told me that the festival began as a highly theoretical, "hipster" event, in their words "preaching to the choir" about games. They soon realized, however, that the event had broad appeal and didn't have to be obscure or "indie." Families and random strangers—that is, "non-gamers" who passed by on the streets—would readily join in and have made up a growing portion of attendees each year. Fortugno and Trefry said they have consciously removed "pretentious, alienating elements" and focused instead on popular appeal, shifting promotion efforts as well to a diversity of outlets that could reach a broader audience.

With the exception of the second year when it took place in Amsterdam, Come Out & Play has been held at various indoor and outdoor areas in New York City, including Times Square and Park Slope. For the past four years, parts of the festival have been held on Governor's Island, which provides open space for large, physical games. The festival has developed into a three-day event consisting of "After Dark" on the first night, followed by "Field Day" and "Family Day."

The majority of games are physical, focusing on "real-world interaction" with limited use of digital elements. Fortugno told me that as curators they are interested in "tool-enabled play" rather than just a "new iPhone game," looking for new and different things and trying to avoid doing the same thing twice. Additionally, some games each year are created by students in game design courses at New York University and Parsons, where Trefry and Fortugno themselves teach, respectively.

The event is "boot-strapped" each year, receiving little to no public or private funding and made possible through the uncompensated time and labor of volunteers. Despite the limited budget, Trefry and Fortugno clearly take pride in the event's "do-it-yourself" aesthetic, claiming that it gives them greater freedom in what they do.

They added that the event has benefited greatly from the "ready-to-go" population of participants and promotional media unique to New York City, recognizing that similar events might not be possible in other cities. As one of the earliest festivals of street games, however, and perhaps because it is located in a city known for cutting edge trends, Come Out & Play has served as a major inspiration for other events, and Fortugno and Trefry said they have been contacted by people who want to hold Come Out & Play in other cities. Though they are open to this type of expansion, they also believe that catering to the unique situation of one's own city is key in reaching a broader audience beyond the community of active creatives. Due to this and their own limitations of time and location, Come Out & Play has so far expanded only to San Francisco, California.

Come Out and Play SF: San Francisco, USA, 2010 to Present

Catherine Herdlick began working with Fortugno and Trefry on organizing Come Out & Play in New York during its early years, but in 2009 she moved to San Francisco, California. At first she continued working on Come Out & Play remotely; however, since a number of the festival's game designers each year were flying in from San Francisco, she decided to launch a west coast version of the festival in 2010. Over the years since then Come Out & Play SF's locations have ranged from a middle school black top (an open, paved area) to an art gallery to sectioned off blocks of city streets.

In terms of curating the festival, Heather Browning, the current Executive Director, emphasized the importance thing of games that involve "interacting with the real world in creative ways" uniquely suited to the festival's site. Just as in New York, most of the games are physical, though Browning mentioned that having a digital element can help set expectations for people who are less familiar with games; it lets them know that they are "about to have a new experience" and that "this is not just a field day with sack races."

One continually popular game at Come Out & Play SF is *Journey to the End of the Night* (Kizu-Blair, Lavigne, & Mahan, 2006). It was in fact featured at the very first Come Out & Play in New York in 2006 but is now held every year in San Francisco to start the festival. Drawing thousands of players, the game involves racing between secret checkpoints in the city while being chased, and becoming a chaser oneself if caught. Praising its "artistic vision, innovation, and openness," Herdlick said that *Journey to the End of the Night* is "an institution in San Francisco."

Some games each year also come from professional design groups that create games and game-like experiences as their normal business, including creators of "escape rooms" and those who run games for "corporate team-building." In some cases, Browning said they invite games that have been featured at IndieCade.

In 2012 the festival organizers applied for and received a curatorial residency with SOMArts, which included a grant and a home for that year's festival in SOMArts' gallery. Over the years they have received other financial support based on the backgrounds and connections of the shifting team of organizers. Still, Browning told me that the festival "barely scrapes by" every year, claiming that it is even more "scrappy" than its New York counterpart. They now hold regular fundraising events throughout the year, recognizing that doing so and staying connected to their community suits their skills and needs better than continually applying for one-time grants.

In 2013, some members of the organizing team began to hold "Sandbox," a monthly playtesting event where designers experiment with ideas for games. These include physical versions of digital game mechanics, party games, and board games, with different themes each month. Sandbox also serves as an opportunity for those who don't necessarily see themselves as game designers to recognize that they too can create games. Browning said she has seen a pattern in which people attend Sandbox out of interest in Come Out & Play SF, design and test a game there, and finally submit it to and end up having it featured in the festival.

w00t: Copenhagen, Denmark, 2013 to 2015

In May of 2015, I attended w00t, held in Copenhagen for the third consecutive year. As a collaboration between a collective of game designers, a school, and a production company, it offers a unique model for a festival of games and play.

With a theme of "playful structures," the festival took place mainly at a public park in downtown Copenhagen, where games and interactive installations were arranged around a grassy lawn. Physical games were regularly held in surrounding areas, including zombie tag along city streets, human foosball on a basketball court, and a party game using glow sticks in a nearby building.

Creation and curation of games for the festival was handled by the Copenhagen Games Collective, which was founded in 2008 after members met at IndieCade while presenting a game. Other members met through the IT University of Copenhagen, which has graduate and post-graduate courses in game design. The Collective has grown over the years and now serves mainly as a loose umbrella organization through which members can create games or events together.

Some of w00t's games were created by Copenhagen Games Collective members themselves, while others were curated from submissions from designers outside Denmark, and some interactive installations were made by local students. When choosing games for the festival, Collective member Lena Mech explained that she and other creative directors sought submissions from people in a variety of fields outside of game design, as this makes for more varied and interesting content. This year, for example, a sculptor created two interlocking metal sculptures that could be taken apart, resembling a life-size puzzle (Vecerova, 2013).

Production and promotion of w00t was handled by Indgreb, a local production company that held music festivals in the past but became interested in game festivals through contact with the Copenhagen Games Collective. The company managed the business side of w00t each year, but, as is the case with many of these festivals, they invest more time and energy than could be considered profitable.

On-site staffing was provided by students from Vallekilde, a unique type of Danish school offering a six-month program for people aged 18-25 to gain experience and skills in certain fields, including game design in Vallekilde's case. As part of its "Game Academy" course, students managed the practical details of making w00t happen, including construction and other manual labor.

More so than other festivals I have attended, there were many families with young children at w00t. They gathered around some of the more popular games, such as a digital soccer game that could be played by jumping on a trampoline (Arnvig, 2015), while their parents waited nearby. Overall, attendees seemed to be a mix of game designers, students, and families with young children.

In October of 2015 the Copenhagen Games Collective announced that they would not be holding w00t again the following year. Collective member Patrick Jarnfelt told me that the many partners involved in w00t made for a complex event with practical and creative limitations. Though still interested in festivals of games and play, the Collective decided to re-evaluate what such a festival should look like.

Plaython: Athens, Greece, 2012 to 2014

Though I have not had the chance to attend Plaython, it presents a unique case where organizers created an urban game design community in Athens, Greece amidst an economic crisis.

Chloe Varelidi, a Greek game designer, moved to New York City to attend graduate school in 2006. There she met Trefry and Fortugno and became familiar with Come Out & Play, where one of her games was featured in 2008. In 2011, she had the idea to bring something like Come Out & Play back to Greece and reached out to Maria Saridaki, an academic studying games, and Artemis Papageorgiou, an architect, to attempt to organize a game festival of their own.

Varelidi and Saridaki told me that they wanted to avoid presenting games as a solution to any of the problems facing Greece, focusing instead on playfulness for people of all ages as a way to relieve the stress felt throughout the city. Although they saw great potential for a festival of urban games in the capital, whose public spaces had become sites of tension and social uprisings, there was virtually no urban game design community in the city on which to draw. So, leading up to the first Plaython in 2012, they held a series of workshops and events to introduce people to game design and give them a chance to develop their own games.

The events and the festival itself turned out to be very popular, garnering enough attention to fund a second edition of the festival in 2013 with a one-time grant from the European Union. Once again, organizers held a series of workshops in the months beforehand to train people in game design skills and expand the game design community in Athens.

These new game designers came from a broad range of professional backgrounds, from architects and lawyers to unemployed young people eager to gain new skills that might lead to work opportunities. Saridaki mentioned that some of the most active and enthusiastic participation during workshops and playtesting came from people over the age of 50, contrary to the perception of game development as something for younger people.

The games created through these workshops were submitted to and often featured in the festival. Other Plaython games were submitted by established game designers, while the organizers specifically invited some designers from abroad whose work they knew from other festivals of games and play.

Saridaki told me that versatility and adaptability were a major focus in developing and curating games for Plaython—that is, they wanted games that could be played and enjoyed by people of all ages and ability levels. One example she gave was *All For One* (Gkion, 2013), a game where players perform a variety of tasks while tied together. She said it drew positive responses from a variety of players, including those who were blind or restricted to wheelchairs.

Another game called *CITYgories* (Kolovou, 2012) involved finding objects in a category that begin with a certain letter and capturing them with a photo or drawing. Designed by an architect who had never before made a game, *CITYgories* won a contest held at the second Plaython and as a result was later presented at GameCity in the United Kingdom. Saridaki said that the game's designer has, since discovering her new interest through Plaython, become a freelance project manager and location-based game designer.

The second Plaython in 2013 drew over 2,000 people, including many from education and business who simply wanted to learn more about games in addition to families and game designers. Having generated considerable interest in urban games, Varelidi and other organizers were contacted by people all over Greece who wanted to see Plaython or something similar held locally in their cities. As a result they decided, rather than hold the festival in Athens again in 2014, to instead provide the tools for people to hold mini-festivals across the country under the title "Playthonakia."

Plaython organizers provided local Playthonakia organizers with a how-to guide for creating a game festival, including example games as well as a game that taught the basics of game design. In the end, Playthonakia was held in ten locations around Greece with a theme of Greek mythology. These mini-festivals included an event where 200 teenagers created Greek mythological artifacts at a campsite, and another held by a library on a beach with books about mythology. Some went so well that local organizers decided to unofficially run them again in 2015, though Plaython itself went on hiatus so that organizers could focus on community building.

Other Festivals

There are more festivals than can be described here in sufficient detail, but a few additional events deserve special notice. GameCity in Nottingham, England, founded in 2006, focuses mainly on video games but is unique in that it is funded and run almost completely by Trent University. Similarly, "Playin' Siegen" in Germany, an urban games festival held for the first time in 2015, was organized as a project by Master's students in Media Culture at Siegen University.

The biannual Playful Arts Festival in the Netherlands, organized by Zuraida Buter and Iris Peters in 2012 and 2014, is focused on play and "playful culture" in relation to other disciplines and art forms. Buter is involved in a number of other events in the Netherlands related to games and play, including a "Playful Jam," which is based on the idea of a game jam (in which programmers, artists and sound designers form teams to make games over a short period of time) but focused on physical play rather than digital games. Buter is also the former director of the Global Game Jam, which is coordinated worldwide each year with participants in 73 countries.

Outside of the US and Europe, there is "Fresh Air," a street games festival in Melbourne, Australia that has been held every year since 2013. The BitSummit Festival in Japan, though focused on video games, is also notable as the first major festival to give a platform to independent Japanese developers despite Japan's long history of video game production. It has been held annually in Kyoto since 2012.

SYNTHESIS

Sites for "Fun, New Experiences"

As is evident from the cases above, these festivals involve games across a broad spectrum, varying mainly in the degree to which they lean towards digital or physical games and how far their range of content extends in each direction. It was also clear from the numerous references in interviews that Come Out & Play played a major role in showing people what could be possible with a festival of games and play. Game designers and event organizers took this inspiration and applied it to their own situations, broadening an event to include more types of games in the case of IndieCade, founding a game design collective that would become a major player in the European festival scene in the case of Invisible Playground, and finding a way to bring urban games to their own country in the case of Plaython.

Each festival found a unique course to funding and support through one-time grants, academia, and governmental support, and yet nearly every organizer mentioned the continual struggle for financial viability. Events like IndieCade and Playpublik are able to achieve greater financial support than many others due to their unique situations, yet they still rely heavily on volunteers and are essentially not for profit.

In terms of organizers' approaches to game curation, terms like "fun," "new," and "creative" came up again and again when describing desired experiences. "Fun, new experiences" could very well be the mantra of these festivals, and based on my own experiences there are in fact many fun, new experiences to be had there.

However, more notable than the quality of individual games was, for me, the atmosphere created by this focus. Though hard to quantify, there is something powerful about hundreds of strangers walking around looking for joyful, new experiences with others. This kind of open, welcoming, and playful space is both very real and very different from most spaces in which we find ourselves in day-to-day life.

Game designer Shawn Pierre noted that after playing a few rounds of his games he often sees people, formerly complete strangers, laughing and hugging one another. This ability of games with physical elements to establish bonds of intimacy over the course of just a few minutes also contributes a lot to the atmosphere at these festivals.

Most organizers also spoke about trying to be as open and inclusive as possible both in terms of what can be considered a "game" and in the backgrounds of those submitting games. Within the thematic scope of their festivals, they spoke about providing a "big tent" where participants can gain greater exposure together than they could alone. This is clear in the professional backgrounds of the people whose games are presented, including fine artists, hobbyists, professors, students, game design collectives and game development studios.

In the case of Plaython, there was an additional focus on making games that were playable and enjoyable regardless of age or ability. I found this refreshing given that many urban games involve running around city streets or other physically intense activities that are not necessarily safe, comfortable, or physically possible for all players.

Finally, the festivals often led to the creation of secondary events such as the mini-festivals of Playthonakia across Greece or Sandbox in San Francisco. These events are focused on the same themes but do not fit into the framework of an annual game festival. Instead they serve to expand the community of game designers and generate more interest in the festivals themselves.

RELATED TRENDS

In terms of broader trends that may have influenced the emergence and spread of festivals of games and play, nearly everyone I spoke with agreed that "something changed in the past ten years." Specifically, people pointed to the following: the widespread use of the Internet, people's "tiredness" with technology and screens, the blurring of distinctions between different types of games, the rise of the "gamer generation" and the normalization of video games, and greater accessibility of the tools of game development.

Internet and Related Technology

There was broad agreement that the Internet has brought about major changes in the way people live and in doing so helped to make these festivals possible. David Hayward, who has contributed to GameCity and is now in charge of his own festival Feral Vector, proposed that the Internet has granted niche interests—such as non-commercial video games—greater visibility and thus enabled the formation of new communities that can reach a broader audience. Doug Wilson also pointed out that the Internet makes it easier for people with similar interests to connect and form coherent communities. Tadhg Kelly, game design consultant and author of the blog "What Games Are," pointed out that the Internet makes both promotion and finding an audience easier, which in turn makes some events possible that couldn't have happened otherwise. Zuraida Buter of the Playful Arts Festival added that social media has made it easier to follow others' work around the world and to communicate about her own events.

Celia Pearce of IndieCade spoke in the most detail about the Internet and its effects on game development. She argued that the exploratory and participatory nature of Internet culture has encouraged people to "reappropriate mass culture and make it their own," these festivals being one form of that reappropriation. She also emphasized that the Internet and its open distribution channels have removed the need for the "gate-keepers and taste-makers" who controlled production and release of content in the past, letting games become a "folk form" instead and thus more varied and accessible.

In terms of related technologies, Trefry and Fortugno said that general familiarity with "smart" devices has made new types of games possible. The increasing population of people with smartphones, for example, makes it possible to run mobile games on larger scales than were possible in the past.

"Tiredness" With Technology

At the same time that they recognized the role the Internet and related technologies have played in benefiting festivals like theirs, Trefry and Fortugno mentioned "tiredness" with technology and a desire to "connect with real people in real life" as reasons for the popularity of events focused on physical games. Hütter also mentioned people's being "tired with digitalization" as a reason for the positive response to Invisible Playground's work.

Kelly, however, criticized such "politicization," questioning whether this is a significant social trend and pointing out that sales of digital devices like iPads are "doing just fine." It is certainly hard to determine to what degree people have stopped "going outside" or "connecting with other people," or how much this might have affected people's willingness to play games in the streets.

Rather, perhaps a sharp distinction between playing "inside" and "outside" is not appropriate; especially for younger people, there may simply be less of a division between real and virtual worlds. Pearce of IndieCade explained that people who grew up with video games and the Internet are accustomed to embodying other worlds that exist alongside the "real world," and for them it feels natural to play a game while walking through one's city on the way to school or work. This suggests that, rather than seeing "digital" and "physical" as being at odds with one another, today's players of a certain age are more willing and able to enjoy games that combine elements of both.

Blurring Divisions Between Games

Similarly, many people brought up the historical divisions that have existed between different fields of design, saying that in the past, one had to be either a commercial video game designer, for example, or an artist creating games for museums, or an urban game designer working in city streets. This is precisely why Fortugno and Trefry wanted to establish one festival for all types of games. In terms of now being able to create across a broad range of media with fewer restrictions, multiple people cited the game *Killer Queen* (DeBonis & Mikros, 2011), which began as a physical game and was later turned into an arcade game.

Shawn Pierre, whose games have been featured at both IndieCade and Come Out & Play, made it clear that he does not see a sharp distinction between games based on the format of their interaction. Pierre explained that he had always loved and wanted to make video games but that the time-consuming process of programming and debugging made it difficult. The rules for a card game or physical game, on the other hand, could be created and tested right away. He thus began making games in 2010 with the card game *These French Fries Make Terrible Hot Dogs*, which, after positive response from the game design community in Philadelphia, he took to IndieCade and then raised nearly USD 20,000 on Kickstarter to produce. Next, he created *Henka Caper Twist*, a game using PlayStation Move controllers and combining physical and digital elements that has been featured at IndieCade and Come Out & Play.

Echoing the theme of "fun, new experiences," Pierre said he wants people to "go outside their comfort zone" and get "dumb and silly," judging a game's success by whether players come back to play again. Pierre's comments and personal history show that the ease of production and response from players matter more to him than a game's format or strict categorical definition.

Similarly, David Hayward of Feral Vector told me that in his early days of organizing indie game events it made sense to focus only on video games, as at that time "things were really divided between digital and analog." Now, however, people are "progressing through the divide and a new focus is emerging on play." Play, indeed, may be key in understanding what is happening at and through these festivals, which I will discuss in the second and third sections.

The "Gamer Generation" and the Normalization of Video Games

Many people mentioned changes in the general familiarity with games that have occurred as the "gamer generation" (those who grew up playing video games) became adults, started families of their own, and continued to be interested in making and playing games. Video games are now a normal part of life for more people than ever before, considerably removed from the childish or dangerous sub-culture as which they were once characterized.

Trefry and Fortugno told me how it is natural for members of the "gamer generation" to play together with the whole family after getting married and having children, and that these families make a natural audience for Come Out & Play. These "grown-up millennials" also make it easier to show games that are meant to be played by adults, allowing for further diversity in the games created.

Many also spoke of how independent video games' increased visibility and success in the past six to seven years helped make games and play more accessible and familiar to the general public.[1] Most major video game events now include sections for indie or physical games; as one example, many American interviewees pointed to the board game section at Penny Arcade Expo, a major series of video game festivals that takes place across the United States and in Australia.

This can be seen as well in the receptivity of major institutions to games and game-related events. I spoke about this with Joe Salina, an event coordinator at Babycastles, a game exhibition and cultural space in Manhattan. Salina explained that in the mid-2000s large museums were not an option as venues for game-related events. However, receptivity to games has since increased and in recent years Babycastles has had the opportunity to hold events at the Natural History Museum and Museum of Modern Art.

Holly Gramazio was a game designer at Hide & Seek, a pioneering game and event production company in the UK until it closed in 2013, and during her time there she said they often received inquiries from companies curious about games. They also created games and game-related events for major organizations like Kensington Palace, the Natural History Museum, and *Sesame Street*.

Mathias Poulson, who has worked with games in education and organizes the CounterPlay festival in Denmark, recalled that around 2008 he often had to defend games and "push back against fear-mongering." However, with the "explosion of interest in games" and their increased acceptance, he no longer needs to defend games' value. He said that at some point games became a "magic solution" to problems in many people's eyes, and he now actually spends time trying to convince people of the opposite—that games alone cannot fix everything.

Trefry and Fortugno summarized all of this by saying that with increased interest in games from the fields of healthcare, education, academia, business, and art, games face less adversity than ever before, thus making festivals of games and play more accessible and viable than in the past. In game designer

Doug Wilson's words, "more people are interested in games, have higher hopes for games, and are accustomed to strange indie games."

Accessibility of Game Development

In terms of changes to games' position in society, many people also brought up the lowered costs and greater ease of use of the tools of video game development as well as increased support for game developers in terms of communities and funding—in short, greater access to game development.

Kelly pointed specifically to the game development engine Unity as "lowering the bar by about 80%" and making experimentation with video game development considerably less intimidating. The availability of open sources projects, Wilson added, also greatly aids developers.

The creation of new communities through the Internet and the surge in indie game development also provide aspiring game developers with stronger support and educational networks. Kelly said that it is now easier to self-publish and to connect with others thanks to websites like, in the case of board games, boardgamegeek.com. Shawn Pierre, like many other young developers, was able to find opportunities for playtesting in his local indie game development community in Philadelphia, using the card-printing site "Ad Magic," the same used by the successful indie card game *Cards Against Humanity*, to print copies of his own game on demand. Similarly, the Global Game Jam offers an opportunity for people in cities all over the world to obtain game development experience and see themselves as part of a worldwide video game development community.

In short, it is easier than ever before to experiment with video game development, see oneself as a game designer, and find communities of like-minded people online if not in real life. New types of events such as Come Out & Play SF's Sandbox and game design courses at universities offer further opportunities to create the games seen at these festivals.

The "Gravity" of Games

The themes above paint a clear picture of broader familiarity with games, greater ease of development, and fewer divisions between different types of games, all supported by the connective power of the Internet. Thus, it is easy to view the spread of festivals of games and play as a natural extension of the independent video game movement, especially in cases like IndieCade.

Starting as a space for independent video games, the organizers of IndieCade began to include other types of games, and the festival now accepts all types of innovative interactive experiences. There are games about physically punching custard (Buckenham, 2014) and playing tag on city streets alongside console games using screens and controllers. Furthermore, the event is funded by video game industry giants like Nintendo and Sony, who are searching for new indie video games to feature on their platforms.

However, considering the details of the other festivals described above, IndieCade appears to be something of an anomaly in its direct emergence from independent video games. Other festivals and their organizers have various backgrounds in theater, art, and academia, drawing on many different communities and funding sources. Even in the case of IndieCade, there is a kind of "awkward alliance," as Wilson put it, in terms of the diverse backgrounds and goals of the designers whose games are featured. Some are trying to create financially sustainable companies or "the next big indie game," while others are losing money by paying out of pocket to attend the festival to show a non-commercial passion project, and still others are supported by their academic institution to attend and present a graduate project.

Thus, though it is tempting to see the festivals as a natural extension of the indie video game movement, this does not capture the diversity of the communities and individuals involved. A more accurate assessment may be that, as Wilson described, the "gravity" of indie video games provided the focus and fuel for other cultural forms—which had until then remained separate and peripheral—to come together and gain greater exposure in a shared space focused on inclusivity and fun, new experiences. That is, the normalization and broad acceptance of video games has provided a space for other types of games and play to reach the general public in an environment where participants are open to new experiences and looking for fun. On a similar note, Kunal Gupta, founder of Babycastles, described one function of games as a "shield" behind which new ideas, cultural forms, and political issues could be brought into the public eye and public space.

In research on play and playfulness there have been similar claims about the ability of play to broaden people's perspectives and expose them to new ideas. In his essay "Orderly and Disorderly Play," Thomas Hendricks (2009) discusses how it has been shown that "imaginative players open up new cognitive territories for themselves" (p. 30). As an individual function of his "disorderly play," he claims that "personally instigated creativity constitutes the means by which people realize they can oppose the world and expose its society as an artifice constructed by people like themselves" (p. 36). Defining "playfulness" as a mental state as opposed to the physical act of play, Stenros (2015) similarly writes that "playfulness can be connected to power structures and it can be especially useful as tactical undermining of existing power structures" (p. 74), though he also highlights the dark side of this power in the case of online "trolls" and "griefers." Rachel Shields (2015) identifies the unique value of play in a contemporary context, claiming that "a prerational notion of play" has the "capacity to interrupt moral and cultural forms that arise in late capitalist context" (p. 312).

Their views point to the politically and socially transformative potential of play. In this light, it is no surprise that games, as a structured form of play that can be commodified and shared with others, would serve as the fuel for the creation of new communities, unprecedented events, and alliances of people from different backgrounds. Indeed, far from surprising, it is *sensible* that people in Greece, for example, would be drawn to play and games in a time of crisis and social unrest.

In addition to being politically and socially transformative, and in fact at the heart of this transformative potential, Shields describes play as being a mystic experience:

Although play is conventionally seen as, and studied for, the many forms it takes, as the expression of a broader metaphysical force, it seeks always to transcend these forms and thus necessarily reaches into unknown and unimagined realms. For lack of a better term, I call such a moment, or affective state, the **feeling of Otherwise,** *or the uneasy state of embodied mind as it treads into new territory without the support of—or frame that is provided by—language. Such states alternate between unleashing a complex, multifaceted flow of ideas, memories, and sensations and arresting this flow into forms that can be clearly thought and communicated. This process of flow followed by cessation, I suggest, may be the mechanism by which cultural forms, intertwined as they are with language, ideology, and power, are frozen into place, appearing momentarily as brittle and jagged, and allowing us to feel the ways in which our political and cultural horizons are limited. (Shields, 2015, p. 300) [Emphasis by Shields]*

In her analysis, this "metaphysical play force" is key to transformation in that it enables the reimagining of one's world in ways that cannot be captured by language or rational thought. Through confrontation with the unknown—her "feeling of Otherwise"—play offers a glimpse of alternatives. She concludes that play can be a valuable aesthetic in and of itself:

What is missing is a turn to the idea of play as an aesthetic, as both a culturally informed thing that is practiced and goes nominally by "play," and a thing that captures the dimension of sensation, as an ideal state of indulgence in the body-mind's capacity for breaking free from patterns. It is in this way that the body itself, the potential of sensation, figures centrally within the conditions of political possibility. (Shields, 2015, p. 319)

In terms of the development of such an aesthetic of play and of a refocusing of attention on the body at play, festivals of games and play are of great value and potential. Further research is needed on the roles and uses of games, play and festivals both within society and within the individual's experience of the world.

CONCLUSION: WHAT DOES THIS MEAN FOR GAMES?

It is clear that we are in the middle of a shift in games' position in society and their significance in people's lives. In the context of these festivals, however, how can we define games that fall somewhere between "physical" and "digital" in order to capture the nuances of today's game landscape?

Wilson, for one, told me that he identifies strictly as a video game developer and sees other video game developers as his peers, rather than the general community of designers seen at these festivals. However, given that his *Johann Sebastian Joust* received considerable attention as a physically intense game without a screen, the fact that he sees himself as an indie video game developer reflects a clear shift in the definition of "video game."

The most tangible impact of these festivals may be something I heard from Greg Trefry and Nick Fortugno of Come Out & Play and Christiane Hütter of Invisible Playground: their explicit goal to "create an audience." These festivals serve as an opportunity for both video game fans and people with no personal experience with games to play together in a public space, and their continued growth despite a lack of financial stability reflects the degree to which people value the experiences they have there and to which they want more.

Thanks to these festivals, more and more people each year are accustomed to and eager to engage in public play across a broad range of physical and digital games, which alone constitutes a major change in games' cultural position and warrants further inquiry from a variety of fields and perspectives. At the same time, these festivals reach only a small section of the population in a limited number of Western countries; it is important to recognize that far from being global, they are for now a very limited and local phenomenon.

I propose that the festivals' focus on "fun, new experiences" amidst changing definitions of games be understood as an "emerging focus on play." If the card games, live-action role-playing games, virtual reality games, mobile games, and party games are understood together as "forms of play," it follows that their categorical divisions would blur as people focus on the core experience that they all share: play. When presented together in one space such as at these festivals, their similarities become more obvious than their differences—that is, they all provide people with an opportunity to play together, albeit with different structures and degrees of technology.

Similar thoughts were voiced by a number of the people with whom I spoke, including David Hayward, who, in addition to his earlier comments, noted that people are beginning to think about what play means in the lives of adults. Zuraida Buter also said that in the last five years she has seen more of a focus on the idea of play, adding that although there is a growing international community of people who "get" play, the concept can be hard to convey locally at each festival. The term "games" is thus useful when promoting an event or applying for grants, but for her the ultimate focus is on playfulness and creating "playful culture."

Gwen Gordon, an independent play scholar and producer of an upcoming public television special about play, said that "the possibility to break through the alienation of our hyper-individualistic society and connect to strangers through play was unlocked by video games," suggesting that this is "spilling over into the rest of society" through street games and festivals. According to her, every sector of society—healthcare, business, community development, education, and even spirituality—is beginning to "tap into the power of play." Gordon claimed, however, that play is bigger than any of these applications and argued that it is the basis of a more life-affirming society, a "playground instead of a proving ground." These sentiments were echoed by Bernie De Koven, who urged game creators to reflect on the political significance of creating one's own game and playing together with others in public.

Central to all of this is the definition of play. It does not suit my purposes to attempt to propose an all-encompassing definition of play, but in terms of describing these festivals and the experiences that players have in practical terms, psychologist Peter Gray's definition is worth noting. He analyzed the many definitions of play that have been offered and identified five common characteristics:

(1) Play is self-chosen and self-directed; (2) Play is activity in which means are more valued than ends; (3) Play has structure, or rules, which are not dictated by physical necessity but emanate from the minds of the players; (4) Play is imaginative, non-literal, mentally removed in some way from "real" or "serious" life; and (5) Play involves an active, alert, but non-stressed frame of mind. (Gray, 2008)

These five characteristics generally describe the experiences that can be had through the games at these festivals when they are at their best. Of course, "playing" a game can also feel like "work" in some cases. This is precisely why Stenros (2015) highlighted the difference between play as an activity that can be observed and defined from the outside and playfulness as a mental state, which can and does occur even during activities typically defined as "work" (pp. 64-72).

For my purposes, I would like to use the notion of "play" in order to understand these festivals as reaching towards and embracing something bigger than games, an experience and mindset that exists beyond games. Understanding the focus on fun, new experiences across the digital-physical spectrum as a focus on play gives cohesion to the festivals and offers an explanation for the changing definitions of and attitudes towards games seen there.

Still, it is important to recognize that many divisions remain between the communities involved in games and between different types of games. Heather Browning of Come Out & Play SF said that although she appreciates games that combine the real and virtual in new ways, designers themselves are still very much split into two communities. Based on my experiences at video game jams and being part of video game development communities, I have also noticed confusion towards physical games that seems to stem from a high valuation of programming skills and the perceived superiority of digital game mechanics. At the same time, for physical game designers who do not have programming ability, digital game development can seem intimidating despite the greater accessibility of the tools of creation.

Holly Gramazio of Hide & Seek additionally pointed out that, despite the increased interest in games from companies and museums, there are still virtually no artist residences or similar positions aimed at game designers. While games are seen as something new and interesting, she said, they are not yet fully embraced alongside other forms of culture. For example, games are usually only included at events through a conscious decision to focus on games rather than being seen as one of many options with equal value.

For now, these festivals are creating a "new public" of people seeking fun experiences with friends and strangers in public spaces, and towards this end, the various games found there should be recognized as belonging together as "forms of play." Similarly, the communities created through these festivals could be seen as "play communities," a term developed by Bernie De Koven (2014) and Celia Pearce (2011). The term refers to communities where maintaining the fun for all players is more important than the type or even rules of the game being played. These communities embrace all players no matter their background and all types of games no matter their format. This brings to mind Plaython, with its explicit focus on accessibility and its spread across the country to a variety of locations and players. Recognizing these festivals as spaces for communities of play and embracing play and playfulness as their core elements could contribute to the festivals' sustained growth and offer a means for the transformative value of play to reach more people around the world.

REFERENCES

Arnvig, N., Barbagallo, L., Christiansen, N., Dick, A., & Hansen, S. (2015). *Physical Soccer Physics* [video game].

Baranowski, K., Reiche, M., & Wood, W. (2014). *Hidden Krakow* [mobile game]. Krakow, Poland: Studio Martin Reiche.

Beavertoad Software (2013). *Cafe Murder* [mobile game].

Buckenham, G. (2014). *Punch the Custard* [video game].

De Koven, B. (2014). *A Playful Path*. Available from: http://press.etc.cmu.edu/files/A-Playful-Path_DeKoven-web.pdf

DeBonis, J. & Mikros, N. (2011, 2012, 2013). *Killer Queen* [physical game, video game, arcade game].

Die Gute Fabrik. (2014). *Sportsfriends* [video game]. Copenhagen, Denmark: Die Gute Fabrik.

Fernandez, H. (2014). *Fluff Eaters* [mobile game].

Fono, D. (2013). *The Brief and Frightening Reign* [live-action role-playing game].

Gkion, T. (2013). *All for One* [physical game].

Gray, P. (2008). *The value of play I: The definition of play gives insights*. Retrieved July 1st, 2015 from https://www.psychologytoday.com/blog/freedom-learn/200811/the-value-play-i-the-definition-play-gives-insights

Henricks, T. S. (2009). Orderly and disorderly play: A comparison. *American Journal of Play*, 2(1), 12–40.

Hyde, J. (2013). *Object Get* [urban game].

Kizu-Blair, I., & Lavigne, S. (2006). *Mahan*. Journey to the End of the Night. [urban game]

KnapNok Games. (2013). *Bumpie's Party* [video game]. KnapNok Games.

Kolovou, E. (2012). *CITYgories* [urban game]. Athens, Greece: bIZZ.

Pearce, C. (2011). *Communities of play: Emergent cultures in multiplayer games and virtual worlds.* Cambridge: MIT Press.

Pierre, S. (2013). *These French Fries Make Terrible Hot Dogs* [card game]. Netcong, New Jersey: Ad Magic.

Rafinski, A. (2013). *Church of Play* [alternate reality game].

Ryan, M. L., Emerson, L., & Robertson, B. (Eds.). (2014). *John Hopkins Guide to Digital Media.* Baltimore, MD: John Hopkins University Press.

Shields, R. (2015). Ludic ontology: Play's relationship to language, cultural forms, and transformative politics. *American Journal of Play*, *7*(3), 298–321.

Stenros, J. (2015). *Playfulness, play, and games: A constructionist ludology approach.* Tampere: Tampere University Press.

Straeubig, M. (2014). *Kling Klang Klong* [mobile game].

Vecerova, V. (2015). *Body Teaser* [interactive sculpture].

Wilson, D. (2011). *Johann Sebastian Joust* [video game].

Wood, W. (2014). *Curse of Play* [physical game].

KEY TERMS AND DEFINITIONS

Community of Play: A community prioritizing the shared experience of play for all members over the types of games being played or the preservation of certain rules.

Digital Game: A game relying exclusively on interaction with digital media to be played. Physical interaction goes no further than the limited use of the hands to press buttons or keys on a controller or keyboard, or to manipulate a joystick or mouse. A digital game may or may not involve a screen. See "physical game" and "video game" for comparison.

Festivals of Games and Play: Events focused on presenting a broad range of games and forms of play to the public. The games are generally independently produced and may include digital games, physical games, urban games, mobile games, or other types of games that do not fit in these categories.

Independent ("Indie") Game: A term that has come to refer to an independently produced video game (that is, one developed outside of a large commercial enterprise).

Mobile Game: A video game that is played on a mobile device, such as a smartphone or tablet.

Physical Game: A game relying solely on physical activity to be played. It may involve physical implements like balls, cards, or costumes, but no digital equipment or devices. See "digital game" for comparison.

Play: For the purpose of conveying what occurs at festivals of games of play, play can be understood as an activity with the following five characteristics as identified by Peter Gray (2008): 1) It is voluntary and can be quit at any time; 2) It is intrinsically motivated, the process mattering more than the goal; 3) It is guided by rules agreed upon by everyone involved; 4) It is imaginative and in some way unreal; and, 5) It is performed in an alert state of positive tension.

Urban Game: A game played in or around city streets and in which the urban environment plays a central role. Urban games generally require physical interaction among players or between players and their environment. They may involve digital equipment or devices.

Video Game: A game requiring the use of a video game console, electronic device or computer together with its accompanying screen in order to be played. Video games may involve varying degrees of physical movement and interaction. See "digital game" for comparison.

Western World: A geographically disparate but politically and culturally similar group of industrialized countries located mainly in North America and Europe.

ENDNOTE

[1] For a more detailed discussion on changes that have affected independent games' viability, see Celia Pearce's chapter "Independent and Art Games" in *John Hopkins Guide to Digital Media* (Ryan, Emerson, & Robertson, 2014).

Compilation of References

(DC)Draco-Dawgg. (2000, September 23). *Dawgg clan elite*. [War2.Warcraft.Org] Retrieved December 28, 2015 from http://war2.warcraft.org/forum/viewtopic.php?t=22

~summoner. (2001, February 13). *Get a life please*. [War2.Warcraft.Org] Retrieved November 27th, 2015 from http://war2.warcraft.org/forum/viewtopic.php?t=485

11 Bit Studios. (2014). *This war of mine* [Microsoft Windows/OS X/Linux video game]. Warsaw, Poland: 11 bit studios.

11. Bit Studios. (2014). *This War of Mine*. [PC game].Warsaw: 11 bit studios.

1Up. (n.d.). *Beyond the mushroom kingdom*. Retrieved 15 December, 2015, from http://www.1up.com/features/essential-50-tomb-raider

2D Boy. (2008). *World of goo* [Wii, Windows, OS X video game]. San Francisco, CA: 2D Boy.

2K Boston and 2K Australia. (2007). *BioShock* [Microsoft Windows (et al.) video game]. Novato, CA: 2K Games.

2K Games. (2007). *Bioshock* [Microsoft Windows video game]. New York, NY: Take Two Interactive.

2K Marin. (2010). *Bioshock 2* [Windows, PS3, Xbox 360 video game]. Novato, CA: 2K Games.

2K. Boston. (2007). *Bioshock* [Xbox 360, PlayStation 3 video game]. Oklahoma City, OK: 2K Games.

Aarseth, E. (2001). Computer game studies, year one. *Game Studies, 1*(1).

Aarseth, E. (2000). Allegories of space: The question of spatiality in computer games. In M. Eskelinen & R. Koskimaa (Eds.), *Cybertext Yearbook 2000*. University of Jyväskylä.

Aarseth, E. (2004). Genre trouble: Narrativism and the art of simulation. In N. Wardrip-Fruin & P. Harrigan (Eds.), *First person: New media as story, performance, and game* (pp. 45–55). Cambridge, MA: MIT Press.

Aarseth, E. J. (1997). *Cybertext: Perspectives on ergodic literature*. London: Johns Hopkins University Press.

Abbott, E. A. (1991). *Flatland: A romance of many dimensions*. Princeton, NJ: Princeton University Press.

Abrams, J. J., & Burk, B. (Producers), & Reeves, M. (Director). (2008). Cloverfield. United States: Paramount Pictures.

Abt, C. C. (1970). *Serious games*. New York, NY: The Viking Press, Inc.

AcademySoft. (1986). *Tetris* [MS-DOS video game]. AcademySoft.

Adams, E. (2013). *Fundamentals of Game Design*. New Riders.

Adcock, C. E., & Turrell, J. (1990). *James Turrell: The art of light and space*. Berkeley: U of California P.

Adelmann, R., & Winkler, H. (2014). Kurze Ketten. Handeln und Subjektkonstitution in Computerspielen. In S. Böhme, R. F. Nohr, & S. Wiemer (Eds.), Diskurse des strategischen Spiels: Medialität, Gouvernementalität, Topografie (pp. 69–82). Münster, Germany: Lit Verlag.

Afterschool Alliance. (2009). *America after 3pm: Key Findings.* Retrieved from http://www.afterschoolalliance.org/documents/AA3PM_Key_Findings_2009.pdf

Afterschool Alliance. (2012). *Afterschool Essentials: Research and Polling.* Retrieved from http://www.afterschoolalliance.org/documents/2012/Essentials_4_20_12_FINAL.pdf

Agosto, D. (2004). Design vs. content: A study of adolescent girls' website design preferences. *International Journal of Technology and Design Education, 14*(3), 245–260. doi:10.1007/s10798-004-0776-y

Ahern, T. C. (2002). Learning by design: Engineering the learned state. In N. Callaos & W. Lesso (Eds.), *6th World Multiconference in Systemics, Cybernetics and Informatics* (pp. 308-313). Orlando, FL: International Institute of Informatics and Systemics.

Ahern, T. C. (2009, October). Bridging the gap: Cognitive scaffolding to improve computer programming for middle school teachers. In *Frontiers in Education Conference, 2009. FIE'09. 39th IEEE* (pp. 1-5). IEEE.

Alberti, J. (2008). The game of reading and writing: How video games reframe our understanding of literacy. *Computers and Composition, 25*(3), 258–269. doi:10.1016/j.compcom.2008.04.004

Alden. (2015, April 27). Removing payment feature from *Skyrim* workshop. [Web log]. *Steam Community.* Retrieved from http://steamcommunity.com/games/SteamWorkshop/announcements/detail/208632365253244218

Alexander, J. (2009, April 21). *Broken Steel* DLC makes *Fallout 3* endless on May 5. *Engaget.* Retrieved from http://www.engadget.com/2009/04/21/broken-steel-dlc-makes-fallout-3-endless-on-may-5/

Alexander, L. (2013, September 20). *The tragedy of Grand Theft Auto V.* Retrieved January 15, 2016, from http://www.gamasutra.com/view/news/200648/Opinion_The_tragedy_of_Grand_Theft_Auto_V.php

Alfieri, L., Brooks, P. J., Aldrich, N. J., & Tenenbaum, H. R. (2011). Does discovery-based instruction enhance learning? *Journal of Educational Psychology, 103*(1).

Alientrap. (2015). *Apotheon* [PlayStation 4 video game]. Saskatoon, Saskatchewan, Canada: Alientrap.

Alison. (2009). Calling all gamer girls. *Dance Spirit, 13*(2), 24.

American Association of University Women. (2000). *Tech-savvy: Educating girls in the computer age.* Washington, DC: AAUW.

American Association of University Women. (2015). *Solving the equation: The variables for women's success in engineering and computing.* Washington, DC: AAUW.

Ames, C. (1992). Classrooms: Goals, structures, and student motivation. *Journal of Educational Psychology, 84*(3), 261–271.

Amnesty International. (2015). *Human rights education.* Retrieved July 12, 2015, from https://www.amnesty.org/en/human-rights-education

Andersen, C. (2014). Game of drones: The uneasy future of the soldier-hero in *Call of Duty: Black Ops II. Surveillance & Society, 12*(3), 360–376.

Anderson, B. (2006). *Imagined communities: Reflections on the origin and spread of nationalism* (Revised ed.). New York, NY: Verso.

Anderson, C., & Bushman, B. (2001). Effects of violent video games on aggressive behavior, aggressive cognition, aggressive affect, physiological arousal, and prosocial behavior: A meta-analytic review of the scientific literature. *Psychological Science, 12*(5), 353–359. doi:10.1111/1467-9280.00366 PMID:11554666

Anthropy, A. (2012). *Dys4ia* [Flash game]. Newgrounds. Retrieved 3 August 2015 from http://www.newgrounds.com/portal/view/591565

Anthropy, A. (2012). *Rise of the videogame zinesters: How freaks, normals, amateurs, artists, dreamers, drop-outs, queers, housewives, and people like you are taking back an art form*. New York, NY: Seven Stories Press.

Antonisse, J. (2008). *Hush* [Flash game]. Southern California: USC.

Ape Inc. (1995). *Earthbound* [Super NES/Game Boy Advance video game]. Kyoto, Japan: Nintendo.

Apogee Software. (1991). *Duke Nukem* [DOS (et al.) video game]. Garland, TX: Apogee Software.

App Camp for Girls. (2015). *Home*. Retrieved from http://appcamp4girls.com/

Apperley, T., & Walsh, C. (2012). What digital games and literacy have in common: A heuristic for understanding pupils' gaming literacy. *Literacy, 46*(3), 115–122. doi:10.1111/j.1741-4369.2012.00668.x

Apple. (2015). *App store review guidelines - Apple developer*. Retrieved July 7, 2015, from https://developer.apple.com/app-store/review/guidelines/#objectionable-content

Arakawa, M. (1991). The man behind Mario. In Mario mania: Nintendo player's strategy guide. Redmond, WA: Nintendo of America.

Arcade Kids. (n.d.). *AxK manifesto*. Retrieved December 16, 2015, from http://arcanekids.com/manifesto

Archangel. (2005, October 10). *Archangel's war2 history*. [Web.Archive.Org] Retrieved December 28, 2015 from http://web.archive.org/web/20060518133918/http://www.winnieinternet.com/games/war2/reports/ArchangelHistory.htm

Armitage, D. (2012). What's the big idea? Intellectual history and the Longue Durée. *History of European Ideas, 38*(4), 493–507. doi:10.1080/01916599.2012.714635

Armitage, D., & Guldi, J. (2014). *The history manifesto*. Cambridge, UK: Cambridge University Press; doi:10.1017/9781139923880

Arnold, D. S., Lonigan, C. J., Whitehurst, G. J., & Epstein, J. N. (1994). Accelerating language development through picture-book reading: Replication and extension to a videotape training format. *Journal of Educational Psychology, 86*(2), 235–243. doi:10.1037/0022-0663.86.2.235

Arnvig, N., Barbagallo, L., Christiansen, N., Dick, A., & Hansen, S. (2015). *Physical Soccer Physics* [video game].

Atari Inc. (1972). *Pong* [Arcade video game]. Sunnyvale, CA: Atari Inc.

Atari Inc. (1979). *Asteroids* [Arcade video game]. Sunnyvale, CA: Atari Inc.

Atari Inc. (1980). *Battlezone* [Arcade video game]. Sunnyvale, CA: Atari Inc.

Atari Inc. (1983). *Star wars* [Arcade video game]. Sunnyvale, CA: Atari Inc.

Atari, Inc. (1982a). *Dig dug* [Arcade video game]. Sunnyvale, CA: Atari, Inc.

Atari, Inc. (1982b). *ET* [Atari 2600 video game]. Sunnyvale, CA: Atari, Inc.

Atari, Inc. (1983). *Krull* [Atari 2600 video game]. Sunnyvale, CA: Atari, Inc.

Atlus. (2011). *Catherine* [PlayStation 3/XBox 360 video game]. Setagaya, Tokyo, Japan: Atlus.

Azerrad, M. (2014). Krist Novoselic: '*Meat Puppets II*' inspired me because 'there were no barriers'. *Billboard*. Retrieved from http://www.billboard.com/articles/news/6296973/1984-krist-novoselic-on-meat-puppets-II-influence

Azerrad, M. (2012). *Our band could be your life: Scenes from the American indie underground, 1981-1991*. New York, NY: Little, Brown, and Company.

Baggaley, J. (2014). MOOC postscript. *Distance Education*, *35*(1), 126–132. doi:10.1080/01587919.2013.876142

Baird, R. (2000). The startle effect: Implications for the spectator cognition and media theory. *Film Quarterly*, *53*(3), 13–24. doi:10.2307/1213732

Bally Midway. (1982a). *Ms. pac-man* [Arcade video game]. Chicago, IL: Bally Midway.

Bally Midway. (1982b). *Tron* [Arcade video game]. Chicago, IL: Bally Midway.

Banchoff, T. F. (1990). Dimension. In L. Steen (Ed.), *On the shoulders of giants: New approaches to numeracy* (pp. 11–59). Washington, DC: National Academy Press.

Bandura, A. (1977). Self-efficacy: Toward a unifying theory of behavioral change. *Psychological Review*, *84*(2), 191–215. doi:10.1037/0033-295X.84.2.191 PMID:847061

Banks, J. (2013). *Human-technology relationality and self-network organization: Players and avatars in World of Warcraft*. (Unpublished doctoral dissertation). Colorado State University.

Banks, J., & Humphreys, S. (2008). The labour of user co-creators. *Convergence*, *14*(4), 401–418.

Baranowski, K., Reiche, M., & Wood, W. (2014). *Hidden Krakow* [mobile game]. Krakow, Poland: Studio Martin Reiche.

Barker, L. J., & Aspray, W. (2006). The state of research on girls and IT. In J. M. Cohoon & W. Aspray (Eds.), *Women and information technology: Research on underrepresentation* (pp. 3–54). Cambridge: The MIT Press. doi:10.7551/mitpress/9780262033459.003.0001

Barlow, S. (2015). *Her story* [Microsoft Windows/OS X/iOS video game].

Barthes, R. (1977). *Image, Music, Text* (S. Heath, Trans.). New York: Hill and Wang.

Barthes, R. (1977). *Image-music-text* (S. Heath, Trans.). New York: Hill and Wang.

Barthes, R. (2002). *S/Z* (R. Miller, Trans.). Malden, MA: Blackwell. (Original work published 1973)

Bartle, R. (1996). Hearts, clubs, diamonds, spades: Players who suit MUDs. *Journal of MUD Research*, *1*(1), 19.

Barton, M. (2010, March 27). *Matt Chat 55:* Daikatana *with John Romero*. December 28, 2015 from https://www.youtube.com/watch?v=lQMtVbz_JuE

Bassett, N. (2011, November 18). *Literature Review: Remediation of Ideology and Narrative, From Old To New*. Retrieved July 29, 2012, from Academia.edu: http://newschool.academia.edu/NathanaelBassett/Papers/1158418/Lit_Review_Remediation_of_Ideology_and_Narrative_From_Old_To_New

Basu, S. (2010). *5 cool edutainment games you can play and also donate to charitable causes*. Retrieved July 10, 2015, from http://www.makeuseof.com/tag/5-cool-edutainment-games-play-donate-charitable/

Batchelor, G. (2016, March 10). *Hot date*. Retrieved March 30, 2016, from https://georgebatch.itch.io/hot-date

Bateman, C. (2015). Implicit game aesthetics. *Games and Culture*, *10*(4), 389–411. doi:10.1177/1555412014560607

Beach, R. (2012). Uses of digital tools and literacies in the English language arts classroom. *Research in the Schools*, *19*(1), 45–59.

Beard, M. (2014). The public voice of women. *London Review of Books*. Retrieved November 28, 2015 from http://www.lrb.co.uk/v36/n06/mary-beard/the-public-voice-of-women

Beavertoad Software (2013). *Cafe Murder* [mobile game].

Beavis, C., & Charles, C. (2005). Challenging notions of gendered game play: Teenagers playing the Sims. *Discourse (Abingdon)*, *26*(3), 355–367. doi:10.1080/01596300500200151

Beesley, A., Clark, T., Barker, J., Germeroth, C., & Apthorp, H. (2010). Expeditionary learning schools: Theory of action and literature review of motivation, character, and engagement. *Mid-continent Research for Education and Learning (McREL)*.

Belew, R. K. (1990). Evolution, learning, and culture: Computational metaphors for adaptive algorithms. *Complex Systems*, *4*(1), 11–49.

Benedetti, W. (2007, April 20). Were video games to blame for massacre? *MSNBC*. Retrieved from: http://www.nbcnews.com/id/18220228/#.U-HgNfmSzSY

Bessiere, K., Seay, F., & Kiesler, S. (2007). The ideal Elf: Identity exploration in *World of Warcraft*. *Cyberpsychology & Behavior*, *10*(4), 530–535. doi:10.1089/cpb.2007.9994 PMID:17711361

Bethesda Game Studios. (2008). *Fallout 3*. Bethesda Softworks.

Bethesda Game Studios. (2011). *The elder scrolls V: Skyrim* [Microsoft Windows, PlayStation 3, XBox 360 video game]. Rockville, MD: Bethesda Softworks.

Bettie, J. (2003). *Women without class: Girls, race, identity*. Berkeley, CA: University of California Press.

BioWare. (2002). *Neverwinter Nights* [Microsoft Windows video game]. Lyon, France: Infogrames/Atari.

BioWare. (2003). *Star wars: Knights of the old republic* [XBox video game]. San Francisco, CA: LucasArts.

BioWare. (2007). *Mass Effect* [Microsoft Xbox 360 video game]. Redmond, WA: Microsoft Game Studios.

BioWare. (2007). *Mass effect* [Xbox 360 video game]. Redmond, WA: Micorsoft Game Studios.

BioWare. (2012). *Mass effect 3*. Electronic Arts.

BioWare. (2014). *Dragon age: Inquisition* [Microsoft Windows/Playstation 3 video game]. Redwood City, CA: Electronic Arts.

Black Girls Code. (2014). *Home*. Retrieved from https://www.blackgirlscode.org

Blanchard, J., Stock, W., & Marshall, J. (1999). Meta-analysis of research on a multimedia elementary school curriculum using personal and video game computers. *Perceptual and Motor Skills*, *88*(1), 329–336. doi:10.2466/pms.1999.88.1.329

Blizzard Entertainment. (2004). *World of warcraft* [Windows, OS X video game]. Irvine, CA: Blizzard Entertainment.

Blizzard Entertainment., (2012). *Diablo III* [Microsoft Windows, OS X video game]. Irvine, CA: Blizzard Entertainment.

Blizzard Entertainment. (2014). *Hearthstone: Heroes of warcraft* [Microsoft Windows, OS X, iOS, Android video game]. Irvine, CA: Blizzard Entertainment.

Blizzard Entertainment. (2015). *Heroes of the Storm* [Microsoft Windows video game]. Irvine, CA: Blizzard Entertainment.

Blue Öyster Cult. (1976). "(Don't fear) The reaper". On Agents of Fortune [Vinyl]. New York: Columbia Records.

Bogost, I. (2007). *Procedural rhetoric: The expressive power of video games* [Amazon Kindle version]. Retrieved from http://www.amazon.com

Bogost, I. (2008). The rhetoric of video games. *The Ecology of Games: Connecting Youth, Games, and Learning*, 117–140.

Bogost, I. (2014, July 17). You are Mountain. *The Atlantic*. Retrieved from http://www.theatlantic.com/entertainment/archive/2014/07/you-are-mountain/374543/

Bogost, I. (2015, March 13). Video games are better without characters. *The Atlantic Monthly*. Retrieved May 4, 2015 from http://www.theatlantic.com/technology/archive/2015/03/video-games-are-better-without-characters/387556/

Bogost, I. (2006). *Unit Operations*. Cambridge, MA: MIT Press.

Bogost, I. (2007). *Persuasive games: The expressive power of videogames*. Boston: MIT Press.

Bogost, I. (2007). *Unit operations: An approach to videogame criticism*. Cambridge, MA: MIT Press.

Bogost, I. (2011). *How to do things with videogames*. Minneapolis: University of Minnesota Press. doi:10.5749/minnesota/9780816676460.001.0001

Bogost, I., Ferrari, S., & Schweizer, B. (2010). *Newsgames: Journalism at play*. Cambridge, MA: MIT Pr.

Bolter, J. D., & Grusin, R. (2000). *Remediation: Understanding New Media*. Cambridge, MA: The MIT Press.

Boluk, S., & LeMieux, P. (2012). Stretched skulls: Anamorphic games and the memento mortem mortis. *Digital Humanities Quarterly, 6*(2).

Borko, H., Whitcomb, J., & Liston, D. (2009). Wicked problems and other thoughts on issues of technology and teacher learning. *Journal of Teacher Education, 60*(3), 3–7. doi:10.1177/0022487108328488

Bosker, B. (2012, October 23). *'Girls Who Code' sets sights on teaching 1 million girls to code*. Retrieved from http://www.huffingtonpost.com/2012/10/23/girls-who-code_n_2005659.html

Bourdieu, P. (1989). Social space and symbolic power. *Sociological Theory, 7*(1), 14–25. http://www.soc.ucsb.edu/ct/pages/JWM/Syllabi/Bourdieu/SocSpaceSPowr.pdf doi:10.2307/202060

Bowers, A. J., & Berland, M. (2013). Does recreational computer use affect high school achievement? *Educational Technology Research and Development, 61*(1), 51–69. doi:10.1007/s11423-012-9274-1

Bowman, N. D. (2016). Video Gaming as Co-Production. In R. Lind (Ed.), *Produsing 2.0: The intersection of audiences and production in a digital world* (Vol. 2, pp. 107–123). New York: Peter Lang Publishing.

Bowman, N. D., & Banks, J. (in press). Playing the zombie author: Machinima through the lens of Barthes. In K. Kenney (Ed.), *Philosophy for multisensory communication*. New York: Peter Lang.

Bowman, N. D., Kowert, R., & Ferguson, C. (2016). The impact of video game play on human (and orc) creativity. In G. Green & J. Kaufman (Eds.), *Video games and creativity* (pp. 41–62). Waltham, Mass: Academic Press.

Bowman, N. D., Westerman, D. K., & Claus, C. J. (2012). How demanding is social media? Understanding social media diets as a function of perceived costs and benefits-A Rational Actor Perspective. *Computers in Human Behavior, 28*(6), 2298–2305. doi:10.1016/j.chb.2012.06.037

Boyan, A., Grizzard, M., & Bowman, N. D. (2015). A massively moral game? *Mass Effect* a case study to understand the influence of players' moral intuitions on adherence to hero or antihero play styles. *Journal of Gaming and Virtual Worlds, 7*(1), 41–57. doi:10.1386/jgvw.7.1.41_1

boyd, d. (2014). *It's complicated: The social lives of networked teens*. New Haven, CT: Yale University Press.

Boyer, B., & Alexander, L. (2007). *MIGS 2007: Jonathan Blow on the WoW drug, meaningful games*. Retrieved from http://www.gamasutra.com/view/news/107343/MIGS_2007_Jonathan_Blow_On_The_WoW_Drug_Meaningful_Games.php

Bracken, C. C., & Skalski, P. (2006), 'Presence and video games: The impact of image quality and skill level', *Proceedings of the Annual International Meeting of the PresenceWorkshop*. Cleveland, OH: Cleveland State University.

Brander, P., De Witte, L., Ghanea, N., Gomes, R., Keen, E., Nikitina, A., & Pinkeviciute, J. (2012). *Compass. Manual for human rights education with young people*. Strasbourg: Council of Europe Publishing.

Bransford, J., Brown, A., & Cocking, R. (Eds.). (2000). *How people learn: Brain, mind, experience, and school*. Washington, DC: National Academy Press.

Branson, J., & Miller, D. (2002). *Damned for their difference: The cultural construction of deaf people as disabled*. Washington: Gallaudet University Press.

Brice, M. (2013, October 29). The Death of the Player. [Web log]. *Alternate Ending*. Retrieved from http://www.mattiebrice.com/death-of-the-player/

Brin, D., & Jackson, S. (1998). *Tribes* [roleplaying game]. Austin, TX: Steve Jackson Games.

Bröckling, U. (2007). *Das unternehmerische Selbst. Soziologie einer Subjektivierungsform*. Frankfurt: Suhrkamp Verlag.

Brooker, C. (2012, April 15). Some people are gay in space. Get over it. *The Guardian*. Retrieved from http://www.theguardian.com/commentisfree/2012/apr/15/charlie-brooker-gay-video-game

Brookey, R. A. (2010). *Hollywood gamers: digital convergence in the film and video game industries*. Bloomington, IN: Indiana University Press.

Brooks, P. (1992). *Reading for the Plot*. Cambridge, MA: Harvard University Press.

Brown, A. L. (1992). Design experiments: Theoretical and methodological challenges in creating complex interventions in classroom settings. *Journal of the Learning Sciences, 2*(2), 141–178. doi:10.1207/s15327809jls0202_2

Brown, J. S., Collins, A., & Duguid, P. (1989). Situated cognition and the culture of learning. *Educational Researcher, 18*(1), 32–42. doi:10.3102/0013189X018001032

Brown, L. M., & Gilligan, C. (1992). *Meeting at the crossroads: Women's psychology and girls' development*. Cambridge, MA: Harvard University Press. doi:10.4159/harvard.9780674731837

Bruce, A. (2013). *Antichamber* [Windows video game].

Bruner, J. S. (1966). *Toward a theory of instruction* (Vol. 59). Harvard University Press.

Bubsy 3D: Bubsy visits the James Turrell retrospective [Computer Software]. (2013). Los Angeles: Arcane Kids. Available from Bubsy3d.com

Buckenham, G. (2014). *Punch the Custard* [video game].

Bungie. (2014). *Destiny* [PlayStation 3, PlayStation 4, Xbox 360, Xbox One video game]. Santa Monica, CA: Activision.

Burke, K. (1969). *A grammar of motives*. Berkeley, CA: University of California Press. (Original work published 1945)

Butler, J. (2006). *Gender trouble: feminism and the subversion of identity*. New York, NY: Routledge Classics.

Caillois, R. (1990). *Os jogos e os homens: a máscara e a vertigem*. Lisboa: Cotovia.

Caillois, R., & Barash, M. (1961). *Man, play, and games*. Champaign, IL: University of Illinois Press.

Cameron, P. (13 Feb. 2012). *Dear Esther review*. Retrieved 15 December, 2015, from http://www.videogamer.com/pc/dear_esther/review.html

Campbell, C. (2013, March 7). *Fired for Making a Game: The Inside Story of I Get This Call Every Day*. Retrieved February 10, 2016, from http://www.polygon.com/features/2013/3/7/4071136/he-got-fired-for-making-a-game-i-get-this-call

Campbell, G. (2010, May 05). *Alan Wake: We speak with Remedy's Matias Myllyrinne*. Retrieved from Gameplanet. co.nz: http://www.gameplanet.co.nz/xbox-360/features/i134842/Alan-Wake-We-speak-with-Remedys-Matias-Myllyrinne/

Campbell, H. A., & Grieve, G. P. (2014). Introduction: what playing with religion offers digital game studies. In H. A. Campbell & G. P. Grieve (Eds.), *Playing with religion in digital games* (pp. 1–24). Bloomington, IN: Indiana University Press.

Campbell, J. (2008). *Pathways to Bliss: Mythology and Personal Transformation: Easyread Large Edition*. Surry Hills, NSW: Accessible Publishing Systems.

Campbell, J. (2008). *The Hero with a Thousand Faces (Collected Works Edition)*. Novato, CA: New World Library.

Campo Santo. (2016). *Firewatch* [Microsoft Windows, OS X, Linux, PlayStation 4 video game]. Portland, OR: Panic.

cancer. (2001, February 14). *Summoner is fucking gay*. [War2.Warcraft.Org] Retrieved December 28, 2015 from http://war2.warcraft.org/forum/viewtopic.php?t=483

Canossa, A. (2014). Reporting from the snooping trenches: Changes in attitudes and perceptions towards behavior tracking in digital games. *Surveillance & Society*, *12*(3), 433–436.

Capcom. (1996). *Resident evil* [PS 1 video game]. Chuo-ku, Osaka, Japan: Capcom.

Capcom. (2006). *Dead rising* [Xbox 360 video game]. Chuo-ku, Osaka, Japan: Capcom.

Caplan, S., & Wallace, W. (Producers), Travis, J., & Johnson, D. (Directors). (2007). *Flatland: The movie* [DVD]. United States: Flat World Productions.

Carlson, M. (2009). *Performance: um introdução crítica*. Belo Horizonte: Editora da UFMG.

Carmack, J., & Romero, J. (1993). Doom [PC game]. Mesquite, TX: id Software.

Carmack, J., & van Waveren, J. P. (1999). Quake III Arena [PC game]. Mesquite, TX: id Software.

Carnes, M. C. (2014). *Minds on fire: How role-immersion games transform college*. [Amazon Kindle edition]. Retrieved from http://www.amazon.com

Carnes, M. C. (2014). *Minds on fire: How role-immersion games transform college*. Cambridge, MA: Harvard University Press. doi:10.4159/harvard.9780674735606

Carr, D. (2002). Playing with lara. InScreenPlay: cinema/ videogames /interface (pp. 171-180). London: Wallflower Press.

Carr, D. (2009). *Textual analysis, digital games, zombies.* DiGRA digital library.

Cassell, J., & Jenkins, H. (Eds.). (1998). *From Barbie to Mortal Kombat: Gender and computer games.* Cambridge, MA: MIT Press.

Castronova, E. (2005). *Synthetic worlds: The business of culture and of online games.* Chicago, IL: University of Chicago Press.

Catrambone, R. (1998). The subgoal learning model: Creating better examples so that students can solve novel problems. *Journal of Experimental Psychology. General, 127*(4), 355–376. doi:10.1037/0096-3445.127.4.355

Cawthon, S. (2013). *Five nights at freddy's* [PC]. Desura.

CD Projekt RED. (2007). *The witcher* [Microsoft Windows/OS X video game]. New York, NY: Atari, Inc.

Center for Gender Equity in Science and Technology. (2015). *CompuGirls.* Retrieved from https://cgest.asu.edu/compugirls

Certeau, M. (1984). *The practice of everyday life* (S. Rendall, Trans.). Berkeley: U of California P.(Original work published 1980)

chalupa. (2000, October 26). *Warcraft language.* [War2.Warcraft.Org] Retrieved December 28, 2015 from http://war2.warcraft.org/forum/viewtopic.php?t=123

Chang, J. [Wicked Al] (2001, August 6). *Wicked al's war2 history.* [Web.Archive.Org] Retrieved December 28, 2015 from http://web.archive.org/web/20060518133759/http://www.winnieinternet.com/games/war2/reports/WickedAlHistory.htm

Charles, A. (2009). Playing with one's self: Notions of subjectivity and agency in digital games. *Eludamos. Journal for Computer Games Culture, 3*(2), 281–294. Retrieved from http://www.eludamos.org/index.php/eludamos/article/viewArticle/vol3no2-10/139

Chen, J. (2006). Flow in games (Master of Fine Arts Thesis/Game). Los Angeles, CA: University of Southern California; Retrieved from http://www.jenovachen.com/flowingames/introduction.htm

Chen, H.-J. H., & Yang, T.-Y. C. (2013). The impact of adventure video games on foreign language learning and the perceptions of learners. *Interactive Learning Environments, 21*(2), 129–141. doi:10.1080/10494820.2012.705851

Chen, S.-Y., & Fu, Y.-C. (2009). Internet use and academic achievement: Gender differences in early adolescence. *Adolescence, 44*(176). PMID:20432601

Chess, S., & Shaw, A. (2015). A conspiracy of fishes, or, How we learned to stop worrying about #gamergate and embrace hegemonic masculinity. *Journal of Broadcasting & Electronic Media, 59*(1), 208–220. doi:10.1080/08838151.2014.999917

Cheung, G., & Huang, J. (2011). *Starcraft* from the stands: understanding the game spectator. In *Proceedings of the SIGCHI Conference on Human Factors in Computing Systems* (pp. 763–772). doi:10.1145/1978942.1979053

Christensen, N. C. (2006). Doing masculinity in an online gaming site. *Reconstruction: Studies in Contemporary Culture, 6*(1). Retrieved June 28, 2015 from http://reconstruction.eserver.org/Issues/061/christensen.shtml

Chutes and Ladders [board game]. (2005). New York: Hasbro Toy Co.

Climax Studios. (2010). Silent hill: Shattered memories [Wii, Playstation 2, Playstation Portable video game]. Minato, Tokyo, Japan: Konami Digital Entertainment.

Clover Studio. (2006). Okami [PlayStation 2 video game]. Chuo-ku, Osaka, Japan: Capcom.

Clover Studio. (2008). Okami [Wii video game]. Chuo-ku, Osaka, Japan: Capcom.

Cobb, J. (2008). *Learning games - 26 serious games to change the world*. Retrieved July 10, 2015, from http://www.missiontolearn.com/2008/04/learning-games-for-change/

Coffee Stain Studios. (2014). *Goat simulator* [Microsoft Windows/OS X/Linux/iOS/Android video game]. Skövde, Sweden: Coffee Stain Studios.

Cohen, J. (1988). *Statistical power analysis for the behavioral sciences* (2nd ed.). Hillsdale, NJ: LEA.

Coiro, J. (2003). Reading comprehension on the internet: Expanding our understanding of reading comprehension to encompass new literacies. *The Reading Teacher*, *56*(5), 458–464.

Coldwood Interactive. (2016). *Unravel* [Microsoft Windows/PlayStation 4/Xbox One video game]. Redwood City, CA: Electronic Arts.

Collins, K. (2013). *Playing with sound: A theory of interacting with sound and music in video games*. Cambridge, MA: MIT Press.

Comstock, M. (2001). Grrrl zine networks: Re-composing spaces of authority, gender, and culture. *Jac*, *21*(2), 383–409.

Connolly, T. M., Boyle, E. A., MacArthur, E., Hainey, T., & Boyle, J. M. (2012). A systematic review of empirical evidence on computer games and serious games. *Computers & Education*, *59*(2), 661–686. doi:10.1016/j.compedu.2012.03.004

Conradi, K., Jang, B. G., Bryant, C., Craft, A., & McKenna, M. C. (2013). Measuring adolescents' attitudes toward reading: A classroom survey. *Journal of Adolescent & Adult Literacy*, *56*(7), 565–576. doi:10.1002/JAAL.183

Consalvo, M., & Dutton, N. (2006). Game analysis: Developing a methodological toolkit for the qualitative study of games. *The International Journal of Computer Game Research*, *6*(1). Retrieved from http://gamestudies.org/0601/articles/consalvo_dutton

Cooper, J., & Weaver, K. D. (2003). *Gender and computers: Understanding the digital divide*. Mahwah, NJ: Lawrence Erlbaum.

Copeland, T., Henderson, B., Mayer, B., & Nicholson, S. (2013). Three different paths for tabletop gaming in school libraries. *Library Trends*, *61*, 825–835. doi:10.1353/lib.2013.0018

Cormon, R., Brock, D., & Daniel, D. (Producers), & Brock, D. (Director). (1987). *Slumber party massacre II* [Motion Picture]. United States: New Concorde.

Crafty Games. (2012). *Mistborn adventure game* [roleplaying game]. Author.

Crary, J. (1999). Suspensions of perception: attention, spetacle, and modern culture. Cambridge, MA, and London: MIT Press.

Crawford, C. (1984). *The art of computer game design*. Berkeley, CA: Osborne/McGraw-Hill.

Crawford, C. (1985). *Balance of Power* [Microsoft Windows (et al.) video game]. Northbrook, IL: Mindscape.

Crawford, C. (2003). *The art of interactive design: a euphonious and illuminating guide to building successful software*. San Francisco, CA: No Starch Press.

Crawford, G. (2015). Is it in the game? Reconsidering play spaces, game definitions, theming, and sports videogames. *Games and Culture*, *10*(6), 571–592. doi:10.1177/1555412014566235

Creative Assembly. (2014). Alien: Isolation [PS 4, Xbox One, PC video game]. Shinagawa, Tokyo, Japan: Sega Games.

Critical Distance. (2015, January 1). Retrieved May 4, 2015 from http://www.critical-distance.com/about/

Crofford, K., Lazzo, M., Willis, D., Maiellaro, M., & Edwards, J. W. (Producers). (2000). Aqua teen hunger force [Television series]. Atlanta, GA: Williams Street.

Cronin, M. (2004, December 7). BYU students play Survivor for credit. *The Salt Lake Tribune.* Retrieved from http://sltrib.com

Crosscade. (2012, March 14). *Mass Effect 3*—Ending movie comparison—All the colors. [Online video clip]. *Youtube.* Retrieved from https://www.youtube.com/watch?v=rPelM2hwhJA

Crowe, M. (2003). Jump for the sun II: Can a monthly program change girls' and women's attitudes about STEM? *Journal of Women and Minorities in Engineering, 9,* 323–332.

Csikszentmihalyi, M. (1990). *Flow.* New York: Harper and Row.

Csikszentmihalyi, M. (2000). *Beyond boredom and anxiety: Experiencing flow in work and play.* San Francisco, CA: Jossey-Bass Publishers.

Csikszentmihalyi, M., & Rathunde, K. (1993). The measurement of flow in everyday life: Toward a theory of emergent motivation. In J. E. Jacobs (Ed.), *Current theory and research in motivation* (Vol. 40, pp. 57–97).

Cuarón, A. (2013). *Gravity* [Motion picture]. United States: Warner Bros. Pictures.

Cunningham, C. (2011). Girl game designers. *New Media & Society, 13*(8), 1373–1388. doi:10.1177/1461444811410397

Cyan. (1993). *Myst* [Mac OS video game]. Eugene, OR: Brøderbund Software, Inc.

Cybulski, A. D. (2014). Enclosures at play: Surveillance in the code and culture of videogames. *Surveillance & Society, 12*(3), 427–432.

D'Anastasio, C. (2015, May 15). *Why video games can't teach you empathy.* Retrieved February 10, 2016, from http://motherboard.vice.com/read/empathy-games-dont-exist

Daniel Mullins Games. (2016). *Pony island* [Microsoft Windows, OS X, Linux video game]. Daniel Mullins Games.

Darabont, F., Hurd, G. A., Alpert, D., Kirkman, R., Eglee, C. H., & Mazzara, G. …Luse, T. (Producers). (2010). The walking dead [Television series]. Beverly Hills, CA: AMC Studios.

Davies, M. (2009). *Examining game pace: How single player levels tick* [online] Gamasutra article. Retrieved from http://www.gamasutra.com/view/feature/4024/examining_game_pace_how_.php

Davis, J., Schroeder, A. (Producers), & Trank, J. (Director). (2012). *Chronicle.* United States: 20th Century Fox.

Davis, M. H. (1996). *Empathy: A social psychological approach (Revised.).* Boulder, CO: Westview Press.

Davison, J. (Producer), Abrahams, J., Zucker, D., & Zucker, J. (Directors). (1980). *Airplane!* [Motion picture]. United States: Paramount Pictures.

Davison, J., & Lowry, H. (Producers), Abrahams, J., Zucker, D., & Zucker, J. (Directors). (1984). *Top secret!* [Motion picture]. United States: Paramount Pictures.

De Koven, B. (2014). *A Playful Path.* Available from: http://press.etc.cmu.edu/files/A-Playful-Path_DeKoven-web.pdf

de Saussure, F. (1986). *Course in general linguistics* (C. Bally & A. Sechehaye, Eds., R. Harris, Trans.). La Salle, IL: Open Court. (Original work published 1972)

Dear Esther script. (18 January 2014). Retrieved 15 December 2015, from http://dearesther.wikia.com/wiki/Dear_Esther_Script

DeBonis, J. & Mikros, N. (2011, 2012, 2013). *Killer Queen* [physical game, video game, arcade game].

Deeley, M. (Producer) & Scott, R. (Director). (1982). *Blade Runner* [Motion picture]. United States: Warner Bros.

Dejobaan Games. (2014). *Elegy for a dead world* [Microsoft Windows/OS X/Linux video game]. Dejobaan Games.

DeKoven, B. (1978). *The well-played game: A player's philosophy*. Garden City, NY: Anchor Books/Doubleday.

Deleuze, G. (1992). Postscript on the Societies of Control. *October, 59*, 3-7.

Deleuze, G. (1993). Postscript on the societies of control. *October, 59*(Winter), 3–7.

Denner, J., Bean, S., & Werner, L. (2005). Girls creating games: Challenging existing assumptions about gender content. *Proceeding of DiGRA 2005 Conference: Changing Views-Worlds in Play*.

Denner, J., Werner, L., Bean, S., & Campe, S. (2005). The Girls Creating Games Program: Strategies for engaging middle school girls in information technology. *Frontiers: A Journal of Women Studies, 26*(1), 90-98.

Denner, J., Werner, L., & Ortiz, E. (2012). Computer games created by middle school girls; Can they be used to measure understanding of computer science concepts? *Computers & Education, 58*(1), 240–249. doi:10.1016/j.compedu.2011.08.006

Dery, M. (Ed.). (1994). *Flame wars: The discourse of cyberculture*. Durham, NC: Duke University Press.

Design, D. M. A. (1997). Grand Theft Auto [DOS (et al.) video game]. Darien, CN: ASC Games.

Design, D. M. A. (2001). *Grand theft auto III* [PS2 video game]. New York, NY: Rockstar Games.

developerWorks [Scott Laningham]. (2006, August 22). *developerWorks Interviews: Tim Berners-Lee*. Retrieved November 27, 2015 from http://www.ibm.com/developerworks/podcast/dwi/cm-int082206txt.html

Dewey, J. (1963). *Experience and Education*. Collier Books.

Dewey, J. (1980). *Art as experience*. New York, NY: Perigee Books.

deWinter, J. (2015). *Shigeru Miyamoto: Super Mario Bros., Donkey Kong, The Legend of Zelda*. New York, NY: Bloomsbury.

Dibbell, J. (1993, December 23). A rape in cyberspace: How an evil clown, a Haitian trickster spirit, two wizards and a cast of dozens turned a database into a society. *The Village Voice*. Retrieved June 28, 2015 from http://www.juliandibbell.com/texts/bungle_vv.html

Dickey, M. D. (2005). Brave new (interactive) worlds: A review of the design affordances and constraints of two 3D virtual worlds as interactive learning environments. *Interactive Learning Environments, 13*(1-2), 121–137. doi:10.1080/10494820500173714

Dickey, M. D. (2006). Girl gamers: The controversy of girl games and the relevance of female-oriented game design for instructional design. *British Journal of Educational Technology, 37*(5), 785–793. doi:10.1111/j.1467-8535.2006.00561.x

Dickey, M. D. (2011). The pragmatics of virtual worlds for K-12 educators: Investigating the affordances and constraints of *Active Worlds* and *Second Life* with K-12 in-service teachers. *Educational Technology Research and Development, 59*(1), 1–20. doi:10.1007/s11423-010-9163-4

Dick, P. K. (1968). *Do Androids Dream of Electric Sheep*. London: Gollancz.

Die Gute Fabrik. (2014). *Sportsfriends* [video game]. Copenhagen, Denmark: Die Gute Fabrik.

Digital Games Research Association. (2015). *Cfp: DIGRA 2015—Diversity of play: Games—Cultures—Identities* (updated). Retrieved from http://www.digra.org/cfp-digra-2015-diversity-of-play-games-cultures-identities/

Digital Pictures. (1992). Night trap [Sega CD/Sega 32X video game]. Ōta, Tokyo, Japan: Sega.

Dillon, R. (2013, May). Serious games and fun: An analysis. *International Journal of Innovative Research & Development, 2*(5), 1046–1063.

Dinosaur Polo Club. (2015). *Mini metro* [Windows/OS X/Linux video game]. Tokyo, Japan: Playism.

diSessa, A. (2004). Metareprentational competence: Native competence and targets for instruction. *Cognition and Instruction, 22*(3), 293–331. doi:10.1207/s1532690xci2203_2

Dixon, D. (2015). *Human dignity and the bottom line: Sweatshop*. Retrieved July 8, 2015, from http://gamechurch.com/human-dignity-and-the-bottom-line-sweatshop/

Dixon, W. (1995). *It looks at you: The returned gaze of cinema*. New York: SUNY Press.

Djaouti, D., Alvarez, J., Jessel, J.-P., & Rampnoux, O. (2011). *Origins of serious games*. Retrieved July 6, 2015, from http://www.ludoscience.com/files/ressources/origins_of_serious_games.pdf

Dog, N. (1996). Crash bandicoot [PS video game]. Minato, Tokyo, Japan: Sony Computer Entertainment.

Dog, N. SCE Bend Studio, & One Loop Games. (2007). Uncharted [PS3, PS4, PSVita, PSNow video game]. Minato, Tokyo, Japan: Sony Computer Entertainment.

Dondlinger, M. J. (2007). Educational video game design: A review of the literature. *Journal of Applied Educational Technology, 4*(1), 21–31.

Doom [Computer Software]. (1993). Richardson, TX: id Software.

Double Fine Productions. (2005). *Psychonauts* [Microsoft Windows (et al.) video game]. Edison, NJ: Majesco Entertainment.

Double Fine Productions. (2014). *Hack "n" slash* [Microsoft Windows/OS X/Linux video game]. San Francisco, CA: Double Fine.

Down, E., & Smith, S. L. (2009). Keeping abreast of hypersexuality: A video game character content analysis. *Sex Roles, 62*(11-12), 721–733. doi:10.1007/s11199-009-9637-1

Dreamforge Intertainment. (1998). Sanitarium [PC video game]. Darien, CN: ASC Games.

Dredge, S. (2011). *Apple bans satirical iPhone game* Phone Story *from its App Store*. Retrieved July 7, 2015, from http://www.theguardian.com/technology/appsblog/2011/sep/14/apple-phone-story-rejection

Duke Nukem. (n.d.). Retrieved from Wikiquote: http://en.wikiquote.org/wiki/Duke_Nukem

Duncombe, S. (2014). *Notes from underground: Zines and the politics of alternative culture*. Portland, OR: Microcosm Publishing.

Dunlap, G., Kern, L., dePerczel, M., Clark, S., Wilson, D., & Childs, K. E. (1993). Functional analysis of classroom variables for students with emotional and behavioral disorders. *Behavioral Disorders, 18*, 275–291.

Dunn, K. (2012). "If it ain't cheap, it ain't punk": Walter Benjamin's progressive cultural production and DIY punk record labels. *Journal of Popular Music Studies, 24*(2), 217–237. doi:10.1111/j.1533-1598.2012.01326.x

Dunwell, I., de Freiatas, S., & Jarvis, S. (2011). Four-dimensional consideration of feedback in serious games. In *Digital Games and Learning* (pp. 42–62). London: Continuum.

Durkin, K. (2006). Game playing and adolescents' development. In P. Vorderer & J. Bryant (Eds.), *Playing computer games: Motives, responses, and consequences* (pp. 415–428). Mahwah, NJ: Erlbaum.

Dyer-Witheford, N., & De Peuter, G. (2006). "EA Spouse" and the crisis of video game labour: Enjoyment, exclusion, exploitation, exodus. *Canadian Journal of Communication, 31*(3), 599–617.

Dyer-Witheford, N., & de Peuter, G. (2009). *Games of empire: Global capitalism and video games*. Minneapolis: University of Minnesota Press.

Ebert, R. (2010, April 16). *Video games can never be art* [Web log post]. Retrieved from http://www.rogerebert.com/rogers-journal/video-games-can-never-be-art

Ede, L., & Lunsford, A. (1990). *Singular texts/Plural authors: Perspectives on collaborative writing*. Carbondale, IL: Southern Illinois University Press.

Egenfeldt-Nielson, S., Heide Smith, J., & Pajares Tosca, S. (2008). *Understanding Video Games: The Essential Introduction*. New York: Routledge.

Eidos Montreal. (2011, August 23). *Deus Ex: Human Revolution* [Microsoft Windows video game]. Skinjuku, TKY: Square Enix.

Ekaputra, G., Lim, C., & Eng, K. I. (2013). Minecraft: A game as an education and scientific learning tool. *Information Systems, 2*(4), 237–242.

Ekaputra, G., Lim, C., & Eng, K. I. (2013). Minecraft: A Game as an Education and Scientific Learning Tool. *Information Systems, 2*, 4.

Elbow, P. (1998). *Writing with power: Techniques for mastering the writing process*. Oxford University Press.

Electronic Arts. (2010). Dante's Inferno [Playstation 3 video game]. Redwood City, CA: Visceral Games.

Elias, N. (1978). *The civilizing process: The history of manners* (E. Jephcott, Trans.). Oxford, UK: Blackwell. (Original work published 1939)

Ellison, C. (2013). Anna Anthropy and the Twine revolution. *The Guardian*. Retrieved from http://www.theguardian.com/technology/gamesblog/2013/apr/10/anna-anthropy-twine-revolution

Ender-Wiggin. (2001, February 9). *Summoner is caught hacking*. [War2.Warcraft.Org] Retrieved December 28, 2015 from http://war2.warcraft.org/forum/viewtopic.php?t=548

Eno, B. (1996, June). *Generative music*. Presented at the Imagination Conference, San Francisco, CA.

Ensslin, A. (2014). *Literary Gaming*. Cambridge, MA: MIT Press.

Entertainment Software Association. (2007). *Game player data*. Entertainment Software Association.

Entertainment Software Association. (2014). *2014 Sales, demographic and usage data: essential facts about the computer and video game industry*. Retrieved in March 8, 2015, from http://www.theesa.com/wp-content/uploads/2014/10/ESA_EF_2014.pdf

Entertainment Software Association. (2015). *2015 Sales, demographic and usage data: essential facts about the computer and video game industry*. Retrieved in April 27, 2015, from http://www.theesa.com/wp-content/uploads/2015/04/ESA-Essential-Facts-2015.pdf

Entertainment Software Association. (2015). *Essential facts about the computer and video game industry*. Retrieved July 6, 2015, from http://www.theesa.com/wp-content/uploads/2015/04/ESA-Essential-Facts-2015.pdf

Entertainment, H. (1995). *Clock tower* [SNES video game]. Tokyo, Japan: Human Entertainment.

Epic Games. (2006). *Gears of War* [Microsoft Xbox 360 (et al.) video game]. Cary, NC: Microsoft Game Studios.

ESA. (2014, October). *Essential facts about the computer and video game industry*. Retrieved from: http://www.theesa.com/wp-content/uploads/2014/10/ESA_EF_2014.pdf

Escher, M. C. (1953). *Relativity* [Lithograph print]. Retrieved from https://en.wikipedia.org/wiki/Relativity_(M._C._Escher)

Eskelinen, M. (2004). Towards computer game studies. In N. Wardrip-Fruin & P. Harrigan (Eds.), *First person: New media as story, performance, and game* (pp. 36–44). Cambridge, MA: MIT Press.

Evil Hat Productions. (2013). *FATE Core System* [roleplaying game]. Author.

Exact Co. Ltd. (1995). Jumping flash! [PS video game]. Minato, Tokyo, Japan: Sony Computer Entertainment.

Fallout 4. [Computer Software]. (2011). Rockville, MD: Bethesda.

Fancsali, C. (2002). *What we know about girls, STEM, and afterschool programs: A summary*. Washington, DC: Educational Equity Concepts, Inc. Retrieved from http://www.afterschool.org/sga/pubs/whatweknow.pdf

Farber, M. (2015). *10 educational games that teach kids about social issues*. Retrieved from http://content.easybib.com/10-educational-games-that-teach-kids-about-social-issues/

Felinto, E. (2001). "Materialidades da Comunicação": por um novo lugar da matéria na Teoria da Comunicação. In *Revista Ciberlegenda*, Niterói, n. 5. Retrieved from http://www.uff.br/ciberlegenda/ojs/index.php/revista/article/view/308

Felman, S., & Laub, D. (1992). *Testimony: Crises of witnessing in literature, psychoanalysis, and history*. New York: Routledge.

Feminist Frequency. (n.d.). Retrieved November 16, 2015, from http://feministfrequency.com/

feministfrequency [Screen name]. (2013). *Damsel in distress: Part 1 - Tropes vs women in video games* [Video file]. Retrieved from https://www.youtube.com/watch?v=X6p5AZp7r_Q

Feng, J., Spence, I., & Pratt, J. (2007). Playing an action video game reduces gender differences in spatial cognition. *Psychological Science*, *18*(10), 850–855. doi:10.1111/j.1467-9280.2007.01990.x PMID:17894600

Ferguson, C. J., Rueda, S. M., Cruz, A. M., Ferguson, D. E., Fritz, S., & Smith, S. M. (2008). Violent video games and aggression: Causal relationship or byproduct of family violence and intrinsic violence motivation? *Criminal Justice and Behavior*, *35*(3), 311–332. doi:10.1177/0093854807311719

Ferkany, M., & Whyte, K. P. (2011). Environmental education, wicked problems, and virtue. *Philosophy of Education, 16*, 331-339. Retrieved from http://ojs.ed.uiuc.edu/

Fernandez, H. (2014). *Fluff Eaters* [mobile game].

Fernández, J. (Producer), Balagueró, J., & Plaza, P. (Directors). (2007). *[REC]* [Motion picture]. Spain: Filmax International.

Fernández-Vara, C. (2014). *Introduction to game analysis*. New York, NY: Routledge.

Ferraz, M. C. F. (2010). *Homo deletabilis: corpo, percepção, esquecimento: do século XIX ao XXI*. Rio de Janeiro: Garamond/FAPERJ.

Ferri, G., & Fusaroli, R. (2009). *Which narrations for persuasive technologies? Habits and procedures in Ayiti: The Cost of Life*. Retrieved July 6, 2015, from http://www.aaai.org/Papers/Symposia/Spring/2009/SS-09-06/SS09-06-007.pdf

FigureFromThePast. (2004, January 4). *My return.vs arch and more!!!!* [War2.Warcraft.Org] Retrieved December 28, 2015 from http://war2.warcraft.org/forum/viewtopic.php?t=7372

Filipowich, M. (2013, November 29). From game to play: Roland Barthes, video games, and criticism. [Web log]. *Big-tallwords*. Retrieved from http://big-tall-words.com/2013/11/29/from-game-to-play/

Filipowich, M. (2015, May 1). *April roundup: 'Palette swaps' | Critical Distance*. Retrieved May 4, 2015 from http://www.critical-distance.com/2015/05/01/april-roundup-palette-swaps/

Flanagan, M. (2005). Troubling 'games for girls': Notes from the edge of game design. *Proceeding of DiGRA 2005 Conference: Changing Views-Worlds in Play*.

Flanagan, M., & Nissenbaum, H. (2014). *Values at play in digital games* (1st ed.). Cambridge, Massachusetts: Mit Press.

Flower, L., & Hayes, J. R. (1981). A cognitive process theory of writing. *College Composition and Communication*, *32*(4), 365–387. doi:10.2307/356600

Flying Mollusk. (2015). *Nevermind* [PC video game]. Glendale, California: Flying Mollusk.

Fono, D. (2013). *The Brief and Frightening Reign* [live-action role-playing game].

Foucault, M. (1969/1977). What is an author? In *Language, counter-memory, practice* (D. F. Bouchard & S. Simon, Trans.). Ithaca, NY: Cornell University Press.

Foucault, M. (1972). *The archaeology of knowledge and the discourse on language* (A. M. Sheridan Smith, Trans.). New York, NY: Pantheon Books. (Original work published 1969)

Foucault, M. (1975). *Discipline and punish: The birth of the prison*. New York: Penuin.

Foucault, M. (2010). *The government of self and others: Lectures at the Collège de France 1982-1983* (A. I. Davidson, Ed.). New York, NY: Palgrave Macmillan. doi:10.1057/9780230274730

Fraizer, G. [Shlonglor] (1997). *Shlonglor presents: The original war 2 story page*. [Nathandemick.com] Retrieved December 28, 2015 from http://nathandemick.com/warcraft2-stories/story.shtml

Frasca, G. (2003). Simulation versus narrative. In M. J. P Wolf & B. Perron (Eds.), The video game theory reader (pp. 221-36). New York: Routledge.

Free Range Studios. (2008). *Homeland Guantanamo* [Flash game]. Washington D.C.: Free Range Studios. Retrieved August 12, 2015 from http://www.homelandgitmo.com/

Freeman, N. (2015). *Freshman year* [Windows, OS X video game].

Freire, P. (1994). The "banking" concept of education. In D. H. Richter (Ed.), *Falling into theory: Conflicting views on reading literature* (pp. 68–84). Boston: Bedford Books of St. Martin's Press.

Frictional Games. (2007). *Penumbra: Overture* [PC video game]. Helsingborg, Sweden: Frictional Games.

Frictional Games. (2010). *Amnesia: The dark descent* [PC video game]. Helsingborg, Sweden: Frictional Games.

Friedlander, L. (2008). Narrative strategies in a digital age. In K. Lundby (Ed.), *Digital storytelling, mediatized stories: Self-representations in new media*. New York, NY: Peter Lang Publishing.

FrielFan. (2005, October 10). *My warcraft 2 history*. [Web.Archive.Org].

Frima Studio. (2012). *Half The Sky Movement: The Game* [Facebook app]. Quebec: Frima Studio. Retrieved September 23, 2015 from https://www.facebook.com/HaIftheGame

Fullbright. (2013). *Gone home* [Windows, OS, Linux video game]. Portland, OR: Fullbright.

Funk, J. (2010, May 18). John Romero apologizes for trying to make you his bitch. *Escapist Magazine*. Retrieved June 28, 2015 from http://www.escapistmagazine.com/news/view/100748-John-Romero-Apologizes-for-Trying-to-Make-You-His-Bitch

Furger, R. (1998). *Does Jane compute?: Preserving our daughters' place in the cyber revolution*. New York, NY: Warner Books.

Fusion. (2015). *Bad Paper* [Browser game]. Doral, FL: Fusion. Retrieved September 3, 2015 from http://static.fusion.net/badpaper/

Galactic Cafe. (2013). *The stanley parable* [Windows/OS X video game]. Galactic Cafe.

GameAxis Unwired. (2008). *Valhalla and Back*. Game Axis Unwired, 69.

Games, H. (2013). *Risk of rain* [Windows video game]. London: Chucklefish Games.

GameTheNews. (2012). *Endgame: Syria* [HTLML5, Android].:GameTheNews. Retrieved August 10, 2015 from http://gamethenews.net/wp-content/games/endgamesyria/

Gee, J. P. (2004). *Situated language and learning: A critique of traditional schooling*. New York: Routledge.

Gee, J. P. (2005). Pleasure, learning, video games, and life: The projective stance. *E-Learning and Digital Media*, 2(3), 211–223.

Gee, J. P. (2005). Semiotic social spaces and affinity spaces: From *The Age of Mythology* to today's schools. In D. Barton & K. Tusting (Eds.), *Beyond communities of practice: Language, power and social context* (pp. 214–232). Cambridge: Cambridge University Press. doi:10.1017/CBO9780511610554.012

Gee, J. P. (2005). *What video games have to teach us about learning and literacy*. New York: Palgrave MacMillan.

Gee, J. P. (2005). *Why video games are good for your soul: Pleasure and learning*. Champaign, IL: Common Ground Publishing.

Gee, J. P. (2007). *Good video games and good learning: Collected essays on video games, learning and literacy* (1st ed.). New York: Lang, Peter New York.

Gee, J. P., & Hayes, E. (2010). *Women gaming: The Sims and 21st century learning*. New York, NY: Palgrave. doi:10.1057/9780230106734

Geek Girl. (2015). *About*. Retrieved from http://geekgirlcamp.com/about-geek-girl

genocider. (2000, November 11). *Parents*. [War2.Warcraft.Org] Retrieved December 28, 2015 from http://war2.warcraft.org/forum/viewtopic.php?t=220

Gentile, D. A., Lynch, P. J., Linder, P. J., & Walsh, D. A. (2004). The effects of violent video game habits on adolescent hostility, aggressive behaviors, and school performance. *Journal of Adolescence*, 27(1), 5–22. doi:10.1016/j.adolescence.2003.10.002 PMID:15013257

Gentile, D., & Anderson, C. (2003). Violent video games: The newest media violence hazard. In D. Gentile (Ed.), *Media Violence and Children*. Westport, CT: Praeger.

George, N. (2003). *The death of rhythm and blues*. New York, NY: Penguin.

George, S. (2012). The Performed Self in College Writing: From Personal Narratives to Analytic and Research Essays. *Pedagogy, 12*(2), 319–341. doi:10.1215/15314200-1503613

Gerber, H. R., & Price, D. P. (2013). Fighting baddies and collecting bananas: Teachers' perceptions of games-based literacy learning. *Educational Media International, 50*(1), 51–62. doi:10.1080/09523987.2013.777182

Gibbs, J. C. (2014). *Moral development & reality: Beyond the theories of Kohlberg, Hoffman, and Haidt* (3rd ed.). New York, NY: Oxford University Press.

Gibson, A., & Dziff. (2016). *Oases* [Windows, OS X video game]. itch.io. Retrieved from https://armelgibson.itch.io/oases

Gibson, J. J. (2015). The ecological approach to visual perception (Classic ed.). New York, NY: Psychology Press

Gibson, J. J. (1979). *The ecological approach to visual perception*. Boston, MA: Houghton Mifflin.

Girl Scouts, Girl Scout Research Institute. (2015). *Generation STEM: What girls say about science, technology, engineering, and math*. Retrieved from https://www.girlscouts.org/research/pdf/generation_stem_summary.pdf

Girl Scouts. (2015). *Imagine STEM*. Retrieved from http://www.girlscouts.org/program/basics/science/

Girls Who Code. (2015). *Home*. Retrieved from https://girlswhocode.com

Gkion, T. (2013). *All for One* [physical game].

Global Arcade. (1999). *Maria Sisters - Clean Room* [Flash game]. San Francisco, CA: Global Arcade. Retrieved September 10, 2015 from http://www.globalarcade.org/sv/

Global Kids & Game Lab. (2006). *Ayiti: The Cost of Life* [Flash game]. Global Kids. Retrieved September 23, 2015 from https://ayiti.globalkids.org/game/

Gold Extra. (2010). *Frontiers* [PC game]. Salzburg: Gold Extra.

Golding, D. (2013). Listening to *Proteus. Meanjin Quarterly, 72*(2). Retrieved from http://meanjin.com.au/essays/listening-to-proteus/

Golding, D. (2013). *Videogames and politics: Why was Escape from Woomera so divisive?* [text]. Retrieved July 9, 2015, from http://www.abc.net.au/arts/blog/Daniel-Golding/videogames-politics-Escape-From-Woomera-130901/

Gone home [Computer Software]. (2013). Portland, OR: Fullbright.

Good-Feel. (2010). *Kirby's epic yarn* [Wii video game]. Kyoto, Japan: Nintendo.

Good-Feel. (2015). *Yoshi's woolly world* [Wii U video game]. Kyoto, Japan: Nintendo.

Goodman, N. R. (2012). The power of witnessing. In N. Goodman & M. Meyers (Eds.), The power of witnessing: Reflections, reverberations and traces of the holocaust (pp. 3-26). New York: Routledge.

Gordon, L., & Silver, J. (Producers) & McTiernan, J. (Director). (1988). *Die Hard* [Motion picture]. United States: 20th Century Fox.

Gosling, V. K., & Crawford, G. (2011). Game scenes: Theorizing digital game audiences. *Games and Culture, 6*(2), 135–154. doi:10.1177/1555412010364979

Gottschalk, S. (1995). *Videology: Video-games as postmodern sites/sights of ideological reproduction.* Academic Press.

Gramsci, A. (1971). *Selections from the prison notebooks of Antonio Gramsci* (Q. Hoare & G. N. Smith, Trans. & Eds.). London: Lawrence & Wishart. (Original work published 1955)

Grant, C. (2014, September 15). *Minecraft's immense popularity, broken down by platform.* Retrieved January 14, 2016, from http://www.polygon.com/2014/9/15/6154437/minecraft-platform-xbox-ps3-ios-android-pc-mac

Grant, J. P. (2011, July 29). Life after death. *Kill Screen Daily.* Retrieved from www.killscreendaily.com/articles/life-after-death

Gray, P. (2008). *The value of play I: The definition of play gives insights.* Retrieved July 1st, 2015 from https://www.psychologytoday.com/blog/freedom-learn/200811/the-value-play-i-the-definition-play-gives-insights

Gray, K., & Huang, W. (2015). More than addiction: Examining the role of anonymity, endless narrative and socialization in prolonged gaming and instant messaging practices. *Journal of Comparative Research in Anthropology & Sociology,* *6*(1), 133–147.

Grayson, N. (16 Feb. 2012). *Dear Esther review.* Retrieved 15 December, 2015, from http://pc.gamespy.com/pc/dear-esther/1218914p1.html

Grayson, N. (2013, November 22). Blizzard on *Heroes of the Storm,* female designs in MOBAs. *Rock, Paper, Shotgun.* Retrieved April 1, 2015 from http://www.rockpapershotgun.com/2013/11/22/blizzard-on-heroes-of-the-storm-female-designs-in-mobas/

Green, S. C. (2014). The perceptual and cognitive effects of action experience. In F. C. Blumberg (Ed.), Learning by playing: Video gaming in education (pp. 29–41). New York: OUP.

Green, C. S., & Bavelier, D. (2003). Action video game modifies visual selective attention. *Nature,* *423*(6939), 534–537. doi:10.1038/nature01647 PMID:12774121

Green, C. S., & Bavelier, D. (2007). Action-video-game experience alters the spatial resolution of vision. *Psychological Science,* *18*(1), 88–94. doi:10.1111/j.1467-9280.2007.01853.x PMID:17362383

Green, M. C., Brock, T. C., & Kaufman, G. F. (2006). Understanding media enjoyment: The role of transportation into narrative worlds. *Communication Theory,* *14*(4), 311–327. doi:10.1111/j.1468-2885.2004.tb00317.x

Greeno, J. (1998). The situativity of knowing, learning, and research. *The American Psychologist,* *53*(1), 5–26. doi:10.1037/0003-066X.53.1.5

Gregory, J. (2009). *Game engine architecture.* Wellesley, MA: AK Peters Ltd.

Griffiths, M. (1999). Violent video games and aggression: A review of the literature. *Aggression and Violent Behavior,* *4*(2), 203–212. doi:10.1016/S1359-1789(97)00055-4

Grixti, J. (1989). *Terrors of uncertainty: The cultural contexts of horror fiction.* London, New York: Routledge.

Grodal, T. (2003). Stories for eye, ear, and muscles: Video games, media, and embodied experiences. In M. Wolf & B. Perron (Eds.), The video game theory reader (pp. 129-155). New York: Routledge.

Grodal, T. (2000). Video games and the pleasures of control. In D. Zillmann & P. Vorderer (Eds.), *Media entertainment: The psychology of its appeal* (pp. 197–214). Mahwah, NJ: Lawrence Erlbaum Associates.

Gulla, B. (2008). *Icons of R & B and soul: An encyclopedia of the artists who revolutionized rhythm* (Vol. 1). Westport, CT: Greenwood Press.

Gumbrecht, H. U. (2004). *Production of Presence: what meaning cannot convey*. Stanford, CA: Stanford University Press.

Haight, G. (Producer), & Montgomery, R. (Director). (1947). *Lady in the lake* [Motion picture]. United States: Metro-Goldwyn-Mayer.

Hale, G., & Cowie, R. (Producers), Myrick, D., & Sánchez, E. (Directors). (1999). The Blair Witch Project [motion picture]. United States: Artisan Entertainment.

Half The Sky movement game: From oppression to opportunity – raising awareness and funding. (2015). Retrieved July 10, 2015, from http://designtoimprovelife.dk/half-the-sky-movement-game-from-oppression-to-opportunity-raising-awareness-and-funding/

Half-life [Computer Software]. (1998). Bellevue, WA: Valve.

Hall, C. (2014, July 30). What it's like to attend Girls Make Games, the all-girls game dev summer camp. *Polygon*. Retrieved from http://www.polygon.com/2014/7/30/5952139/the-hole-story-girls-make-games-all-girls-game-camp-the-negatives

Hall, C. (2015, April 10). Obsidian's CEO on *Pillars of Eternity* backer's hateful joke. *Polygon*. Retrieved from http://www.polygon.com/2015/4/10/8383627/pillars-of-eternity-transphobic-kickstarter-hate-feargus-urquhart

Hamilton, W. A., Garretson, O., & Kerne, A. (2014, April). Streaming on Twitch: Fostering participatory communities of play within live mixed media. In *Proceedings of the SIGCHI Conference on Human Factors in Computing Systems* (pp. 1315-1324). ACM. doi:10.1145/2556288.2557048

Haraway, D. (1991). A cyborg manifesto: science, technology and Socialist-Feminism in the late twentieth century. In D. Bell & B. M. Kennedy (Eds.), The Cybercultures Reader (pp. 291-324). New York, NY: Routledge.

Hargittai, E. (2010). Digital na(t)ives? variation in internet skills and uses among members of the "Net generation". *Sociological Inquiry*, *80*(1), 92–113. doi:10.1111/j.1475-682X.2009.00317.x

Harmon, J. (2011). *Unlocking literacy with iPad*. Retrieved from http://www.throughstudentseyes.ort/ipads.Unlocking_Literacy_with_iPads/iPads_files/Unlocking_Literacy_iPad.pdf

Harmonix. (2005). *Guitar hero* [PlayStation 2 video game]. Mountain View, CA: RedOctane.

Harmonix. (2007). *Rock band* [Xbox 360/PS3 video game]. Redwood City, CA: Electronic Arts.

Harrer, S. & Schoenau-Fog, H. (2015). *Inviting grief into games: The game design process as personal dialogue*. DiGRA digital library.

Harrer, S. (2013). From losing to loss: Exploring the expressive capacities of videogames beyond death as failure. *Culture Unbound*, *5*(35), 607–620. doi:10.3384/cu.2000.1525.135607

Harrington, S., Malencyzk, R., Peckham, I., Rhodes, K., & Yancey, K. B. (2001). WPA outcomes statement for first-year composition. *College English*, *63*(3), 321–325. doi:10.2307/378996

Harris, T. (1998). *Hobson's Choice* [Browser game].

Hartmann, T., & Klimmt, C. (2006). Gender and computer games: Exploring females' dislikes. *Journal of Computer-Mediated Communication*, *11*(4), 910–931. doi:10.1111/j.1083-6101.2006.00301.x

Harvey, A., & Fisher, S. (2013). Making a name in games: Immaterial labour, indie game design, and gendered social network markets. *Information Communication and Society*, *16*(3), 362–380. doi:10.1080/1369118X.2012.756048

Harvey, D. (2005). *A brief history of neoliberalism*. Oxford: Oxford U P.

Hathaway, J. (2014, October 10). What is Gamergate and why? An explainer for non-geeks. *Gawker*. Retrieved June 28, 2015 from http://gawker.com/what-is-gamergate-and-why-an-explainer-for-non-geeks-1642909080

Hayward, V., Astley, O., Cruz-Hernandes, M., Grant, D., & Robles-De-La-Torre, G. (2004). Haptic interfaces and devices. *Sensor Review*, 24(1), 16–29. doi:10.1108/02602280410515770

Hegarty, M. (2010). Components of spatial intelligence. *Psychology of Learning and Motivation*, 52, 265–297. doi:10.1016/S0079-7421(10)52007-3

Hegarty, M., & Waller, D. (2004). A dissociation between mental rotation and perspective-taking spatial abilities. *Intelligence*, 32(2), 175–191. doi:10.1016/j.intell.2003.12.001

Heibert, J., & Stigler, J. W. (2004). A world of difference: Classrooms abroad provide lesson in teaching math and science. *Journal of Staff Development*, 24(4), 10–15.

Heidegger, M. (2013). *What is metaphysics? An interpretive translation* (T. Sheehan, Trans.). Stanford University. Retrieved March 29, 2015 from http://religiousstudies.stanford.edu/wp-content/uploads/1929-WHAT-IS-METAPHYSICS-2013-NOV.pdf (Original work published 1929)

Heidegger, M. (1996). *Being and Time*. New York, NY: State University of New York Press.

Heimburger, M. Y. (1994). *No university is an island: Implications of the Daedalus Project for BYU and American higher educational philosophy at large.* (Unpublished undergraduate honors thesis). Brigham Young University, Provo, UT.

Henricks, T. S. (2009). Orderly and disorderly play: A comparison. *American Journal of Play*, 2(1), 12–40.

Hern, A. (2015, January 13). Gamergate hits new low with attempts to send SWAT teams to critics. *The Guardian*. Retrieved June 28, 2015 from http://www.theguardian.com

Hernandez, P. (2012, December 21). *I'm glad I played this depressing game about working in a call center*. Retrieved February 10, 2016, from http://kotaku.com/5970524/im-glad-i-played-this-depressing-game-about-working-in-a-call-center?tag=i-get-this-call-every-day

Heron, M., & Belford, P. (2014). 'It's only a game' - ethics, empathy and identification in game morality systems. *The Computer Games Journal*, 3(1), 34–52.

Hickey, D. T., McWilliams, J., & Honeyford, M. A. (2011). Reading *Moby Dick* in a participatory culture: Organizing assessment for engagement in a new media era. *Journal of Educational Computing Research*, 45(2), 247–263. doi:10.2190/EC.45.2.g

Higinbotham, W. (1958). *Tennis for two* [Analog computer/Oscilloscope video game]. Upton, NY.

Hodgson, D. (2010). *Alan Wake Official Survival Guide*. Roseville: Prima Games.

Hoey, C., & Smith, P. (2011). *The Great Gatsby*. Retrieved July 10, 2012, from http://greatgatsbygame.com/

Hofmeier, R. (2011). *Cart life* [Microsoft Windows video game]. self-published.

Holbein, H. (1533). *The ambassadors* [Painting]. Retrieved from https://en.wikipedia.org/wiki/The_Ambassadors_(Holbein)

Holkins, J. (Writer), & Krahulik, M. (Illustrator). (2008, May 2). *Making an impression* [Cartoon]. Retrieved April 4, 2016, from https://www.penny-arcade.com/comic/2008/05/02/making-an-impression

Hollwitz, J. (2001). The Grail Quest and Field of Dreams. In C. Hauke & I. Alister (Eds.), *Jung and Film: Post-Jungian Takes on the Moving Image* (pp. 83–94). Hove: Brunner-Routledge.

Holpuch, A. (2013). Half the Sky *Facebook game launches with women's empowerment at core.* Retrieved July 10, 2015, from http://www.theguardian.com/technology/2013/mar/04/facebook-game-half-the-sky

Houser, R., & Deloach, S. (1998). Learning from games: Seven principles of effective Design. *Technical Communication: Journal of the Society for Technical Communication, 45*(3), 319–329.

Howald, B. S. (2009). A quantitative perspective on the minimal definition of narrative. *Text & Talk, 29*(6), 705–727. doi:10.1515/TEXT.2009.036

Hsu, H., & Wang, S. (2010). Using gaming literacies to cultivate new literacies. *Simulation & Gaming, 41*(3), 400–417. doi:10.1177/1046878109355361

Huang, H. (2001). The spatialization of knowledge and social relationships: A study on the spatial types of the modern museum.*Proceedings of the Third International Space Syntax Symposium.*

Huberts, C. (2014). Insufficient funds. Prekäre Leben im Computerspiel. *WASD Bookazine Für Gameskultur*, (5), 76–83.

Hudson, C. (2010, June 15). Interview: BioWare's Case Hudson on the making of *Mass Effect 2* [Interview conducted by J. McElroy]. *Engaget.* Retrieved from http://www.engadget.com/2010/06/15/interview-bioware-casey-hudson-on-the-making-of-mass-effect-2/

Hudson, L. (2014, November 19). Twine, the video-game technology for all. *The New York Times Magazine.* Retrieved from http://www.nytimes.com/2014/11/23/magazine/twine-the-video-game-technology-for-all.html?_r=0

Hug, S. (2007). *Developing technological fluency in a community of digital storytelling practice: Girls becoming tech-savvy* (Doctoral dissertation). Retrieved from ProQuest. (3256474.)

Huizinga, J. (1949). *Homo ludens A study of the play-element in culture.* London: Routledge & Kegan Paul.

Huizinga, J. (1955). *Homo Ludens: A study of the play element in culture.* Boston, MA: Beacon Press. (Original work published 1938)

Huizinga, J. (1955). *Homo Ludens: A Study of the Play-elememt in Culture.* Beacon Press.

Huizinga, J. (1980). *Homo ludens: a study of the play-element in culture.* London: Routledge & Kegan Paul.

Huizinga, J. (2014). *Homo ludens Ils 86.* New York, NY: Routledge.

Huntemann, N. B., & Aslinger, B. (Eds.). (2012). *Gaming globally: Production, play, and place.* New York, NY: Palgrave Macmillan. doi:10.1057/9781137006332

Hunter, J. (2013). *World peace and other 4th-grade achievements* [Amazon Kindle edition]. Retrieved from http://www.amazon.com

Hunt, L. (1986). French history in the last twenty years: The rise and fall of the Annales paradigm. *Journal of Contemporary History, 21*(2), 209–224. doi:10.1177/002200948602100205

Hurd, G. A. (Producer) & Cameron, J. (Director). (1984). *The Terminator* [Motion picture]. United States: Orion Pictures.

Hutchins, B. (2008). Signs of meta-change in second modernity: The growth of e-sport and the world cyber games. *New Media & Society, 10*(6), 851–869. doi:10.1177/1461444808096248

Hutchison, A., & Woodward, L. (2014). A planning cycle for integrating digital technology into literacy instruction. *The Reading Teacher, 67*(6), 455–464. doi:10.1002/trtr.1225

Hyde, J. (2013). *Object Get* [urban game].

id Software. (1992). *Wolfenstein 3D* [DOS video game]. Garland, TX: Apogee Software.

id Software. (1993). *Doom* [MS-DOS, Mac video game]. New York, NY: GT Interactive.

id Software. (1996). *Quake* [DOS video game]. New York, NY: GT Interactive Software.

id Software. (1996). *Quake* [MS-DOS video game]. New York, NY: GT Interactive.

IDResearch. (2012). *Immigropoly* [Flash game]. Hungary: IDResearch. Retrieved August 20, 2015, from http://en.immigropoly2.ittvagyunk.eu/auth

Ihde, D. (1993). *Postphenomenology: Essays in the postmodern context*. Evanston, IL: Northwestern University Press.

Illiger, A. (2011). *Tiny Wings* [iOS game]. Kiel, Germany: Andreas Illiger.

iMinds. (2010). *P.I.N.G. Poverty Is Not a Game* [PC game]. Gent-Ledeberg: iMinds.

Indie MEGABOOTH. (2015). *Indie MEGABOOTH* [Company website]. Retrieved from http://indiemegabooth.com/

Infinity Ward,. (2003). *Call of duty* [Windows video game]. Santa Monica, CA: Activision.

Infocom. (1977). *Zork* [PDP-10 video game]. Cambridge, MA: Infocom.

Institute for the Future. (2012). *Catalysts for Change*. Palo Alto, CA: Institute for the Future.

Intelligent Systems. (2007). *Super paper mario* [Wii video game]. Kyoto, Japan: Nintendo.

Interactive, S. (1993). Star wars arcade [Arcade video game]. Ōta, Tokyo, Japan: Sega.

Interplay Productions,. (1985). *The bard's tale (Version Apple Macintosh, Atari ST, Commodore 64 video game)*. Redwood City, CA: Electronic Arts.

Jackson, Z. A. (2002). Connecting video games and storytelling to teach narratives in first-year composition. *Kairos: A Journal of Rhetoric, Technology, and Pedagogy, 7*(3). Retrieved from: http://kairos.technorhetoric.net/7.3/coverweb/jackson/index.htm

Jakobsson, M. (2007). Playing with the rules: Social and cultural aspects of game rules in a console game club. In *Situated Play, Proceedings of the Digital Games Research Association (DiGRA) Conference*.

Jameson, F. (1997). *Postmodernism, or the cultural logic of late capitalism*. Durham, NC: Duke U P. (Original work published 1992)

Jansz, J. (2011). Preface. In K. Poels & S. Malliet (Eds.), *Vice city virtue: Moral issues in digital game play* [EPUB version]. Retrieved from http://acco.be

Jansz, J. (2005). The emotional appeal of violent video games for adolescent males. *Communication Theory, 15*(3), 219–241. doi:10.1111/j.1468-2885.2005.tb00334.x

Jansz, J., Avis, C., & Vosmeer, M. (2010). Playing the *Sims2*: An exploration of gender differences in players' motivations and patterns of play. *New Media & Society, 12*(2), 235–251. doi:10.1177/1461444809342267

Jansz, J., & Martis, R. G. (2007). The Lara phenomenon: Powerful female characters in video games. *Sex Roles, 56*(3), 141–148. doi:10.1007/s11199-006-9158-0

Jaszi, P. (1994). On the author effect: Contemporary copyright and collective creativity. In M. Woodmansee & P. Jaszi (Eds.), *The construction of authorship: Textual appropriation in law and literature*. Durham, NC: Duke University Press.

Jenkins, H. (1998). "Complete freedom of movement": Video games as gendered play spaces. In J. Cassell & H. Jenkins (Eds.), *From Barbie to Mortal Kombat: Gender and computer games*. Cambridge, MA: The MIT Press.

Jenkins, H. (2004/2006). Game design as narrative architecture. In K. Salen & E. Zimmerman (Eds.), *The game design reader: A rules of play anthology*. Cambridge, MA: MIT Press.

Jennings, S. C. (2015). Passion as method: Subjectivity in video games criticism. *Journal of Games Criticism*, 2(1). Retrieved from http://gamescriticism.org/articles/jennings-2-1

Jolivette, K., Wehby, J. H., Canale, J., & Massey, N. G. (2001). Effect of choicemaking opportunities on the behavior of students with emotional and behavioral disorders. *Behavioral Disorders*, 26, 131–145.

Jonassen, D. H. (2011). *Learning to solve problems: A handbook for designing problem-solving learning environments*. New York, NY: Routledge.

Jonnes, D. (1990). *The Matrix of Narrative: Family Systems and the Semiotics of Story*. New York: Mouton de Gruyter.

Jorgensen, K., Kostroff, L., & Weiss, R. K. (Producers), & Landis, J. (Director). (1977). *Kentucky fried movie* [Motion picture]. United States: KFM Films.

Juul, J. (2007, February 1). *Guitar hero II: Playing vs. performing a tune*. Retrieved March 28, 2016, from http://www.jesperjuul.net/ludologist/guitar-hero-ii-playing-vs-performing-a tune

Juul, J. (2005). *Half-Real*. Cambridge: MIT Press.

Juul, J. (2010). *A casual revolution*. Cambridge, London: The MIT Press.

Juul, J. (2011). *Half-real: Video games between real rules and fictional worlds*. Cambridge, MA: MIT Press.

Kafai, Y. B. (1998). Video game design by girls and boys: Variability and consistency of gender difference. In J. Cassell & H. Jenkins (Eds.), *From Barbie to Mortal Kombat: Gender and computer games* (pp. 90–114). Cambridge, MA: MIT Press.

Kafai, Y. B. (2008, June). Considering gender in digital games: Implications for serious game designs in the learning sciences. In *Proceedings of the 8th international conference on International conference for the learning sciences-Volume 1* (pp. 422-429). International Society of the Learning Sciences.

Kafai, Y. B., Heeter, C., Denner, J., & Sun, J. Y. (2008). Preface: Pink, purple, casual, or mainstream games: Moving beyond the gender divide. In Y. B. Kafai, C. Heeter, J. Deener, & J. Y. Sun (Eds.), *Beyond Barbie and Mortal Kombat: New perspectives on gender and gaming* (pp. xi–xxv). Cambridge, MA: MIT Press.

Kalinchuk, A. (2012). *Apple bans artistic game based on Foxconn suicides from App Store*. Retrieved July 7, 2015, from http://www.digitaltrends.com/mobile/apple-bans-game-based-on-foxconn-suicides/

Kanaga, D., & Key, E. (2013). *Proteus* [Computer Software]. London: Curve Digital.

Karlsen, F. (2007). Emergence, game rules and players. *Nordisk Medieforskerkonference*. Retrieved from http://www.ipd.gu.se/digitalAssets/873/873905_karlsen.pdf

Kaytoue, M., Silva, A., Cerf, L., Meira, W., & Raïssi, C. (2012). Watch me playing, I am a professional: A first study on video game live streaming. In *Proceedings of the 21st international conference companion on World Wide Web* (pp. 1181–1188). doi:10.1145/2187980.2188259

Kearney, M. (2006). *Girls make media*. New York: Routledge.

Ke, F., & Abras, T. (2013). Games for engaged learning of middle school children with special learning needs. *British Journal of Educational Technology*, *44*(2), 225–242. doi:10.1111/j.1467-8535.2012.01326.x

Kennedy, H. W. (2002). Lara Croft: Feminist icon or cyberbimbo? On the limits of textual analysis. *Game Studies*, *2*(2). Retrieved from http://www.gamestudies.org/0202/kennedy/

Kennewell, S. (2001). Using affordances and constraints to evaluate the use of information and communications technology in teaching and learning. *Journal of Information Technology for Teacher Education*, *10*(1-2), 101–116. doi:10.1080/14759390100200105

Keogh, B. (2015). Between tripleA, indie, casual, and DIY. In K. Oakley & J. O'Connor (Eds.), The Routledge Companion to the Cultural Industries (pp. 152-162). New York, NY: Routledge.

Keogh, B. (2014). Across worlds and bodies: Criticism in the age of video games. *Journal of Games Criticism*, *1*(1). Retrieved from http://gamescriticism.org/articles/keogh-1-1

Kerr, A., Whitson, J. R., Harvey, A., Shepherd, T., & O'Donnell, C. (2013). Strategies and tactics for promoting indie game design. *Selected Papers of Internet Research*. Retrieved from http://spir.aoir.org/index.php/spir/article/view/874

Kerr, A. (2006). *The business and culture of digital games: Gamework/gameplay*. London: Sage.

Key, E. (2013, February 1). *What are games* [Blog]. Retrieved from http://www.visitproteus.com/

Key, E. (2013, February 1). *What are games* [Web log post]. Retrieved from http://www.visitproteus.com/

Key, E., & Kanaga, D. (2013). Proteus.[Linus, OS, Windows, PS3, PSVita video game].

Kirkland, E. (2009). *Horror videogames and the uncanny*. DiGRA digital library.

Kirkpatrick, G. (2012). Constitutive tensions of gaming's field: UK gaming magazines and the formation of gaming culture 1981-1995. *Game Studies*, *12*(1).

Kittler, F. (1999). *Gramophone, film, typewriter*. Stanford, CA: Stanford University Press.

Kizu-Blair, I., & Lavigne, S. (2006). *Mahan*. Journey to the End of the Night. [urban game]

Klein, B. (2005). Dancing about architecture: Popular music criticism and the negotiation of authority. *Popular Communication*, *3*(1), 1–20. doi:10.1207/s15405710pc0301_1

Klepek, P. (2013, August 15). *Gone home review*. Retrieved January 15, 2016, from http://www.giantbomb.com/reviews/gone-home-review/1900-591/

Klepek, P. (2015, November 13). *Beautiful Game Pays Tribute To Grandfather Lost In a Plane Crash*. Retrieved January 8, 2016, from http://kotaku.com/a-game-that-imagines-a-happy-ending-for-a-tragic-loss-1742203440

Klimmt, C. (2009). Serious games and social change. Why they (should) work. In U. Ritterfeld, M. Cody, & P. Vorderer (Eds.), Serious games. Mechanisms and effects. New York: Routledge. Retrieved from https://books.google.at/books/about/Serious_Games.html?hl=de&id=eGORAgAAQBAJ

Klimmt, C., & Hartmann, T. (2006). Effectance, self-efficacy, and the motivation to play computer games. In P. Vorderer & J. Bryant (Eds.), *Playing video games: Motives, responses, and consequences* (pp. 143–177). Mahwah, NJ: Erlbaum.

Klopfer, E., Osterweil, S., & Salen, K. (2009). *Moving learning games forward*. Academic Press.

KnapNok Games. (2013). *Bumpie's Party* [video game]. KnapNok Games.

Koehler, M. J., & Mishra, P. (2008). Introducing TPACK. In American Association of Colleges for Teacher Education Committee on Innovation and Technology (Ed.), Handbook of Technological Pedagogical Content Knowledge (TPACK) for Educators (pp. 3-29). New York: Routledge.

Kollar, P. (2014, June 12). *'Her'* game creator releasing a mountain simulator. *Polygon*. Retrieved from http://www.polygon.com/2014/6/12/5804478/mountain-simulator-david-oreilly

Köln International School of Design. (2014). *Outcasted*. Köln: Köln International School of Design.

Kolovou, E. (2012). *CITYgories* [urban game]. Athens, Greece: bIZZ.

Konami Computer Entertainment Japan. (1998). *Metal gear solid* [PlayStation/Microsoft Windows video game]. Tokyo, Japan: Konami.

Konami. (1981). *Frogger* [Arcade video game]. Minato, Tokyo, Japan: Konami.

Konami. (1986). *Castlevania* [Nintendo Entertainment System video game]. Tokyo, Japan: Konami.

Konami. (1998). *Dance Dance Revolution* [Coin-operated video game]. Tokyo, Japan: Konami.

Konami. (1999). *Silent hill* [PS 1 video game]. Minato, Tokyo, Japan: Konami Digital Entertainment.

Konami. (2004). *Silent hill 4: The room.* [PS 2, Xbox, PS 3, PC video game]. Minato, Tokyo, Japan: Konami Digital Entertainment.

Kondrat, X. (2015). Gender and video games: How is female gender generally represented in various genres of video games? *Journal of Comparative Research in Anthropology & Sociology, 6*(1), 171–193.

Konijn, E. A., Walma van der Molen, J. H., & Hoorn, J. F. (2011). Babies versus bogeys: In-game manipulation of empathy in violent video games. In K. Poels & S. Malliet (Eds.), *Vice city virtue: Moral issues in digital game play* [EPUB version]. Retrieved from http://acco.be

Kopstein, J. (2012). *Apple removes iPhone game based on Foxconn suicides from App Store*. Retrieved July 7, 2015, from http://www.theverge.com/2012/10/12/3495466/apple-bans-another-objectionable-iphone-game-about-foxconn-workers

Koster, R. (2010). *A theory of fun for game design* [Amazon Kindle version]. Retrieved from http://www.amazon.com

Koster, R. (2013). *Theory of fun for game design*. Sebastopol, CA: O'Reilly Media, Inc.

Krzywinska, T. (2002). Hands-On horror. In H. Wu (Ed.), Axes to grind: Re-Imagining the horrific in visual media and culture. Academic Press.

Kuehn, K., & Corrigan, T. F. (2013). Hope labor: The role of employment prospects in online social production. *The Political Economy of Communication, 1*(1), 9–25.

Küklich, J. (2005). Precarious playbour: Modders and the digital games industry. *The Fiberculture Journal, 5*. Retrieved from http://five.fibreculturejournal.org/fcj-025-precarious-playbour-modders-and-the-digital-games-industry/

Kushner, D. (2003). *Masters of doom: How two guys created an empire and transformed pop culture*. New York, NY: Random House.

Labov, W., & Waletzky, J. (1967). Narrative analysis: Oral versions of personal experience. In J. Helm (Ed.), Essays on the Verbal and Visual Arts, (pp. 12-44). Seattle: University of Washington Press.

Labov, W. (1972). The transformation of experience in narrative syntax. In *Language in the Inner City* (pp. 354–396). Philadelphia: University of Pennsylvania Press.

Labov, W. (2013). *The language of life and death*. Cambridge, UK: Cambridge University Press. doi:10.1017/CBO9781139519632

Lacan, J. (1990). *Televison: A challenge to the psychoanalytical establishment* (J. Copjec, Ed., D. Hollier, R. Krauss, A. Michaelson, & J. Mehlman, Trans.). New York: Norton.

Lamorisse, A. (1995). *RISK: The game of global domination*. Pawtucket, RI: Hasbro Brands.

Landow, G. (1992). *Hypertext: The convergence of contemporary critical theory and technology*. Baltimore, MD: Johns Hopkins University Press.

Lang, D. J. (2015, May 13). *"Minecraft"* most streamed video game in YouTube's history. *Associated Press*. Retrieved from https://www.yahoo.com/tech/s/minecraft-most-streamed-video-game-youtubes-history-140023346.html

Lange, A. (2014). "You're just gonna be nice": How players engage with moral choice systems. *Journal of Games Criticism, 1*(1).

Larabee, K., Burns, M., & McComas, J. (2014). Effects of an iPad-supported phonics intervention on decoding performance and time on-task. *Journal of Behavioral Education, 23*(4), 449–469. doi:10.1007/s10864-014-9214-8

Latour, B. (1993). *We have never been modern* (C. Porter, Trans.). Boston, MA: Harvard University Press. (Original work published 1991)

Lave, J., & Wenger, E. (1991). *Situated learning: Legitimate peripheral participation*. Cambridge, UK: Cambridge University Press.

Lavender, T. J. (2011). *Video games as change agents -- the case of Homeless: It's No Game - viewcontent.pdf*. Retrieved July 8, 2015, from http://s3.amazonaws.com/academia.edu.documents/30989963/viewcontent.pdf?AWSAccessKeyId=AKIAJ56TQJRTWSMTNPEA&Expires=1436335381&Signature=7jOataOgmbFnnFdUKP%2BpXQhKylo%3D&responsecontent-disposition=inline

Lavoie, R. (2002). *Self-esteem: The cause and effect of success for the child with learning differences*. Retrieved from http://www.ricklavoie.com/Self-esteem.pdf

Lazzaro. (2015). *The 4 keys 2 fun | Nicole Lazzaro's Blog*. Retrieved from http://www.nicolelazzaro.com/the4-keys-to-fun/

Lazzo, M., Crofford, K., Fortier, J., & Willis, D. (Producers). (2005). Squidbillies [Television series]. Atlanta, GA: Williams Street.

Lee, D., & Schoenstedt, L. J. (2011). Comparison of eSports and traditional sports consumption motives. *ICHPER-SD Journal of Research, 6*(2), 39–44.

Lee, J. J., & Hoadley, C. M. (2007). Leveraging identity to make learning fun: Possible selves and experiential learning in massively multiplayer online games (MMOGs). *Journal of Online Education, 3*(6).

Lefebvre, H. (1991). *The production of space* (D. Nicholson-Smith, Trans.). Malden, MA: Blackwell. (Original work published 1974)

Lehtinen, S. (2010). *Alan Wake: Light and Dark Presentation*. Retrieved from GDCvault.com: http://www.gdcvault.com/play/1013666/Alan-Wake-Light-and

Lenhart, A., Kahne, J., Middaugh, E., Macgill, A. R., Evans, C., & Vitak, J. (2008). Teens, video games, and civics: Teens' gaming experiences are diverse and include significant social interaction and civic engagement. *Pew Internet & American Life Project*. Retrieved from http://eric.ed.gov/?id=ED525058

Levine, J. (2008). Broadening our definition of gaming: Tabletop games. *Library Technology Reports*, *44*(3), 7–11.

Lien, T. (2013). *The Apple obstacle for serious games*. Retrieved July 7, 2015, from http://www.polygon.com/2013/6/21/4449770/the-apple-obstacle-for-serious-games

Lien, T. (2014, May 16). Escape from Woomera *still highlights Australia's shame 11 years on*. Retrieved July 6, 2015, from http://www.polygon.com/2014/5/16/5717520/escape-from-woomera-immigration-australia

Limperos, A. M., Downs, E., Ivory, J. D., & Bowman, N. D. (2013). Leveling up: A review of emerging trends and suggestions for the next generation of communication research investigating video games' effects. *Communication Yearbook*, *37*, 348–377.

Lindsey, M.-V. (2015). The politics of Pokémon: Socialized gaming, religious themes and the construction of communal narratives. *Heidelberg Journal for Religions on the Internet*, *7*(1), 107–138. doi:10.11588/rel.2015.0.18510

Link, J. (2013). *Versuch über den Normalismus. Wie Normalität produziert wird* (5th ed.). Göttingen, Germany: Vandenhoeck & Ruprecht. (Original work published 1997)

Lipkin, N. (2012). Examining indie's independence: The meaning of "indie" games, the politics of production, and mainstream cooptation. *The Journal of the Canadian Game Studies Association*, *7*(11), 8–24. Retrieved from http://journals.sfu.ca/loading/index.php/loading/article/viewArticle/122

Littleloud. (2011). *Sweatshop*. [Flash game]. Retrieved July 12, 2015, from http://www.playsweatshop.com/

Locke, E. A., & Latham, G. P. (1990). *A theory of goal setting and task performance*. Englewood Cliffs, NJ: Prentice Hall.

Logas, H. L. (2011). *Meta-rules and complicity in Brenda Brathwaite's* Train. Paper presented at Think Design Play: The fifth international conference of the Digital Games Research Association (DIGRA), Utrecht, Netherlands.

Lucasfilm Games. (1990). *The Secret of Monkey Island* [Amiga (et al.) video game]. San Fransco, CA: LucasArts.

Lucas, K., & Sherry, J. L. (2004). Sex differences in video game play: A communication-based explanation. *Communication Research*, *31*(5), 499–523. doi:10.1177/0093650204267930

Lukacs, G. (1974). *The theory of the novel* (A. Bostock, Trans.). Cambridge, MA: MIT Press. (Original work published 1920)

MacCallum-Stewart, E. (2014). "Take that, bitches!" Refiguring Lara Croft in feminist game narratives. *Game Studies*, *14*(2). Retrieved from http://gamestudies.org/1402/articles/maccallumstewart

MacCallum-Stewart, E. (2008). Real boys carry girly epics: Normalising gender bending in online games. *Eudamos. Journal for Computer Game Culture*, *2*(1), 27–40.

Maia, A. (2013). *A materialidade de jogar no Kinect: o terror ganha outras proporções. Anais do XXII Encontro Anual da Compós*. Salvador: Universidade Federal da Bahia.

Malone, T. W., & Lepper, M. R. (1987). Making learning fun: A taxonomy of intrinsic motivations for learning. *Aptitude, Learning, and Instruction, 3*(1987), 223-253.

Manovich, L. (2001). *The language of new media*. London: The MIT Press.

Marchiafava, J. (2012, March 30). Why changing the *Mass Effect 3* ending is a mistake. *Game Informer*. Retrieved from http://www.gameinformer.com/b/features/archive/2012/03/30/why-changing-the-mass-effect-3-ending-is-a-mistake.aspx

Marcotte, A. (2012, June 13). *Online misogyny: Can't ignore it, can't not ignore it*. Slate.com.

Marcus, S. (2010). *Girls to the front: The true story of the riot grrrl revolution*. New York, NY: HarperCollins.

Margathe, J. (2013, August 16). *Review:* Papers, Please. Retrieved from http://blog.jovinomargathe.com/2013/08/16/review-papers-please/

Martin, G. (2013, September 30). *Grand theft auto V review (Multi-platform)* [Magazine]. Retrieved January 15, 2016, from http://www.pastemagazine.com/articles/2013/09/grand-theft-auto-v-review-multi-platform.html

Martin, N. K. (2007). *Sexy thrills: Undressing the erotic thriller*. Chicago: University of Illinois Press.

Mass Effect 3 Debacle. (2012). *GameFAQs.* [Post by user nospacesinmyname as a repost of an original post by BioWare Social Network user cato_84, which has since been removed].

Mass Effect 3 extended cut. (2012, April 5). [Web log]. *BioWare Blog*. Retrieved from http://blog.bioware.com/2012/04/05/mass-effect-3-extended-cut/

Maxis. (2000). *The Sims*. Electronic Arts.

Maxis. (2008). *Spore* [Microsoft Windows/Mac OS X video game]. Redwood City, CA: Electronic Arts.

Mayer, B., & Harris, C. (2010). *Libraries got game: Aligned learning through modern board games* [Amazon Kindle version]. Retrieved from http://amazon.com

Mayrath, M. C., Traphagan, T., Heikes, E. J., & Trivedi, A. (2011). Instructional design best practices for Second Life: A case study from a college-level English course. *Interactive Learning Environments, 19*(2), 125–142. doi:10.1080/10494820802602568

McCormack, D. (2014). *Queer postcolonial narratives and the ethics of witnessing*. London: Bloomsbury.

McDonald, K. (2012). *Dear Esther review*. Retrieved 15 December, 2015, from http://www.ign.com/articles/2012/02/13/dear-esther-review

McGee, M. (2012). *Dear Esther review*. Retrieved 15 December, 2015, from http://www.gamespot.com/reviews/dear-esther-review/1900-6349936/

McGonigal, J. (2011). *Reality is broken* [Amazon Kindle version]. Retrieved from http://amazon.com

McGonigal, J. (2011). *We don't need no stinkin' badges: How to re-invent reality without gamification* [Video file]. Retrieved from http://www. gdcvault. com/play/1014576/We-Don-t-Need-No

McGonigal, J. (2011). *Reality is broken: Why games make us better and how they can change the world*. New York: Penguin Press.

McGowan, T. (2007). *The real gaze: Film theory after Lacan*. Albany: State University of New York Press.

McLuhan, M. (1994). *Understanding media: the extensions of man*. London: The MIT Press.

McShaffry, M., & Graham, D. (2013). *Gaming coding complete* (4th ed.). Boston, MA: Cengage Learning.

McWhertor, M. (2015, April 23). Valve now lets modders sell their work through Steam, starting with *Skyrim. Polygon*. Retrieved from http://www.polygon.com/2015/4/23/8484743/steam-mod-sales-workshop-skyrim

McWilliams, W. C., & Piotrowski, H. (2009). *The world since 1945: A history of international relations* (7th ed.). Boulder, CO: Lynne Rienner Publishers, Inc.

Meadows, M. S. (2003). *Pause & effect: The art of interactive narrative*. Indianapolis, IN: New Riders.

Media Molecule. (2013). Tearaway [PlayStation Vita video game]. Minato, Tokyo, Japan: Sony Computer Entertainment Europe.

Meehan, E. R. (2005). *Why TV is not our fault: Television programming, viewers, and who's in control.* Lanhan, MD: Rowan & Littlefield.

Meier, S. (2012. March). *Interesting decisions.* Presentation and the Game Developers Conference, San Francisco, CA.

Meier, S., & Shelley, B. (1991). *Civilization* [DOS video game]. Hunt Valley, MD: MicroProse.

Melhuish, K., & Falloon, G. (2010). Looking to the future: M-learning with the iPad. *Computers in New Zealand Schools: Learning, Leading. Technology (Elmsford, N.Y.), 22*(3).

Mellamphy, D. (2013). Dead eye: The spectacle of torture porn in Dead Rising. In G. Papazian & J. M. Sommers (Eds.), Game on, Hollywood! Essays on the intersection of video games and cinema (pp. 35-46). London: McFarland & Company.

Menagerie [Computer Software]. (2014). oleomingus. Available from olelomingus.itch.io/menagerie

Merleau-Ponty, M. (1981). *Phenomenology of perception* (C. Smith, Trans.). Humanities.

Merleau-Ponty, M. (2013). *Phenomenology of Perception.* New York, NY: Routledge.

Messhof. (2014). *Nidhogg* [Windows, OS X, PS4, PSVita video game]. Messhof.

Metacritic.com. (n.d.). *Dear Esther for PC.* Retrieved 15 December, 2015, from http://www.metacritic.com/game/pc/dear-esther

Meyer, R. (2013, December 16). Facebook Advice: Don't Mistake Anti-Racist Satire for Patriotism. *The Atlantic.* Retrieved from http://www.theatlantic.com/technology/archive/2013/12/facebook-advice-dont-mistake-anti-racist-satire-for-patriotism/282406/

Meyers, R. E. (2014). *In search of an author: from participatory culture to participatory authorship* (Masters Thesis). Brigham Young University.

Michael, D., & Chen, S. (2005). *Serious games: Games that educate, train, and inform.* Mason: Course Technology PTR. Retrieved from http://www.amazon.de/Serious-Games-That-Educate-Train/dp/1592006221

Millar, R. (1994). *Warcraft II: Tides of Darkness* [PC game]. Irvine, CA: Blizzard Entertainment.

Miller, R., & Miller, R. (1993). *Myst* [Computer Software]. Mead, WA: Cyan.

Miller, T. (2006). Gaming for beginners. *Games and Culture, 1*(1), 512. doi:10.1177/1555412005281403

Mills, K. A., & Exley, B. (2014). Narrative and multimodality in English language arts curricula: A tale of two nations. *Language Arts, 92*(2), 136–143.

Mishra, P., & Koehler, M. J. (2006). Technological Pedagogical Content Knowledge: A framework for teacher knowledge. *Teachers College Record, 108*(6), 1017–1054. doi:10.1111/j.1467-9620.2006.00684.x

Moberly, K. (2008). Composition, computer games, and the absence of writing. *Computers and Composition, 25*(3), 284–299. doi:10.1016/j.compcom.2008.04.007

Mojang. (2011). *Minecraft* [Windows, OS, Linux, Android, iOS video game]. Stockholm, Sweden: Mojang.

Molleindustria. (2011). *Phone Story.* [Flash game]. Retrieved July 12, 2015, from http://phonestory.org/

Moore, R. (2004). Postmodernism and punk subculture: Cultures of authenticity and deconstruction. *The Communication Review, 7*(3), 305–327. doi: 10.1080/10714420490492238

Morgan, P. L. (2006). Increasing task engagement using preference or choicemaking: Some behavioral and methodological factors affecting their efficacy as classroom interventions. *Remedial and Special Education, 27*(3), 176–187. doi:10.1177/07419325060270030601

Moriarty, C. (2012, March 12). *Mass Effect 3: Opinion video.* [Online video clip]. IGN. Retrieved from http://www.ign.com/videos/2012/03/13/mass-effect-3-opinion-video

Morpheus. (2005 October 10). *Burning Blade's War2 History.* [Web.Archive.Org] Retrieved December 28, 2015 from http://web.archive.org/web/20060518133933/http://www.winnieinternet.com/games/war2/reports/BurningBladeHistory.htm

Mottier, V. (2009). "Talking about music is like dancing about architecture": Artspeak and pop music. *Language & Communication, 29*(2), 127–132. doi:10.1016/j.langcom.2009.01.003

Mulvey, L. (1989). Visual and other pleasures. London: Palgrave Macmillan. doi:10.1007/978-1-349-19798-9_3

Murray, D. (1972). Teach writing as a process not product. *The Leaflet, 71*(3), 11–14.

Murray, J. H. (1997). *Hamlet on the holodeck: The future of narrative in cyberspace.* New York: The Free Press.

Mustich, E. (2012, March 10). *Video games as multi-player art projects.* Retrieved March 28, 2016, from http://www.salon.com/2012/03/10/video_games_as_multi_player_art_projects/

Nakamura, L. (1995). Race in/for cyberspace: Identity tourism and racial passing on the Internet. *Work and Days, 13,* 181-193. Retrieved June 28, 2015 from http://www.humanities.uci.edu/mposter/syllabi/readings/nakamura.html

Nakamura, L. (1995). Race in/for cyberspace: Identity tourism and racial passing on the Internet. *Works and Days, 25*(26), 13.

Nakamura, L., & Chow-White, P. A. (2012). Introduction–race and digital technology: code, the color line, and the information society. In L. Nakamura & P. Chow-White (Eds.), *Race after the Internet.* New York, NY: Routledge.

Namco Bandai. (2009). *Noby noby boy* [PlayStation 3 video game]. Tokyo, Japan: Namco Bandai.

Namco. (1980). *Pac-man* [Arcade video game]. Chicago, IL: Midway.

Namco. (1985). *Dig dug II* [Arcade video game]. Minato, Tokyo, Japan: Namco.

Namco. (2004). *Katamari damacy* [PlayStation 2 video game]. Tokyo, Japan: Namco.

Namco. (2004). *Katamari Damacy* [PlayStation 2 video game]. Tokyo, Japan: Namco.

Naone, E. (2008). Jenova Chen, 26. *MIT's Technology Review, 111*(5), 64.

Narcisse, E. (2010, June 25). Press "B" to Skip: A Brief History of the Cutscene. *Time.* Retrieved from http://techland.time.com/2010/06/25/press-%E2%80%9Cb%E2%80%9D-to-skip-a-brief-history-of-the-cutscene/

Nasscom.in. (2015). *Exciting times ahead for the Indian gaming industry. NASSCOM.* Retrieved 30 March 2015, from http://www.nasscom.in/exciting-times-ahead-indian-gaming-industry?fg=159176

National Center for Education Statistics. (2013). *Digest of educational statistics 2013.* Washington, DC: U.S. Department of Education.

National Research Council. (2006). *Learning to think spatially: GIS as a support system in the K-12 curriculum*. Washington, DC: National Academies Press.

Naughty Dog. (2013). The last of us [PlayStation 3]. Minato, Tokyo, Japan: Sony Computer Entertainment.

Necrophone Games. (2014). *Jazzpunk* [Microsoft Windows/OS X/Linux/PlayStation 4 video game]. Atlanta, GA: Adult Swim Games.

Neh.gov. (2015). *About The National Endowment For The Humanities | National Endowment For The Humanities*. Retrieved from http://www.neh.gov/about

Neigher, E. (2012, May 29). *Alan Wake's American Nightmare Review*. Retrieved from IGN.com: http://uk.ign.com/articles/2012/05/29/alan-wakes-american-nightmare-review-2

Neuendorf, K. A. (2001). *The content analysis handbook*. Thousand Oaks, CA: SAGE.

New Games Foundation. (1976). *New games book*. New York, NY: Doubleday/Dolphin.

Newberry, E. (1790). *The New Game of Human Life* [Board game]. England: J. Wallis & E. Newberry.

Newcombe, N. S., & Frick, A. (2010). Early education for spatial intelligence: Why, what, and how. *Mind, Brain, and Education*, 4(3), 102–111. doi:10.1111/j.1751-228X.2010.01089.x

Newsgaming. (2003). *September 12th: A Toy World* [Macromedia Shockwave]. Uruguy: Newsgaming. Retrieved July 12, 2015, from http://www.newsgaming.com/ newsgames.htm

Nicholls, S. (2003). Escape game wires the minister. *Sydney Morning Herald*. Retrieved from http://www.smh.com.au/articles/2003/04/29/1051381951157.html

Nickerson, R. S. (2005). Technology and cognition amplification. In R. J. Sternberg & D. D. Preiss (Eds.), *Intelligence and technology: The impact of tools on the nature and development of human abilities*. Mahwah, NJ: Lawrence Erlbaum Associates.

Nintendo EAD Group No.4. (2015). *Super mario maker* [Wii U video game]. Kyoto, Japan: Nintendo.

Nintendo Power, 80 (January, 1996). The game guys. 24–25.

Nintendo R & D4. (1985). *Super Mario Bros.* [NES/Famicom video game]. Kyoto, Japan: Nintendo.

Nintendo R & D4. (1986). *The Legend of Zelda* [NES/Famicom video game]. Kyoto, Japan: Nintendo.

Nintendo R&D1. (1984). *Excitebike* [Nintendo Entertainment System video game]. Kyoto, Japan: Nintendo.

Nintendo. (1981). *Donkey kong* [Arcade video game]. Kyoto, Japan: Nintendo.

Nintendo. (1985). *Super mario bros.* [NES/Famicom video game]. Kyoto, Japan: Nintendo.

Nintendo. (1986). *Metroid* [NES video game]. Kyoto, Japan: Nintendo.

Nintendo. (1987). *Super Mario Bros.* [NES]. Kyoto: Nintendo.

Nintendo. (1996). *Super mario 64* [Nintendo 64, iQue Player video game]. Kyoto, Japan: Nintendo.

Nintendo. (2002). *Metroid prime* [Nintendo GameCube video game]. Kyoto, Japan: Nintendo.

Nintendo. (2007). *Super mario galaxy* [Wii video game]. Kyoto, Japan: Nintendo.

Nintendo. (2012). *Style Savvy: Trendsetters Sarah Hyland TV commercial* [Television commercial]. Retrieved from https://www.youtube.com/watch?v=4RU3EuoIl8M

Nintendo, E. A. D. (1991). *Pilotwings* [Super Nintendo Entertainment System video game]. Kyoto, Japan: Nintendo.

Nintendo, E. A. D. (1995). *Super mario world 2: Yoshi's island* [Super Nintendo/Game Boy Advance video game]. Kyoto, Japan: Nintendo.

Nintendo, E. A. D. (1998a). *The legend of zelda: Ocarina of time* [Nintendo 64 video game]. Kyoto, Japan: Nintendo.

Nintendo, E. A. D. (1998b). *Yoshi's story* [Nintendo 64 video game]. Kyoto, Japan: Nintendo.

Nitsche, M., & Thomas, M. (2003). In O. Balet, G. Subsol, & P. Torquet (Eds.), *Stories in space: The concept of the story map* (pp. 85–94). Graz, Austria: Springer Verlag.

Noble, J. (2009). *Programming interactivity*. Sebastopol: OReilly Media.

Nooney, L. (2013). A pedestal, a table, and a love letter: Archaeologies of gender in videogame history. *Game Studies, 13*(2). Retrieved from http://gamestudies.org/1302/articles/nooney

Norman, D. (2013). *The design of everyday things*. New York, NY: Basic Books.

Norris, E. (2012, March 13). 3 severe cases of gamer entitlement. *CraveOnline*. Retrieved from http://www.craveonline.com/gaming/articles/184645-3-severe-cases-of-gamer-entitlement

Number None, Inc. (2008). *Braid* [Xbox Live Arcade video game]. Number None, Inc.

Numinous Games. (2016). *That dragon, cancer* [Microsoft Windows, OS X, Ouya video game]. Numinous Games.

Oakes, K. (2009). *Slanted and enchanted: The evolution of indie culture*. New York, NY: Macmillan.

Obsidian Entertainment. (2015). *Pillars of Eternity*. PC: Paradox Interactive.

O'Donnell, C. (2013). Wither *Mario Factory?:* The role of tools in constructing (co)creative possibilities on video game consoles. *Games and Culture, 8*(3), 161–180. doi:10.1177/1555412013493132

OED Online. (2015, September). *myth,* n. Retrieved from OED Online: http://www.oed.com.ezproxy.lancs.ac.uk/view/Entry/124670?rskey=whPmFn&result=1#eid

Ohannessian, K. (2012). *Game Designer Jenova Chen on the Art Behind His 'Journey'*. Retrieved from fastcocreate.com: http://www.fastcocreate.com/1680062/game-designer-jenova-chen-on-the-art-behind-his-journey

Oleomingus.itch.io. (2015). *Menagerie by Studio Oleomingus*. Retrieved 28 December, 2015, from http://oleomingus.itch.io/menagerie

Oliver, K. (2001). *Witnessing: Beyond recognition*. Minneapolis: University of Minnesota Press.

Oliver, K. (2003). Witnessing and testimony. *Parallax, 10*(1), 79–88.

Oliver, M. B., Bowman, N. D., Woolley, J. K., Rogers, R., Sherrick, B., & Chung, M.-Y. (2015). Video games as meaningful entertainment experiences. *Psychology of Popular Media Culture*. doi:10.1037/ppm0000066

Online, S. (1986). Space quest: Chapter 1 - The Sarien encounter [DOS, Macintosh, Apple II, Apple IIGS, Amiga, Atari ST video game]. Fresno, CA: Sierra Online.

Onyett, C. (2012). *Alan Wake Review*. Retrieved from IGN.com: http://uk.ign.com/articles/2012/02/15/alan-wake-review

OReilly, D. (2014). Mountain [iOS and PC game]. Los Angeles, CA: Double Fine.

Osborne, J. (2015, April 7). Video Games without characters. *Medium*. Retrieved May 4, 2015 from https://medium.com/@jmarquiso/video-games-without-characters-3e99856cd0e4

Ouyang, J., & McKeown, K. (2014, May). Towards automatic detection of narrative structure.*Proceedings of the 9th International Conference on Language Resources and Evaluation*, Reykjavik.

Owens, S. L., Smothers, B. C., & Love, F. E. (2003). Are girls victim of gender bias in our nation's schools? *Journal of Instructional Technology, 30*(2), 131-138.

Owlchemy Labs. (2011). *Snuggle Truck* [Android, iOS]. Austin, TX: Owlchemy Labs. Retrieved July 12, 2015, from http://snuggletruck.com/

Packer, J. (2010). The Battle for Galt's Gulch: Bioshock as Critique of Objectivism. Journal of Gaming and Virtual Worlds, 209-224.

Painter, C., Martin, J. R., & Unsworth, L. (2013). *Reading visual narratives: Image analysis of children's picture books.* London: Equinox.

Pajot, L., & Swirsky, J. (Directors) (2012). Indie game: The movie. Canada: BlinkWorks Media.

Palacios, M., & Cunha, R. (2012). A tactilidade em dispositivos móveis: Primeiras reflexões e ensaio de tipologias. *Contemporânea, Salvador, 10*(3), 668–685.

Palumbo, D. E. (2014). *The Monomyth in American Science Fiction FIlms: 28 Visions of the Hero's Journey.* Jefferson: McFarland & Co.

Papale, L. (2014, June 22). *Beyond identification: Defining the relationships between player and avatar.* Retrieved July 8, 2015, from http://gamescriticism.org/articles/papale-1-2/

Parkin, S. (2006). Darfur is Dying. *When videogames discovered ethics.* Retrieved July 10, 2015, from http://www.eurogamer.net/articles/i_darfurisdying_pc

Parkin, S. (2013). *A serious game about sweatshops … you won't find it in Apple's App Store.* Retrieved July 7, 2015, from http://www.theguardian.com/commentisfree/2013/mar/22/sweatshop-game-apple-app-store

Paul, H., Bowman, N. D., & Banks, J. D. (2015). The enjoyment of griefing in online games. *Journal of Gaming and Virtual Worlds, 7*(3), 243–258. doi:10.1386/jgvw.7.3.243_1

Pearce, C. (2008). Spatial literacy: Reading (and writing) game space. In *Proceedings, Future and Reality of Gaming (FROG)*. Retrieved from http://lmc.gatech.edu/~cpearce3/PearcePubs/Pearce_FROG_FINAL.pdf

Pearce, C. (2011). *Communities of play: Emergent cultures in multiplayer games and virtual worlds.* Cambridge: MIT Press.

Peirce, C. S. (1932-58). In C. Hartshorne, P. Weiss, & A. W. Burks (Eds.), Collected papers of Charles Sanders Peirce (Vols. 1–8). Cambridge, MA: Harvard University Press.

Pellegrini, A. D. (1995). *The future of play theory: A multidisciplinary inquiry into the contributions of Brian Sutton-Smith.* Albany, NY: SUNY Press.

Peng, W., Lee, M., & Heeter, C. (2010). The effects of a serious game on role-taking and willingness to help. *Journal of Communication, 60*(4), 723–742. doi:10.1111/j.1460-2466.2010.01511.x

Peracchio, L. A., & Escalas, J. E. (2008). "Tell me a story": Crafting and publishing research in consumer psychology. *Journal of Consumer Psychology, 18*(3), 197–204. doi:10.1016/j.jcps.2008.04.008

Pereira, V. A. (2008). *G.A.M.E.S. 2.0: Gêneros e Gramáticas de Arranjos e Ambientes Midiáticos Mediadores de Experências de Entretenimento, Sociabilidades e Sensorialidades. Anais do XVII Encontro Anual da Compós.* São Paulo: UNIP.

Perron, B. (2004). *Sign of a threat: The effects of warning systems in survival horror games. COSIGN 2004.* Croatia: University of Split.

Persson, M. (2009). *Minecraft* [Computer Software]. Stockholm: Mojang.

Peters, J. (2007, June 27). World of Borecraft. *Slate.com.* Retrieved November 11, 2015 from: http://www.slate.com/articles/technology/gaming/2007/06/world_of_borecraft.html

Peters, J. D. (2001). Witnessing. *Media Culture & Society, 23*(6), 707–723. doi:10.1177/016344301023006002

Phillips, T. (2015). "Don't clone my indie game, bro": Informal cultures of videogame regulation in the independent sector. *Cultural Trends, 24*(2), 143–153. doi:10.1080/09548963.2015.1031480

Phillips, W. (2015). *This is why we can't have nice things: Mapping the relationship between online trolling and mainstream culture.* Cambridge, MA: The MIT Press.

Picado, B., & Araújo, J. (2013). *A performatividade da experiência estética: modulações rítmicas e tensivas da sensibilidade. Anais do XXII Encontro Anual da Compós.* Salvador: UFBA.

Picard, M. (2013). The foundation of *Geemu*: A brief history of early Japanese video games. *Game Studies, 13*(2). Retrieved from http://gamestudies.org/1302/articles/picard

Pierre, S. (2013). *These French Fries Make Terrible Hot Dogs* [card game]. Netcong, New Jersey: Ad Magic.

Pinchbeck, D. (2008). *Dear Esther*: An interactive ghost story built using the source engine. In U. Spierling & N. Szilas (Eds.), Lecture Notes in Computer Science: Vol. 5443. *Interactive storytelling* (pp. 51–54). Berlin: Springer. doi:10.1007/978-3-540-89454-4_9

Pipher, M. (1994). *Reviving Ophelia: Saving the selves of adolescent girls.* New York: Putnam Books.

Playdead. (2010). *Limbo* [Xbox Live Arcade video game]. Redmond, WA: Microsoft Studios.

Plough, I. (2014). Development of a test of speaking proficiency in multiple languages. *Papers in Language Testing and Assessment, 3*(2), 27-52. Retrieved from http://www.altaanz.org

Plunkett, L. (2012, March 14). Charitable donations don't give you the right to ask for changes to *Mass Effect 3. Kotaku.* Retrieved from http://kotaku.com/5893119/charitable-donations-dont-give-you-the-right-to-demand-changes-to-mass-effect-3

Poe, E. A. (1843). The tell-tale heart. *The Pioneer, 1*(1), 29–31.

Poe, E. A. (1846). The cask of Amontillado. *Godey's Lady's Book, XXXIII*(5), 216–218.

Poels, K., & Malliet, S. (2011a). Moral issues in digital game play: A multi-disciplinary view. In K. Poels & S. Malliet (Eds.), *Vice city virtue: Moral issues in digital game play* [EPUB version]. Retrieved from http://acco.be

Poels, K., & Malliet, S. (2011b). *Vice city virtue: Moral issues in digital game play* [EPUB version]. Retrieved from http://acco.be

Polytron Corporation. (2012). *Fez* [Xbox 360 video game]. Montreal, Canada: Trapdoor.

Ponce, H. R., Mayer, R. E., & Lopez, M. J. (2013). A computer-based spatial learning strategy approach that improves reading comprehension and writing. *Educational Technology Research and Development*, *61*(5), 819–840. doi:10.1007/s11423-013-9310-9

Poole, S. (2012, March 9). Bang, bang, you're dead: How *Grand Theft Auto* stole Hollywood's thunder. *The Guardian*. Retrieved May 20, 2015 from http://www.theguardian.com/technology/2012/mar/09/grand-theft-auto-bang-bang-youre-dead

PopCap Games. (2001). *Bejeweled* [PC game]. Seattle: PopCap Games.

PopCap Games. (2009). *Plants vs. zombies* [IOS video game]. Redwood City, CA: Electronic Arts.

Pope, L. (2013). *Papers, Please* [Microsoft Windows video game]. n.c.: self-published.

Pope, L. (2013). *Papers, please* [Windows, OS X video game].

Pope, L. (2013). *Papers, Please* [PC game]. Lucas Pope.

Portal [Computer Software]. (2007). Bellevue, WA: Valve.

Poynter, B. (2013). *In a permanent save state* [Android]. Reno: Benjamin Poynter.

Prensky, M. (2006). *"Don't bother me mom, I'm learning!": How computer and video games are preparing your kids for twenty-first century learning*. St. Paul, MN: Paragon House.

Prensky, M. (2006). *Don't bother me mom – I'm learning*. Saint Paul: Paragon House.

Prey [Computer Software]. (2006). Madison, WI: Human Head Studios.

Priestman, C. (2015). *The videogame trying to change how we treat the homeless*. Retrieved July 10, 2015, from http://killscreendaily.com/articles/outcasted/

Productions, P. T. V. (2010). *Inside the Haiti Earthquake* [Flash game]. PTV Productions. Retrieved 20 August 2015 from http://www.insidedisaster.com/experience/Main.html

Propp, V. (1968). *The Morphology of the Folktale*. Austin: University of Texas Press.

Provelengios, P., & Fesakis, G. (2011). Educational applications of serious games: The case of the game *Food Force* in primary education students. In *Proceedings of the 5th European conference on games based learning* (pp. 476–485). Retrieved from https://books.google.at/books/about/Proceedings_of_the_5th_European_Conferen.html?hl=de&id=5CoJBAAAQBAJ

Provenzo, E. (1991). *Video kids*. Cambridge, MA: Harvard University Press. doi:10.4159/harvard.9780674422483

Quantic Dream. (2010). Heavy Rain [PS 3 video game]. Minato, Tokyo, Japan: Sony Computer Entertainment.

Question. (2015). *The magic circle* [Microsoft Windows/OS X/Linux video game]. Question.

Rafinski, A. (2013). *Church of Play* [alternate reality game].

Raha, M. (2005). *Cinderella's big score: Women of the punk and indie underground*. New York, NY: Seal Press.

Ramsey, C. (2015, August 17). *The stormy world of Three Fourths Home has drama, cornfields*. Retrieved January 14, 2016, from https://killscreen.com/articles/stormy-world-three-fourths-home-has-drama-cornfields/

Rand, A. (2007). *Atlas Shrugged*. London: Penguin Modern Classics.

Raphael, C., Bachen, C., Lynn, K.-M., Baldwin-Philippi, J., & McKee, K. A. (2006). Portrayals of information and communication technology on world wide web sites for girls. *Journal of Computer-Mediated Communication, 11*(3), 771–801. doi:10.1111/j.1083-6101.2006.00035.x

reaverlisk. (2000, October 20). *Trash talking.* [War2.Warcraft.Org] Retrieved December 28, 2015 from http://war2. warcraft.org/forum/viewtopic.php?t=112

Red Barrels. (2013). *Outlast* [PC, PS 4, Xbox One video game]. Montreal: Red Barrels.

Red Barrels. (2014). *Outlast: Whistleblower* [PC, PS 4 Xbox One video game]. Montreal: Red Barrels.

redpaw. (2000, January 16). *Welcome to the internet.* [Web.Archive.Org] Retrieved December 28, 2015 from http://web. archive.org/web/20001110014700/http://deeplight.net/editorials/redpaw/welcome.shtml

Rehak, B. (2003). Playing at being: Psychoanalysis and the avatar. In M. J. P. Wolf & B. Perron (Eds.), The video game theory reader (pp. 103-128). Routledge: New York and London.

Reid, E. (1999). Hierarchy and power: social control in cyberspace. In P. Kollock & M. Smith (Eds.), *Communities in cyberspace* (pp. 107–134). New York, NY: Routledge.

Reigeluth, C., & Stein, R. (1983). Elaboration theory. *Instructional-design theories and models: An overview of their current status*, 335-381.

Reimann, M., & Schilke, O. (2011). Product differentiation by aesthetic and creative design: A psychological and neural framework of design thinking. In H. Plattner, C. Meinel, & L. Leifer (Eds.), *Design thinking: Understand—improve—apply* (pp. 45–60). New York, NY: Springer. doi:10.1007/978-3-642-13757-0_3

Re-Logic. (2011). *Terraria* [Windows video game]. Indiana: Re-Logic.

Remedy Entertainment. (2010). Alan Wake [Xbox 360, Microsoft Windows video game]. Redmond, WA: Microsoft Studios.

Remedy Entertainment. (2012, February 22). *Alan Wake's American Nightmare* [Xbox 360, Xbox One, Microsoft Windows video game]. Redmond, WA: Microsoft Studios.

Reviews for Antique Road Trip: American Dreamin'. (n.d.). Big Fish Games. Retrieved May 4, 2015 from http://forums. bigfishgames.com/posts/list/257559.page

Rheingold, H. (1991). *Virtual reality: Exploring the brave new technologies of artificial experience and interactive worlds from cyberspace.* London: Seeker and Warburg.

Rieber, L. P. (1996). Seriously considering play: Designing interactive learning environments based on the blending of microworlds, simulations, and games. *Educational Technology Research and Development, 44*(2), 43–58. doi:10.1007/BF02300540

Rigby, S., & Ryan, R. M. (2011). *Glued to Games: How Video Games Draw Us In and Hold Us Spellbound: How Video Games Draw Us In and Hold Us Spellbound.* ABC-CLIO.

Riot Games. (2009). *League of legends* [Microsoft Windows, OS X video game]. Los Angeles, CA: Riot Games.

Robison, A. J. (2008). The design is the game: Writing games, teaching writing. *Computers and Composition, 25*(3), 359–370. doi:10.1016/j.compcom.2008.04.006

Rockstar North. (2008). *Grand theft auto IV* [PS3, Xbox 360, Windows video game]. New York, NY: Rockstar Games.

Rockstar North. (2013). *Grand theft auto V* [PS 3, Xbox 360 video game]. New York, NY: Rockstar Games.

Rockstar San Diego. (2010). *Red dead redemption* [Playstation 3/XBox 360 video game]. New York, NY: Rockstar Games.

Rollins, H. (2004). Get in the van. New York, NY: 2.13. 61 Publications.

Romero, J. (2000). *Daikatana* [PC game]. Dallas, TX: Ion Storm.

Room of 1000 snakes [Computer Software]. (2013). Los Angeles: Arcane Kids. Available from http://arcanekids.com/snakes

Rose, M. (2013, February 1). *Opinion: It's totally OK to not like "anti-games"* [Web log post]. Retrieved from http://www.gamasutra.com/view/news/185885/Opinion_Its_totally_OK_to_not_like_antigames.php#.UQ0vR0pERpY

Rossi, A. (2013, October 10). *Fixing Broken Links on the Internet.* [Blog Post]. Retrieved June 28, 2015 from https://blog.archive.org/2013/10/25/fixing-broken-links/

Roy, D. (2015). Fighting heroic hegemony with *ennui*: The remarkable everyday in *World of Warcraft. Journal of Gaming and Virtual Words, 7*(2).

Ruggiero, D. N. (2014). *Spent: Changing students' affective learning toward homelessness through persuasive video game play.* ACM Press; doi:10.1145/2556288.2557390

Ruiz, S. (2006). *Darfur is Dying* [Flash game]. Take Action Games. Retrieved 23 September 2015 from http://www.darfurisdying.com/index.html

Rusch, D. (2009). *Mechanisms of the soul: Tackling the human condition.* DiGRA digital library.

Rusch, D. C. (2009). *Mechanisms of the soul: Tackling the human condition in videogames. In Proceedings from DiGRA 2009: Breaking new ground: Innovation in games, play, practice and theory.* London: Brunel University.

Ryan, M. (2011). The interactive onion: Layers of user participation in digital narrative texts. In R. E. Page & B. Thomas (Eds.), *New narratives: Stories and storytelling in the digital age.* Lincoln, NE: University of Nebraska Press.

Ryan, M. L., Emerson, L., & Robertson, B. (Eds.). (2014). *John Hopkins Guide to Digital Media.* Baltimore, MD: John Hopkins University Press.

SaBiQ. (2000, October 11). *haha sailormoon ide own u in chess =/.* [War2.Warcraft.Org] Retrieved December 28, 2015 from http://war2.warcraft.org/forum/viewtopic.php?t=115

Sadker, M., & Sadker, D. (1995). *Failing at fairness: How our schools cheat girls.* New York: Touchstone.

Sadowski, J., Seager, T. P., Selinger, E., Spierre, S. G., & Whyte, K. P. (2013). An experiential game-theoretic pedagogy for sustainability ethics. *Science and Engineering Ethics, 19*(3), 1323–1339. doi:10.1007/s11948-012-9385-4 PMID:22895636

Salen, K. (2008). *The ecology of games: Connecting youth, games, and learning.* Cambridge, MA: MIT Press.

Salen, K., & Zimmerman, E. (2004). *Rules of play: game design fundamentals.* Cambridge, London: The MIT Press.

Salen, K., & Zimmerman, E. (2004). *Rules of play: Game design fundamentals.* Cambridge, MA: The MIT Press.

Salen, K., & Zimmerman, E. (2006). *The game design reader: A rules of play anthology.* Cambridge, MA: MIT Press.

Samantha. (2012). *This House of Dreams.* Retrieved from blogger.com: http://thishouseofdreams.blogspot.co.uk/

Sandel, M. J. (2009). *Justice: What's the right thing to do?* New York, NY: Farrar, Straus and Giroux.

Sandoval, W. A., & Bell, P. (2004). Design-based research methods for studying learning in context: Introduction. *Educational Psychologist, 39*(4), 199–201. doi:10.1207/s15326985ep3904_1

Sappy. (2000, October 8). *Valkrie*. [War2.Warcraft.Org] Retrieved December 28, 2015 from http://war2.warcraft.org/forum/viewtopic.php?t=60

Sappy. (2005, October 10). *Sappy's war2 history*. [Web.Archive.Org] Retrieved December 28, 2015 from http://web.archive.org/web/20060518133833/http://www.winnieinternet.com/games/war2/reports/SappyHistory.htm

Saussure, F. d. (1959). *Course in general linguistics* (C. Bally, A. Sechehaye, & A. Reidlinger, Trans. & Eds.). New York: Philosophical Library. (Original work published 1916)

Sc~Nixon. (2005, October 10). *Nixon's war2 history*. [Web.Archive.Org] Retrieved June 18, 2015 from http://web.archive.org/web/20060518133812/http://www.winnieinternet.com/games/war2/reports/NixonHistory.htm

Schechner, R. (2006). *Performance Studies: an introduction* (2nd ed.). New York, NY: Rouledge.

Schell, J. (2015). *The art of game design: A book of lenses* (2nd ed.). Boca Raton, FL: CRC Press.

Schiesel, S. (2008, January 26). Author Faults a Game, and Gamers Flame Back. *The New York Times*. Retrieved from http://www.nytimes.com/2008/01/26/arts/television/26mass.html

Schilling, D. R. (2013). *Knowledge doubling every 12 months, Soon to be every 12 hours. Industry tap into news*. Retrieved from http://www.industrytap.com/knowledge-doubling-every-12-months-soon-to-be-every-12-hours/3950

Schoenbrodt, F. D. (2013, June 6). At what sample size do correlations stabilize? *Nicebread.de* [personal blog]. Retrieved from: http://www.nicebread.de/at-what-sample-size-do-correlations-stabilize/

Schoenbrodt, F. D., & Perugini, M. (2013). At what size do correlations stabilize? *Journal of Research in Personality*, *47*(5), 609–612. doi:10.1016/j.jrp.2013.05.009

Schofield, J. (2013). Modeling choices in nuclear warfighting: Two classroom simulations on escalation and retaliation. *Simulation & Gaming*, *44*(1), 73–93. doi:10.1177/1046878112455488

Schreier, J. (2012a, March 27). Gamers send BioWare 400 cupcakes. *Kotaku*. Retrieved from http://kotaku.com/5896847/gamers-send-bioware-400-cupcakes

Schreier, J. (2012b, February 23). *Mass Effect 3* DLC triggers fan outrage, BioWare response. *Kotaku*. Retrieved from http://kotaku.com/5887626/mass-effect-3-dlc-triggers-fan-outrage-bioware-response

Schulzke, M. (2011). Reflective play and morality: Video games as thought experiments. In K. Poels & S. Malliet (Eds.), *Vice city virtue: Moral issues in digital game play* [EPUB version]. Retrieved from http://acco.be

Schwartz, D. L., Chase, C. C., Oppezzo, M. A., & Chin, D. B. (2011). Practicing versus inventing with contrasting cases: The effects of telling first on learning and transfer. *Journal of Educational Psychology*, *103*(4), 759–775. doi:10.1037/a0025140

Schwartz, D. L., Lin, X., Brophy, S., & Bransford, J. D. (1999). Toward the development of flexibly adaptive instructional designs. In C. Reigeluth (Ed.), *Instructional-design theories and models: A new paradigm of instructional theory* (pp. 183–213). Mahwah, NJ: Erlbaum.

Schwarz, E., & Stolow, D. (2006). Twenty-first century learning in afterschool. *New Directions for Youth Development*, *110*(110), 81–99. doi:10.1002/yd.169 PMID:17017259

Schwarzer, R., & Jerusalem, M. (1995). Generalized self-efficacy scale. In J. Weinman, S. Wright, & M. Johnston (Eds.), *Measures in health psychology: A user's portfolio. Causal and control beliefs* (pp. 35–37). Windsor, UK: Nfer-Nelson.

Scott, J. W. (1986). Gender: A useful category of historical analysis. *The American Historical Review, 91*(5), 1053–1075. doi:10.2307/1864376

Seager, T. P., Selinger, E., Whiddon, D., Schwartz, D., Spierre, S., & Berady, A. (2010). Debunking the fallacy of the individual decision-maker: An experiential pedagogy for sustainability ethics. In *Proceedings of the 2010 IEEE International Symposium on Sustainable Systems & Technology (ISSST)*. doi:10.1109/ISSST.2010.5507679

Seel, M. (2014). No escopo da experiência estética. In B. Picado, C. M. C. Mendonça, & J. Cardoso Filho (Eds.), *In Experiência estética e performance*. Salvador: EDUFBA.

Sega. (1982). *Zaxxon* [Arcade video game]. Ōta, Tokyo, Japan: Sega.

Seiter, E. (1993). *Sold separately: Children and parents in consumer culture*. New Brunswick, NJ: Rutgers University Press.

Selfe, C. (2009). The movement of air, the breath of meaning: Aurality and multimodal composing. *College Composition and Communication, 60*(4). Retrieved from http://www.ncte.org/cccc/ccc/issues/v60-4

Selzer, E. (Producer), & Jones, C. M. (Director). (1953). *Duck amuck*. [Motion picture]. United States: Warner Bros.

Shaffer, D. W., Halverson, R., Squire, K. R., & Gee, J. P. (2005, April). *Video games and the future of learning*. Retrieved July 7, 2015, from http://files.eric.ed.gov/fulltext/ED497016.pdf

Shah, N. (2011). Special education pupils find learning tools in iPad applications. *Education Week, 30*(1), 16–17.

Shapiro, A. (Host). (2016, January 15). In "That Dragon, Cancer," "Unshakeable Empathy Gives Game Life" [Radio program]. All Things Considered. National Public Radio.

Shapiro, J. (2015, August 16). Something is wrong with '*Minecraft*.' This game has a solution. *Forbes*. Retrieved from http://www.forbes.com/sites/jordanshapiro/2015/08/16/something-is-wrong-with-minecraft-this-game-has-a-solution/

Shapiro, J. R., & Williams, A. M. (2012). The role of stereotype threats in undermining girls' and women's performance and interest in STEM fields. *Sex Roles, 66*(3), 175–183. doi:10.1007/s11199-011-0051-0

Shaw, A. (2014). *E-sport Spectator Motivation* (Doctoral dissertation).

Sheffield, B. (2014, October 19). When quality comes before making money: developing *Monument Valley. Gamasutra*. Retrieved from http://gamasutra.com/view/news/228094/When_quality_comes_before_making_money_Developing_Monument_Valley.php

Shepherd, R. P. (2015). FB in FYC: Facebook use among first-year composition students. *Computers and Composition, 35*, 86–107. doi:10.1016/j.compcom.2014.12.001

Shields, R. (2015). Ludic ontology: Play's relationship to language, cultural forms, and transformative politics. *American Journal of Play, 7*(3), 298–321.

Shumow, L., & Schmidt, J. A. (2014). *Enhancing adolescents' motivation for science*. Thousand Oaks, CA: Corwin.

Shweder, R. A., & Haidt, J. (1993). The future of moral psychology: Truth, intuition, and the pluralist way. *Psychological Science, 4*(6), 360–365. doi:10.1111/j.1467-9280.1993.tb00582.x

Sicart, M. (2009). *The ethics of computer games* [Amazon Kindle version]. Retrieved from http://www.amazon.com

Sicart, M. (2011). Against procedurality. *Game Studies, 11*(3). Retrieved from http://gamestudies.org/1103/articles/sicart_ap

Sicart, M. (2011). Against procedurality. *Game Studies, 11*(3). Retrieved June 6, 2015, from http://gamestudies.org/1103/articles/sicart_ap

Sierra Entertainment. (1984). *King's quest* [IBM PC/Apple II video game]. Fresno, CA: Sierra Entertainment.

Sierra On-Line. (1983). *King's quest I* [IBM PCjr video game]. Armonk, NY: IBM.

Silicon Knights. (2002). *Eternal darkness: Sanity's requiem* [Nintendo Game Cube video game]. Kyoto, Japan: Nintendo.

Sinclair, B. (2015, April 22). *Gaming will hit $91.5 billion this year.* Retrieved January 15, 2016, from http://www.gamesindustry.biz/articles/2015-04-22-gaming-will-hit-usd91-5-billion-this-year-newzoo

Sinders, C. (2015). *Twitter has a UX problem.* Paper Presented at the Fifth Annual Conference on Theorizing the Web, New York, NY.

Singer, B. (2001). Modernidade, hiperestímulo e o início do sensacionalismo popular. In L. Charney & V. Schwartz (Eds.), *O cinema e a invenção da vida moderna.* São Paulo: Cosac Naify.

Skartveit, H.-L. (2010). *Changes in museum practice.* Berghahn Books. Retrieved from https://books.google.at/books/about/Changes_in_Museum_Practice.html?hl=de&id=4OoBXAMKZJsC

sLuGGo. (2000, October 14). *Ash = War2 god.* [War2.Warcraft.Org].

Smith, P., & Riley, A. (2009). *Cultural Theory: An Introduction.* Oxford: Blackwell Publishing.

SNK. (1988). *Lee Trevino's Fighting Golf* [Nintendo Entertainment System video game]. Suita, Japan: SNK.

Sojo Studios. (2012). *WeTopia* [Facebook App]. Sojo Studios. Retrieved April 23, 2014 from https://www.facebook.com/WeTopiaOfficial

Sontag, S. (2013). *Against interpretation and other essays.* New York: Picador. (Original work published 1966)

Spence, I., & Feng, J. (2010). Video games and spatial cognition. *Review of General Psychology, 14*(2), 92–104. doi:10.1037/a0019491

Spivak, G. C. (1988). Can the Subaltern speak? In G. Nelson (Ed.), *Marxism and the interpretation of culture* (pp. 271–316). Champaign, IL: University of Illinois Press. doi:10.1007/978-1-349-19059-1_20

Squire, K. (2011). *Video games and learning: Teaching and participatory culture in the digital age.* New York: Teacher's College Press.

Staples, W. G. (1997). *The culture of surveillance: Discipline and social control in the United States.* New York: St. Martin's Press.

Star Maid Games. (2015). *Cibele* [Microsoft Windows video game].

Starbreeze Studios. (2013). *Brothers: A tale of two sons* [Xbox 360/Microsoft Windows/PlayStation 3 video game]. Milan, Italy: 505 Games.

StarLogo [computer program]. (2005). *MIT Scheller Teacher Education Program.* Cambridge, MA: MIT University. Available at http://education.mit.edu/portfolio_page/starlogo-tng/

Steam Game Forums. (n.d.). *Dear Esther Forum.* Retrieved 15 December, 2015, from https://steamcommunity.com/app/203810/discussions/

Steam. (2016, April 1). *Steam search - simulator.* Retrieved April 2, 2016, from http://store.steampowered.com/search/?snr=1_4_4__12&term=simulator

Steinke, J. (1999). Women scientist role models on screen: The case of contact. *Science Communication, 21*(2), 111–136. doi:10.1177/1075547099021002002

Stenros, J. (2015). *Playfulness, play, and games: A constructionist ludology approach.* Tampere: Tampere University Press.

Sterling, J. (2012, March 10). *Mass Effect 3* fans petition BioWare to change the ending. *Destructoid.* Retrieved from http://www.destructoid.com/mass-effect-3-fans-petition-bioware-to-change-the-ending-223615.phtml

Sterling, J. (2016, January 12). *That dragon, cancer review – Betwixt "game" and "experience".* Retrieved from http://www.thejimquisition.com/that-dragon-cancer-review/

Stern, S. (2004). Expressions of identity online: Prominent features and gender differences in adolescents' world wide web home pages. *Broadcast Education Association, 48*(2), 218–243.

Steuer, J. (1992). Defining virtual reality: Dimensions determining telepresence. *Journal of Communication, 42*(4), 73–93. doi:10.1111/j.1460-2466.1992.tb00812.x

Steve Jackson Games. (2008). GURPS (4th ed.) [roleplaying game]. Author.

Stobbart, D. (2012, August). *The Darkness and the Light: Traditional Tales in a Modern Environment.* Retrieved from academia.edu: https://www.academia.edu/3622550/The_Darkness_and_the_Light_Traditional_Tales_in_a_Modern_Environment

Stokes, B., Seggerman, S., & Rejeski, D. (2011). *For a better world: Digital games and the social change sector.* Retrieved July 7, 2015, from http://www.gamesforchange.org/g4cwp/wp-content/uploads/2011/06/g4cwhitepaper.pdf

Storm, I. (2000). Deus ex [Windows, OS video game]. Wimbledon, London, United Kingdom: Eidos Interactive.

Straeubig, M. (2014). *Kling Klang Klong* [mobile game].

Street Fighter [Computer Software]. (1987). Osaka: Capcom.

Stuart, K. (2016, January 14). That dragon, cancer and the weird complexities of grief. *The Guardian.* Retrieved from http://www.theguardian.com/technology/2016/jan/14/that-dragon-cancer-and-the-weird-complexities-of-grief

Studios, W. (1995). *Command & Conquer* [DOS, Microsoft Windows, Mac OS video game]. Las Vegas, NV: Virgin Interactive.

Subrahmanyam, K., & Greenfield, P. M. (1998). Computer games for girls: What makes them play? In J. Cassell & H. Jenkins (Eds.), *From Barbie to Mortal Kombat: Gender and computer games* (pp. 46–71). Cambridge, MA: The MIT Press.

super radish. (2000, December 5). *The good thing about 24-7 being back up.* [Web.Archive.Org] Retrieved December 28, 2015 from http://war2.warcraft.org/forum/viewtopic.php?t=296

Superbrothers & Capybara Games. (2011). *Sword & Sworcery EP* [iOS, Android, PC game]. Quebec, Canada: Capybara Games.

Supermassive Games. (2015). Until dawn [PlayStation 4 video game]. Minato, Tokyo, Japan: Sony Computer Entertainment.

Sutton-Smith, B. (2009). *The ambiguity of play.* Cambridge, MA: Harvard University Press.

Swain, C. (2007). *Designing games to effect social change.* Retrieved September 18, 2015, from http://www.digra.org/wp-content/uploads/digital-library/07311.09363.pdf

Swain, C. (2010). *The mechanic is the message: How to communicate values in games through the mechanics of user action and system response.* Retrieved July 12, 2015, from http://www.irma-international.org/viewtitle/41321/

Swain, E. (2014). *Choice and consequence in "Papers, Please"*. Retrieved July 8, 2015, from http://www.popmatters.com/post/183289-papers-please-morality/

Swalwell, M. (2003). *The meme game:* Escape from Woomera. Retrieved July 6, 2015, from http://www.realtimearts.net/article/issue55/7103

Sweeney, J. (2015). *Indie implosion: Walking simulators*. Retrieved 15 December, 2015, from https://supernerdland.com/indie-implosion-walking-simulators/

Sylvester, T. (2013). *Designing games: A guide to engineering experiences*. Sebastopol, CA: O'Reilly Media, Inc.

Sypher. (2005, October 10). *Sypher's war2 History*. [Web.Archive.Org] Retrieved December 28, 2015 from http://web.archive.org/web/20060518133848/http://www.winnieinternet.com/games/war2/reports/SypherHistory.htm

Taito. (1978). *Space invaders* [Arcade video game]. Shinjuku, Tokyo, Japan: Taito.

Tamborini, R., & Skalski, P. (2006). The role of presence in the experience of electronic games. In P. Vorderer & J. Bryant (Eds.), *Playing video game: Motives, responses, and consequences* (pp. 225–240). Mahwah, NJ: LEA.

Tassi, P. (2014, January 27). Riot's '*league of legends*' reveals astonishing 27 million daily players, 67 million monthly. *Forbes*. Retrieved October 12, 2015, from http://www.forbes.com

Taylor, T. L. (2009). *Play between worlds: Exploring online game culture*. London: MIT Press.

Taylor, T. L. (2012). *Raising the stakes: E-sports and the professionalization of computer gaming*. Cambridge: The MIT Press.

Team Ico. (2005). Shadow of the colossus [PlayStation 2 video game]. Minato, Tokyo, Japan: Sony Computer Entertainment.

Team Meat. (2010). *Super meat boy* [Xbox 360, Windows video game]. Team Meat.

Team Ninja. (2003). *Dead or alive: Extreme volleyball* [Xbox video game]. Tokyo, Japan: Tecmo.

Tecmo & Grasshopper Manufacture. (2001-2014). *Fatal Frame* [PS 2 video game series]. Kyoto, Japan: Nintendo.

Telltale Games. (2012). *The walking dead* [PlayStation 3/Xbox 360 video game]. San Rafael, CA: Telltale Games.

Terlecki, M. S., Newcombe, N. S., & Little, M. (2008). Durable and generalized effects of spatial experience on mental rotation: Gender differences in growth patterns. *Applied Cognitive Psychology*, *22*(7), 996–1013. doi:10.1002/acp.1420

thatgamecompany. (2009). *Flower* [PlayStation 3 video game]. Minato, Tokyo, Japan: Sony Computer Entertainment.

Thatgamecompany. (2009). *Flower* [PS3, PS4, PSVita game]. Los Angeles, CA: Sony Computer Entertainment.

thatgamecompany. (2012). *Journey* [PlayStation 3 video game]. Minato, Tokyo, Japan: Sony Computer Entertainment.

Thatgamecompany. (2012). *Journey* [PS 3 video game]. Minato, Tokyo, Japan: Sony Computer Entertainment.

Thatgamecompany. (2012). *Journey* [PS3, PS4 game]. Los Angeles, CA: Sony Computer Entertainment.

thatgamecompany. (2012). *Journey*. Retrieved April 19, 2012, from thatgamecompany.com: http://thatgamecompany.com/games/journey/

The Astronauts. (2014). *The vanishing of Ethan Carter* [Windows video game]. The Astronauts.

The Chinese Room, & SCE Santa Monica Studio. (2015). *Everybody's gone to the rapture* [PlayStation 4 video game]. Minato, Tokyo, Japan: Sony Computer Entertainment.

The Chinese Room. (2012). *Dear Esther* [Windows, OS X video game]. Brighton, United Kingdom: The Chinese Room.

The Chinese Room. (2015). Everybody's Gone to the Rapture [PS 4 video game]. Minato, Tokyo, Japan: Sony Computer Entertainment.

The elder scrolls V: Skyrim [Computer Software]. (2011). Rockville, MD: Bethesda.

The Fullbright Company. (2013). *Gone Home* [PC video game]. Portland, Oregon: The Fullbright Company.

The Giant Beastcast. (2015, August 28). *The giant beastcast: Episode 14* [Audio podcast]. Retrieved from http://www.giantbomb.com/podcasts/download/1332/ep14_thegiantbeastcast-08-28-2015-3863808300.mp3

The Giant Beastcast. (2015, August). *The Giant Beastcast - Episode 14*. Retrieved from http://www.giantbomb.com/podcasts/download/1332/ep14_thegiantbeastcast-08-28-2015-3863808300.mp3

The sims 4 [Computer Software]. (2014). Redwood City, CA: Maxis.

Thompson, C. (2002). Violence and the political life of videogames. In L. King (Ed.), Game on: The history and culture of videogames (pp. 22-31). London: Laurence King Publishing Ltd.

Thornham, H. (2011). *Ethnographies of the Videogame: Gender, Narrative and Praxis*. New York, NY: Ashgate Press.

Tiltfactor. (2009). *Layoff* [Flash game]. Hanover, NH: Tiltfactor. Retrieved July 8, 2015, from http://tiltfactor.org/play-layoff

Timbre Interactive. (2015). *Sentris* [Linux/Microsoft Windows/OS X/Ouya/PlayStation 4 video game]. Seattle, WA: Timbre Interactive.

Tobatabai, D., & Shore, B. M. (2005). How experts and novices search the Web. *Library & Information Science Research*, *27*(2), 222–248. doi:10.1016/j.lisr.2005.01.005

tobyfox. (2015). *Undertale* [Microsoft Windows/OS X video game]. tobyfox.

Tondello, G. (2015). *The use of games and play to achieve real-world goals*. Gamification Research Network. Retrieved from http://gamification-research.org/2015/06/the-use-of-games-and-play-to-achieve-real-world-goals/#sthash.7IZaAkdn.dpuf/

Totals | Freerice.com. (2015). Retrieved July 10, 2015, from http://freerice.com/frmisc/totals

Totilo, S. (2015, March 3). *He saw her face - Why we still love metroid prime* [Web log post]. Retrieved from http://kotaku.com/he-saw-her-face-why-we-still-love-metroid-prime-1691270398

Treyarch. (2013). *Call of Duty: Black Ops II* [PC, PS3, Xbox 360, Wii U video game]. Santa Monica, CA: Activision.

Triada Studio Games. (2015). *Shadowmatic* [IOS video game]. Triada Studio Games.

Triggs, T. (2006). Scissors and glue: Punk fanzines and the creation of a DIY aesthetic. *Journal of Design History*, *19*(1), 69–83. doi:10.1093/jdh/epk006

Tripp, S. (1998, Spring). On a wing and a prayer. *BYU Magazine*. Retrieved from magazine.byu.edu

Tucker, A. (2012). The art of video games. *Smithsonian Magazine*. Retrieved 15 December, 2015, from http://www.smithsonianmag.com/arts-culture/the-art-of-video-games-101131359/?no-ist]

Tucker, A. (2012, March). *The art of video games*. Retrieved March 28, 2016, from http://www.smithsonianmag.com/arts-culture/the-art-of-video-games-101131359/

Tudor, A. (1997). Why horror? The peculiar pleasures of a popular genre. *Cultural Studies*, *11*(3), 443–463. doi:10.1080/095023897335691

Turi, T. (13 Feb. 2012). *Dear Esther: A haunting indie story worth listening to.* Retrieved 15 December, 2015, from http://www.gameinformer.com/games/dear_esther/b/pc/ archive/2012/02/13/a-haunting-indie-story-worth-listening-to.aspx

Turkle, S. (1997). *Life on the screen: Identity in the age of the Internet.* New York, NY: Simon & Schuster.

Twitch. (2016, April 5). *Twitch.* Retrieved April 5, 2016, from https://www.twitch.tv/

Twitch.tv. (2015). Retrieved July 15, 2015, from http://www.twitch.tv/

TwitchPlaysPokémon. (2016, April 5). *Twitch plays pokémon.* Retrieved April 5, 2016, from http://www.twitch.tv/twitchplayspokemon

Ubisoft Montpellier. (1995). *Rayman* [PlayStation (et al.) video game]. Montpellier, France: Ubisoft.

Ubisoft Montpellier. (2006). *Rayman Raving Rabbids* [Nintendo Wii (et al.) video game]. Montpellier, France: Ubisoft.

Ubisoft Montreal. , (2003). *Prince of Persia: The sands of time* [Playstation 2, Xbox, GameCube video game]. Montral, Canada: Ubisoft.

Ubisoft Montreal,. (2014). *Far cry 4* [Windows, PS3, PS4, XBox 360, XBox One video game]. Montreuil, France: Ubisoft.

Ubisoft Motion Pictures. (2013). *Rabbids Invasion* [Television series]. Montreuil, France: Ubisoft.

Ukieri.org. (2015). *UKIERI: UK-India Education and Research Initiative.* Retrieved 1 November 2015, from http://www.ukieri.org/program-background.html

United Nations High Commission on Refugees. (2005). *Against All Odds* [Flash game]. UNHCR. Retrieved 10 August 2015 from http://www.playagainstallodds.ca/ game_us.html

United Nations High Commission on Refugees. (2012). My Life As a Refugee [iOS, Android]. Genève: UNHCR.

United Nations World Food Programme. (2007). *Free Rice* [Browser game]. UNWFP. Retrieved September 20, 2015 from http://freerice.com

United Nations. Human Rights. (2015). *World programme for human rights education.* Retrieved December 18, 2015, from http://www.ohchr.org/EN/Issues/Education/Training/Pages/Programme.aspx

United States Department of Education. (2015). *Science, technology, engineering and math: Education for global leadership.* Retrieved from http://www.ed.gov/stem

Unity Technologies. (2015). *Unity Manual.* Retrieved from http://docs.unity3d.com/Manual/index.html

Unity3d.com. (2012). *Zines, screens, and all in betweens.* Retrieved 28 December, 2015, from https://unity3d.com/showcase/case-stories/arcanekids-zineth

Ustwo. (2014). *Monument Valley* [iOS game]. New York, NY: Ustwo.

Ustwo. (2014). *Monument valley* [IOS, Android video game]. Ustwo.

Uttal, D. H., Meadow, N. G., Tipton, E., Hand, L. L., Alden, A. R., Warren, C., & Newcombe, N. S. (2013). The malleability of spatial skills: A meta-analysis of training studies. *Psychological Bulletin, 139*(2), 352–402. doi:10.1037/a0028446 PMID:22663761

Uttal, D. H., Miller, D. I., & Newcombe, N. S. (2013). Exploring and enhancing spatial thinking links to achievement in science, technology, engineering, and mathematics? *Current Directions in Psychological Science, 22*(5), 367–373. doi:10.1177/0963721413484756

Vagle, M. D. (2010, May). *A post-intentional phenomenological research approach.* Paper presented at the American Educational Research Association, Denver, CO.

Valentine, K. D. (2014). *Problematizing space and perspective: A middle school mathematics experience* (Doctoral dissertation, The University of Georgia). Retrieved from The University of Georgia Library Electronic Theses and Dissertations. (Record No. 13472).

Valkenberg, P. M., & Peter, J. (2013). Five challenges for the future of media-effects research. *International Journal of Communication, 7,* 197-215. doi: 1932-8036/2013FEA0002

Valve. (1998). *Half Life* [PC game]. Bellevue: Valve.

Valve. (1998). *Half-life.* Sierra Entertainment.

Valve. (1999). *Counter-strike.* Valve Corporation.

Valve. (2007). *Portal* [PlayStation 3 (et al.) video game]. Bellevue, WA: Valve Corporation.

Valve, L. L. C. (1998). *Half-Life* [PC video game]. Fresno, CA: Sierra Entertainment.

Van Ditmarsch, J. (2013). *Video games as a spectator sport.* Thesis.

Van Eck, R. (2006). Digital game based learning: It's not just the digital natives who are restless. *EDUCAUSE Review, 41,* 16–30. Retrieved from http://net.educause.edu/ir/library/pdf/erm0620.pdf

van Manen, M. (1990). *Researching lived experience: Human science for an action sensitive pedagogy.* Albany, NY: State University of New York Press.

Van Roessel, L. (2014). *Do Apple's policies impede the growth of serious games?* Retrieved July 7, 2015, from http://policyreview.info/articles/news/do-apples-policies-impede-growth-serious-games/305

Vecerova, V. (2015). *Body Teaser* [interactive sculpture].

Venturelli, M., & Studio, K. (2009). *Space of possibility and pacing in casual game design–A Pop Cap case study.* Paper presented at VII Brazilian Symposium on Games and Digital Entertainment, Rio de Janeriro. Retrieved from http://www.sbgames.org/papers/sbgames09/artanddesign/60345.pdf

Vermeer, D. (2014, October 25). *The decline of women in computer science* [Web log post]. Retrieved from http://daniellelvermeer.com/blog/women-computer-science

Verve. (1997). Bitter sweet symphony. On *Urban Hymns* [CD]. London: Hut Records.

Vidler, A. (1999). *The architectural uncanny: Essays in the modern unhomely.* London: MIT Press.

Vogel, J. J., Greenwood-Ericksen, A., Cannon-Bowers, J., & Bowers, C. A. (2006). Using virtual reality with and without gaming attributes for academic achievement. *Journal of Research on Technology in Education, 39*(1), 105–118. doi:10.1080/15391523.2006.10782475

Vygotsky, L. S. (1966). *Play and its role in the mental development of the child* (C. Mulholland, Trans.). (Original work published in 1933). Retrieved from the Psychology and Marxism Internet ArchiveWeb site: www.marxists.org/archive/vygotsky/works/1933/play.htm

Wagner, M. (2007). Identitätsrückprojektion in aktiven Medien. Wann können Computerspiele unser reales Verhalten beeinflussen? *E-Beratungsjournal.net, 3*(2). Retrieved from http://www.e-beratungsjournal.net/ausgabe_0207/wagner.pdf

Wagner, M. G. (2006, January). On the scientific relevance of eSports. In *Proceedings of the 2006 International Conference on Internet Computing & Conference on Computer Games Development, ICOMP 2006*, (pp. 437-442).

Wagner, R. (2014). The importance of playing in earnest. In H. A. Campbell & G. P. Grieve (Eds.), *Playing with Religion in Digital Games* (pp. 192–213). Bloomington, IN: Indiana University Press.

Wai, J., Lubinski, D., & Benbow, C. P. (2009). Spatial ability for STEM domains: Aligning over 50 years of cumulative psychological knowledge solidifies its importance. *Journal of Educational Psychology, 101*(4), 817–835. doi:10.1037/a0016127

Walker, A. (2015, April 3). *Three Fourths Home: Extended Edition Review*. Retrieved January 14, 2016, from http://www.gamespot.com/reviews/three-fourths-home-extended-edition-review/1900-6416087/

Walkerdine, V. (2007). *Children, gender, video games: Toward a relational approach to multimedia*. New York: Palgrave MacMillan. doi:10.1057/9780230235373

Walz, S. P., & Deterding, S. (2014). *The gameful world. Approaches, issues, applications*. Cambridge, MA: MIT Press.

Wanzek, J., Vaughn, S., Wexler, J., Swanson, E. A., Edmonds, M., & Kim, A.-H. (2006). A synthesis of spelling and reading interventions and their effects on the spelling outcomes of students with LD. *Journal of Learning Disabilities, 39*(6), 528–543. doi:10.1177/00222194060390060501 PMID:17165620

Wardrip-Fruin, N., & Harrigan, P. (Eds.). (2004). *First person: New media as story, performance, and game*. Cambridge, MA: MIT Press.

Wark, M. (2009). *Gamer theory*. Cambridge, MA: Harvard University Press.

Warner, M. (2014). *Once Upon a Time: A Short History of Fairy Tale*. Oxford: Oxford University Press.

Warren, S. J., Stein, R. A., Dondlinger, M. J., & Barab, S. A. (2009). A look inside a MUVE design process: Blending instructional design and game principles to target writing skills. *Journal of Educational Computing Research, 40*(3), 295–321. doi:10.2190/EC.40.3.c

Waugh, P. (2013). *Metafiction*. Routledge.

Webster, A. (2014, April 3). Explore the impossible architecture of '*Monument Valley*'. *The Verge*. Retrieved from http://www.theverge.com/2014/4/3/5573812/monument-valley-mc-escher-ipad-game

Webster, A. (2016, February 19). *Video game stories don't have to suck | The Verge*. Retrieved March 5, 2016, from http://www.theverge.com/2016/2/19/11056794/video-game-storytelling-writing-firewatch-the-witcher

West Virginia Department of Education. (2015). *Eighth grade science objectives*. Retrieved from http://wveis.k12.wv.us/Teach21/public/cso/popUp.cfm

Wetcoast Games. (2006). *Homeless: It's No Game* [Flash game]. Wetcoast Games. Retrieved 10 February 2014 from http://www.wetcoastgames.ca/homeless/homeless.swf

Wild, K. et al. (2004). *Escape from Woomera* [PC game].

Williams, D., Martins, N., Consalvo, M., & Ivory, J. (2009). The virtual census: Representations of gender, race and age in video games. *New Media & Society, 11*(5), 815–834. doi:10.1177/1461444809105354

Williams, R. (1976). *Keywords: A vocabulary of culture and society*. London: Fontana.

Williams, R. (1996). *Roberta Williams' Anthology* [DOS video game]. Fresno, CA: Sierra Online.

Wilson, B. (2006). Why America's disadvantaged communities need twenty-first century learning. *New Directions for Youth Development, 110*, 47-54.

Wilson, C. (2015, April 9). *Against "indie": New albums from Modest Mouse, Sufjan Stevens, and more show it's time to eliminate the racist term for good.* Retrieved from http://www.slate.com/articles/arts/music_box/2015/04/against_indie_new_albums_from_modest_mouse_sufjan_stevens_and_more_show.html

Wilson, D. (2011). *Johann Sebastian Joust* [video game].

Wilson, B., & Cole, P. (1992). A critical review of elaboration theory. *Educational Technology Research and Development, 40*(3), 63–79. doi:10.1007/BF02296843

Wilson, K. A., Bedwell, W. L., Lazzara, E. H., Salas, E., Burke, C. S., Estock, J. L., & Conkey, C. et al. (2009). Relationships between game attributes and learning outcomes: Review and research proposals. *Simulation & Gaming, 40*(2), 217–266. doi:10.1177/1046878108321866

Winn, W. (2002). Current trends in educational technology research: The study of learning environments. *Educational Psychology Review, 14*(3), 331–351. doi:10.1023/A:1016068530070

Witkowski, E. (2012). On the digital playing field: How we "do sport" with networked computer games. *Games and Culture, 7*(5), 349–374. doi:10.1177/1555412012454222

Wolf, M. J. P. (2002). *The medium of the video game.* Austin, TX: University of Texas.

Wolonick, J. (2013). *The* Half the Sky *movement: Is a Facebook game the next step toward global social justice?* Retrieved July 10, 2015, from http://www.minyanville.com/sectors/media/articles/Half-the-Sky-Movement253A-Improving-Foreign/3/12/2013/id/48644?refresh=1

Women in Games International. (2015). *Home.* Retrieved from http://wigigsprogram.org/

Wong, K. C. (2010). Interpretation of correlation coefficients. *Hong Kong Medical Journal, 16*(3), 237. PMID:20519766

Wood, W. (2014). *Curse of Play* [physical game].

Woolf, N. (2014, December 3). *Star Citizen* sets crowdfunding record as players spend $65m on spaceships. *The Guardian.* Retrieved from http://www.theguardian.com/technology/2014/dec/03/star-citizen-crowd-funding-record-65m-game

Woolgar, S. (1986). On the alleged distinction between discourse and praxis. *Social Studies of Science, 16*(2), 309–317. doi:10.1177/030631278601600200006

World Food Programme. (2005). *Food Force* [PC game].

World of Warcraft [Computer Software]. (2004). Irvine, CA: Blizzard Entertainment.

Wreden, D. (2011). *The Stanley parable* [Computer Software]. Austin, TX: Galactic Café.

Wright, W. (1984). *Raid on Bungeling Bay* [Commodore 64 video game]. Eugene, OR: Brøderbund.

Xu, Y., Park, H., & Baek, Y. (2011). A new approach toward digital storytelling: An activity focused on writing self-efficacy in a virtual learning environment. *Journal of Educational Technology & Society, 14*(4), 181–191.

Yacht Club Games. (2014). *Shovel knight* [Windows, Nintendo 3DS, Nintendo Wii U, OS X, Linux video game]. Valencia, CA: Yacht Club Games.

Yarouze, G., & Studio, J. (2008). Echochrome [PS3, PSPortable, PSStore video game]. Minato, Tokyo, Japan: Sony Computer Entertainment.

Yin, R. (1994). *Case study research: Design and methods* (2nd ed.). Thousand Oaks, CA: Sage Publications.

York Zimmerman Inc. (2010). *People Power: The Game of Civil Resistance.* Washington, DC: York Zimmerman Inc.

Young Horses. (2014). *Octodad: Dadliest catch* [Microsoft Windows/OS X/Linux video game]. Young Horses.

Young, N. (2015, January 17). Why empathy is the next big thing in video games. *Spark.* CBC. Retrieved from http://www.cbc.ca/radio/spark/286-empathy-games-intangible-art-and-more-1.3073000/why-empathy-is-the-next-big-thing-in-video-games-1.3074676

Yuke's Media Creations. (2004). Berserk [PlayStation 2 video game]. Minato, Tokyo: Sammy Corporation.

Zackariasson, P., & Wilson, T. L. (2012). Marketing of video games. In P. Zackariasson & T. L. Wilson (Eds.), *The video game industry: Formation, present state, and future* (pp. 57–75). New York, NY: Routledge.

Zacny, R. (2014). *The uneasy brilliance of "This War of Mine".* Retrieved July 9, 2015, from http://www.pcgamesn.com/this-war-of-mine/the-uneasy-brilliance-of-this-war-of-mine

Zichermann, G., & Cunningham, C. (2011). *Gamification by design: Implementing game mechanics in web and mobile apps.* Sebastopol, CA: O'Reilly Media, Inc.

Zimmerman, E. (2012, February 7). *Jerked around by the magic circle - Clearing the air ten years later.* Retrieved March 28, 2016, from http://www.gamasutra.com/view/feature/135063/jerked_around_by_the_magic_circle_.php

Zimmerman, L. (2009). *2008 U.S. presidential election: Persuasive YouTube interactions about war, health care and the economy.* (Unpublished Master's Thesis). Georgia State University, Atlanta, GA.

Zimmerman, E. (2004). Narrative, interactivity, play, and games: Four naughty concepts in need of discipline. In N. Wardrip-Fruin & P. Harrigan (Eds.), *First person: New media as story, performance, and game* (pp. 154–164). Cambridge, MA: MIT Press.

Zineth [Computer Software]. (2012). Los Angeles: Arcane Kids. Available from http://zinethgame.tumblr.com/

Zipes, J. (2012). *The Irresistable Fairy Tale. Woodstock.* Princeton University Press.

Zizek, S. (2002). Big Brother, or, the triumph of the gaze over the eye. In T. Y. Levin, U. Frohne, & P. Weibel (Eds.), Ctrl space: Rhetorics of surveillance from Bentham to Big Brother (pp. 224-227). Cambridge, MA: MIT Press.

About the Contributors

Keri Valentine is an Assistant Professor of Mathematics Education in the department of Curriculum and Instruction at West Virginia University's College of Education and Human Services. In addition to her role in the Mathematics Education program, she contributes to (Science, Technology, Engineering, Art, Mathematics) STEAM education transdisciplinary research endeavors as part of the WVU Center for Excellence in STEM Education. She earned her Ph.D. in Learning, Design, and Technology at The University of Georgia in 2014 where she conducted both design-based and postphenomenological research projects. One project includes designing a middle school mathematics learning environment integrating cases as alternative perspective with the goal of conveying complex relationships during the process of learning mathematics (see Space and Perspective http://spaceandperspective.com/). Her research is motivated by phenomenological questions that seek to understand how learning (especially shifts in perspective) manifests, especially related to complex spatial phenomenon. Recently, Keri collaborated with co-editor, Dr. Lucas Jensen, to both design, teach, and investigate summer game design camps for grades 5-12 learners, seeking to understand the design practices of young learners in these informal spaces. In addition to investigating learning and the design of formal and informal learning spaces, she also contributes to the field of qualitative inquiry, such as considering new ways we might conceptualize reflexive practice in living inquiry research.

Lucas John Jensen is an Assistant Professor of Instructional Technology in the department of Leadership, Technology, and Human Development at Georgia Southern University. He has a B.A. in Political Science from Mississippi State University as well as two M.Eds from the University of Georgia in Social Science Education and Instructional Design and Development. For his Ph.D research in Learning, Design, and Technology at the University of Georgia he studied the use of Twitter hashtags in the classroom. His research interests include video game design in education, motivating online students, and instructional social media usage. Lucas has taught educational media development, innovative technology usage, instructional design, and visual literacy. He also cooked crawfish in a gas station in Mississippi for a while. For the past seven years, he has been an instructor and counselor for a series of design-based summer and after-school youth programs dedicated to video game design electronic and hip-hop music, creative entrepreneurship, tabletop and role-playing games, among other subjects. Before coming to academia and education, Lucas worked for over a decade as a music industry professional, primarily in publicity and public relations. He has been playing video games since 1979 and has no intention of stopping. His favorite game of all time is *Super Metroid*.

* * *

Terence C. Ahern is an Associate Professor in Instructional Design and Technology in the College of Education and Human Resources at West Virginia University. He coordinates the Instructional Design and Technology program in the Department of Learning Sciences and Human Development. His research interests are in the design, development and the deployment of instructional technology in the classroom. Additionally, he is interested in the intersection between learning and instruction. He has published extensively in the areas of distance education, social network media and innovative software apps. Currently, he is using his expertise in instructional design and software development to create game-based learning environments for the middle school classroom.

Christine J. Anderson, PhD, has 15 years of teaching experience (K-12), specifically instructing students with disabilities. She received a Bachelor of Arts from Charleston Southern University, a Master of Arts from the University of South Florida, and a doctorate from the University of Iowa. At the university level, Dr. Anderson has worked at Arizona State University, the University of Iowa, and is currently an Associate Professor in the Curriculum and Instruction Department at Western Illinois University where she also serves as the Graduate Special Education Coordinator. Her research interests include the benefits of art for individuals with disabilities; educational technology, specifically as it relates to teacher preparation and training; and effective interventions for individuals with behavior disorders including the population identified as juvenile offenders. She and her husband are the parents of six children and the grandparents of eight.

Sandy Baldwin is Associate Professor of English at the Rochester of Technology. He is author or editor of eleven books, including *The Internet Unconscious* (Bloomsbury), winner of the 2015 N. Katherine Hayles prize for criticism. He is vice president of the Electronic Literature Organization; Managing Editor of *Electronic Book Review*, one of the oldest all-online peer-reviewed journals; and editor in chief of the *Computing Literature* book series, the only academic book series focused on electronic literature. He has received numerous externally-funded grants, including several to study the culture of video games. In addition, he makes hybrid performance/mod/game hacks that have been shown and exhibited at conferences and art galleries around the world.

Daisyane Barreto is an Assistant Professor of Instructional Technology at the University of North Carolina at Wilmington (UNCW). Dr Barreto has worked for educational organizations and corporations as a multimedia developer, instructional designer, and educational game consultant. Her interests involve game-based learning, technology integration, and multimedia design and production.

Nick Bowman (Ph.D., Michigan State University) is Associate Professor of Communication Studies at West Virginia University. His primary research focuses on how people use and interact with communication technologies, including social media and video games. He has published over four dozen research articles and presented over 100 conference papers at regional, national, and international associations. He maintains an active research agenda in the United States, Germany, and Taiwan, and serves on the editorial board of several journals such as *Media Psychology* and the *Psychology of Popular Media Culture*.

Tobias Conradi is a postdoctoral researcher at ZeM – Brandenburgisches Zentrum für Medienwissenschaften in Potsdam. He received his PhD in media studies from the Universität Paderborn, where he held a scholarship with the Graduiertenkolleg Automatismen. His research focuses on the connection between crisis, critique and decisions, the politics of representation, and the history of games and play. His recent publications include *Breaking News. Automatismen in der Repräsentation von Krisen- und Katastrophenereignissen* (Paderborn: Wilhelm Fink, 2015) and (Ed. with Florian Hoof, Rolf F. Nohr) *Medien der Entscheidung* (Münster, Lit 2016).

Steven Conway is a convener and lecturer in the area of Games & Interactivity at Swinburne University of Technology. Steven received his doctorate from the University of Bedfordshire in 2010 on an Arts Humanities Research Council National Award Scholarship. He is interested in the philosophical principles underlying play and games, and his research investigates object relations and aesthetics of games, play and sport across all media. He is co-editor with Jennifer deWinter of *Video Game Policy: Production, Distribution, and Consumption*, which was published by Routledge in 2015. It is the sixth book in the Routledge Advances in Game Studies series.

Carolyn M. Cunningham is an Assistant Professor in the Masters Program in Communication and Leadership Studies Program at Gonzaga University, where she teaches classes in social media, multimedia, communication theory, and women and leadership. She received her PhD from the Department of Radio-Television-Film at the University of Texas at Austin. Her research explores the intersections of gender and technology, with a specific focus on girls. She is the editor of *Social Networking and Impression Management* (Lexington Books, 2012). Her work also has been published in several journals, including *New Media & Society* and the *Journal of Children and Media*.

Jennifer deWinter is an Associate Professor of Rhetoric and faculty in the Interactive Media and Game Development program at Worcester Polytechnic Institute. She teaches courses on game studies, game design, and game production and management. She has published on the convergence of anime, manga, and computer games both in their Japanese contexts and in global markets. Her work has appeared in numerous journals and edited collections, and her recent book, *Shigeru Miyamoto: Super Mario Bros., Donkey Kong, The Legend of Zelda* (Bloomsbury), is the first published in the Influential Game Designer book series. She is also the editor of *Videogames* (Fountainhead), and co-editor of *Computer Games and Technical Communication: Critical Methods and Applications at the Intersection* (Ashgate) and *Video Game Policy: Production, Distribution, and Consumption* (Routledge).

Angela Dowling has a Master's in Secondary Education and a Doctorate of Education in Instructional Design and Technology from West Virginia University. She is also an adjunct faculty member at West Virginia University and has taught 8th grade Science at Suncrest Middle School in Morgantown, West Virginia for 19 years. Angela has written and presented at state and national conferences on the various uses of technology in the science classroom. Her current research involves the use of game-like curriculum design and its effect on student achievement, engagement, and motivation. Angela currently resides in Grafton, West Virginia and can be reached at adowling@.k12.wv.us or adowlingsms@gmail.com.

Jason A. Engerman is a Ph.D. candidate in the Learning, Design and Technologies program, at The Pennsylvania State University. His research interests focuses on the interactions between disenfranchised populations and their sociocultural uses of digital media (such as video games) within their native learning ecologies. In particular Jason investigates how disenfranchised populations use indigenous knowledge to impact educational reform efforts. His boys and gaming research focuses on the learning impact of video games within boy culture. He is involved with the Bring Back the Boys Initiative that seeks to re-engage boys back into classroom settings. Jason interviews established scholars and thought leaders in both games based learning and masculinity. This work gives insight on boy development for parents, researchers and instructional designers. Jason is also in involved in non-profit organizational leadership. He is one of the directors of Designers for Learning. This virtual service-learning platform supports graduate student instructional designers by helping them to connect with non-profit organizations. The student instructional designers gain authentic learning experience while addressing client needs. Soon this platform will evolve to a MOOC platform.

Jorge Cardoso Filho is a Professor of Universidade Federal do Recôncavo da Bahia - UFRB and of the Programa de Pós-Graduação em Comunicação e Cultura Contemporâneas - PosCóm, UFBA

Sonja Gabriel is deputy head of Research & Development at University College of Teacher Education Vienna/Krems, doing research on digital media and game-based learning. She received her Ph.D. at PH Weingarten in Germany with her thesis on knowledge management at secondary schools. Sonja also garnered a Master's from Danube University Krems in Austria in Applied Game Science abnd another in Education Media from University Duisberg/Essen. Her bachelor's work in German and English was conducted the University Vienna in Austria.

Spencer P. Greenhalgh is a PhD candidate in the Educational Psychology and Educational Technology program at Michigan State University. He holds a BA in French Teaching from Brigham Young University, where he also taught undergraduate-level French and participated in organizations promoting the study of the humanities. Prior to beginning his graduate work, he taught French, debate, and keyboarding at the secondary level. He has worked with Michigan State University's Master of Arts in Educational Technology program and with MSU's Residential College in the Arts and Humanities. His research focuses on the use of games in education and the application of Internet research methods to educational inquiry. A summary and updates of his work can be found at spencergreenhalgh.com.

Chris Hanson completed a BA in Media Studies at Carleton College, worked for a number of years in video game and software development, and later assisted with the planning and production of an educational series and content for PBS. Chris returned to academia in Los Angeles and received his MA and PhD in Critical Studies at the University of Southern California School of Cinematic Arts, where his dissertation focused on replay and repetition in video games, television, and avant-garde film. Chris has been a HASTAC Scholar (Humanities, Arts, Science, and Technology Advanced Collaboratory) and his work has appeared in *Film Quarterly*, *Spectator*, and *Discourse*.

Robert James Hein is a former High School English teacher and competitive gamer. He has taught literature, poetry, and creative writing both aboard in Dublin, Ireland and domestically. Between 2006 and 2011, he traveled the east coast of the United States participating in e-sports tournaments and building relationships with fellow gamers. Robert is currently interested in researching narrative-driven video games and student literacy skills. He still enjoys playing *World of Warcraft* in his free time… and when he should be doing work instead.

Stephanie C. Jennings is a graduate student in the Department of Communication and Media at Rensselaer Polytechnic Institute. She researches video games and games criticism, with interests in player subjectivity, player agency, and feminist theory. Lately, she has been particularly preoccupied with examining the survival-horror and roguelike genres. Jennings's other writings have focused on developing subjective methods of games criticism. Currently, her work has specifically come to center on gender performance through acts of play, feminine subject positions in games, and resistant play. She has previously been published in the *Journal of Games Criticism* and has contributed to *Critical Distance* and *Cyborgology*.

John Jones is an Assistant Professor of Professional Writing and Editing in the Department of English at West Virginia University. His research addresses the impact of tools, particularly digital tools, on writing and other communication practices. His previous work examined the revision patterns of Wikipedia contributors, how Twitter users create ad hoc networks on the social media site, and the influence of networks on writing and rhetorical practices. His most recent research has appeared in *Computers and Composition*, *Kairos*, and the *Journal of Business and Technical Communication*, and he is now working on a collaborative project studying the rhetorical aspects of wearable technologies, from activity monitors to medical monitoring devices.

Laura Kieran has 17 years (K-12) teaching experience, 14 of which has been in Special Education settings. In her last 3 years in K-12 settings she was the assistive technology coordinator for Duluth Public Schools in Duluth, MN. She has taught at the university level for Concordia College, Western Illinois University, and is currently an Assistant Professor at Drake University. Her research interests include Universal Design for Learning, the application of assistive and instructional technologies, and increasing social justice for marginalized populations in education. Toward this end, she has recently begun research in South Africa with faculty at the University of KwaZulu Natal in Durban, SA.

Carly A. Kocurek is Assistant Professor of Digital Humanities and Media Studies and Director of Digital Humanities at the Illinois Institute of Technology. She is cofounder and co-editor of the Influential Game Designers book series (Bloomsbury). Her book, *Coin-Operated Americans: Rebooting Boyhood at the Video Game Arcade* (University of Minnesota Press, 2015) excavates the early cultural history of coin-op video games in the United States. Her work has appeared in journals such as *Game Studies*, *The Journal of Gaming and Virtual Worlds*, and *Visual Studies*, and in anthologies including *Before the Crash: An Anthology of Early Video Game History* (Wayne State University Press, 2012), *Technical Communication and Computer Games* (Ashgate, 2014), and *Debugging Game History: A Critical Lexicon* (The MIT Press, Forthcoming), among others. She is also a game designer, and her interactive fiction game *Choice: Texas* (2014) was called one of the best games of 2014 by *Paste Magazine*.

Marley-Vincent Lindsey is a graduate student in the History Department of Brown University. He is primarily focused on royal grants of land and labor in sixteenth-century New Spain and the Caribbean and the influence of such grants on the development of modern ideas about race and gender. He is also interested in extending historical analysis to digital culture and continually working on ways to make the discipline more accessible. Currently, he is working on a manuscript on the ways that the Internet and digital consciousness transform the production of knowledge in the twenty-first century. He received his undergraduate degree form the University of Chicago in 2014. He is best contacted on Twitter: @ MarleyVincentL.

Ken S. McAllister specializes in the early history of Western rhetorics, rhetorics of technology, and computer game studies. He has authored or co-authored six books, three edited collections, and dozens of articles and book chapters on media history, theory, and analysis. In his role as Co-Director of the Learning Games Initiative Research Archive he has also published and lectured widely on the politics and processes of digital artifact archiving and preservation. Ken is currently serving as the Associate Dean of Research and Program Innovation in the College of Humanities, is Co-Chair of the Research Computing Governance Council's Data Visualization Committee, and is a founding partner of the UA iSpace, a campus-located maker lab accessible to all students, staff, and faculty interested in exploring immersive VR, augmented reality, 3D modeling and additive manufacturing, motion capture, Arduino and Raspberry Pi development, and other innovative tools for transdisciplinary scholars and teachers.

Kevin Moberly is an Associate Professor of Rhetoric, Digital Media, and Game Studies at Old Dominion University in Norfolk, Virginia. His research focuses on understanding how computer-enabled manifestations of popular culture reflect, contribute to, and transform contemporary cultural and political discourses. In particular, he is interested in the way that contemporary computer games encode labor, often blurring already uneasy distinctions between work and play. He is currently working on a number of academic projects, including a book-length study about medieval-themed computer games, which he is co-authoring with his brother, Brent Moberly. His scholarship has been published in a wide variety of books and journals.

Hazel E. Monforton received her MSt in Women's Studies from the University of Oxford in 2012. In 2013 she began a PhD at the University of Durham in English studies, supervised by Patricia Waugh. Her thesis explores the depiction, consequence, and use of violence within women's writing, particularly the works of Virginia Woolf and Angela Carter. While she writes primarily on 20th century women's literature, she has a strong interest in emerging media and the creative capacity of video games. Despite her doctorate coming to a close, video games seem to take up more of her time than is strictly wise.

Randy Nichols is an Assistant Professor in the School of Interdisciplinary Arts and Sciences at the University of Washington Tacoma. His research focuses on the critical political economy of media, particularly the production of video games. He serves as an editor of the online journals *Eludamos: Journal of Computer Game Culture* and *The Political Economy of Communication*. He has written a number of chapters on the impact of the production of video games, as well as on the relationship between the game industry and other institutions including Hollywood film and the U.S. military. His book, *The Video Game Business*, was published in 2014 by the British Film Institute.

Rolf F. Nohr is Dean and Professor of Media Aesthetics and Culture at Hochschule für Bildende Künste Braunschweig. His research is focused on game studies, media theory, and critical discourse analysis. He was head of the research project Play Strategy: Steering Techniques and Strategic Action in Popular Computer Games (On the Example of Economic, Military, and Reconstruction Simulations), and currently heading a project on German business games (from 1950-1970) as cultural techniques. More information about the business games project can be found at www.strategiespielen.de. His most recent book is *"The cake is a lie!" Polyperspektivische Betrachtungen des Computerspiels am Beispiel von 'Portal'* (Münster: LIT, 2015).

Kwabena Opoku-Agyemang is a Doctoral Candidate at West Virginia University's English Department, where he teaches a selection of courses in Literature and Composition. He has an MPhil in Literature from the University of Ghana, as well as an MA in English Literature from West Virginia University. He is currently working on a dissertation that examines various intersections between electronic literature and African literature in the context of oral tradition, using Ghana as a focal point. His publications vary from social media through gaming in electronic literature to gender issues in African women's writing.

Marc A. Ouellette is an Assistant Professor of English at Old Dominion University. He is the managing editor of *Reconstruction: Studies in Contemporary Culture*, as well as co-editor with Jason Thompson (University of Wyoming) of *The Game Culture Reader* (Cambridge Scholars Publishing, 2013). He is widely published, and his work has appeared in *Game Studies, Eludamos: Journal for Computer Game Culture, TEXT Technology*, and elsewhere. He is also an award-winning educator in the fields of cultural, media, and gender studies, and serves on the editorial advisory board for *Dialogue: The Interdisciplinary Journal of Popular Culture and Pedagogy* (ISSN 2378-2323, ISSN 2378-2331).

Dibyadyuti Roy is a Doctoral Fellow and Instructor in the Department of English and Cultural Studies at West Virginia University, where he teaches courses in advanced literature and writing. He came to West Virginia by way of the University of Glasgow where he completed his M.Litt in Modern Literature, Theory and Culture. His dissertation project explores performances of masculinity within nuclear discourses and has led to him discovering the far-reaching effects of the atomic age on our daily existence. He has current and forthcoming publications on varied fields ranging from Video Game Studies to British Theater. Besides his scholarly pursuits, he particularly enjoys immersing himself and his students in the wondrous world of speculative fiction and fantasy literature.

Judd Ethan Ruggill is an Associate Professor of Computational Media at the University of Arizona. He co-directs the Learning Games Initiative, a transdisciplinary, inter-institutional research group that studies, teaches with, builds, and archives computer games. His essays have appeared in a variety of journals, anthologies, and periodicals, and his most recent book, which he co-authored with Ken S. McAllister (University of Arizona), is titled *Tempest: Geometries of Play* (University of Michigan Press, 2015).

Dawn Stobbart researches at Lancaster University's English Department, focusing on the way that videogames function as a carrier for narrative and its role within this medium. She has an interest in contemporary Literature, and especially the way this translates to the videogame. Within videogame studies, she has conducted research into Gothic fiction, Posthuman fiction, folklore, focusing on how videogames construct narratives for these genres. She is also interested in contemporary Gothic fiction.

Felippe Calazans Thomaz is a master and PhD student at the Programa de Pós-Graduação em Comunicação e Cultura Contemporâneas in the Federal University of Bahia - UFBA (Brazil). Among his research interests are Digital Games, Theory of Materialities, Perception, Presence, Experience and other topics concerning Game Studies, Communications and Philosophy. He is also a Professor at UNIFACS - Laureate International Universities and the director of Flip-o Video Lab company.

Harrington Weihl is a PhD student in English Literature at Northwestern University whose publications include an article on space and architecture in modernist fiction in *Studies in the Novel* and an article on the politics and form of MMOs in *The Journal of Gaming and Virtual Worlds*. His larger project will engage with representations of space – broadly construed – in modernist fiction and subsequent cultural production. He has an abiding interest the link between politics and aesthetics that undergirds his work.

William Zachary Wood received a Bachelor of Arts in East Asian Studies from Stanford University in 2007 and studied at Kyoto Seika University in Japan from 2010 to 2011 as a research student in the Story Manga Department. Since 2013 he has been conducting practical and theoretical research on festivals of games and play in the United States and Europe. He believes that having a practical understanding of play is crucial for researchers of games, play and playfulness, and he continues to explore play as an "open-ended playful experience designer." His other research interests include imagination, spirituality, the creative process, and collaborative creativity. Currently based in Berlin, Wood is not affiliated with any academic institution, and the research presented in this chapter was carried out independently.

Index

2Thread 193

A

AAA Video Games 341
Actions 4, 8-11, 15-16, 20-21, 37, 40, 42-43, 58-60, 65,
    67, 97-98, 110-111, 136, 139, 141, 143, 146, 177-
    179, 203-205, 208, 232, 251, 257, 275, 277, 290,
    310, 321, 332, 347, 349-351, 353, 359, 374-375
Adolescents 155, 260, 263, 272, 331
Aesthetic Experience 343-345, 349, 351, 354, 359
Affinity spaces 238-239, 241-242, 248
Affordance 226, 237, 249, 353-354
Analog Game 226, 232, 237
Anti-theory 95, 112
Arcane Kids 73-74, 83-86, 88-89
Art Games 380
Authorship 63, 123-128, 130-143, 146
Autoethnography 379

B

Baba Yaga 38, 42, 44, 48-50
Bangor University 364, 367, 371, 376
Bernie De Koven 393-394
bodily functions 344-345
Branching Narratives 319

C

Capitalism 25, 88-89, 106, 315, 373-374
Casual Games 248, 279, 347, 352
Censorship 134
Civic Engagement 150, 159, 164, 196
Cognitive Apprenticeships 239, 247, 249, 251-252
Collective Action 135
Come Out and Play 382-383
Commodification 95, 114, 121
Community of Play 395
Computer Games Across Cultures 364

Constraint 232, 237
Constructivism 149, 169
Crowdfunding 134
Cultural Contexts 157, 238, 372-374, 376
Cultural Rationales 159, 161-162, 169
Curriculum 149, 151, 220, 261-262, 273-275, 280,
    283, 300, 305, 308, 331, 369-370, 372

D

Democratic Rationales 148, 159-160, 162-164, 169
Design Model 308
Digital Communities 170, 174-175, 182, 186-188
Digital Game 129, 175, 195, 207, 217, 220, 232, 237,
    348-349, 359, 383, 393, 395-396
Digital Learning 262, 271
Digital Space 160, 174-176, 181-183, 186-188
Discipline 56, 64, 97, 105-106, 108-109, 111-112,
    116, 121, 188
Discourse 24, 64, 95-99, 106-109, 111, 113, 121, 124,
    126, 170-171, 174, 181-183, 185, 188, 368
Distributed Authorship 123-124, 132-134, 137-139,
    141-143, 146
Doom 15, 79, 170, 172, 176-177, 182, 286, 326-327
Doxxing 182, 193
Dramatis Personae 42-43, 45-46

E

Economic Rationales 148, 159-161, 163-164, 169
Educational Technology 219, 222-223, 232, 237, 262
Eighth Grade 292, 323
electronic games 237, 344, 347, 349-352, 355
Emergent Gaming 2, 10, 23
Emergent Narrative 128, 136, 142, 146
Empathy 24-27, 149, 196, 201, 203-204, 210-212, 217
E-Sports 2, 27-28, 170, 180, 238, 240-253, 255-256
Ethics Education 219-224, 228, 231-234, 237
Ethics Game 223, 228, 233, 237
Experimental Games 5, 73, 319

F

Festivals of Games and Play 377, 384-385, 387, 389-390, 392, 395
Fictional World 41, 55, 224-225
Film studies 61, 108
First-Year Writing 282-283
Flaming 193
Folklore 38-39, 49-50, 53
Formal Education 220-221, 237
Forums 49, 105, 133, 172, 174, 178, 180, 182, 187, 193, 241
Foucault 56-57, 62, 64, 90, 101, 110, 125-126, 132

G

Game Development 7, 12, 18-19, 26-27, 83, 99-100, 115, 129, 131, 310, 314, 317-319, 334, 377, 380, 382, 385, 387, 390, 393
Game Elements 195, 198, 201, 210-212, 306, 329, 346
Game Mechanics 1-4, 10, 12-13, 15, 23, 27, 54, 59, 199, 202-203, 212, 233, 279, 306, 308, 310, 315, 320, 383, 393
Game Players 98, 105, 152, 211, 220, 241, 283, 285, 347, 375
Game Studies 5, 95-99, 104-106, 108-110, 112-116, 121, 128, 174, 188, 347, 365
Game-like Design 304-305
Gamer 4, 18, 96-99, 101-104, 109-114, 116, 121, 140, 153-154, 175, 177, 197, 206, 241, 250-251, 266-267, 276, 283, 323, 326, 358-359, 387, 389
Games for Change 153, 195, 199, 217
Gaming 1-2, 4, 6, 10-11, 18, 23, 26-28, 38, 77, 97, 100, 106, 110, 115, 129, 138, 148, 153-155, 162, 164, 170, 174-175, 177, 180, 234, 238-243, 247, 249, 251, 255, 258, 260-265, 267-269, 273, 275-279, 281, 283-286, 310-311, 318, 322, 327, 333-334, 348, 354, 364-370, 372-376
Gaming Spaces 375-376
Gaze 54-64, 66-67, 101-102
Geometric Transformations 341

H

Hearthstone 28, 240-241, 243, 245-246, 250, 256
Hero 14, 38-46, 48, 50-51, 53, 306, 364
Human Rights Education 195-196, 217

I

Ideology 121, 169, 373, 391
independent (indie) games 19, 21, 312, 317-321, 323, 326, 333-334, 347, 380, 389-390

Indie Gaming 334
Indie Video Games 309, 311, 317-318, 333, 341, 390-391
Informal Learning 149, 169, 241, 255, 334
Institutionalization 54, 62-65, 95, 108
Interactive Fiction 9, 19, 27
Interactivity 3-4, 14, 18, 27, 38, 50, 54, 109, 126-128, 130, 135, 146, 195, 204, 260, 263, 380
Internet Archive 172, 179
Intertextuality 38, 53

J

Jamming Econo 309, 315, 317, 341
Jawaharlal Nehru University 364, 367, 376
Joseph Campbell 38-39, 43

L

Lacan 57, 62, 64
Language Arts 258-260, 262-267, 269
Lexicon 251
Lifelong Learning 197
Lived-Experience 324, 342
Live-streaming 238-239, 241-242, 250, 252-253, 255

M

Magic Circle 20-22, 37, 100, 103, 108, 115, 295, 303, 346-347, 351, 357
Mass Effect 3 134, 138-141
Materialities 347-349, 351-352, 354-355, 359
Mathematization 329, 342
Meaningful Play 103
Media Consumption 239, 278
Message Boards 18, 106-107, 241, 244, 251, 255, 323
Metafiction 20-22, 37
Middle School Science 296
Mobile Game 321, 379, 381, 395
Mobile Gaming 28
Modding 129, 133, 334
Mods 12, 128-129, 133, 146, 334
Monomyth 42-43, 45, 53
Monument Valley 309, 311, 314-315, 321, 327-332, 343-344, 346-347, 351-355, 358-359
Morality 8, 21, 212, 220, 234, 237
Morphology 38-43, 46, 48
Motivation 99, 259-260, 262, 264, 267, 275, 295-296, 303, 305
Mountain 343-344, 346-347, 351, 355-359
Multi-User Dungeons (MUD) 170, 173, 193, 309
Myth 38, 40-41, 45-46, 48, 50, 53, 67, 104, 125-126, 130, 132, 135, 138, 140-141

N

New Media 39-40, 53, 105, 371
non-hermeneutic field 348-349, 351, 355
Non-Playable Character 203-204, 206, 208, 217

O

oleomingus 74, 83, 85-87, 89
Open World (Sandbox) Game 2, 37
Oral tradition 41, 373
Outlast 54-55, 59-68

P

Pacing 2, 294, 296, 302, 305, 308
Pedagogy 126, 184, 239, 285, 368, 372-373
Perspectival Shift 310, 321, 342
Persuasion 195
Physical Games 379-382, 384, 386, 388-389, 393, 395
Player Choice 205, 212
Playfulness 346, 349, 377, 379, 385, 391, 393-394
Politics 64, 160, 182, 188, 219, 223, 233, 316, 319, 334, 364, 375
Postphenomenology 312, 342
Procedurally Generation 37

R

Reacting to the Past 221, 226-227, 231, 268, 271
Recursion 95, 105, 107, 121, 295
Remediation 38-41, 50, 53, 261
Remedy Entertainment 39, 43-46, 48-50
Rochester Institute Of Technology 369
Roleplaying Game 219-220, 223, 237

S

Scratch 40, 43, 45, 131, 147, 381
Self-effectiveness 95, 110
Self-Expression 3, 26-27, 154-155, 158-159, 161-162, 169
Sequencing 304, 308
Serious Games 24, 37, 115, 149, 164, 195-198, 200-203, 209-211, 217, 221, 261, 269, 304, 380
Simulator 7, 18, 23-25, 37, 89, 275, 319, 322-323, 327, 356
Social Construction 74
Social History 170, 175

Social Media 18, 107, 134, 240, 246, 258-260, 262-263, 265, 267-268, 271, 279, 387
Spatial Thinking 309, 330-333, 342
STEM 148-151, 158-163, 169, 228, 273, 297, 306, 331-332, 393
Stereotype Threat 150, 157, 169
Storytelling 1-2, 4, 6-7, 14, 19, 37, 49, 53-54, 63, 153, 262-263, 274, 373
Street Games 382, 386, 393
Student-Centered Learning 271
Super Smash Brothers: Melee 241, 243, 248, 256

T

Tension 55, 57, 61-63, 65, 78, 86, 188, 205, 226, 272-273, 280-283, 286, 290, 294, 351, 385, 396
Trauma theory 55-56, 61
Trilateral Collaboration 364-365, 376
Troll 6, 193, 250
Turn 13, 23, 38, 55, 59, 64-65, 75, 88, 102-103, 106, 108, 114, 138, 179, 182, 188, 193, 248, 272-273, 280-283, 286, 290, 294, 296, 313, 344-345, 350, 353, 369, 387, 392
Twenty-First Century Skills 149, 159, 169
Twitch.tv 239-253, 255, 257

U

Universal Design for Learning 271
Urban Games 377, 385-387, 395-396

V

Video Game Design 89, 147-149, 154-155, 157-164, 169, 218, 311, 315, 318
Video Game Text 146
Video Game Work 131, 137, 146
Vladimir Propp 38-39

W

Warcraft II 170, 172, 174-175, 177-180, 183, 185-186
Western World 67, 201, 377-378, 396
Witnessing 56-57, 60-61, 65-68
World of Warcraft 3, 74, 162, 242-243, 247, 256, 276, 284, 310, 368, 370
Writing 7, 19, 43, 106-107, 125-128, 130-131, 138, 143, 177, 179, 251-253, 258, 260-265, 267-268, 272-275, 277-286, 329, 369, 371, 373, 380

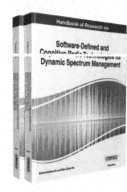

Printed in the United States
By Bookmasters